The World and Its People
EUROPE, AFRICA, ASIA, AND AUSTRALIA

EUROPE,

SERIES AUTHORS

Val E. Arnsdorf, Professor,
   College of Education, University of Delaware,
   Newark, Delaware

Carolyn S. Brown, Late Principal,
   Robertson Academy School, Nashville, Tennessee

Kenneth S. Cooper, Professor of History, Emeritus,
   George Peabody College for Teachers, Vanderbilt
   University, Nashville, Tennessee

Alvis T. Harthern, Professor of Education,
   University of Montevallo, Montevallo, Alabama

Timothy M. Helmus, Classroom Teacher,
   City Middle and High School, Grand Rapids,
   Michigan

Bobbie P. Hyder, Elementary Education Coordinator,
   Madison County School System, Huntsville,
   Alabama

Theodore Kaltsounis, Professor and Associate Dean,
   College of Education, University of Washington,
   Seattle, Washington

Richard H. Loftin, Director of Curriculum and Staff
   Development,
   Aldine Independent School District, Houston, Texas

Norman J.G. Pounds, Former University Professor of
   Geography,
   Indiana University, Bloomington, Indiana

Edgar A. Toppin, Professor of History and Dean of the
   Graduate School,
   Virginia State University, Petersburg, Virginia

GRADE–LEVEL CONTRIBUTORS

Sandra Breman, Teacher,
   Weisser Park Magnet School, Fort Wayne, Indiana

Sharon Gaydon, Teacher
   Thompson Middle School, Alabaster, Alabama

Jan Talbot, Teacher,
   Del Paso Manor School, Sacramento, California

William Tucker, Assistant Principal,
   White Oaks Elementary School, Virginia Beach, Virginia

Sister Catherine Zajac, S.S.J., Teacher,
   St. Mary's Elementary School, Westfield, Massachusetts

AFRICA, ASIA, AND AUSTRALIA

KENNETH S. COOPER Professor of History, Emeritus

George Peabody College for Teachers

Vanderbilt University, Nashville, Tennessee

SILVER BURDETT COMPANY Morristown, New Jersey

Glenview, Ill. • San Carlos, Calif. • Dallas • Atlanta

Agincourt, Ontario

ACKNOWLEDGEMENTS

Page 22: Map, Weather Forecast for Selected U.S. Cities and surrounding information from THE NEW YORK TIMES, Friday, February 1, 1980. © 1980 by the New York Times Company. Reprinted by permission. Page 53: Diagram of early writing adapted courtesy of The Oriental Institute, University of Chicago. Page 56: Excerpt reprinted from THE SUMERIANS by Samuel Noah Kramer by permission of The University of Chicago Press, 1963. Page 231: Excerpt from THE RUSSIANS by Hedrick Smith. Copyright © 1976 by Hedrick Smith. Reprinted by permission of Times Books, a division of Quadrangle/The New Times Book Co., Inc. Page 398: Illustration from the article "Chinese Oracle Bones" by Hung-hsiang Chou in SCIENTIFIC AMERICAN, April, 1979. Used by permission.

CONTENTS

MAPS

ATLAS

GRAPHS

DIAGRAMS

TABLES

TIME LINES

SPECIAL INTEREST MATERIALS

END–OF–CHAPTER SKILLS DEVELOPMENT

A LETTER TO YOU FROM THE AUTHOR

Dear Student,

I am writing this letter in my study where I have written most of this book. The book is about a very large subject. It is a book about most of the people of the world. They live in Europe, Africa, Asia, and Australia. It is also about peoples of different times—some long ago, some very recent.

A book on such a large subject could be very big—far bigger than I could write or you could read. If this book tried to tell all that could be told about the subject, it would not be a single book but a whole library of books. To try and learn all about these lands and peoples would be like trying to look at each tree in a huge forest. You would never see the forest because of the trees. Perhaps you have visited a forest and seen lookout towers. Forest rangers need lookout towers above the trees so that they can see the forest. This book is a kind of lookout tower. By learning some of the most important things about different lands, you can get a view of half the world and more than half its peoples.

These peoples of the other continents share the earth with us. What we do affects them, and what they do affects us. We use each other's products and borrow each other's ideas. We need to know something about the people with whom we live.

We also depend on ideas and inventions of people who lived in earlier times. At this moment you and I are making use of a very old invention—the alphabet. The letters of the alphabet make it possible for me to write these words in my study and for you to read them in your school or home. The alphabet also made it possible for me to read and put into this book some sayings of people who lived long ago. We not only share the world with people living now, we share the ideas of those who once lived.

As I worked on this book, I often thought of you. I kept asking the question: what will interest you? It is not an easy question to answer because different people are interested in such different things. What seems interesting to some seems deadly dull to others. For example, some of you would be interested in the gray tabby cat that likes to sit on my desk as I write. But I am sure that there are others who cannot stand cats, and they would prefer to read nothing more about the subject. All of us find some subjects more interesting than others. I think fish a dull subject, and I can not imagine why anyone wants to keep fish. (I should add that my gray tabby has an interest in fish.) It may be that you keep fish and think them very interesting. If you ask, do I know much about fish? I would admit that I do not. That may be the reason for my lack of interest in fish. You have to know something about a subject in order to find it interesting.

You will not find much about either cats or fish in this book. But you will find a lot about other subjects. You are already interested in some of them, but you may think others quite dull. You probably have not yet learned much about the subjects you think dull. Once you begin to learn, you may discover that dull subjects begin to get interesting. That is one reason for this book. It is not so much to tell you about the world in which you live as it is to interest you in that world.

Sincerely,

Kenneth S. Cooper

Knowledge That Helps You Learn

1 Learning About Maps, Continents, and Climate

Maps Old and New

VOCABULARY

astronomy	Equator
sphere	hemisphere
symbol	parallels
elevation	meridians
altitude	Prime Meridian
cartographer	projection
geography	natural
grid	resource
latitude	population
longitude	density

Early ideas and models of the earth
Have you ever visited a museum? There are many different kinds. In some museums you can learn about everything from sports to space travel. Would you like to know about art? Asia? Baseball? Clocks? Or gold miners? There are museums where you can find information on these subjects and a great many others as well.

The name *museum* is a good one for places where you can learn so much. The word means "place of the muses." Who were the muses? They were Greek goddesses of art and knowledge. The Greeks of long ago believed that each art or field of knowledge had its own goddess. There were muses of poetry, music, history, and **astronomy,** the study of the stars and planets. (Words in heavy type are in the Glossary at the end of the book.) A place for the muses was one set aside for art and knowledge. That is what our museums are today.

One of the world's first museums was in Egypt in the city of Alexandria. It was built by a Greek king who ruled Egypt more than 2,300 years ago. The king's name was Ptolemy. (You forget the *P* and pronounce Ptolemy as if it were spelled tol′ ə mē.)

King Ptolemy's museum differed from most museums today. It was not a place to teach visitors. It was a place for scholars (skol′ ərz) and artists to work. They lived at the museum, wrote books, and discussed everything from plants to planets. There were meeting rooms and shaded walks and gardens where they could talk and work.

Most important of all, the museum had a library. King Ptolemy and later rulers used their power to get books for the library. They bought books from other lands. In those days there were no printing machines. Every book was carefully written and bound by hand. Anyone entering Egypt with a book had to give it up if the library did not already have it. All that people got in return were copies of their own books. This was one reason why the museum had the greatest library in the world at that time.

The Apollo space capsule and these airplanes are in the "Milestones of Flight" exhibit at the National Air and Space Museum in Washington, D.C.

At the bottom of this page, you will read that the distance around the earth is 24,859 miles, which is about the same as 40,008 kilometers (kil′ ə mē tərz). Kilometers and miles are both units of measure used to express distance or length. One kilometer and a little more than half a mile are about the same distance. A kilometer is a unit of measure in the metric system.

This system is used for measuring distance. It is also used for measuring such things as weight, capacity, and heat. The metric system is in use or being introduced in all the major countries of the world except the United States. Some day the United States will probably "go metric" also.

To prepare you for this change, we have used both U.S. and metric measurements in this book. When a U.S. measurement appears in this book, it is followed in parentheses ( ) by the metric measurement that is about equal to it. Inches are changed to centimeters (cm), feet and yards to meters (m), miles to kilometers (km), and acres to hectares (ha). Pounds are changed to kilograms (kg), and quarts to liters (L). Degrees Fahrenheit (°F) are changed to degrees Celsius (°C).

The drawing at the beginning of this unit shows a person with a globe on a stand. He is Eratosthenes (er ə tos′ thə nēz), one of the Greek scholars at the museum in the city of Alexandria. The scholars knew then that the earth is a **sphere,** shaped like a round ball. Eratosthenes had worked out a careful guess of the distance around the sphere. His guess was surprisingly close to what we know today to be the actual distance of 24,859 miles (40,008 km).

Eratosthenes was the head librarian and interested in many different subjects. He wrote poetry and history. He improved the calendar, and he studied mathematics. He made a map of the world that probably was better than any made earlier. He knew so much about so many things that other people called him the "all-rounder."

An ancient map   Maps were nothing new in Eratosthenes' time. People had been making maps for hundreds—even thousands—of years. The picture at the top of the next page shows the oldest known map in the world. It was made more than 4,000 years ago. That is more than 2,000 years before Eratosthenes lived. It was drawn on damp clay with a sharp stick and then allowed to harden. This map was found in what is now the country of Iraq (i räk′). (Find Iraq on the map of Eurasia (yùr rā′ zha) on pages 466 and 467.)

Map symbols   On the next page you will find a modern map of Iraq. The old clay map and the modern map are quite different. But they are alike in one important way. Both maps use **symbols**. Symbols are marks on a map that stand for real places or real features on the earth's surface. On the clay map, the lines that run across the tablet stand for a river and its branches. The humps at the top and bottom stand for hills or mountains. The circles show where cities were located. The symbols on the modern map are

4

The top of this old clay map is east. North is at the left. Circles stand for cities. Although the clay is damaged in places, the map has lasted for more than 4,000 years.

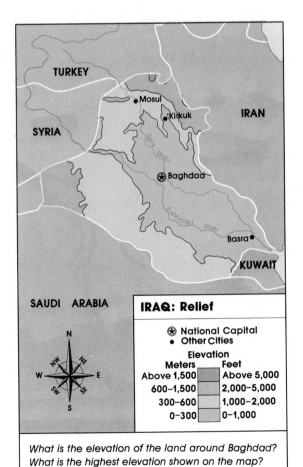

IRAQ: Relief

⊛ National Capital
• Other Cities

Elevation

Meters	Feet
Above 1,500	Above 5,000
600–1,500	2,000–5,000
300–600	1,000–2,000
0–300	0–1,000

What is the elevation of the land around Baghdad? What is the highest elevation shown on the map?

explained in the map key. Some of these symbols are very much like those on the clay map.

Showing elevation There are some important differences between the two maps. The top of the clay map is east. The top of the modern map is north. The modern map uses colors rather than humps to show different levels of land. The height of land is called its **elevation**, or **altitude**. Elevation is measured from sea level, which is the average level of the oceans. Different colors stand for different ranges in elevation. Land shown in the same color may have hills, valleys, and mountains. But the elevation does not become lower or higher than the range shown in the map key. Dark green shows land that is between sea level and 1,000 feet (300 m) above sea level. The next lighter shade of green is land that is more than 1,000 feet (300 m) but less than 2,000 feet (600 m) above sea level.

From photographs to maps Many of the early mapmakers, or **cartographers** (kär tog′ rə fərz), had to guess about the shapes of the places they showed. It is amazing that some of the early maps are as accurate as they are. Today it is much easier to draw a map than it was 4,000 years ago. Remember, a map is a kind of drawing of the earth. It shows the earth, or part of it, as it might look from high above the earth's surface.

It is no longer necessary to guess what the earth's surface looks like. Most major parts of the world have been explored. Also, airplanes and satellites, flying high above the earth, have photographed its entire surface.

5

FROM PHOTOGRAPH TO MAP

Woods
Other Land
Water
Roads
Bridges

Other Buildings
Parking Lots
Swimming Pool
Houses

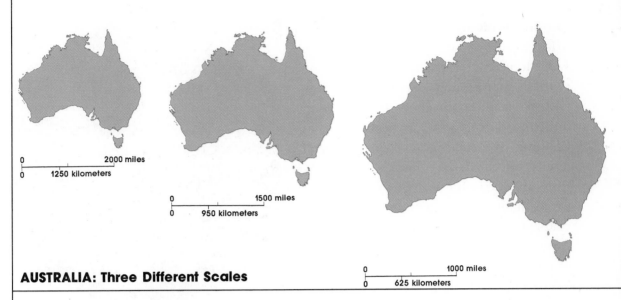

AUSTRALIA: Three Different Scales

Map scales tell how to figure distance from one place to another. Map scale is a ratio between distances on the earth's surface and distances on a map.

Study the photograph on page 6. Now look at the map made from that photograph. The map is a simplified drawing of the picture. Unlike the photograph, the map has a key. The map uses symbols to stand for real things and places on the earth. The map key tells what the symbols stand for. Find the symbol used for houses. Now pick out a house in the photograph and find that house on the map. Can you locate a parking lot?

Scale shows distance There is no way to judge distances on the clay map because it does not have a scale. Map scales tell how to find out how far it is from one place to another on the earth's surface. The scale line on a map shows how much an inch (or centimeter) on the map stands for in real distance on earth. A map can be drawn at many different scales. The three maps on this page show

Australia. But each map is drawn at a different scale. Put a ruler under the scale line of the left-hand map. You will see that 1 inch stands for about 2,000 miles. (One centimeter stands for about 1,250 kilometers.) Now measure how many inches (or centimeters) it is across Australia on the left-hand map. It is about 1.25 inches (3.2 cm) across. To find out how many actual miles (or kilometers) it is across Australia, you multiply 1.25 times 2,000 (or 3.2 times 1,250). By doing this, you will see that Australia is about 2,500 miles (4,000 km) wide. Go through the same steps with each of the other two maps of Australia. You will find that the number of inches (or centimeters) changes from map to map. However, when you use the scale for each map to figure miles or kilometers on the earth's surface, the distance across Australia stays the same in each case.

Maps are simplified drawings of the earth's surface. Map symbols stand for real things and places on the surface of the earth.

7

Another Ptolemy Scholars at Alexandria continued to study and map the earth long after Eratosthenes' time. One of these later scholars, Claudius Ptolemy, had the same last name as the king who built the museum. It has been said that Claudius Ptolemy came from the royal family, but this is very doubtful. We know little about his life except that he wrote books that people studied for hundreds of years. One book was about astronomy. Another was about **geography**, the study of the earth and its life.

The picture on this page shows an old stone carving of Claudius Ptolemy. The carving is old, but it was made long after Ptolemy's lifetime. The artists did not know what he looked like, but they did know why he was important. They carved a man observing the stars, and they carved a globe on his desk.

In his geography book, Ptolemy gave instructions for making maps that are still followed today. He said to put north at the top. Modern mapmakers usually do.

About A.D. 150, Claudius Ptolemy stated that the earth is round. He also said that the earth was at the center of the universe.

How to locate a place Ptolemy also showed an easy way that we still use to locate places on a map. The plan is much the same as locating seats in a theater. The drawing on this page shows the plan of a theater with 195 seats. The rows have

The system used to show the location of a seat in a theater or sports stadium is similar to the way we state the location of a place on the surface of the earth.

THEATER SEATING PLAN

This map is based on Claudius Ptolemy's view of the world. North is at the top. Can you find the Mediterranean Sea and the three continents that he knew about?

letters and the seats in each row are numbered. A ticket gives two facts about a particular seat. It gives the letter of the row and the number of the seat in that row. This is all you need to know. Can you locate the seats for the two tickets shown? Can you tell which letter and number will be on the ticket for the seat that has been shaded?

Pictured above is an old map based on Ptolemy's instructions. It shows the lands of the globe about which he knew. The pattern of lines, called a **grid**, was drawn to help locate places. The lines that run west and east—left and right—are lines of **latitude**. Those that run north and south—top to bottom on the map— are lines of **longitude**. On pages 466 and 467, there is a modern map that shows the same part of the world. The modern map also has lines of latitude and longitude. The grid is made up of lines that are all imaginary. But they make it possible to state the location of any spot on earth.

Some maps have a grid system of letters and numbers to help you find places. On page 179 find the letter and number given for Paris in the list of cities. Using the letter and number, find the square on the map where Paris is located.

9

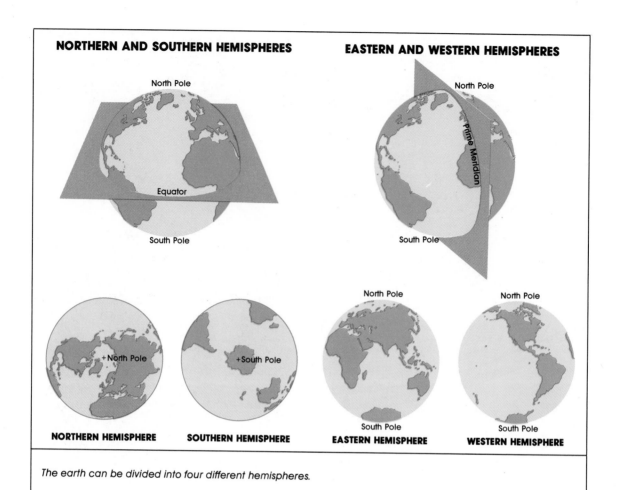

The earth can be divided into four different hemispheres.

Hemispheres and parallels The **Equator** is one of the imaginary lines of latitude that run east and west. It circles the earth an equal distance from the North and South Poles. So the Equator divides the earth's sphere into two halves. The Greek word for half is *hemi*, so half of the earth's sphere is called a **hemisphere**. The Equator divides the world into a Northern Hemisphere and a Southern Hemisphere. Later you will read that the world can also be divided into an Eastern Hemisphere and a Western Hemisphere. The maps above show how we usually divide the world into these four hemispheres.

Lines of latitude are called **parallels**. They run around the earth parallel to the Equator. Like the Equator, these lines form whole circles. This means that if you trace a parallel with your finger, your finger will always be the same distance from the Equator as it moves around the earth.

The parallels measure distances from either side of the Equator toward the poles. The whole way from the Equator to either of the poles is a quarter of a circle. This is measured in degrees. A whole circle has 360 degrees. So the quarter of a circle north from the Equator to the North Pole is 90 degrees. Also, there are 90 degrees south from the Equator to the South Pole. These units of measure are written ° N and ° S. We think of having a parallel for every degree. This is why we say there are 90 parallels north of the Equator and 90 parallels south of it. But mapmakers draw different numbers of parallels for different maps and globes. Turn to the Atlas map of the world on pages 452 and 453. You can see that every twentieth parallel appears on this map.

Meridians   Mapmakers draw imaginary lines of longitude from the North Pole to the South Pole. They are called **meridians** (mə rid′ ē ənz). Each meridian crosses the great circle formed by the Equator. It is customary to have a meri-dian for each degree in the circle of the Equator. That means there are 360 lines of longitude, or meridians. But mapmakers usually do not show every meridian on a small-scale map.

Meridians are numbered from a line called the **Prime Meridian**, which runs through Greenwich, England. Find this line on the map below at the left. The meridians are counted both east and west from the Prime Meridian. Halfway around the world is the 180° meridian. This and the Prime Meridian form a full circle, which divides the world into the Eastern Hemisphere and the Western Hemisphere. Study a globe to see how these meridians meet at the North Pole and South Pole to form a full circle.

The Prime Meridian is 0° longitude.   *The Equator is 0° latitude.*

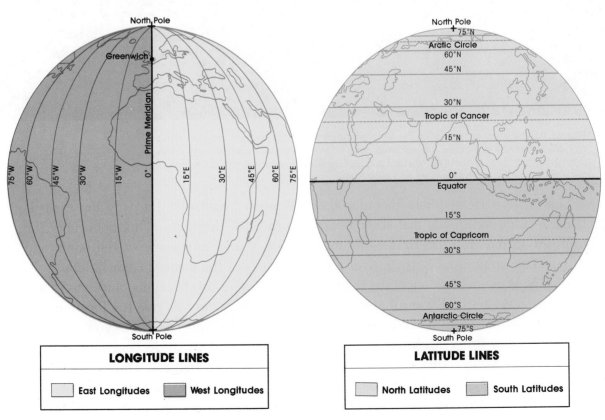

Naples, Italy, is a major seaport on the Mediterranean Sea. Here you can see part of the city along the Bay of Naples. The volcanic cone of Mount Vesuvius can be seen in the background. Naples is about 40°N, which is about the same distance from the Equator as the American cities of Philadelphia and New York.

The Eastern Hemisphere includes the lands of four continents that stretch east from the Prime Meridian to the 180° meridian. They are Europe, Africa, Asia, and Australia. When we talk about the Eastern Hemisphere, we usually mean also to include the parts of Europe and Africa that lie west of the Prime Meridian. You can see why this makes good sense if you look at the map on page 13. Australia, which is part of the Eastern Hemisphere, cannot be seen because of the way the earth is turned in this map. This book tells the history and geography of the lands and peoples of the Eastern Hemisphere.

The grid of parallels and meridians makes it as easy to give the location of a place on the earth as it is to find a seat in a theater. You need only two facts: latitude and longitude. To find the city of Leningrad on the map on page 13, find 60 degrees of latitude north of the Equator and 30 degrees of longitude east of the Prime Meridian. To locate Leningrad find where these two lines come together. The short way to write these facts is 60°N, 30°E. You do not need to write 60°N *latitude* or 30°E *longitude* because only latitude lines are counted north and south. Only longitude lines are counted east and west. Knowing this, you need only to learn that Naples, Italy, is about 40°N, 15°E to find it on the map below. Can you state the location of Port Sudan in Africa?

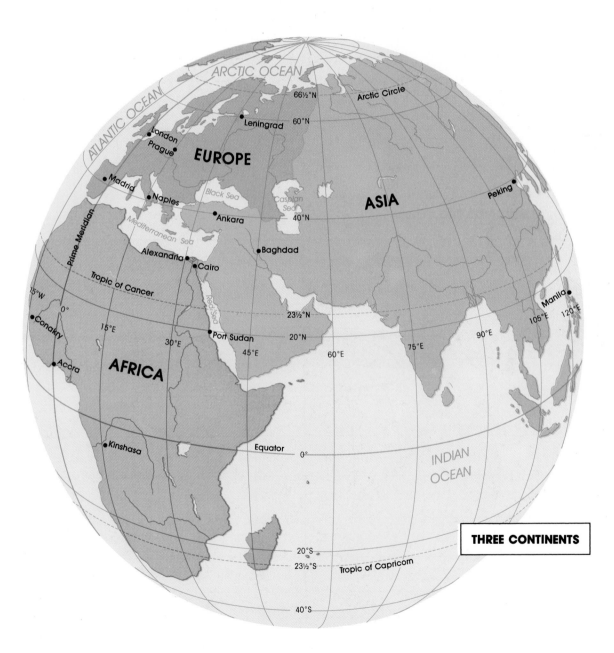

Lines of latitude and longitude help us to locate places on the earth's surface.

13

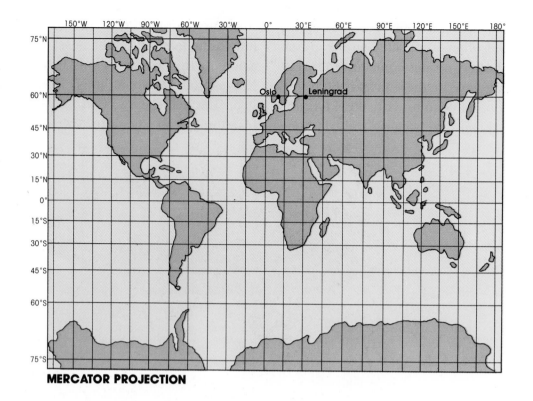

MERCATOR PROJECTION

A Mercator projection is good for showing directions on a map.

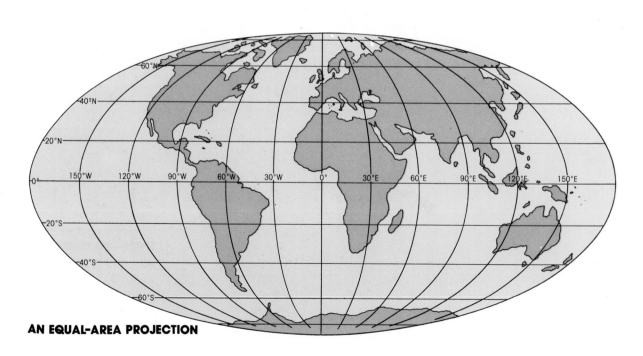

AN EQUAL-AREA PROJECTION

An equal-area projection is good for showing the sizes of land and water areas.

Flat maps of a round earth   Mapmakers ever since Ptolemy have faced a problem: how to make a map of the round earth on a flat page. If it were possible, they would make a flat map that would show the surface of the earth as it really is. The map would have the following four properties:

1.   Lands would have their true shapes.

2.   The scale of distance would be the same for all parts of the map. If one inch stood for 1,000 miles at the Equator, it would stand for 1,000 miles at the North Pole.

3.   It would be an equal-area map. This means that the size of a place on the map would be drawn to represent accurately its real size on the earth. So equal areas on the map would stand for areas of equal size on the earth's surface.

4.   Directions would be accurate and would be the same for all points on the map. North and south would always be up and down. And east and west would always be right and left. For this to happen, lines of latitude and longitude would curve as the earth's surface curves, yet they would have to cross at right angles as they do on a globe.

There is no way to make a flat map that has all these characteristics. Only a globe can have them, and so only a globe gives a completely accurate view of the earth. But flat maps are so useful that we need them even if no one of them gives a completely accurate view of the earth's surface.

Try to recall the last time you used a map. Do you remember why you needed the map? People use flat maps for many purposes. Can you name five different uses of flat maps?

Projections   Mapmakers, or cartographers, have different ways to show the round earth. These ways are called **projections**. No projection has all of the four characteristics. In order to show one thing, it cannot show another. The projection you choose depends on the use you make of a map. A projection useful for sailing across the ocean may not be good for comparing the size of countries.

One of the most famous map projections was invented 400 years ago by Gerhardus Mercator (je rärd′ əs mėr kā′ tər). The map at the top of the facing page is a Mercator projection. The parallels and meridians cross at right angles, so that north and south are always up and down. And east and west are always right and left. This makes it easy to see that Oslo, Norway, is straight west of Leningrad in the Soviet Union. Both are located near 60°N. The Mercator map is good for finding directions because they do not shift on the map.

However, this map does not show an equal-area projection. It stretches the size of lands north and south of the Equator. Between the 50th parallels and the Equator, the stretching is not too great. But north or south of the 60th it is quite another matter. You can see that Greenland appears as large as Africa, but really Africa is more than 13 times the size of Greenland. If we wanted to show land sizes the way they really are, we would use an equal-area projection, such as the one at the bottom of the facing page. Areas of equal size on the earth's surface are shown equal in size on equal-area maps. The Atlas maps on pages 452 to 469 at the back of this book are equal-area maps.

Other facts from maps   The two maps of Eurasia in the Atlas present different kinds of facts. The one on pages 464 and 465 gives facts about the earth's natural surface. It shows rivers, plateaus, mountains, and seas. It is called a physical map. The map on pages 466 and 467 shows the lines, or boundaries, between countries. These are political facts. Boundaries are made by governments. It is called a political map.

There are other kinds of maps that present still other kinds of facts. **Natural resource** maps show where you would find things made by nature that people use, such as trees, water, soil, coal, and oil. The map on this page tells important facts about oil and natural gas. What do the symbols stand for on this map? Knowing about these facts is important for understanding the world, as you will learn in later chapters.

Maps that tell about people   Maps give facts about people. The world map on page 17 tells where people live. It is called a population density map. **Population density** tells how closely together people live in a set area of land. It states the number of people for each square mile or square kilometer of land. We find the population density of a place by dividing the total number of people who live there by the land area of the place.

The population density map shows that people are not evenly spread over the earth. What parts of North America have the highest density of people?

Oil and natural gas are two of the earth's most important natural resources.

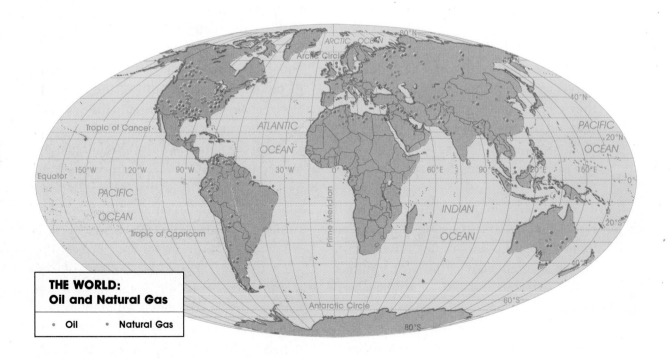

THE WORLD:
Oil and Natural Gas

· Oil   · Natural Gas

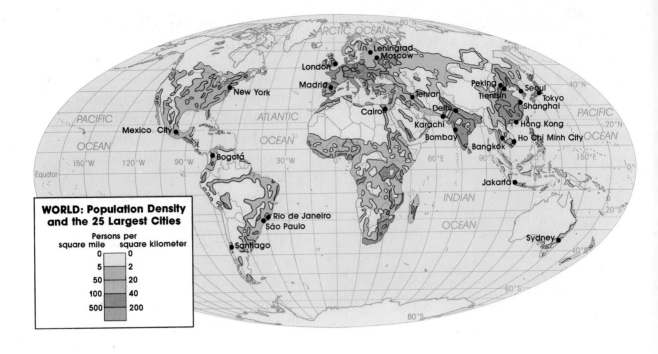

WORLD: Population Density and the 25 Largest Cities

Persons per
square mile | square kilometer
0 | 0
5 | 2
50 | 20
100 | 40
500 | 200

One of the 25 largest cities in the world is located in the United States. What is the name of the city?

You can see there are maps for many different uses. You have learned about physical maps, political maps, maps that show population density, and others that show natural resources. You will study other maps later in this book. Can you name some different kinds of maps that show other kinds of facts?

CHECKUP

1. What did scholars know about the shape of the earth 2,000 years ago?
2. From what point is the elevation of land measured?
3. Why are lines of latitude called parallels?
4. In what direction do the meridians run? What is the Prime Meridian?
5. What four characteristics of the earth's surface can be shown accurately on a globe but not together on a flat map?
6. What is population density a measure of?

This is a morning rush-hour crowd waiting for a subway in Tokyo, Japan. People live and work close together in crowded cities all over the world.

The Mediterranean Sea (upper left) is connected by the Suez Canal to the Red Sea (center). Asia is to the right and Africa is to the left of this waterway. Find the Nile River at the lower left. The Suez Canal is located at about 31°N, 32°E. Find it on the map on page 249.

Continents, Weather, and Climate

Continents and oceans Ptolemy thought that the lands of the world could be divided into three **continents**: Africa, Asia, and Europe. You can better understand his reason if you look at Africa on the map on page 13. Locate Alexandria in Egypt where Ptolemy lived. Looking at the world from the city of Alexandria, it was easy to think of the three continents as

Major movements of water in the oceans are called ocean currents. Currents that move away from the Equator are warm. Those moving toward the Equator are cold.

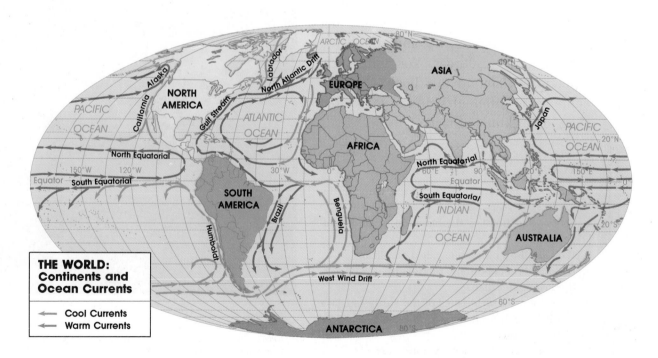

THE WORLD:
Continents and Ocean Currents

← Cool Currents
← Warm Currents

landmasses divided by seas. The Mediterranean (med ə tə rā′ nē ən) and Red seas separate Africa from Europe and Asia except for a small strip of land—known as an **isthmus**—near the Sinai Peninsula (sī′ nī pə nin′ sə lə). Today the Suez Canal runs across that isthmus. Europe is partly separated from the other two continents by the Mediterranean, Aegean (ē jē′ ən), and Black seas. You can see this clearly by looking at the map of Eurasia on pages 464 and 465. You can also see that north of the Black Sea no large bodies of water divide Europe and Asia. It is hard to say just where Europe ends and Asia begins. As viewed from Asia, Europe appears to be a **peninsula** of the larger continent. That is the reason why we sometimes speak of the two continents as the single landmass of Eurasia.

Ptolemy did not know a great deal about the land north of the Black Sea. As his map on page 9 shows, he thought the land was narrower than it actually is. We know more about that part of the world today, but we still follow his way of dividing the land. We speak of Europe as a continent, and we usually think of the Ural Mountains as the boundary between Europe and Asia.

Today we know about other parts of the world not even shown on Ptolemy's map. Counting Europe and Asia separately, there are seven continents in all. The other five continents are Africa, North America, South America, Australia, and Antarctica. Find each continent on the world map on page 18. Which continent is the largest? Which is the smallest? Does most of the world's land lie in the southern or northern latitudes?

The seven continents add up to a lot of land area: more than 57 million square miles (149 million sq km) in all. But did you know that more than twice as much of the earth's surface is covered by water? The world's oceans cover about 70 percent of the earth. Although their waters form a continuous body around the world, we divide them into the Pacific, Atlantic, Indian, and Arctic oceans. There are also lakes and seas. But you can see from the Atlas map on pages 454 and 455 that these make up only a small part of the total water surface of the earth.

Hot, cold, and in between   Ptolemy borrowed some ideas from another Greek named Strabo (strā′ bo) who had written about geography at an earlier time. Strabo divided the world into hot, cold, and in-between zones. The hot zone was near the Equator. Strabo called it the **torrid** zone, which means very hot. He called the zones at the far north and south **frigid** zones, which means very cold. The zones in between, which Strabo believed were neither very hot nor very cold, were named the **temperate** zones. Altogether there were five zones: northern frigid, northern temperate, torrid, southern temperate, and southern frigid.

Strabo made some mistakes. He thought that no one could live in the torrid or frigid zones. But many people really do live near the Equator in what Strabo called the torrid zone. And some people live in the Arctic, one of his frigid zones. The names of the zones are not very good ones. The frigid zone is not always frigid. The short Arctic summer may be very warm or even hot. On the other hand, the temperate zones are sometimes very hot or very cold.

Today we divide the earth into lands similar to Strabo's temperature zones. They are the low, middle, and high latitudes, which are shown on the map at the bottom of this page.

Changing seasons   Can you imagine moving at 67,000 miles (107,800 km) an hour? That is more than 1,000 times the top speed that most cars travel. You may never have guessed that right now you *are* moving at 67,000 miles (107,800 km) an hour. This is the speed of the earth's journey—or revolution—around the sun. This revolution, once every 365¼ days, has a lot to do with the change of seasons on earth.

Strabo reasoned that the seasons in the Southern Hemisphere were the opposite of those in the Northern Hemisphere. This is true because the tilt of the earth never changes as the earth travels around the sun. Look carefully at the diagram on page 21. On June 22 the northern part of the earth is tilted toward the sun. This is the first day of summer and the longest day of the year for the Northern Hemisphere. The direct rays of the sun are as far north as they ever get.

This same day is the first day of winter and the shortest day of the year for the Southern Hemisphere. The southern part of the earth is tilted as far away from the sun as it ever gets, so the sun's rays fall on the Southern Hemisphere at a slant.

Half a year later, on December 22, summer begins south of the Equator and the first day of winter comes to the Northern Hemisphere. During this half revolution around the sun, the tilt of the

The low latitudes are located between two special parallels—the Tropic of Cancer at 23½°N, and the Tropic of Capricorn at 23½°S. Find these lines of latitude on the map.

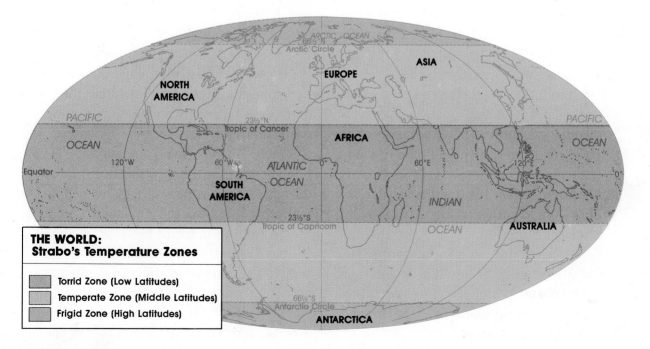

THE WORLD:
Strabo's Temperature Zones

- Torrid Zone (Low Latitudes)
- Temperate Zone (Middle Latitudes)
- Frigid Zone (High Latitudes)

The weather map also shows the location of highs and lows with the letters **H** and **L**. On this particular day there were two high pressure areas over the United States. You will see that there are some lines with points and semicircles strung along them. These lines mark **fronts.** A front is a strip of changing weather. Fronts form between a mass of cold air and a mass of warm air. When the cold air pushes against a mass of warm air, it is called a cold front. It generally brings stormy and cooler weather. The line for a cold front has pointed symbols. When warm air moves over a mass of cold air, it is called a warm front. As it brings warmer weather to a place, a warm front is often led by rain or snow. The line for a warm front has semicircle symbols along it. You can often know the kind of weather to expect by noting the location and movement of fronts.

What is climate? The weather in the year 1816 was very unusual. People in the United States and Europe called it "the year without a summer." Snow fell in Connecticut on June 7. There were killing frosts in July and August.

The cause of the odd weather was a volcano half way around the world. In 1815 Mount Tambora in Indonesia erupted. You can find Indonesia on the Atlas world map on pages 452 and 453. It lies on the Equator between 100°E and 140°E. Mount Tambora's eruption threw huge amounts of dust into the upper air. The dust circled the earth, and it kept some of the sun's rays from reaching the earth's surface. That was the reason for

Are the coldest parts of the world near the Equator or near the North Pole and the South Pole? Where are the hottest parts of the world?

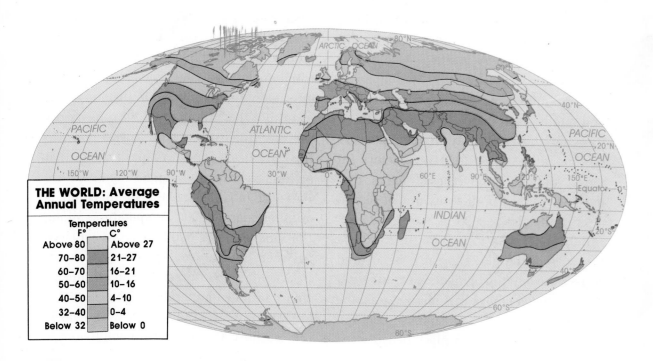

THE WORLD: Average Annual Temperatures

Temperatures	
F°	C°
Above 80	Above 27
70–80	21–27
60–70	16–21
50–60	10–16
40–50	4–10
32–40	0–4
Below 32	Below 0

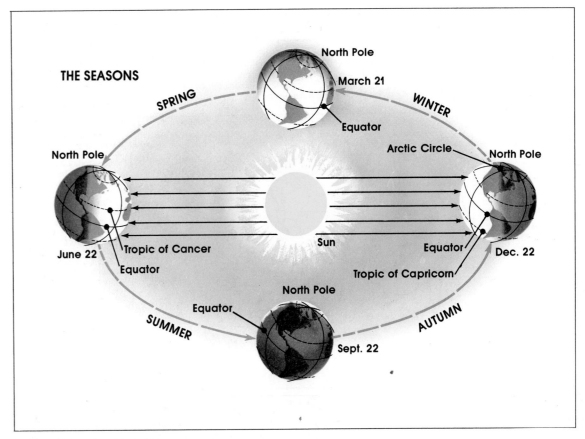

THE SEASONS

In the Northern Hemisphere, the most direct rays of the sun never reach beyond the Tropic of Cancer. In the Southern Hemisphere, the most direct rays of the sun never reach beyond the Tropic of Capricorn.

earth has caused a change in seasons from one extreme to the other for all parts of the world.

What is weather? Strabo thought a great deal about weather, and many people still do. We find it an interesting subject. Radio and television stations broadcast the weather news many times a day. Newspapers print weather reports and maps, such as that on page 22. What is weather? What is it that we learn when we hear or read the weather news?

Weather is the condition of the air at a particular time and place. A weather report usually answers these questions: (1) What is the temperature—is it hot, warm, cool, or cold? (2) Is the sun shining or is it cloudy? (3) Has there been any **precipitation**—rain, snow, hail, or sleet? (4) How windy is it, or is it calm? (5) Is there much **humidity**—dampness—in the air?

Measuring weather Today weather reports give exact answers to the questions. We do not just say that the day is hot. We say how hot. We are able to measure temperature and other conditions of the air. Strabo could not do this because he did not have a thermometer or the other instruments we use today.

National Forecast for February 1, 1980

Snow flurries are expected from northern New England into the lower lake region with extremely cold temperatures predicted for the North Atlantic States. Showers will be scattered across portions of southern Texas and rain is expected in the Pacific Northwest. The rest of the nation should have mostly sunny skies.

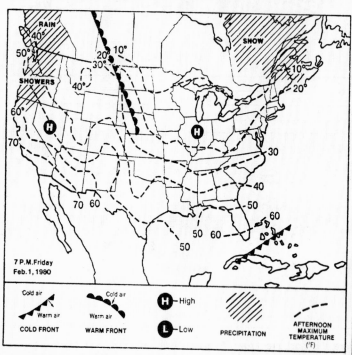

7 P.M. Friday
Feb. 1, 1980

Cold air — COLD FRONT
Warm air — WARM FRONT
H — High
L — Low
PRECIPITATION
AFTERNOON MAXIMUM TEMPERATURE (°F)

Recreational Forecast

Boating

Winds: North to northwesterly winds at 15 to 25 knots today and tonight. **Visibility:** Generally 5 miles or better. **Wave heights:** 3 to 4 feet on the sound and 5 to 10 feet on the ocean.

High Tides

Sandy Hook	7:51 A.M.	8:17 P.M.
Willets Point	11:59 A.M.	12:22 A.M.
Shinnecock Canal	11:57 A.M.	12:25 A.M.
Fire Island	7:12 A.M.	7:38 P.M.
Montauk Point	8:11 A.M.	8:39 P.M.

Ski Area Forecast

Adirondacks, Green and White Mountains: Breezy and very cold today through tomorrow with a chance of a few flurries. High: 5-15. **Catskills and Berkshires:** Windy and very cold through tomorrow with a chance of a few flurries. High: 5-15. **Poconos and Northwest New Jersey:** Windy and cold today, fair tonight and tomorrow. High: 17-24.

Weather Forecast for Selected U.S. Cities

The following forecast for today shows the projected weather conditions and the expected range of temperatures (°F), from the afternoon high to the evening low.

Atlanta: Mostly sunny. 32-17.
Boston: Mostly sunny. 21-5.
Chicago: Mostly sunny. 15-0.
Cleveland: Snow likely. 15-2.
Dallas: Mostly cloudy. 37-34.

Denver: Mostly sunny. 44-15.
Houston: Mostly cloudy. 45-33.
Kansas City: Partly cloudy. 22-13.
Las Vegas: Mostly fair. 62-38.
Los Angeles: Partly cloudy. 72-55.
Miami: Mostly fair. 58-43.
Minneapolis: Partly cloudy. 16 to -1.
New Orleans: Mostly fair. 49-33.

Philadelphia: Mostly windy. 20-6.
Phoenix: Partly cloudy. 74-50.
Pittsburgh: Snow likely. 14-1.
St. Louis: Partly cloudy. 20-11.
San Francisco: Mostly cloudy. 59-52.
Seattle: Rain likely. 50-42.
Washington: Mostly windy. 27-18.

Yesterday's Weather in Selected Foreign Cities

Following are the temperatures (°F) and weather conditions in foreign cities yesterday at the local time indicated:

City	Time	Temp	Condition
Amsterdam	1 P.M.	50	Clear
Athens	2 P.M.	57	Clear
Auckland	Midnt.	68	Clear
Bangkok	2 P.M.	93	Clear
Belgrade	2 P.M.	54	Clear
Berlin	1 P.M.	41	Rain
Brussels	1 P.M.	48	Pt.cldy.
Cairo	2 P.M.	63	Clear
Casablanca	Noon	65	Pt.cldy.
Copenhagen	1 P.M.	30	Cloudy
Dublin	1 P.M.	39	Rain
Frankfurt	2 P.M.	45	Rain
Geneva	1 P.M.	48	Rain
Helsinki	2 P.M.	-3	Clear
Ho Chi Minh City	8 P.M.	82	Pt.cldy.
Hong Kong	9 P.M.	48	Cloudy
Jerusalem	2 P.M.	45	Clear
Johannesburg	2 P.M.	75	Snow
Lisbon	Noon	57	Clear
London	1 P.M.	45	Rain
Madrid	1 P.M.	54	Cloudy
Manila	8 P.M.	81	Clear
Moscow	3 P.M.	10	Snow
New Delhi	5 P.M.	72	Clear
Nice	1 P.M.	46	Clear
Oslo	1 P.M.	18	Cloudy
Paris	1 P.M.	52	Cloudy
Peking	8 P.M.	23	Cloudy
Rome	1 P.M.	59	Cloudy
Seoul	9 P.M.	10	Clear
Stockholm	1 P.M.	19	Pt.cldy.
Sydney	10 P.M.	77	Pt.cldy.
Taipei	9 P.M.	45	Drizzle
Teheran	3 P.M.	34	Pt.cldy.
Tel Aviv	2 P.M.	59	Clear
Tokyo	9 P.M.	45	Clear
Vienna	1 P.M.	37	Haze
Warsaw	1 P.M.	39	Cloudy

This weather map and the national forecast are part of the weather information for February 1, 1980, that was printed in the newspaper called The New York Times.

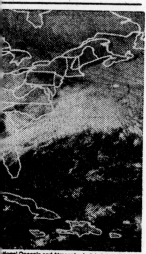

National Oceanic and Atmospheric Administration/UPI
...tic States into the Gulf States. An ...thwest Desert region. High and mid... ...Pacific Northwest and the Central

Hayden Planetarium

Sun, Moon and Planets

Sun rises today 7:07 A.M., sets 5:12...

Records

cold dry air into the region contin... ...opolitan area today. A low pressure ...rce the northwesterly flow of arctic

---

the United States annual production of some 300 million tons of grain and oil-seeds. But this country's exportable surplus of wheat, corn, soybeans, sorghum and other feed materials is over 15 million tons.

President Carter sent Gen. Andrew J. Goodpaster, the superintendent of the United States Military Academy, here last week to try to persuade the military

House Votes to Loosen Rules on Jetliner Noise

WASHINGTON, Jan. 31 (AP) — The House easily overcame opposition from environmentalists and some local citizen groups today and approved, 285 to 122, a compromise bill that would relax noise control regulations for two-engine jetliners.

The measure also provides $57 million more for airport development, including $13 million for smaller airports that serve private planes, and appropriates $15 million for planning new noise-reduction projects.

The bill is a product of a Senate-House conference committee compromise. Last year the Senate approved a version that was more lenient toward the airlines. The compromise measure is expected to be passed in the Senate.

Proponents of the bill said that forcing airlines to refit their planes with heavier, quieter engines would use more fuel. Opponents criticized provisions of the bill that would extend the time airlines may continue to fly two-engine jets that lack noise controls.

The jets were to be replaced or refitted with quieter engines by 1983. The bill provides that two-engine jets with 100 or fewer seats will be exempt until 1988, and those with more than 100 seats will be exempt until at least 1985. The larger two-engine jets could fly for an additional year if replacements are ordered by 1983 and delivered by 1986.

The word *thermometer* means "heat-meter." It is used to measure temperature. There are two temperature scales. Both are named after the people who invented them. Gabriel Fahrenheit (far′ ən hīt) described the Fahrenheit scale in 1724. Anders Celsius (sel′ sē əs) made the Celsius scale about 18 years later. The freezing point of water on the Fahrenheit scale is 32 degrees. The boiling point is 212 degrees. These are usually written 32°F and 212°F. An air temperature of 100°F is very hot. This is the same as 38°C. When a Fahrenheit thermometer measures below 32°, it is cold. Temperatures below 0°F are written with negative signs, such as −3°F. Most people find temperatures in the 70's on the Fahrenheit scale pleasant.

Anders Celsius had fewer degrees on his scale than Fahrenheit. Celsius used 0 degrees for the freezing point of water and 100 degrees for the boiling point. These are written 0°C and 100°C. Temperatures below 0°C are written with negative signs. A very warm 95°F would be 35°C. A cold 4°F is the same as −16°C.

We also have instruments that measure the amount of precipitation. The weather news tells how many inches of rain or snow fell during the day. We can measure the speed of the wind. **Hygrometers** (hī grom′ ə tərz) are wetness meters that measure humidity, the amount of dampness in the air.

Barometers (bə rom′ ə tərz) record the pressure of the air. The earth is covered by an ever-moving blanket of air. Air pressure is the weight of this blanket pushing down on the earth. The pressure is not the same from place to place because the blanket of air changes and moves. Where the weight is great, there is a high pressure area called a *high*. A *low* is an area of low pressure where the blanket of air pushes down less. Highs generally bring fair weather. A low often means clouds and wet weather. The air usually flows from a high toward a low. For this reason it helps to know where highs and lows will be when forecasting the weather.

Weather maps Weather maps provide facts about the weather in different places on a particular day. There are different kinds of weather maps. Some show more facts than others. The map on page 22 shows what the weather was over the United States on February 1, 1980. This is but one of several different kinds of weather maps. This map gives facts about precipitation, temperatures, air pressure, and weather changes. The shaded areas show where there was precipitation. Showers fell in the northwestern states. There was snow on the other side of the continent. The broken lines running across the country tell temperatures. The numbers of the lines mean the highest afternoon temperature for that day. For example, the line marked 40 runs across the country from the northwest coast to the southeast coast. This means that along this line the highest temperature was 40°F (4°C). Above the 40° line there is another marked 30. Temperatures along that line only reached 30°F (−1°C). Places between the lines will generally have in-between temperatures. Central Florida on this day had temperatures between 50°F (10°C) and 60°F (16°C). How warm was it on February 1, 1980, where you live?

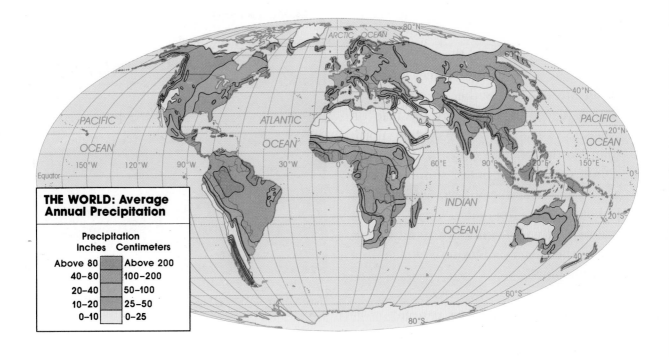

THE WORLD: Average Annual Precipitation

Precipitation
Inches   Centimeters

Above 80   Above 200
40–80   100–200
20–40   50–100
10–20   25–50
0–10   0–25

Precipitation includes rain, snow, sleet, and hail.

the cold summer halfway around the earth the following year.

It is interesting to know about the unusual summer of 1816. But it is more important to know what kind of weather is the normal, or usual, pattern for a place over a period of years. We call this pattern the **climate** of an area. Climate includes the temperature, humidity, precipitation, wind, and days of sunshine that are normal for the different seasons of a place.

Maps are sometimes the clearest way to state facts about climate. Look at the map on page 24. It shows annual average temperatures for the world. What is the average temperature for your part of the United States? The map above shows average annual precipitation around the world. What do you learn from this map about the amount of rain in lands crossed by the Equator? Do lands near the North Pole and South Pole get much precipitation? How much rain falls in Florida?

What affects climate? Strabo thought that the distance from the Equator determined climate. That is why he divided the world into zones from torrid to frigid. It is true that lands near the Equator tend to be warmer throughout the year than those at the poles. But there are other things that affect climate too. A high elevation, or altitude, makes a place cool even in the low latitudes. Mount Kilimanjaro (kil ə mən jär′ ō), in eastern Africa, is very near the Equator, yet snow covers its peak throughout the year. If you were to climb this or some other mountain, you could feel the air becoming colder. The temperature drops about 3°F (1.7°C) for every 1,000 feet (305 m) of elevation going from sea level to the higher points of land.

Oceans and seas cool the air in summer and warm it in winter. Places near the water are usually neither so cold nor so hot as places inland. Study the map on page 18. Great Britain is farther north than North Dakota, yet North Dakota has colder winters and hotter summers. Britain is an island country, while North Dakota is far from any large body of water. You will learn more about the effect of the ocean on Europe's climate in a later chapter.

How does climate affect people? A Greek thinker, Aristotle (ar′ is tot l), believed that climate greatly affected people. Aristotle lived before King Ptolemy built the museum, but Aristotle's ideas were well known there. His many books were in the great library at Alexandria. Aristotle wrote that a cold climate made people active and "full of spirit." But he also said that the cold made them lack skill and "brainpower." On the other hand, people in hot climates had skill and brainpower but lacked spirit. Aristotle thought that Greece had the best of climates. It was neither too cold nor too hot, so the Greeks had just the right mixture of spirit, skill, and brainpower. Of course, Aristotle was a Greek. Is it possible that this affected his view?

Not all Greeks agreed with Aristotle about the effects of climate. Strabo was Greek, but he did not think climate had much to do with skill or brainpower. He believed a people's customs and education shaped their character for the most part. He pointed out that the peoples of

In cold-winter climates, people have learned how to grow crops year round in garden beds like this.

Athens and Sparta, two Greek cities, were very different. Yet they lived in the same climate.

Most scholars today agree with Strabo rather than Aristotle. Climate does not make us what we are, although it affects how we live. The kind of clothes we wear depends in part on the climate. Where we live affects the kinds of houses we have. People do not build igloos in the desert heat of the Sahara. Climate certainly has much to do with the kinds of crops people grow. They do not raise corn in the short Arctic summers.

Perhaps the best way to describe the effects of climate is to say that climate may limit what we do. The climate of Antarctica limits what people can do in that cold desert. In fact, the limits are so great that no one has ever lived there except for short periods, even though Antarctica is larger than Europe.

Although climate is limiting, people sometimes invent ways to get around the

This is a modern aqueduct in Israel. For at least 5,000 years, people have known how to move water along channels like this to dry areas where it is needed.

limits. The first people who learned to use fire set aside one of the limits of climate. A desert climate, which at one time kept people from growing crops, no longer limited them when they learned to irrigate the land. And at one time, no one could ice-skate in hot climates. Now, because of ice-making machines, places that have no frosts do have ice rinks. People have learned to get around many limits of climate. In later chapters you will learn how people have often used brainpower to do what once seemed impossible.

CHECKUP

1. Name the seven continents.
2. What kinds of facts do we want when we ask, What is the weather?
3. What is the freezing point of water on the Fahrenheit scale? On the Celsius scale?
4. What is the difference between weather and climate?
5. In what way does climate affect people?

KEY FACTS

1. Maps show facts about the earth and people on the earth. Facts are shown with symbols, color, scale, and grid lines.

2. Climate is the usual weather for a particular place over a period of years.

3. Distance from the Equator, elevation, and nearness of large bodies of water affect climate.

4. Climate limits what people can do, but people find ways to get around the limits.

VOCABULARY QUIZ

On a sheet of paper, write the numbers of the following statements. Then write the letter of the ending that best finishes each sentence.

1. A sphere is shaped like (**a**) a round ball, (**b**) a flat plate.

2. The elevation of a place is its (**a**) value, (**b**) height above sea level.

3. Symbols on a map (**a**) are counted both east and west of the Prime Meridian, (**b**) stand for real places and things on earth, (**c**) give a representation of real distance on earth.

4. The study of the stars and planets is known as (**a**) geography, (**b**) astronomy.

5. Parallels (**a**) cross the Equator, (**b**) run in the same direction as the Equator.

6. Population density is the (**a**) number of people for each square mile, (**b**) total number of people in a country.

7. A very hot climate is (**a**) torrid, (**b**) frigid, (**c**) temperate.

8. A hemisphere is (**a**) the northern part of the world, (**b**) half of the world.

9. Precipitation is (**a**) the dampness of air, (**b**) water that falls to earth as rain or snow.

10. A barometer measures (**a**) humidity, (**b**) air pressure.

REVIEW QUESTIONS

1. In what ways is the world's oldest map like a modern map? In what ways is it different?

2. What can you learn from (**a**) a physical map? (**b**) a political map? (**c**) a natural resource map?

3. What is the difference between weather and climate?

4. In what ways does climate limit people in the place where you live?

5. Explain the ideas of each of the following, and then tell if most people today agree with them: (**a**) Eratosthenes' ideas about the shape of the earth, (**b**) Strabo's ideas about the seasons in the Southern Hemisphere, (**c**) Aristotle's ideas about the effects of climate on people.

ACTIVITIES

1. Using the map of the United States on pages 456 and 457, classify the cities below according to elevation. Use the elevations shown in the map key as headings for your chart. List each city under the correct heading. (**a**) Washington, D.C., (**b**) Albuquerque, N. Mex., (**c**) Denver, Colo., (**d**) Chicago, Ill., (**e**) Great Falls, Mont., (**f**) Portland, Oreg., (**g**) Madison, Wis., (**h**) Atlanta, Ga., (**i**) Portland, Maine.

2. The map of the United States shows every fifth parallel and meridian. Locate each city below by giving the two parallels and meridians between which it is located. For example, Los Angeles is between 30°N and 35°N, and 115°W and 120°W. (**a**) Washington, D.C., (**b**) Oklahoma City, Okla., (**c**) Detroit, Mich., (**d**) Tampa, Fla., (**e**) the capital of your state.

3. Watch the weather news on television. Make a list of the facts given.

1/SKILLS DEVELOPMENT

USING CONTEXT CLUES

A DICTIONARY GIVES THE MEANINGS OF WORDS

If we do not know the meaning of a word, we may look up the word in a dictionary. Sometimes we find more than one meaning. We then have to choose the meaning that fits the way the word is being used.

SKILLS PRACTICE: Part I

Listed below are statements based on what you have read in Chapter l. One word is underlined in each statement. Listed also are two meanings you would find if you looked up that word in a dictionary. In each case, read the statement. Then choose the meaning that fits the way the word is used in the statement. Write on a separate sheet of paper.

1. The museum scholars at Alexandria knew that the earth is a <u>sphere</u>.
   a. A round object shaped like a ball
   b. The place or range of action
2. Symbols are marks that stand for places and <u>features</u> on the earth's surface.
   a. Any part of the face
   b. The makeup, shape, or outward appearance of something
3. There is no way to judge distances on the clay map because it has no <u>scale</u>.
   a. Thin, flat plates that cover some fish
   b. A series of marks along a line used for measuring
4. Ptolemy wrote a famous <u>geography</u>.
   a. The study of the earth
   b. The natural features of a certain part of the earth
5. Oil, coal, timber, and iron are natural <u>resources</u>.
   a. Supplies of something that people use
   b. Skills in solving problems

6. Looking at the world from Alexandria, it was easy for Ptolemy to think of the three continents as <u>landmasses</u> divided by seas.
   a. The common people
   b. Things of great size
7. Strabo divided the world into torrid, frigid, and <u>temperate</u> zones.
   a. Exercising self-control
   b. Neither very hot nor very cold
8. The weather map shows a <u>front</u> running from Texas to the Great Lakes.
   a. The part that faces forward
   b. A boundary between two large masses of air
9. Aristotle wrote that a cold climate made people active and "full of <u>spirit</u>."
   a. Strength and energy
   b. A being not of this world, such as a ghost
10. Strabo believed that a people's customs and education shaped their <u>character</u> for the most part.
   a. The total of things that make one person or group different from others
   b. The total of things a person does and thinks that are thought of as good

SKILLS PRACTICE: Part II

Suppose you are a wake-up disc jockey at a radio station. Write what you would have told your listeners about the weather this morning. What facts would you have given them? Be sure to write the weather report so that your listeners will know the meanings of difficult words by the way you use them.

Measuring Time

VOCABULARY

reign	circa
Olympiad	decade
era	century
monk	modern
anno Domini	ancient
calendar	time line

Dating events　　The coin shown at the left on the next page has no date, yet we know that it is about 2,300 years old. The lifelike head on one side is the image of King Ptolemy. This is the same King Ptolemy who established the museum at Alexandria. We are sure that it is he because the words on the other side of the coin read: Ptolemy the King. At that time, rulers often put their own images on their coins during their lifetime. Perhaps they thought it impressed people with their greatness. Since we know that this is Ptolemy's coin and that he ruled Egypt nearly 2,300 years ago, we have an idea of the coin's age.

We have no trouble knowing the age of modern coins because they have dates. The date on a penny or quarter tells us the year it was issued. We usually pay little attention to the dates unless we are coin collectors. After all, there are dates on so many things. Newspapers and

magazines have dates. We date the letters we write and, sometimes, school reports. Even books have dates. If you turn to the title page of this book, you will find its date on the other side. Some buildings, such as courthouses and churches, have cornerstones with dates. Do your report cards have dates? Can you think of other things in your classroom or things you use at home that have dates?

A date is a fairly exact idea about time—an idea of *when*. Not all statements about time are dates. To say that Columbus arrived in America "a long time ago" does not give the event a date. The statement is not exact. The date of Columbus's landing was 1492 or, still more exactly, October 12, 1492. Dating an event means giving the year or the day it happened.

Ways to measure time　　To state exactly when an event happened, people needed some way to measure time. Otherwise they could say only that an event happened "in the past" or "a long time ago." They needed some point from which to count days or months or years.

People have invented different systems for measuring time. When King Ptolemy lived, it was common to date events by the years of a king's or queen's **reign** (rān)—the years of his or her rule. They would

A date is a fairly exact idea about time. Find the dates that are on many of the objects pictured on the opposite page. What do these dates tell us?

LIBERTY · IN GOD WE TRUST · 1981 · UNITED STATES · E·PLURIBUS·UNUM · ONE D[OLLAR]

1901

NEW AMSTERDAM

1882

WASHINGTON IRVING
BORN
April 3, 1783,
DIED
Nov. 28, 1859.

BURLINGTON JUNIOR HIGH SCHOOL

BURLINGTON, VERMONT

PERIOD, SEMESTER, AND ANNUAL REPORTS
OF:

Schneider, William

Grade __9__ Division or Course __R. 38__

For the School Year Beginning __Sept. 7, 1960__

L. E. Dyke

Home Room Teacher

[HOS]PITAL BIRTH CERTIFICATE

that Donald Henry Kinkle

[Was]hington County Memorial Hospital of Bartlesville, Oklahoma

[fo]urth day of November A. D. 1935

Witness Whereof the said Hospital has caused this Certificate to

[be s]igned by its duly authorized officer and its Corporate Seal to be here-
[unt]o affixed.

[Direct]or

[Hos]pital

[Numb]er 91

Dorothy Henderson R. n.
Superintendent

This archway leads to the track at Olympia where the ancient Greeks held the Olympian Games every 4 years. The Greeks called each block of 4 years an Olympiad.

say that the army won a battle during the third year of Ptolemy's reign or that he conquered Cyprus (sī′ prəs) in the eleventh year. When a new king or queen came to the throne, people would date by the years of that person's reign beginning with the first.

We still sometimes think this way about time. Perhaps you date an event by remembering that it happened when you were in the third grade. Of course, this means little to others unless they know when you entered the first grade. There was the same difficulty in dating events by reigns—the years that different rulers were in power. One had to know who the kings and queens were and how many years each had ruled.

Eratosthenes, the "all-rounder" of the museum at Alexandria, wanted a better system, one that would not change with each king's or queen's reign. He worked out a system for always counting from the same point in time. The year he chose was that of the first Olympian Games. Eratosthenes realized that most Greek-speaking people, even those in Egypt, knew about the Olympian Games. These were athletic contests held every 4 years at Olympia in Greece. Each block of 4 years was called an **Olympiad.**

Eratosthenes numbered the Olympiads from the first to the most recent. He could then speak of a particular year as the first, second, third, or fourth year of a numbered Olympiad. For example, he could date an event in the second year of Olympiad 34. The next year would be the third year of Olympiad 34. It would still be possible to use Eratosthenes' system. Instead of calling a year 1985, we could speak of it as the first year of Olympiad 691. What would the year 2000 be called?

Eratosthenes drew up a table of dates of important events based on the Olympiads. It is not surprising that he worked out this measurement of time. After all, he tried to measure the size of the earth and made a map of the world. Eratosthenes had a great desire to make knowledge clear and exact. A world map helped him to think more accurately about *where* places were. A table of dates made it possible to think more accurately about *when* events happened.

The man who invented A.D. There have been other systems that number years based on other **eras** (ir′ əz). An era is a stretch of years counted from a set point in history. The Romans, for example, counted from the founding of their city. If we still used the Roman system, the year 1985 would be 2738.

The system we do use today was invented by a man named Dionysius Exiguus (di ə nish′ ē əs eg zig′ yù əs) in the year we call A.D. 525. *Exiguus* means "the Little." We do not know much about Dionysius—not even why he was called Dionysius the Little. We do know that he was a Christian monk. **Monks** were men who belonged to a religious group and lived under rules in a monastery. As a Christian, Dionysius believed that the birth of Christ was the most important moment in history. He decided to number years from that point in time. The year that came 525 years after the birth of Christ he called **anno Domini** (an′ ō dom′ə nī) 525. The Latin words mean "in the year of the Lord." We usually shorten this and use only the letters A.D., so that we write A.D. 525.

Dionysius did not use this system for dating events before the birth of Christ, but others did so. Years were counted back from the birth of Christ. The year before A.D. 1 was numbered 1 before Christ, written as 1 B.C. The year before that was 2 B.C., and so on. By this system of dating, the first Olympian Games took place in 776 B.C. The second, 4 years later, was in 772 B.C. Remember that for dates before Christ's birth, the larger a number is, the earlier is the year it stands for. The smaller the number, the later the year. The date 146 B.C. is earlier than 101 B.C. For years after the birth of Christ, it is the other way. A.D. 101 is earlier than A.D. 146. We ordinarily do not write A.D. before a modern date. It is understood that a year such as 1969 is numbered from A.D. 1.

Dates before Christ can be written in the same way as negative numbers. Some people use a negative sign rather than B.C. They date the first Olympian Games as −776 rather than 776 B.C.

Some writers do not use A.D. or B.C. at all. They prefer to date years as Common Era or Before Common Era. These terms are usually shortened to C.E. and B.C.E. Instead of giving the time of Strabo's life as 63 B.C. to A.D. 24, they write 63 B.C.E. to 24 C.E. This system is clear, but as yet dating by the Common Era is not common. In this book, we use B.C. and A.D. When no letters are given, the date is A.D.

Calendars   The system of dating by the Christian era is not the only way people count time today. Some people use other **calendars** to measure and number months and years differently. Jews count the years of their religious seasons from a year that would be called 3760 B.C. by the Christian calendar. Moslems count time from A.D. 622 by the Christian calendar. Something that took place in January 1985 of the Christian calendar would be in 5745 by the Jewish calendar. This would be 1405 by the Moslem calendar because it has a shorter year than the Christian calendar.

Today the Christian calendar is the most widely used all over the world. Dionysius may have been "the Little," but his invention had a big effect on later times. Every time we write a date, we make use of his system. Even people who use C.E. and B.C.E. measure time from the same year as Dionysius.

These ruins are part of Stonehenge, a structure built in England about 4,000 years ago. At sunrise on the first day of summer every year, the shadow of the distant stone is cast through the center of this arch.

This ancient Roman calendar stone shows 7 days of the week across the top and 12 months in a year around the circle at the center.

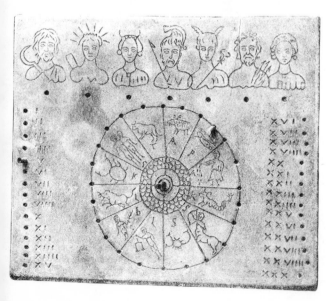

Useful terms about time   We do not always know the exact year of an event even though we know about when it happened. We are not exactly sure of the year Eratosthenes was born. In such a case we write ca. or c. before the date that is our best guess. These letters stand for **circa** (sėr′ kə), a Latin word meaning "about." To show that our knowledge is not exact, we date Eratosthenes's birth as ca. 276 B.C. This practice would surely have pleased him because he valued accurate knowledge so highly. To be accurate we must admit that an uncertain date is uncertain.

Decades and centuries   We can date by 10-year blocks of time as well as by years. A stretch of 10 years is called a **decade.** It is useful to speak of a decade, such as the 1930s or 1960s, when we refer to events that took place over several years.

We also use blocks of 100-year periods, called **centuries,** to date the past. We number centuries as we number years. The 100-year stretch of time starting with A.D. 1 and continuing to the end of A.D. 100 is the first century. The years from A.D. 101 to A.D. 200 are the second century and so on. We now live in the years between 1901 and 2000, so we live in the twentieth century of the Christian (or Common) Era. Note that except for the year 2000, the twentieth century is the 1900s. In the same way, the 1800s were the nineteenth century, the 1700s the eighteenth, and so on.

It is useful to date by centuries when thinking of things that happen over many years. We say that the Americans moved west in the nineteenth century, the 100 years starting with 1801 and going to the end of 1900. We date some people's lives only by the century in which they lived. We cannot even make a careful guess as to the dates of their birth and death. Such is the case with Claudius Ptolemy, the scholar of Alexandria. Even though Ptolemy wrote very important books, we know only that he lived in the second century A.D.

Ancient and modern times   There are certain terms about time that although not exact are useful. One of these is the

There are 10 years in a decade and 10 decades in a century.

A CENTURY HAS 10 DECADES AND 100 YEARS

CENTURIES (A.D. 1001 to 2000)	DECADES (of the 20th Century)	YEARS (of the 1980s)
A.D. 2000 / A.D. 1901 — 20th Century A.D.	A.D. 2000 — 1990s	A.D. 1990 — 1990
A.D. 1801 — 19th Century A.D.	1980s	1989
18th Century A.D.	1970s	1988
A.D. 1701 — 17th Century A.D.	1960s	1987
A.D. 1601 — 16th Century A.D.	1950s	1986
A.D. 1501 — 15th Century A.D.	1940s	1985
A.D. 1401 — 14th Century A.D.	1930s	1984
A.D. 1301 — 13th Century A.D.	1920s	1983
A.D. 1201 — 12th Century A.D.	1910s	1982
A.D. 1101 — 11th Century A.D.	A.D. 1901 — 1900s	A.D. 1981 — 1981
A.D. 1001		

word **modern.** *Modern* means the present or recent, so we say we are living in modern times. But how far back does the present or recent go? Were your parents born in modern times? They certainly think so—even if you do not. It may seem strange, but in history the last several centuries are called modern times. They are called modern because they are much closer to now than to the period long past called **ancient** times.

How long ago must something have been to be ancient? It, too, is not an exact term. But it gives us a way to say that Eratosthenes, Strabo, and Claudius Ptolemy lived a very long time age. They did not live at the same time, but they all lived in ancient times. Gabriel Fahrenheit lived much nearer to our own day even though he developed his thermometer scale about 1724. We call Fahrenheit's thermometer a modern invention.

Time lines   You read in Chapter 1 that a map is a chart that shows facts about

places. There are also charts, such as that below and the one on the opposite page called **time lines.** They show facts about time. A time line, like a map, has a scale. A map scale measures distance; a time line scale measures time.

Both time lines have scales that run from the left of the page to the right. The scale for the time line on this page states that 1 inch (2.54 cm) stands for 500 years. The whole time line shows 3,000 years, from 1000 B.C. to A.D. 2000, still in the future. Along the line are listed people and events that are placed next to their time. The time line makes it easy to see the order of events. It shows that the Olympian Games began long before King Ptolemy established the museum.

The time line makes clear how very long is the stretch of years we call ancient. The time between the first Olympian Games and Claudius Ptolemy is shorter than that between his lifetime and our own. You can see why Gabriel Fahrenheit is said to be a modern man.

The shaded area on this time line represents the same period of years shown on the time line at the top of the next page.

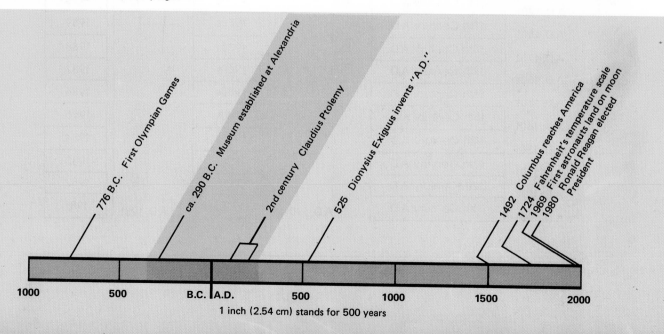

776 B.C. First Olympian Games

ca. 290 B.C. Museum established at Alexandria

2nd century Claudius Ptolemy

525 Dionysius Exiguus invents "A.D."

1492 Columbus reaches America
1724 Fahrenheit's temperature scale
1969 First astronauts land on moon
1980 Ronald Reagan elected President

1000   500   B.C. | A.D.   500   1000   1500   2000

1 inch (2.54 cm) stands for 500 years

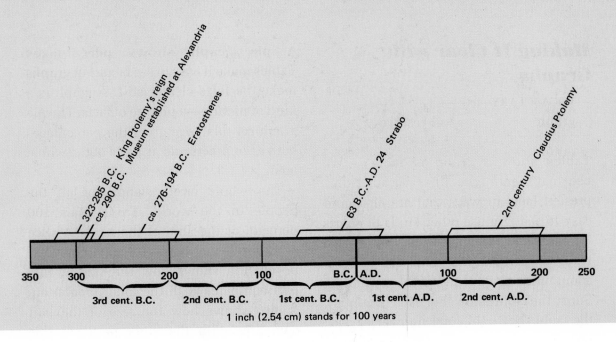

323-285 B.C. King Ptolemy's reign
ca. 290 B.C. Museum established at Alexandria
ca. 276-194 B.C. Eratosthenes
63 B.C.-A.D. 24 Strabo
2nd century Claudius Ptolemy

| 350 | 300 | 200 | 100 | B.C. | A.D. | 100 | 200 | 250 |

3rd cent. B.C.   2nd cent. B.C.   1st cent. B.C.   1st cent. A.D.   2nd cent. A.D.

1 inch (2.54 cm) stands for 100 years

This time line is drawn at a larger scale than the time line at the left.

The above time line shows a much shorter length of time. The scale for it shows that 1 inch (2.54 cm) stands for 100 years. The period shown along this line is marked on the longer time line. The top time line has a larger scale so it is possible to show shorter periods of time in greater detail. It is easy to see that although Eratosthenes, Strabo, and Claudius Ptolemy lived in ancient times, they did not live at the same time.

You will find time lines throughout this book. They will help you understand ideas about time and the order of people and events more clearly. Maps will help you know where people lived; time lines will help you know when they lived. Remember, in using a chart it is always important to think about scale.

A plaque just like the one pictured here was left on the moon by the first astronauts to land there. Find the date on the plaque and locate this event on the time line at the left.

HERE MEN FROM THE PLANET EARTH
FIRST SET FOOT UPON THE MOON
JULY 1969, A. D.
WE CAME IN PEACE FOR ALL MANKIND

NEIL A. ARMSTRONG
ASTRONAUT

MICHAEL COLLINS
ASTRONAUT

EDWIN E. ALDRIN, JR.
ASTRONAUT

RICHARD NIXON
PRESIDENT, UNITED STATES OF AMERICA

CHECKUP

1. Name three things in your classroom that have dates on them.
2. What are two ways to number years besides the one commonly used today?
3. What does ca. 1850 mean?
4. How many years in a decade? How many years in a century? How many decades in a century? In which decade do you live? What century is the 1500s?
5. Which is the earliest date? (a) 744 B.C., (b) 768 B.C., (c) 124 B.C., (d) A.D. 1. Strabo lived from 63 B.C. until A.D. 24. How many years did he live?

37

Making It Clear with Graphs

Tables show a group of facts We use maps and time lines because they present facts in ways that are clear and easy to see. We use other kinds of charts for the same reason. Let us look at two ways to present the same set of facts about where the peoples of the world live. Study the table below. For each continent, the table shows the total number of people and the percentage of the total world population. Often percentages are easier to grasp than raw numbers. (Remember that 58 percent is 8 percent more than half because 100% always stands for the total. That is a way of saying 58 percent equals 58 of 100.) It is easier to understand that about 58 percent of the world's people live in Asia than to know that 2,670,000,000 out of 4,585,000,000 people in the world are Asians. The table is one way to make it easy to compare figures.

A pie graph shows percentages Tables make it easy to see facts, but **graphs** make the facts clearer still. A graph is a kind of picture—a picture of facts. The pie graph on this page gives the percentages both as numbers and as parts of the whole area.

The whole circle stands for all the people in the world. This equals 100 percent, or the sum of the parts. A slice of the circle that stands for part of the total population shows how the size of that part compares with the total population. It also shows how the size of the part compares with the other parts. In this way, a pie graph makes it quick and easy to see facts and to understand what the facts have to do with each other. It also shows a clear way to represent figures as parts of a total.

This pie graph makes it easy to see how large one part is compared with the other parts.

POPULATION OF THE WORLD BY CONTINENT
(Figures are rounded)

Continent	Number of people	Percent of world's population
Africa	498,000,000	10.9
Asia	2,671,000,000	58.3
Australia and Oceania	24,000,000	.5
Europe	758,000,000	16.5
North America	381,000,000	8.3
South America	252,000,000	5.5
Total	4,585,000,000	100.0

WHERE THE WORLD'S PEOPLES LIVE

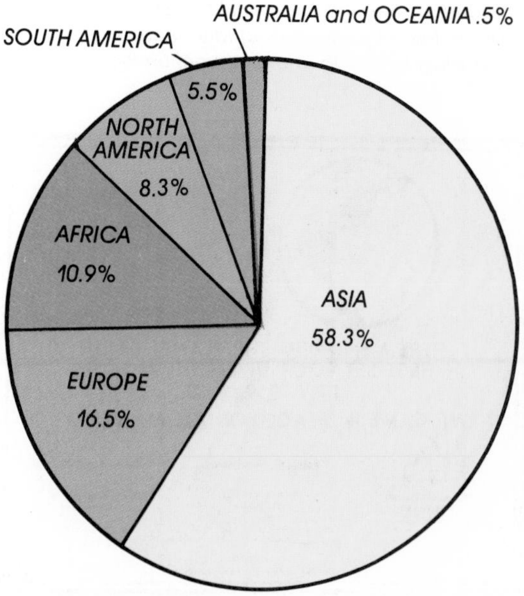

AUSTRALIA and OCEANIA .5%
SOUTH AMERICA 5.5%
NORTH AMERICA 8.3%
AFRICA 10.9%
EUROPE 16.5%
ASIA 58.3%

Pictographs A pictograph is a chart that uses picture-symbols to stand for fixed amounts of some selected thing. On this graph, the picture of a barrel stands for 10,000,000,000 barrels of **oil reserves.** Oil reserves are the amount of oil known to be still in the ground in a country.

This pictograph shows the amount of oil reserves located in each country listed. To find the size of a country's reserves, count the number of barrels pictured for that country and multiply by the amount of oil that the barrel symbol represents.

In the pictograph below, the barrel is a symbol that stands for 10 billion barrels of oil. The bar graph to the right gives two kinds of information about the populations of Sweden and Upper Volta. It shows total population. It also shows the number of people under 15 years of age.

Bar graphs show comparisons Each of the bars on a bar graph stands for a fact or set of facts. Since they are placed alongside each other, it is easy to compare these facts. The bar graph below shows two sets of facts about the populations of two countries. The countries are Sweden in Europe and Upper Volta in West Africa.

A glance at the bar graph tells which country has more people. But the bars tell more. Each pair of bars shows what part of the population is under 15 years of age in each country. By comparing the bars, you quickly see that Sweden has more people. But you also learn that Upper Volta has more people under the age of 15. Can you think of ways that this would affect the services each country needs?

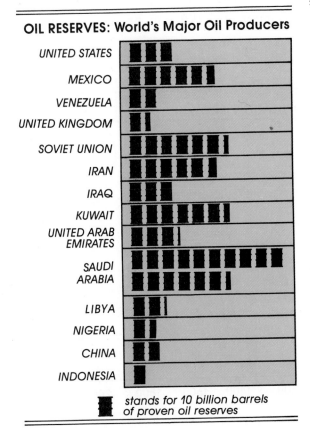

OIL RESERVES: World's Major Oil Producers

■ stands for 10 billion barrels of proven oil reserves

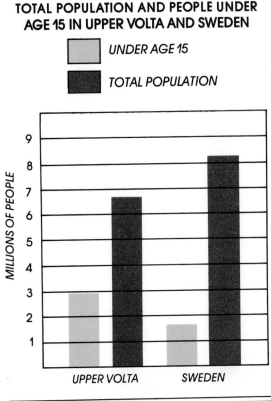

TOTAL POPULATION AND PEOPLE UNDER AGE 15 IN UPPER VOLTA AND SWEDEN

Line graphs tell stories It is also easy to compare things clearly on a line graph. Generally it is the best kind of graph for showing the change in something over a stretch of time. You would use a line graph to show how much you grow or how your weight changes from week to week during the year. A line graph could show the second-by-second change in the speed of a rocket from blastoff to splashdown. In fact, you could use a line graph to show almost anything as it keeps on changing: the size of a block of ice as it melts, or the daily temperature from season to season.

Let us look at how a line graph is a good way to show something as it becomes more or less as time passes. One of the most important facts about the world during the last 200 years has been the rapid increase in the total number of people. For centuries the world's population had increased at a very slow rate. There were periods during which it probably did not grow at all. All this changed after 1800. The world's population began shooting up at an increasing rate. It has continued to do so. The line graph below tells this important story.

The graph has two scales. The bottom scale stands for years, somewhat like a time line. The scale on the right measures total number of people. Even a quick look at the line shows what happened. The world's population did, indeed, shoot up. It does not take long to tell this story with a line graph.

By adding lines to a line graph it is possible to show more sets of facts. The line graph on page 41 gives two sets of facts about the climate of two cities: Copenhagen (kō pən hā gən), Denmark,

On this line graph, you can tell how quickly the world population grew during any period of years. A sharper rise in the line stands for greater growth.

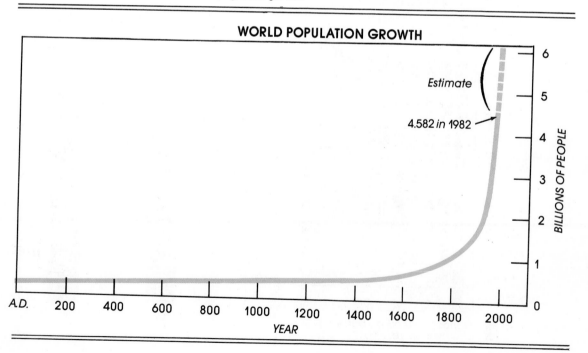

WORLD POPULATION GROWTH

Estimate

4.582 in 1982

BILLIONS OF PEOPLE

A.D. 200 400 600 800 1000 1200 1400 1600 1800 2000

YEAR

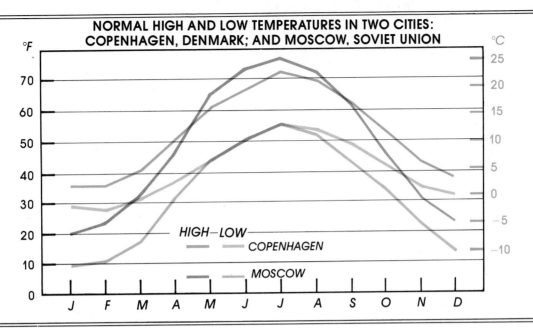

**NORMAL HIGH AND LOW TEMPERATURES IN TWO CITIES:
COPENHAGEN, DENMARK; AND MOSCOW, SOVIET UNION**

°F

°C

HIGH—LOW
COPENHAGEN
MOSCOW

J F M A M J J A S O N D

*This line graph gives two sets of facts about the cities of Copenhagen and Moscow. It
shows the usual high and the usual low temperatures for each month of the year.*

and Moscow, Soviet Union. Both cities are 55.4 degrees north of the Equator. But Copenhagen is near a large body of water, and Moscow is in the middle of Eurasia. Find these cities on the map of Eurasia on pages 466 and 467. The graph shows changes in temperature during the year.

In Chapter 1 you read that places near the ocean are usually neither as cold in winter nor as hot in summer as places far inland. The lines on the graph show that location near the water makes a great deal of difference. The lines show the usual high and low temperatures for each month in the two cities. The two shades of red lines are for Moscow. The two shades of blue lines are for Copenhagen. Since the lines rise and fall with the temperatures, the graph makes the facts easy to see. You may want to make a line graph showing the usual high and low temperatures for where you live. How

would a graph like this one help you see the differences between your climate and that of Copenhagen or Moscow?

In this book you have pictures, maps, graphs, tables, and charts to read as well as words. They help you learn about who, what, when, where, how, and why. All of these are ways to tell a story about peoples and the world in which they live. What are some interesting facts about where you live that would be easy to show on a graph or chart?

CHECKUP

1. What is a pie graph? Why might it be called "a picture of percentages"?
2. What is a pictograph?
3. What is a bar graph?
4. After studying the bar graph on page 39, how do you answer the question, "Are more people in Sweden younger than age 15 or are more people age 15 and older?"
5. What is the advantage of a line graph?

41

KEY FACTS

1. To date events there must be a system for measuring time.

2. People have invented and used different systems to measure time: the reigns of kings and queens, the Olympiads, the Common and Christian eras, and many different calendars.

3. There are 10 years in a decade, and 100 years in a century.

4. Time lines show the order of events and different lengths of time.

5. Graphs present facts so that comparisons can be quickly and clearly shown.

6. A line graph is a good way to show how something changes over a period of time.

VOCABULARY QUIZ

Choose the word in the list below that could be used in place of the underlined words in the statements that follow. Write your answers on a sheet of paper.

a. era   **f.** oil reserves

b. decade   **g.** ancient

c. monk   **h.** Olympiads

d. century   **i.** anno Domini

e. circa   **j.** reign

1. The Greeks measured time by 4-year periods.

2. Socrates was born about 470 B.C.

3. The rule of King Louis the Fat of France lasted from A.D. 1108 to 1137.

4. Although Eratosthenes lived in long-ago times, he knew the earth is a sphere.

5. In the year of the Lord 1979, the Soviet Union had more oil reserves than all but one country.

6. The date in question 5 is given in the Christian period of time.

7. The man who lived in a monastery kept a record of each year's events.

8. There are 10 decades in 100 years.

9. Many Middle Eastern countries have large amounts of oil that are still in the ground.

10. Television became common in the United States during the 10-year period of the 1950s.

REVIEW QUESTIONS

1. Why is the year of the first Olympian Games called 776 B.C.? Would people living then have called it that? Explain your answer.

2. Hypatia, a scholar in Egypt, was born A.D. 370 and lived 45 years. When did she die? In which century did Hypatia die?

3. Caesar Augustus, a Roman emperor, was born in 63 B.C. and lived 77 years. When did he die? In which century did he die?

4. Which continent has the second largest number of people?

5. Is it true that the world's population has more than tripled since 1800?

ACTIVITIES

1. Make a time line to show your family's history or the history of your community. First make a list of the things that you will show. Decide how many years you want to show and choose a scale so that you can fit everything on one sheet of paper. Now use a ruler to place the events in the order that they occurred at the right places along the line.

2. Make a graph comparing the populations of France, Great Britain, West Germany, East Germany, Italy, and Spain. You may make whichever kind of graph you think will show the facts clearly. Population figures are given in the tables beginning on page 486.

2/SKILLS DEVELOPMENT

READING TIME LINES

SCALE SHOWS LENGTH OF TIME

A time line shows when events took place. Some time lines also show for how long something took place, such as the number of years King Ptolemy ruled. It is also easy to tell the length of time between two events on a time line. To find this information you must read the scale of the time line. The scale tells you how many years are represented by an inch or a centimeter on the time line.

SKILLS PRACTICE

The time lines on pages 36 and 37 have two different scales. Read the scale at the bottom of each time line and then answer the following questions.

1. How long must the line be to show 500 years on the scale on page 36? On the scale on page 37?

2. How many years does 2 inches (5.08 cm) stand for on the first scale? How many years does the same length stand for on the second scale?

3. How many years did Eratosthenes live?

4. How many years passed between the time of the first Olympian Games and when Columbus reached America?

5. Tell which time period was longer: (**a**) between the first Olympian Games and the establishment of the museum at Alexandria or (**b**) between Fahrenheit's invention and today.

PUTTING EVENTS IN SEQUENCE

The time of events shown on a time line are put in the order, or sequence, in which they occurred. Listed below are ten events in the typical day of a student. The events are not listed in the order in which they would happen. Study the events.

Go to bed at night
Leave for school
Eat dinner
Leave school for home
Do homework

Eat breakfast
Change to play clothes
Get up in the morning
Eat lunch at school
Begin schoolwork

SKILLS PRACTICE

1. On a piece of paper, write these events in the order in which you would do them.

2. On the same sheet of paper, draw two time lines like those shown below. Each space on the lines stands for one hour of a day. Mark on the time lines the times at which you would do the ten events.

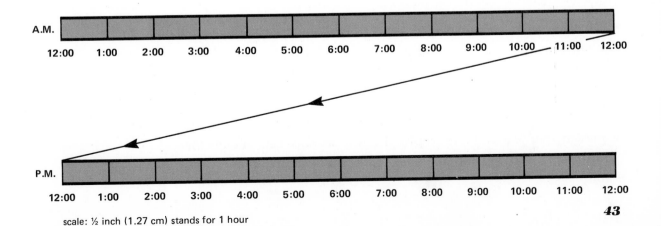

scale: ½ inch (1.27 cm) stands for 1 hour

1/UNIT REVIEW

1. Knowledge of maps, graphs, special terms, and ways to measure time makes it easier to find and understand other information. This knowledge is like a tool because of how it helps you. — *What two kinds of information can be clearly shown on a time line?*

2. A map is a drawing that uses symbols to stand for real places and features of the earth's surface. Map scale tells the ratio between distances on the map and real distances on the earth. — *What different kinds of information can be found in a map key? If you made a map of your community, what places and features would you show by using symbols? How would you use color on your map?*

3. The invention of latitude and longitude makes it easier to locate places on both flat maps and globes of the earth. — *What is the latitude and longitude of Alexandria, Egypt?*

4. Maps also show facts about people and what they do. Other maps show information about weather and climate. — *If you wanted to go mountain climbing in August, what kinds of maps do you think would be useful to plan your trip?*

5. We divide the landmasses of the earth into seven continents, and the earth's water into four major oceans. — *What are the names of the continents and oceans? Which hemispheres is each in?*

6. Weather is a condition of the air at a set time and place. Climate is the usual weather for a place over a period of years. — *What conditions make up weather? How is climate affected by elevation and the location of a place on the earth's surface?*

7. People find ways to get around the limits of weather and climate. — *After studying your community, what examples can you give for the ways people have gotten around the limits of your climate?*

8. To date events, we must count years from some fixed point, such as the first Olympian Games or the birth of Christ. — *What eras besides the Christian era have been used to number years? Make a list of different eras by looking up "calendar" in the* World Almanac *or an encyclopedia.*

9. Graphs are ways to present facts clearly. A pie chart illustrates portions or percentages. Bar and line graphs give two or more sets of facts for comparison. — *What kind of comparison can be clearly shown on a line graph?*

Beginnings of Western Civilization

3 Cities and Kingdoms in Mesopotamia and Egypt

The Advantages of City Life

┌─VOCABULARY─────────────┐
| silt | token |
| citadel | cuneiform |
└────────────────────────┘

Nippur on the Euphrates River   The picture on the opposite page shows all that is left of the city of Nippur (nip ůr′). There is nothing there but the mound of crumbling brick. A modern building stands on top. It was built about 80 years ago by scholars searching the ruins. The ruins of Nippur are left from the city that began more than 4,000 years ago. Before 2000 B.C. thousands of people lived there. A gleaming temple stood on the brick platform that is now only a crumbling mound. What is now desert was then a place of gardens and green fields of barley and wheat. Now all that is left are these ruins in southern Iraq, a country of southwest Asia.

What happened to bring so great a change? For one thing, a river changed its course. Today, as in ancient times, much of Iraq is a desert. But it is watered by two great rivers, the Tigris (tī′ grəs) and the Euphrates (yü frā′ tēz). They flow from the mountains and highlands of Turkey across Iraq to the Persian Gulf. Find these rivers on the map on page 49. In 2000 B.C. the waters of the Euphrates ran alongside the walls of Nippur. The people of Nippur had built canals from the river through the city. Small boats could dock inside the walls. Other canals carried water to irrigate the fields outside the walls. But today, the Euphrates is 20 miles away. The remains of Nippur bake in the desert sun.

Why did the Euphrates River change course? When the springtime floods rush down from the highlands, the Euphrates washes tons of soil down to the flat river plain. As the river flows across the flatlands the water moves more slowly. The soil in the water, called **silt**, settles to the bottom. The riverbed gradually fills up until the stream flows over the plain, cutting new channels. Both the Tigris and the Euphrates have changed their courses a number of times in the past 4,000 years.

Before there were cities   Not all people lived in cities, nor have there always been cities to live in. Before people learned how to grow crops and raise animals for food, families and small groups of people lived on wild food. People gathered nuts, fruits, and grains. They also caught fish and other wildlife to eat. When a certain place no longer could yield enough food, the group moved. Roaming was a way of life. People searched for enough to eat and places to stay that were protected from danger and bad weather.

The ruins of Nippur are in the country of Iraq. Find Nippur on the map on page 49.

As people learned how to raise their own food they could stay in one place. Planting crops and keeping animals became a new way of life. The work to be done also changed. People no longer had to prepare to move or to look for new and sheltered places to live. Homes were built to last longer and to give better protection. People lived together in some places that became growing villages. As people learned more about growing crops, there was enough food for more people. People discovered the advantages of city life as some of these villages grew into cities such as Nippur.

Other early cities in southwest Asia Nippur was only one of a number of cities in southwest Asia 4,000 years ago. Other cities grew up along the Tigris and the Euphrates. The Greeks later called this land Mesopotamia (mes ə pə tā′ mē ə). The name means "land between the rivers." But Mesopotamia became the name of the whole river plain. A people known as the Sumerians (sü mir′ ē ənz) built the first cities in Mesopotamia before 3000 B.C., more than 5,000 years ago. Ur (ər) and Uruk (ü′ rùk) were two of the Sumerian cities. Other peoples who invaded Mesopotamia copied the Sumerians and built cities of their own, such as Akkad (ak′ ad) and Babylon (bab′ ə lən). The cities of the Sumerians, Akkadians, and Babylonians were much alike. We call all of these people Mesopotamians. It is interesting to note that Ur, Uruk, Akkad, and Babylon are all mentioned in the Bible.

There were also cities in other parts of southwest Asia. Near the eastern end of the Mediterranean Sea, cities grew up where people farmed fertile land. Jericho (jer′ i kō) was in the Jordan River valley. It was, perhaps, one of the world's first cities. Ebla (eb′ lə) grew up in the country we now call Syria (sir′ ē ə). Ebla had more than 22,000 people living within its walls 4,000 years ago.

The stretch of land from Jericho up to Ebla and around through Mesopotamia is often called the Fertile Crescent. Look at

How many years are there between the rise of Akkad and the rise of Babylon?

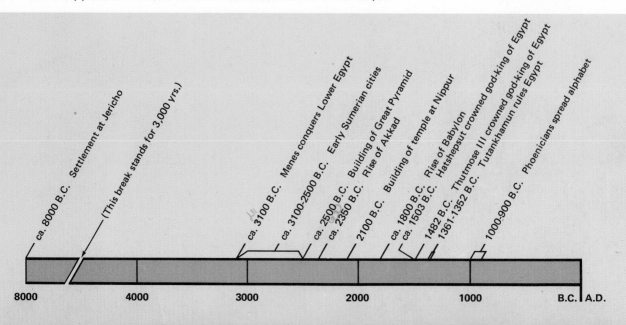

the map below. If you put your finger on Jericho and move it north to Ebla, then down the Tigris and Euphrates rivers to the Persian Gulf, you will make a curved shape, or crescent, on the map.

Cities of mud brick   The rivers and canals that supplied water for Mesopotamia also supplied building material for its cities. There was no building stone on the flat river plain. There were also very few trees for lumber. The rough trunks of the date-palm tree could be used for posts or beams, but there were not enough date palms to build whole houses. Wood was precious. Most of it had to be brought down from the mountain forests to the north. But another material was plentiful on the plain—mud.

This aerial view of the Tigris River shows that the river has made several courses in its plain.

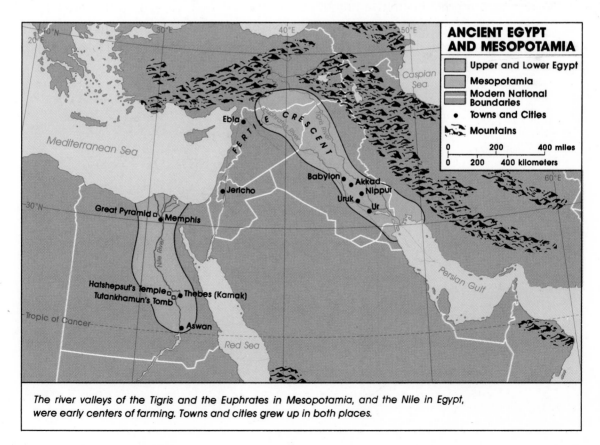

The river valleys of the Tigris and the Euphrates in Mesopotamia, and the Nile in Egypt, were early centers of farming. Towns and cities grew up in both places.

49

People dug sticky clay mud from the banks of the rivers and ditches. They shaped it into flat bricks that they dried in the sun. The sun-baked bricks became hard enough to be stacked for walls of houses. They could be piled together to make a solid platform such as the base of the temple that once stood at Nippur.

The sun-dried bricks served well enough in dry weather. But heavy rains sometimes beat on the plains of Mesopotamia during winter months. The downpours softened the sun-dried bricks. Walls weakened and fell. People discovered that when clay bricks were first dried and then baked in a fire they did not soften in the rains. Sometimes the Mesopotamians laid a layer of fire-baked bricks over sun-dried ones.

Wood was too precious to use much of it to fuel fires for baking bricks. So Mesopotamians used fire-baked bricks mostly for important buildings such as temples. Other buildings were simply repaired or replaced after the rains. When walls fell, the people trampled the old bricks into the earth, and built on top of them. By building again and again on top of fallen walls, they gradually raised the levels of their cities.

The advantages of living behind walls Today, American cities spread over large areas. People no longer live crowded together within city walls. People have moved farther and farther out from the old centers as towns have grown larger. It is often hard to know where a city ends unless you see a city limits sign.

Ancient cities were very different. Thick walls surrounded the city like a fort. The protected area was called the **citadel**, and people wanted to live within the walls. In fact, living within the walls was one of the

A model of part of the city of ancient Ur shows a street and the inside of a house.

main reasons why people lived in cities. Walls meant protection from bandits. Walls kept out the bands of raiders from the desert who came seeking food.

Walls also meant greater safety in times of war. Wars were common among the cities, and those people captured were either killed or made slaves. The citadel was the safest place to live at that time. The protection of the wall was one of the main advantages of city life.

The advantage of doing each other's work Another advantage of living in a city was that each family did not have to gather or grow all of its own food. Some families grew enough food for others to eat. Farm villages nearby produced grain, turnips, onions, and lettuce, which city dwellers ate. Other people caught fish and brought them to the city. Shepherds kept flocks of sheep for meat and wool.

Since city dwellers could count on others for much of their food, they were free to do other kinds of work. Some made wooden benches. Some made cooking pots. Others spun and wove wool into cloth. People who grew food depended on other workers for these kinds of goods. The weaver made cloth for those who kept sheep. The potter made pots for those who grew food. The bench maker depended on others, and others depended on him.

Because people spent most of their time doing one kind of work, they became good at it. Shepherds learned more about caring for sheep. Weavers produced more and better cloth. This was one of the advantages of city life.

One bad part about people doing each other's work is that some jobs were less desirable than others. It was tiresome to sit all day weaving cloth. It was also hard

Diners attend a banquet at Ur. Other people bring animals and supplies.

work in the hot fields to stand all day breaking the earth with a hoe. The kind of work a person did was mainly a matter of luck. A girl or a boy born into a family of field workers grew up to work in the fields. Children of weavers usually became weavers. Perhaps this was unfair, but city life depended on people working for each other. It still does, and some jobs are still harder than others.

This golden bull's head, its hair and beard made out of blue stone, shows the skill of Mesopotamian artists. The memory aid tokens below stand for: 1. cloth; 2. oil; 3. sheep; 4. cattle; and 5. metal.

An important invention: making marks for words   One job in the city was keeping accounts of how much barley, wool, and other goods were put into the storehouses. We call people who do this work bookkeepers.

To keep their records straight, bookkeepers needed some way to help them remember each account. The use of memory aids was not new even then. The picture on this page shows some very old memory aids. Small pieces, or **tokens,** of baked clay were used to represent particular things. One kind of token stood for a sheep, another for a cow, a third for a bundle of wool. To remember how many sheep were in a flock, a person could put the same number of sheep tokens into a bag or pot. As the flock increased, more sheep tokens were added. If sheep were lost, tokens could be taken away.

Mesopotamian bookkeepers invented a somewhat similar way to keep accounts. Instead of keeping tokens, the bookkeepers made marks on smooth tablets of soft clay mud. They wrote the records of their cities on the same material from which they built them.

Writing develops   There were three steps in the invention of writing. First the bookkeepers made pictures of *things*. To write the word ox, they drew the head of an ox, as the chart shows. Three trees meant "orchard". The bookkeepers took the second step by making marks that stood for *actions* rather than things. Some of these marks were pictures too. The drawing of a mouth meant "speaking." Pictures of a mouth and food together meant "eating."

The third step was the greatest. It was the use of marks to stand for sounds. Sometimes the mark was a picture, but it did not mean the thing pictured. It stood for the *sound* of the name. Perhaps you have worked puzzles in which pictures stood for sounds. A picture of a bee stands for the sound *B* rather than the insect. A picture of a leaf stands for the sound, not what grows on a tree. When the two pictures are put together, you get the following result:

🐝 + 🍃 = **belief**

Writers in Mesopotamia made their marks on clay tablets with three-cornered sticks. The writing material affected how they wrote. In time they gave up drawing line pictures. They simply pushed the end of the stick into the clay to make wedge-shaped marks. This kind of writing is

HOW EARLY WRITING DEVELOPED				
Meaning	Picture Writing		Cuneiform	
	early symbol	in a different position	early	later
Bird				
Fish				
Ox				
Sun/Day				
Grain				
Orchard				

Early writing changed from actual pictures of things—such as a bird or fish—to symbols.

This cuneiform tablet from Ebla shows a writing exercise done by a student.

called **cuneiform** (kyü nē ′ ə fôrm). The word means "wedge form." The cuneiform words did not look like the pictures of things. The chart shows how much they changed.

Today when we write, we generally use marks that stand for sounds. All the words on this page were written with the 26 sound marks that we call the alphabet. The people of Mesopotamia did not invent an alphabet. That is a story told in Chapter 5. But the city dwellers of that land did invent the main idea of writing—making marks for words.

Ancient words of wisdom preserved
Writing began as a memory aid for bookkeepers, but people found many other uses for this invention. Rulers sent orders to officials. People made written contracts,

or agreements, to carry on their business. Kings and queens had laws written down on clay or stone. Stories and poems could be passed along even when people died or forgot them.

We know what people wrote about because scholars have read thousands of the clay tablets. Writing on clay lasts longer than printing on paper, such as in this book. In 1975 scholars found nearly 15,000 tablets in the ruins of the city of Ebla in Syria. Ebla was not a Mesopotamian city, but the tablets were written in cuneiform. The Ebla tablets were part of a library that had burned ca. 2250 B.C. A fire in a modern library would destroy the books, but it baked the clay tablets. They are as hard as fire-baked bricks.

Because modern scholars can read clay tablets, we can know what ancient people thought. Their words have lasted longer than their cities. Nippur is a crumbling mound, but here are some of the wise sayings found in cuneiform on tablets from this ancient Mesopotamian city:

He who eats too much can't sleep.
If you tell a lie today, people will not believe the truth you tell tomorrow.
A kind word is everybody's friend.
A loving heart builds the home; a hating heart destroys the home.

CHECKUP

1. Why did the Tigris and Euphrates rivers change courses from time to time?
2. Why did people in Mesopotamia build cities of mud brick?
3. Why did cities in Mesopotamia have walls?
4. Why was it an advantage for people to depend on the work of each other?
5. What is writing? Why do we still have material that was written more than 3,000 years ago in southwest Asia?

The Beginning of Governments and Laws

VOCABULARY
empire

Keeping order   In a city someone must be in charge. Some person, or group of persons, must manage the affairs of the city. They must direct the work of others, since all depend on each other. Someone must settle disputes so that the city is not upset by fighting. Someone must keep people from robbing or harming others. In ancient Mesopotamia both priests and kings were in charge of the cities.

Priests and temples   Priests had very important positions, for they were in charge of the city's temple. The people of Mesopotamia believed in many gods. They believed certain gods controlled the weather, crops, health, love, and almost everything else. Each city— even each village—had its own god and a house for the god. In a village the god's house would be only a small room. In a city the god's house was a temple, usually built on top of a solid brick platform.

Priests were also in charge of the temple property. Part of the land around the city belonged to its god. The priests managed the land and saw to it that grain and livestock were brought to the temple storehouses. The priests also collected grain, wool, and cattle from the city dwellers as offerings to the god. These offerings and the products of the temple lands supported the priests and others who served the god. The priests also gave food to orphans and other people in need.

Why did people build costly temples and make offerings to the god? The reason is much the same as for building city walls. People thought their safety depended on these practices. They believed that if the god was pleased, then the city would be safe and enjoy good times. If the god was not pleased, there would be troubles, such as hunger, sickness, and defeat in battle.

Wars, rulers, and empires   When cities first began, each ruled itself. There was no one government over all Mesopotamia. Sometimes cities quarreled over land and there was war. That was one reason for city walls.

In time of war, cities often chose one person to be their leader, whom they called the "Big Man." They gave the Big Man power over the whole city because they feared defeat. As noted before, defeat in war often meant death or slavery.

Once a Big Man got power he did not always give it up. He continued to rule the city even when danger had passed. In city after city the Big Man became a king. One such city king, Sargon the Great, ruled Akkad from ca. 2334 to 2279 B.C. What was so great about Sargon? He was a great war leader. He was not content to rule his city of Akkad only. He made war against other cities and brought all Mesopotamia under his rule.

Sargon the Great created the world's first empire. An **empire** is many different lands brought under the rule of one government. You may not think that this was such a great deed. But Sargon was not the last person to be called great because he conquered an empire.

Kings and laws   Some of the kings were not just war leaders. They also gave the people laws. City life required—and still requires—laws. People who live and work together closely need rules so that they know what they may and may not do. They need laws that make them do what they should do. The laws of the Mesopotamian kings did both.

We know about many of the ancient laws because they were written on clay and stone. We know most about the laws of King Hammurabi (häm ù rä′ bē), who became king of Babylon ca. 1700 B.C. Hammurabi's laws were carved on a pillar of hard stone.

Some of Hammurabi's laws now seem as hard as the stone on which they were carved. Some of them required that a per-

Hammurabi is given the right to rule by a god. You can see Hammurabi's laws carved on the stone pillar below. The pillar, found broken, has been repaired.

son who caused an injury receive the same injury.

> If a man put out the eye of a noble, they shall put out his eye.
> If he breaks the bone of a noble, they shall break his bone.
> If he knocks out the tooth of a noble, they shall knock out his tooth.

This hard "eye for an eye" rule applied only if the wronged person was of the highest, or noble, class. It did not apply if he was a common man. Hammurabi's laws did not treat people as equals.

> If a man has knocked out the eye of a common man or broken the bone of a common man, he shall pay one large piece of silver.

Hammurabi's laws held people responsible for careless acts that did harm:

> If a man causes the loss of goods, he shall pay back what he has destroyed.
> If a man leaves an irrigation ditch open and destroys another's crop, he must pay damages.
> If a boatman loses another's goods, he must pay for them.

We still think these laws fair. They are much like our laws.

Hammurabi declared that the Babylonians should keep his laws "to the end of time." Babylon did not last that long. Today Hammurabi's city is in ruins. It has gone the way of Nippur. But the idea that people should be held responsible for what they do has lasted. It is as important today as it was 4,000 years ago.

CHECKUP

1. Why did people in the Mesopotamian cities build temples and make offerings in them?
2. Why did the Mesopotamian cities have rules?
3. Who was Sargon the Great?
4. What was the "eye for an eye" rule?

Egypt's Gifts from the Nile

> **VOCABULARY**
>
> | | |
> |---|---|
> | pyramid | papyrus |
> | delta | scroll |
> | irrigate | |

Ancient pyramids The people of ancient Egypt (ē′ jəpt), like those of Mesopotamia, built their houses of mud bricks. But they also knew how to build from stone, which was plentiful in the desert near the Nile River. Find Egypt on the map on page 49. The Egyptians built stone temples for their gods and stone tombs where they buried their rulers.

The largest of the tombs were the **pyramids.** There are a number of pyramids in Egypt, but the largest was that built as a tomb for a ruler named Khufu (kü′ fü). This tomb, called the Great Pyramid, is the largest stone building in the world. It rises about 450 feet (137 m) above

Life in Egypt has always depended upon the Nile River.

Khufu's Great Pyramid rises in the background above. In front is the Sphinx, with the head of a man and the body of a lion. Both monuments were built over 4,500 years ago. The diagram below shows a cross section of Khufu's pyramid. The grand hall leading to the king's burial room is 153 ft (47 m) long and 28 ft (8.5 m) high.

the desert west of the Nile. It contains 2,300,000 stone blocks, some weighing as much as 5,000 pounds (2,270 kg). The Great Pyramid is almost solid stone except for passageways leading to different rooms. In the drawing on this page, find where the ruler's body was placed. But Khufu's body is not in the room. The tomb was robbed long ago.

Many tourists and travelers to Egypt have seen the ancient stone buildings. They visit the pyramids and other tombs, some of them cut deep into stone cliffs near the Nile. They view the remains of temples, such as that at Karnak (kär′ nak) with its giant columns. The picture on page 58 shows the size of these columns.

CROSS SECTION OF KHUFU'S GREAT PYRAMID

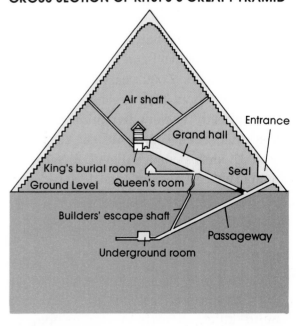

These great columns in the temple at Karnak, at Thebes, are 76 ft (24 m) high. The carvings show a beautiful system of picture writing invented by the ancient Egyptians.

Among the visitors over the centuries was a man from Sicily (sis′ ə lē) named Diodorus (dī ō dō′ rəs). The size of Khufu's tomb deeply impressed him. He wrote about what he saw. It was a sight that filled him "with wonder and astonishment." He marveled that its builders cut so much hard stone, "which is difficult to work but lasts forever." The stone does last well and the pyramids are very old. Even 2,000 years ago Diodorus wondered about their great age, yet they were already ancient pyramids. Khufu's tomb had been completed ca. 2500 B.C. And Diodorus visited Egypt in 60 B.C., which we call ancient times! More years passed between Khufu's time and Diodorus's visit than have passed since.

Egypt, like Mesopotamia, is an ancient land. Long before Khufu, the Egyptians had discovered the advantages of people working for each other. They did not build cities as early as the people of southwest Asia, but they did live and work together in communities before 3000 B.C. They, too, invented a system of writing in which pictures stood for words. It was a beautiful way to write, as you can see by the writing carved on the columns above.

"Egypt consists only of riverland." Strabo, the Greek geographer, also visited Egypt in ancient times. Strabo wrote that "Egypt consists only of riverland." In a way, Strabo was right. Much of Egypt is a desert where very few people can live. Most Egyptians live along the Nile River and its **delta**. A delta is the land that is formed by mud and sand as it is deposited by a large river at its mouth. It is called a delta because it is shaped somewhat like the Greek letter for delta (Δ) turned upside down.

Life in Egypt depends on the Nile and its gifts. The Nile is not only the longest river in Africa, it is the longest river in the world. The Nile flows north from the highlands of East Africa down to the Mediterranean Sea. Ancient Egyptians called the lowlands of the delta Lower Egypt. Upper Egypt was the land up the river south of Memphis. These names sometimes confuse people, since Lower Egypt is nearer the top of the map. But, of course, although the Nile flows north, it does not flow uphill. It flows down to the sea like all rivers. Remember, when thinking about Egypt and the Nile River, it is always north *down* the river to the sea and south *up* the river.

In the picture at the top, an Egyptian farmer plows riverland along the Nile in the same way it was done 3,000 years ago. In the ancient Egyptian painting at the bottom, a couple harvest wheat and flax, and plow and sow their fields. Notice the orchard and the canals that bring Nile water to irrigate the farmland.

Black soil—a gift from the Nile   The Nile is a river with rather regular habits. However, a dam at Aswan (a swän′) has somewhat changed its ways. Each June the river rises. In ancient times it spread its water over the narrow valley and the delta. It was not a fast, rushing flood that washed the soil away. Instead, the water rose with a gentle flow, carrying with it rich silt from upstream. As floodwaters went down in September and October, they left behind a rich gift of black soil on the fields of Egypt. Diodorus thought a country was fortunate to have its fields enriched each year. Another ancient writer called Egypt "the gift of the Nile."

As soon as the water was off the fields, farmers scattered grain over the mud. Then they drove pigs or goats across the field to push the seeds into the soil. Grain grew rapidly in the warm, moist silt. By the time the fields were thoroughly dry, the grain was ripe and ready to be cut.

The Egyptians **irrigated** their crops in other ways too. As the flood went down, some water was held back by dams. Later it was let out as needed to irrigate fields of onions, cucumbers, melons, and other vegetables. When there was no more floodwater, the Egyptians drew water from the river a bucketful at a time. It was very hard work, but the farmers grew two or three crops a year on their land. Diodorus thought the skill of Egypt's farmers was equal to that of its builders. He wrote that they, more than any other people, had the "most exact knowledge of the nature of the soil, the use of water in irrigation, the times of sowing and reaping, and the harvesting of crops."

The Nile flooded every June, but the height of the flood varied from year to year. Because the flood was so important, the Egyptians became experts at measuring the river. They could tell by the height of the Nile far upstream how high the

This wooden model shows a census taker counting the number of cattle belonging to a rich person. Cattle were a valuable form of wealth in ancient Egypt. Such models were put in tombs so that people could have their wealth in the next life. Cattle were valuable and useful in ancient Egypt because they were used to farm the Nile riverland.

This papyrus comic strip shows animals, usually enemies, working and playing together.

flood would rise downstream. The height of the flood meant the difference between good times and bad. If the water was too high, it flooded villages and destroyed mud brick houses. If the water was too low, it meant smaller fields of rich black soil and less water behind the dams. By knowing what to expect, the Egyptians were able to prepare for it.

Other gifts of the Nile   Black soil was only one of the Nile's gifts to Egypt. There was also **papyrus** (pə pī′ rəs), a large reed that grew wild along the river. The papyrus marshes partly took the place of forests in the desert land. Egyptians built papyrus boats by binding the reeds together in bundles. They wove baskets and mats and made sandals from split reeds. They twisted the tough fibers into ropes.

The Egyptians also made writing material from papyrus that looked somewhat like paper. We get our word *paper* from papyrus. They cut thin strips of papyrus stalk and glued them together in sheets. The Egyptians wrote on the sheets with reed brushes dipped in ink. Papyrus sheets ordinarily do not last as long as clay tablets, but the dry Egyptian climate has preserved some sheets in long rolls, or **scrolls.** The comic strip on this page comes from a scroll 3,000 years old. The artist must have had a sense of humor. In this strip, wolves herd goats and a cat takes care of geese.

Today a visitor to Egypt can go to the museum of Cairo (kī′ rō) to see papyrus growing. But the land along the river is too thoroughly farmed to leave space for papyrus to grow wild. What was once a free gift of the Nile is now a museum exhibit.

The Nile was home to many kinds of fish. Diodorus reported that they were "in numbers beyond belief." This gift was to be had for the taking. There were other creatures in the Nile, such as crocodiles, which were not so useful. Diodorus said that crocodiles sometimes caught animals. There was an old saying that "dogs run when they drink from the Nile for fear that a crocodile will get them." This was probably no more true than a lot of old sayings, but it made a good story to tell visitors.

CHECKUP

1. What was the purpose of the pyramids?
2. Since Egypt is a desert land, why did Strabo call it a river land? How did the Nile flood help the Egyptians?
3. What is the delta in Egypt?
4. What is papyrus and what uses were made of it?

61

A Land Ruled by God-Kings

Working together   Many people had to work together to make the kind of life ancient visitors found in Egypt. The Nile offered gifts, but it took a lot of work to use them well. The flood rose without human effort, but many people needed to work together to make use of the water and black soil. People dug ditches, built dams, and raised dikes. It also took many people working together for decades to build the pyramids and temples. They had to cut hard stone without tools of iron or steel. They had to move large blocks of stone without machines.

When many work together, someone has to direct the work. In Egypt those who directed were officials of the government. Those officials, in turn, were under the king who ruled the whole land.

Changes in Egypt under the first king   Egypt came under the rule of one king much earlier than Mesopotamia. At one time each village along the Nile had its own chief, but some chiefs grew more powerful and conquered their neighbors. In time there were but two rulers on the Nile, one for Upper Egypt and one for Lower Egypt. The advantages of working together made it easier for a strong chief to bring more land and people under one rule.

About 3100 B.C. a king of Upper Egypt names Menes (mē′ nēz) conquered Lower Egypt to the north and brought the whole land under his rule. We do not know much about how all of this happened. All we have are some old stories that were told in later times. According to an old story, Menes built his palace, the "Great House," at Memphis (mem′ fəs), where Upper and Lower Egypt met. Find Memphis on the map on page 49. The Egyptian word for "Great House" was **pharaoh** (fãr′ ō). The word was later used to refer to the rulers themselves much as Americans speak of the White House when referring to the Presidents.

One old story says that Menes did two other things.

> He taught people to worship gods.
> He taught people to supply themselves with tables and couches. In a word, he introduced luxury.

The statement about luxury is very interesting. A luxury is something not needed. We hardly think of tables and couches as luxuries, but of course people could live without them. Indeed, they had done so for many centuries. Probably almost anything new when it first comes into use may be thought of as a luxury.

We cannot be sure how true are the old stories about Menes. It is likely that there is some truth in the story mentioned above. It suggests that great changes took place when one king came to rule the whole land. This is probably true. One sign of the change was that more and more Egyptians began to worship some of the *same* gods. This was important because it meant that they were becoming more alike in the ways they thought.

When people came under the rule of one government, it is also likely that villages traded more with each other.

It Happened in Other Places Too

The people of Mesopotamia were not the only ones to discover the advantages of living and working together. People in other parts of the world made the same discovery. There were cities along the Indus (in′ dəs) River in present-day Pakistan. The pharaohs of Egypt were not the only rulers to govern a great river valley. Kings ruled the valley of the Hwang Ho (hwäng hō) in North China when Tutankhamun ruled the valley of the Nile.

The peoples of these different lands all had systems of writing 4,000 years ago. As the map shows, cities developed in the river valleys of the Indus and Hwang Ho in Asia. Carved stone seals have been found in great numbers in the Indus valley. When they are pressed against soft clay, such seals show animals and other signs. The signs were a form of writing. But we do not know what they say. No one can read them now. The picture shows a piece of bone with marks on it. Thousands of such bones and tortoise shells have been found in North China. The marks were an early form of Chinese writing. People seem to have used these bones and shells for some sort of fortune telling.

The stone seal and the writing on the bones tell us that eastern and southern Asia have histories that go back thousands of years. You will read more about the early history of these lands in Unit 7.

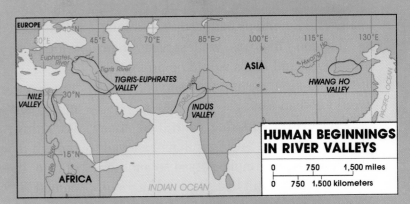

HUMAN BEGINNINGS IN RIVER VALLEYS

EUROPE, ASIA, AFRICA, TIGRIS-EUPHRATES VALLEY, NILE VALLEY, INDUS VALLEY, HWANG HO VALLEY, Euphrates River, Tigris River, PACIFIC OCEAN, INDIAN OCEAN

0   750   1,500 miles
0   750   1,500 kilometers

Craftworkers could spend their time on one kind of job and so become more skilled at it. As a result of trade, people had a greater variety of goods. The Egyptians owned more luxuries such as tables and couches. These changes were somewhat like what had happened in the early cities of Mesopotamia. The truth in the story about King Menes may be that he helped these changes to take place. He taught the people to worship the same gods and he introduced luxury.

In a gold coffin, King Tutankhamun's mummy is guarded by painted gods and goddesses.

Kings who were gods The Egyptians were like the people of Mesopotamia in that they believed in many gods. But there was an important difference. The Egyptians believed that their kings were gods. It was partly because of this belief that they obeyed the king and the king's officials. The Egyptians believed that so long as the god-king was well served, their well-being and lands would be protected. If the god-king was not well served, there would be bad times.

Service to a god-king continued after the ruler's death. The Egyptians believed that a god-king simply passed to another kind of life and still had the power to help them. They prepared a ruler for long life in the next world. The body was made into a mummy and placed in the tomb along with the ruler's fine jewels and clothing. Some mummies have kept as long as the stone tombs have.

A ruler's tomb became his or her palace after death. That was the reason for building the great tombs. They had to be fit for a god-king.

Life in the tomb was believed to be much like life in this world. The Egyptians put fine beds, chairs, chests, and even musical instruments into the tomb with the king's body. They made statues of all sorts of people. These statue-people were to serve the god-king in the new life.

The woman who was king Egypt had many god-kings during its long history. We know the names of most of them even though there were nearly a hundred. One of the most interesting was a woman named Hatshepsut (hat shep′ süt).

Hatshepsut was the daughter of one king and the wife of another. Her husband died as a young man, leaving a small stepson named Thutmose III (thüt mō′ sə). Since Thutmose was only a young boy, Hatshepsut took over the government. At first she ruled for her stepson. But not much later, she seems to have decided that she had a right to rule Egypt for herself and in her own name.

Hatshepsut was crowned king—not queen—of Upper and Lower Egypt ca. 1503 B.C. It was declared that she was the daughter of a god so that she was a god-king. Some statues showed her wearing a false beard as other god-kings had done.

Hatshepsut was a builder like many of the god-kings who came before her. She repaired temples that had become run down. She completed temples that had been begun but not finished. She had two stone **obelisks** (ob′ ə lisks) raised at the temples at Karnak in Thebes.

An obelisk is a four-sided stone pillar. Egyptian obelisks were carved from one piece of hard stone. Some of them were more than 105 feet (32 m) tall. Most were made at Aswan, more than 100 miles (160 km) south of Thebes.

A statue of Hatshepsut as pharaoh, or god-king

This drawing from the early 1800s shows two obelisks before another temple near Karnak. We do not know today how the Egyptians raised obelisks upright in their places.

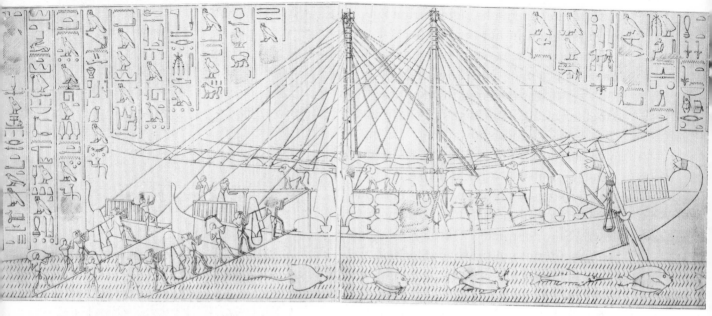

Two of Hatshepsut's trading ships in Punt are loaded with plants and animals.

Hatshepsut ruled in peace Hatshepsut began building her tomb while she was still living, as other rulers had done. She also built her temple near the tomb as was the practice of god-kings. Carvings on the temple walls usually showed a god-king's great deeds. A king who had conquered an enemy would have a battle scene carved on the walls of his temple. Hatshepsut fought no wars; she ruled in peace. Instead of sending armies to foreign lands, she sent trading ships to the land of Punt (pùnt). Punt was a country on the east coast of Africa.

The carvings on Hatshepsut's temple show the trading ships. The drawing on this page is a copy of one carving. It shows ships being loaded in Punt, and we can see the kinds of things brought back. Notice that the men are loading growing trees in pots. These were myrrh (mèr) trees. The Egyptians valued the sap of this tree, from which they made incense, per-

fume, and medicines. Hatshepsut wanted to plant these rare trees in the temple gardens.

The sacks stacked on board held many things such as rare animal skins, gold, and sweet-smelling woods. If you look closely, you will see a stack of pointed ivory tusks. You will also notice three baboons climbing around the ship. They, too, were among the goods brought back from Punt along with dogs and small monkeys. An account on the wall of the temple mentions "two live panthers that followed Her Majesty about." The panthers may have helped convince doubters that Hatshepsut was really a god-king.

Hatshepsut ruled Egypt for about 20 years. She lost her crown to her stepson Thutmose III in 1482 B.C. We do not know how this came about or why. All we know is that Thutmose III wanted people to forget the woman god-king. He had her name chiseled from the carvings on her temple. He had her statues smashed. The statue shown on page 65 was put together from pieces. He even built stone walls to cover the carvings on her obelisks. Fortunately, the walls later fell down so that her work can again be seen.

Thutmose III became one of Egypt's most powerful kings. He conquered an empire in southwest Asia. Yet he was not powerful enough to remove Hatshepsut's name from history.

Tutankhamun the boy god-king Today a king named Tutankhamun (tüt ängk ä′ mən) is even more famous than either Thutmose III or Hatshepsut. More people know about him than can pronounce his name. They usually shorten it to "King Tut." Tutankhamun actually had very little chance to do much during the 9 years of his short reign from 1361 to 1352 B.C. He was only 9 or 10 years old when he became king, and died before he was 20. It was his death and his tomb that make him famous today.

Things for another life   When young Tutankhamun died, his body was laid in a solid gold coffin in a hidden tomb. As was the custom, all sorts of things for his use were put into the tomb. People believed that he would live in another life, like all god-kings. They put in a bed, chairs, and chests decorated with gold and ivory. A fine game board went into the tomb. God-kings supposedly played games in the next life as they did in this one. There were statues of the young king, such as the one pictured, which shows him standing in a boat holding a spear. The king was supplied with precious jewelry and jars filled with sweet-smelling oils. The picture below shows one such jar with a lion on its cover.

A lion rests on the lid of this oil jar of Tutankhamun.

Tutankhamun, spear in hand, stands in a papyrus boat.

The treasures put in Tutankhamun's tomb were not greater than those placed in the tombs of other kings. There may well have been fewer treasures because the tomb was much smaller than others. He had not had time to build a large tomb.

What is unusual about Tutankhamun's tomb is that it was not robbed of all its treasures. The belief that god-kings lived in their tombs did not keep robbers away. They broke into almost all the ancient kings' tombs in ancient times. Twice thieves went into Tutankhamun's tomb, but they seem to have left in a hurry, taking very little. Tomb guards may have frightened them away. Later the entrance was accidentally buried under piles of rock and dirt.

Discovered treasures　　It was not until 1922 that an English scholar named Howard Carter found the long hidden entrance to Tutankhamun's tomb. As he entered the tomb holding a candle, he was asked if he could see anything. He could only reply, "Wonderful things!" Wonderful things they were, indeed. There were wonderful things made of gold and precious stones, and beautiful works of art. These works showed the fine skills of Egyptian artists and craftworkers who had lived more than 3,000 years ago.

The ancient treasures were moved from the tomb to the Egyptian Museum at Cairo. Visitors to Egypt can see them there. In the 1970s the Egyptian government allowed some of the most unusual objects to be shown in museums in Europe and the United States. Millions of people have now seen these treasures.

Measuring the year by the sun　　The pyramids show that the Egyptians built large buildings. The tomb treasures show that they made fine works of art. They also produced ideas that have lasted as long as the pyramids. Some of their ideas, which were new and useful to them, were borrowed by other groups of people who followed. One such idea was a calendar based on the sun rather than the moon.

Most ancient peoples measured time by moon months. A moon month is the time between one new moon and another. Our word *month* comes from *moon*; a month is a "moon-th." A moon month is about 29½ days. Twelve moon months make a year of 354 days. Such a short year does not fit the yearly cycle of seasons. To keep the season and years roughly together, an extra month may be added every two or three years. This is what people did in Mesopotamia.

The Egyptians needed a calendar that would tell when the Nile would rise, because their lives depended so much on the floodwaters. The flood came regularly with the summer season. Egyptian scholars discovered that a year measured by the sun fitted the cycle of seasons. A sun year is called a solar year. We now know that a solar year is the time it takes for the earth to go around the sun. The ancient Egyptians did not know this. But their scholars had learned to tell the exact length of a solar year by watching the position of a star known as the dog star.

There are 365¼ days in a solar year. The Egyptians divided their calendar year into 12 months of 30 days each with 5 extra holidays added at the end of the year. This 365-day calendar was still one fourth of a

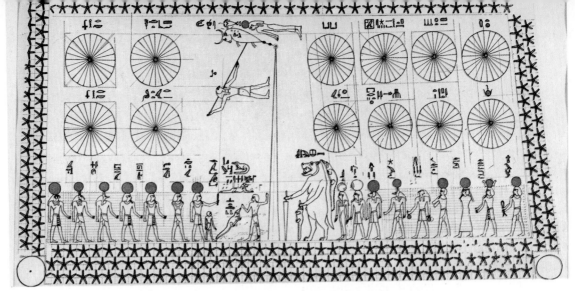

This ancient painting represents the heavens and the twelve months of the Egyptian calendar year. The red dots show the dog star's changing position in the sky.

day shorter than a solar year. As a result, one full cycle of seasons was not the same length as their calendar year. So summer started one fourth of a day later every year. Today we take care of this by adding an extra day to every fourth year. We call these leap years. The Egyptians did not have leap years, but they knew when to expect the summer flood. They could tell the beginning of the solar year by the dog star.

Our calendar today is not quite the same as that of the Egyptians. Someone invented the idea of the leap year so that we do not need to watch the position of the stars. We also do not have the five extra holidays. Instead we have some months with 31 days. But our calendar is based on the ideas of those Egyptian scholars who knew how to measure the year by the sun rather than by the moon.

Other ideas that have lasted   In time, the Egyptians came to believe that all people, not just god-kings, lived after death. They believed that the gods judged all people by how they had lived. The gods rewarded the good and punished the bad.

Who were good people? Old papyrus scrolls tell quite clearly. A good person is one who can stand before the gods and truthfully say

> I have not told lies.
> I have not stolen.
> I have not cheated.
> I have not taken property from a temple.
> I have not been quarrelsome.

Have you been taught ideas like these about what is good or bad? Most people today agree with the ancient Egyptians about what is good. Even though many things have changed since the times of Hatshepsut and Tutankhamun, these ideas have lasted very well.

CHECKUP

1. Why did life in ancient Egypt require that many people work together?
2. According to the old stories, what did Menes do? What truth may there be in these stories?
3. Why did Egyptians serve the god-kings?
4. What were some of the things that Hatshepsut did as ruler?
5. Why did the Egyptians come to use a solar rather than a moon calendar?

KEY FACTS

1. The first cities were built in southwest Asia and were ruled by priests and kings.
2. City life gave people safety and more goods.
3. People in Mesopotamia invented writing.
4. The Egyptians built large stone buildings 4,500 years ago.
5. The Nile floods provided both water and fertile soil for Egypt.
6. The Egyptians invented a solar calendar.

VOCABULARY QUIZ

On a sheet of paper write the words from the list below to fill the blanks in the statements that follow:

a. tokens   **e.** pharaoh   **h.** silt
b. pyramid   **f.** empire   **i.** scrolls
c. cuneiform   **g.** obelisk   **j.** delta
d. irrigate

1. The _____ is the land at the mouth of the Nile.
2. This land has been built up by soil, or _____, deposited by the river.
3. Before the invention of writing, people used small clay _____ as memory aids.
4. An early form of writing used wedge-shaped marks called _____.
5. Thutmose III was the Egyptian _____ who conquered an empire in southwest Asia.
6. The Washington Monument is a four-sided, tall stone structure in the shape of an Egyptian _____.
7. Sargon created the world's first _____ when he brought all of Mesopotamia under his rule.
8. In order to grow crops after the flood, the Egyptians had to _____ their fields.
9. The Egyptians wrote about judgment by the gods on papyrus _____.

10. A _____ was built for Khufu's tomb.

REVIEW QUESTIONS

1. What were some advantages of city life in ancient times?
2. What were three steps in the invention of writing?
3. What were some of the laws that Hammurabi gave the Babylonians?
4. What gifts did Egypt receive from the Nile?
5. Who brought Egypt together under a single king? Why do you think this was possible? What were the results?
6. What changes took place in Egypt under Menes?
7. Why did the Egyptians build great tombs for their rulers?
8. What did Hatshepsut do as ruler of Egypt?
9. How did the Egyptians measure years?
10. How did their calendar differ from ours?

ACTIVITIES

1. Early forms of writing used pictures of things to stand for sounds. In a rebus puzzle, pictures also stand for sounds which are combined with letters. For example:

☆ + ling = starling

Can you read the meaning of the following:

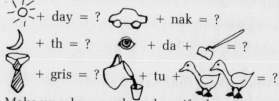

Make up rebus words and see if others in your class can read them.
2. Find out how many football fields will fit on the floor of the great pyramid.

3/SKILLS DEVELOPMENT

IDENTIFYING MAIN IDEAS AND TOPIC SENTENCES

A TOPIC SENTENCE STATES THE MAIN IDEA

The sentence that states the main idea of a paragraph is called the topic sentence. The first sentence of a paragraph usually states the main idea. Turn to the section "The advantage of doing each other's work," on page 51. Write this heading on a sheet of paper. Under it, copy the first sentence of each of the four paragraphs. You now have a summary of the main ideas of that section. Now read the section for the details.

In some paragraphs the first sentence does not state the main idea. For example, the first paragraph of the section "Kings and laws," on page 55, begins: "Some of the kings were not just war leaders. They also gave the people laws. City life required—and still requires—laws." The third sentence states the main idea of this paragraph. Are there any other paragraphs on page 55 in which the first sentence does not state the main idea?

SKILLS PRACTICE: Part I

In the passage that follows, each sentence has been numbered. Read the passage. Think of where you would divide it to make three paragraphs. On a sheet of paper, write the number of each sentence that you think should begin a paragraph. Does each of those sentences state the main idea of the paragraph it begins? Explain your answer for each paragraph. Now write the passage on your paper by copying all the sentences in each of the three paragraphs.

(**1**) Most Egyptians worked on the land, but every town had workshops for craftworkers. (**2**) In the workshops, shoemakers made san-

dals, and smiths hammered out tools and weapons. (**3**) Skilled woodworkers made fine furniture of wood and ivory brought from foreign lands. (**4**) The tools of the Egyptian craftworkers differed from modern tools, yet modern carpenters would not be lost in an Egyptian shop. (**5**) They could probably use the saws, mallets, hammers, and chisels, for the shapes of these tools have changed little in 4,000 years. (**6**) People have not had to change them because ancient craftworkers discovered the best shapes for the tools. (**7**) Egyptian workers also mastered the art of weaving linen. (**8**) Making linen from the fibers of the flax plant required much labor. (**9**) Workers soaked flax stalks in water until the outer layer was loose. (**10**) Then they dried the stalks and pounded them with wooden mallets to break the outer layer away from the tough center fibers. (**11**) After they combed these fibers clean, they spun them into thread which they wove into cloth.

SKILLS PRACTICE: Part II

The topic sentence of a paragraph states the main idea. The other sentences supply details that support the main idea. They are called supporting sentences. After you have copied the passage on this page into these paragraphs, answer the following questions.

1. In the first paragraph, how many sentences give details? What crafts are mentioned? Are any other details given?

2. What sentences give details in paragraph two? What are the details?

3. How many supporting sentences are there in the third paragraph? What details do they give?

71

4 Ancient Times in Greece

The Land and Seas of Ancient Greece

---VOCABULARY---
navigate

Our Greek heritage   There are 15 cities, towns, and villages named Athens in the United States. There are 10 Spartas and 6 places named Corinth. The people who named these American places probably hoped they would be great like the Greek cities. About 2,500 years ago Athens and Sparta were the greatest cities in ancient Greece. For most of the decade in the 320s B.C., Greek armies controlled one of the largest empires the world has ever seen.

People still know the names and history of these cities because so many things in our world began in ancient Greece. The very word *history* comes from the Greek word *historía*, which means history or story. About 12 percent of the words in our language come from the language of the ancient Greeks. We write our words with an alphabet that the Greeks gave to the Romans. The word *alphabet* is made up from the names of the first two letters of the Greek alphabet, *alpha* and *beta*. These are just a few of the things that connect our world with that of ancient Greece.

The Greek peninsula   Greece is a land quite unlike Egypt or Mesopotamia. It is not a land of great rivers. The streams are small, and most dry up during the summer. Greece is a land of mountains, narrow plains, and islands. Study the map on page 75. Greek cities in ancient times grew up mostly in the plains and valleys along the lengthy coastline. This explains how the Greeks came to be great sailors and settlers of other coast lands.

The Greek mainland is a peninsula that extends into the Mediterranean Sea. The southern part, called the Peloponnesus (pel ə pə nē′ səs), is almost an island. Peloponnesus means "Island of Pelops." Only the isthmus of Corinth joins the Peloponnesus to the rest of the Greek mainland. Today, a narrow canal, called the Corinth Canal, has been cut through the isthmus.

The importance of the sea   A string of islands, including Crete and Rhodes, form a chain between the Peloponnesus and the coast of Asia Minor. Asia Minor is the part of eastern Mediterranean land that we now call Turkey. In ancient times there were Greek cities on that coast and on the islands. The chain of islands encloses the branch of the Mediterranean

Temple ruins overlook the sea at Lindos, a Greek city on Rhodes, the easternmost island in the Aegean Sea. The rugged coast is typical of Greece.

Sea known as the Aegean (ē jē′ ən) Sea. The Aegean separates the two continents of Europe and Asia. Our names for these continents were given by Greek sailors. The land east of the Aegean they called *Asia*, which meant "land of the sunrise." *Europe* meant "land of the sunset."

The Aegean was important to the Greeks in several ways. They fished for much of their food. Water was a way both to travel and to ship goods. Many Greek cities used their ships to defend themselves and to settle other lands, called colonies. A home city and its colonies had close ties through trade, and shared ways and beliefs. Find the Greek homeland and colonies on the map on page 77.

The Greeks carried on trade with many lands near and far. It was easier and faster to ship goods by sea than to carry them overland on the mountainous peninsula. It was safer to sail on the Aegean Sea, which was protected from high winds, than on the open waters of the rest of the Mediterranean. Also, the ancient sailors had no compass to tell directions. Islands dot the Aegean and served as welcome landmarks. The Greeks could sail, or **navigate**, by sight. They sailed from island to island by daylight.

Rough mountains and narrow plains
The mountains of Greece are by no means the tallest in Europe, but they seem very high because they rise so near the sea. The peak of Mt. Olympus, the tallest in Greece, reaches 9,570 feet (2,917 meters) less than 15 miles (24 kilometers) from the shore. Europe's highest peak is twice that altitude.

Between the mountains and along the coast are valleys and plains that are good farmlands. But the plains are mostly small and narrow. Farming these lands in ancient times differed from the farming along the irrigated valley of the Nile River. Unlike Egypt, Greece receives some rain. In most of Greece the rain falls mostly during the fall and winter. Summers are hot and dry except for an occasional storm. Winters are not very cold. Snow falls only in the mountains.

How many years did Athens and Sparta fight during the Peloponnesian War?

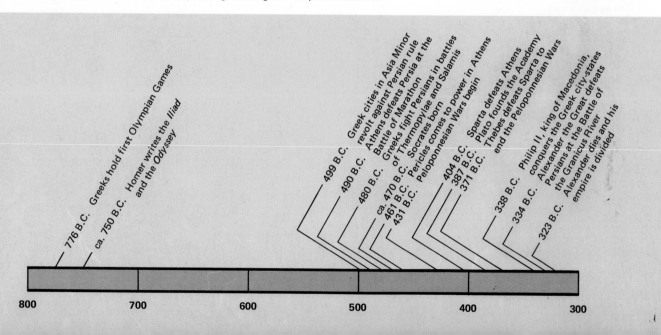

776 B.C. Greeks hold first Olympian Games

ca. 750 B.C. Homer writes the *Iliad* and the *Odyssey*

499 B.C. Greek cities in Asia Minor revolt against Persian rule

490 B.C. Athens defeats Persia at the Battle of Marathon

480 B.C. Greeks fight Persians in battles of Thermopylae and Salamis

ca. 470 B.C. Socrates born

461 B.C. Pericles comes to power in Athens

431 B.C. Peloponnesian Wars begin

404 B.C. Sparta defeats Athens

387 B.C. Plato founds the Academy

371 B.C. Thebes defeats Sparta to end the Peloponnesian Wars

338 B.C. Philip II, king of Macedonia, conquers the Greek city-states

334 B.C. Alexander the Great defeats Persians at the Battle of the Granicus River

323 B.C. Alexander dies and his empire is divided

800   700   600   500   400   300

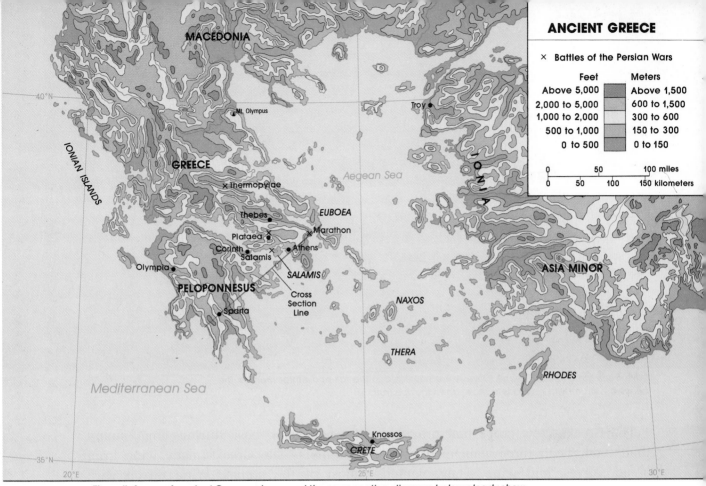

ANCIENT GREECE

× Battles of the Persian Wars

Feet		Meters
Above 5,000		Above 1,500
2,000 to 5,000		600 to 1,500
1,000 to 2,000		300 to 600
500 to 1,000		150 to 300
0 to 500		0 to 150

0   50   100 miles
0   50   100   150 kilometers

MACEDONIA

40°N

IONIAN ISLANDS

Mt. Olympus

Troy

GREECE

Aegean Sea

× Thermopylae

IONIA

Thebes

EUBOEA

Plataea

Marathon

Corinth   Athens

Salamis

ASIA MINOR

Olympia   SALAMIS

PELOPONNESUS

Cross
Section
Line

NAXOS

Sparta

THERA

RHODES

Mediterranean Sea

Knossos

CRETE

35°N

20°E   25°E   30°E

The relief map of ancient Greece above and the cross section diagram below clearly show
the mountains, narrow coastal plains, and little valleys of Greece. A cross section shows an
area of land as though the earth had been cut away to sea level.

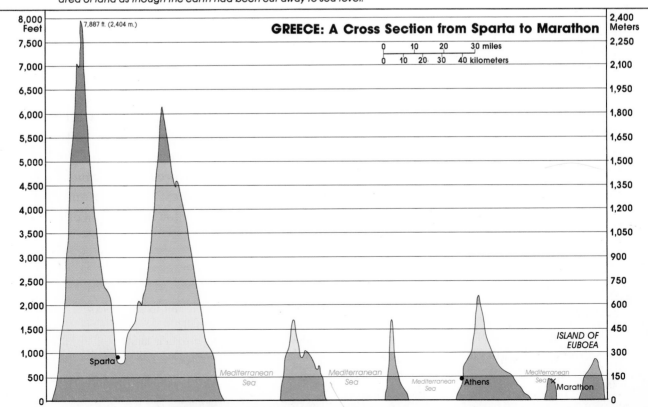

GREECE: A Cross Section from Sparta to Marathon

Feet		Meters
8,000	7,887 ft. (2,404 m.)	2,400
7,500		2,250
7,000		2,100
6,500		1,950
6,000		1,800
5,500		1,650
5,000		1,500
4,500		1,350
4,000		1,200
3,500		1,050
3,000		900
2,500		750
2,000		600
1,500		450
1,000		300
500		150
0		0

0   10   20   30 miles
0   10   20   30   40 kilometers

Sparta

Mediterranean Sea

Mediterranean Sea

Mediterranean Sea

Athens

Mediterranean Sea

ISLAND OF EUBOEA

Marathon

Olive trees grow well in Greece. Olives were harvested in the fall and winter months. The trees were struck with long rods to shake down the ripe fruit.

The Greeks grew crops that provided their food. Their three main foods were bread, olives, and wine. They planted wheat on the plains in the fall. Winter rains watered the crop, which grew rapidly and ripened in the spring. Farmers cut wheat in May. They threshed it, which means to separate the grain from the straw, during the dry summer when there was little other work in the fields.

Olive trees grow well along the coast in Greece. There are few killing frosts in winter. And the trees can stand the long, dry summers. Greeks harvested the olives for the fruit and to make oil. Olive oil was used for food, soap, and lamp fuel. The ancient Greeks used the best oil as modern Americans use butter, cooking oil, and shortening. They also used the best oil as hand cream, and they burned the poorer grades in lamps.

Greek farmers grew grapes, mostly on the slopes of the hills and mountainsides.

Grapes grow best during long, sunny summers. The Greeks made wine from most of the grapes. Wine mixed with water was their most common drink. After the fall harvest, some grapes were dried to be raisins.

Greek farmers had too little good land to use it for pastures or growing hay. Few cattle were raised but oxen were kept for plowing and drawing heavy loads. Instead, the Greeks raised sheep and goats, which could feed on rocky land where cattle would starve. The sheep were shorn for their wool and some were raised for meat. Goats also provided meat, as well as milk both for drinking and for making cheese.

CHECKUP

1. Why was the sea important to the Greeks?
2. How did the Greeks sail?
3. How did the Greeks use their land?
4. What did the ancient Greeks eat?

The Cities of Ancient Greece

Citizens of free cities   Governments in Greece were different from the government of ancient Egypt. The Egyptians had one government over all their land. The Greeks lived in or near a number of separate cities, called city-states. Each Greek city was **independent**. Each was a little nation or state with its own government and laws.

The Egyptians were **subjects** of their god-king. A subject is a person under the power of another. The Greeks were **citizens** of their free cities. Citizens are members of a city or nation. They belong to it as people belong to a club or team.

To say that the Greeks were citizens of free cities does not mean that all Greeks were equal. Some citizens had more power than others. Being a citizen was somewhat like being a member of a basketball team. Some team members start the game; some do not. Some play most of the time; some sit on the bench. Yet both starters and bench warmers belong to the team.

The Greek cities were also the homes of people who were not citizens. Prisoners taken in wars with other lands were

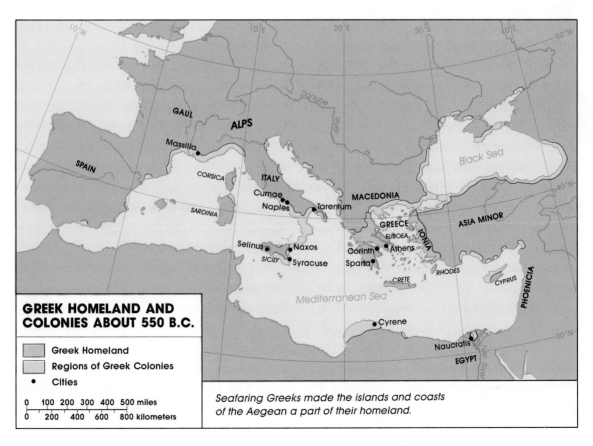

GREEK HOMELAND AND COLONIES ABOUT 550 B.C.

☐ Greek Homeland
☐ Regions of Greek Colonies
• Cities

0   100 200 300 400 500 miles
0   200   400   600   800 kilometers

Seafaring Greeks made the islands and coasts of the Aegean a part of their homeland.

brought home as slaves. They were neither citizens nor free. People who were free but not citizens included **immigrants.** They were people who came from another land or another Greek city.

Different Greek cities had different kinds of government. In some cities, a few families had most of the power. The Greeks called a government by a few an **oligarchy** (ol′ ə gär kē). In other cities all the citizens ruled. Their word for rule by the people was **democracy.** Oligarchy and democracy are two more of the many Greek words in our language. We also use the Greek word **monarchy,** which means "rule by one," such as a king or queen. Under the god-kings, ancient Egypt was a monarchy.

What freedom meant in Sparta   The cities of Greece were free, but this did not mean that all individuals had great freedom. It depended on the city. Spartans had many limits on how they lived. Sparta was ruled by very strict laws that could not be changed. Only a small group of people were in power to uphold these laws. Spartans were not, for example, free to travel to other cities or to carry on trade.

Look up *Spartan* in a dictionary; you will find that it means, "A person who is brave, obeys orders, and lives without luxuries." Such persons are called Spartans because the citizens of ancient Sparta were supposed to be like that.

Growing up in Sparta   The laws of the Spartans had one main purpose: to make good soldiers. Training for a young Spartan began at an early age. When a boy

was 7, he joined a troop with other boys his own age under the command of a young man.

The boys learned to obey orders without asking questions. They learned to take care of themselves. The young Spartans had to know how to live on little food and how to keep warm with little clothing. They had to be able to sleep out-of-doors in all kinds of weather. The boys exercised their bodies and learned to use swords and spears.

When a boy became a man, he continued to train with his troop. He ate with them rather than in his own house. His troop of companions would fight together in time of war, so they kept together in time of peace. When a man became 60 years old, he could retire from service as a soldier.

Girls in Sparta did not join troops as the boys did. They stayed home with their mothers, but girls did take part in sports. They threw darts, ran races, danced, and wrestled. The Spartans wanted women as well as men to be strong and healthy. The women were the mothers of soldiers. They also took charge of family affairs when their husbands went to war.

Some Spartan women became wealthy. At one time, women owned more than a quarter of the city's land.

There was a reason why the Spartans had so little freedom in their private lives. The reason was fear—fear of **revolt,** or attack by people they ruled. In earlier times the Spartans had conquered their neighbors in the Peloponnesus. The Spartans had made slaves of the conquered people, whom they called helots (hel′ əts). They made the helots work the land. That

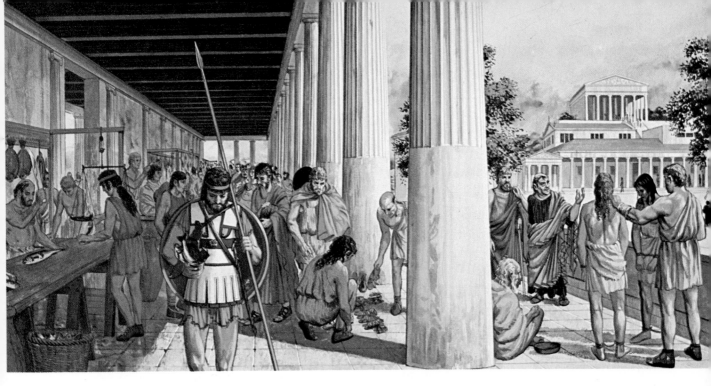

The marketplace of Athens, called the agora, was a place to buy and sell things. It was also a place to meet friends and talk about politics.

left the Spartans free to train for war. The Spartans had to train for war because they feared that the helots would revolt. It was a strange situation. The Spartans were citizens of a free city, but they had little freedom because they feared the people they ruled.

Trading goods and ideas in Athens
Life in Athens differed from life in Sparta. The Athenians traded with other lands. Unlike the Spartans, Athenians wanted traders from other places to come to their city. Pericles (per′ ə klēz), a leader of the Athenians, proudly declared, "Our city is open to the world."

The marketplace of Athens, called the agora (ag′ ər ə), was the busiest place in the city. It was a place where more than just Athenian farmers sold olives, lettuce, onions, and other vegetables. Merchants from other lands and cities brought goods to the agora. Traders from Asia had brightly colored cloth, fine jewelry, and purple dye. Other traders, from the island of Cyprus, sold copper vessels. Merchants from Corinth, another Greek city, offered perfumes and sweet-smelling oils.

Athenians sold fresh fish from the nearby sea. But they could also buy pickled fish in clay pots brought from the Black Sea or the Mediterranean island of Sicily. They could also choose either smoked or dried fish wrapped in fig leaves. Pericles boasted, "All the good things from all over the world flow in to us, so that it seems just as natural to enjoy foreign goods as our own local products."

The agora was more than a place to buy and sell goods. The Athenians spent a lot of time there. It was a place to meet people and talk. Men gathered in open-air barber shops and exchanged jokes.

Some talk in the agora was much more serious. A merchant from Cyprus named Zeno became so interested in the talk that he moved to Athens. Zeno gave up his business and spent the next 40 years of his life trading ideas in the agora. He became the teacher of a group that gathered there in a covered walkway called the stoa. The Athenians called Zeno and his followers the Stoics.

Growing up in Athens   A very wise Greek named Aristotle (ar' is tot'l) thought that a baby's rattle was a great invention. Babies cannot be expected to remain still. Rattles give them something to do and keep them out of trouble. Aristotle noted that as children grew, they needed other ways to keep busy. "For older children, education is their rattle."

Athenian girls were kept busy in their homes, where they got their education. They did not go to school. Their mothers, grandmothers, and aunts taught them the things that the Athenians thought women should know. Girls learned Greek beliefs about their gods and about people of past times. They learned the skills of running a house and how to spin and weave. Some mothers may even have taught their daughters to read and write.

Boys received part of their education outside the home. When a boy was 6 or 7 years old, he was sent to a schoolmaster. The master taught him to read, write, and do arithmetic. Boys also began to learn stories and poems about Greek beliefs and history. The Athenians believed that the stories about the old heroes set a good example for the young. One Athenian wrote, "My father, eager that I become a good man, made me learn all the poems of Homer." Later in this chapter you will read more about the poet Homer.

Boys also went to gymnasiums each day. There they learned to run, jump, wrestle, and throw the javelin, a type of spear. The Athenians, as well as the Spartans, believed that a strong city needed men with strong bodies. The exercises in the gymnasiums made boys strong. The skills they learned as boys were the ones needed in battle in a day when soldiers fought hand to hand.

Athenian education was not so harsh as in Sparta. But Athenian education was not gentle. Athenian schoolmasters were expected to whip any lazy or disobedient pupil. As one Athenian wrote, "They straighten him with threats and beatings, like a warped and twisted plank."

Democracy of Athens: "Rule by the many"   The Athenian leader Pericles was proud that his people did not spend their whole lives training for war. They

In this old painting boys are taught music and writing. At right sits the slave who brought the boys to class.

did far more pleasant things. Yet, Pericles declared, "we are just as ready ... to face danger as the Spartans." The Athenians were brave because they enjoyed a great deal of freedom in the way they lived. They knew that "happiness depends on being free, and freedom depends on being brave."

Pericles said that Athens was a democracy "because it is in the hands of the many rather than the few." All male citizens in Athens could take part in the government when they became 18 years old. Indeed, they were expected to do so. Pericles explained, "We do not say that a man who takes no interest in politics is a man who minds his own business; we say that he has no business here at all."

The male citizens of Athens met together in the Assembly. There they made the laws and decided questions of war and peace. Thousands of men attended the Assembly, which met about three times a month. Any male citizen could speak and vote. When a **majority**—more than half—of them agreed on some questions, they could decide what to do. It was, in fact, "rule by the many" because the many—the majority—made decisions for the city.

Pericles was elected general and leader by the Athenians almost every year for 30 years.

The Athenians elected ten generals each year. The generals led the city in time of peace as well as war. Pericles was a great leader for a long time in Athens because the people elected him general nearly every year for 30 years. Many people called this period "The Golden Age of Pericles."

Most Athenian officials were chosen by drawing from among all male citizens. For example, every year Athenians drew the names of 500 men to serve on the Council. The Council had charge of the city's day-to-day business. Since no one could serve on the Council more than twice, the job was passed around. Sooner or later almost every Athenian male citizen took a turn on the Council.

"The many" did not mean everyone When Pericles spoke of "rule by the many," he meant only male citizens. He did not mean women. Women could be citizens, but they could not take part in the Assembly nor sit on the Council.

Athenian citizens were tried by juries that were chosen by drawing names. Our juries usually have 12 members. Athenian juries sometimes had 500. Shown below are jurors' ballots. The ballot with the hole in the center meant guilty. The others meant not guilty.

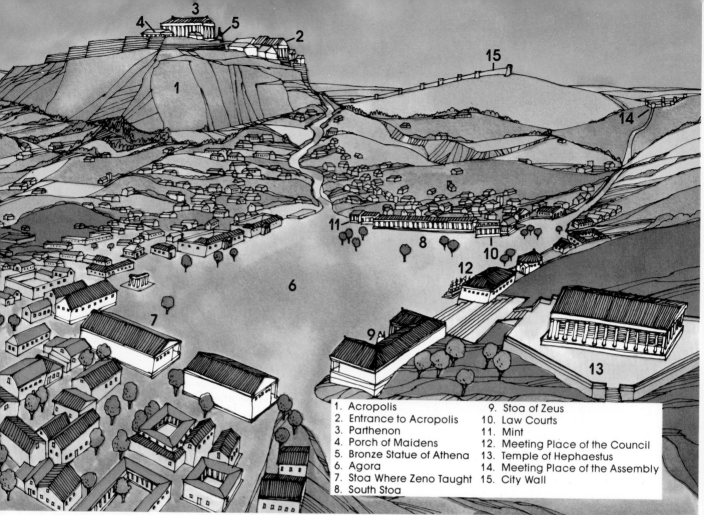

1. Acropolis
2. Entrance to Acropolis
3. Parthenon
4. Porch of Maidens
5. Bronze Statue of Athena
6. Agora
7. Stoa Where Zeno Taught
8. South Stoa
9. Stoa of Zeus
10. Law Courts
11. Mint
12. Meeting Place of the Council
13. Temple of Hephaestus
14. Meeting Place of the Assembly
15. City Wall

This drawing shows Athens at the time of Pericles. Use the key to find the following: Agora, Parthenon, Mint, and Meeting Place of the Assembly.

Pericles did not even mean that all men who lived in Athens could take part in government. Not all were citizens. Citizenship depended on birth. Only children of citizens were citizens. Children of immigrants, even though born in Athens, could not take part in the democracy.

Athens also had slaves—possibly one third of the population. They also could not take part in Athens's government by the many. Many were slaves simply because their parents were slaves. Some were prisoners of war. Still others had been brought to Athens by slave-trading pirates. Slaves were so valuable that pirates made a regular business of stealing people from poorly defended places. Slavery was a common evil in ancient times. It existed almost everywhere. Athenians believed that some people were just meant to be slaves. Needless to say, people who held this view were probably not slaves.

CHECKUP

1. What is the difference between a subject and a citizen?
2. How are a democracy, an oligarchy, and a monarchy different?
3. How did the Spartans live and why?
4. What was it like to grow up in Athens?
5. How could an Athenian citizen take part in government?

Greek Cities and Foreign Lands

War with the Great King of Persia
Sometimes the Greek cities fought each other. Sometimes they joined together as **allies** and fought an outside enemy. Such was the case in the war against Darius (də rī′ əs), Great King of the Persians. The Persians were a people who had come from the country now called Iran. Find Persia on the map below.

The Greeks never forgot the war against the Persians. We, too, know a great deal about it because a man named Herodotus (hə rod′ ə təs) wrote its history. Herodotus' work is one of the world's oldest histories. It is also one of the best, for Herodotus was a natural storyteller.

Darius was called the Great King for good reason. He ruled a vast empire, as the map on this page shows. Notice that Egypt and Mesopotamia were only parts of this huge empire. The empire also included the Greek cities on the coast of Asia Minor. The Great King treated these Greeks as his subjects. He forced them to pay him **tribute** money. This was money, like a tax, paid for protection. He also made them serve in his army and navy.

In 499 B.C. the cities in Asia Minor rose against Darius and refused to pay tribute. The Greeks in Asia Minor asked the cities on the Greek peninsula for help. Athens and a few other cities sent ships, but they were not enough.

The Persians put down the revolt, but Darius did not forget what Athens had done. He decided that someday he would punish the free cities of Greece. He would

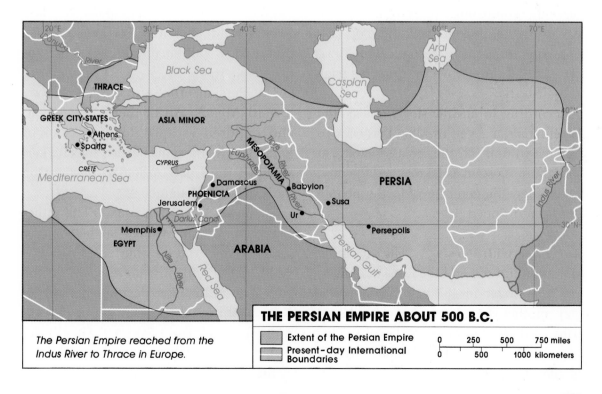

The Persian Empire reached from the Indus River to Thrace in Europe.

THE PERSIAN EMPIRE ABOUT 500 B.C.

- Extent of the Persian Empire
- Present-day International Boundaries

0   250   500   750 miles
0   500   1000 kilometers

conquer the lands in the west so that his empire would have "no limits but the sky."

Battle of Marathon   Darius sent a large army to Greece in 490 B.C. The Persians landed at Marathon, a level plain about 20 miles (32 km) from Athens. The Persians had far more men than the Athenians and their allies. Even so, the Greeks attacked. The Persians could not believe their eyes when they saw the Greeks running straight at them. But the Athenians had some advantages. They fought with longer spears, and they moved together as a team.

The Athenians had very strong reasons for fighting. This may have been their greatest advantage. They knew that they were fighting for the freedom of their families and their city. They knew what was most likely to happen if they lost. The Persians would burn the city and make slaves of the people they did not kill. Knowing this, the Athenians fought so fiercely that they drove the Persians back to their boats.

According to an old story, one of the Athenians ran 24 miles (38.6 km) back to Athens to tell of the great victory at Marathon. As soon as he reached the city, he shouted the good news to the people and then dropped dead.

More war with Persia   The victory at Marathon did not end the Persian danger. Ten years later in 480 B.C. Xerxes (zėrk' sēz), another Great King, sent a still larger army and fleet to conquer Greece. This time all the Greek cities banded together against the Persians.

Led by the Spartan Leonidas, a Greek army of 6,000 held the Persians at Thermopylae. When the Greeks were betrayed, Leonidas sent most of them away. He and a small band fought to the last soldier rather than give up.

A small army led by the Spartans met the Persians in a narrow pass at Thermopylae (thər mäp' ə lē). Find Thermopylae on the map on page 75. The Greeks held back the Persians until a traitor showed them another way through the pass.

The Persian army and fleet advanced toward Athens. All of the men, women, and children escaped to the island of Salamis. The Persians burned the city and attacked the small Athenian fleet in the narrow bay of Salamis.

That was a great mistake. The Athenians knew these waters far better than the Persians. And the shorter Greek ships could move and turn more easily in the bay. The Athenians destroyed many of Xerxes' ships. The rest of his fleet withdrew to Asia. The next year, Greeks defeated what was left of the Persian army at the Battle of Plataea near Corinth.

Sparta, Athens, and the other free cities acted together to defeat the Persians. They did not act together to keep the peace they had won. The cities made war against each other. The wars between the Greek city-states were called the Peloponnesian Wars. Sparta defeated Athens, and Thebes defeated Sparta.

The Peloponnesian Wars so weakened the Greek city-states that in 338 B.C. a king, Philip of Macedonia, conquered them all. Macedonia was a land in northern Greece. King Philip planned to lead the Greeks in a new war against the Persians. But he was killed before he could do so. His son Alexander carried out the plan.

Alexander conquers an empire   Alexander was one of those who have been called great because he conquered a large empire. You remember that Sargon of Akkad, who conquered the first empire in Mesopotamia, was also called great. Alexander's empire was far larger than Sargon's had been. Alexander conquered all the lands from Greece to the Indus River in the country we know as Pakistan. Today there are a dozen different countries within what was Alexander's empire.

Alexander dreamed of more than conquest. He wanted to unite the different peoples of his empire. To make them one people he needed their support. He tried to get it by fitting into their ways. In Egypt he became a god-king. In Persia he married a princess. He offered to pay the debts of his soldiers who would marry Persian women. Alexander established cities throughout his empire, each called Alexandria. The most famous Alexandria was on the Nile Delta in Egypt.

In 323 B.C. Alexander died at the age of 33. He died before he could carry out his plans. After his death, several generals

At Salamis 300 Greek ships defeated a much larger Persian fleet of 1,000 ships. Most ships in both fleets had three banks of oars and a ram at the front. The Greeks tricked the Persian ships into entering the narrow bay, only 1 mile (1.6 km) wide, then attacked them from both sides. Most of the Persian ships were sunk.

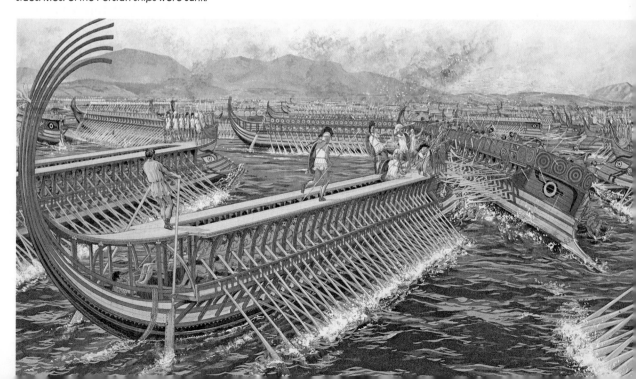

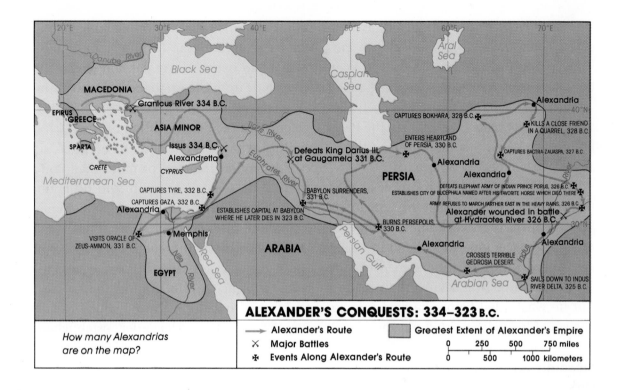

ALEXANDER'S CONQUESTS: 334–323 B.C.

How many Alexandrias are on the map?

→ Alexander's Route
✕ Major Battles
✠ Events Along Alexander's Route

Greatest Extent of Alexander's Empire

0   250   500   750 miles
0   500   1000 kilometers

Map labels:
MACEDONIA
EPIRUS GREECE
ASIA MINOR
SPARTA
CRETE
CYPRUS
Mediterranean Sea
Black Sea
Caspian Sea
Aral Sea
Granicus River 334 B.C.
Issus 334 B.C.
Alexandretta
Defeats King Darius III at Gaugamela 331 B.C.
CAPTURES TYRE, 332 B.C.
CAPTURES GAZA, 332 B.C.
Alexandria
ESTABLISHES CAPITAL AT BABYLON WHERE HE LATER DIES IN 323 B.C.
BABYLON SURRENDERS, 331 B.C.
VISITS ORACLE OF ZEUS-AMMON, 331 B.C.
Memphis
ARABIA
EGYPT
Nile River
Red Sea
Tigris River
Euphrates River
Persian Gulf
PERSIA
BURNS PERSEPOLIS, 330 B.C.
ENTERS HEARTLAND OF PERSIA, 330 B.C.
CAPTURES BOKHARA, 328 B.C.
KILLS A CLOSE FRIEND IN A QUARREL, 328 B.C.
CAPTURES BACTRA-ZAUASPA, 327 B.C.
Alexandria
Alexandria
Alexandria
DEFEATS ELEPHANT ARMY OF INDIAN PRINCE PORUS, 326 B.C.
ESTABLISHES CITY OF BUCEPHALA NAMED AFTER HIS FAVORITE HORSE WHICH DIED THERE
ARMY REFUSES TO MARCH FARTHER EAST IN THE HEAVY RAINS, 326 B.C.
Alexander wounded in battle at Hydraotes River 326 B.C.
Alexandria
Alexandria
CROSSES TERRIBLE GEDROSIA DESERT.
SAILS DOWN TO INDUS RIVER DELTA, 325 B.C.
Arabian Sea
Indus River

At the Battle of the Granicus River, Alexander and his soldiers crossed the river to attack the Persians.

divided up the empire. You read in Chapter 1 about one of those generals, King Ptolemy of Egypt.

Ptolemy made Alexandria a Greek city outside of Greece. That was the reason he built the museum. But Alexandria could never truly be like the free cities of Greece that had once ruled themselves. People could go to the museum library to read Pericles' speech to the Athenian Assembly. But they could not take part in such an assembly. They were subjects of Ptolemy, not citizens.

CHECKUP

1. Why did King Darius of Persia attempt to conquer Greece?
2. What advantages did the Athenians have in the war with Persia?
3. How did the Greek cities come to be conquered by the Macedonians?
4. What plans did Alexander have for his empire?

Greek Works That Have Lived On

Athenian love of beauty Pericles proudly declared that the buildings of Athens "cheer the heart and delight the eye." We have some idea of what he had in mind, because the remains of some of these buildings still stand. People everywhere will recognize the marble building shown in the picture below. This is the Parthenon on the Acropolis (ə krop′ ə lis), the rocky hill in the midst of the city of Athens. In Pericles' day the Athenians built the Parthenon as a temple for Athena, goddess of the city. The temple later served other purposes. Christians used it as a church for many years. Three hundred years ago, the Parthenon was used as a place to store gunpowder. When the gunpowder exploded, the building blew up. Yet even the ruins "cheer the heart and delight the eye."

The temples on the Acropolis in Athens, Greece, are some of the most beautiful buildings in the world. Athens is located at 38°N, 23°E.

In this temple on the Acropolis a lamp was kept burning in honor of the goddess Athena. Its south porch, called the Porch of the Maidens, has columns carved in the shape of young women.

Works of art both large and small The Parthenon was only one of the beautiful public buildings in Athens. Athenians built other temples and many public buildings, such as theaters, markets, and government buildings. The builders tried to make each one a true work of art.

The Greeks made small works of art as well as large ones. They thought that a vase, pot, or coin ought to "delight the eye" as much as a temple. The picture of the Greek vase on this page suggests how well Greek artists did the job.

Poems about gods and humans The Greeks believed in many gods and goddesses. They were thought to be much like men and women except that gods and goddesses never grew old nor died. They were more powerful than humans, but they acted and felt much as humans did. Gods and goddesses fell in love, grew angry, quarreled, and sometimes played tricks on each other.

Each god and goddess had special functions or jobs. Zeus was god of the sky. His brother, Poseidon (pə sī′ dən), had charge of the sea. Zeus was the ruler of the gods. This was no easy job, for the gods and goddesses had strong wills of their own. Athena was the goddess of wisdom. Wisdom was especially honored in Athens, and the city chose Athena as its goddess.

Hera, wife of Zeus, had charge of marriage and the birth of children. The beautiful Aphrodite (af rə dī′ tē) was goddess of love and beauty. Apollo was both the god of the sun and of music. Statues of Apollo often show him holding a stringed musical instrument called a lyre (līr). Ares was the god of war. The other gods were not

A vase like this one, with Athena's picture on one side, was often a winner's prize at athletic games. The vase would usually be filled with olive oil.

The war between the Greeks and Troy ended when the goddess Athena told the Greeks to build a large wooden horse in which soldiers could hide. The Greeks burned their camp outside the walls of Troy, and pretended to sail away. The people of Troy pulled the horse into the city. During the night the Greeks climbed out and opened the city gates to the Greek army. Troy fell.

fond of Ares who, it was said, "enjoyed nothing but strife, war, and battle."

Long before the time of Pericles, a blind poet named Homer told how the gods and goddesses took sides in the lives of the Athenians. One of Homer's poems is called the *Iliad* (il′ ē əd). It tells how gods and goddesses played a part in a long war between the Greeks and the city of Troy. Homer also created another long poem called the *Odyssey* (od′ ə sē). It tells about the later adventures of Odysseus, one of the Greek heroes of the Trojan War.

Today, each of these poems fills a book, but Homer never wrote them down. He kept the poems in his memory and spoke and sang them. Other people also mem-

orized Homer's works. The *Iliad* has 15,693 lines, and the *Odyssey* is still longer. Do you think you could memorize so long a poem? Fortunately you do not have to do so. About 200 years after Homer's time both poems were written down. Today people still read them.

The Greeks had many poets. Among them was a woman named Sappho (saf′ ō). Her poems do not tell tales of gods and wars. Sappho sang of human feelings—of love and friendship. The following lines are rewritten from one of her poems.

Some think a gallant navy on the sea, and some an army on foot or horse, to be Earth's most beautiful thing, but I say the one we love is more beautiful.

Unfortunately we know very little about Sappho's life. It is sometimes said that she started the first school for girls, to whom she taught poetry and music. But we do know that the Greeks thought her one of their greatest poets. People in Greece thought so highly of Sappho that they often put her likeness on coins, such as the one below.

Stories that have lived   Have you ever heard of "The Tortoise and the Hare"? If so, you know something about an old Greek story told at least 2,500 years ago. A slave named Aesop (ē′ səp) told the story of the hare who was so far ahead in a footrace with the tortoise that he stopped for a nap. The slower, yet steady, tortoise passed the sleeping hare and crossed the finish line first.

Aesop told many stories about animals and birds that talk like people. The tales are called **fables,** because they usually teach a lesson. They also teach us something about the ideas of the ancient Greeks.

The face of Sappho is found on this old Greek coin.

Today we use many expressions based on Aesop's fables. Do you know about "sour grapes," "the dog in the manger," or "the grasshopper and the ant"? These expressions come from Aesop. His fables, unlike the Parthenon, are not in ruins. They are as good as ever, and we still enjoy the wisdom in them.

The ancient Greeks liked plays, which they performed in open-air theaters. The picture on page 91 shows the old theater at Epidauris (ep ə dôr′ əs). The stone seats are hard, but as many as 15,000 people at one time would go to see the plays. Many Greek plays have lasted, and people still perform them all over the world.

The curiosity of the Greeks   Many Greeks had a great deal of **curiosity.** Curiosity is the desire to know or learn. Herodotus, who wrote the history of the Persian wars, had a great deal of curiosity. He traveled to Egypt, Mesopotamia, and other lands just "to see what he could see."

Herodotus liked to hear stories that people told about their countries. For example, he tells a story he heard about gold-digging ants. The Persians told him that in India there were

> ants somewhat smaller than dogs but bigger than foxes.... The ants make dwellings under the ground, and in so doing they carry up sand in the same way they do in Greece, and the sand that is carried up contains gold.

Sometimes Herodotus admits he did not believe what people told him. He would say, "I give the story as it was told to me—but I do not believe it." He felt much the same when he saw a large gulch that

Ancient Greek plays are still given in this theater at Epidauris, an ancient seaport town in southern Greece.

The moon had mountains and plains and reflected the sun's light. Anaxagoras also said it was likely that other bodies besides the earth were **inhabited,** meaning they were homes for living things.

Socrates, the great questioner Socrates (sok′ rə tēz) of Athens had a great desire to understand things. He believed that people were the most important subject to study and understand. His motto was "Know thyself." Above all else, Socrates wanted to know what a truly good person would be like. He would study something by asking questions. What is good? Why is something beautiful? This became his method of teaching as well.

people said had been made by a god. Herodotus decided that an earthquake had caused it.

Anaxagoras (an ak sag′ ō rəs) was another Greek who refused to accept old stories. People commonly said the sun and moon were living things. Anaxagoras said that the sun was a large flaming rock.

Socrates wrote no books, but he was a good teacher with many followers. One follower, Plato (plā′ tō), wrote accounts somewhat like plays about Socrates and

Some Athenians hated Socrates' teachings. They accused him of being an enemy of Athens. A jury of 500 found Socrates guilty. He was sentenced to die by drinking poison.

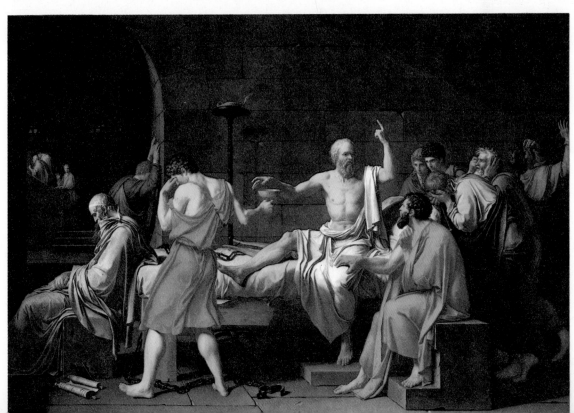

Games and Gods

Sports and religion went together in ancient Greece. The Greeks believed that the gods themselves enjoyed sports. They said that Zeus, greatest of their gods, had established their greatest sporting event, the Olympian Games. Of course, this was a very old tale, but it is true that the Greeks held the Olympian Games in honor of Zeus.

The Olympian Games took place every four years near the temple of Zeus at Olympia in western Greece. The Greeks held the first Olympian Games in 776 B.C., and they continued for nearly 12 centuries.

People from all over Greece came to the Olympian Games. The stadium could seat as many as 45,000 people. One of the top events was the pentathlon, a series of five contests in which each athlete took part. Each had to run, jump, wrestle, and throw both the discus and the javelin. The Greeks favored this event because only an all-around athlete could win the pentathlon.

The Greeks thought that good athletes made good soldiers. Some games tested skills useful in war. In one race the athletes wore helmets and carried heavy shields.

The games also included horse and chariot races. Chariot races were dangerous but very popular with the crowds. Drivers and chariots often tipped over on the sharp turns. Teams of horses sometimes ran into each other. Most of the starters did not finish. Greek crowds, like many of later times, enjoyed dangerous sports.

It was a great honor to win an Olympian event, although the prize was only a crown woven from the branches of a wild olive tree. But the athlete who received one of these olive leaf crowns received many gifts and favors when he returned home.

The modern games are called the Olympic Games and they have nothing to do his students. People read Plato's books today to learn what Socrates and his students talked about when the Parthenon was new.

Plato's Academy   After Socrates' death Plato started a school of his own. He taught his students in an olive grove called the academy near the city of Athens. Plato's school became so famous that the name of the olive grove came to mean a place of learning. Some schools are still called academies.

For years, tourists in Athens were shown an old olive tree and told that it was one of the original trees in Plato's grove. In 1977 a bus ran into the tree and split it into pieces. It was a shame to wreck an old tree, but Plato's wisdom was not destroyed.

Aristotle, a great thinker   One day a young man named Aristotle came to Plato's Academy to study. He remained there for many years, and later he opened a school of his own. Aristotle liked to walk

with Zeus or any religion. They began in 1896 and are held every 4 years in different countries all over the world. The games are divided into the Winter Olympics and the Summer Olympics. They include many more sports than the ancient Olympian Games. But there are still contests in jumping, throwing, wrestling, and running. There is now a decathlon in which the athletes take part in ten events.

The events now include a long-distance race called the marathon. It was given that name in honor of the Greek soldier who ran 24 miles (38.6 km) back to Athens from the Battle of Marathon to bring news of the Greek victory in 490 B.C.

Curiously enough, the ancient Olympian Games had no marathon race. In fact, the distance of the modern race is somewhat longer than the distance run by the Greek soldier. The length of the present race was not fixed until 1924 at the London Olympics in the United Kingdom. The race started at Windsor Castle and ended in front of the royal box in the London stadium. The distance from start to finish was 26 miles, 385 yards (42,195 m). Since 1924, that has been the official length of the Olympic marathon in our modern games.

about as he talked, so his students nicknamed him "the walker." He believed that people "naturally desire to know." Sometimes Aristotle is called the world's first scientist because he observed and thought so carefully. He had great curiosity about animals, birds, poetry, laws, stars—almost everything.

Aristotle became so famous that King Philip invited Aristotle to come to Macedonia to teach his 13-year-old son, Alexander. For 3 years Aristotle taught the boy who later conquered a great empire. Alexander showed much curiosity about the lands and peoples he conquered. Perhaps he owed his desire to know to his old teacher.

CHECKUP

1. Why did the Athenians build the Parthenon?
2. What did the Greeks believe about their gods and goddesses? Name some of them.
3. Who was Homer? Who was Sappho?
4. What kind of stories did Aesop tell?
5. What things were each of the following Greeks curious about: Herodotus? Anaxagoras? Socrates? Aristotle?

KEY FACTS

1. The ancient Greeks were citizens of free cities rather than subjects of a monarch.

2. The purpose of Spartan life was to make good soldiers and to defend the city.

3. The government of Athens was a democracy. All male citizens were expected to take part in making decisions.

4. Alexander the Great wanted to make one people of the many within his empire.

5. The Greeks had many gods and goddesses who they believed took sides in human affairs.

6. Socrates, Plato, and Aristotle were great thinkers; Homer and Sappho, great poets.

7. During Pericles' time, Athenians built beautiful buildings whose ruins still stand.

VOCABULARY QUIZ

If you know the meanings of the underlined words, you can tell which of the statements below are true and which are false. On a sheet of paper, write **T** for the true statements and **F** for the false statements.

1. A democracy is governed by the people.

2. When the Greek cities in Asia Minor became subjects of Persia, they lost their freedom.

3. An oligarchy is government by one.

4. In ancient Athens, only male citizens were allowed to vote in the Assembly.

5. Aesop's fables amuse and teach lessons.

6. At the Battle of Marathon, the Persians led a revolt against the Greek city-states.

7. Greek cities in Asia Minor collected tribute money from the kings of Persia.

8. Immigrants who came to live in Athens were not citizens of the city.

9. Even though the Greek cities fought each other at many different times, they joined together as allies to defeat the Persians.

10. Greek thinkers had so little curiosity that they cared little for learning.

REVIEW QUESTIONS

1. How was the sea important to the Greeks?

2. How did the Greeks use their land?

3. What was the difference between life in Sparta and life in Athens?

4. What did Pericles say about life in Athens? How does this show what the Athenians thought was important? Mention four things.

5. What were some of the things about which the Greeks were curious?

6. How did the word *academy* come to mean "a school or place of learning"?

ACTIVITIES

1. The top part of a column is called the capital. The drawings below show three types of capitals used by Greek builders. Find buildings where you live or pictures of buildings that use these capitals. Make a list for each type.

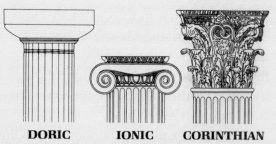

DORIC   IONIC   CORINTHIAN

2. Read some of Aesop's fables and discuss what lessons they tell. Then write your own fable.

4/SKILLS DEVELOPMENT

LOOKING FOR THE ORIGINS OF WORDS

WORDS HAVE ONE OR MORE PARTS

You can often understand the meaning of a new word by knowing the meaning of its word parts. Many of our English words come from Greek words. For example, the word *democracy* is made up of the Greek word *demos* and the Greek word part *cracy* that comes from the Greek word for *rule*. So democracy is rule by the people.

demos + cracy = democracy

If you look up a word in a large dictionary you will usually find a list of the older words from which the word comes. Such older words are often called the roots of our English words. If you like puzzles, you will find that looking up the roots of words makes an interesting game. Below is a list of words and word parts that come from Greek.

ROOTS FROM GREEK

anthropos = human being
aristos = best
auto = self (oneself)
bios = life
cracy = rule
demos = people
ge(o) = earth
graphy = writing
logy = study (science) of
monos = one
philos = loving
phobia = fear
sophia = wisdom

SKILLS PRACTICE

Below is a list of English words and their meanings. These words are formed from the Greek words and word parts listed at the left. Complete the following steps in this exercise:
1. Copy the English words on a sheet of paper.
2. Study the Greek words and word parts.
3. Write the letter of the correct meaning for each word on your list.

English words formed from Greek words

1.	biology	**7.**	monarchy
2.	biography	**8.**	autobiography
3.	geology	**9.**	anthropology
4.	autograph	**10.**	philanthropy
5.	aristocracy	**11.**	philosophy
6.	geography	**12.**	demophobia

English word meanings

a. writing about one's own life by oneself
b. study of human beings
c. rule by one person
d. rule by the best
e. writing about a person's life
f. fear of people
g. love and pursuit of wisdom
h. study of living things
i. study of the earth
j. love of human beings as shown by helping people through gifts of money
k. something written in a person's own hand-writing, especially his or her own name
l. writing about the earth

Growth of the Roman World

VOCABULARY

consul	plebeian
dictator	tribe
republic	civil war
patrician	

When Rome began The ancient Romans told a story of how their city began. They said that a man named Romulus (rom′ yə ləs) built the city's first wall and ruled as its first king. That was the reason for the city's name. Rome was the city of Romulus. This was said to have happened in the eighth century B.C. The Romans said that Romulus had a twin brother Remus. According to the old story, the two boys had been left by the Tiber River as babies. A friendly female wolf found and fed them. You can read this story in an old history of Rome written long ago by Livy (liv′ i), a Roman historian.

Ancient Rome was located on the peninsula of Italy in the western Mediterranean Sea. This peninsula is shaped like a boot kicking the island of Sicily. Look at the map on page 100. Rome was near, but not on, the sea. The city grew up by a crossing of the Tiber River at the place where the wolf supposedly found Romulus and Remus.

A republic, not a democracy Livy's history tells us that, at first, kings ruled Rome. Some ruled wisely; others did not. By experience the Romans discovered the dangers of monarchy—rule by one. When a monarch held all power, he could do as he pleased. It pleased some kings to do cruel and unfair things.

In 509 B.C., some of the Romans decided that they had had enough. They rebelled and drove their king from the city. Some Romans thought there was then nothing to do but to choose another king.

Other Romans wanted to set up a new kind of government. They suggested that the people choose two leaders to be called **consuls**. Each consul would have the powers of a king, but for a year only. Because each consul would have the same power, one could keep the other from misusing the power of the office. If a single leader was needed in time of danger, the people could choose a **dictator.** A dictator would be given complete power, but the person could hold office for only 6 months. The Romans wanted to keep some control over those who governed.

The Romans called their new government a **republic.** The word means "a public thing" or "the people's affair." A republic is a government in which the citizens choose those who are to run the

Ruins of the Colosseum in Rome show the skill of ancient Roman builders. The Colosseum held about 45,000 people. Awnings could be hung from its walls to provide shade.

country. We still have republics. Have you ever recited these words: "I pledge allegiance to the flag of the United States of America and to the republic for which it stands"?

The Roman Republic was "the people's affair," but not all people had the same voice in it. Only men who were citizens could take part in the government. Women citizens had no share in the government. There also were many slaves in Rome. These men and women were not citizens, nor were they allowed any part in the government.

There were even two classes of citizens in ancient Rome—the upperclass, called **patricians,** and the common people, called **plebeians.** Both patricians and plebeians took part in the assembly, which elected the consuls. The patricians, though fewer in number, controlled the assembly. And only patricians served as consuls or as members of the council of elders. The Romans called this council the Senate. It was a body of older men. In time, the plebeians won a greater voice. But the Roman Republic never became a government of all the people.

The growing power of a city　When Rome first became a republic, it was no larger than the Greek cities. It was only one of a number of free cities and clusters of people called **tribes** in Italy. As in Greece, each city had its own laws and had to defend itself. Disputes between neighboring cities often led to wars.

The Romans were probably no more warlike than their neighbors, but they had more success. As a result the city on the Tiber came to rule more and more land. Rome brought first central Italy and then the whole peninsula under its rule.

The conquest of Italy did not end Rome's disputes with its neighbors. But now its neighbor was Carthage, a city in North Africa. Find Carthage on the map on page 100.

For how many years was Rome a republic?

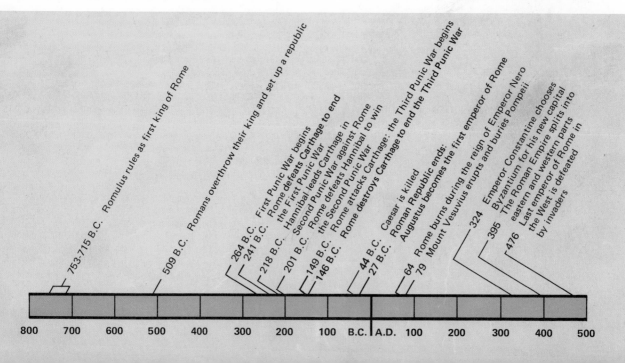

Carthage was a rich trading city that had grown powerful at sea. The Carthaginians had control of the western Mediterranean and they intended to keep it. It was said that they would drown any foreign sailor they caught in "their sea."

Carthage and Rome both had settlements on the island of Sicily, which lies 10 miles (16 km) from the toe of the Italian boot. Warily, they kept a close watch on each other. The Carthaginians did not want the Romans on an island in "their sea." The Romans did not want the Carthaginians so near to Italy. Carthage feared the power of Rome. Rome feared the power of Carthage. Such fears easily lead to war.

War with Carthage   War began in 264 B.C. This was the first of three struggles which the Romans called the Punic Wars.

Hannibal led the Carthaginians in the Second Punic War, which was fought from 218–201 B.C. Hannibal was Rome's bitter enemy. When he was 9 years old, his father made him promise to make war against Rome until it was defeated. Hannibal kept his word. He spent his whole life either preparing to fight or fighting the Romans.

In the land now called Spain, which Carthage controlled, Hannibal organized and trained an army. It was a large force including thousands of men, hundreds of horses, and 37 elephants. What were elephants doing in an army? These large animals served as "walking tanks" against an enemy's soldiers on foot.

Hannibal did not take his large force to Italy by crossing the Mediterranean Sea. Instead, he marched. It was a dangerous

Hannibal's army sometimes came under attack as it made its way through the passes of the Alps.

march across the Pyrenees (pir′ ə nēz) Mountains and over the Alps. There were no good roads through the mountains. In the narrow mountain passes, people attacked the Carthaginians by pushing rocks down on them. Hannibal lost many soldiers and animals, yet he brought his army and a few elephants into northern Italy.

For nearly two decades, Hannibal won battles, but he could not take the walled city of Rome. Hannibal's forces grew weaker while the Romans patiently waited. Then in 202 B.C. the Roman army boldly crossed by sea to North Africa. Carthage, now in danger, called its best general home. It was too late. The Romans defeated Hannibal, and Carthage surrendered. Rome was now the most powerful city in the western Mediterranean.

Rome and Carthage later fought the Third Punic War. Finally in 146 B.C. Rome conquered Carthage for the last time and took over all its lands along the northern and southern shores of the Mediterranean Sea.

A city gains an empire   As the power of Rome grew, the foreign lands that it ruled came to include more than ancient Carthage. See the map on this page. Along the eastern Mediterranean, kings who ruled Alexander's old empire fought among themselves. Some of the warring kings turned to Rome for support. They discovered that those whom Rome helped, Rome also controlled.

Beyond the Alps, Rome conquered all of Europe north to the Rhine and Danube rivers. North of the Danube, the Romans ruled Dacia. Today Dacia is the country called Romania, land of the Romans. They also ruled most of Britain.

The map below shows all of the lands that Rome ruled. It also shows the Roman roads, which knit the scattered lands together. It was an empire on three continents: Europe, Africa, and Asia. Today there are 27 countries within what was one empire. The Roman Empire surrounded the Mediterranean Sea. "Mediterranean Sea" means sea in the middle of land. For the Romans, the

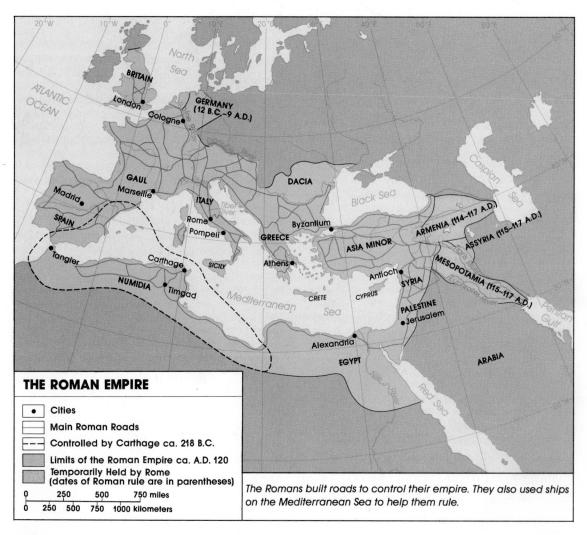

THE ROMAN EMPIRE

- • Cities
- Main Roman Roads
- --- Controlled by Carthage ca. 218 B.C.
- Limits of the Roman Empire ca. A.D. 120
- Temporarily Held by Rome (dates of Roman rule are in parentheses)

0   250   500   750 miles
0   250 500 750 1000 kilometers

The Romans built roads to control their empire. They also used ships on the Mediterranean Sea to help them rule.

The Romans built cities all over their empire. Timgad in Algeria, North Africa, begun in
A.D. 100, was a colony for veteran soldiers. Its theater held 4,000 people.

Mediterranean was truly the "middle sea" of their great empire.

The end of the Republic   Rome was a small city when the republic began. This kind of government worked well enough so long as Rome remained small. Consuls elected for 1 year could rule when they governed only the city itself. Consuls could even lead armies when an army was nothing but an armed band of citizens who fought near home.

All of this changed as Rome's empire grew. Soldiers served for years rather than a few months. Generals who con-quered kingdoms in North Africa and Asia became powerful and popular heroes. When they returned with their soldiers to Rome, they were able to control elections. One general had himself elected consul seven times even though it was against the constitution. **Civil war**—which means fighting within the country—broke out. General fought general for control of the government. No longer did the citizens of Rome govern Rome. The soldiers did.

Julius Caesar (jül′ yəs sē′ zər) was one of the most successful generals. He de-feated his rivals in battle. By 46 B.C. he was master of Rome. Many Romans, weary of

101

the civil war, gladly accepted Caesar's rule. They hoped that a strong leader could bring peace to Rome. They made Caesar dictator, not for 6 months, but for life.

Julius Caesar wanted fame and glory, but he also wanted peace for Rome and its empire. He tried to win the support of those who had fought against him and his bid for power. Caesar wanted a fair government for the Roman people, one that would work. Caesar gave Roman citizenship to conquered peoples. And he replaced dishonest officials with good leaders.

Caesar planned many changes. He tried to help poor people in the cities. He also offered free land to workers and farmers who wanted to move to unsettled parts of the empire. You will read about more of Caesar's plans later in this chapter.

Despite Julius Caesar's good works and government reforms, many people in Rome feared him. After he was made dictator for life, he was assassinated.

Some people thought that Caesar was too powerful and planned to make himself king. Perhaps he did. His rivals spoke of the dangers of monarchy. They recalled how the Romans once drove a king from their city. They warned that a man who would be king was as much an enemy of Rome as an enemy on the battlefield. A true Roman should be ready to kill an enemy of either kind. On March 15—called the ides of March—in 44 B.C., a group of patricians acted on this advice. They killed Caesar in the Senate House.

Monarchs but not kings The death of Caesar did not bring the old republic back to life. It brought more civil war. Caesar's nephew Octavian won the war.

The Romans hailed Octavian as Emperor, an old title which meant "commander." And the Senate gave him the name Augustus, meaning "honored." Augustus became as powerful as a king, but he wisely avoided that title. He knew how the Romans felt about kings.

Emperor Augustus not only gained the same powers as his uncle, Augustus also wanted to carry out his uncle's plans. And he lived long enough to do so. Caesar had been killed 5 years after he came to power. Augustus ruled the empire for 40 years as a monarch.

Some writers call the reign of Augustus the golden age of Rome. Livy and other important Roman thinkers and writers lived during this time. Many roads and beautiful buildings and other works were created. Augustus said that he had "found Rome brick and left it marble." You will read about more of these great works later in the chapter.

This model of the Roman Forum was made as a movie set. The Forum was a busy place. Armies paraded here, and the Senate House was located here.

Augustus was the first of many emperors who ruled the Roman Empire during the next 5 centuries. His reign marked the beginning of a long period of peace. After he died in A.D. 14, other emperors also ruled with great skill and wisdom. And some ruled badly. Just as the old kings had misused the powers of monarchy, some emperors abused their power under the new monarchy.

Constantinople—"The New Rome"
One of Rome's great emperors was Constantine, who rose to power nearly 300 years after the reign of Augustus. In A.D. 324 Emperor Constantine decided to build a new capital for the Roman Empire in the East. The eastern part of the empire had come to have more people and greater wealth than the western part. Constantine chose the ancient Greek city of Byzantium as his capital. Find Byzantium on the map on page 100. Constantine rebuilt Byzantium

This arch in the Roman Forum was built to honor the victories of the emperor Titus (A.D. 4–81).

into a much larger and grander city. He called it New Rome. But it came to be known as Constantinople—the city of Constantine.

Constantine's New Rome required Romans. The emperor ordered a number of important Roman families to move to the East. Each family brought a handful of soil from the old city of Rome to the new. The emperor had statues and monuments brought from Old Rome. He built palaces, public baths, stadiums, and government buildings like those of the old capital. He even build a Senate House, although Senators no longer had any part in the government.

Constantine built no temples to the old Roman gods in his new capital. He built Christian churches for the people of New Rome, because he was the first Roman emperor to adopt that religion. The greatest of his churches stood near the Imperial Palace and the Senate House. It was called Hagia Sophia in Greek, the Church of Holy Wisdom. Fire destroyed Constantine's church, but a later emperor replaced it with a grander structure. This later Hagia Sophia still stands after more than 1,450 years. It is probably the best known building in the modern city of Istanbul, the name by which Constantinople is now called. Hagia Sophia is no longer a church. Today it is a museum.

In time this Eastern Roman Empire became quite different from the empire that had been ruled from Rome. Today scholars usually call the eastern empire the Byzantine Empire. The name is taken from the ancient Greek city of Byzantium where Constantine had built his New Rome.

Hagia Sophia was built between 532 and 537. Its dome, damaged by an earthquake, was rebuilt in 563. The towers, called minarets, were added 900 years later.

The rulers who came after Constantine continued to call themselves emperors even though their empire became smaller and smaller. The map on page 274 shows the extent of the Byzantine Empire about 400 years after Constantine founded New Rome. In time, all that was left was the city itself and a small part of Greece. Finally in 1453, the city was conquered by the Ottoman Turks. The last fragment of the once great Roman Empire had disappeared. Yet few governments have lasted this long.

CHECKUP

1. What limits did the Romans put on a consul? On a dictator?
2. Why did Rome and Carthage go to war?
3. When did the Third Punic War end?
4. How did Rome gain an empire?
5. Why was Julius Caesar able to become so powerful? Why was he killed?

The Ways of the Romans

"First of the cities"   As Rome's empire grew, so did the city itself. Perhaps a million people lived in and about the city at the time of the later emperors. No Greek city had been nearly so large. People marveled at the grandeur, or greatness, of Rome. One poet called it "Golden Rome, first of the cities." Others thought it not so grand. Another poet wrote of Rome's "thousand dangers." He thought a person who was wise would move out of the city to a quiet country place. There were good reasons for both views.

Rome had many attractions. It was the capital and the center of a great empire. Something was always going on there. Today, we still use a saying about the importance of the old city: "All roads lead to Rome." People and goods from all over the empire came to Rome. It was said, "Whoever wishes to see all the goods of the world must either journey throughout the world or stay in Rome."

Rome had many problems as well. They were similar to those of large cities today: crowding, dirt, noise, and heavy traffic.

Food and water for a large city   A city of a million people needs a lot of food. The nearby farms could not feed so many people. Grain ships from Egypt and other parts of North Africa brought wheat for Rome's daily bread. Spain supplied fine olive oil and dried fish. Greece also sent olive oil along with wine and honey. The "first of the cities" depended on other places for much of its food. Large cities always do.

A large city needs water. The Tiber River runs through Rome, but the city itself made the water too dirty to drink.

Roman engineers built waterways, called **aqueducts,** to bring clean water

This Roman aqueduct is still in use. It brings water to the city of Segovia in Spain. The water flows in a channel along the top of the aqueduct.

from distant streams and springs. The water flowed through the aqueducts to fountains and tanks in the city. Find the aqueducts on the map of the city of Rome on page 109.

The water moved through the aqueducts without pumps. To keep the water flowing, engineers had to tunnel through hills in some places. In other places they had to build stone arch bridges to support the waterway. Pipes carried the water into the first floor of some of the houses. The Romans used pipes made of earthenware or lead.

A large city also needs sewers. Sewers are waterways that carry the wastes away from the city. One of Rome's early rulers built the Great Sewer, which 2,500 years later still empties into the Tiber. The Romans were proud of their ability to build useful things such as roads, aqueducts, and sewers.

Life in a crowded city   In spite of its aqueducts and sewers, Rome was a dirty and rather smelly city. Garbage was thrown into open pits within the city. The open fish and meat markets gave forth

Building an aqueduct took large numbers of workers, many of whom were slaves. Large cranes and pulleys were used to lift huge blocks of stone into place.

Streets in Rome, especially in parts of the city where poor people lived, were narrow, crowded, and often filled with garbage. Some streets were unpaved.

odors in a day when no one had refrigerators. A leather **tannery,** a place where hides are prepared, gave forth other bad odors into the air.

Streets through the city were narrow and crooked. Some were paved with stone, others were not. They were little more than dirt lanes, dusty in dry weather and muddy when it rained. Traffic became so bad that Julius Caesar ordered the carts and wagons to stay out of the city until late afternoon. Goods had to be brought into the city after the crowds got off the streets. Cart wheels rumbling over the stone pavements did not make it easy to sleep at night.

Roman roads can still be seen in many countries that were once part of the Roman Empire. On the left below is the Appian Way, a Roman road just outside modern Rome. The drawing, below right, shows how Roman roads were built.

CROSS SECTION OF A ROMAN ROAD

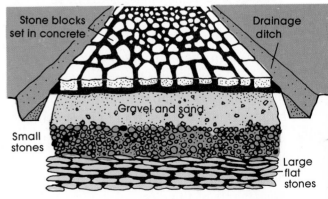

Stone blocks set in concrete

Drainage ditch

Gravel and sand

Small stones

Large flat stones

Most of Rome's people lived crowded together in four- and five-story apartment buildings. Many of these buildings were made of brick and wood. When a fire got started, it would spread rapidly through the crowded city.

A fire during the reign of Emperor Nero in A.D. 64 destroyed a large part of the city. Perhaps you have heard that "Nero fiddled while Rome burned." The saying is based on an old story. Nero supposedly had the fire set because he did not like the old buildings and narrow, crooked streets. According to the old story, Nero wanted to build a grander city. While much of Rome burned to the ground, the emperor sang and played.

This story is probably not true. But after the fire, Nero ordered that there be "regular rows of streets and broad thoroughfares" instead of narrow, winding lanes. He limited the height of buildings. He ordered that all buildings be at least partly made of stone so that they would not burn so easily. Some people thought that Nero made Rome a more beautiful city. Others said that the old neighborhoods had been better. Officials who rebuild old cities often make things both better *and* worse.

Rome had some open spaces in spite of the crowding. One such space was the Field of Mars where citizen soldiers had gathered in the early days of Rome. The Field of Mars in later times became a sort of public park. People went there to play ball, roll hoops, wrestle and, in general, to enjoy themselves. The grassy field must have been a welcome relief to many Romans from the crowded streets and apartments of the city.

This Roman bath, dating from the first century A.D., is in Bath, England. Behind the bath can be seen a church built in the early sixteenth century.

The great baths   Romans could also go to one of the city's many public baths by paying a small fee. A Roman bath was a great deal more than a place to get clean. It was more of a recreation center. It was also a place to meet people and talk. Some baths even had libraries.

There were many small baths and several very large ones built by emperors for the people of the city. The large baths had beautifully decorated lounges, dressing rooms, and swimming pools. A man who lived near a bath wrote that he could hear the noise of "those who jump into the pool with a mighty splash." He also wrote about the puffing and groaning of the "stronger fellows exercising and swinging heavy lead weights in their hands."

People could play games in the exercise hall. Bowling with stone balls was one of the favorite games. People could also use the steam room, the hot tubs, and the chilling cold pool.

A Roman circus   The Romans liked to go to the circus, but a Roman circus was not like any circus you may have seen. The Great Circus in Rome, called the Circus Maximus, was a place for chariot races. It was a huge U-shaped stadium which could seat as many as 200,000 people. It was often filled, for the races were free. The emperor or another wealthy person paid for them as a sort of party for the whole city.

People of all sorts crowded into the Great Circus. An ancient historian declared that it was the "true temple" of the Romans. On race days people rushed to get seats as if they would outrun the

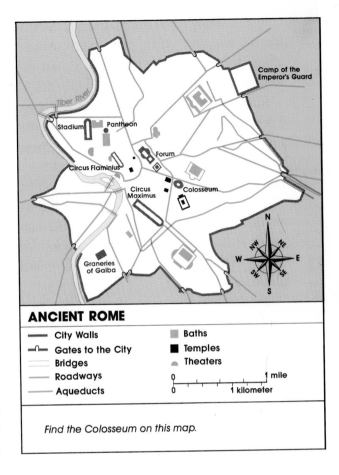

ANCIENT ROME

- ‖‖‖‖ City Walls
- ⊣▢⊢ Gates to the City
- Bridges
- Roadways
- Aqueducts
- ▢ Baths
- ■ Temples
- ▲ Theaters

0 —————— 1 mile
0 —————— 1 kilometer

Find the Colosseum on this map.

Chariot races were exciting to watch. The two-wheeled chariots were pulled by two or four horses. If a chariot overturned its driver could be badly hurt or even killed.

chariots. They gathered to discuss the different drivers with great seriousness. They acted as if the future of Rome depended on who won the race.

Successful drivers became famous. They were even honored with monuments put up by the Romans. These words were carved on a monument for a man named Diocles: "The champion of all charioteers. He drove chariots for 24 years, ran 4,257 starts, and won 1,462 victories." It was rather like the modern "halls of fame" for football and baseball players.

Chariot races were both fast and dangerous. Chariots often upset on the sharp turns at either end of the track. To keep from being dragged along the ground, drivers carried knives to cut themselves free from the horses' reins. Such accidents made the races more thrilling for the crowd.

Roman games   In the early days of the republic, Romans held public games in honor of their gods. In time, the games came to be held more to give the people a free show.

The Romans liked the excitement of danger. They preferred the rougher sports at the games. They liked boxing rather than running or jumping. Roman boxing was particularly brutal because the boxers wore gloves with strips of metal on them.

The athletes who took part in these contests were mostly professionals. They fought for pay. They had their own organization, and they toured the cities of the empire. Some fighters became popular heroes, at least as long as they kept winning. But they paid a high price for their fame. They sometimes received permanent injuries. A doctor of the time reported that they also usually ate too much, became overweight, and died young.

Boxing was not the most brutal Roman sport. Crowds also gathered to watch both animals and armed men fight to death. Many such events took place in the **Colosseum** (kol ə sē′ əm), a large arena in

Exits in the Colosseum were so well designed that the building could be emptied of people in minutes. Since the arena floor no longer exists we can look into the basement where the wild animals were kept.

Rome, part of which still stands. In the Colosseum different kinds of animals were made to fight each other. Tigers attacked bulls. Lions fought bears. Lightly armed men had to do battle with frightened wild animals. Sometimes the man killed the animal. Sometimes the animal killed the man.

The Romans had at least one story about a happy outcome in the arena. There was once a slave named Androcles (an′ drə klēz) who ran away from a cruel master and hid in a cave. A wild lion entered the cave with a thorn in its badly swollen paw. Androcles gently removed the thorn, and the lion became quite friendly.

Later, Androcles was captured and sent into the arena to fight for his life. A cage was opened and out came the same lion. The grateful animal recognized Androcles. It rubbed its head against Androcles and licked his hand. The crowd was so surprised by the unusual turn of events that it demanded freedom for both Androcles and the lion. It is said that Androcles afterwards went about Rome showing the friendly lion in taverns.

Not only did people fight animals in the Colosseum, they fought each other. Men and sometimes women who fought to entertain the crowds were called **gladiators.** They were usually slaves or criminals condemned to death. The fight in the arena gave them a chance to escape their fate. A gladiator who fought especially well might be given freedom. Those who lost a fight usually lost their lives as well.

Gladiators killed each other to thrill and amuse the crowds. Only a few Romans protested that it was wrong to kill people

In Roman games gladiators fought each other for life or death. They were trained in special schools, and were often armed with different kinds of weapons.

"for sport and amusement." It was one of the cruel facts of life in the "First of the cities."

Pompeii—another ancient Roman city
Today, visitors to Pompeii see in the doorway of a house a sign that warns, *CAVE CANEM*, which is Latin for "beware of dog." But they need not worry about being bitten. The sign was put there more than 1,900 years ago. The dog that watched the house probably died on August 24 in the year A.D. 79. On that day a great cloud of fire and smoke burst from nearby Mount Vesuvius (və sü′ vē əs). Rocks and ashes fell like hail and snow on Pompeii. By the time the mountain grew quiet again, a 12-foot blanket of ashes buried the city. Many of its people—and their dogs—lay dead under that layer of ashes.

111

Business in Pompeii   Before ashes covered it, Pompeii was a busy city of 20,000 people. It was south of Rome on the western coast of the peninsula. Like most cities in the Roman Empire, Pompeii could be reached by water as well as by road. People came from Rome to vacation in Pompeii. Traders and other travelers came on business.

Shops and houses were crowded together along Pompeii's narrow streets. Most of the shops were small family businesses run by men and women. Butchers, sandal makers, leather workers, and wine sellers all sold their goods from small shops that opened on the streets.

Every neighborhood had its bakery. All the work of making bread from wheat and barley was done within each bakery. The baker ground the flour, mixed the dough, shaped the loaves, and baked them in an oven. The bakeries made different kinds of bread. Some even made dog biscuits, perhaps for the dogs that watched the doorways.

Pompeii had a number of fullers' shops. Fullers finished the rough woolen cloth woven by peasants in the nearby

Most streets in Pompeii were narrow. They were lined with shops and paved with large stone blocks. Stepping stones let people cross the street without getting dirty.

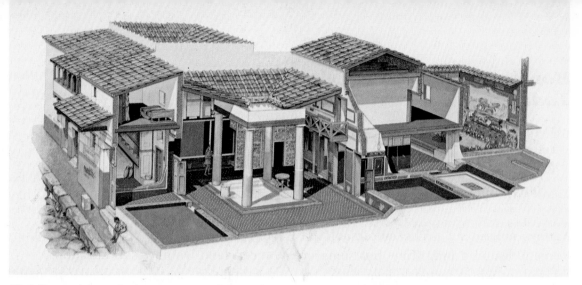

Most Roman houses had rooms grouped around an open court. This drawing of a Pompeian house has walls and roof cut away to show this. The street entrance is on the left.

villages. The fullers washed and thickened the cloth. They bleached it in the sun and then dyed it. The materials used for cleaning and dying were rather smelly. So was a fish sauce made in Pompeii for which the city was well-known. Perhaps that is why there were also a number of perfume shops in Pompeii.

Public places and private houses
One of the busiest places in Pompeii was the forum. The forum was somewhat like a modern shopping mall. It was a paved open area where people could walk without having to dodge vehicles. There was a town hall at one end and a temple at the other. A two-story covered walkway supported by stone columns ran along each side. Shops and offices were located on the walkway. Farmers selling fruit and vegetables sat in the shade of the walkway. Potters spread pots and plates on the pavement for buyers to see.

Today thousands of visitors go to see what remains of this once-busy city. They look at tracks worn by chariot wheels in the stone streets. They see a bakery that had bread in the oven when Pompeii was buried. They sit in the stadium where 20,000 people once watched gladiators fight. Visitors walk through the rooms of a public bath. Most interesting of all, they enter the houses where people were living on that August morning so long ago. They go into the rooms where the Romans slept and the kitchens where they cooked. Most of the rooms are built around pleasant open courtyards. There are few outside windows. Scenes were painted on the walls so that the small rooms seem large and open.

Visitors to Pompeii can easily imagine the busy forum and streets, barking dogs, and children at play even though the city was destroyed over 19 centuries ago.

CHECKUP

1. Why were food and water brought from great distances to Rome? How were they brought?
2. What were some of the problems of life in crowded Rome?
3. What was a Roman bath? A Roman circus?
4. Who were the gladiators? Why did they fight?
5. What shops and businesses were in Pompeii?

Roman Works That Live Today

VOCABULARY

reform	justice
Romance languages	

A new calendar   The empire of the Romans lasted a long time, but some of their other works lasted longer. They are part of the modern world. Some of these great works include new ideas and **reforms,** which are changes made for the better or to improve something. The Romans were also great builders. Because they ruled an empire, there are Roman works in Europe, Asia, and Africa.

One reform brought about by Julius Caesar was a new calendar. Caesar realized that the Egyptian calendar was better than that used at Rome. But he thought it too could be improved. He asked a Greek scholar at Alexandria to work out a calendar year that would be the same as the solar year of 365¼ days. The scholar suggested a plan that Caesar and later Augustus adopted for the Roman calendar.

The improved calendar was almost the same as our calendar. The year was made up of 365 days divided into 12 months. Every fourth year had 366 days. A day was added at the end of February.

In our calendar February has 28 days. Every fourth year it gains an extra day. We call this a leap year. It takes care of the extra ¼ day in the solar year. Two of our months remind us how our calendar began. July was named for Julius Caesar, August for Augustus.

The alphabet—a good idea that spread   The Romans did not invent the alphabet they used. They borrowed it from the Etruscans (i trus′ kənz), a neighboring people who, in turn, had borrowed their alphabet from the Greeks. But the Greeks were borrowers too. They borrowed from the Phoenicians (fə nish′ ənz), a people from the Eastern Mediterranean land we now call Lebanon.

Alphabets were borrowed so many times that we do not know just who invented the first one. You read in Chapter 3 that people in Mesopotamia used marks for sounds. But they had different marks for each syllable. This meant that a person had to memorize hundreds of marks in order to learn to write.

By 1200 B.C. some people in the eastern Mediterranean lands developed a simpler kind of writing. They discovered that if each mark stood for a single, simple sound, they could write using far fewer marks. This is the main idea of an alphabet. You can write all the words in our language with only 26 letters.

The Phoenicians were one of the peoples who adopted and developed an alphabet. The Phoenicians were sea traders who did business all around the Mediterranean. The Phoenicians often sailed to Greece to sell all sorts of precious goods. The Greeks bought their purple cloth, pearls, and gold jewelry. But they borrowed something much more valuable— their alphabet. The Greeks started using Phoenician letters to write their own language. Later the Etruscans and Romans borrowed from the Greeks.

Each borrower of the alphabet made changes. The Greeks changed the Phoeni-

Writing about his war in Gaul, Caesar tells how he had great ramps and towers built to attack a city. His soldiers reached the city's walls through covered walkways.

cian, and the Romans changed the Greek. For example, the Greek Δ became the Roman "D." The Greek π became Roman "P." The Roman alphabet is the most widely used alphabet in the world today. You are using it as you read this book.

Living Latin   Latin, the language of the Romans, lasted much longer than their empire. People still study Latin in order to read the writings of the ancient Romans. You will read about some of those writings in the next section.

Ancient Latin also lives in languages people speak every day. Spanish, Portuguese, French, Italian, and Romanian all grew out of Latin. They are called **Romance languages** because they came from the language of the Romans. Nearly one tenth of the people in the world today speak one of these Latin-based Romance languages. Spanish and Portuguese are the main languages of Central and South America. That is why they are called Latin America.

English does not come directly from Latin, but English borrows nearly half its words from Latin. Most of the borrowed words are slightly changed, but some are not. For example, here are a few Latin words which are also English words: arena, circus, index, senior, stadium, veto, virus, viaduct. If you do not know any of these words, you can find their meanings in either an English or a Latin dictionary.

Living books by dead authors   Some of the Romans who made the empire also wrote books that people still read. Julius Caesar wrote *The Gallic War*, an account of his war in Gaul, the land we call France. Caesar wrote so clearly that students learn Latin by reading his history.

115

Cicero (sis′ ə rō), a Roman lawyer who lived at the same time as Caesar, wrote many books. His writings have been read by so many people that some of Cicero's sayings have become common sayings. Did you know that all of the following were the words of Cicero, a man who died in 43 B.C.?

Where there is life there is hope.
He is his own worst enemy.
One does not have to believe everything he hears.
He added insult to injury.
Not to know what happened before you were born is to remain forever a child.

What do you think is meant by this last saying? Both girls and boys were taught to read and to write. Some children learned mathematics and the ideas of Greek and Roman scholars. But not many Romans grew up to write works that lasted along with the writings of Cicero, Caesar, and a few other great thinkers.

Lasting ideas of Roman builders
The Romans built well in stone, brick, and concrete. They built cities, roads, bridges, and aqueducts in all parts of their empire. Visitors still view the remains of their temples, theaters, baths, and other buildings in Europe, North Africa, and western Asia.

Some of the Roman buildings, such as the Pantheon, have held up very well. Its huge concrete dome has lasted, as have the ideas of those who planned and built it. Compare the Pantheon with the building in the United States designed by Thomas Jefferson. A look at the pictures below makes it clear where Jefferson got his idea.

The pictures of the ancient Roman Colosseum on pages 97 and 110 tell the same

The Pantheon, on the left below, was built in Rome as a temple to all the Roman gods. It was finished in A.D. 126. On the right below is the Rotunda, one of the buildings designed by Thomas Jefferson between 1819 and 1825 for the University of Virginia. As the pictures show, Jefferson was much influenced by the Roman Pantheon.

story. Many modern stadiums have been designed after it. The ideas of ancient builders live in modern buildings. Are there any buildings where you live that show how people have used Roman ideas?

Laws: "The art of the good and fair"
Many different peoples lived within the Roman Empire. There were Egyptians, Babylonians, Greeks, North Africans, Gauls, and a great many others. Each of these peoples had their own customs and laws. Yet each could not just follow their own rules. To live together in peace, the different peoples of the empire had to live by some of the same laws.

Rome ruled the empire, so the Romans laid down the laws of the empire. But the Romans paid some attention to the ideas and customs of other peoples. The Romans knew that all peoples share the ability to reason. The Romans thought that if they made reasonable laws, *all* peoples could see that the laws were reasonable.

A Roman law book said that laws should give people **justice.** What is justice? Justice gives every person her or his due. By due, the book meant that which rightfully belongs to a person. If someone gets justice, that person receives what is deserved. How can we know what is rightfully due a person? That was and is the business of judges and courts. A judge should decide what is good and fair in each individual case. The law book said that law was "the art of the good and fair."

Roman law had a number of rules to guide judges in the practice of this art. These were rules that the Romans thought any reasonable person would find "good and fair." Listed below are some of the rules. Do they seem "good and fair" to you?

> It is wrong for one person to attack another without cause.
> No one should gain wealth through harm or injury to another.
> A person should not be punished for what he or she thinks.
> It is better for a crime to be left unpunished than for an innocent person to be punished.
> A person accused of a crime should have a chance to face one's accusers and defend oneself.
> There should be no ex *post facto* law.

The last statement means that no law can be used to punish someone for something done before the law was made.

Roman law developed over a long period of time. It grew out of what many peoples in different times found "good and fair." The law systems of a number of modern countries are based on Roman law. The United States is not one of them, but Roman ideas about law found their way into our system. The Latin words *ex post facto* became part of our language and the rule part of our law. The Constitution of the United States reads: "No ex post facto law shall be passed." Here again, a great work from Rome outlasted the Roman Empire.

CHECKUP

1. Describe the calendar that Julius Caesar and Augustus adopted for Rome.
2. What is the main idea of an alphabet?
3. Why is Latin called a living language?
4. Why can the writings of Caesar and Cicero be called living books?
5. According to Roman law books, what is justice?

KEY FACTS

1. Ancient Rome had a republic but not a democracy.

2. Rome's conquest of an empire helped lead to the destruction of its republic and the beginning of a monarchy.

3. Rome, the capital city of the Roman Empire, had many of the same attractions and problems as large cities in the world today.

4. The Romans were very good at building useful things, such as roads, aqueducts, sewers, bridges, and stadiums.

5. People in the modern world still use the Roman calendar, alphabet, language, and law.

VOCABULARY QUIZ

On a separate sheet of paper, write the letter of the term next to the number of its description. Be careful. Two of the statements describe words that are not in the list.

a. dictator   **f.** aqueduct
b. justice   **g.** consul
c. plebeian   **h.** reform
d. tannery   **i.** patrician
e. civil war   **j.** republic

1. A citizen of ancient Rome who was a member of the upper class

2. A waterway that carries water from a stream or spring to where the water is used

3. A change that makes something better

4. A place where hides are prepared for clothing and other uses

5. A leader of ancient Rome chosen by the people to rule for 1 year

6. Fighting between different groups within the same country or empire

7. A citizen of ancient Rome who was in the class of common people

8. A place where rough woolen cloth was cleaned and dyed

9. A leader of ancient Rome chosen to rule for 6 months during times of danger

10. A war between two different countries

11. A government in which the people choose leaders to rule

12. Something that gives a person what is rightfully his or hers

REVIEW QUESTIONS

1. Why can it be said that the Romans had a republic but not a democracy?

2. Why did the early Romans want to keep some control over those who governed?

3. How did Rome's conquest of an empire help lead to the destruction of its republic?

4. What did Julius Caesar want to do for Rome?

5. What is meant by "All roads lead to Rome"?

6. What were some of the attractions and problems of life in the city of Rome?

7. Why did Rome want people under its rule to think that Roman laws were reasonable?

8. What works of the Romans have lasted until modern times?

ACTIVITIES

1. Look up the history of the letters of your initials in an encyclopedia or a dictionary. Write the Phoenician, Greek, and Roman forms of your initials on a piece of paper. Now make a chart to show the history of six other letters in the alphabet.

2. Use the library to find pictures of ancient Roman buildings. Then collect pictures of modern buildings that in some way look like those found in Roman architecture.

5/SKILLS DEVELOPMENT

USING A GAZETTEER

A GEOGRAPHICAL DICTIONARY

A gazetteer is a geographical dictionary. It lists places in alphabetical order and gives their locations and descriptions. It gives the latitude and longitude of places such as cities and mountain peaks. For places such as regions, seas, and rivers, a gazetteer describes the locations.

The Gazetteer for this book is on pages 470–479. Turn to page 470. Information about the first entry is given in this order:

1. The name of the place is Accra.

2. Its latitude and longitude is 6°N/0° long.

3. The place is described as the capital and most populated city in the country of Ghana. It is a port city on the Atlantic Ocean.

4. The page number tells you there is a map on page 355 where Accra may be found.

SKILLS PRACTICE

Your Gazetteer is a useful tool for locating places. The historical map below shows the limits of the Roman Empire about A.D. 120. Complete the following steps to show where places were located in the Roman Empire.

1. Trace this map on a sheet of paper.

2. Look up the places below in the Gazetteer.

3. Find each place on the map on the page number given for the entry in the Gazetteer.

4. Use the latitude and longitude or the location described in the Gazetteer to locate and label each place on your map.

a. Pompeii   **f.** Black Sea

b. Dacia   **g.** Rome

c. Rhine River   **h.** Gaul

d. Athens   **i.** Alexandria

e. Danube River   **j.** Mediterranean Sea

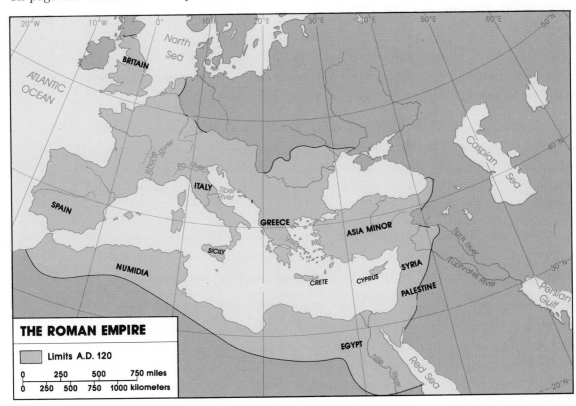

THE ROMAN EMPIRE

Limits A.D. 120

0 250 500 750 miles
0 250 500 750 1000 kilometers

2/UNIT REVIEW

1. Much of the modern world has its roots in the past. The beginnings of how we live and think today go back thousands of years to people who lived in Mesopotamia and the lands around the Mediterranean Sea. — *Name five or more ideas or practices in use today that began among some of the people who lived in these ancient times.*

2. Living in cities offered people greater protection and more goods and services because people depended upon each other's work. — *In what different ways have you benefited from the work of other people during the past 24 hours?*

3. City peoples invented writing, which made it possible for laws to be written down, and for ideas to be passed along and stored in books. — *How have you made use of written or printed words during the past week? In what ways does television offer some of the same benefits?*

4. Farming in the Nile River valley in ancient Egypt made it necessary for people to live and work closely together. The whole land came under the rule of god-kings. — *How was it easier for one ruler to gain control over all the land because the people were working together?*

5. Each Greek city-state ruled itself as nations do today. Sparta made laws to prepare strong soldiers. Athens had a democracy. — *What is the difference between the democracy of ancient Athens and democracy in the United States?*

6. The curiosity of Greek thinkers such as Socrates, Plato, and Aristotle produced ideas and books that people still study. — *How were their ideas passed along in ancient times? What other Greek writers do we read today? Name some other works of the ancient Greeks that have lasted.*

7. The Greek Alexander the Great and the emperors of the Roman world ruled vast empires that included many different lands. — *How did the rulers travel, trade, and move their armies throughout the empires?*

8. The alphabet, language, and laws of Rome lasted longer than their empire. — *Prepare a report on either the beginnings of numerals or the alphabet that is used to write the English language. For information on these topics, use an encyclopedia and other reference books to look up the following subjects: "numeration systems, history" or "alphabet."*

Western Europe

6 Nature and People in Western Europe

A Most Favorable Continent

VOCABULARY
conifers	soil
deciduous	abundance

Strabo's geography Strabo was a Greek scholar who wrote about geography 2,000 years ago. He wrote when the Emperor Augustus ruled an empire that spanned three continents—Europe, Africa, and Asia.

Strabo thought that Europe was the best of these continents. He wrote that it was the one "best suited for the development of excellence" in people.

Of course, Strabo did not know everything about these continents. He knew very little about East Asia. He knew nothing about Africa south of the Sahara. Strabo did not even know that there were four other continents.

Strabo knew far less about the world than today's geographers. Yet a modern geographer has written that "Europe may be looked upon as the most favorable continent" for people. This is the same idea that Strabo had, but it was written almost 2,000 years later.

Why have scholars living in such different times had the same idea? It is probably because of the gifts that nature has given the continent of Europe.

When we speak of "nature's gifts" to a continent, we mean those things not made by human beings. Climate, rivers, mountains, soil, and minerals are all gifts of nature. The first part of this chapter tells about nature's gifts to Western Europe. The second part of the chapter describes what the people of Western Europe have done with these gifts.

Western and Eastern Europe Since the end of World War II in 1945, many people have thought of Europe as a divided continent. The divisions are commonly called Western and Eastern Europe, but are not based only on geographic location. What happened politically after World War II has had much to do in deciding whether a country is considered part of Western or Eastern Europe.

Many countries fought against Germany during World War II. These countries included the United States, the United Kingdom, France, and the Soviet Union.

The countries that joined together to fight against Germany did not remain united after Germany was defeated. These countries had many important differences among themselves as to what should be done thoughout the world, and especially in Europe.

Western Europe is a richly varied area with many high mountain ranges and fertile river valleys. It is a land with many gifts from nature.

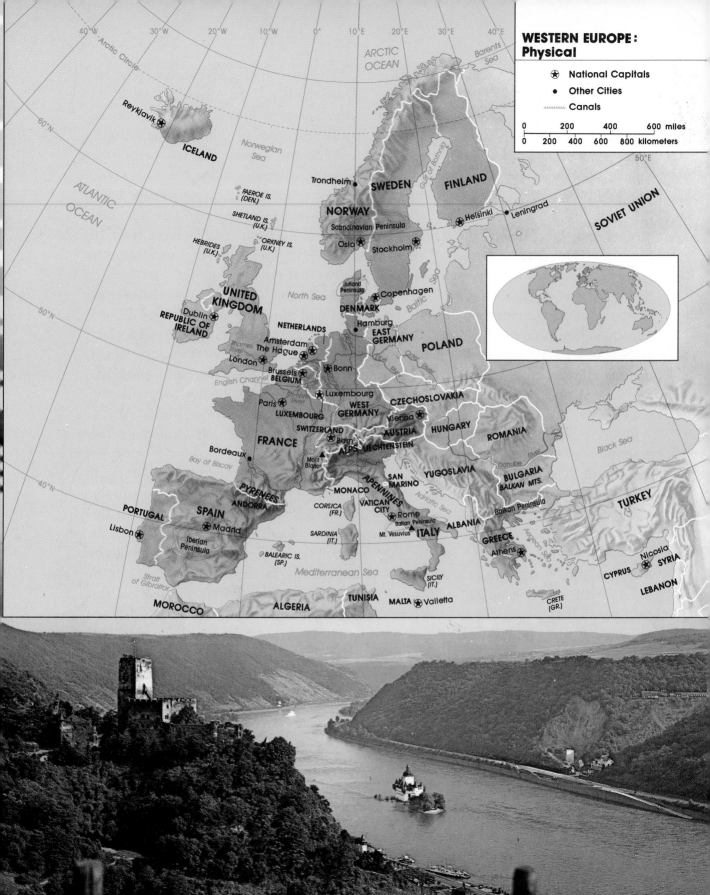

⍟ National Capitals

● Other Cities

⊷⊷⊷ Canals

0	200	400	600	miles
0 200	400	600	800	kilometers

ARCTIC
OCEAN

Barents
Sea

Arctic Circle

SOVIET UNION

Reykiavik
ICELAND

Norwegian
Sea

Trondheim
SWEDEN
FINLAND

Gulf of Bothnia

Helsinki
Leningrad

ATLANTIC
OCEAN

FAEROE IS.
(DEN.)

SHETLAND IS.
(U.K.)

ORKNEY IS.
(U.K.)

NORWAY
Scandinavian Peninsula

Oslo
Stockholm

HEBRIDES
(U.K.)

Baltic
Sea

UNITED
KINGDOM

North Sea

Jutland
Peninsula
Copenhagen

Dublin
REPUBLIC OF
IRELAND

NETHERLANDS

DENMARK

Hamburg
EAST
GERMANY

POLAND

Amsterdam
The Hague

Thames River
London

Brussels
BELGIUM

Bonn

English Channel

Luxembourg

WEST
GERMANY

CZECHOSLOVAKIA

Paris
LUXEMBOURG

SWITZERLAND

Vienna

AUSTRIA
HUNGARY

ROMANIA

FRANCE
Bern
LIECHTENSTEIN
ALPS

Bordeaux

Mont
Blanc

YUGOSLAVIA

Danube River

Black Sea

Bay of Biscay

APENNINES

SAN
MARINO

BULGARIA
BALKAN MTS.

PYRENEES
ANDORRA

MONACO

CORSICA
(FR.)

VATICAN
CITY
Rome

Balkan Peninsula

TURKEY

PORTUGAL
SPAIN
Madrid

SARDINIA
(IT.)

Italian Peninsula

ITALY
ALBANIA

Adriatic Sea

Aegean Sea

GREECE

Lisbon

Iberian
Peninsula

BALEARIC IS.
(SP.)

Mt. Vesuvius

Athens

Nicosia

Strait
of Gibraltar

Mediterranean Sea

SICILY
(IT.)

CRETE
(GR.)

CYPRUS
SYRIA

LEBANON

MOROCCO
ALGERIA
TUNISIA
MALTA Valletta

The Soviet Union, a Communist country, made sure that most of the countries close to its borders in Europe had Communist governments. These countries have become known as Eastern Europe. You will read about the Communist countries of Eastern Europe in a later unit in this book.

Most—but not all—of the European countries that remained free of Soviet power were located in the western part of the continent. Just as Eastern Europe came to mean Communist lands, the non-Communist countries came to be known as Western Europe. But not all of these non-Communist European countries are located on the western part of the continent.

For example, Greece is usually considered part of Western Europe. But geographically, Greece is located in southeastern Europe. This chapter is about the non-Communist European lands generally called Western Europe.

Nature's gifts   Europe is a large peninsula with many smaller peninsulas. You remember that a peninsula is a piece of land extending into water from a larger body of land. Europe is a peninsula on the larger landmass of Eurasia. You can clearly see this if you look again at the physical map of Eurasia in the Atlas on pages 464 and 465. If you sailed from the Black Sea in southeastern Europe to the Barents Sea in northern Europe, you would sail around all sides of Europe except one.

If you look at the map of Europe on page 123, you can see the smaller peninsulas on the larger European peninsula.

The Balkan (bôl′ kən) Peninsula lies between the Black and Adriatic (ā drē at′ ik) seas. Greece is located on the tip of the Balkan Peninsula. Notice that the Adriatic Sea, like the Aegean Sea, is a part of the larger Mediterranean Sea.

West of the Adriatic, you see the boot-shaped peninsula of Italy. Italy is so narrow that no major city is more than 70 miles (112 km) from the sea. Most of these cities are much closer.

The Iberian (ī bir′ ē ən) Peninsula forms the tip of the peninsula of Europe. Strabo thought that the Iberian Peninsula looked like an ox hide with the "neck part" joined to the rest of the continent. Only the narrow Strait of Gibraltar separates the Iberian Peninsula from North Africa. Spain and Portugal are located on the Iberian Peninsula.

The peninsula called Jutland (jət′ lənd) is located between the North Sea and the Baltic Sea. The North Sea is part of the Atlantic Ocean. The Baltic Sea is the long arm of the Atlantic that reaches into Eastern Europe as far as the Russian city of Leningrad. Denmark is located on the peninsula of Jutland.

The large, hook-shaped peninsula called Scandinavia (skan də nā′ vē ə) encloses the northern side of the Baltic Sea. Finland borders the northeastern part of this peninsula. Sweden and Norway are located on the peninsula of Scandinavia. Notice that the elbow of the peninsula's hook is north of the Arctic Circle.

After looking at these peninsulas of Europe, we can understand why Strabo said that Europe had the "most irregular shape" of any continent. But the irregular shape is, in fact, one of Europe's gifts from nature. The irregular shape of the continent means that many parts of Western Europe are close to the sea. This is an advantage because large bodies of water tend to cool the air in summer and warm it in winter. As a result, people in Western Europe can grow crops nearer the Arctic Circle than people in non-European countries near the Arctic Circle. Trondheim (trän′ hām), the ancient capital of Norway, is a city of more than 100,000 people but is only about 200 miles (320 km) south of the Arctic Circle.

Although located near the Arctic Circle, Trondheim is a thriving city.

Many climates   All the countries of Western Europe do not have the same type of climate. Italy, Spain, and Greece have a relatively warm climate with hot, dry summers and mild winters. Germany and Austria have cold winters and warm summers. Sweden and Finland have long, cold winters and mild summers.

Which climate is the best climate?

There is no satisfactory way to answer this question. People like different climates just as they like different seasons. Is summer better than winter? Is spring or fall the best time of year? Your answer may depend on whether you like sledding better than swimming, or baseball better than football.

Some of the ancient Romans certainly did not like the cool climate of northern Europe. A Roman historian named Tacitus (tas′ i tùs) strongly disliked Germany and its climate. Tacitus was sure that the Germans had always lived in that land because he could not imagine anyone moving there from another place.

"Who would leave Asia, Africa, or Italy to go to Germany with its unlovely scenery, its bitter climate, and general dreariness?" wrote Tacitus. Many people must have agreed with him at that time because "sunny Italy" had twice as many people as Germany in Roman times. Today it is quite different. Modern-day East and West Germany have more people than Italy.

Europe's variety of climates does not prevent people from living on almost every part of the continent. There are no great deserts, no hot tropical forests, and little polar wasteland. This is why the world's second *smallest* continent has the world's second *largest* population.

Ocean currents and climate   Europe is a northern continent. You can see how far north it lies by comparing the locations of European cities with those in North America. Rome, in southern Europe, is as far north as Cleveland or Chicago in the United States. But Rome has much warmer winters than Chicago or Cleveland. London, England, is farther north than all the major cities of Canada. But the average January temperature in London is higher than that in Montreal or Quebec.

Relatively mild winters in some Western European countries are not just because of the nearness of the ocean. Halifax (hal′ ə fax), Canada, has a seaside location, as you can see on the map of North America on page 459. Halifax is about as far south as Bordeaux (bôr dō′) on the west coast of France. But the average January temperature in Halifax is twice as cold as in Bordeaux.

Ocean currents and air movements make the difference. The currents are great streams that flow in the oceans. They have sometimes been called rivers in the oceans, although they are far larger than any river.

The map on page 18 shows ocean currents. Look at the North Atlantic. The Gulf Stream flows north and east from the warm waters of the Gulf of Mexico. The Gulf Stream moves into the Atlantic, where it joins other currents flowing from the south to form the North Atlantic Drift. This huge stream of warmer water moves toward Western Europe. Winds blowing off the ocean usually give this part of Europe fairly mild winters in spite of the continent's northern location.

Mountain walls   The three large peninsulas of southern Europe are partly walled off from the rest of the continent by mountain ranges. The Balkan Mountains cover much of the Balkan Peninsula. In fact, the peninsula gets its name from a Turkish word for mountains.

The Alps stand like a wall at the northern part of Italy. The wall provides some protection to Italy from cold, north winds during the winter. A number of peaks in the Alps rise more than 13,000 feet (3,962 m) above sea level. Mont Blanc (mōN bläN′), the highest peak, located between France and Italy, is 15,771 feet (4,807 m) high. The Alps are the highest mountains in Europe, but they are not as high as the Caucasus, which form the border between Europe and Asia.

The Alps are rugged mountains. Even so, people have long been able to cross this mountain wall. The Romans built roads that made crossing the Alps easier.

The Alps form a mountain wall in northern Italy.

The Pyrenees are a mountain range that runs from the Mediterranean to the Atlantic at the base of the Iberian Peninsula. The Pyrenees peaks are not as tall as those of the Alps. The range is narrow with few good passes. As viewed on a map, the Pyrenees look as if the range were designed as a wall to separate the Iberian Peninsula from the rest of Europe. No wonder a French king once spoke of the Pyrenees wall as a "natural boundary" between France and Spain. Today modern airplanes fly over this natural boundary with ease.

Major rivers   Four of Western Europe's important rivers begin in the Alps. These rivers are the Rhine (rīn), Danube (dan' yüb), Po (pō), and Rhone (rōn). Each river flows in a different direction. The Rhine flows north and west to the North Sea. The Danube flows east and south to the Black Sea. Together these two rivers form a line that runs across the continent. The Rhine-Danube line served as the boundary of the Roman Empire. In those days, three fourths of Europe's population lived south and west of the Rhine-Danube line. Today more of Europe's population lives north and east of the Rhine-Danube line than in Roman times.

The Po River begins as a tiny stream in the Alps but becomes a broad river as it flows across northern Italy on its way to the Adriatic Sea.

The Rhine is farther north of the Equator than the St. Lawrence River in North America, but the Rhine freezes only in the coldest winters. The St. Lawrence is usually frozen for several months every year. Since the Rhine seldom freezes, it can be used for year-round shipping.

The Rhone also begins in the Alps. It forms Lake Geneva, the largest of the Alpine lakes, before flowing south into France on the way to the Mediterranean Sea.

Italy's largest river, the Po, begins in the Alps. It flows southeast across Italy to the Adriatic Sea. The valley of the Po has the richest farming land in Italy.

Forests, soil, and minerals Tacitus complained that the lands east of the Rhine were covered with woods. Actually, forests covered most of Europe at one time, including the Mediterranean lands that Tacitus favored. It is also true, however, that the Mediterranean forests were generally not as thick as those north of the Alps. The northern forests got rain and snow throughout the year. This made them thicker than the Mediterranean forests that got rain and snow only part of the year. It is also true that many of the forests in Mediterranean lands had disappeared by Tacitus's time.

Most of the forests of Western Europe are a mixture of **conifers** (kō′ nə fərz) and **deciduous** (di sij′ u əs) trees. Conifers

Petroleum beneath the waters of the North Sea is one of nature's gifts to Western Europe. Oil wells like the one shown help people get petroleum from beneath the ocean floor.

are evergreen trees that have cones. Pine, fir, and spruce are conifers.

Deciduous trees are broad-leaved trees such as oak, beech, elm, and maple. Deciduous trees shed their leaves every year. The forests themselves have been useful to people, and so has the soil where the mixed forests grow.

It is curious that people speak of dirt as a thing of little value. They call an object "dirt cheap" when they mean that it is worth little. But dirt is another word for **soil,** and soil is among the most valuable of nature's gifts.

Soil is the top layer of the earth where plants grow. Without plants there can be no life. Good soil is not found everywhere. Western Europe has plenty of good soil. The soil where thick forests once grew was used to grow crops after the forests were cleared.

There are also valuable materials beneath the surface of the forests and mountains in Western Europe. There is an **abundance** of stone in many places. Stone is valuable—not because it is rare—but because it is useful. People have made everything from tools to buildings out of stone.

Western Europe also has deposits of coal, iron, lead, and other minerals beneath the earth's surface. There is also some petroleum, not only under the land, but also under the water of the North Sea.

CHECKUP

1. What is meant by the term "gifts of nature"?
2. Why is Europe called a peninsula with peninsulas?
3. Why do some parts of Western Europe have a mild climate?

People Change the Face of Europe

┌─VOCABULARY──────────────┐
│ scrub   flint   │
│ mature   ore   │
│ pollution   │
└──────────────────────────┘

Using nature's gifts People change the earth. They change it by growing crops where there was once forest, swamp, or desert. They change it by keeping livestock where there were once only wild animals. Above all, they change it by building cities, roads, and dams.

People have been changing the looks of Western Europe for thousands of years. They sometimes changed it in ways they did not intend. This is what happened in Greece more than 2,300 years ago. The Greeks cut down the best trees for timber and fuel. Since slow-growing trees like oaks had the best wood, they were the first to be cut. They were also the slowest to grow back, and less useful **scrub** bushes replaced oaks on the steep hills and mountainsides. Even the scrub did not grow well because of goats and their eating habits.

Goats are very useful animals. They are better than sheep at protecting themselves from wild animals. They provide people with milk, meat, and hides. Goats would, no doubt, prefer to feed in pastures of thick, green grass. But they also will eat many kinds of rough plants if there is no thick, green grass. This was good in a rocky, hilly land like Greece. Any land rich enough for pastures was used to grow crops. Farmers could keep goats on the steep hills where they fed on whatever grass they could find. But the goats also chewed leaves, twigs, and the bark from young trees. Hungry goats made it almost impossible for the forest to replace itself, particularly in a land with long, dry summers. Woodchoppers in ancient Athens complained that they had to go farther and farther into the mountains to get good wood.

People and their animals helped change a land of forested hills into a land of bare hills. As the hills lost their cover of trees and shrubs, they also lost soil. Without tree roots to hold the soil, heavy winter rains washed it away. Without soil, new trees could not take root. This continued for many years, and today Greece is still a land with many barren hills.

By eating grass and shrubs that kept soil in place, goats helped change parts of Greece into barren hills.

People in Western Europe cut down forests in many parts of the land to make room for cultivated fields.

The Athenian scholar Plato knew that the land had changed. Plato told the students at his Academy that at one time "the mountains were covered by thick woods." Plato said, "Some mountains, which today will only support bees, once produced trees that provided roof beams for huge buildings." When trees grew on the hills, "the soil benefited from the yearly rainfall, which did not run to waste off the bare earth. . . ."

According to Plato, as the soil washed away, the Greeks were left "with something rather like the skeleton of a very sick man; the rich, soft soil has all run away leaving the land nothing but skin and bones."

People, farms, and forests   The larger part of Europe's population lived in the Mediterranean lands in Plato's time. But there were also many people living north of the Alps and Pyrenees. These people were also changing the looks of the continent. They cleared trees from much of the best land and grew crops instead. They kept cattle and sheep in woodland pastures. They raised pigs that fed on roots and acorns in the forest. Pigs, like goats, are useful, but they tend to destroy new growth.

The people north of the mountains cleared the forest without steel axes or saws. They cleared it by the "slash-and-burn" method. First they slashed the bark around the trees to kill them. After the trees had dried out, they were set on fire. Fire not only cleared the land, it also left ashes that fertilized the earth for a time. When a field wore out, the people slashed and burned other trees in the forest.

Much of Western Europe today is farmland. France is an important agricultural country that grows enough wheat to sell to other countries. French farmers grow crops on about 33 percent of the land and use another 25 percent for pasture. Farms cover about 70 percent of the land in the small country of Denmark. You will read more about the importance of farming in individual countries in a later chapter in this book.

But the forests are not all gone from Western Europe. They still cover the greater part of Finland and Scandinavia. About one fourth of East and West Germany is still covered by forests.

The Germans have worked out ways to use forests without destroying them. Trees are grown and harvested much like any other crop. They are cut as they **mature,** leaving space and sunlight for young trees to grow. The total amount of wood cut at any time is never greater than the new growth.

People in Western Europe made many changes to the land nature had given them. They built towns, roads, and bridges and learned how to farm the land.

Cities Cities are not gifts of nature. They are the works of people. When people build a city, they change the earth's surface with materials taken from the earth. They take wood, clay, and stone to make houses, shops, and streets. They use stone, sand, iron, and asphalt to build roads and railways that connect the cities. They build bridges over streams and dig ditches to drain away water.

Most people in Western Europe did not live in cities in Plato's day. They were farmers and herders. There were no cities north of the mountain walls.

Today there are many cities in all of Europe, and the cities are far larger than they were in ancient times. Athens now has at least seventeen times as many people as it did when Plato lived there.

The largest European cities are now north of the mountains. Paris is four times larger than modern Athens; London is nearly three times as big. Almost every country in Western Europe today has cities with more than a million people.

People change the air Cities not only change the earth's surface, but they also change the air above the surface. The stoves, factories, and automobiles of today's cities put tons of waste matter into the air. Putting these wastes into the air is called air **pollution.**

Ever since people started building fires, they have polluted the air. But the amount of pollution has grown very rapidly in recent years. Take the case of pollution caused by lead. Lead is harmful to living things. Burning coal and making metals have always put some small particles of lead into the air. But the amount of

In many parts of Western Europe, smoke from factories has caused air pollution.

lead in the air has greatly increased during the last 50 years. This happened because lead is added to gasoline that is burned in automobile engines. Never before has there been so much lead in the air around us.

But lead is only one of the harmful substances that has polluted the air in growing amounts. Such pollution shows that some changes made by people may be harmful.

Air pollution can ruin works of art made out of stone. For some time, the officials in charge of the Acropolis in modern Athens have been worried about damage being done by air pollution to the ancient buildings located there. Chemicals in the air mix with moisture and fall in the form of rain. The chemicals in the rain slowly eat away at stone columns and statues.

The statues on the Porch of Maidens were moved after air pollution damaged them.

In 1979 the officials removed the stone statues that had stood on the Porch of the Maidens for 2,400 years. They placed the statues indoors, where they were partly protected from the pollution that had already seriously damaged them. The rains of 50 years in a modern city had done them more harm than the rains of many centuries.

Improving transportation People have traveled on rivers for a very long time. They were, perhaps, the first highways. Rivers do not usually flow in straight lines. They twist and bend back and forth, so that you may travel a long way but only cover a short distance. In some places a river may be deep. In other places it may spread out and grow shallow so that heavily loaded boats and barges get stuck on sandbars.

People sometimes change a river by straightening and deepening it. Changing a river in this way makes it more useful for travel and shipping. It does not necessarily make it more beautiful.

Many rivers in Western Europe have been improved so that they can carry large boats and barges. The mouths of the rivers have been deepened so that large ships can sail into river harbors. Today ships sail 68 miles (109 km) up the Elbe (el′ bə) River to the West German city of Hamburg (ham′ bərg). It is Europe's largest seaport even though it is miles from the open sea.

Canals are not natural waterways. They have to be dug. A canal can make it possible to travel by water from one river to another. A Roman general connected the Rhine with the Meuse (myüz) River 1,900 years ago. Today there are miles and miles of canals in Western Europe. They connect inland cities with large rivers. They link great river systems together in a network of waterways. Canals connect the Rhone with the Rhine, and the Rhine with the Danube. Today it is possible to travel across Europe by water from the Black Sea to the North Sea by using canals and rivers.

People have always been able to cross the mountains that separate the southern peninsulas of Europe from the rest of the continent. But it is easier today. You can take trains in Italy that climb the slopes and then go through tunnels in the Alps. One of the train tunnels is 12½ miles (20 km) long.

Ships pass through the locks of the Volkerak, a large important canal in the Netherlands.

You can also drive a car or ride a bus through the mountain passes. It is also possible to drive through tunnels under parts of the Alps. The first highway tunnel opened under Mont Blanc in 1965. The tunnel is 7 miles (11.3 km) long, but it shortened the driving distance from Paris to Rome by 125 miles (201 km). If you travel through the tunnels, you miss some mountain scenery, but you do not have to worry about snow on the road in the winter and spring.

Mining   People dug beneath the surface of Western Europe long before they had iron shovels or picks. They dug with shovels made from the shoulder blades of oxen and picks made from reindeer antlers. They mined the earth for **flint** because they used this hard, brittle stone to make knives, axes, and spearheads. Sometimes they dug an open pit and separated the flint from softer stone with the antler picks. At times they tunneled into the side of a hill to get at flint.

135

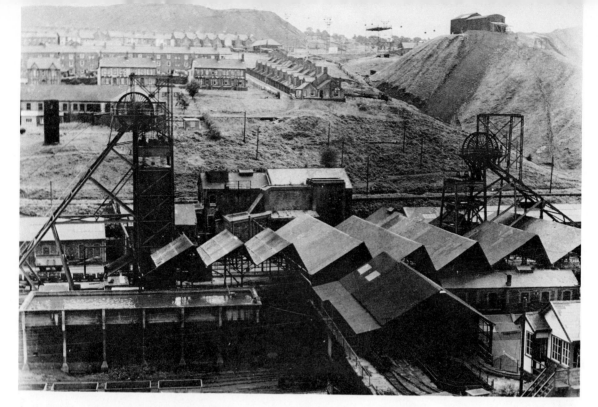

A coal mine in Wales shows how people have changed the face of the land by digging for nature's gifts below the surface of the earth.

In the mountains of Austria, people mined for rock salt with tools made of wood, stone, bone, and antler. Salt is useful for seasoning food and preserving it. The salt miners tunneled into the mountains 1,000 feet (304.8 m) or more. Deep in such passageways, the miners worked by the uneven light of pine torches.

Digging for flint and salt was only the beginning of mining. Miners in Western Europe have also taken great amounts of other useful materials from beneath the earth's surface. They have dug out coal, iron, copper, zinc, lead, and other **ores.** Oil drillers have drilled wells in the floor of the North Sea.

Mining and drilling under the earth's surface changes the surface, too. Mining sometimes leaves large stacks of waste materials on the land after coal has been mined. The pile of mining waste shows one of the problems people face in using the earth. In order to do something desirable, they often do something undesirable. To get coal to heat homes or make steel, people have dumped large amounts of mining waste on the earth's surface.

Few people think that these dumps improve the scenery. Yet few people want to live in cold homes or do without steel tools. It is a difficult choice, but it is only one of many choices people have had to make. Indeed, as people's power to change the earth has increased, so has the number of difficult choices.

CHECK UP

1. How did woodchoppers and goats affect the land of ancient Greece?
2. Name three ways that people have changed the land to improve transportation.
3. In what ways have people changed the forests, air, and rivers of Western Europe?

A Trip to 300 B.C. in A.D. 1977

In 1977, a group of people in England tried to find out what it would be like to have lived in 300 B.C. The group consisted of 12 adults and 3 children. These people went to live in a forest completely set apart from the rest of the country. They planned to live for a year in the same way the ancient Britons had lived about 2,300 years ago.

The group started out with the same simple tools and the same kinds of animals their ancestors had. They took 2 dogs, 3 cows, 4 pigs, 9 goats, 25 sheep, 40 chickens, and some bees. They built the same kind of shelter used in 300 B.C.—a round single-room house made of mud and thatch. The hut had no chimney. Smoke escaped through a hole in the roof.

The Britons of 1977 raised the same kinds of crops as those raised in 300 B.C. They hunted rabbits and squirrels. They killed their farm animals as needed and preserved the meat by exposing it to smoke.

The modern-day Britons clipped wool from their sheep, but found it hard to clean the wool without modern chemicals. The clothing they made from the wool was greasy. In fact, the modern-day Britons generally found it hard to be clean, especially during the long, muddy winter. They also had no clocks or watches to keep time. They got up and went to bed when the sun rose and set. They ate their meals when the food was ready to be eaten, not when clock hands pointed at certain numbers.

There was one very important difference between this village of 1977 and those scattered in the forest 2,300 years ago. Twice each week, a television crew came to film the experiment. That was the reason for the whole project. They were making a television series.

There was also another tie to the modern world. Government officials were concerned that the children would miss school for a year. The officials insisted that the children take school books with them on their trip back in time.

What was it like to live in 300 B.C.? These modern-day Britons tried to find out.

6/CHAPTER REVIEW

KEY FACTS

1. Europe, the world's second smallest continent, has the world's second largest population partly because of the gifts of nature.

2. Europe is a peninsula with peninsulas.

3. Parts of Western Europe have a mild climate partly because of warm currents in the North Atlantic.

4. The Balkan Mountains, Alps, and Pyrenees separate Europe's southern peninsulas from the rest of the continent.

5. Forests once covered most of Europe.

6. People have changed Western Europe by clearing forests, building cities, and making roads, railroads, and waterways.

7. Western Europe is a rich farming area, but forests still cover much of the surface.

8. Some changes of the earth have had harmful or unpleasant effects, such as pollution.

VOCABULARY QUIZ

Choose the word from the list below that best completes each sentence that follows. Write your answers on a sheet of paper.

a. soil   **f.** conifers

b. Strabo   **g.** deciduous

c. pollution   **h.** ore

d. flint   **i.** abundance

e. scrub   **j.** mature

1. _____ is a hard, brittle stone that was used to make tools and weapons such as knives, axes, and spearheads.

2. _____ trees lose their leaves every year.

3. Adding lead to gasoline caused greater _____ of the air.

4. Trees that are fully grown are said to be _____.

5. The top layer of the earth's surface is usually called _____.

6. _____ are evergreen trees such as pine, fir, and spruce.

7. _____ contains useful minerals, such as iron or zinc.

8. _____ bushes replaced the trees that were cut down in Greece.

9. There was once an _____ of forests in Italy.

10. _____ wrote his geography about 2,000 years ago.

REVIEW QUESTIONS

1. Name five of the peninsulas in Europe. How does the continent's irregular shape affect Europe's climate?

2. What are the Gulf Stream and the North Atlantic Drift? How do they affect Western Europe?

3. What mountain ranges separate the three southern peninsulas of Europe from the rest of the continent? Why are these ranges no longer serious barriers to travel and shipping?

4. How have people changed the look of the land in Western Europe?

5. How have cities affected the air?

6. How have people improved waterways in Western Europe?

7. Why have people dug below the earth's surface.

ACTIVITIES

1. Make a list of the "gifts of nature" in the place where you live. Make another list of changes that people have made to these gifts. Compare your lists with those of others in your class.

2. Draw a cartoon strip that illustrates how Plato described what had happened to the soil of ancient Greece before his time.

MAKING OUTLINES

OUTLINES LIST IMPORTANT IDEAS

Outlines are useful for reviewing what you have learned. An outline lists important ideas in an orderly manner. Shown below is the beginning of an outline of Chapter 6. Look it over to see how an outline should be made.

Nature and People in Western Europe
I. A Most Favorable Continent
    A. Strabo's geography
        1. Strabo's idea
        2. Europe's resources
    B. Western and Eastern Europe
        1. Europe since World War II
        2. Eastern Europe
        3. Western Europe

In the above example, the chapter's title serves as the title of the outline. The first major part of the chapter is *A Most Favorable Continent*. This is shown after the Roman numeral **I**. Each major part of this section is further broken down into smaller parts. There are eight smaller parts in the first main section of Chapter 6. The headings for the first two of these parts appear in the outline as the capital letters **A** and **B**.

Additional information found under each capital letter is shown by using the Arabic numerals **1** and **2**.

If the outline above were complete, it would show the second major part of Chapter 6, listed as **II**. *People Change the Face of Europe*. This section would also be subdivided.

MORE COMPLETE OUTLINES

It is sometimes better to make a more complete outline, expressing the divisions in complete sentences rather than using single words or short terms.

For example, the fourth subtopic under Roman numeral **II**, which appears on pages 133—134, could be outlined as follows:
    D. People change the air.
        1. Cities change the air.
        2. Pollution has grown rapidly in recent times.
        3. Pollution can be harmful to works of art as well as to people.

Sometimes each piece of additional information is the first sentence of each paragraph following a topic. *But this is not always so.* You cannot simply copy the first sentence of each paragraph when making an outline. You must ask yourself, "What is the main fact or idea of this paragraph?"

SKILLS PRACTICE

It is useful to make an outline when you are making a report. Suppose you were preparing a report on the sports of different seasons. An outline of your report would list the title and the main topics like this:
The Sports of Different Seasons
    I. Winter
    II. Spring
    III. Summer
    IV. Fall

1. On a sheet of paper write the subtopics you would list under each season.
2. Now prepare a sentence outline for the same subject.
3. Prepare either a topical or sentence outline for a report on one of the following subjects:
    Forms of Transportation
    Uses of the Wheel
    Video Games
    My Home Town

7 The Birth of Modern Europe

The Middle Ages

VOCABULARY

knight	guild
fief	monopoly
vassal	apprentice
feudalism	monastery
manor	abbot
serf	convent

Periods of history   The word *modern* comes from a Latin word meaning "just now." We say we are living in modern times, but so did the German writer, Cellarius (se lär′i us), who lived nearly 300 years ago.

Cellarius wrote books in Latin. One of his books, *Modern History*, came out in 1696. It told the story of Europe from 1453 to his own times.

You may think it strange that Cellarius called the times he lived in "modern" because he lived so long ago. But will people living 300 years from now think we lived in "modern" times?

The fact is that people always think of their own times as modern, or "just now." Socrates and Julius Caesar did not think they lived in ancient times. It is we who call their times ancient.

Cellarius also wrote two other histories. He called one *Ancient History*. It told of events before A.D. 337. The other book was a history of the period between ancient and modern times. He called this book *History of the Middle Ages*. We have continued to use Cellarius's labels for these periods of history, but not all people who study history agree with the dates Cellarius picked.

Cellarius may have chosen A.D. 337 as the end of ancient times because that was the year the great Roman Emperor Constantine (kon′ stan tēn) died. Cellarius chose 1453 as the end of the Middle Ages because that was the year Turkish armies conquered the city of Constantinople (kon stant′ ən ō pəl). Other historians have chosen different dates, but most use the name he invented. They call the period between ancient and modern times the Middle Ages.

Life in the Middle Ages   What was life like in the Middle Ages? The answer to that question depends on what part of the Middle Ages you are talking about, what part of Europe you mean, and what kind of people you are studying.

Life in the early part of the Middle Ages was different from life in the later part of the Middle Ages. The lives of the peasants who worked the land were very different from the lives of the nobles who owned the land.

Religion played an important role in the lives of people who lived in the Middle Ages. How does this painting show the importance of religion in the Middle Ages?

It also made a difference where you lived. Europe is a continent with many different types of land and climates. Life in southern France was different from life in Scandinavia.

Most of Europe was Christian during the Middle Ages. But Moslem armies from North Africa invaded Spain. The Moslems were stopped when an army led by Charles Martel defeated them at the Battle of Tours (tùr) in A.D. 732. You will read more about Moslems in Unit 5.

Charles Martel's grandson, Charlemagne (shar' le mān), became a great emperor. He ruled much of Western Europe, but his empire came apart when he died in A.D. 814. Western Europe broke into many small states. It remained divided until strong rulers came to power later in the Middle Ages.

A king who conquered his kingdom William the Conqueror was fat, bald, strong, and brave. Few people could bend his bow, which he used with ease. Few warriors showed a greater bravery in battle. William was a fierce fighter. He had to be, for he lived in warlike times.

William was the son of the Duke (the lord or ruler) of Normandy, a part of France. William's father died when William was 7. In those warlike times, it seemed doubtful that young William would live long enough to rule Normandy.

One night enemies broke into the castle where William slept. They would have killed him if his uncle had not slipped him out of the castle and hidden him with woodchoppers in a forest. It was a dangerous time for William because he was too young to defend himself in battle and protect his lands.

That soon changed. William grew up and at the age of 19 he led his loyal followers in putting down a rebellion.

William now ruled Normandy, but he had his eyes on a bigger prize. His cousin, King Edward of England, had no children.

What events took place on the dates Cellarius chose for the beginning and end of the Middle Ages?

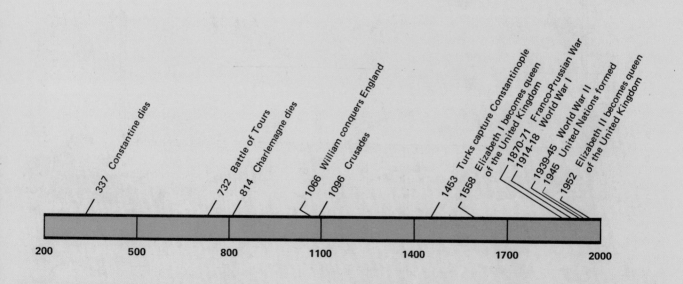

In this section of the Bayeux Tapestry, William lifts his helmet to show his face to his men.

When Edward died, William claimed to be the king of England. The English leaders did not accept William. Instead, they crowned Harold, an English noble, as king. William decided he would try to conquer England.

In September 1066, William sailed for England with an army. King Harold was fighting other enemies in the north, so no one stopped the landing of William's army.

William was the first to come ashore. As he stepped on the beach, he stumbled and fell flat on his face. His followers might have taken this for an unlucky sign, but William was a quick thinker. He grabbed two handfuls of dirt, and as he got up he shouted, "I now take hold of the land of England!"

The armies of Harold and William met at the Battle of Hastings on October 14, 1066. William's army defeated the English, and King Harold was killed.

There is a very unusual record of the Battle of Hastings. It is a 231-foot (70.4 m) strip of cloth known as the Bayeux Tapestry (bā yū′ tap′ə strē). The Bayeux Tapestry was made 11 years after the Battle of Hastings. It shows the story of William's conquest in pictures and words, much like a modern comic strip.

The part of the tapestry shown on this page illustrates one event in the Battle of Hastings. William had a horse killed from under him. Word spread that William was also killed. William quickly got another horse and rode into the thick of the fight. He boldly lifted his helmet and shouted. "Here I am! Look at me! I live and will conquer yet!"

The tapestry shows that the Normans fought mostly on horseback while the

English fought on foot. In the scene shown, William has raised his helmet so that his men can see he is not dead.

After his victory at Hastings, William and his army went to London. The English crowned him king. Duke William of Normandy was now also *King* William the Conqueror of England.

Raising an army without taxes William had won a great prize, but he had to reward those who had helped him win it. William gave his soldiers lands taken from Harold's followers. But William did not give away the land without getting something in return. Each person who got land had to swear loyalty to William as lord. Each had to promise to give William a certain number of armed men with horses for service to the king every year. These mounted fighting men were known as **knights.**

Knights formed the warrior class of the Middle Ages.

Knights formed the backbone of most fighting forces in the Middle Ages. Their main purpose in life was fighting, and they spent many years learning their trade. Young boys from noble families studied the art of fighting under the keen eyes of older knights. The boys learned how to ride and how to use a sword and lance. After serving older knights for a period of time, the young men were knighted by their lords.

The land granted to William's followers was known as a **fief** (fēf). The people who got fiefs were called the king's **vassals.** Granting fiefs made it possible for William to have a fighting force at hand when he needed it without having to pay money for it.

A vassal who promised knights to the king got them by giving parts of his fief as smaller fiefs to other people who would promise to supply knights. The king's vassals became lords of their own vassals. These vassals, in turn, would grant parts of their fiefs to still others, and so on. The smallest fief was usually granted to a single knight who promised to serve his lord each year.

Feudalism The system of granting fiefs for the service of knights is called **feudalism** (fyü′ də liz əm). It divided the power to govern among a number of nobles. Each lord ruled his vassals just as he was ruled by his lord. This meant that each lord protected his own vassals and settled their disputes in his courts.

Feudalism was the system of government in much of Western Europe during the Middle Ages. If all went well, the feudal

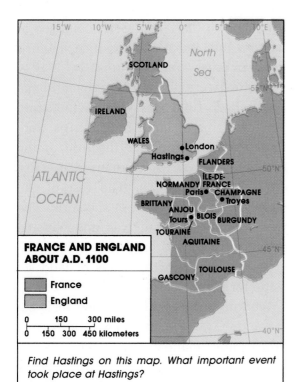

FRANCE AND ENGLAND
ABOUT A.D. 1100

France

England

0   150   300 miles
0   150 300 450 kilometers

Find Hastings on this map. What important event took place at Hastings?

Manors   Almost all ways of life during the Middle Ages depended on the work of the people who lived on manors. A **manor** was a large farm or estate. The peasants on the manors plowed its fields and raised animals and crops. Their long, hard work put the food on the tables of kings and nobles.

A king or queen usually had many manors in different parts of the kingdom. It was said in the Middle Ages that "the king should live on his own." This meant that the royal manors should supply food and other things needed by the royal household. The royal household included knights, officials, and servants, as well as

arrangement should have kept order. But things rarely went smoothly. Vassals sometimes grew more powerful than their lord. Oaths of loyalty were not always kept. Vassals fought against vassals, and lords could not stop them. Vassals often revolted against their lords.

There could hardly be peace in a time when so many people had small private fighting forces and their own private forts—their castles.

You may think it would be fine to live in a castle. But castles in the Middle Ages were built mainly for protection, not comfort. Thick stone walls might keep out an enemy, but not the damp winter weather. Small windows served well for lookouts, but they let in little sunshine. Castles were usually built in hard-to-reach places. If possible, a water-filled ditch called a moat surrounded a castle. A moat helped protect a castle from attack.

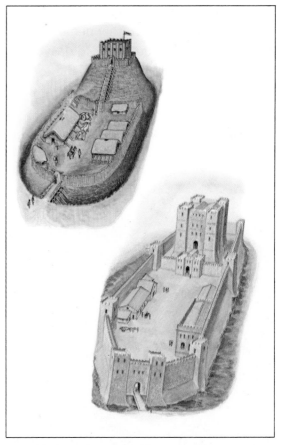

Compare these two castles. Which one do you think was built first? How are the castles different?

the king and queen and their family. The household needed so many things that it generally moved about the kingdom from one royal manor to another during the year. One manor could not possibly feed so many people and animals throughout the year. William the Conqueror usually spent Christmas at his manor in Gloucester (gläs′ tər) and Easter at his manor in Winchester (win′ ches tər).

The fiefs granted by the king or queen to great vassals usually had a number of manors. The great vassals would grant some of these manors as fiefs to others in order to get the knights they had promised the king.

Life of the serfs   Many of the peasants who worked on the manors were **serfs.** Serfs were not free to leave the manor without the consent of the lord of the manor. It was said that serfs were "attached to the land." Serfs belonged to manors just like the trees in a manor's forest or grass in its pastures.

Manors were divided into several large fields. Each field was then divided into narrow strips of land. Some strips were used to grow crops for the lord of the manor. Other strips were used to raise crops for the church. The rest of the strips were for the use of the serfs. The work on all the land was done by the serfs, but they got only that part of the crop that grew on the strips of land set aside for them.

We know the names of some serfs because they were written down in the records some manors kept. Some serfs' names were William Sparrow, Roger Mouse, William Littlefair, John Stoutlook, Agnes Redhead, and Margaret Merry. We have records of their names, but we know little about the lives of the serfs who had

A large manor was like a village, complete with its own church.

these names. No one wrote down their stories, and serfs themselves could not read or write. We only know in general what their lives were like.

Serfs usually lived in a village on the manor. It was safer in those warlike times to live in a village than to live alone in the countryside.

The serfs worked long, hard hours with simple tools. They had to do many kinds of things besides working in the fields. They cut and carried wood that would be burned in fireplaces in the lord's home. They gathered nuts and berries from the forest for the lord's dinner table. They took care of the lord's cows, goats, and horses.

When serfs killed one of their own animals, they had to give the lord some of the best parts of the animal. Serfs had to give eggs to the lord's kitchen. They had to grind the grain they raised at the lord's mill. They paid for using the mill by giving the lord part of the grain.

The life of a serf was hard, but it was the life led by many people in the Middle Ages. There were far more serfs than nobles. If you had lived then, it is very likely that you would have been a serf rather than a noble.

Living in cities   Not everyone who lived in the Middle Ages lived in a manor house, in castles, or in villages. Nor was everyone a serf, a noble, or a knight. Many people also lived in cities.

Cities in the Middle Ages were often crowded and dirty. The picture on this page shows how narrow some of the streets were in some European cities in the Middle Ages. Life must have been very crowded on this street, which is only about 10 feet wide. The buildings are very close together, and very little sunlight enters the street. This street, built so long ago, still exists in Europe.

Many of the people who lived in cities were known by their trade or business. There was Richard le Barbier (ba′byā) and Thomas le Potier (pō′ ty ā). In England they would have been known as Richard Barber and Thomas Potter. As you can tell by looking in a telephone book, many names today go back to the time when

Many European cities still have narrow streets and stone houses built in the Middle Ages.

Two workers, a stone mason and a carpenter, show their skills before a kingly figure representing the power of medieval guilds. Workers had to show they could work well before they were allowed to join guilds.

people were known by their trade. Some examples are Butcher, Baker, and Weaver.

People who had a trade in a city did not have to travel to work every morning because they usually lived where they worked. Tailors, for instance, might have their shops on the first floor of their house and live upstairs.

Goods were sold in the shops where the goods were made. People did not go to a clothing store to buy a hat. They went to a hatmaker's shop. Therefore, the person who sold hats could not blame someone else if the hats were not made well.

A person with a trade belonged to a trade **guild**. These guilds were organiza-

tions of people who had the same trade. Shoemakers, tailors, and bakers all had their own guilds.

The guilds controlled the making and selling of goods. This kind of control is called a **monopoly.** Guilds set rules for making and selling goods. All guild members had to follow the rules set down by the guilds. Tailors had to use a certain type of cloth. People who worked with gold had to measure the gold honestly. Guilds also ruled such things as what time guild members could open their shops. No one in a trade run by a guild could open shop before other guild members did.

A person who wanted to learn a trade was called an **apprentice** (ə pren′ tis). Guilds limited the number of apprentices in a trade. Apprentices learned their trade from someone who already was a guild member. These people were called masters. By limiting the number of apprentices a master might have, the guilds made sure there would never be too many people in their line of business.

Apprentices agreed to work for a certain number of years for a master. In some trades, apprentices had to work 4 years. In others, apprentices had to work as long as 12 years.

The master agreed to feed and clothe the apprentice during these years. But more importantly, the master agreed to teach the apprentice a trade.

After putting in the time promised, apprentices might seek to become masters. The apprentices would have to present to the guild statements from their masters saying that the apprentices were good people who had learned the trade. Sometimes, apprentices would have to show a sample of their work. These samples were called masterpieces. A masterpiece would have to meet guild standards.

When apprentices showed that they could practice the trade according to guild standards, they became masters and swore that they would uphold the guild's rules. They would follow the guild's standards and help it keep its monopoly.

Not all apprentices became masters. There was a middle level called journeyman. These people practiced a certain trade and usually worked for a master. Journeymen were no longer apprentices, but had not yet become masters.

A strong-willed woman   During the Middle Ages men and women were not usually treated equally. Men usually had more power than women. When a vassal died, his oldest son would usually get his father's fief if the son swore loyalty to his father's lord.

There was once a Duke of Aquitaine (ak′ wə tān) who had no son. He did have a daughter named Eleanor. Aquitaine was one of the largest fiefs in France. The French king and the duke worried about what would happen to Aquitaine when the duke died. The king and the duke agreed that Eleanor should get the fief and that she should marry the king's son, Louis.

The old duke died in 1137. Eleanor married Louis that same year. The king died a month after the wedding. Eleanor's new husband became King Louis VII. The numeral after his name means that he was the seventh king of France named Louis. The young girl was now Queen of France as well as ruler of Aquitaine.

If the former king had thought that Louis could control both Eleanor and her fief, he was wrong. Eleanor was not easy to control. She certainly was not one to remain shut up in a royal palace. Louis discovered this when he decided to go on a crusade.

Crusades were religious wars between Christians and Moslems. *Crusade* means "war for the cross." During the First Crusade (1096–1099), knights from Europe captured the holy city of Jerusalem and set up a Christian kingdom there. They found it hard to hold the kingdom. From time to time the Moslems tried to recapture it.

The Second Crusade began in 1147. Louis VII decided that he would take an army to help the Christians. Eleanor decided that she would go on the crusade, too. When Louis and his army set out on the crusade, Eleanor and a group of her ladies set out on horseback with them. Eleanor and Louis quarreled while they were on the crusade. They were divorced after they returned to France.

Eleanor went back to Aquitaine. She was no longer Louis's wife, but she was still his vassal.

Eleanor did not remain unmarried long. She soon became the wife of Henry, the great-grandson of William the Conqueror. Henry later became King Henry II of England, and the former Queen of France now became Queen of England. But Eleanor still ruled Aquitaine. Under feudalism it was possible to be a king or queen in one country and a vassal in another.

It would be nice to say that Eleanor and Henry lived happily ever after, but that was not the case. They, too, quarreled and separated after many years of marriage. But Eleanor continued to play an important part in English affairs because two of her sons became kings of England. Her daughters married other European kings and dukes. By the time she died at the age of 80, people called her the "grandmother of Europe."

The religious life   Religion played a big role in life during the Middle Ages. Christianity was very powerful and many people led religious lives. Bernard of Clairvaux (klär vō′) was one such person. Bernard's father was a knight but Bernard followed a very different way of life. He was a monk.

Monks devoted their whole lives to religion. They lived together in houses called **monasteries.** When a man became a monk, he gave away all that he owned. He made a vow, or promise, that he would never marry. He vowed that he would obey the **abbot,** or head of the monastery. Monks gave up their property and families to spend their lives in prayer and work.

Women who wished to follow this sort of life were called nuns. They lived in houses called **convents.** Nuns made the same kinds of promises that monks made. They gave up everything they owned and never married. They obeyed the abbess who was in charge of the convent. The life of a nun was also a life of prayer and work.

Bernard entered the French monastery Cîteaux (si tō′) in 1112 when he was 21. He picked Cîteaux because the monks there strictly followed the rules of a religious life. Bernard scorned those who took vows as monks but did not keep them strictly.

Life at Cîteaux was a joy to a man like Bernard, although it may sound very hard to others. The monks got up at 3 o'clock every morning for their first prayer service of the day. The monks then worked between 6 o'clock and 10 o'clock. Bernard weeded the garden, swept the floor, and worked in the fields where the monks grew their own food. At 10 A.M. there was another prayer service. Then Bernard was free to read or study until noon.

After noon prayers, the monks ate a simple meal. Usually the monks ate only

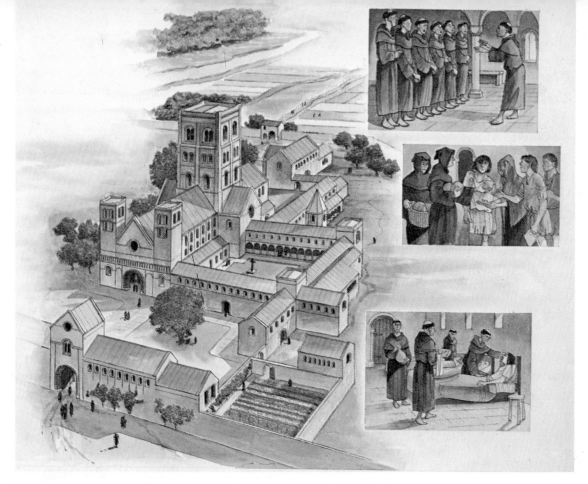

Larger monasteries had many buildings where monks lived, prayed, and worked.

once a day. But during the summer when there was hard work to do in the fields, they did have a second meal. The monks ate simple foods. Only the sick got meat or eggs. Bernard did not mind the simple food. He said that fine food might be good for the body, but it did not help the soul, or spirit. "The soul is not fattened out of frying pans," Bernard wrote. What do you think he meant by this?

After dinner there was time for more study, or a monk might rest if necessary. At 3 P.M. there was another prayer service, and then more work until time for prayers and bed at sundown. The monks went to bed early in order to get up again at 3 A.M. to begin another day of prayer and labor.

Work in both monasteries and convents included helping other people. The monks and nuns fed the poor. They gave travelers shelter for the night. They taught children, and they cared for the ill. It was a way of life very different from that of kings, queens, and knights.

CHECKUP

1. What do we mean by the term *Middle Ages*? What do we mean by *modern*?
2. What was feudalism? How did it enable William the Conqueror to raise an army without taxes?
3. What did a serf do in return for using land on a manor?
4. In what ways did guilds control a trade or business?
5. What vows, or promises, did a monk or nun make when he or she entered a monastery or convent?

The Beginnings of Modern Nations

Using money to pay taxes and other debts brought about many changes in the feudal system.

VOCABULARY

taxes	Renaissance
shield money	engineer
rent	sculptor

A new age   About the year 1450, a man in Italy wrote that he was thankful for being born "in this new age, so full of hope and promise." Cellarius later looked back at the 1450s and considered that period the beginning of modern times. The period seemed new because of all the changes that were taking place. These changes produced ways of living that were very different from life in the Middle Ages.

Taxes raise money   One great change was the way rulers began to raise armies. The feudal promise to give service for land did not always work well. Those who owed service lived in many parts of the kingdom. It took time to bring them together when the king needed them. The knights were not trained to fight together as a group. They had to serve only a few months every year. Kings and queens found it better to hire soldiers, especially for long wars.

But rulers needed money to pay an army. Today governments raise the money they need to fight wars by having their people pay **taxes**. But you will remember that under feudalism a king was supposed to "live on his own," not tax others for support.

In order to get money, some kings and queens began to give up the system that required vassals to provide knights. The kings and queens let their vassals pay **shield money** in place of providing knights when needed. The shield money became a form of tax.

Many vassals welcomed this change. They preferred to pay money rather than to serve in the king or queen's army. Shield money gave queens and kings more freedom and power. They could hire soldiers just when they needed them.

Kings and queens soon began collecting other forms of taxes. These taxes helped change feudal governments into governments more like those of modern times. What started out as a new way to raise an army became a way to pay for everything that governments do today.

Free peasants instead of serfs   Money payments also brought changes on the manors. Lords of the manor wanted and needed money, too. They had their serfs pay **rent** for the land they used rather than work for the lord for a certain number of days each week. Paying rent for using land brought about great changes in the way of life on the manors. Lords of the manors now became landlords, and serfs became peasant renters.

The change often gave both serfs and nobles greater freedom. But freedom also brought troubles, especially to those who were once serfs.

As renters, the serfs no longer "belonged" to an estate. They no longer could be made to work. But they also no longer had the right to use the land on a manor. They could work the land only if they paid rent.

A landlord no longer had to keep peasants he did not want or need. The change that made the serfs free from the land also made the lords free from the duty to keep the peasants on the land which could now be used for purposes other than farming.

Some landlords in England found that they could make more money raising sheep on their land than by raising crops. Wool from sheep could be sold at a good price, and raising sheep required fewer workers than farming. This meant that some peasants had no work to do. And if they had no work and no land, they had to leave the village. Sheep pastures took the place of fields of crops. One writer complained that the sheep were eating up the villages.

Some of the peasants forced to leave their villages found land in other places. Other peasants moved to towns and cities, where some of the peasants did well.

For all the problems that freeing the serfs brought, most people felt it was better not to be a serf. Serfs sometimes revolted and demanded to be free. Free people never revolted in order to become serfs.

One great change that came about in modern times was the spread of the idea that everyone has a right to freedom. In 1574 Queen Elizabeth I of England ordered that all serfs still held on all of her royal estates should be freed. Many people in modern times would probably agree with the reason Elizabeth gave: "Since from the beginning, God created all men free by nature, we believe it to be acceptable to God that those in serfdom should be wholly free."

Raising sheep and selling wool became an important way of earning money for landowners.

A man for modern times As times changed, so did ideas about what was important and useful. New ways of living required new ways of thinking. Many important changes took place as the Middle Ages ended and modern times began. Historians sometimes call this period of change the **Renaissance** (ren′ ə säns). Historians invented this name just as Cellarius invented the name *Middle Ages* for the earlier period.

As gunpowder and guns changed the way wars were fought, rulers changed their ideas about the usefulness of knights. Knights in armor were a poor match against cannons.

Castles were not as safe as they once were. Cannons could blast open castle gates. Explosions set off in tunnels under the ground could bring down even the strongest stone walls of a castle.

People with new skills were needed to fight this new kind of war. In 1481, Leonardo da Vinci (lāō när′ dō dä vēn′ chē) wrote a letter describing these skills.

Leonardo came from the city of Florence, in Italy. He wanted a job with the Duke of Milan (mə län′), the ruler of another city in Italy. In his letter, Leonardo described the things he could do.

He said he could make very light and strong bridges useful for crossing castle moats. He knew how to dig tunnels without making noise. He had ways to destroy a castle "even if it was built on a rock." He could make "big guns" and cannons that shot small stones like a storm.

Da Vinci said he had a plan for "covered chariots" that could be used against an army. These "covered chariots" were a kind of tank moved by men hidden inside.

If it was necessary to fight a war at sea, Leonardo said that he had "many kinds of machines most useful for attack and defense."

Leonardo was an **engineer,** not a knight. Engineers design and build many different types of machines. The skills of an engineer were becoming more useful in warfare than the skills of knights.

Leonardo had interest and skills in many different fields. In his home city of Florence, Leonardo was known mainly as a painter. In fact, he was considered one of the best painters in Italy. But he did have a fault. He was rarely satisfied with the pictures he painted. He would begin a picture again and again, and then leave it unfinished because he did not like what he had done.

Part of Leonardo's trouble came from his desire to experiment—to try out new things. He tried new kinds of paint for one of his most famous pictures, "The Last Supper." Leonardo's new type of paint faded very badly in less than 50 years. We know of this painting today only because it was repainted and copied.

Leonardo was also a **sculptor**—a person who makes statues. He planned to make a large bronze statue of the Duke of Milan seated on a horse. Leonardo made a large plaster model of his statue that stood 26 feet (7.9 m) high. It would have taken 50 tons (45.4 metric t) of bronze to make the real statue. The duke did not provide that much bronze, so another of Leonardo's works remained unfinished.

Leonardo studied many different sciences. Everything seemed to interest him, from the stars in the heavens to the rocks on the earth's surface. He studied the

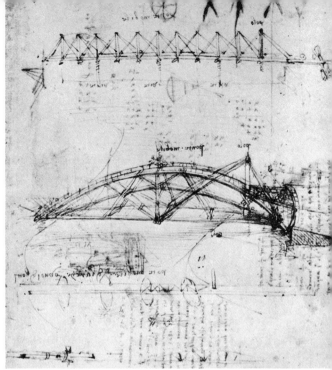

Leonardo da Vinci's most famous painting is the Mona Lisa *(above left).* Leonardo's sketches for a movable bridge *(above right)* and for cannons show his interest in engineering and in warfare.

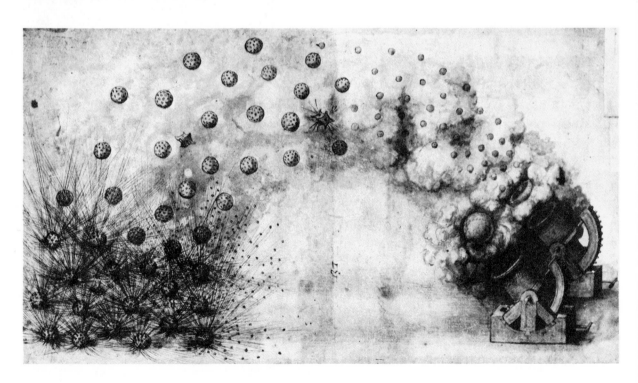

human body and made drawings of the body's different parts. He planned many inventions besides those useful in war. He designed tools, such as a monkey wrench. He had an idea for a parachute, which he described as a closed "tent made of linen." He even thought up plans for a type of helicopter.

Leonardo did not build everything he thought of, but he drew pictures of his ideas in notebooks.

In the last years of his life, Leonardo went to live at the court of the French king. The king enjoyed talking to this very special person. "Never has any man come into this world who knew as much as da Vinci," the French king said.

Perhaps the king went too far in his praise. But people today still admire Leonardo's works. He is considered a good example of a Renaissance person. They admire his paintings and drawings. They are delighted by the ideas he put in his notebooks.

Queen of a nation   During the Middle Ages the countries of Europe were not nations as we know them today. They were collections of feudal fiefs in which a duke might have more power than a king or queen.

Queen Elizabeth I (1533–1603) of England belonged to modern times rather than to the Middle Ages. She was the ruler of a nation rather than the chief of great feudal vassals.

Elizabeth's father and grandfather had done much to reduce the power of the feudal nobles. They increased the power of the monarch over the whole nation. When Elizabeth became queen in 1558, some people wondered if the young unmarried woman could handle such power. They need not have worried. The red-haired young queen was intelligent and wise, and she grew wiser as she grew older. She spoke French and Italian, as well as English. She also knew ancient Greek and Latin. She loved music, danced well, and loved to hunt. She was a good shot with a bow and arrow.

Knowing languages and shooting well do not necessarily make a good ruler. Elizabeth's success as queen was based on her ability to judge people. She usually picked good advisors. She knew how to run a government. Under her leadership

Elizabeth I helped make England a powerful country.

England's smaller, faster ships defeated the larger, slower ships of the Spanish Armada.

England became a powerful nation. Trade with the rest of the world increased and industry grew.

Spain was one of England's enemies during Elizabeth's time. In 1588 her navy defeated a great number of Spanish warships called the Spanish Armada (är mä′də), which had been sent into English water by the Spanish king.

Elizabeth understood that even a powerful queen needs the support of her people. She realized that she was the ruler of a nation, not of just a group of great nobles. For that reason she let the people of the nation see her. Every summer she traveled about her land to see her people and to be seen by them. If she lived today, she would probably appear on television.

The queen's summer trips were big affairs. She traveled with many servants and members of her royal court. The queen rode either on horseback or in a coach. She stopped in many towns or at the houses of nobles. It was a great honor to have the queen as a guest. It was also a great expense. The honored hosts had to feed hundreds of people and animals. They had to provide all sorts of entertainment, such as music, dances, plays, and hunts. It may be that some of the hosts who were glad to see the queen arrive were also glad to see her go.

Elizabeth probably enjoyed the summer trips. She kept making them until she was 70. But she well knew that they were more than vacations. They were part of the business of government. Thousands of people saw her as she rode through the countryside or visited towns. It was probably easier for villagers to think of Elizabeth as *their* queen after seeing her ride by wearing gorgeous clothing and jewels. Elizabeth acted like a queen so that people would think of her as the queen. This was all part of ruling a nation. England belonged to Elizabeth, but she saw to it that the people felt she belonged to England.

National governments instead of feudalism As modern nations developed, queens and kings in other European countries also gained greater powers. Nobles might hold high government offices, but the queens and kings gave them these positions. A king or queen might also choose someone of lesser rank to serve the government.

Cardinal Richelieu was a religious leader who also ran the French Government for King Louis XIII.

In 1624 Cardinal Richelieu (rē′ shė lyü) became the chief adviser of King Louis XIII of France. Cardinal Richelieu promised that he would decrease the "pride of the great." By this he meant that he would reduce the power of the nobles. He took an important step in that direction when he ordered that all castles built like forts must be torn down. It would be harder for nobles to oppose the king if they had no castles to protect them.

Richelieu said that even the greatest nobles had to obey the king's laws. When an important noble broke the law against dueling, Richelieu quickly punished him. Richelieu said to the king: "Nothing so upholds the law as punishment of persons of high rank."

Nobles still held important offices in France, but Richelieu sent other royal officers to keep check on them. The royal government no longer had to depend on the service of nobles. The king hired government officials to serve him just as he hired soldiers.

The royal government in France became a government of a nation. The same thing happened in many countries of western Europe. National governments took the place of feudal governments. In modern times, a person is a member of a nation rather than a vassal of a lord.

CHECKUP

1. Why did taxes take the place of a knight's service in raising an army?
2. How did paying rent change the manors?
3. How did Elizabeth show that she was a national ruler?
4. How did Richelieu deal with the nobles in France?

Coats of Arms

Members of a football team all wear the same colors. This makes it easier to tell different teams apart on a playing field. Team members all wear the same emblem on their helmets. An emblem is a sign that stands for a certain group or person. The American flag is an emblem of the United States.

During the Middle Ages, each knight had his own emblem and colors. These emblems were called coats of arms because they were sewn on cloth coverings, or coats, that knights wore over their armor. Knights also put these emblems on their shields and banners.

There was a good reason to wear a coat of arms. A knight's helmet covered most of his face. Wearing an emblem made it easier to tell one armored knight from another on the field of combat. Knights also used coats of arms to decorate things they owned, such as furniture or jewelry.

A knight's coat of arms was passed on to his children just as his land and other property were. A knight's oldest son received his father's coat of arms. Other sons had to make some changes in the design so they would not be mistaken for their older brother. A knight's daughter used her father's coat of arms until she married. A girl's coat of arms was shaped like a diamond in a deck of playing cards.

When a woman married, her coat of arms appeared on half a shield and her husband's coat of arms was on the other half. Shields could also be divided into four or more parts to show the coats of arms of a number of ancestors.

No two knights could wear the same coat of arms. This meant there had to be many different designs. The designs were of different colors, and the colors were divided in many ways. Birds, animals, and plants were often used as emblems.

Coats of arms are interesting decorations. People continued using them long after knights stopped wearing them.

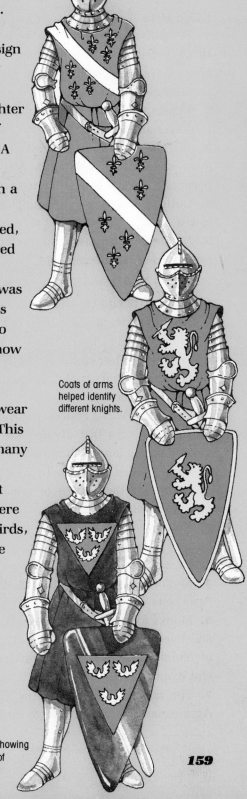

Coats of arms helped identify different knights.

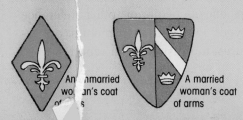

An unmarried woman's coat of arms

A married woman's coat of arms

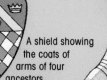

A shield showing the coats of arms of four ancestors

159

7/CHAPTER REVIEW

KEY FACTS

1. Feudalism was a system of government that divided the power to govern among nobles who received land in return for providing the services of knights.

2. Monks and nuns vowed to spend their lives in prayer and work.

3. Serfs were people who worked the land of a manor and were not free to leave without permission of the lord of the manor.

4. Guilds controlled the making of goods in towns.

5. National governments supported by taxes replaced feudal governments.

VOCABULARY QUIZ

Certain key words have been left out of the statements below. Based on your reading in this chapter, select words that will best complete these statements. Write your answers on a sheet of paper.

1. _____ was a system of government in the Middle Ages that divided the power to govern among landholding nobles.

2. Land granted to a noble by a king or queen in return for the service of armed fighting men was called a _____.

3. Nobles who received land from a king or queen were called the king's or queen's _____.

4. Mounted armed men during the Middle Ages were called _____.

5. Monks followed a life of prayer and work and lived in houses called _____.

6. Nuns followed a life of prayer and work and lived in houses called _____.

7. The lands of a noble during the Middle Ages usually had several large estates called _____.

8. Most of the work done on a noble's large estate was carried out by _____.

9. During the Middle Ages, _____ usually had complete control over different trades.

10. Complete control over the making and selling of goods is called a _____.

REVIEW QUESTIONS

1. What is the meaning of the word *modern* as used in this chapter? What is the meaning of the term *Middle Ages*?

2. How was William the Conqueror able to raise an army without collecting taxes?

3. How was it possible for a person to be both a lord and a vassal at the same time?

4. What promises, or vows, did monks and nuns make? What was the title of the person who was in charge of the house where monks lived? What was the title of the person in charge of a house for nuns?

5. What were the duties of a serf?

6. What was a guild and what did it do?

7. What effect did taxes and rent have on feudalism, manors, and the lives of serfs?

8. What were some of the things that Leonardo da Vinci could do?

9. Why did Queen Elizabeth I travel throughout her kingdom every summer?

10. How were feudal governments changed into national governments?

ACTIVITIES

1. Use a telephone directory to find ten names that go back to the time when people were known by their trade or business.

2. Make a report on the training of knights using an encyclopedia or other reference book as your source. Draw a picture, or several pictures, to illustrate your report.

7/ SKILLS DEVELOPMENT

USING SYNONYMS

MORE THAN ONE WAY TO SAY SOMETHING

There is usually more than one way to say the same thing. For example, one sentence in this chapter reads: The system of <u>granting</u> fiefs for the service of knights is called feudalism. You could replace the underlined word with another word without changing the meaning. It would read: The system of <u>giving</u> fiefs for the service of knights is called feudalism.

SKILLS PRACTICE: Part I

Listed below is a series of statements. Each statement is followed by three words. One of the words could be used in place of the underlined word without changing the meaning. On a sheet of paper, write the number of each statement and the term that could take the place of the underlined word. Use a dictionary if you need to look up underlined words.

1. The Bayeux Tapestry <u>gives</u> the story of William's conquest in pictures and words. (finds, presents, gets)

2. A <u>ditch</u> often surrounded a castle. (canal, stream, moat)

3. Knights from Europe captured the city of Jerusalem and <u>organized</u> a Christian kingdom. (defeated, established, destroyed)

4. A monk <u>promised</u> that he would never marry. (vowed, denied, remembered)

5. The king <u>granted</u> land to vassals throughout the kingdom. (took, gave, promised)

6. Life at Citeaux may sound impossibly <u>hard</u> to some people. (strange, difficult, holy)

7. Serfs on manors had to perform various <u>chores</u> besides working in the fields. (tasks, favors, prayers)

8. The guilds carefully <u>guarded</u> their control over the making of goods. (protected, needed, sold)

9. The German historian Cellarius <u>chose</u> the date A.D. 337 to mark the beginning of that period of history he called the Middle Ages. (selected, desired, created)

10. In the Middle Ages, when a vassal died his oldest son usually <u>got</u> his father's estate. (sold, purchased, inherited)

SKILLS PRACTICE: Part II

For the next set of statements, think of a word that could be used in place of the underlined word without changing the meaning of the sentence. Write each statement with the word you think of on a sheet of paper.

1. William of Normandy claimed that he was the <u>rightful</u> king of England after King Edward of England died.

2. During the Middle Ages, lords ruled their vassals who <u>received</u> fiefs in exchange for the service of armed men.

3. A serf was not <u>permitted</u> to leave a manor without the consent of the lord of the manor.

4. An apprentice is a <u>person</u> who learns a trade or business by working for a master for a certain number of years.

5. Guilds set <u>guides</u> for the making and selling of goods, and all guild members had to obey.

6. Leonardo da Vinci claimed that he knew how to dig tunnels without making any <u>noise</u>.

7. The feudal system began to change when vassals began to pay taxes instead of <u>providing</u> armed fighting men.

8. Vassals who owed service to their lord were often <u>scattered</u> throughout the land.

9. Taxes <u>started</u> as a way to raise money for an army but became a way to pay for everything that a government does.

10. The change to renting land on manors gave both serfs and lords <u>greater</u> freedom.

161

The United Kingdom and the Republic of Ireland

┌─VOCABULARY─────────────┐
| Parliament | export |
| import | raw materials |
└────────────────────────┘

The United Kingdom   English is the most common language spoken in the United States. Spanish is also an important language in this country. English and Spanish are European languages. The fact that so many Americans speak these languages shows how much Europe has affected this country.

England has probably had the most important influence on the United States. Not only the English language but also many of our customs and laws can be traced back to England.

Today England is part of a larger country called the United Kingdom of Great Britain and Northern Ireland. This country is located on the British Isles. It unites, or brings together, England, Scotland, Wales, and Northern Ireland under one government. Since the official name of this country is so long, many people shorten it to the United Kingdom. Some people call it Great Britain, and others mistakenly call it England.

The British Isles are the largest of several groups of islands that lie off the western coast of Europe. The British Isles are so close to mainland Europe that they are considered part of the continent. The two largest British Isles are Great Britain and Ireland.

The United Kingdom is one of two countries located on the British Isles. The second country is the Republic of Ireland. If you look at the map on page 164, you will see that this country takes up most of the island of Ireland.

Monarchs then and now   In 1558, Elizabeth I became queen of England. You read about her in Chapter 7. Nearly 400 years later, in 1952, Elizabeth II became queen of the United Kingdom. The powers of the second Elizabeth are very different from those of the first.

Elizabeth I was the real ruler of her country. She had a great deal of power. Elizabeth II is the living symbol of her country. She represents, or stands for, it. She has little political power, but she is greatly respected. Instead of singing about the flag as Americans do, the British sing "God Save the Queen." Instead of pledging allegiance to their flag, the British pledge loyalty to the queen.

The actual business of governing the United Kingdom today is carried on by **Parliament.** Like the United States Congress, Parliament is made up of two houses. Members of the House of Com-

Western Europe is one of the most heavily industrialized areas of the world. Factories such as these in Duisburg, West Germany, are a common sight.

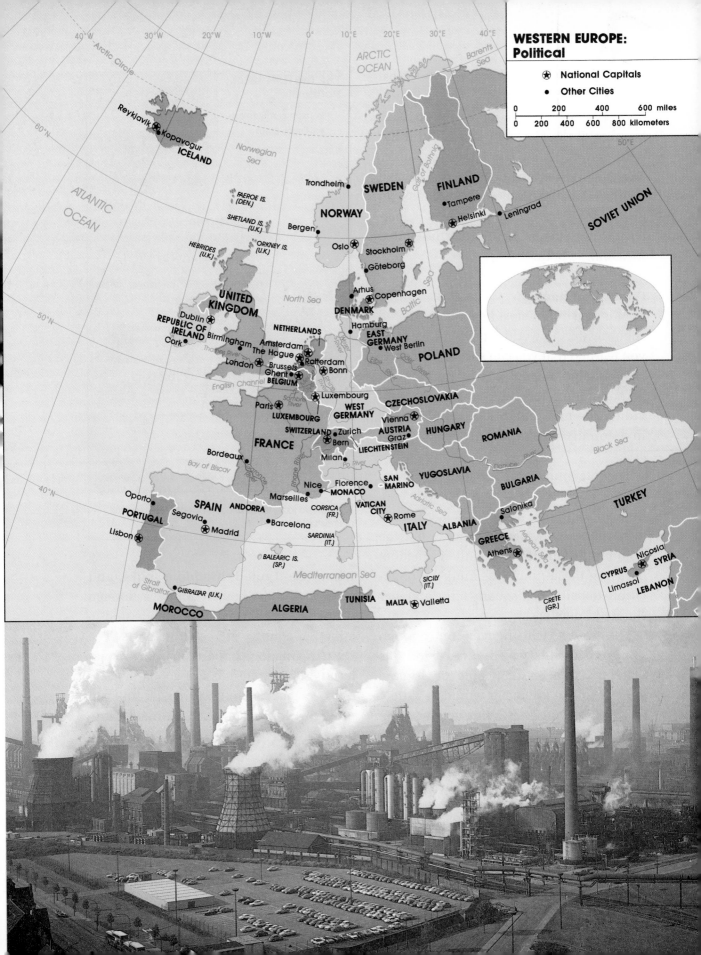

WESTERN EUROPE: Political

⊛ National Capitals
● Other Cities

| 0 | 200 | 400 | 600 miles |
| 0 | 200 | 400 | 600 | 800 kilometers |

ARCTIC OCEAN

Arctic Circle

ATLANTIC OCEAN

Barents Sea

Norwegian Sea

Reykjavik ⊛ Kopavogur
ICELAND

Trondheim ● **SWEDEN** **FINLAND**

● Tampere

NORWAY Helsinki ⊛ ● Leningrad

SOVIET UNION

FAEROE IS. (DEN.)

SHETLAND IS. (U.K.)

Bergen ●

Oslo ⊛ Stockholm ⊛

Göteborg ●

HEBRIDES (U.K.)

ORKNEY IS. (U.K.)

North Sea

Århus ● Copenhagen ⊛

DENMARK

Hamburg ●

EAST GERMANY

● West Berlin

POLAND

UNITED KINGDOM

Dublin ⊛ Birmingham ●

REPUBLIC OF IRELAND

Cork ●

NETHERLANDS

Amsterdam ●
The Hague ● ⊛ Rotterdam

London ● Brussels ⊛ ● Bonn ⊛

Ghent ● **BELGIUM**

Thames River

English Channel

Sambre River

Paris ⊛ ● Luxembourg ⊛

LUXEMBOURG

WEST GERMANY

CZECHOSLOVAKIA

Vienna ⊛

SWITZERLAND ● Zürich

FRANCE Bern ⊛

AUSTRIA
● Graz

HUNGARY

LIECHTENSTEIN

Rhone River

● Milan

Po River

Bordeaux ●

Bay of Biscay

Garonne River

ROMANIA

Black Sea

Nice ● ● Florence

SAN MARINO

YUGOSLAVIA

BULGARIA

Marseilles ● **MONACO**

Oporto ●

SPAIN **ANDORRA**

PORTUGAL

Segovia ●

CORSICA (FR.)

VATICAN CITY

● Rome

Adriatic Sea

Salonika ●

TURKEY

Lisbon ⊛ ● Madrid ⊛ ● Barcelona

SARDINIA (IT.)

ITALY **ALBANIA**

GREECE

Aegean Sea

Athens ⊛

Nicosia ●

Strait of Gibraltar

● GIBRALTAR (U.K.)

BALEARIC IS. (SP.)

Mediterranean Sea

SICILY (IT.)

CYPRUS **SYRIA**

Limassol ●

LEBANON

CRETE (GR.)

MOROCCO **ALGERIA** **TUNISIA** **MALTA** ⊛ Valletta

mons are elected by the people. Most members of the House of Lords inherit their positions. It is an honor to be a member of the House of Lords, but it has little power today. The power to make laws and govern belongs to the elected members of the House of Commons. In Elizabeth I's time, England was a monarchy but not a democracy. Today the United Kingdom is both.

Population density   The United Kingdom is one of the most heavily populated countries in the world today. In Chapter 1 you learned that you can show how heavily populated a country is by figuring out its population density. You do this by dividing the total number of people living in a country by that country's total land area.

The total number of people living in the United Kingdom is about 56,000,000. Its total land area is 94,251 square miles (244,108 sp km). Can you figure out the population density of the United Kingdom by using these numbers? Find the population density per square mile and per square kilometer.

The trouble with figuring out population density this way is that it tells us what the number of people per square mile or square kilometer would be *if* they were spread out evenly in a country. The fact is that people are almost never spread evenly in a country.

Turn back to the population density map of the world on page 17. Notice that the population density on the island of Great Britain is heavier in the southern part of the island than it is in the north. This shows that not all parts of Great Britain are equally populated.

What two independent countries are found on the British Isles?

What the United Kingdom buys and sells   Goods bought from a foreign country are called **imports.** Goods sold to a foreign country are called **exports.** The United Kingdom imports many **raw materials.** Raw materials are goods that are used to make manufactured or finished products. For example, the United Kingdom imports iron, copper, and other metals. These raw materials are used to make airplane engines and cars, which are then exported to other countries throughout the world.

Imports and exports are very important to the United Kingdom. The country has good farmland and pastures but does not raise enough food for all its people. The

London, England, one of the most densely populated cities in Europe, lies at 52°N, 0° longitude. London is a busy port, a cultural center, and the capital of the United Kingdom.

British must import about half their food. They export manufactured goods to help pay for imported food.

Before 1975 oil was the largest and most valuable import into the United Kingdom. Since then the amount of imported oil has gone down. Oil from under the North Sea brought about this change.

In 1958 the countries around the North Sea agreed to divide the rights to any oil or natural gas that might be found under the sea. After spending much money and effort, the British found oil under the North Sea in 1969. It took another 6 years before the British were able to get large amounts of oil from the North Sea. Now pipelines on the floor of the sea carry oil more than 200 miles (300 km) from underwater wells to the coast of the United Kingdom. Some other countries, especially Norway, also get oil from under the North Sea today.

Natural beauty is a crowded country The United Kingdom has many cities and towns. In fact, four out of five people in the United Kingdom live in cities or towns. Yet all of these cities and towns have not destroyed the countryside. There is still much open space in the United Kingdom. There are "picture postcard villages" in the beautiful Cotswold Hills less

165

than 40 miles (64 km) from Birmingham, the United Kingdom's second largest city.

The British have made national parks in some of the most beautiful parts of their country. People who lived and farmed the land where the parks were made did not lose their farms and homes. The British plan was not to destroy country life in order to make recreation areas throughout the United Kingdom. Instead they wished to keep country areas where people could come for recreation.

The British have also tried to bring back some of the beauty of the Thames (temz) River. This river runs through the heart of London, the United Kingdom's capital. The Thames has long served as a waterway from London to the open sea. It has also served as a sewer for the huge city and its industries. By 1960 so much waste was being dumped into the Thames that it had become a "dead river." Fish could not live in it. Few ducks or other water birds came there.

In 1961 the government began to clean up the Thames. London built water treatment plants to clean the water from sewers before letting it flow back into the river.

Industries were no longer allowed to dump harmful wastes directly into the river. All of this cost a great deal of money, but the plan worked. By 1974 salmon were once again swimming in the Thames at London. After 13 years of hard work, the Thames had been changed from a great open sewer into a rather pleasant river. The return of the salmon showed that it was possible for London to be both a large city and a pleasant place to live.

From Empire to Commonwealth

The British began to build an empire during the time of Elizabeth I. England claimed land in North America. British traders went to India to seek trade and power in that part of the world. In the following centuries, the British Empire continued to grow. The British took over land on every continent. It was said that the British ruled an empire "on which the sun never sets." What do you think that meant?

If you look at a map of the world made 80 years ago, you will probably see many parts of the world colored red or pink. This was the color that represented the United Kingdom and its possessions. A map of the world today is much different.

Almost all the countries once ruled by the United Kingdom now rule themselves. Some of these countries have joined with the United Kingdom to form an organization called the Commonwealth of Nations. The Commonwealth is an organization of 43 independent countries. Each Commonwealth country makes its own laws. The United Kingdom does not rule these countries as it did in the days of the British Empire.

The United Kingdom also belongs to another group of countries known as the European Economic Community. This organization, sometimes called the Common Market, was set up to help make trade easier between certain countries in Europe. Today, there are nine other countries besides the United Kingdom in the Common Market. These countries are the Republic of Ireland, France, Italy, Belgium, the Netherlands, Luxembourg, West Germany, Denmark, and Greece.

Working Together

Countries join together in groups for many different reasons. The Common Market is only one example of such a group or *international* organization. International means "between nations."

The Common Market was set up in 1951 for business reasons. Some international organizations are set up to help nations defend themselves. The North Atlantic Treaty Organization, often called NATO, is an example of a group of nations coming together for common defense. NATO was set up in 1950. Most of the countries that belong to the Common Market also belong to NATO. The United States is also a NATO member, but the Soviet Union and the countries of Eastern Europe are not. The Soviet Union and the countries of Eastern Europe have their own business and defense organizations. You will read about these groups in another chapter.

The Common Market and NATO are often called regional organizations. The members of these groups are located in a certain region, or part of the world.

There are other regional organizations for countries in other parts of the world. The Organization of American States, or OAS, is made up of most of the countries in North and South America. The OAS helps these countries deal with their problems.

Some international organizations bring together countries from different parts of the world that have a common interest. The Organization of Petroleum Exporting Countries, or OPEC, has member countries from Asia, Africa, and South America. These countries are very different from each other, but they have one thing in common. They are all important oil producing and exporting countries.

The largest international organization is the United Nations. Countries from all over the world belong to the UN. The UN was set up in 1945 to help keep international peace. It also deals with many other international problems, such as hunger, disease, and lack of education. The UN is divided into special groups that deal with these problems.

The Security Council of the United Nations deals with many international problems.

Green hills and forests are two reasons why Ireland is called the "Emerald Isle".

Old reasons for modern troubles in Ireland   At one time all of Ireland was under British rule. As we have seen, today only Northern Ireland remains part of the United Kingdom. The larger part of the island is a separate country with its own government.

Ireland's troubles go back to the Middle Ages, when England took over Ireland. Many people in Ireland lost their lands and became serfs. In 1541 King Henry VIII of England took the title King of Ireland, too.

For hundreds of years, the people of Ireland fought back. Sometimes they fought battles with the English. At other times they helped the enemies of England.

In order to control Ireland better, England sent people from Scotland and England to live in Ireland. These people were Protestants, while most people in Ireland were Catholics. This difference in religion made each group dislike and distrust each other even more.

This dislike has lasted for centuries. When Ireland finally won its freedom from the British in 1922, the people of Northern Ireland refused to be part of the new country. Northern Ireland remained part of the United Kingdom. The rest of the island became the Republic of Ireland. Some people in Ireland still believe dividing the island was wrong. This view, so deeply rooted in the past, still troubles Ireland today.

CHECKUP

1. In what ways are the positions of Elizabeth I and Elizabeth II different?
2. What is population density?
3. How did the British Empire change?
4. Why is Ireland divided today?

The Nordic Countries

Lands of northern Europe   The word *Nordic* means north. It is often used to describe the countries of northern Europe. These countries are Norway, Sweden, Denmark, and Finland. Iceland is also called a Nordic European country but it is not part of mainland Europe.

Norway, Sweden, Denmark, and Iceland are also called Scandinavian countries. Denmark is not located on the peninsula of Scandinavia as Sweden and Norway are. But the people of all three countries share the same history and speak similar languages. Icelandic, the language spoken by the people of Iceland, is also a Scandinavian language.

Even though Finland borders Norway and Sweden, the Finns are not Scandinavians. Finland's history and language are different from the history and languages of the other Nordic countries.

Homeland of the Vikings   Scandinavia was the homeland of the Vikings a thousand years ago. The Vikings were fierce, warlike people of warlike times. They raided many countries in Europe. The Vikings traveled very far in light ships moved only by sails and oars. They raided Britain, Ireland, and France. They sailed into the Mediterranean Sea and invaded Italy. The Vikings even sailed their open boats out into the North Atlantic Ocean to Iceland, Greenland, and the coast of North America. Greenland is the world's largest island. It was ruled as a colony by Denmark

Viking warriors sailed to lands far beyond Scandinavia.

for many years. Today, Greenland is still part of the Danish kingdom but its people rule themselves.

The modern Scandinavian people are not at all like their fierce Viking ancestors. Sweden has not been at war for more than 160 years. Norway fought in World War II only when it was attacked by the Germans. It is interesting that the descendants of the Vikings now give the Nobel (nō bel′) Peace Prize each year to the person who has done the most for the cause of peace.

169

Per capita income Sweden is the largest Nordic country. It also has the most people, yet its population is less than one sixth that of the United Kingdom. Size and population do not tell us much about how rich or poor a country is. Large countries with many people are not always rich. Small countries with few people are not always poor.

A country's **per capita** (pər kap′ ə tə) **income** gives us a better idea of how rich or poor that country is. Per capita income means that amount of income (money received) each person in a country would have if the country's total income were divided equally among all of its people. When we compare the per capita incomes of countries, we discover that the country's size may have little to do with its wealth.

Denmark is a far smaller country than the United Kingdom and it has far fewer people. But Denmark has a much higher per capita income than the United Kingdom does. So do Norway, Sweden, and even Iceland. In fact, as measured by per capita incomes, Norway, Sweden, Denmark, and Iceland are among the richest

This department store in Stockholm, Sweden, sells products from many countries.

countries in the world. Finland's per capita income is not quite as high as the per capita incomes of the other Nordic countries, but Finland is still among the richest countries of the world.

What the Nordic countries produce
A country's wealth depends not only on the gifts of nature, but also on what people do with these gifts. North Sea petroleum is a gift of nature to Norway. But the petroleum had no value until Norway found ways to pump it from beneath the sea.

The people of Norway found wealth in the sea long before petroleum was discovered. Norway has been a great fishing country for hundreds of years. Today the people of Norway catch and **process** a great deal of fish. To process a product means to get it ready to be used. The fish is canned, frozen, or packed in ice and shipped to other countries. Norway makes good use of its forests too. It ships wood and paper made from wood to other countries around the world.

Sweden has many forests and rich deposits of iron ore. It exports some of these resources to other countries and uses the rest at home. Sweden makes furniture from its wood and steel from its iron ore. The steel is used to make knives and cars, among other things. Sweden ships its cars to many countries, including the United States.

Denmark is a small country, but the Danes have learned to make good use of their land. They raise dairy cattle for milk, and process the milk into butter and cheese. The Danes export butter and cheese to the United Kingdom and other countries. The Danes feed hogs with the liquid left over from making butter. Bacon, ham, and other meat products made from hogs are exported. Even people in American farm states buy canned Danish ham.

In spite of its name, Iceland is not completely covered with ice. Some of the land in Iceland is used to raise crops of potatoes and turnips. Grassland is used to raise many sheep and some cattle. But Iceland's main product comes from the sea, not the land. Fishing is Iceland's major industry.

Finland has important deposits of copper and iron ore. But Finland's greatest wealth comes from its forests. Wood and wood products make up more than half of Finland's exports to other countries of the world.

Products from farms, forests, and industries are only one way to measure a country's wealth. A country can also be rich in its poetry, art, and music. Many famous artists, musicians, and writers have come from Nordic countries. Do you know the story of "The Ugly Duckling" or the tale "The Emperor's New Clothes"? These stories and many more were written by the famous Danish writer, Hans Christian Andersen. Such stories have little to do with per capita income, but they make a country rich in other ways.

CHECKUP

1. Why can all the Scandinavian countries be called Nordic countries, but not all the Nordic countries be called Scandinavian?
2. Why is per capita income a better measurement of a country's wealth than facts about the country's size and population?
3. What kind of wealth may a country have besides wealth measured by per capita income?

West Germany, Austria, and Switzerland

┌─VOCABULARY─────────────────┐
│ tourism   neutrality │
└─────────────────────────────┘

Wars and the map of Germany The map on this page shows changes in the size and shape of Germany over the last century. In 1872 Germany's border with France was west of the Rhine River, and in the east, Germany bordered Russia.

By 1923, however, France had taken some of the land west of the Rhine. Germany itself was divided by Poland. Polish lands separated the eastern part of Germany from the rest of the country.

The map on this page shows that today there is not one Germany, but two—West Germany and East Germany. Both lie west of the Oder (ōd′ ər) River.

Wars brought about these changes in the size and shape of Germany. France and Germany fought the Franco-Prussian War in 1870. Germany won that war and took some French land west of the Rhine.

A much greater war broke out in 1914. This war lasted 4 years. In this war Germany was joined by Austria-Hungary and Turkey to form one group of countries called the Central Powers. France, the United Kingdom, Russia, and Japan formed another group called the Allies. Italy joined the Allies in 1915. The United States joined the Allies in 1917. Because so many countries fought in this war, it was called the World War. We now call it World War I. In 1918 the Central Powers lost the war, and France got back some land west of the Rhine.

Hitler prepares Germany for war In the years after World War I, Germany went through a period of hard times. In 1932 Adolf Hitler and the Nazi party got control of the country.

Hitler was a dictator who prepared Germany for war. He put in jail or killed many people who opposed him. He said that all Jews both inside and outside of Germany were enemies of the country. Some Jews left Germany. Those who did not escape were put in slave labor camps or killed. Before Hitler was stopped, his government killed about 6 million Jewish men, women, and children in Germany and in countries Germany came to control.

World War II Just 21 years after the end of World War I, another war broke out in Europe. We call it World War II because, before the war was over, it involved most of the countries of the world. Hitler started

How has the shape of Germany changed?

HOW GERMANY'S BORDERS CHANGED

- Area lost after World War I
- Area lost after World War II
- East Germany today
- West Germany today
- ✪ National Capitals
- ── Boundary of Germany in 1872

the war by sending the German armies to attack Poland in 1939. France and the United Kingdom entered the war to stop Germany. This time Italy joined Germany. The two countries were known as the Axis. Japan also joined the Axis.

In 1940 it looked as if the Axis might quickly win the war. Germany took over much of France, and the French gave up. German airplanes attacked the United Kingdom. Bombs fell on many cities including London. But the British did not give up. They received weapons and other supplies from the United States.

After its victory over France, Germany attacked the Soviet Union in 1941. The German army pushed deep into the Soviet Union, but it could not defeat the Soviet army. The United States entered the war later in 1941. Four hard years of war followed. In 1945 the United States, the United Kingdom, France, and the Soviet Union defeated the Axis. When Hitler saw that Germany had lost, he killed himself.

Conquering German troops marched past the Arc de Triomphe in Paris, France, in 1940.

Germany is divided into two countries   The countries that defeated Germany wanted to make sure that any new German government would be different from that of the Nazis. But the countries could not agree on how to do this. As a result, the country was divided into West Germany and East Germany.

The official name of East Germany is the German Democratic Republic. It has a Communist government and close ties with the Communist government of the Soviet Union. You will read more about the Communist governments of Eastern Europe in the next unit.

The official name of West Germany is the Federal Republic of Germany. It has a democratic government. The people of West Germany elect government officials much as the other countries in Western Europe do.

Trade and industry in West Germany   West Germany is larger than East Germany. It has twice as much land and three times as many people. Both East and West Germany are now leading industrial countries. Both produce steel, machinery, textiles, and other manufactured goods. West German industry built one of the most popular cars in history, the Volkswagen "Beetle."

West Germany has more and better farmland than East Germany, but West Germany still does not grow enough food to feed its large population. The country imports some of its food and pays for the imports by exporting manufactured products. West Germany also has a higher per capita income than East Germany, but East Germany is not poor.

Austria There was a time when Austria was much larger than it is today. It was once a great empire. All that changed at the end of World War I. Austria had sided with Germany during that war and was defeated. Many of the lands within Austria's empire became free.

Austria has a number of industries that need highly trained workers, such as those who make fine glassware. **Tourism**—the care and feeding of visitors—is an important business in Austria today.

The country has many mountains, including parts of the Alps. The mountains attract tourists (visitors) from all over the world. Another place tourists visit in Austria is its capital city of Vienna. Some people think Vienna is the most beautiful city in Europe. Vienna is also known for its music. The city's opera and orchestra are considered to be among the finest in all of Europe.

Switzerland—the benefits of neutrality Switzerland took no part in World War I or World War II. In fact, Switzerland has not fought a war in a great many years. During all the wars in Europe over the past 100 years, the Swiss have kept their **neutrality.** Neutrality means not taking anyone's side in a war or dispute. Switzerland has kept its neutrality because other, more powerful, European nations agreed a long time ago that they would not try to conquer independent Switzerland.

The Swiss speak several different languages. Four of these languages have been declared national languages. These national languages are German, French, Italian, and Romansh (rō mansh'). Romansh is a language that comes from the Latin once spoken by the Romans. Most Swiss speak German as their first language. French is the second most common language in Switzerland.

The Matterhorn looms over skiers in the Swiss Alps.

Mountains cover about 70 percent of Switzerland. The most important mountains are the Alps and the Jura (jur′ ə). Most Swiss do not live in the mountains. They live on a high plateau between the mountains. Bern, Switzerland's capital, is located on the plateau.

Mountains are very important to Switzerland. They attract thousands of tourists to the country every year. Tourism is one of Switzerland's important industries. But tourism is not Switzerland's only industry. Dairy farming is also an important industry and the Swiss are famous for their cheese. Over the years, the Swiss have also become known for making fine watches and scientific equipment. Since the country has few sources of raw materials, the Swiss have developed industries that require great skill rather than large amounts of raw materials. There is not much metal in a fine Swiss watch or scientific instrument, but it takes a great deal of human skill to make these products.

Since Switzerland has been a neutral nation for so long, people from other nations have found that Switzerland is a good place to keep money. These people feel that their money will be safe in a country that has no wars. As a result, Switzerland has become one of the world's great banking centers.

CHECKUP

1. Why have Germany's borders changed so much during the last 100 years?
2. Give two reasons why Austria has a good tourist business.
3. How has Switzerland's neutrality helped the country?

France and the Low Countries

France—a country with variety   It would be hard to be bored traveling in France. It is such a varied land. It has beaches, mountains, and plains. The beaches are on both the Atlantic Ocean and the Mediterranean Sea. The sunny Riviera on the Mediterranean near the city of Nice (nēs) has long been one of Europe's favorite vacation spots.

One tourist attraction on the Riviera is the tiny country of Monaco. The whole country stretches less than 2 miles (3 km) along the beach.

The mountains of France include parts of the Alps and Pyrenees. Lower mountains, plateaus, and forested hills cover much of the country from the Pyrenees to the Rhine. Rolling plains stretch from the southeast corner of France to its northern border. These plains have some of the best farmland in all of Europe.

France is both a farming and an industrial country. The farms produce enough grain and other crops so that France exports more food than any other country of Western Europe. French industries make many different types of goods, from automobiles to clothing.

The variety of French governments During the last 200 years France has had four kings, two emperors, and five republics. Three of the four kings were named Louis—Louis XVI, Louis XVIII, and Louis

The Eiffel Tower in Paris, France, is 984 feet (300 m) high, and is visited by thousands of tourists every year.

Philippe. Both emperors were named Napoleon. The first Napoleon ruled France from 1795 to 1815. He conquered a large part of Europe. The second Napoleon ruled from 1852 to 1871. He was emperor when France fought Germany in 1870. The Fifth Republic was set up in 1958. Under its constitution the people of France elect the country's president and members of the National Assembly.

The Netherlands—a truly low country Belgium, Luxembourg, and the Netherlands are all called Low Countries because they do not have much high land. The name Low Country best fits the Netherlands. This country is sometimes called Holland, a name that means "hollow land." Part of the Netherlands is, in fact, a land in a hollow in the sea.

The Dutch made the "hollow" in the sea by building **dikes.** A dike is a wall of sand, clay, and stone that holds back water. The Dutch built dikes along the coast of the Netherlands to hold back the sea's high tides. The Dutch put dikes around the flooded land and then pumped the water out. Piece by piece the Dutch made their country larger by pushing back the sea. Today 38 percent of the land in the Netherlands would be covered by the sea if it were not for the dikes.

The Netherlands is a crowded country, one of the most densely populated in Europe. The Dutch must make good use of the land won from the sea with great cost. They are careful farmers and the country is known for its dairy products. The Dutch export butter, cheese, and canned milk. Vegetable growers raise crops of tomatoes and lettuce throughout the year in hothouses. Dutch industries also make many different manufactured goods.

The languages of Belgium and Luxembourg   All people in some countries speak the same language. This is one way to show **nationality,** a feeling of belonging to a certain nation or country. But there is no Belgian language. Both Dutch and French are official languages, and people usually speak of themselves as Flemings or Walloons. The Flemings, who live mostly in northern Belgium, speak Dutch in their schools. The Walloons in the south use French in the schools. But many people speak both languages, especially in Brussels, the capital, where street signs are printed in both Dutch and French.

The Netherlands is famous for its colorful tulips.

There are two correct ways to spell the name of Belgium's neighbor. It may be either Luxembourg or Luxemburg. The first spelling is French and the second is German. Both languages are spoken in this tiny country. A newspaper in Luxembourg may carry stories in both languages on the same page.

High per capita income   The people of Belgium and Luxembourg, like the people of the Netherlands, make careful use of their land. Belgium's farmers grow 85 percent of the country's food even though Belgium is densely populated. Even with careful land use, the Low Countries might be poor if they depended only on farming and dairying for income. For this reason, all three countries make use of the skills and energy of their people in other businesses and in trade.

Amsterdam in the Netherlands and Antwerp in Belgium are centers for the diamond business. Buying, cutting, and selling diamonds does not take a lot of space for factories but does call for very skilled workers. Much of Europe's shipping passes through the Low Countries. Antwerp in Belgium and Rotterdam in the Netherlands are two of Europe's leading ports. Many large, worldwide businesses have offices in the Low Countries. All three countries have high per capita incomes.

CHECKUP

1. What kinds of variety are found in France?
2. How have the people of the Netherlands made their country larger?
3. What languages are spoken in Belgium? What languages are spoken in Luxembourg?

Mediterranean Countries

The Iberian Peninsula   Spain, Andorra, and Portugal are located on the Iberian Peninsula. Of these three countries, only Spain actually borders the Mediterranean Sea. Andorra is a small country located in the Pyrenees between Spain and France. Portugal is on the western side of the Iberian Peninsula.

The peninsula itself is mostly a high plateau. Madrid, the capital of Spain, sits in the middle of this plateau. It is the highest capital city in Europe. It is even higher than Bern, the capital of Switzerland. Portugal has rolling plains south of its capital, Lisbon. But the northern part of the country has mountains.

The east coast of Spain has a **Mediterranean climate**—cool, rainy winters and hot, dry summers. The high Spanish plateau has a different climate. Madrid is both colder in winter and hotter in summer than the city of Barcelona (bär sə lō′ nə) on Spain's Mediterranean coast. Central Spain has the driest land in Western Europe.

Spain takes up about 85 percent of the Iberian Peninsula. The country was once part of the Roman Empire. A Roman aqueduct still carries water to the Spanish city of Segovia (si gō′ vē ə).

For most of its history Spain has been a farming country. During the last 30 years industry has been growing in Spain, but farming is still important. The Spanish raise large amounts of grapes and olives. The grapes are used to make wine. The olives are used to make olive oil. Wine and olive oil are two of Spain's exports.

Tourism is an important business in Spain. Visitors come to Spain to see its castles, view great works of art in its museums, and watch its bullfights.

Tourism is also a major business in tiny Andorra. This country is only about half the size of New York City. Andorra has two languages—French and Spanish.

Portugal, the third country on the Iberian Peninsula, once had a great empire. Hundreds of years ago, Portuguese sailors opened sea routes around southern Africa to India. They also sailed to South America and settled in Brazil. Today almost all the lands once ruled by Portugal are free countries.

The Portuguese are still fine sailors. They sail their small boats far out into the Atlantic Ocean in search of fish. Fishing is a major industry in Portugal. The Portuguese process the fish they catch and export it to many countries.

Modern machines help Spanish farmers with their work in their fields.

WESTERN EUROPE: Natural Resources

Legend:
- ⊛ National Capitals
- • Other Cities
- ⚑ Petroleum
- ◆ Iron Ore
- ▨ Coal

Scale:
0 — 200 — 400 — 600 miles
0 — 200 — 400 — 600 — 800 kilometers

Rich deposits of iron ore and coal have helped make Western Europe an important industrial area. Which country has the most cities with more than one million people?

Portugal today is mainly an agricultural country. Olives and grapes are two important crops raised. Wine made from Portuguese grapes is exported all over the world. The Portuguese also export great amounts of cork.

Portugal's cities have been growing in recent years. Lisbon is Europe's westernmost port. It is often a first or last stop for ships sailing to or from Europe.

Italy The peninsula of Italy is shaped like a boot. The land has many mountains. The Alps are located in northern Italy. South of the Alps is the rich Po River valley, the most important agricultural area in Italy. A chain of mountains, the Apennines (ap′ e nīnz), runs down the center of Italy all the way to the tip of the "boot."

Much of Italy has a Mediterranean climate. This helps attract tourists to the country. Tourism is an important business in Italy. The tourists come not only for the fine climate but also to visit Roman ruins, Italy's museums, and Vatican City.

Vatican City is an independent country right in the center of Rome, Italy's capital. Vatican City covers only .17 square miles (0.44 sq km). It is the smallest country in the world. Visitors come to Vatican City because it is the center of the Roman Catholic Church. Its ruler is the **pope**—the leader of Roman Catholics throughout the world.

Tourists also visit San Marino, another tiny country in Italy. Tourism is San Marino's chief source of income.

Italy is an important industrial country in Europe today. Much of Italy's industry is found in the northern part of the country. The southern part of Italy is mostly agricultural and relatively poor when compared to the north.

Greece The country of Greece is located on the southern part of the Balkan Peninsula. There are many mountains on this peninsula, and there is little good land for farming. However, the Greeks still manage to grow crops of olives, grapes, other fruits, and wheat.

Tourism is a big business in Greece. The tourists like the country's warm, dry summers and its pure blue ocean waters. But probably Greece's major tourist attractions are the remains of the ancient Greek cities.

Greece is one of the world's leading shipping countries. Ships flying the blue and white Greek flag carry the products of many nations.

As seen from the top of St. Peter's Basilica in Vatican City, the city of Rome, Italy, stretches to the far horizon.

The harbor of Mykonos, Greece, is often filled with both fishing and pleasure boats. The blue waters and mild climate of Greece attract many tourists.

Two island nations The island nation of Malta is south of Sicily in the Mediterranean Sea. Malta is very small, but its location has made it important to other countries. People from Greece set up a colony there more than 2,000 years ago. Rome once ruled Malta and so has the United Kingdom.

Malta became an independent nation in 1964. The island is very rocky. Little food is grown there. Most of the food for Malta's people must come from other countries. Two important businesses on Malta are shipping and building ships. The people of Malta speak two languages—Maltese and English. Maltese is made up of Italian and Arabic.

The island nation of Cyprus is located at the eastern end of the Mediterranean Sea. Geographically, Cyprus can be considered part of Asia, not Europe. But for the most part, the history of Cyprus is more closely connected with Europe. The island was settled centuries ago by the Greeks. It was later conquered by the Turks.

Today, Cyprus is an independent country with close ties to Western Europe. About 80 percent of the people in Cyprus are Greek. Most of the remaining 20 percent are Turks. Greek and Turkish are both official languages in Cyprus. There has been trouble on the island between Greek Cypriots and Turkish Cypriots.

About half of the people of Cyprus make their living by farming. The other major industry is mining. Cyprus has rich deposits of asbestos and copper. Cyprus also produces olive oil and wine.

CHECKUP

1. What three countries are located on the Iberian Peninsula today?
2. What are some of the things that attract tourists to Italy?
3. Describe a Mediterranean climate. How does this type of climate affect tourism in most Mediterranean countries?

KEY FACTS

1. The United Kingdom is both a monarchy and a democracy.

2. The United Kingdom is very heavily populated and exports and imports many goods.

3. The British Empire became an organization of independent countries known as the Commonwealth of Nations.

4. Both the Scandinavian countries and the Low Countries have high per capita incomes.

5. Belgium, Luxembourg, and the Netherlands are known as the low countries.

6. Wars have greatly changed the boundaries of Germany during the past century. There are now two Germanys.

7. France is a land of great variety. It is both a farming and an industrial country.

8. Tourism is important in Switzerland, Austria, Greece, Italy, Spain, and Portugal.

9. During the last 30 years, industry has been growing in Spain.

10. Countries with a Mediterranean climate usually have cool, wet winters and hot, dry summers.

VOCABULARY QUIZ

On a sheet of paper write the word or words that will correctly fill in the blanks in each of the statements below.

1. A crowded country has a high population _____.

2. _____ is the care and feeding of people who travel for pleasure.

3. The governing power in the United Kingdom today rests with the elected members of _____ rather than with the monarch.

4. Switzerland kept its _____ in both World War I and World War II.

5. Norway _____ a great deal of fish to other countries.

6. The Danes _____ milk into cheese and butter.

7. The United Kingdom _____ raw materials for its industries.

8. A wealthy country with a small population has a high _____ income.

9. The British import _____ and export manufactured goods.

10. The _____ is the head of the Roman Catholic church.

REVIEW QUESTIONS

1. How did the British Empire change in modern times?

2. What kinds of goods does the United Kingdom export? What does it import?

3. What is per capita income?

4. Does being small make a country poor?

5. Why are there two Germanys?

6. Why can France be called a land of variety?

7. In what ways are the Netherlands and Denmark alike? Switzerland and Austria?

8. How does the Mediterranean climate of Europe's southern countries affect tourism?

9. Name two island countries located in the Mediterranean Sea.

10. What countries belong to the European Economic Community?

ACTIVITES

1. Make a list of seven things in your home that were imported from another country.

2. Read a story by Hans Christian Andersen. Write a short summary of the story. Tell the story to the class, a smaller group, or another person *without using your written summary*.

8/SKILLS DEVELOPMENT

READING FOR UNDERSTANDING

UNDERSTANDING WORDS IN CONTEXT

In 1867 the American author Mark Twain took a trip to Europe. He wrote a book about his travels called *The Innocents Abroad*. Three selections of that book are given on this page. You may find some new words in the selections. If so, see if you can guess the meanings of these words by how they are used before you look them up. There is a list of statements following the selections. *Based on your reading of what Mark Twain wrote*, decide whether each statement is true or false.

THE INNOCENTS ABROAD

Selection A. "At Pisa we climbed up to the top of the strangest structure the world has any knowledge of—the Leaning Tower. As everyone knows, it is in the neighborhood of one hundred and eight feet high . . . yet it leans more than thirteen feet out of the perpendicular. . . . Standing on the summit, one does not feel altogether comfortable (and) . . . to stretch your neck out far enough to see the base of the tower, makes your flesh creep."

Selection B. "The Venetian gondola is as free and graceful, in its gliding movement, as a serpent. It is twenty or thirty feet long, and is narrow and deep, like a canoe. . . . We sit in the cushioned carriage-body of a cabin, with the curtains drawn, and smoke, or read, or look out upon the passing boats, the houses, the bridges, the people, and enjoy ourselves much more than we could in a buggy jolting over our cobble-stone pavements at home. This is the gentlest, pleasantest locomotion we have ever known. But it seems queer—ever so queer—to see a boat doing duty as a private carriage. We see businessmen come to the front door, step into a gondola, instead of a street-car, and go off down-town to the counting room."

Selection C. "[In Florence] we used to go and stand on the bridges and admire the Arno. It is popular to admire the Arno. It is a great historical creek with four feet in the channel and some scows floating around. It would be a very plausible river if they would pump some water in it. They call it a river, and they honestly think it *is* a river. . . . They even help out the delusion by building bridges over it. I do not see why they are too good to wade."

SKILLS PRACTICE

Are the following statements true or false? Write your answers on a sheet of paper.

1. Few people know about the Leaning Tower.

2. The tower is *exactly* 180 feet high.

3. Mark Twain felt somewhat uneasy at the top of the tower.

4. A gondola is a wide, flat boat.

5. Mark Twain thought gondolas a queer way to travel, and he did not enjoy riding in them.

6. People rode carriages and streetcars to work in Venice.

7. The Arno is too wide to build a bridge across it.

8. The people of Florence thought of the Arno as a river.

9. Mark Twain made fun of the Arno's size.

10. Mark Twain made fun of the Leaning Tower of Pisa.

11. The Leaning Tower is found in the Italian city of Venice.

12. Mark Twain's gondola had a cushioned cabin with curtains.

13. Mark Twain could not see the sights of Venice from his gondola.

14. Mark Twain thought that riding in a gondola was much like riding in a carriage in the United States.

15. Mark Twain felt the Arno River was not wide enough to have bridges over it.

183

3/UNIT REVIEW

1. The way people live depends, in part, on the gifts nature has given to the places where people live. — *What are some of nature's gifts to Western Europe?*

2. Over the years, people in Western Europe have used nature's gifts in many ways. By using these gifts, people have changed the land in Western Europe. Sometimes the changes were good; sometimes they were not. — *What changes have people made to the land in Western Europe by using its gifts of nature?*

3. The continent of Europe has been described as a peninsula with peninsulas. — *In what ways have the irregular shapes of Europe's peninsulas affected the continent?*

4. There were many different ways of living during the Middle Ages. People lived on manors, in cities, and in monasteries. — *How did the life of a serf on a manor differ from the life of a guild member in a city?*

5. In modern times, money payments such as taxes helped change feudal governments into national governments. — *What kinds of taxes do people pay? What are some of the things governments pay for with these taxes?*

6. Leonardo da Vinci still interests people living today because of his many skills and interests. — *What were some of the skills and interests Leonardo da Vinci had?*

7. Although the United Kingdom is a major industrial nation today, there are still many beautiful parts in the country. — *What has the United Kingdom done to help keep its land beautiful?*

8. What has happened in the past often affects the present. — *Why is the fact that there are two Germanys today a good example of how the past affects the present?*

9. As measured by per capita income, the countries of Western Europe are among the richest in the world. — *What is per capita income, and how is it figured?*

10. Speaking the same language helps people to think of themselves as a nation, but some countries in Western Europe have two or more official languages. — *What countries in Western Europe have two or more official languages?*

The Soviet Union and Eastern Europe

The Lands and People of the Soviet Union

VOCABULARY

pedestrian	taiga
continental	steppe
climate	tundra
permanent	permafrost
artisan	source

A close relationship   As you learned in Chapter 6, the countries of Eastern Europe are historically linked with the Soviet Union. Eastern Europe includes Poland, East Germany, Czechoslovakia, Hungary, Yugoslavia, Romania, Bulgaria, Albania, and part of the Soviet Union. Find these countries on the map on page 187. This is an important part of the world.

Although these countries have differences, they have much in common. They have a similar form of government. Like the Common Market of Western Europe, the Soviet Union and the countries of Eastern Europe have joined together in an organization to make trade easier among themselves. The Soviet Union and most of these countries also have an agreement to protect each other if one of them should be attacked, or if a war should break out. You will learn more about the history of Eastern Europe and the Soviet Union in the next two chapters.

From sea to sea   The Soviet Union is the largest country in the world today. Throughout history, many people have been curious about the vast lands that are now part of this country.

On Valentine's Day in 1820, Captain John Cochrane of the British Royal Navy set out on a journey. It was not a sea journey, as you might expect. Captain Cochrane traveled on foot. He set out from the coast of France in Western Europe for a country in Eastern Europe called Russia. He then planned to walk all the way across the vast lands of the Russian empire, a country that reached from the Baltic Sea to the Pacific Ocean.

Captain Cochrane later wrote the story of this trip. He called it *Narrative of a Pedestrian's Journey Through Russia and Siberian Tartary*. A **pedestrian** is a walker. Like the Russian empire, the Siberian Tartary is a thing of the past. It was a large region in northern and central Asia that is now part of the Soviet Union. Part of Tartary was in the vast Asian territory known as Siberia (sī bir' ē ə). Siberia stretches across Asia from the Ural Mountains to the Pacific. Since the distance from the Baltic Sea to the Pacific is about 6,000 miles (9,654 km), this would have been quite a walk for Captain Cochrane! That is, if the captain had actually

As the map shows, the Soviet Union spans two continents. It stretches from Eastern Europe to the Pacific Ocean.

National Capitals
Other Cities
Canals

300   600 miles
0   300 600 900 kilometers

North Pole

ARCTIC OCEAN

Bering Strait

Bering Sea

Sea of Okhotsk

JAPAN

Sea of Japan

Vladivostok

NORTH KOREA

Yakutsk

ASIA

SIBERIA

SOVIET UNION

Trans-Siberian Railroad

Amur R.

Lake Baikal

Irkutsk

MONGOLIA

CHINA

Arctic Circle

Yenisei

Ob R.

URAL MOUNTAINS

Lake Balkhash

Aral Sea

Pik Kommunizma
(24,590 ft. 7,495 m)

AFGHANISTAN

Kazan

Trans-Siberian Railroad

Volgograd

Caspian Sea

IRAN

Leningrad

Trans-Siberian Railroad

Moscow

White Sea

FINLAND

NORWAY

Baltic Sea

North Sea

NORTH EUROPEAN PLAIN

Dnieper R.

CRIMEA

Black Sea

Mt. Elbrus
(18,481 ft.
5,642 m)

CAUCASUS
MOUNTAINS

TURKEY

LINE OF INSET

POLAND

Warsaw

Vistula R.

EAST GERMANY

East Berlin

WEST GERMANY

CZECHOSLOVAKIA

Prague

AUSTRIA

HUNGARY

Budapest

HUNGARIAN PLAIN

CARPATHIAN MTS.

ROMANIA

Bucharest

Danube R.

IRON GATE

Danube R.

BALKAN MTS.

BULGARIA

YUGOSLAVIA

Belgrade

Sava R.

Adriatic Sea

ALBANIA

Tirana

GREECE

ITALY

0   100   200 miles
0   100 200 kilometers

Leningrad, formerly St. Petersburg, is one of the Soviet Union's busiest Baltic seaports.

walked all of it. But he did not. He often caught rides in carriages and wagons. He rode on horses and traveled by river boat, canoe, and even dogsled. If the word *hitchhiker* had been invented, he might better have called his book *A Hitchhiker's Journey Through Russia and Siberian Tartary.*

Even though Captain Cochrane did not actually walk all the way, he did get a close look at the lands of Eastern Europe and northern Asia. He saw them as only a walker or a horseback rider can. Those who travel slowly see much more than those who speed across a land in a car or fly over it in an airplane.

Much has changed since Captain Cochrane took his trip. The country he crossed is as large as ever, but the name has changed. It is now the Union of Soviet Socialist Republics. The name is often shortened to Soviet Union or the U.S.S.R. People also sometimes still speak of the whole country as Russia because most of the people live in the part of the Soviet Union called Russia. In the next chapter you will read how the old Russian empire became the Soviet Union.

Across the North European Plain

From the French coast of the Atlantic Ocean into Russia, Captain Cochrane traveled across one of Europe's flatlands called the North European Plain. It stretches from France into Russia. You can see the extent of this plain by looking at the relief map on page 187. Most of the plain lies across the northern part of Eastern Europe, including the present-day countries of East Germany and Poland.

The North European Plain lies along the Baltic Sea. The Baltic is an arm of the Atlantic that reaches far into Eastern Europe. The Baltic Sea is as far north as Hudson Bay in Canada. It is not so cold as Hudson Bay, but its waters are colder than those of the North Sea. Ice freezes in some of its ports during the winter months.

Spring came late in 1820. Captain Cochrane saw ice in Russia's ports on the Baltic even though it was already April. He even got caught in a late snow after entering Russia. He wrote in his journal, "I have traveled faster than the seasons. I found winter still lingering in the northern boundary of Europe."

On the last day of April, Captain Cochrane reached the city of St. Petersburg. He had come about 1,600 miles (2,575 km), most of it on foot. He had averaged about 20 miles (32 km) a day. Later he did better. He once walked 96 miles (154 km) in 32 hours.

You will not find St. Petersburg on a modern map of the Soviet Union. St.

Petersburg is now named Leningrad. Leningrad stands in the midst of swampy forests and lakes on the delta of the Neva River.

In 1820, when Captain Cochrane visited St. Petersburg, it was the Russian capital. Today Moscow is the capital of the Soviet Union. It is an older city, and it had been the capital in earlier times. Moscow is near the center of European Russia. When Captain Cochrane reached Moscow later in his trip, he noted that the city was well located to be a capital of so large a country. He wrote that it was "a sort of central spot between the Caspian and Baltic as well as the White Seas." If you look at the map on page 187, you will see what he meant.

An imaginary line between two continents When Captain Cochrane reached the crest, or top, of the Ural Mountains, he stopped for a short time. The Urals are not high mountains. He wrote that "the traveler would hardly suppose that he was crossing a range of hills." The Ural crest was the boundary between Russia and Siberia. Since Russia was in Europe and Siberia in Asia, it also was considered the boundary between two continents. Had it not been for a marker along the road, he would probably not have known that he was crossing from one continent to another. As he walked, some children gave him wild strawberries. He ate them, standing "with one foot in Asia and the other in Europe."

The Urals are not very high. In some places, as this picture shows, they hardly look like mountains. The Urals are rich in iron, copper, zinc, and other minerals.

Today the Soviet Union no longer has an official border at the crest of the Urals. But the crest is still considered the boundary that divides Eurasia into two continents, Europe and Asia.

Crops and climates A country that stretches across two continents has more than one kind of climate. There are places in the Soviet Union where frosts rarely occur. The lowland coast, east of the Black Sea, is warm enough to grow oranges, lemons, tea, and other warm-weather crops. Part of the Crimea region also has mild winters. The Crimea is a peninsula that juts into the Black Sea. The southern shore of the Crimea is called the "Russian Riviera" because it has a climate somewhat like the Mediterranean coast of France. You learned about Mediterranean climates in Chapter 6.

Such mild winters are not common in most parts of the Soviet Union. In general the country has a **continental climate:** winters are cold, summers are hot. As a rule the farther inland a place is, the more extreme its climate. Leningrad is farther north than Moscow but not so far inland. Leningrad's winters are not so cold nor its summers so hot as in Moscow. Kazan, a city that is even farther inland than Moscow, has still colder winters and hotter summers.

Cities farther east in central Siberia have even more extreme temperatures than do those in European Russia. Irkutsk (ir kùtsk′) is such a city. It is located at 52°N and 104°E. Can you find it on the map on page 187? Irkutsk's latitude is almost the same as that of Moscow, but Irkutsk's winters are a great deal colder.

Temperatures in Irkutsk sometimes fall as low as −58°F (−50°C).

There were only 15,000 people in Irkutsk when Captain Cochrane stopped there. Today it is a large city of half a million people and many industries, offices, and schools. The people of Irkutsk have learned to live with extreme cold. Schools are dismissed when the temperature falls to −30°F (−34°C). People stop working outdoors when it gets to −40°F (−40°C). Steel gets brittle at that temperature and bulldozer blades snap like glass.

Irkutsk is by no means the coldest place in Siberia. There are other places which have reported temperatures below −90°F (−68°C). These same cold spots may also have hot summers. One place, which has reported a record low temperature of −94°F (−70°C), has had summer temperatures as high as 98°F (37°C). Of course, such extremes are not reached every year. The extreme temperatures are just that—unusual temperatures that go into a book of records. Every winter does not have record cold. Nor does every summer have record heat.

Cold enough for an ice palace The winter of 1739–1740 was one of the unusually cold winters in Russia. The Neva River at St. Petersburg, which always freezes, froze thicker than ever. Empress Anne, who ruled Russia at that time, thought it would be fun to build an ice palace on the river. She had it built with as much care as if it were a **permanent** structure, something meant to last a long time.

Workers cut blocks of the clear ice. They were carefully fitted together to

A wedding procession—the bride and groom riding in a cage on the back of an elephant—passes Empress Anne's ice palace. The palace and everything in it was made of ice.

make the walls of the small palace. The ice walls were over 20 feet (6 m) high and nearly 300 feet (90 m) long. The workers formed windows from very thin sheets of ice that could be seen through.

Artists carved statues and other decorations for the front of the palace. They made an ice garden with flowers and trees sculptured in ice. They even carved ice birds to sit in the limbs of the ice trees. Other **artisans,** or skilled craftworkers, made furniture of ice and built an ice fireplace complete with ice logs. To make the fireplace look real, an oil fire was lighted so that the ice logs appeared to burn.

Thousands of people came to see Empress Anne's ice palace. It stood for months, but the unusually cold winter finally came to an end. By late spring there was nothing left of the ice palace but blocks of ice floating down the river.

Mountains, forests, and steppes   The Soviet Union has different kinds of land as well as different climates within its vast territory. There are deserts, swamps, mountains, forests, and plains. The deserts are mostly in Asia east of the Caspian Sea. Parts of this dry region are irrigated for growing cotton.

Except for the Urals, most of the mountains in the Soviet Union lie along the southern and eastern borders. The Soviet Union's western boundary touches the Carpathian Mountains in Europe. The

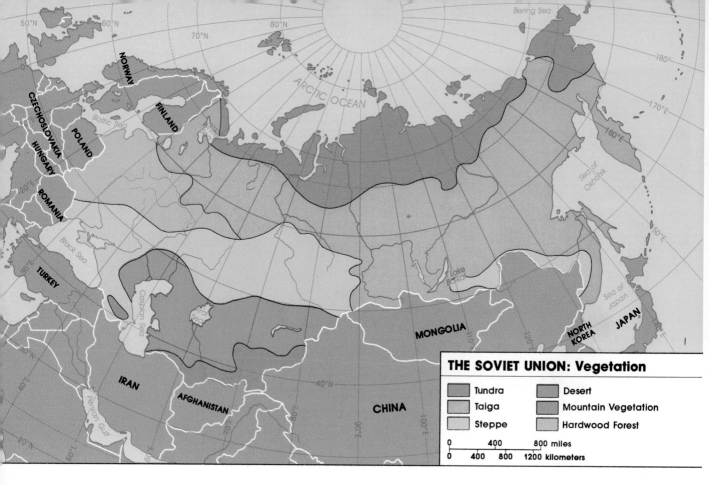

THE SOVIET UNION: Vegetation

- Tundra
- Taiga
- Steppe
- Desert
- Mountain Vegetation
- Hardwood Forest

0   400   800 miles
0   400   800   1200 kilometers

The Soviet Union has six vegetation regions. Which one covers the largest land area?

Caucasus Mountains lie between the Black and Caspian seas. The Caucasus form the southern boundary between Europe and Asia. The peaks of the Caucasus are both rugged and high—higher than the Alps. Mt. Elbrus, the tallest, is 18,481 feet (5,633 m) high. That is nearly 3,000 feet (900 m) higher than Mont Blanc in the Alps. Mt. Elbrus is the highest mountain in Europe, although there are higher mountains in Asia. The tallest mountains in the Soviet Union are near its southern border with the countries of Afghanistan (af gan′ ə stan) and China. The highest peak is Pik Kommunizma (pēk käm u nēz′ mə), or Communism Peak. It is 24,590 feet (7,495 m) high.

In Asia, mountains stretch along most of the Soviet Union's southern and eastern borders. These mountains and plateaus separate the Soviet Union from the countries of Mongolia and China. You can see these groups of mountains clearly on the map at the beginning of this chapter.

The greater part of the Soviet Union is flat and rolling land. Forests cover much of the flatlands and the mountains. The largest forests are made up of conifers such as fir, pine, and larch trees. These forests stretch through northern Russia and most of Siberia. This great forest area is called the **taiga** (tī′ gə).

There are also hardwood forests in the European part of the Soviet Union. These forests include maples, elms, beeches, oaks, and linden trees. Find the two different forest areas on the map on the opposite page.

A great supply of timber has been one of nature's gifts to the Soviet Union. The country has about one fifth of all the timber in the world. Captain Cochrane noted that Russia had "whole forests of fuel." Timber was so plentiful in the forests that the Russians built roads out of logs. Captain Cochrane traveled over a log road on the way to Moscow. He discovered that most of the buildings in Moscow and other cities also were made of wood.

Timber was a cheap and useful material, but it could easily catch fire. Eight years before Captain Cochrane visited Moscow, the city had burned. Captain Cochrane found that much of the city had been rebuilt. He remarked on how quickly Moscow had "risen from its ashes."

South of the forest lie the broad grassy plains which the Russians call the **steppes** (steps). The rich, black soil in parts of the steppes makes them ideally suited for grain crops. This is one of the largest wheat-growing parts of the world. Drier areas of the steppes are grazing lands for cattle and horses. Captain Cochrane traveled over the steppes. He liked these "pasture plains" that extended "as far as the eye could reach." Here was land where "not a tree, nor a shrub, nor a house was to be seen— nothing but grass." The Russian steppes, like the Great Plains of North America, were wide open spaces. At night on the steppes, the traveler could hear only "the barking of wolves and other wild animals."

The Irkutsk-Lake Baikal road winds through taiga forestland in Soviet Siberia. These great taiga forests are mostly made up of conifers.

Nature's Deep Freeze

The permafrost is nature's deep freeze. It preserves the bodies of animals frozen in it for as long as they are left there. In 1977 a man digging for gold in Siberia found the complete body of a baby mammoth frozen in the permafrost. Mammoths were a type of hairy elephant. They were once fairly common in Europe, Asia, and North America, but that was a very long time ago. There are no mammoths on the earth today. There have been none for at least 10,000 years. No one has ever seen a living mammoth, but because of the permafrost it has been possible to see what they looked like.

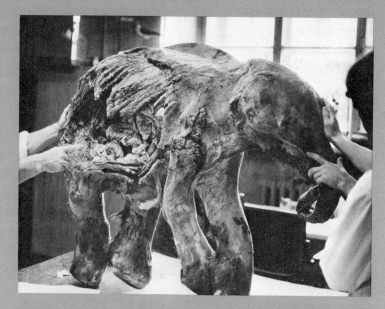

There is no way to know just how this particular baby mammoth came to be in the permafrost. But it was preserved just as it was when it died. Everything was there—hair, skin, trunk, flesh. This was not the first mammoth discovered in the permafrost. A hunter found one in Siberia in 1839, and a number of others have been discovered since then. In earlier times it was usually not possible to preserve the remains once they had been dug out of the frozen earth. There are stories of sled dogs eating unfrozen mammoth meat. In 1977 the discoverer reported his find to authorities who had the animal's body flown to a laboratory. There it was placed in a special refrigerator. Scientists had the chance to study an animal that has not existed on earth for thousands of years. Nature's deep freeze had preserved it.

Tundra and permafrost   Captain Cochrane traveled across Siberia north to the Arctic Ocean. There it was too cold for trees. Even the larch tree that covers much of Siberia did not grow there. The treeless Arctic land is called **tundra**. Mosses and various low bushes grow on the tundra. Here Captain Cochrane's horse had little to eat but the tough tops of scrubby bushes.

Very few people lived in the tundra region. Today it is the region of lowest population density in all of the Soviet Union. The captain visited one northern outpost where people kept several cows for milk. They fed the animals on precious hay brought from fields 80 miles (130 km) to the south. The outpost had wooden buildings made from timber that had been brought in during the short summer. The land in this region is flat or slopes gently to the Arctic Ocean to the north.

Summer days on the tundra can get warm and even hot. But the earth remains frozen all the time just a few feet under the surface. This permanently frozen earth is called **permafrost.** It underlies not only the tundra but much of the northern forests. About half of the Soviet Union has permafrost under the surface. This greatly limits the use of the land for agriculture and for mining.

Rivers and canals   The rivers of the Soviet Union do not provide a water route across the country. Most of the large rivers flow either north or south.

The great Siberian rivers flow north into the Arctic Ocean, as you can see by looking at the map at the beginning of the chapter. The Ob (ōb) River drains the enormous plain of western Siberia. One **source,** or place where a river begins, of the Yenisei (yen ə sā′) is Lake Baikal (bī käl′), the world's deepest lake. In one place it is more than a mile (1.6 km) deep. The Lena (lē′ ·nä) River also begins its northward course near Lake Baikal.

The rivers on the European side of the Urals flow generally southward. The Dnieper (nē′ pèr) and Don rivers empty into the Black Sea. The Volga, Europe's longest river, flows to the Caspian Sea. The Caspian is an inland sea without any outlets.

The Russians have made east-west connections between several of their European rivers. Even in Captain Cochrane's time a canal connected the upper Volga River with water routes to St. Petersburg. There is now a canal that connects Moscow and the Volga. The map at the beginning of the chapter shows that the Don and Volga rivers flow close to each other near the city of Volgograd. A canal runs between them at this point so that barges from the Volga can reach the Black Sea. Find these canals on the map. You can see from the map that the Black Sea connects with the Mediterranean by way of the Aegean Sea. This waterway provides the Soviet Union with a very important shipping route from its Black Sea ports to the Atlantic Ocean.

Canal connections are useful, but water transportation in the Soviet Union faces one great difficulty—the cold of winter. The rivers and canals freeze over for months at a time. Captain Cochrane traveled down the Lena River to the town of Yakutsk (yə kütsk′) early in October in 1820. He was lucky to get so far by boat. Usually the Lena is ice covered by that time. Later that same year he went downstream by dogsled on the frozen river.

A railroad to the Pacific Ocean   If Captain Cochrane had traveled across the Russian empire about 80 years later, he could have chosen yet another way to travel. He could have taken a train. A railroad connected St. Petersburg and Moscow as early as 1851. Forty years later the Russians began building a line across Siberia, the Trans-Siberian Railway. *Trans* means "across" or "over." The railroad followed the same route that Captain Cochrane had taken across the Urals. When it was finally finished, Russia's Trans-Siberian railroad ran close to the southern border of Siberia to the city of Vladivostok (vlad ə vəs täk′) on the coast of the Pacific Ocean.

At one time travelers had a delay when their train reached Lake Baikal. Here they had to stop in the summertime and wait for a boat to ferry the train cars 50 miles (80 km) across the lake. During the winter, when the lake froze over, tracks were laid across the ice. But there was still a delay. It was too dangerous to put the heavy engine car on the ice. Horses pulled the other cars across one at a time. Another locomotive took the train the rest of the

Thawing and freezing of the soil above the Siberian permafrost causes rails to be pulled out of line.

way across the continent. A few years later there was no more wait at Lake Baikal when a loop of tracks was built around the south end of the lake.

In the 1970s the Soviet Union began to build another railroad across Siberia north of Lake Baikal. The new route goes through an area rich in copper, coal, iron, natural gas, and petroleum. The Soviet Union produces more petroleum than any other country in the world.

Most of this northern route has very cold winters. Two thirds of the track is built on permafrost. This creates serious problems, as you can see by the picture on this page. The thawing and freezing of the soil above the permafrost causes the ground to heave and shift. The rails get pushed and pulled out of line.

Different peoples of the Soviet Union In his journey through the Russian empire, Captain Cochrane met peoples of many different nations, or nationalities. The Russians ruled their far-reaching empire from many towns and outposts. Some of the posts in Siberia had few Russians except for the officials and the soldiers.

Some of the empire's peoples adopted Russian ways of living. They lived in towns and learned the Russian language and religion. Others held fast to their own ways. They spoke their own language and kept their own religion. A number of the people in Asia were Moslems, followers of the religion called Islam (is′ ləm). In that part of the empire Captain Cochrane saw both Russian Christian churches and Moslem holy places.

On the steppes of Asia he met people who lived in tents and moved about with their herds of sheep and cattle. In northern Siberia Captain Cochrane visited tribes that lived by herding reindeer. The reindeer herders also fished and hunted. They did not usually kill a reindeer to eat except for special events, or if food was scarce.

The reindeer were very valuable. They gave milk for drinking and making cheese. They were trained to pull and carry heavy loads. People also rode them. If they were killed, the hide was used for tents, clothing, and other wares. A herd of reindeer was like "money in the bank" for the people in this hard climate.

Captain Cochrane stayed with many different people in the course of his journey. He ate and slept in houses and tents that were as clean as any he could find in England. He also stayed in some that were "filthy to an extreme." But clean or filthy, the owners almost always treated him well. People invited Captain Cochrane to share their meals even if there was not much food. Sometimes he ate cabbage soup and bread. Other times he had beef, mutton, elk, or even reindeer. The generous reindeer herders did not hesitate to kill one of their animals for a guest. Captain Cochrane reported that in the Arctic he ate the local favorite, thin slices of frozen raw fish.

Captain Cochrane became convinced that hunters and herders in Siberia were more friendly to strangers than were the people in Europe's finest cities. The people of the steppes and forests often had very little, but they would take no payment for the food they shared. Captain Cochrane wrote that they "freely give that bread which they will not sell."

Soviet citizens of different nationalities watch a parade in Alma-Ata, U.S.S.R. Alma-Ata is located at 43°N, 77°E.

The Soviet Union is still a country with different nationalities. The Russians are the largest group, but there are a number of others, such as the Georgians and Armenians. Americans are sometimes puzzled by the fact that there is a Georgia in the Soviet Union. Only the names are the same; there is no other connection.

Armenia and Soviet Georgia are in the Caucasus Mountains. The people of each of these lands have their own language and ways. They think of themselves as Armenians or Georgians—not Russians. There are a number of other nationalities in both Russia and Siberia who think of themselves as separate peoples. You will read about the government of this country with so many different nationalities in Chapter 10.

CHECKUP
1. What is the present name of the city once called St. Petersburg?
2. What divides European Russia and Siberia?
3. Why does Kazan have a colder winter than Leningrad?
4. What are the steppes?

Countries of Eastern Europe

—VOCABULARY—
strait

Lands of the Danube River The Russian rivers are not the only ones that flow into the Black Sea. It also receives the waters of the Danube, the great river of southeastern Europe. You read in Chapter 6 that the Danube begins in the mountains of West Germany not far from the source of the Rhine River. But the rivers flow in opposite directions. The Rhine runs northwest to the North Sea.

The Danube flows southeast to the Black Sea. Six of the eight countries along its course are in Eastern Europe. Find them on the map on page 187. The only Eastern European countries not touched by the Danube are East Germany, Poland, and Albania.

The Danube runs between two mountainous areas. To the south are the Balkans on one of Europe's southern peninsulas. The Balkan Peninsula includes some of the countries that make up Eastern Europe. They are Albania, Bulgaria, and part of Yugoslavia (yü gō släv′ e ə). Greece, the country at the tip of this peninsula, is part of Western Europe.

The Danube River flows through a gap between the Carpathian and Balkan mountains at the Iron Gate, shown below. The Iron Gate is the deepest gorge in Europe.

To the north of the Danube lie the hook-shaped Carpathian Mountains. Nestled inside the hook is the Hungarian Plain, which includes most of Hungary and parts of other Eastern European countries. They are Czechoslovakia (chek ə slō väk′ ē ə), part of Yugoslavia, and Romania, which, you will remember, was named after the Romans.

The Danube flows across the Hungarian Plain and then through a gap between the Carpathian and Balkan mountain ranges. The gap is known as the Iron Gate. Once through the Iron Gate the river flows more slowly across the Romanian plain to its mouth on the Black Sea.

More than a hundred years ago, an Austrian composer wrote a waltz, "On the Beautiful Blue Danube." The waltz became famous. People all over the world know this piece of music even if they know nothing else about the river. The Danube is a beautiful river. But over the years, wastes have been dumped into its waters. There are large cities and industries on its banks. Diesel-powered boats push barges on it. The Danube is important for transporting both people and goods. Because it is such a useful river, it has become somewhat less beautiful.

Gateway to the Black Sea   There are four countries on the Black Sea, but there is only one way in or out. The map on this page tells the story. The only opening to the Black Sea is a narrow waterway, or **strait**, called the Bosporus. At its narrowest the Bosporus is less than a half mile (1 km) wide. It is so narrow that a bridge has been built across it. Since the Bosporus divides Europe from Asia at this

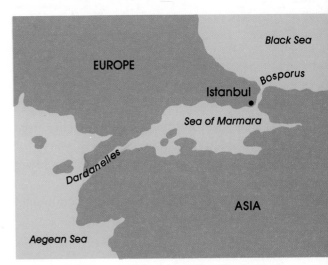

The Sea of Marmara and the two straits of the Bosporus and the Dardanelles connect the Black and Aegean seas.

point, it is now possible to take a bridge from one continent to another.

The Bosporus opens into the Sea of Marmara. This sea, in turn, connects with the Aegean Sea through another, longer strait, the Dardanelles (därd ən elz′). The Aegean, you recall, is a part of the Mediterranean.

It is easy to see the importance of this waterway. Whoever holds it holds the water gateway to a large part of Eastern Europe. The land on either side of the gateway is part of Turkey. Istanbul, Turkey's largest city, is on the Bosporus. In Chapter 5 you learned something about the early history of this city. It is a history that goes back many centuries to ancient Greece and Rome.

CHECKUP

1. Where is the Hungarian Plain located?
2. Where is the source of the Danube River, and where does it flow?
3. What countries make up Eastern Europe?
4. What is the Bosporus? The Dardanelles? Why are they important?

KEY FACTS

1. The North European Plain stretches from France along the Baltic Sea into Russia.

2. The Ural Mountains, located in the Soviet Union, divide Europe from Asia.

3. Most of the Soviet Union has a continental climate: cold winters and hot summers.

4. Much of the Soviet Union is forestland and plains called steppes.

5. Most of the large rivers in the Soviet Union flow north or south.

6. People of many nationalities live within the Soviet Union.

7. The Danube, southeastern Europe's largest river, flows from the Alps to the Black Sea.

8. The Bosporus is the gateway to the Black Sea.

VOCABULARY QUIZ

Write the letter of the word or words that correctly complete each statement.

1. The steppes of Russia are (**a**) mountain passes, (**b**) plains and grasslands, (**c**) canals between rivers, (**d**) frozen earth.

2. The permafrost is (**a**) earth that is always frozen under the surface, (**b**) cold fog that forms over the Arctic Ocean, (**c**) an area too cold for trees, (**d**) mineral-rich earth.

3. Tundra is (**a**) land too cold for trees covered by moss and low bushes, (**b**) a group of people who live by herding reindeer, (**c**) a river in Siberia, (**d**) frozen earth.

4. An artisan is (**a**) an important public official, (**b**) a pedestrian or walker, (**c**) a skilled craftworker.

5. The source of a river is (**a**) its mouth, (**b**) the course it runs from end to end, (**c**) the direction it flows, (**d**) its origin.

REVIEW QUESTIONS

1. What is the present-day name of the land once called the Russian empire? Of the city once called St. Petersburg?

2. What is a continental climate?

3. London, Moscow, and Irkutsk are located at about the same latitude. Which has the coldest winters? Why?

4. Locate the following items on the map on page 187, and list the countries they touch, or where they can be found. (**a**) Mountains: Urals, Carpathians, Caucasus, Balkans. (**b**) Rivers: Don, Volga, Ob, Yenisei, Lena, Danube. (**c**) Seas or lakes: Black, Caspian, Baltic, Aral, Balkhash, Baikal. (**d**) Cities: Leningrad, Moscow, Kazan, Irkutsk, Vladivostok, Istanbul.

5. Why is the Soviet Union called a country with different peoples?

6. What are five of the major crops or resources produced by the Soviet Union?

7. List five countries in Eastern Europe.

8. Why are the Danube River and the Bosporus important waterways?

ACTIVITIES

1. It is said in this chapter that "Those who travel slowly see much more than those who speed across a land in a car." Walk some place to which you usually ride. Make a list of things you noticed when walking that you had not noticed when riding.

2. Read a story or a news article about Eastern Europe or the Soviet Union. On a piece of paper, list the places named in the story. Include cities, countries, mountains, rivers, oceans, and other features. Try to find these places on a map and tell where they are.

TABLES AND GRAPHS GIVE FACTS IN A VISUAL WAY

Tables and graphs present facts in ways that are clear and easy to read. Often when facts are given graphically, we can better understand them and see relations between them. For example, the Soviet Union is the world's largest country in land area. It is more than twice the size of the next largest country in the world. Find the Soviet Union in the table and on the bar graph on this page.

The table and the bar graph give us the land areas of the world's seven largest countries. The huge size of the Soviet Union can be easily seen. But the table and the graph also enable us to compare the Soviet Union at a glance with the other six countries. Find these countries on the map of the world on pages 452–453. Which of these countries are in the Eastern Hemisphere?

SKILLS PRACTICE

The Table of Countries on pages 486–491 gives information about all the countries of the Eastern Hemisphere. Using this table, make up a table and a bar graph that compare the land areas of these Eastern European countries: Albania, Bulgaria, Czechoslovakia, East Germany, Hungary, Poland, Romania, and Yugoslavia.

TABLE

Country	Land Area	
	(sq mi)	(sq km)
Soviet Union	8,649,500	22,402,000
Canada	3,852,000	9,976,000
China	3,691,523	9,561,000
United States	3,618,770	9,408,802
Brazil	3,286,487	8,511,965
Australia	2,966,139	7,682,000
India	1,269,346	3,287,590

LAND AREAS OF THE WORLD'S SEVEN LARGEST COUNTRIES

BAR GRAPH

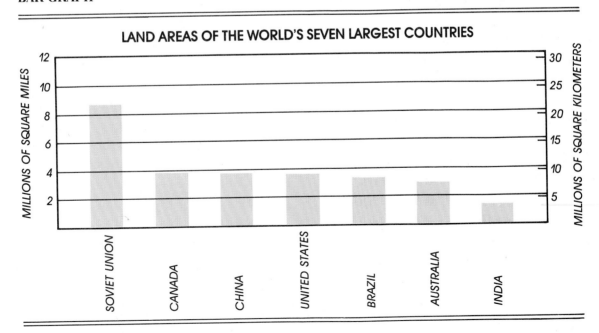

LAND AREAS OF THE WORLD'S SEVEN LARGEST COUNTRIES

From the Vikings to the Tsars

┌─VOCABULARY─────────────────┐
Slav	Mongol
orthodox	khan
authority	tsar
bishop	autocrat
catholic	abolish
└────────────────────────────┘

Vikings come to Russia   Fierce, warlike peoples from Scandinavia, the Vikings, moved along the coast and waterways of Western Europe during the Middle Ages. By the ninth century, other Vikings had sailed east across the Baltic. They began moving up the rivers into the forests of Eastern Europe including Russia, the land we call the Soviet Union. Travel was not difficult. There were no mountains and Viking boats were light enough to carry from river to river.

As the Vikings moved farther inland to the Dnieper River, which flowed south to the Black Sea, the landscape changed. They left the forest behind and came out on vast rolling grasslands. You read about these steppes in Chapter 9.

Most of the people whom the Vikings met along the rivers were **Slavs.** Slavs were among the first tribes of people to live in the hills and plains of Eastern Europe. In the forests, most Slavs cleared trees off patches of land, which they farmed. The Slavs also had log homes similar to those built by early settlers in America.

The Slavs traded some of the furs and food that they hunted and trapped in the forest. Traders carried furs, honey, and beeswax down the rivers to the cities on the Black Sea. Beeswax was in big demand for making candles. It was also used for polishing marble in the fine palaces and churches in Constantinople and other southern lands. The long trip down the Dnieper could be dangerous. Nomads, or roaming herdsmen, who lived in the steppes often attacked traders' boats.

Vikings stay to trade and rule   Some of the bands of Vikings settled along the northern rivers. About 862 a Viking named Rurik became the leader, or prince, of the town of Novgorod. Rurik's brothers and followers took over other towns. Some of them went down the Dnieper and became rulers of Kiev, a town located at the place where forest and steppe meet.

For centuries, most of the princes of the Russian towns were descendants of Rurik. Vikings, Slavs, and several other peoples make up the Russian people.

The princes of Novgorod, Kiev, and the other river towns were mainly concerned

The Mongols, an Asian people, invaded Russia in 1224 and ruled for 250 years. This battle between the Russians (on the left) and the Mongols took place in 1380. In front of the two armies a Russian warrior and a Mongol champion fight on horseback.

with trade. Every winter the prince of Kiev toured the villages in his area, collecting taxes in the form of furs, jars of honey, and pressed cakes of beeswax. During the winter months, when the ground was frozen and covered with snow, sleds carried the tax receipts to Kiev.

When spring arrived, boats were loaded at Kiev for the trip down the Dnieper River to the Black Sea. The Russians sailed to Constantinople, where they found a good market for their forest products. Here, too, they sold as slaves the prisoners who had been captured in war. When they were ready for their return trip, the Russians loaded their boats with fine cloth, sweet wines, and the fruits of the southern lands.

The Russians become Christians Russians who journeyed to Constantinople brought back more than goods. They returned with ideas.

In Constantinople they found themselves in one of the most important Chris-

tian cities. It was a city with many fine churches and monasteries. Most impressive of all was the great domed church of Hagia Sophia, or Holy Wisdom. The church was first built by the Byzantine emperor Justinian between 532 and 537. After witnessing a service at Hagia Sophia, one group of Russians reported, "We knew not whether we were in heaven or on earth, for on earth there is no such splendor or such beauty."

The Christian religion had developed into two branches because of disagreements between two groups of followers. The branch centered in Constantinople became known as the Eastern Orthodox Church, which it is called today. These Christians believed that their church had preserved the true, or **orthodox**, faith. *Orthodox* means having the correct views or teachings.

The greatest disagreement between the eastern and the western branches of Christianity had to do with **authority**— the right to govern the church. Both

How many years of Russian history are covered by entries on the time line below?

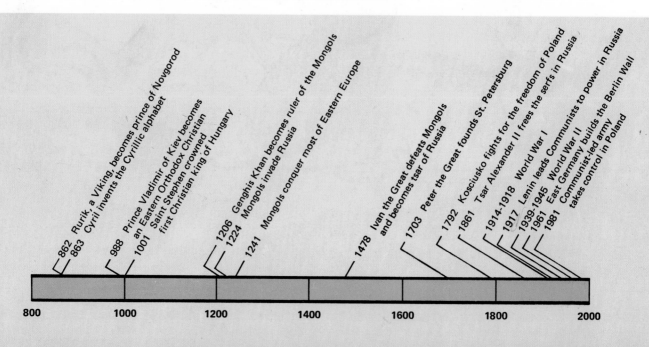

The Cathedral of the Annunciation in Moscow's Kremlin shows Byzantine influence. Its many onion-shaped, or bulbous, domes are typically Russian.

branches had officials called **bishops.** The western branch held that the bishop in Rome, called the pope, had authority over all other bishops. Because followers of the western branch believed in the authority of the Roman pope, that branch came to be called the Roman Catholic Church. **Catholic** means general or universal.

Eastern Christians did not accept the pope's authority. They believed that the bishop in Constantinople, called the patriarch, had as much authority as the bishop in Rome. The eastern branch of Christianity came to be governed by the patriarch.

In about 988 Vladimir, a prince of Kiev, became an Eastern Orthodox Christian. He ordered his followers to pull down the wooden image of a non-Christian god that stood in the city of Kiev. Then Vladimir commanded that all his subjects should also become Christians. Many of the Russian people already knew something about the Christian religion. A few of them complained about being ordered to give up the beliefs of their ancestors. Other people accepted Vladimir's new order. They said: "If this were not good, the prince would not have accepted it." The Russians became Orthodox Christians.

An alphabet for the Slavic languages　With the new religion came the Bible, written with an alphabet that had been developed for the Slavic languages. In the list below, you can see the difference between this alphabet and the one used in Rome and most of the lands of Western Europe. The word *book* is written in four different European languages.

Buch　—　German
libro　—　Spanish
livre　—　French
книга　—　Russian

The first three words are in different languages, but they are each written with the Roman alphabet. It is the same Roman alphabet we use in writing English. The Russian word is written in the Cyrillic alphabet. The reason for the difference goes back to Constantinople.

About 100 years before the Russians became Christians, the Cyrillic alphabet was invented by an Eastern Orthodox monk named Cyril. He and his brother, who was also a monk, lived in Constantinople, but they could speak the Slavic languages. The emperor at Constantinople sent the brothers to help some Slavic-speaking Christians in Eastern Europe. Because these Christians did not speak Greek or Latin, they needed to have the Bible translated—put into their own language.

The brothers first had to invent a way to write the spoken language of these Slavs. Cyril worked out an alphabet of 43 letters for the sounds of the Slavic language. He used the letters of the Greek alphabet and borrowed a few from the Hebrew alphabet as well. The result was

The words above, written in letters of the Cyrillic alphabet, say: "Success to our five-year plan!" Such plans set production goals in the Soviet Union.

an alphabet that was used for the different Slavic languages, including Russian.

The Mongols conquer Russia　The villagers and townspeople of Russia lived in fear of the nomads of the steppes. Time after time these nomads invaded the settled areas, burning villages and capturing people to sell as slaves. The troublesome raids started in the thirteenth century.

In 1206 a young man known as Genghis Khan (jeng′ gis kän′) became ruler of the **Mongols,** a nomadic people of Mongolia. Mongolia was a desert land in the heart of Asia. Within a short time Genghis Khan conquered a large part of Asia. **Khan** means ruler.

In 1224 the Mongols came sweeping out of Asia across the steppes. One of Genghis Khan's armies went beyond the Caspian Sea into Russia.

206

Some of the villagers on the steppes joined the Mongols. Others fled in terror before them. Some of the fleeing people reached Kiev and pleaded for help. "Our land they have taken away today; and yours will be taken tomorrow!"

The prince of Kiev combined his army with those of several other Russian cities and marched forth to meet the Mongols. The Russians fought bravely, but they went down to defeat.

The Mongols did not follow up their victory immediately because just at this time Genghis Khan died. It was not until some years later that Genghis Khan's grandson, Batu, threatened Russia again.

As the Mongol army approached the Russian city of Kiev, Batu demanded: "Give me one tenth of everything, one man in ten, and the tenth part of all your wealth." The Russian prince sent back word: "We will give you nothing; when we are dead, then you can have it all."

The Mongols brought up battering rams to break down the city gates and catapults to put stones and even explosives over the city walls. It took them 5 days to take the city, and then the destruction began. When the raiders were finished, an old chronicle says, "No eye was left open to weep for the dead."

Batu's army then moved on to other Russian cities. After they took the main city in each district, they spread out over the countryside. Some villagers fled as the Mongols approached. Others came out and knelt on the ground before them.

The Mongols not only swept over Russia, they conquered much of Eastern Europe. In 1241 their armies almost reached Germany.

How the Mongols ruled   Batu made his camp on the steppe east of the Volga River. From this place he sent orders to all the Russian princes. "Your land is now conquered and you are subjects of Batu Khan." All princes had to go to learn what the conquering khan demanded of them.

When a prince arrived at Batu's camp, he was taken to Batu's great white tent. Upon entering the tent, the prince fell down on his knees and pressed his forehead to the ground. In this position he listened while Batu spoke. Batu told the princes that he did not want their cities. He could never be cooped up within brick and wooden walls. However, the princes must send payments, called tribute, each year to their Mongol lords. "Each year you will bring your tribute: one tenth of your harvest, one tenth of your flocks and your horses, one tenth of all your produce."

For almost 300 years the Russian princes continued to rule their people while making payments to the Mongols.

The prince of Moscow becomes tsar of all the Russians   About a hundred years after Batu's conquest, Prince Ivan of Moscow suggested that he collect the tribute for the Mongols and save them the trouble. The Mongol khan agreed, and the ruler of Moscow became the most important of the Russian princes. Ivan seems to have done very well for himself while gathering tribute for the Mongols. He became wealthy and came to be known as Ivan Kalita, a nickname meaning "Ivan Moneybags."

Later rulers of Moscow brought more and more land under their rule. However, they still continued to pay tribute to the Mongols. They did this until the time of Ivan III—usually called Ivan the Great. He became prince of Moscow in 1462, and ruled until 1505.

Ivan III decided that Moscow need no longer fear the Mongols. He knew that Moscow had grown stronger and the Mongols had grown weaker. They had given up the ways of Batu. They no longer dwelled in tents on the steppes, but in their own city at Kazan.

In 1478, when Mongol agents came to Moscow demanding the yearly tribute, Ivan refused to pay. He then acted as a Mongol might have done. He killed all but one of the Mongols and sent him back to

Ivan III, called the Great, was the first Russian ruler to use the title of tsar. He began to unite all Russian lands under Moscow's leadership.

Kazan with the message: "Tell your master what you have seen! Tell him that if he troubles me again the same thing will happen to him!"

The Mongol khan sent an army against Moscow, but this time it met defeat. The great days of the Mongols in Russia were ended.

The rulers of Moscow were no longer just princes of a city as in the old days. They were rulers of a country. Ivan the Great was called "Tsar of all the Russias." The word **tsar** (zär) is sometimes spelled *czar*. It is the Russian form of the name Caesar. The emperors of ancient Rome had been known as the Caesars. The Russians thought it a fitting title for those who ruled their growing empire. Ivan the Great liked to speak of Moscow as the "Third Rome." He meant that it had taken the place of Rome and Constantinople. Tsars ruled Russia until 1917. The map on the next page shows the growth of the territory under Russia's rule from the time of Ivan the Great.

Russia and the ways of Western Europe
In spite of the claim that Moscow was the "Third Rome," Russia seemed behind the times to most visitors from Western Europe. For example, Russia had no printing press until nearly a century after its invention. Even then, so many powerful people opposed the printing of books that the press was closed down.

The fear of outside ways did not keep ideas out of Russia. Merchants from Germany, England, and the Netherlands continued to find their way to Russia. They brought with them not only goods but ideas as well.

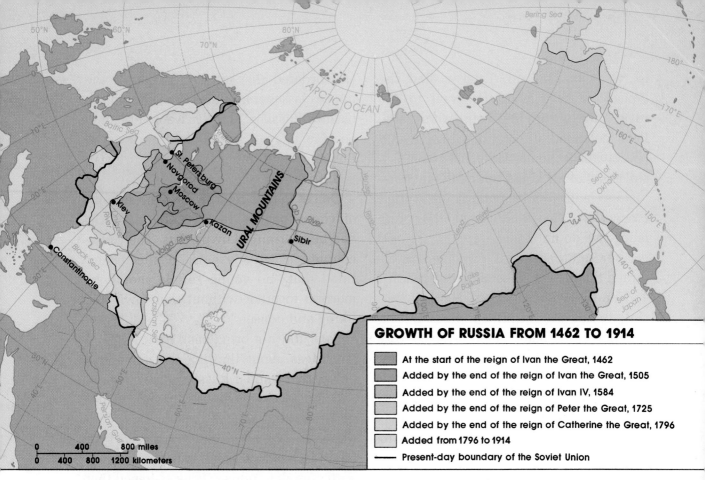

GROWTH OF RUSSIA FROM 1462 TO 1914

- At the start of the reign of Ivan the Great, 1462
- Added by the end of the reign of Ivan the Great, 1505
- Added by the end of the reign of Ivan IV, 1584
- Added by the end of the reign of Peter the Great, 1725
- Added by the end of the reign of Catherine the Great, 1796
- Added from 1796 to 1914
- —— Present-day boundary of the Soviet Union

From the time of Ivan the Great to the present day, the Soviet Union has grown from a small principality to the largest country in the world.

Tsar Peter works to change Russia
Perhaps the one who did most to bring western ways to Russia was a young tsar named Peter, called Peter the Great.

Peter's interest in the western countries began when he was still a boy and spent long hours talking with foreign merchants and others about their homelands. He was especially interested in what they told him about the workshops. Peter himself liked to work with his hands, and machines and tools fascinated him.

One day while hunting through an old storeroom, Peter came across a boat. He asked a Dutch friend about the boat and he learned that it was an English boat that could sail against the wind as well as with

it. Peter had the boat repaired and fitted with new sails. His Dutch friend took the boat to a nearby lake and showed Peter how it was possible to sail against the wind.

Peter never lost his interest in ships and boats. Later he built Russia's first navy. The little old English boat, which still exists, came to be known as the "grandfather of the Russian navy."

When Peter was 25, he decided to visit Western European countries. Among other things, he wanted to see how they built their ships.

Peter and his party traveled to the Netherlands, where the tsar worked in the shipyards for about 5 months. After that he went to England. Peter visited the houses of Parliament. He went to the royal mint to learn how coins were made. Peter collected all sorts of things, which he sent back home. He bought compasses, tools of all kinds, sailcloth, anchors, pistols, and—oddly enough—a stuffed crocodile. Why this caught the tsar's fancy, we do not know.

Peter returned to his own land determined that he would establish a powerful and up-to-date government. He paid special attention to his armed forces, but he did not stop there. Peter believed that every Russian should serve Russia "by labor of hand or brain." He made the people pay many new taxes in order to pay for his army and other changes that he planned. He built canals. He tried to establish modern industries, though he did not have much success.

Peter also wanted to change Russian ways of thinking. He established schools and ordered that all young men of the upper classes should learn some language besides Russian. The tsar wanted them to be able to read the books from France, England, and other Western European countries.

One of Peter's reforms won the support of young people. In the past, marriages had been arranged by parents. The young couple was usually not consulted. Peter ruled that "no young couple should be married together without their own free liking and consent."

Peter did *not* bring back from England any ideas about limiting the monarch's power. He wanted Russia to have a navy and modern workshops, but he did not desire a Russian parliament. He continued to rule according to his will. Like other tsars he was an **autocrat,** a ruler with complete power. Peter believed that the people did not always know what was good for them.

In the picture on the left below, Tsar Peter the Great is shown talking with Dutch shipbuilders. On the right below, Tsar Peter oversees the building of his new capital city of St. Petersburg that was to be his port on the Baltic Sea.

Peter's city on the Baltic Peter wished to enlarge his empire. He particularly wanted Russian ports on the Black Sea in the south and on the Baltic Sea to the west. The Ottoman Turks at that time ruled the land around the Black Sea. Peter failed to win a southern port on the Black Sea. But he began a long war against Sweden, and took a piece of the marshy Baltic coast.

In 1703 Peter decided to build a new capital city at the mouth of the Neva River, where it flows into the Baltic. It was to be his port on the Baltic Sea. Peter had supplies brought from great distances. He forced thousands of people to work at building a city on this marshy coast. Many died. Almost all suffered from cold and disease.

Whatever the cost, Peter built his new city. He called it St. Petersburg in honor of the saint for whom he was named. Today it is known as Leningrad, and is the Soviet Union's second largest city.

Peter the Great died in 1725. After Peter, Catherine II, also called "the Great," was the ruler who did most to bring Western ways to Russia. As the map on page 209 shows, under Catherine the Great, Russia reached the Black Sea and took a large part of Poland.

Many Russians were not free people Ivan the Great and the later tsars freed Russia from the Mongols, but they did not free the Russian people. Many Russians were serfs. You read about serfs in Western Europe in Chapter 7.

Indeed, laws governing Russian serfs became more harsh as the tsars became more powerful. At a time when serfs elsewhere gained freedom, their number increased in Russia. By 1800 more than half of the people were serfs.

Like serfs in the Middle Ages, Russian serfs worked their lord's lands a number of days each week. Each year they paid the lord a share of their livestock, grain, and other produce.

Serfdom in Russia was very much like slavery. Lords could punish their serfs as they saw fit. A lord could sell a serf just as a piece of property is sold. An advertisement in the *Moscow Gazette* in 1801 tells a great deal about Russian serfdom. The advertisement announced:

> TO BE SOLD—Three coachmen, well trained and handsome, and two girls, the one eighteen and the other fifteen years of age, both of them good-looking, and well acquainted with various kinds of handiwork. In the same house there are for sale two hairdressers; the one, twenty-one years of age can read, write, play on a musical instrument, and act as huntsman; the other can dress ladies' and gentlemen's hair.

The end of serfdom In 1861, Tsar Alexander II ruled that in Russia serfdom was "forever abolished." **Abolished** means done away with. Serfs had been freed in other European countries at an earlier time. Alexander's law came 2 years before slavery was ended in the United States.

Freeing the serfs did not change life for the peasants as much as they had hoped. Lords still held large parts of the estates. Serfs did not get much new land to work. And it cost them more to use the small piece they had farmed before.

Serfs had to pay for their freedom. They had to pay taxes that were higher than the lords ever had paid. This was because the government taxed the serfs to

Even after the Russian serfs were freed, their life was hard. The former serfs did not get much new land to work and they had to pay heavy taxes for their freedom.

pay the lords for the loss of their property. As a result, a villager worked about as hard without much more to eat or better clothes to wear.

About 50 years after the freeing of the serfs, an English traveler asked a villager if things were better or worse than they had been in the old days. The villager thought a bit and answered that in some ways things were better and in some ways they were worse. The Englishman then asked if he would like to be a serf again. "Oh no!" the man replied without hesitation. He evidently had no doubt that it was better to be a free man than a serf in Russia, even though freedom brought many burdens.

The harsh government of the tsars   The tsars who brought an end to Mongol rule were sometimes as cruel as the rulers they had defeated. Ivan IV, the grandson of Ivan the Great, earned the nickname "Ivan the Terrible" because of the number of people he had tortured and executed.

The people did not choose the officials in the days of the tsars, and the officials paid little attention to the people. Officials were chosen either by the tsar or by someone he had selected.

The people had little freedom to say what they liked. Newspapers printed nothing that might displease the tsar.

The Russians move east across Asia   The Mongols had come out of Asia into Europe. After their defeat, the tide began to run in the other direction. Ivan the Terrible took the Mongol city of Kazan. He encouraged bands of Russians called Cossacks (kos′ aks) to cross the Ural Mountains and to spread into Asia.

The Cossacks were bands of frontierspeople who lived on the steppes. Some Cossacks were serfs who had fled to freedom. They were rough, fighting people who knew how to ride and shoot.

They had to fight to survive on the open grasslands.

Yermak, the leader of one Cossack band, was wanted for robbery. Ivan agreed to pardon Yermak if he would lead his band against the Mongol town of Sibir on the eastern side of the Urals. It was a tough job that required a tough band of fighters.

Yermak's Cossacks built boats and traveled down a river on the eastern slope of the Urals. As they neared Sibir, their scouts reported an ambush ahead. According to an old story, Yermak had his Cossacks put logs upright in the boats with their hats upon the logs. The Cossacks let the boats float on downstream while they advanced quietly along the bank. The people who hid in the ambush shot arrows at the wooden soldiers in the boats while the Cossacks slipped up to attack them from behind.

The Cossacks wiped out the ambush and then went on to take Sibir. It became the first Russian stronghold in Asia. The town also gave its name to the great stretch of land across northern Asia that is known as Siberia.

In later years, groups of Russians advanced all the way across Siberia to the Pacific Ocean. For centuries, only a few settlers came to live in this vast land. Those who did settle there were almost cut off from the outside world. There were only trails connecting the few scattered settlements with each other and with Russia west of the Urals.

To travel overland from Europe to the Pacific was an adventure. Captain Cochrane made his trip from sea to sea in the 1820s, when the tsars still ruled this vast Russian empire. You may remember that in 1891, the tsars started to build a railroad across Siberia. When finished, it connected Vladivostok on the Pacific Ocean with St. Petersburg on the Baltic Sea.

CHECKUP

1. What was the "third Rome"?
2. How were Russia's rivers useful for the Vikings and the Slavs?
3. What is an autocrat? What powers did the tsars have as autocrats?
4. What did Tsar Peter do for Russia?
5. Why did freeing the serfs not put an end to discontent?

Russia Under the Communists

VOCABULARY
revolution	communism
socialism	collective

Lenin   As you have read, St. Petersburg no longer appears on the map of the Soviet Union. It is now the city of Leningrad. The name was changed to honor Lenin, a man whose real name was Vladimir Ulyanov, (vlad' i mir ŭl ya' nof). Lenin (len' ən) was the name he adopted to confuse the tsar's police.

Lenin wanted to confuse the police because he spent his life working for a **revolution** in the government of Russia. A revolution is a complete change in government, in a way of thinking, or in a way of life. The American Revolution in 1776 changed 13 British colonies into an independent country. The revolution that Lenin worked for would come to change Russia.

Lenin was a forceful speaker and a skilled leader. He led the Russian Communists to power in 1917 and ruled the Soviet Union until his death in 1924.

Vladimir's older brother had been a revolutionary also. In 1887, the brother was hanged because of his part in a plot to kill Tsar Alexander III. Vladimir was in high school at the time. A few years later he joined a secret organization that worked against the government. He was arrested, jailed, and sent to Siberia for 3 years.

It was after his release that Vladimir took the name Lenin. He left Russia and went to live in Western Europe. There he published a newspaper and wrote other works that were smuggled into Russia. He organized another group that worked for revolution. A man who knew him at that time said that Lenin thought of revolution 24 hours a day. "Even when he sleeps, he dreams of nothing but revolution."

Lenin's idea of revolution   Lenin dreamed of a revolution that would change a great deal more than the government. He wanted a revolution to take land, factories, and other businesses away from those who owned them. Lenin accepted the ideas of a Socialist named Karl Marx. Socialists are people who believe that land and industry should be owned and controlled by the government rather than by individuals.

Marx said that there had always been a struggle between the people who owned property and those who did not. He believed that **socialism**—ownership by the government—would end the struggle.

Lenin had a group of followers who came later to be called Communists. Their ideas became known as **communism.** They chose that name because they favored the *common* ownership of land and industry by people as a group.

Lenin believed that a Communist revolution would be for the people's benefit. But like Peter the Great, he also believed that the people did not always know what was good for them. For that reason the Communists did not work for winning free elections.

The end of the tsar's government
The autocratic government of the tsars was usually thought to be a strong government. The tsar had no limits on his power. He could choose his officials and remove them as he wished. He could issue orders that became laws. But there was a great weakness: the tsar was blamed for whatever went wrong. This weakness became plain during World War I when Nicholas II was tsar.

214

Russia, later joined by France and Britain, went to war against Germany in 1914. The war went badly for the Russians. The army lacked guns and other supplies. Thousands were killed. Food was hard to get, especially in the cities. By 1917 people grumbled and blamed the tsar for their troubles.

In March 1917 the once-powerful tsar found himself powerless. Some of the troops rebelled. There were strikes and disorders in the capital city. At the battle-front, Nicholas II sent orders, but they were not obeyed. More and more people said openly that the tsar should give up his crown. Finally, Nicholas II agreed to do so. Rule by the tsar came to an end, but it was not the end of autocratic government.

The Communist revolution Lenin took no part in the March revolution that overthrew the tsar. He was then living in Switzerland. The sudden end of the tsar's government caught him by surprise. Lenin returned to Russia, not to support

Lenin and his followers used groups of workers and soldiers to take control of the government. This picture shows Communist revolutionaries in Vladivostok, U.S.S.R.

the new government, but to overthrow it. Lenin did not think that other groups would carry out the true revolution that he believed was needed.

The Communists were only a small group when Lenin returned to Russia. He freely admitted at the time, "We are a very small minority." But Lenin was a very skilled leader. He and his followers got control of groups of workers and soldiers in the capital city. A terrible bloody struggle took place in the streets.

In November 1917 the Communists and their supporters overthrew the new government. They declared that they were now the government of the country. The Communists also managed to get control of Moscow, which they made the capital.

The Communists had control of the two main cities, but they did not yet control the country. Many people fought against them. The country suffered through 2 years of a terrible civil war. Many people were killed, among them Tsar Nicholas, his wife, and his five children. Many more people starved to death. The revolution cost Russia a great deal of suffering.

By 1922 the Communists had firm control of the country, but Lenin became ill. He died 2 years later. The Communists regard him as Russia's great hero. Today his picture appears in schools and public buildings. His body was preserved and is still displayed in his tomb in Moscow.

Rule by the Communists   The Communists established a new government, which they called the Union of Soviet Socialist Republics. As explained in Chapter 9, it is often called Russia, the Soviet Union, or the U.S.S.R. The Soviet Union was supposed to be a group of self-governing republics. As it worked out, the separate republics had almost no independence. This is also the case today. Now there are 15 republics. Find these republics on the map on page 223. Russia is the largest of these.

The Communists called their form of government a republic. You may recall from Chapter 5 that a republic is a government in which the citizens choose the people who run the country. The Soviet Union was not then, nor is it today, like the republics of Western Europe or North America or ancient Rome.

The people do not truly choose those who govern. To be sure, the people vote, but there is only one party allowed—the Communist party. People have no chance to vote for anyone who opposes the Communists. They have very little chance to hear any ideas discussed except those approved by the Communists. The government controls newspapers, magazines, radio, and television. A large secret police force keeps watch on those suspected of opposing the government.

The Communist leaders who came after Lenin shared his view of opponents. Anyone thought to be against the party was considered "an enemy of the people." The Communist government treated such persons much as the tsar's government had done in the past. They were arrested, sent to prison camps, and—in many cases—killed. The Soviet leader Stalin started the Great Purge to crush his opponents. Purge means to clear out opponents. During the worst years, in 1937 and 1938, as many as 40,000 people a month were killed. The revolution had brought many changes to Russia, but it had not changed the way of treating those who opposed the government.

Government-owned industries   The Communists set about making Russia into a Socialist country. The government took over banks, factories, mines, and other industries. The owners received nothing for their property. The government also began developing a large number of new industries. It built large tractor factories, steel mills, and electrical power plants.

Government officials decided what should be produced in the government-owned plants. For example, they decided that Russia needed coal, steel, and machines to become a strong industrial country. Consumer goods—goods that people use up—such as soap, clothing, furniture, and food, were produced in lesser amounts.

Government officials also set production goals for each industry and for farming. Those in charge of a factory or mine set goals for the individual workers. Workers received their regular pay only if they reached their goals. If they produced more or less than their goals, they got extra or less pay.

Russia had only just begun to develop industries in the time of the tsars. The Communists made Russia a leading industrial country in less than 40 years.

Under the Communists, the Soviet Union began many new industries. Much of the steel from the new factories was used to put up new buildings in Soviet cities.

Land for the peasants   When the tsar's government fell in 1917, peasants took over the estates of many large landholders. They divided the land into small family holdings. Lenin and the Communists encouraged this taking of land. The Communists declared again and again, "Land for the peasants."

Most peasants understood that "land for the peasants" meant land for each family. They learned differently 10 years later. The Communists believed in the common ownership of land. They thought that the peasants should hold land as groups rather than as individuals or families.

The Communists forced the peasants to combine their individual plots of land into large **collective** farms. The members of a collective farm worked the land together. They owned machinery and other equipment as a group. They divided what the collective farm produced according to the work each had done.

The Communists preferred collective farms for other reasons too. The government could control the peasants better on collectives than on millions of small farms. The Communists also thought that the family farms were too small and poor to use machinery. On the collective farms people were supposed to have tractors and machines. Fewer people could do more work and produce more food. This would free many people to work in the new mines to be opened and in the new factories to be built.

Many peasants did not want to give up their small holdings. The Communists called these farmers "enemies of the people." Millions were herded into prison camps. Large numbers were killed. These people had hardly expected that prison would be the result of the Communist promise of "land for the people."

World War II and Eastern Europe
Russia grew into the world's largest country under the rule of the tsars. They added one territory after another in both Asia and Eastern Europe. During the reign of Peter the Great, the Russian empire stretched from the Baltic Sea to the Pacific Ocean. Russia lost some territory in Eastern Europe after World War I. Eastern European nations such as Poland and Finland became independent countries. The Soviet Union took back some of this territory after World War II.

World War II began in Eastern Europe. In August 1939, Germany and the Soviet Union secretly agreed to divide Eastern Europe between them. The next month Germany and the Soviet Union took over Poland.

The German leader Adolf Hitler really did not plan to share any of Europe with the Soviet Union or any other power. In 1941 Germany attacked the Soviet Union. German forces came within 20 miles (32.2 km) of Moscow. They also reached the Volga River in the south. Hilter thought the war would be short, but he was wrong. The Soviet armies did not give up, and the Germans faced a winter in the Soviet Union. If you have forgotten how cold the weather becomes, remember the winter of the ice palace in St. Petersburg.

The cold weather proved to be a powerful enemy of the Germans. One of the tsars said that Russia had two great generals, General January and General Feb-

Like an overturned turtle, a German tank rests bottom up and helpless in the snow of a Russian winter during World War II. In the background is another damaged tank.

ruary. These two were on the Soviet side during three winters of World War II.

By 1944 the Germans were being pushed back by the Soviet armies in the east and the American and British armies in the west. The Germans finally gave up in May 1945.

At the end of World War II, Soviet armies held Eastern Europe. The Soviet Union did not give up all of these lands. Three Baltic countries—Estonia (e stō′ nē ə), Latvia (lat′ vē ə), and Lithuania (lith ə wā′ nē ə)—were made part of the Soviet Union. They have become 3 of the 15 Soviet republics. The Soviets also took over parts of 5 other countries.

In the decades that followed, the Soviet Union made certain that neighbors had friendly governments. "Friendly" meant ruled by Communists. In the next chapter you will read more about the Soviet Union and these other countries of Eastern Europe.

CHECKUP
1. What do Socialists believe?
2. How did World War I affect the tsar's government?
3. What two revolutions took place in Russia in 1917?
4. How did the Communist government change industry in Russia?
5. What is a collective farm? Why did the Communist government favor this kind of farm?

KEY FACTS

1. The Eastern Orthodox Church converted the Russians to Christianity. Cyril's alphabet spread to Russia from Eastern Europe.

2. The Russian tsars, who were autocrats, defeated the Mongols and united Russia.

3. Serfdom lasted longer in Russia than in Western Europe.

4. The first Russian revolution in 1917 overthrew the tsar; the second brought the Communists into power.

5. The Communist revolution did not give the Russian people freedom to choose their government nor freedom of expression.

VOCABULARY QUIZ

On a piece of paper, write the word that correctly fills in each blank below.

1. The western branch of Christianity believed that the pope of Rome had _____ over the whole church.

2. The Western Church held that it was the universal church. For that reason it was called the Roman _____ Church.

3. The Eastern Church believed that it preserved the correct or accepted Christian teachings. It was called the Eastern _____ Church.

4. Among the first tribes of people in Russia were ____.

5. The rulers of the Mongols were called ____.

6. As the power of the princes of Moscow grew, these rulers became ____ of all Russia.

7. Peter the Great was an _____, a ruler with complete, unchecked powers.

8. Alexander II _____ serfdom in Russia in 1861.

9. Communism is one form of _____, the view that the government should own and control land and industry.

10. The _____ farms of the Soviet Union are held and worked by groups of people.

REVIEW QUESTIONS

1. When the Vikings moved into Russia, how did they travel and what did they find?

2. Why did separate eastern and western branches of Christianity develop?

3. Why does the author say that differences between the alphabets of Western Europe and Russia go back to Constantinople?

4. How did the tsars come to power in Russia and what power did they have as rulers?

5. What part did Cossacks play in spreading Russian power east of the Ural Mountains?

6. How did the end of serfdom change the life of the Russian peasants?

7. What kind of revolution did Lenin want?

8. In what ways were the ideas of Lenin somewhat like those of Peter the Great?

9. What changes did the Communists make in building and running industry in Russia?

10. What changes did the Communists make on Russian farms? Why did they make them?

ACTIVITIES

1. This chapter tells that the Russian people, past and present, have had little freedom. Make a set of notes listing ways in which freedom has been denied the Russian people from the time of the Vikings to the present.

2. Look up Peter the Great in a reference book and make a report about his trip to Europe. Include information about the ideas and goods that he took back to Russia.

IO / SKILLS DEVELOPMENT

USING TIME LINES

PRACTICE IN THINKING ABOUT TIME

It is often hard to keep the times of people and events straight in our minds. We know about George Washington and Peter the Great, but we are not sure if one lived before, after, or at the same time as the other. We are often confused about time partly because we do not pay attention to dates as we read. It takes practice in paying attention to dates.

The time line below gives you a number of people and events with dates. The dates before each ruler or President shows when he or she governed. The date or dates before an event states when it took place. Study the time line carefully. It gives you all the information you need to do the following exercise.

SKILLS PRACTICE

Use the information in the time line below to decide if the statements at the right are true or false. Write your answers on a sheet of paper.

1. Alexander II freed Russian serfs 2 years after Abraham Lincoln freed American slaves.

2. Catherine the Great ruled Russia when George Washington was President.

3. The United States landed people on the moon 20 years after the Soviet Union launched the first earth satellite.

4. The Russian revolutions took place during World War I.

5. Nicholas II was tsar from 1881 to 1894.

6. World War II lasted twice as long as World War I.

7. Napoleon I ruled France while Alexander I was tsar of Russia.

8. The British abolished slavery in their empire 29 years before American slaves were freed.

9. There were still serfs in Russia when Captain Cochrane visited that country.

10. The Russian revolutions began 150 years after the French Revolution.

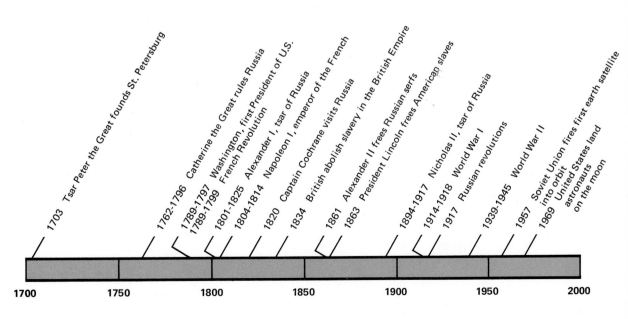

CHAPTER

11 The Soviet Union and Eastern Europe Today

The Soviet Union—A Country That Spans Two Continents

> **VOCABULARY**
>
> | | |
> |---|---|
> | Slavic language | plot |
> | military alliance | kremlin |
> | annex | candidate |
> | consumer goods | foreign aid |

Different countries with similar histories Most but not all of the peoples of Eastern Europe and the Soviet Union speak one of the **Slavic languages.** As you read in Chapter 10, the Slavic languages come originally from the first Slavs, who lived more than 5,000 years ago in Eastern Europe and the Soviet Union. People who understand one Slavic language do not necessarily understand another. There are even different ways to write these languages. Some use the Cyrillic alphabet invented in the Middle Ages. Others use the Roman alphabet.

Many of the people of Eastern Europe and the Soviet Union also have common religious backgrounds. Either the Eastern Orthodox Church or the Roman Catholic Church was the official religion of most of the countries in this part of the world before Communist parties took over their governments.

The countries of Eastern Europe have many differences, but in recent times they have had similar histories. Partly because of the Soviet Union, the other eight countries also have had Communist governments since World War II.

The Soviet Union and Eastern European countries share other ties. All of these countries except for Yugoslavia have joined COMECON, an organization to make trade easier among the member countries. Most of these countries have a defense agreement called the Warsaw Pact. This is a **military alliance** by which they have promised to help each other in case of war. *Military* means having to do with soldiers or war. *Alliance* means an agreement to join together for some purpose. Yugoslavia never joined the Warsaw Pact, and Albania has not been a member since 1968. In this chapter you will read about the Soviet Union and each of the Eastern European countries.

The growth and population of the Soviet Union The Soviet Union is the largest country in the world. During World War II, the Soviet Union won part of Finland's territory and took over three small countries on the Baltic seacoast. They are Estonia, Latvia, and Lithuania. Later the Soviet Union took other pieces

The map on the next page shows the 15 republics that make up the Soviet Union. Locate the 15 capitals of these republics.

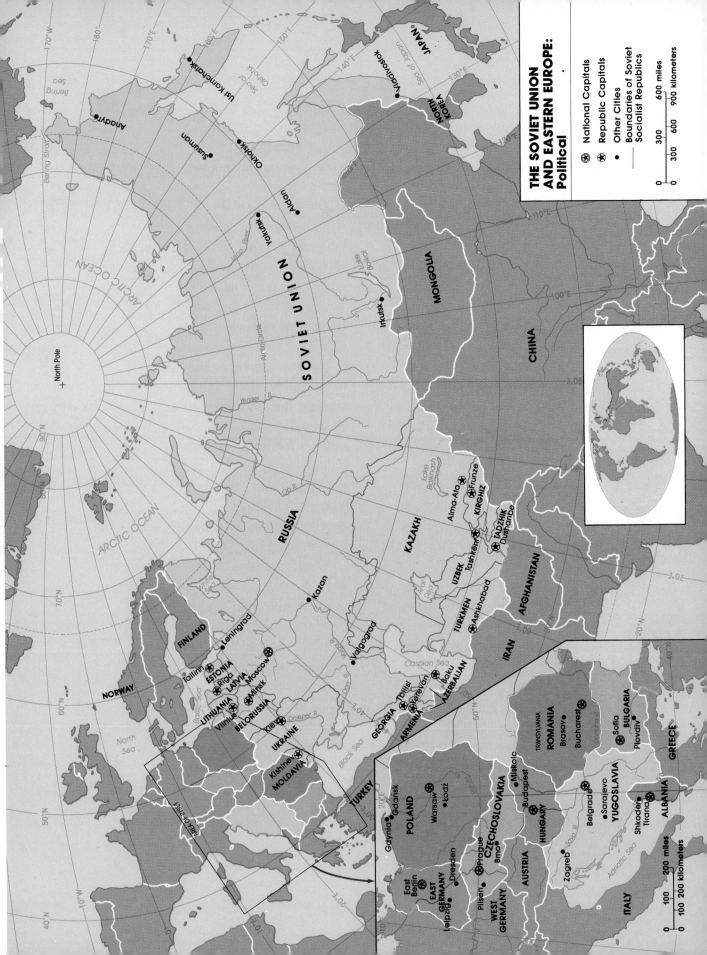

THE SOVIET UNION
AND EASTERN EUROPE:
Political

* National Capitals
⊛ Republic Capitals
• Other Cities
— Boundaries of Soviet
Socialist Republics

0   300   600 miles
0   300   600   900 kilometers

North Pole

ARCTIC OCEAN

90° N

70° N

60° N

50° N

40° N

Bering Strait

Bering Sea

Sea of Okhotsk

Anadyr

Susuman

Okhotsk

Ust Kamchatsk

Aldan

Yakutsk

Vladivostok

JAPAN

NORTH KOREA

Sea of Japan

SOVIET UNION

RUSSIA

Irkutsk

Lake Baikal

MONGOLIA

CHINA

Yenisei R.

Ob R.

Arctic Circle

Kazan

Volgograd

Don R.

KAZAKH

Lake Balkhash

Alma-Ata

⊛Frunze

KIRGHIZ

TADZHIK

⊛Dushanbe

Tashkent⊛

UZBEK

Aral Sea

TURKMEN

Ashkhabad⊛

Caspian Sea

AFGHANISTAN

IRAN

FINLAND

NORWAY

Leningrad

Tallinn
ESTONIA

Riga
LATVIA

⊛Moscow

Minsk⊛

BELORUSSIA

Vilnius
LITHUANIA

Kiev⊛

UKRAINE

Dnieper R.

Kishinev⊛
MOLDAVIA

Black Sea

TURKEY

GEORGIA
Tbilisi⊛

ARMENIA
⊛Yerevan

Baku⊛
AZERBAIJAN

White Sea

Baltic Sea

North Sea

ARCTIC OCEAN

AREA OF INSET

POLAND

Gdynia
Gdansk⊛

Warsaw⊛

Łódź

EAST GERMANY

East Berlin⊛

Leipzig

Dresden

WEST GERMANY

Pilsen

CZECHOSLOVAKIA

Prague⊛

Brno

AUSTRIA

HUNGARY

Budapest⊛

Miskolc

Zagreb

Sava R.

YUGOSLAVIA

Belgrade⊛

Sarajevo

ITALY

Adriatic Sea

ALBANIA

Tirana⊛

Shkoder

GREECE

ROMANIA

TRANSYLVANIA

Brasov

Bucharest⊛

BULGARIA

Sofia⊛

Plovdiv

0   100   200 miles
0   100   200 kilometers

Time Zones

12:00 Noon
Greenwich,
England

11:00 A.M.
Reykjavik,
Iceland

10:00 A.M.
Praia, Cape Verde Is.
(Portugal)

9:00 A.M.
Brasília,
Brazil

8:00 A.M.
Halifax, Nova Scotia,
Canada

7:00 A.M.
New York, N.Y.,
U.S.

6:00 A.M.
Chicago, Ill.,
U.S.

5:00 A.M.
Helena, Mont.,
U.S.

4:00 A.M.
San Francisco, Calif.,
U.S.

3:00 A.M.
Whitehorse, Yukon,
Canada

2:00 A.M.
Anchorage, Alaska,
U.S.

1:00 A.M.
Nome, Alaska,
U.S.

A day is the time it takes the earth to spin around once on its axis. An hour is a twenty-fourth part of a day, so the earth is divided into 24 standard time zones, each covering approximately 15° of longitude. The time of day depends on where you are on the earth.

Look at the clocks on this page. You will see that when it is 12 o'clock noon in Greenwich, England, it is 1 o'clock in the afternoon in Berlin, and 7 o'clock in the morning in New York City.

Hours are numbered from the Prime Meridian, or 0° longitude, which passes through Greenwich, England. Time zones east of the Greenwich zone are *ahead* of Greenwich time. This is because the earth spins toward the east, so that lands to the east get the sun earlier than Greenwich does. Berlin is in the first zone east of Greenwich, so when it is noon in Greenwich, it is 1 o'clock in Berlin. Leningrad lies two time zones east of Greenwich. When it is noon

in Greenwich, it is 2 o'clock in the afternoon in Leningrad according to standard time.

Time zones west of Greenwich are *behind* Greenwich time. New York City is five zones west, so when it is noon in Greenwich, it is 7 o'clock in the morning in New York City.

The boundaries of the time zones usually follow straight lines over the oceans. Every fifteenth degree of longitude marks a different time zone. On the continents time zone boundaries usually zigzag. People living in the same region or country find it convenient to live by the same time.

Some countries are so large that they are in more than one time zone. As you can see from the clocks showing times in Soviet cities, the Soviet Union stretches across 11 time zones. From the state of Maine to the state of Hawaii, the United States spreads across 7 of them.

12:00 Midnight
Anadyr,
U.S.S.R.

11:00 P.M.
Ust-Kamchatsk,
U.S.S.R.

1:00 P.M.
Berlin,
Germany

2:00 P.M.
Leningrad,
U.S.S.R.

3:00 P.M.
Baku,
U.S.S.R.

4:00 P.M.
Sverdlovsk,
U.S.S.R.

5:00 P.M.
Tashkent,
U.S.S.R.

6:00 P.M.
Novosibirsk,
U.S.S.R.

7:00 P.M.
Irkutsk,
U.S.S.R.

8:00 P.M.
Aldan,
U.S.S.R.

9:00 P.M.
Okhotsk,
U.S.S.R.

10:00 P.M.
Susuman,
U.S.S.R.

of land from Poland, Czechoslovakia, and Romania. If all the territory taken over and **annexed**—which means added to one's own country—by the Soviet Union were in one piece of land, it would equal the size of Spain.

The Soviet Union is truly a vast land. As you read in Chapter 9, it includes a large part of Eastern Europe and stretches eastward across Asia to the Pacific Ocean. If you were to cross it from coast to coast, you would travel halfway around the world. Leningrad, on the west coast of the country, is closer to New York City than it is to the city of Vladivostok on the east coast of the Soviet Union.

The population of the Soviet Union is about 270 million. About 62 percent of these people live in cities. There are 18 cities in the country with 1 million or more people. Moscow, the capital and largest city, has nearly 8 million people. Only China has more cities of 1 million or more. Our country has 6 such cities.

Mining and Manufacturing   As you would expect, a country so large has a big share of the world's natural resources. The Soviet Union has large deposits of petroleum, coal, iron ore, and other minerals. It has huge supplies of timber. One third of the country is covered by forests. The coniferous forest, the taiga, is the largest in the world. Unfortunately, the taiga and many other Soviet resources are in Siberia. Severe climate and great distance make it difficult to use some of the country's natural wealth.

The Soviet Union has become one of the world's industrial giants. Only the United States produces more goods than the Soviet Union. Most Soviet goods are heavy-industry and mining products. The Soviet Union leads the world in the production of steel, oil, iron ore, and manganese. Manganese is a metal needed to make steel. Coal deposits found in the Ukraine and Siberia make the Soviet Union second only to the United States in coal mining. Iron ore also is mined in the Ukraine, Siberia, and the Ural Mountains. Large petroleum fields are in the Caucasus Mountains. The Baku (bä kü') field is the most famous of these. Important new petroleum fields have been developed in the Ural Mountains. The Soviet Union also has petroleum fields in western Siberia. Locate these natural resources of the Soviet Union on the resource map on page 234.

The Soviet Union is also the world's second largest producer of electricity, natural gas, copper, aluminum, nickel,

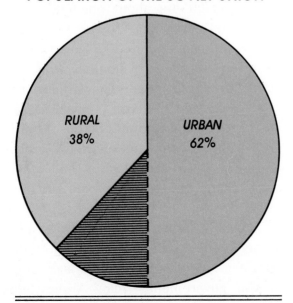

POPULATION OF THE SOVIET UNION

RURAL 38%

URBAN 62%

The striped area shows the 12 percent of the Soviet urban population that lives in cities of 1 million or more.

lead, zinc, silver, and tungsten. Tungsten is used in making light bulbs. It is also added to other metals to harden them. The Soviet Union's great supplies of almost every resource needed for industry mean that the country does not have to import many natural resources.

Industries in the Soviet Union also make **consumer goods**—products that get used up—such as clothing and housewares. Factories in Moscow and Leningrad make automobiles, chemicals, electronic equipment, processed food, textiles, and other consumer goods.

Moscow and Leningrad are the oldest and the largest industrial centers in the country. Other factories have been built in many smaller cities and industrial centers. Many of these centers are nearer the supplies of coal and oil that are used in manufacturing. Some port cities have fish-packing factories. The Soviet Union is the second largest producer of fish.

Automobiles are popular consumer goods in the Soviet Union, just as they are in our own country.

The Soviet Union is a Socialist country All resources belong to the government. The government owns and controls all of the main industries. It is against the law in the Soviet Union to strike against the industries owned by the government. Government officials decide what the people need and what shall be produced. Officials set prices and wages.

Large farms and small plots Much of the Soviet Union is too cold or too dry to be good farmland. However, the Soviet Union is a leading crop producer in the world. Most of the best cropland is in the steppe. About one tenth of the total country is farmed. The Soviet soil is generally not as fertile as in the United States. Also, much of the farmland in the Soviet Union has a short growing season because it is near the Arctic Circle.

There are two kinds of large farms—state-owned farms, which average about 112,000 acres (45,320 ha), and collective farms, which are about one-tenth that size. The government owns the state farms and runs them like government factories. Hundreds of families work together on these farms. The farmers are paid wages and the farm is given a goal each year for the amount of crops it must grow. The government owns the crops and ships them to the cities and other areas. State livestock farms are run the same way.

Collective farms own their crops and animals. These farms rent their land from the government, and produce according to the government's plan. Wages are lower than on state farms, but the farmers share in the profits from the crops

Huge combines, or harvesting machines, are used to bring in the wheat crop on the large collectives and state-owned farms of the Soviet Union.

that the government buys from the collective. Profit is what is gained from the sale of something. The collective farms make up about one third of the total farmland in the Soviet Union. The average collective farm is 10,500 acres (4,249 ha) and supports about 300 families.

Large farms produce most of the main crops, such as grain crops, cotton, and sugar beets. The Soviet Union is the largest producer of wheat, barley, oats, and potatoes. In some years these farms have not produced enough to feed the country. The Soviet government has had to buy grain from other countries, such as the United States and Canada. This has usually happened in years with bad weather.

Even in good years an important part of the country's food supply comes from small **plots** of land worked by individuals. The government permits people to have small plots. The plots cannot be bigger than 1 acre (.4 ha). People may also keep chickens and a cow or two. The government allows them to sell what they raise on their small plots in farmers' markets. There are thousands of these markets in cities and towns throughout the country.

The small plots make up less than 2 percent of the farmland, yet they provide much of the food. They supply one third of the vegetables, milk, and meat, nearly half of the eggs, and more than half of the potatoes.

Moscow, the Kremlin, and Red Square Moscow, the Soviet Union's capital and its largest city, grew up around an old fortress, called a **kremlin,**

227

Long lines of people wait in Moscow's Red Square to visit the tomb of Lenin outside the Kremlin wall. At the far end of the square stands St. Basil's Cathedral.

on the Moskva River. *Kremlin* is the old Russian word for fortress. Moscow's kremlin was only one of many such fortresses. But it became the center for Russia's government. When people speak of the Kremlin today, they usually mean the Soviet government.

Inside the Kremlin's red brick walls, there are a number of famous old churches, including the Cathedral of the Assumption, where many tsars were crowned. Just outside the walls, on a public plaza called Red Square, stands St. Basil's Cathedral. The picture above shows this many-towered church of brick and white stone built more than 400 years ago. It is probably the most photo-

graphed building in the city of Moscow today.

The government has carefully preserved St. Basil's and the churches within the Kremlin's walls. But the Communist government discourages religion. People are not allowed to practice many of their religious traditions. Most of the old church buildings in Soviet cities are preserved as museums rather than as places of worship.

Probably every visitor to Moscow goes to Red Square. There they can also see the tomb of Nikolai Lenin. The Soviet's largest department store, known as GUM is located on Red Square. Like most other large businesses GUM is owned by the government. About 350,000 people go to GUM every day. Many of the people are tourists from other countries. The large store is a kind of showcase for the country, where people can buy food and other consumer goods that the Soviet Union produces. Often there is a shortage of consumer goods, such as meat and other foods, in the Soviet Union. Sometimes people have to stand in long lines for scarce items even at GUM.

Lenin—the official hero Lenin's Tomb on Red Square is only one of many reminders of that past leader's importance in the Soviet Union. Lenin is the country's official hero. A Russian friend of an American writer warned him, "You can joke about many things here but not about Lenin."

There are a great number of streets, squares, factories, schools, and other institutions named for Lenin. His statues are seen all over the Soviet Union. His picture appears in offices, factories, schools, and public buildings, as well as in most homes and apartments.

From the earliest years, children in school are taught to think of Lenin as the ideal person. Teachers encourage kindergarten children to decorate his classroom picture with flowers and ribbons on holidays. Older students are taught that he was one of the world's great thinkers. They study his writings and speeches. Writers and leaders still repeat his words to prove their arguments. All nations honor heroes, but few countries in modern times go so far as the Soviets do to honor their official hero.

GUM, Moscow's busiest and largest department store, is on Red Square. Its covered galleries, or walkways, and its many shops are filled with shoppers.

The government and the party The Communist party, which took over the country in 1917, still rules it. The most important leaders are always members of this one party. The government does not allow people to form other parties. The Communists are strict about whom they let join their party. It is an honor to be a member, and many people are not allowed to join.

Elections in the Soviet Union There are elections in the Soviet Union. In fact, the government does a great deal to get people to vote. The government says that as many as 99 percent of the people turn out to vote. But the voters have very little choice in these elections. They are very different from elections in Western Europe or the United States. There is only one name for each office on the ballot. That name is always someone approved by the Communist party. People can only vote for or against the party's **candidate.** A candidate is one who runs for office. People have no chance to vote for anyone who opposes the Communists.

Books and newspapers The people in the Soviet Union read a great deal. But they are allowed to read only what is approved by the government. Government publishing houses turn out a large number of books each year. More newspapers are printed in the Soviet Union than in the United States. But neither books nor newspapers print material against the Communists or the government.

The Communist party publishes *Pravda* (präv′ də), the country's leading newspaper. *Pravda* gives the news that the party thinks people ought to read. It criticizes only those whom the government wants criticized. *Pravda* seldom prints news about crime in the Soviet Union because that would make the country look bad. The Communist party newspaper is so much the official voice of the government that people in other countries read it to learn about the government's views.

A young American girl in a Soviet school Hedrick Smith, an American newspaper writer, and his family lived in Moscow for 4 years during the 1970s. His daughter Laurie attended a Soviet school during the year she was in the sixth grade. Mr. Smith described that year in a book about the Russian people.

Laurie went to school 6 days a week, and she discovered that sixth graders in

This Soviet newsstand has magazines on many topics. There are magazines on architecture, music, women, science, aviation, Vietnam, and Bulgaria.

Soviet pupils listen closely to their teacher. On the board are the words "John," "willow tree," and "catch."

the Soviet Union have a lot of homework. Fortunately Laurie found a good Russian friend in her class who helped her to keep up with her work. In his book, Laurie's father wrote:

> Laurie's sixth grade had a dozen set subjects: math, physics, biology, Russian literature, Russian grammar, Russian medieval history, geography, English, drawing, singing, physical culture, and work (sewing for girls, shop for boys).

Note that the Soviet sixth graders were studying a foreign language, English, in this class. Of course, Russian was a foreign language for Laurie.

In her father's book, Laurie tells about some of the differences between her Russian school and those she had attended in the United States.

> In an American school sometimes you wander off the subject and get into a discussion that is interesting, but it seemed as though that never happened in a Russian

school. You know how you can have some games, like spelling bees or mathematical puzzles or games? Well, they don't do that.

Laurie's father added: "The emphasis was on drill, drill, drill and straight memory work." Mr. Smith admitted that the Russian school did seem to get results, especially in science and mathematics.

The Soviet Union in the world   As you read in Chapter 10, Communist parties have come to power in the countries of Eastern Europe with the help of the Soviet Union. The Soviet Union had also aided Communist groups in many other countries. For example, in 1979 the Soviet Union sent armies into one of its southern neighbors, Afghanistan. This military action helped to support a government that was friendly to the Soviet Union.

The Soviet Union also gives many other kinds of aid around the world, just as the United States does. It sends food, money, machinery, and experts who know how to solve many difficult problems. This is called **foreign aid.** *Foreign aid* means "aid given outside one's own country." In the decades since World War II, the Soviet Union has helped Communist groups or countries on every continent in the world.

CHECKUP

1. Who owns the natural resources, land, and main industries in the Soviet Union? How are farms and factories run in the Soviet Union?
2. Why are the individual plots of land important in the Soviet Union?
3. What is the Kremlin? In what city is it?
4. What are elections like in the Soviet Union? How are they different from those in the United States?
5. What is school like in the Soviet Union?

Poland, East Germany, and Czechoslovakia

VOCABULARY

independence   boundary

Poland's long struggle for independence   In 1776 a young man from Poland named Thaddeus Kosciusko (thad′ ē əs kos ē us′ kō) came to America. He came to help the Americans in their struggle for **independence.** He joined the army of General George Washington and served throughout the Revolutionary War. He had been trained as a military engineer, and he built a fort at West Point on the Hudson River in New York State. Today the United States Military Academy uses this fort.

The American Revolution was Kosciusko's first war for independence but not his last. In 1792 he fought for the freedom of his own land of Poland. At that time, Poland had three powerful neighbors. They were Russia, Prussia, and Austria. They had already taken over part of Poland. Kosciusko and his fellow Poles fought to save what was left. They lost, and Poland's neighbors divided up the rest of the country in 1795. The independent country of Poland disappeared from the map of Eastern Europe.

It was not until 1918, at the end of World War I, that Kosciusko's homeland again became completely free. It remained independent for only 21 years. Hitler's Germany and the Soviet Union conquered Poland at the beginning of World War II.

Later Germany declared war on the Soviet Union and took over all of Poland. This was a dreadful time for the Poles. In Chapter 8, you read about how Hitler treated people who opposed him. Over 3 million Polish Jews died in the "death camps" established by Hitler's government. Nearly 3 million other Poles were also sent to death camps or as slave labor to Germany. Most of these people also died.

Poland appeared on the map again at the end of World War II. But it was a smaller country, and its eastern **boundary** was farther west because the Soviet Union took a strip of eastern Poland. The Poles received part of Germany to make up for the loss. Kosciusko's hometown is no longer a part of his homeland. It is now part of the Soviet Union.

Poland is the world's fourth largest coal producer. Coal mining is hot, dirty, often dangerous work.

When Poland became an independent country again, the Soviets made sure that Polish Communists took control. The Soviets had troops in Poland, which made it easier for the Communists to set up a government like that of the Soviet Union.

Groups of Poles have shown from time to time that they want more freedom than the Communists permit. There were riots in 1956, and the Communists chose new leaders in the hope that this would satisfy the people. But the Communist party remained in control. In 1980, shipyard workers at Gdańsk went on strike. The strikers forced the government to allow workers to form unions free from government control. No such freedom exists in any other Communist country.

Many Polish workers welcomed their new freedom and joined a union called Solidarity. As the union grew, its leaders wanted still more freedom. On December 12, 1981, Solidarity demanded that the people of Poland be allowed to vote on whether they wanted to keep Communist rule. The government leaders would not allow this freedom. The very next day, army leaders declared that Solidarity was trying to destroy the country. The Communist-led army took over the country. Many of the leaders of the Solidarity union were arrested and imprisoned.

Poland—Europe's second largest Communist country Poland is on the great North European Plain, which lies south of the Baltic Sea. At one time, forests covered this land. There are still patches of woodland, but the best land was cleared long ago and turned into fields. The name *Poland* means "field country."

Farmers bring in a harvest of sugar beets, an important crop in Poland. Although Poland's government is Communist, many farms are small and privately owned.

Nearly three fifths of Poland's land area is under cultivation. The main crops are rye, potatoes, and sugar beets. Polish farmers also raise a lot of livestock, including pigs. Polish hams and sausages are famous. But under Communist rule Polish farms have produced less. In fact, Poland has had to import part of its food from other countries, particularly the United States.

Poland's wealth comes from its mines as well as its fields. After World War II, Poland gained one of Europe's most important coalfields when the coal region of Silesia (sə lē′ sh) was taken from Germany. Poland is now the fourth largest coal producer in the world. But coal production declined during the struggle between Solidarity and the government.

The Vistula (vis′ chə lə) River is Poland's own river. It crosses no national boundaries. The Vistula drains most of the

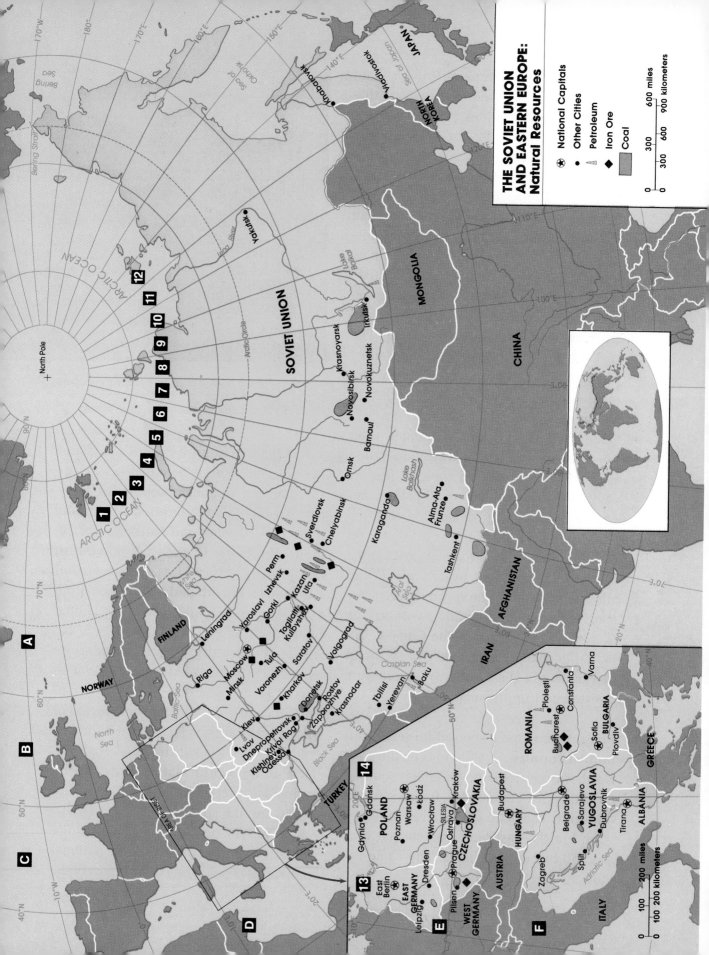

THE SOVIET UNION
AND EASTERN EUROPE:
Natural Resources

⊛ National Capitals
• Other Cities
⚑ Petroleum
◆ Iron Ore
▒ Coal

	300	600 miles
0	300	600	900 kilometers

North Pole

ARCTIC OCEAN

NORWAY

FINLAND

SOVIET UNION

MONGOLIA

CHINA

JAPAN

NORTH KOREA

Bering Sea
Bering Strait
Sea of Okhotsk
Sea of Japan

Yakutsk

Khabarovsk

Vladivostok

Irkutsk

Lake Baikal

Krasnoyarsk

Novosibirsk

Novokuznetsk

Barnaul

Omsk

Karaganda

Lake Balkhash

Alma-Ata
Frunze

Tashkent

Aral Sea

AFGHANISTAN

IRAN

Caspian Sea

Baku

Yerevan

Tbilisi

Krasnodar

Rostov

Volgograd

Saratov

Kuibyshev

Togliatti

Ufa

Kazan

Izhevsk

Perm

Sverdlovsk

Chelyabinsk

Gorki

Yaroslavl

Moscow

Tula

Voronezh

Kharkov

Donetsk

Zaporozhye

Dnepropetrovsk

Krivoi Rog

Kiev

Lvov

Kishinev

Odessa

Minsk

Riga

Leningrad

White Sea

Baltic Sea

North Sea

Black Sea

TURKEY

North Pole

ARCTIC OCEAN

Arctic Circle

Lena River

Ob River

AREA OF INSET

1 2 3 4 5 6 7 8 9 10 11 12

13 14

POLAND

Gdynia
Gdansk

Poznan

Warsaw

Łódź

Wrocław

SILESIA

Kraków

Ostrava

Prague

Pilsen

CZECHOSLOVAKIA

EAST
GERMANY

East
Berlin

Dresden

Leipzig

WEST
GERMANY

AUSTRIA

HUNGARY

Budapest

ROMANIA

Bucharest

Ploiești

Constanța

BULGARIA

Sofia

Plovdiv

Varna

YUGOSLAVIA

Belgrade

Sarajevo

Zagreb

Split

Dubrovnik

ALBANIA

Tirana

GREECE

ITALY

Adriatic Sea

	100	200 miles
0	100	200 kilometers

The key on the map on page 234 shows the coal, petroleum, and iron ore resources of the Soviet Union and the countries of Eastern Europe. Using the map key, locate on the map the petroleum resources of the Soviet Union and Romania.

broad Polish plain. Warsaw, the capital and largest city, is located on the Vistula.

More than 60 percent of Poland's 35 million people live in city areas. Since World War II, many industries have been built in these areas. Polish factories make mostly heavy machinery. Poland's port cities of Gdańsk (gə dän′ sk) and Gdynia (gə din′ ē ə) are important for shipping the machinery and coal exports to other countries.

Religion in a Communist country
Poland has been a Roman Catholic country for more than a thousand years. The Polish Communists, like other Communist parties, would like to do away with religious practices. At one time the government tried to do so. But the Communist rulers discovered that a great many Poles remained fiercely loyal to their religion. The government decided that attacking the Roman Catholic Church

in Poland was a hopeless job. The Communists still discourage religion, but they no longer try to do away with it.

One of the Polish church leaders, Karol Wojtyla (voi tē′ wə), was chosen head of the Roman Catholic Church in 1978. He took the title Pope John Paul II. The next year Pope John Paul II paid a 9-day visit to his homeland. It was the first time a pope had ever visited a Communist country. Millions of his fellow Poles saw him during those days and heard his words. According to Pope John Paul II, religion remains strong in Poland because it is "very closely bound up with the entire people." Many people seem to feel that to be a Pole is to be a Roman Catholic regardless of the kind of government.

East Germany and the Berlin wall
In Chapter 8 you read about the division of Germany after World War II. The German Democratic Republic, usually

called East Germany, is Poland's neighbor. In spite of its official name, East Germany does not have a democratic government. It is another of the Eastern European countries ruled by a Communist party with the support of the Soviet Union. There are no free elections such as those in West Germany.

Berlin, the old German capital, is now a city divided between two countries. It is entirely surrounded by East German territory. But the city itself is divided between East and West Germany. The East German capital is in the part of Berlin held by East Germany.

In the years after World War II many people left East Germany because they did not want to live under Communist rule. About one out of five East Germans decided to leave their homes. The East German police guarded the boundary between the two Germanys, but people kept slipping across the line into West Berlin. In 1961 the East German government built a concrete wall through the heart of Berlin topped with glass and barbed wire. There were only eight places where people could cross from one part of the city to the other. These were closely guarded, and the stream of East Germans leaving the country slowed to a trickle. In recent years the government has allowed more people to travel back and forth beyond the wall.

The Berlin wall cannot keep out television broadcasts from West Berlin. Unlike most people in Eastern Europe, the East Berliners can watch news and other programs that come from outside Communist countries. It is easier for people in East Berlin to know more than their gov-

ernment tells them. Most of the rest of Eastern Europe can also tune in to radio broadcasts from Western Europe.

East Germany is less than half as large as West Germany. Its population is less than one-third that of West Germany. Per capita income is not so high as that of West Germany, but it is higher than that of any other Eastern European country. Even though it is not large, East Germany has become one of the world's leading industrial countries. The cities of Dresden and Leipzig (līp′ sig) are the major industrial centers.

The land of the Czechs and Slovaks Czechoslovakia is a fairly small country with a long name. The name tells that this is a country of two peoples, the Czechs and the Slovaks. These two groups speak slightly different languages.

Czechoslovakia did not appear on maps of Europe until 1919, after World War I. This does not mean that there were no Czechs or Slovaks before that time. These peoples have a history going back to the Middle Ages. They have stories about their good King Wenceslas who lived about a hundred years before William the Conqueror, the King of England. According to the stories, Wenceslas "used to rise secretly at night and with only one servant attending him, go to his forest; and bearing wood thence on his shoulders, used to lay it secretly at the doors of widows and poor people."

It has been hard for Czechoslovakia to remain independent because of its location. It has many neighbors. Its boundaries touch Austria, Hungary, Poland, both Germanys, and the Soviet Union.

Czechoslovakia, one of the industrial countries of Eastern Europe, has many steel mills like the one above.

Hitler's Germany took over most of the country before World War II. Czechoslovakia became independent again after the war, and the Czechoslovak Communist party took control of the government.

In the spring of 1968, the Communist leaders began to give the people more freedom. They said that they would create a new kind of Communist country, one in which people could speak and write freely. Leaders in the Soviet Union did not think such a Communist government was possible. The Soviet army was sent into Czechoslovakia and new Czechoslovak Communists were put in charge of the government. These leaders once again established tight controls over the people.

Although Czechoslovakia is not large, it has a variety of lands. There are mountains along the German border, and the rugged Carpathians reach into the eastern part of the country. Prague (präg), the capital, is located on one of the country's plains. Like East Germany, Czechoslovakia is one of the industrial countries of Eastern Europe. Large ironworks are located around Pilsen and Ostrava. The rich coalfields of Silesia, mainly in Poland, also extend into Czechoslovakia.

CHECKUP

1. What happened to Poland during World War II?
2. Why is Poland called "field country"? What other kinds of wealth do the Poles get from the earth?
3. What is the position of the Roman Catholic Church in Poland?
4. What are the effects of Berlin being a city in two countries?
5. What happened to Czechoslovakia in World War II and in 1968?
6. Which countries touch the boundaries of Czechoslovakia?

Communist Southeastern Europe

┌─VOCABULARY─────────────────┐
Magyar   **vault**
└────────────────────────────┘

The crown and country of the Hungarians   The Hungarians usually call themselves **Magyars** (mag' yärs). That is also their name for the language they speak. The Magyar tongue is not related to the Slavic languages of their neighbors.

Today Hungary has a Communist government, but kings ruled this land for hundreds of years. For more than 30 years after the Communists came to power in 1945, the crown of the Hungarian kings was kept in an underground **vault** at Fort Knox, Kentucky. The Hungarians call this crown the Holy Crown of Saint Stephen. According to their old histories, Saint Stephen was the first Hungarian Christian king. The crown was sent to him by the pope for the king's crowning in 1001. For centuries after that date, king after king wore the Holy Crown of Saint Stephen. Indeed, a king was not considered a true ruler unless he had been crowned with it. The Hungarians used to say, "He who has the crown has Hungary."

Communists come to power in Hungary   How did Saint Stephen's crown ever get to the United States? At the close of World War II, the Soviet army took over Hungary, along with the rest of Eastern Europe, and set up Communist governments. The Hungarian keepers of the crown did not want it to fall into the hands of the Communists. They smuggled it out of the country and asked the American army to keep it for the Hungarian people. The United States government agreed to hold the crown for a time. It was put in the safest place possible, the underground vault at Fort Knox, where the United States government stores much of its gold.

Farming is an important business in Hungary. Wheat is one of the chief crops grown.

During the early period of the Hungarian Communist government, a revolt broke out against it. In 1956 the government called on the Soviet army for help. Many Hungarians lost their lives. Many more fled the country. And the Communists remained in power.

Hungary has no king under the Communists, but the government kept asking to have the crown of Saint Stephen returned. They wanted it because the old crown was the symbol of the country. It was returned in 1978. Since then hundreds of thousands of Hungarians have viewed the Holy Crown of Saint Stephen. Like people everywhere, the Hungarian people love and honor things that remind them of their country's past.

The farmlands of Hungary   Hungary was mostly an agricultural country before World War II. The Hungarian Plain, which makes up most of the country, is good farmland. The Danube flows through the center of this plain. Hungary's farms are still very important. Most of the farms are run as collectives. The chief crops are wheat, rye, sugar beets, corn, potatoes, and paprika—a red spice much favored by Hungarian cooks. Paprika is used in many dishes including the most famous, which Americans call Hungarian goulash.

Livestock is an important part of Hungary's farm business. More hogs and chickens are raised than any other animals. There are also wide grasslands where hard-riding Hungarian cowhands tend cattle, horses, and sheep. Dairy products also are important. Hungary's exports include some of the livestock and processed food.

Industry in Hungary Today Hungary is described as an "industrial-agricultural" country. More Hungarians now work in industries than on farms. The industries produce such things as farm machinery, buses, television sets, radios, and shoes. One of Hungary's chief resources is bauxite, the ore from which aluminum metal is made. Aluminum products rank among the country's important exports.

Hungary's chief industrial center is the capital city of Budapest (büd ə pest'). Near the north end of its course down the middle of Hungary, the Danube River flows through Budapest.

At one time there were two cities, one on either side of the Danube. Buda, a well-fortified city with a castle, was on the west. Pest, a busy industrial city, lay on the east. In 1872 the two cities and the two names were combined to form Budapest. The modern capital is by far the country's largest city. About one fifth of Hungary's population lives in Budapest. Hungarians and many tourists alike think that Budapest is one of the most beautiful Eastern European cities.

Yugoslavia—land of southern Slavs
Yugoslavia has had several official names, and the different names tell much about that country's history. In 1918 at the close of World War I, most of the present-day country became united and independent. It was called the Kingdom of Serbs, Croats, and Slovenes (slō' vēnz).

As the name suggests, the country was home of several different nationalities. All of them were southern Slavs, as they are today. The Serbs and Croats speak the same Slavic language. But they use dif-

The Danube River, which flows through Hungary, also flows through the middle of its capital, Budapest.

ferent alphabets. The Serbs used the Cyrillic alphabet, and the Croats the Roman one. The Slovenes speak a different Slavic language and also use the Roman alphabet. There also are Macedonians who live in the southern part of Yugoslavia. They speak yet another Slavic language, which they write with the Cyrillic script.

The differences in alphabets are connected with differences in religion. Serbs and Macedonians follow Eastern Orthodox Christianity. The Croats and Slovenes are Roman Catholics. About 10 percent of the people of Yugoslavia believe in the Moslem religion.

The Kingdom of Serbs, Croats, and Slovenes became the Kingdom of Yugoslavia in 1929. The name means land of the southern Slavs. Today there are about 25 different daily newspapers published in many of the different languages. Many Yugoslavs today prefer to think of themselves as Serbs, Croats, Slovenes, or Macedonians.

239

Communist Yugoslavia The country's official name today is the Socialist Federal Republic of Yugoslavia. As this name suggests, it is another of the Eastern European countries taken over by Communists after World War II.

Yugoslavia is the only Communist-ruled country where private ownership of businesses and land is allowed to a great extent. The government owns most industries, but individuals own about one fourth of the stores. Most of the land belongs to the private farmers rather than the government.

The Soviet Union does not approve of much that the Yugoslav Communists have done. But the Yugoslav government has been strong enough to go its own way. It is the only country in Eastern Europe that never joined COMECON and the Warsaw Pact.

Countryside and cities in Yugoslavia The greatly varied geography of Yugoslavia makes it a beautiful country. The Danube River cuts across the north-eastern corner of Yugoslavia and flows by Belgrade (bel' grād), the capital and largest city. *Belgrade* means "white fortress." It is named after an old fort that was built here.

South of the Danube plain rise the highlands that fall to the Adriatic Sea. Yugoslavia has a scenic, rocky coast. A growing tourist trade has become one of the country's important industries.

Today about half of the 22 million Yugoslavs live in cities. There are eight cities in addition to Belgrade that have more than 100,000 people. In one of these cities, Sarajevo (sär' ə ye vô), tourists can find the site of the 1984 Winter Olympics.

The economy of Yugoslavia depends on many kinds of business. The mountainous highlands have mineral resources that make mining an important industry. Manufacturing and shipping are also important parts of the economy. Some of the goods the Yugoslavs make are automobiles, textiles, many kinds of metal goods, and forest and food products. Still Yugoslavia has to spend more money on

The ancient walled city of Dubrovnik, on Yugoslavia's Adriatic coast, draws many tourist visitors. Dubrovnik is located at 42°N and 18°E.

This ski lift is near Sarajevo, Yugoslavia. Sarajevo is the site of the 1984 Winter Olympics.

imports than it earns from exports to other countries. For this reason, the spending by tourists is an important aid to keeping the flow of money back into the country.

About two fifths of the working people in Yugoslavia are farmers, but the number was larger before World War II. Today farmers grow corn, grain crops, vegetables, and fruits. Yugoslavia grows more plums than any other country in Europe.

Albania—land of the eagles Albania is the smallest country in Eastern Eruope—one of the smallest on the whole European continent. It is almost entirely covered by rugged mountains and hills. Albanians call their country the "land of the eagles." Perhaps they chose this name because eagles build their nests in high, hard-to-reach places. Or perhaps the Albanians like the name because they think of eagles as being good at taking care of themselves. In any case, Albania is a high, mountainous country with fiercely independent people. They have their own language, which is not one of the Slavic group.

Albania's Communist party has ruled the country since the end of World War II. The Communists, too, have shown the Albanian spirit of independence. For that reason they have not always remained friendly with other Communist countries. Albania quarreled with Yugoslavia because Albanian leaders thought this Communist neighbor intended to take them over.

Later the Albanians quarreled with the Soviet Union and asked China for support. China, the world's second largest Communist country, had its own quarrel with the Soviet Union. The Chinese helped Albania develop its industries.

Today Albania remains the poorest country in Europe. There are few large cities. Only the capital, Tirana (ti rän′ ə), has a television station. The rough mountains make transportation difficult. More than three fourths of the people are farmers. Most of these use very old methods to work the land. Their diets are mostly bread, and milk and cheese from sheep and goats.

The government has worked hard to make some changes in Albania. It began a program to teach most people how to read and write. Electric power plants have been built to be run by the falling waters of some of the many rivers that flow down to the Adriatic Sea.

At one time, seven out of ten Albanians were Moslems, two were Eastern Orthodox, and one was Roman Catholic. The large number of Moslems was the result of 500 years of Turkish rule under the Ottoman Empire. No one knows for sure how many Albanians hold fast to these religions today. The Communist government does not allow public religious services. The Communists say that people are free to believe any religion they like so long as they do not go to a church or mosque. This would not be thought of as religious freedom in Western Europe or the United States.

Romania—land with rubber boundaries Romanians trace the history of their country back to the time when it was part of the Roman Empire. You will remember that *Romania* means "land of the Romans." There was a Roman settlement where Bucharest (bü′ kə rest), the capital, now stands. The Romanians do not speak a Slavic language. Their language comes from the Latin of the Romans. They also use the Roman alphabet. But religion and alphabet did not go together in this case. Most Romanians belong to the Eastern Orthodox Church rather than the Roman Catholic Church.

Romania has been called a land with "rubber boundaries" because its borders have changed so many times. They were stretched larger after World War I and drawn smaller after World War II.

The mouth of the Danube lies in Romania, so that part of the land is river plain and delta. The Danube comes out of the mountains in Romania at the Iron Gate, where Europe's largest power project has been built.

If you look at the map on page 187, you will see that the Carpathian Mountains form a great hook in the midst of the country. Enclosed within the hook is the part of Romania that is called Transylvania (tran səl vān′ yə). A number of German and Hungarian-speaking peoples live in Transylvania. It was part of Hungary before World War I. Many Hungarians think that Transylvania should still be part of their country. That is one of the troubles with having rubber boundaries.

The economy of Communist Romania
The Soviet army went into Romania after World War II and helped the Romanian Communists take control. But the Romanian Communist government has not always acted as the Soviets wished. For example, Romania built a new steel plant, which the Soviet Union did not think was needed. The Soviets wanted the Romanians to buy more steel from the Soviet Union or East Germany.

The Soviets wanted Romania to produce grain and petroleum for Eastern Europe. Romania has the Ploieşti (plô yesht′ē) petroleum field, which was the largest in Europe outside the Soviet Union. But Romanians did not want to become Eastern Europe's supplier of grain and petroleum. Romanian leaders knew that the more petroleum they produced for other countries, the less there would be for Romania. Indeed, by the 1980s Romania's petroleum production had declined.

Romania also has large crop and pasturelands that are run as collective and state-owned farms. Corn and wheat are leading crops. Sheep are the chief livestock raised.

Romania encourages trousits to come and spend money at its resorts on the Black Sea coast. The government has also developed other tourist attractions—including Count Dracula's castle. You probably know the story of Count

As the picture above shows, Romania not only produces petroleum but is also a farming country.

Dracula. There really was a Dracula, but he was not like the character in the story. The real person was Prince Vlad Dracula who is a warrior-hero of Romania. However, the story has become more famous than the facts. So the Romanians restored an old castle and called it "Count Dracula's castle."

Bulgaria and the Soviet Union   The first Bulgars (bul′ gärs) came from Asia during the Middle Ages. They conquered the peoples in the land now called Bulgaria. The name is about all that remains of the original Bulgars. They married the people they conquered and adopted their Slavic language.

Constantinople greatly influenced the Bulgarians. They became Eastern Orthodox in religion. Sofia, Bulgaria's capital, has the same name as an old church in Constantinople. *Sofia* is simply another way to spell *sophia*, a word that means "wisdom."

The Soviet Union has had close relations with Bulgaria for many years. The Russians helped the Bulgarians win independence from Turkey more than a hundred years ago. After World War II, the army of the Soviet Union helped set up a Communist government in Bulgaria. The Bulgarian government has followed the Soviet Union more closely than has its neighbor Romania. For this reason, the Soviets have not kept troops in Bulgaria since 1974.

Bulgaria's chief natural resource is its fertile soil in the river plains of the Danube and Maritsa. Nearly half of the country's 9 million people farm. Leading crops are corn, wheat, tobacco, grapes, and other fruits. Roses are grown for their oil, to make perfume. Bulgarian rose oil is well known because it is exported to many countries.

Bulgaria also has some important mineral resources and industries. The Soviet Union has an agreement with Bulgaria to buy its uranium. Uranium is used in making nuclear power.

Bulgaria lies along the Black Sea, where it has fine beaches and leading seaports. The Soviet Union and Romania are Bulgaria's Communist neighbors that share the advantages of this coastline. The Balkan mountains rise in the middle of the country, dividing it into its northern and southern parts.

CHECKUP

1. What was the Holy Crown of Saint Stephen?
2. Which country is the land of the southern Slavs? Which peoples live there?
3. Why is "land of the eagles" a good name for Albania?
4. What is the meaning of *Romania*?
5. Which country has had close relations with Bulgaria? Why?

243

II / CHAPTER REVIEW

KEY FACTS

1. Most people in Eastern Europe speak one of the Slavic languages.

2. The nine countries of Eastern Europe have Communist governments. The Soviet Union is the largest of the group.

3. In the Soviet Union, government controls or owns land, industry, and most business.

4. East Germany is a leading industrial country with the highest per capita income in Eastern Europe.

5. People of different Slavic languages were united to form Czechoslovakia and Yugoslavia.

6. Hungary is mostly a great plain. Yugoslavia, Bulgaria, and Albania are mountainous.

7. Communist governments in Yugoslavia, Albania, and Romania have not always followed the leadership of the Soviet Union.

VOCABULARY QUIZ

On a sheet of paper, write each word from the list below next to its definition.

a. Slavic languages
b. plot
c. Kremlin
d. candidate
e. independence
f. military alliance
g. boundary
h. Magyars
i. consumer goods
j. annex

1. Center of the Soviet Union's government
2. An agreement between countries to join together in times of war
3. A person seeking office
4. Freedom from the control of others
5. People of Hungary
6. To add territory to one's own country
7. A small piece of land
8. The outside limit of a country
9. Russian, Polish, and many others
10. Things that get used up when put to use

REVIEW QUESTIONS

1. Who owns the land, natural resources, large businesses, and industries in the Soviet Union? How are they managed?

2. How does voting in the Soviet Union differ from voting in the United States?

3. What is the Berlin wall? Why was it built?

4. What do the names of each of the following countries tell about them: Poland, Czechoslovakia, Yugoslavia, Albania, and Romania?

5. What are two or three important products or businesses in the Soviet Union and in four other countries of Eastern Europe?

ACTIVITIES

1. Make a bar graph like the one on page 39 to compare populations of eight Eastern European countries. Do not use the Soviet Union. Population figures are on pages 486–491.

2. You have read about nine different countries in this chapter. Making a table such as the one shown below will help you to remember what you have read.

COUNTRY	CAPITAL	KIND OF LAND	INTERESTING FACTS
Albania	Tirana	Mostly rugged mountains and hills	—Only European country in which majority once were Moslems —Strongly independent —Has not remained friendly with other Communist countries

II /SKILLS DEVELOPMENT

USING SYLLABLES/USING MAPS

SYLLABLES MAKE UP THE SOUNDS OF NAMES

The names of some Eastern European countries are long, but they are not hard to spell if you divide them into syllables. Make a list of the names of these nine countries and study how they are spelled. Then put your list away.

SKILLS PRACTICE

In the exercise below, the names of eight of the countries have been divided into syllables and some letters left out. Try to guess each name and pronounce it. Next write each name on a sheet of paper, including the letters that have been left out. For example, B–l/g–r/–/a is Bulgaria. See if you can solve the other words without looking them up.

B–l/g–r/–/a

1. P–/l–nd
2. East G–r/m–/–y
3. S–/v–/–t U–/–on
4. A–/b–/–i/a

5. R–/m–/n–/a
6. H–n/g–/r–
7. Y–/g–/sl–/v–/a
8. –z–ch/o/sl–/v–/k–/a

USING PHYSICAL MAPS

It is often easier to learn facts about the geography of a country from a map than from a written description. Listed below are statements about countries of Eastern Europe. In each statement there are blanks, each with a letter in it.

SKILLS PRACTICE

Using the maps on pages 187 and 468, find the correct words to go in the blanks. On a sheet of paper, complete each statement by writing the missing place names or figures after the letter of the blank. For example, the first answer is as follows:

1. a. Warsaw **b.** Vistula **c.** Baltic

1. a. _____, the capital of Poland, is on the **b.** _____ River, which flows into the **c.** _____ Sea.

2. Poland's boundaries touch three countries: **a.** _____, **b.** _____, and **c.** _____.

3. The capital of Czechoslovakia is **a.** _____. If you went straight south from this city, you would reach the country of **b.** _____. If you went straight west, you would reach **c.** _____.

4. The Carpathian mountains extend through four countries: **a.** _____, **b.** _____, **c.** _____, and **d.** _____.

5. a. _____ is the capital of Hungary. If you went down the Danube River from this city, you would reach **b.** _____, the capital of Hungary's southern neighbor, **c.** _____.

6. The Danube empties into the **a.** ____ Sea.

7. Yugoslavia has more neighbors than any other country in Europe. Its boundaries touch those of the following countries: **a.** ___, **b.** _____, **c.** _____, **d.** _____, **e.** _____, **f.** _____, and **g.** _____.

8. Traveling south from Albania, you would reach the **a.** _____ Sea. If you traveled west across the sea, you would reach **b.** ____.

9. a. _____ is the capital of Romania. **b.** ____ is the capital of Bulgaria. Which city is farther east? **c.** _____.

10. The elevation of central northern Yugoslavia is at the most about **a.** __ feet, or **b.** __ meters, above sea level. Most of southern Yugoslavia is at least **c.** ____ feet, or **d.** __ meters, above sea level.

4/ UNIT REVIEW

1. The old Russian empire, which became the Soviet Union, includes a great variety of lands and peoples. — *Name four different kinds of land within the Soviet Union. Use an encyclopedia to make a list of parts of the United States that are somewhat like the different kinds of land in the Soviet Union.*

2. The Danube is the main river of southeastern Europe. — *Where is the source of the Danube, and where is its mouth? Name the countries that the Danube touches along its course.*

3. People from Constantinople spread Eastern Orthodox Christianity and their alphabet among the Slavic peoples of Eastern Europe during the Middle Ages. — *How does your answer to "2" above also show the importance of Constantinople?*

4. Russia under the tsars was a land with little freedom. Serfdom existed until 1861. — *Peter the Great said that people had to be forced to adopt changes that were for their own good. Do you agree or not? Give reasons for your answer.*

5. The Communists made Russia a Socialist country. — *What is socialism?*

6. The Communists promised "land for the peasants," but instead they set up collective farms. — *How is a collective farm run? Why are small individual plots of land still important in the Soviet Union?*

7. The Soviet Union under the Communists remained a land with little freedom. — *What are some of the things that people can do in the United States that they cannot do in the Soviet Union?*

8. Communists took control of eight Eastern European countries after World War II. — *Name the eight countries. Make a report on the three Baltic "lost countries": Estonia, Latvia, and Lithuania.*

9. The Soviet Union has aided Communist groups all over the world. It also has used its army to put down revolts in some of the Eastern European Communist countries. — *Which Eastern European countries have become somewhat independent of the Soviet Union?*

10. The countries of Eastern Europe are similar in some ways, but they differ in others. . — *Tell something that is special about each of the Eastern European countries.*

The Middle East and North Africa

12 Nature and People in the Middle East and North Africa

The Land and Climate

VOCABULARY

desert	wadi
caravan	oasis
journal	evaporate

Where is the Middle East? The countries of southwestern Asia are often called the Middle East. This name was invented by people from Europe because these lands are east of Europe. Other lands in Asia such as China and Japan are farther east from Europe and are often called the Far East. This name was also invented by people from Europe.

Sometimes the countries of northeastern Africa are thought of as part of the Middle East. In this unit we will study all the countries of North Africa—not just those in the northeast—as well as the countries of southwestern Asia.

All these lands and peoples have much in common. The region stretches from Morocco (mə räk′ ō) in the west to Iran in the east, and from Turkey in the north to the two Yemens on the southern part of the Arabian Peninsula.

The word *middle* describes these lands very well. The Middle East and North Africa are located in the middle of a great mass of land formed by the continents of Africa, Asia, and Europe. You can see this if you look at the map of the world in the Atlas on pages 454 and 455.

Dry, hot lands Most of the Middle East and North Africa is very dry. You can see how dry by looking at the rainfall map on page 25. Compare the rainfall of these lands with that of Europe. Which area, on the whole, gets more precipitation?

Most of the Middle East and North Africa gets less than 10 inches (25.4 cm) of rain a year. Lands that get this little rain are usually called **deserts.** Some of the world's driest deserts are in the Middle East and North Africa.

The world's largest desert, the Sahara, covers much of the land in the countries of North Africa. *Sahara* means "desert" in Arabic. Almost all of the Arabian Peninsula is a desert. Riyadh (rē (y) äd′), the capital of Saudi Arabia (sä üd′ e ə rā′ bē a), gets only about 3 (7.6 cm) inches of rain a year. In some parts of the deserts in the Middle East and North Africa there is no rain for years at a time.

People often think of deserts as lands covered with sand where no plants grow. Actually, only about 30 percent of the world's deserts are covered with sand. About 70 percent of the world's deserts are covered with rocks, stones, or gravel. Geographers call a sand desert erg.

An oasis in the Sahara in Algeria provides some water and a few trees in the largest desert in North Africa. Locate the Sahara on the map.

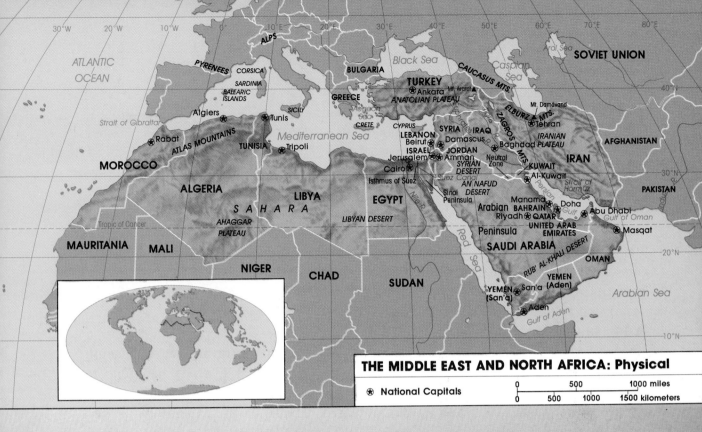

THE MIDDLE EAST AND NORTH AFRICA: Physical

⊛ National Capitals

0		500		1000 miles
0	500	1000		1500 kilometers

Map labels:

ATLANTIC OCEAN
SOVIET UNION
Aral Sea
Black Sea
Caspian Sea
ALPS
PYRENEES
CORSICA
SARDINIA
BALEARIC ISLANDS
SICILY
CRETE
CYPRUS
BULGARIA
GREECE
Aegean Sea
TURKEY
⊛ Ankara
Mt. Ararat ▲
ANATOLIAN PLATEAU
CAUCASUS MTS.
Mt. Damávand
ELBURZ MTS.
⊛ Tehran
IRANIAN PLATEAU
AFGHANISTAN
ZAGROS MTS.
SYRIA
Damascus ⊛
IRAQ
Baghdad ⊛
IRAN
PAKISTAN
Strait of Hormuz
Strait of Gibraltar
Algiers ⊛
⊛ Tunis
LEBANON
Beirut ⊛
ISRAEL
Jerusalem ⊛
Rabat ⊛
ATLAS MOUNTAINS
TUNISIA
Tripoli ⊛
JORDAN
⊛ Amman
SYRIAN DESERT
Neutral Zone
KUWAIT
Al-Kuwait ⊛
Mediterranean Sea
Cairo ⊛
Isthmus of Suez
Suez Canal
Sinai Peninsula
AN NAFUD DESERT
Manama ⊛
⊛ Doha
Abu Dhabi ⊛
Persian Gulf
MOROCCO
ALGERIA
LIBYA
EGYPT
Nile
SAHARA
LIBYAN DESERT
Arabian
BAHRAIN
Riyadh ⊛
QATAR
UNITED ARAB EMIRATES
Masqat ⊛
Gulf of Oman
Tropic of Cancer
AHAGGAR PLATEAU
Peninsula
SAUDI ARABIA
OMAN
MAURITANIA
MALI
NIGER
CHAD
SUDAN
Red Sea
RUB' AL-KHALI DESERT
YEMEN (San'a)
San'a ⊛
YEMEN (Aden)
⊛ Aden
Gulf of Aden
Arabian Sea

Only parts of the deserts in the Middle East and North Africa are covered with sand. There are large areas of sand in the Sahara, but they cover only about one fifth of the desert. Sand dunes cover about one third of the deserts on the Arabian Peninsula. Various plants grow in many parts of these deserts.

Daytime temperatures in the deserts of the Middle East and North Africa can get very hot—especially in the summer. Sometimes summer temperatures in the deserts on the Arabian Peninsula reach 120°F (49°C) in the shade. The dry desert air cools very fast after the sun goes down. Winter temperatures are much more pleasant in the daytime. Winter nights sometimes have temperatures below freezing.

No railroad has ever been built across the Sahara, but people have been crossing the desert for hundreds of years. Today the trip is made easily by airplane or more slowly by truck or jeep. Until modern times, the only way to make the long and difficult trip was by camel **caravan.** A caravan is a group of people traveling together. There were well-used routes that travelers knew well even if the trail was not easy to see. Today some traders still make the trip by caravan.

Crossing the Sahara   In 1850 a British explorer named James Richardson crossed the Sahara with a camel caravan. Richardson kept a **journal** describing what he saw. A journal is a daily record of something. A reader of Richardson's journal learns very quickly how much more there is in the Sahara besides sand dunes.

Camel caravans still cross the Sahara.

Richardson's caravan set out south from Tripoli in Libya. He had time to keep accurate records because camels travel about 2 or 3 miles (3–5 km) an hour. At first he saw land where people grew olives, figs, wheat, and barley. The land grew drier as the caravan moved inland. Richardson traveled through scattered grass and bush at the edge of the desert. There were few crops except "tiny fields of barley fed by irrigation from wells." The camels found less grass, so they fed on bushes.

The caravan usually camped in sandy **wadis** (wä′ dēz). A wadi is the bed of a stream that is dry most of the time. Only during a rare rain does water flow in the wadi. In the southwestern United States, such a dry streambed is called an arroyo (ə roi′ ō). By digging down into the bottom of a wadi, the travelers sometimes found underground water for themselves and their camels.

Here and there along the wadis Richardson saw small **oasis** settlements. These were green places in the desert where people grew a few crops in their small "garden-fields," which they irrigated from wells. Richardson wrote that the water was good but that "the surface of the land is covered with salt." The oases had many date trees, which attracted thousands and thousands of flies. Insects were some of the few creatures that could live in the desert.

The land changed to a high, stony plateau where the caravan journeyed for days. The days were hot, but the nights were cold. "One morning," Richardson wrote, "the desert was covered with a shining frost." Daytime temperatures rose higher than 110°F (43°C).

The caravan reached an area of sand dunes. Richardson wrote, "This is our first day of sand. I had almost forgotten that there was such a thing as sand in the desert." Here the trail seemed to disappear. But the camel drivers told him, "The trail is in our heads."

One night a hard 10-minute rain shower fell. Richardson remembered how much people back in England hated to get caught in a sudden shower. It was very different in the desert. Here people thought that a downpour was "a heaven-sent gift." Most of the Sahara gets less than 8 inches (20 cm) of rain a year. Many areas in this desert get less than 1 inch (2.5 cm).

Lands near the sea   The Middle East and North Africa is not only a place of dry lands and deserts, but also a region of lands near the sea. The countries of North Africa border the Mediterranean Sea. Many countries of southwestern Asia also border the Mediterranean. The coastal parts of these lands have a Mediterranean climate much like the climate of the countries of Western Europe that border the Mediterranean Sea.

A large catch of fish is hauled in along the coast of Oman. People in the Middle East and North Africa have long used the nearby seas for food and transportation.

The Red Sea, the Arabian Sea, and the Persian Gulf border the Arabian Peninsula. Iran lies between the Persian Gulf and the Caspian Sea. People in the Middle East and North Africa have fished and sailed for thousands of years because their lands are close to the sea.

Mountains and climate Although most of the Middle East and North Africa is hot and dry, there are places in this region that do get a fair amount of rain. These places are either mountainous or near mountains.

The Atlas Mountains stretch across three countries in North Africa—Morocco, Algeria (al jir′ ē ə), and Tunisia (tü nē′ zhē ə). During the winter moist winds from the Atlantic Ocean blow over these mountains. High altitudes are generally cooler than low altitudes and cool air does not hold as much moisture as warm air. As the warm, moist air from the Atlantic rises over the Atlas Moun-

tains, it cools. As the moist air cools, it drops rain and snow. People are able to ski in the Atlas Mountains, which serve as a wall between the coastal areas of northwestern Africa and the Sahara.

Mountains also make a difference in the climate of the lands at the eastern end of the Mediterranean. Hills and mountains in Israel (iz′ rē əl), Lebanon (leb′ ə nən), and Syria (sir′ ē ə) catch moisture dropped by westerly winds off the Mediterranean during the winter. The highest peaks in the mountains of Lebanon are covered with snow during most of the year. These snowy mountains are only about 25 miles (40 km) from Lebanon's Mediterranean coast, where oranges grow.

The southwestern part of the Arabian Peninsula also has mountains and rugged highlands. It is one part of the Arabian Peninsula that is not a desert. Two countries named Yemen (yem′ ən), are located here. San'a (sä na′), the capital of the Yemen Arab Republic, is 7,750 feet (2,362 m)

The Atlas Mountains stand like a wall in Morocco, separating the coast from the Sahara.

higher than the Red Sea, which is only about 100 miles (161 km) away. This is a half-mile (0.8 km) higher than Denver, Colorado, which boasts that it is the "mile high city." Moist summer winds blowing off the Indian Ocean bring rain to San'a and the Yemen highlands. Winters are usually dry and cool. Temperatures fall below freezing in this southern part of the Middle East.

Mountains also affect the climate of other countries in the Middle East. Most of Turkey is a peninsula called Anatolia (an ə tō′ lē ə). This peninsula is a rugged plateau with hills and mountains. The only level or gently sloping land lies along its coasts. The highest part of the plateau is in the east around Mount Ararat (ar′ ə rat).

The high Anatolian Plateau has a direct effect on Turkey's climate. The middle part of Anatolia is dry but not dry enough to be a desert. Winters on the northeastern part of Anatolia are as cold as winters in North Dakota. On the other hand, winters along Turkey's coast on the Aegean Sea are as mild as those in southern California.

Iran is another plateau country. The Zagros (zag′ rəs) Mountains run along the western edge of this plateau. These mountains separate Iran's highlands from the low plain of the Tigris and Euphrates rivers. Another mountain range, the Elburz (el burz′), forms a wall along the northern edge of the plateau. The highest and lowest parts of Iran are close together in the northern part of the country. The Elburz Mountains are close to the Caspian Sea. This sea is completely surrounded by land and is about 92 feet (28 m) *below* sea

This small village in Iran is in the highlands near the Zagros Mountains.

level (the levels of the world's oceans). The Caspian Sea is the largest inland body of water in the world. It is larger than all the Great Lakes put together. From the low shores of the Caspian you can see the snowy top of Mount Damāvand (dam′ ə vand), 18,386 feet (5,604 m) *above* sea level. Mount Damāvand is the highest mountain in Iran and in the Middle East.

Iran, like Turkey, has a variety of climates. Cities along the Persian Gulf are hot all year long. Tehran (tā ə ran′), the capital of Iran, is on the plateau. This city has hot summers and cool winters. Snow falls in Tehran in the winter.

Most of Iran is dry except for a narrow plain near the Caspian Sea. Winds off the sea drop heavy rains on the plain as they blow against and over the Elburz. Some parts of this plain get as much as 78 inches (198 cm) of rain a year. The desert southeast of Mount Damāvand gets less than 4 inches (10 cm) of rain a year.

253

A bather enjoys the warm waters of the Dead Sea while large pieces of solid salt formed from the water's high mineral content float around her.

The Dead Sea The Dead Sea is another inland sea like the Caspian, but the Dead Sea is much lower than the Caspian. It is nearly one fourth of a mile (395 m) below sea level.

The Dead Sea is located between Israel and Jordan (jord′ ən). Water from the Jordan River flows into the Dead Sea but no water flows out. Because this part of Jordan and Israel is so hot, the water in the Dead Sea **evaporates** (turns into water vapor in the air) about as fast as it comes in from the Jordan River.

As the water evaporates, salts and minerals are left behind in the sea. It is easy to float in water that is very salty. People float on their backs in the Dead Sea as if they were lying on a great big water bed. After floating in the Dead Sea, people must shower with fresh water to wash off the salty crust that has formed on their skin.

The Dead Sea is about seven times saltier than the oceans. If you evaporate a cup of Dead Sea water, you will have about one-fourth cup of salt left. The Dead Sea is so salty that fish cannot live in it. This is probably how the Dead Sea got its name.

Winters at the Dead Sea are warm. People come here to enjoy the desert sun in winter and to soak in the nearby hot mineral springs. Summers near the Dead Sea get very hot. Temperatures often reach 104°F (40°C) and can go as high as 124°F (51°C).

CHECKUP

1. How did the lands of southwestern Asia get the name Middle East?
2. Name and locate the major seas and deserts in the Middle East and North Africa.
3. How do mountains affect the climate in northwestern Africa, Lebanon, and the Yemen Arab Republic?
4. In what ways are the Caspian Sea and the Dead Sea alike?

Using the Land

VOCABULARY

groundwater	petroleum
qanat	asphalt
dromedary	renewable
Bactrian camel	resource
Bedouin	land bridge
nomad	

Skillful ways to farm dry lands   The Middle East and North Africa do not have much good farmland when compared to Europe and North America. Much of the level land in the Middle East and North Africa is too dry for farming. Much of the land that gets enough rain is too hilly or mountainous for farming. Yet the Middle East is where farming began thousands of years ago.

People first learned how to raise wheat and barley in the Middle East. Vegetables such as peas and onions were first raised in that part of the world. People in the Middle East were the first to raise melons and date palm trees. Most of the world's dates still come from the Middle East, and so do some of the world's best oranges and lemons.

It takes knowledge, skill, and hard work to grow crops in the dry lands of the Middle East. You have already learned how people in ancient Egypt and Mesopotamia irrigated their fields with river water. Today people in the Middle East still irrigate their fields with river water. The Nile River valley is a green strip of irrigated fields and gardens running through the desert. Irrigation ditches still carry water from the Tigris and Euphrates rivers over the plain once known as Mesopotamia where great cities flourished in ancient times.

Irrigation of crops is vital in the dry lands of the Middle East and North Africa.

Water from underground   There are not many large rivers in the Middle East and North Africa. Some rivers dry up in the dry seasons when water is most needed. In many places farmers get water from under the ground.

Not all the water that comes from rain or snow runs off in streams and rivers. Some of this water soaks into the ground and collects in layers of soil, sand, and rock. This water under the earth's surface is called **groundwater.** Wells are holes that are dug or drilled into the earth to get at this groundwater. Buckets or pumps bring the groundwater to the surface.

People in Iran invented a way to get groundwater 3,000 years ago. They dug wells and tunnels called **qanats** (kwän′ ats).

The builders of a *qanat* first dug a well into the groundwater layer of soil under the side of a hill. Workers then dug a tunnel from a field downhill from the well up to the bottom of the well. The workers dug uphill so that the water from the well would flow downhill through the tunnel. Every 50 feet or so, the workers dug a hole down to the tunnel from the surface. These holes provided air and a way to take out dirt and rock from the tunnel. Once the workers reached the well, the water began to flow downhill to the field.

There are thousands of *qanats* in Iran. Some are only a mile or two (1.6 to 3.2 km) long. Most are about 6 to 10 miles (10 to 16 km) long. One *qanat* carries underground water more than 18 miles (25 km). Altogether there are about 170,000 miles (273,530 km) of these tunnels.

Qanats in Iran are used to carry water from wells dug in hillsides down to land where there is not enough groundwater for wells.

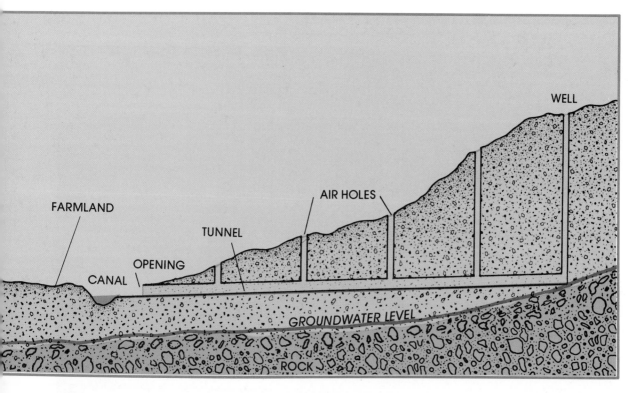

What seem to be lines of craters are actually the tops of air holes marking the paths of qanats in this aerial photo of a hillside in Iran.

A *qanat* needs no pumps because the water simply runs down through the tunnel. It saves water because little evaporates in the tunnel.

It took great skill and a lot of hard work to build a *qanat*. The people who built it had to measure both the direction and slope of the tunnel as they dug back toward the bottom of the well, or they might miss it. The workers had to move great amounts of dirt and rock to make the tunnel and air holes. They had to work in low tunnels that might cave in. All the dirt and rocks had to be lifted up through the air holes, one bucket at a time.

The *qanats* show how human brains and muscles made it possible to grow crops in dry lands. People still use *qanats*, but not many are being built today. Instead machines are used to drill deep wells. Powerful pumps bring the groundwater up to the earth's surface. This is another way that human skill and work make it possible to farm dry lands.

Cooling without air conditioners Most of the Middle East and North Africa has long, hot summers. Strong dry winds often blow during the summer months. Modern air conditioners can cool off a house or building in hot weather. But modern air conditioners cost a lot and use much electricity.

Long before air conditioners were invented, people in the Middle East and North Africa found ways to make their homes more comfortable during the summer. They made use of the oldest type of cooling—shade. They built the houses in their villages close together so that the shade from one house would cool the house next door during the early morning and late afternoon. People also planted trees and shrubs close to their houses. The trees and shrubs shaded house walls, and shaded walls meant cooler rooms.

People in the Middle East and North Africa found ways to make cooler buildings. They built their houses with thick walls, because thick walls help keep out heat. They painted these walls white because this color reflects the sun's rays and keeps a building cooler. They dug basements under their houses because basements are below the earth's surface and cooler than rooms above the surface. In some places people still live in basements during the hottest part of the year.

People in Iran built a type of wind tower as part of some houses. These towers use summer winds to help cool houses. The wind tower is something like a tall chimney. It has an opening on the top facing the direction from which the summer wind usually blows. There is another opening in the basement of the house. The opening at the top catches the wind, which then moves down the tower and comes out through the opening in the basement. The flow of air from the basement creates a breeze as it blows through the other rooms in the house. Sometimes a small water fountain is placed in the basement near the bottom opening of the wind tower. The air from the tower is made cooler as it blows over the water in the fountain before passing to the other rooms in the house.

Camels and the desert People have often joked about camels. The American writer Mark Twain made fun of them when he visited the Middle East more than a hundred years ago. He did not think the camel with its hump and long neck was a beautiful animal. He thought they had strange eating habits. "They are not particular about their diet," Twain wrote. "They would eat a tombstone if they could bite it."

Twain said that camels seemed to like to eat plants with sharp needles "that would pierce leather." For this reason, Twain supposed "it would be a real treat for a camel to have a keg of nails for supper."

The type of camel Mark Twain saw in the Middle East was a **dromedary** (drom′ ə der ē). A dromedary is a camel with one hump. Camels with two humps are called **Bactrian** (bak′ trē ən) **camels.** They are found mainly in Central Asia.

The funny-looking humps that Mark Twain joked about are actually very useful. A hump is a pile of fat under the skin. A camel stores energy from the food it eats in its hump. This stored energy makes it possible for a camel to go without food for days if necessary.

The houses in this village in Algiera were built close together so they can shade each other.

How can you tell these are dromedaries?

Camels can also go without water for long periods of time. A camel may drink 15 to 25 gallons (57 to 95 L) of water at one time, and then not drink again for several days or even a week. It is possible for a camel to go without drinking for up to 20 days if it can find food.

People in the Middle East have raised camels for a long time. Camels provide milk, meat, and hides for people of the Middle East, much as cattle do for people in other parts of the world. Special camel saddles were invented to fit over a dromedary's hump. With a saddle a camel can carry a rider or a load of goods weighing up to 500 pounds (227 kg).

Camels have been a major means of transportation in the Middle East and North Africa for a long time. Camels can cross deserts where other animals might die for lack of food and water. Even the desert sand does not stop camels because they have feet well suited for walking on sand. Mark Twain made fun of the camel's "flat, forked cushions of feet." He said they made tracks in the sand "like a pie with a slice cut out."

Mark Twain was joking, but he pointed out one of the good things about camels. Those large "cushions of feet" make it possible for camels to walk across sand without sinking into it as horses and mules do.

Groups of people called **Bedouins** (bed′ ü ins) have raised camels and depended on them for thousands of years. Bedouins are **nomads**—people who move about rather than have permanent homes. The Bedouins live in tents. They raise goats, camels, and sheep. They move about the deserts of North Africa and the Middle East in a never-ending search for water and pastures. Camels provide Bedouins with food, clothing, and transportation. Through their knowledge and skill, the Bedouins make use of the desert. There are not as many wandering Bedouins today as there were years ago. Many have settled down in villages and towns.

Much has changed in recent years in the Middle East and North Africa. Trucks and cars are taking the place of camels. More and more roads are replacing the old camel trails. Camels can live on desert plants and water. The trucks and cars need gasoline and oil.

An important gift of nature Oil is one of nature's gifts to the Middle East and North Africa. Most of the oil lies deep under the earth's surface in beds of sand and rock. However, in some places oil seeps out through cracks in rocks on the earth's surface. Many years ago people named this oil **petroleum** (pǝ trō′ lē ǝm), a Latin word that means "rock oil." We still use this name although we often simply call petroleum "oil" as if there were no other kinds of oil such as olive oil, corn oil, and whale oil.

When many people think of the Middle East, they also think of oil. You have already studied a chart on page 39 that explains why. The graph shows that the Middle East is very rich in oil. The lands around the Persian Gulf are a great source of oil. There is also much oil in some countries of North Africa. This oil has become very important to the people of the Middle East and to people living on other continents.

The ancient and modern story of oil The story of oil in the Middle East is a very old one. People in ancient Mesopotamia knew about the oil that seeped from rocks. Some of this oil mixed with sand and rock to form natural **asphalt.** This asphalt is much like the asphalt made today for paving roads and parking lots. The people of Mesopotamia used blocks of asphalt along with clay bricks to make buildings.

Some of the oil turned into tar—a thick, sticky material that the people of Mesopotamia spread on boats to stop leaks. They also burned oil in clay lamps, though it gave off a black smoke.

People of other lands learned about the oil and asphalt of the Middle East, but did not think it was very important. Strabo wrote about the way asphalt was used to make buildings in Babylon, a large city in Mesopotamia. He thought the use of asphalt was just a strange fact that might interest his readers.

About 1272 an Italian named Marco Polo visited Persia, the land we now call Iran. Marco Polo continued across Asia, traveling all the way to China. When he returned to Italy, he wrote a book about the things he had seen in Asia. He said that in Persia he saw "a fountain from which oil springs in great abundance." The oil was not like Italian or Greek olive oil. "It is not good to use with food," Marco Polo wrote, "but it is good to burn." He also said that "people come from vast distances to get it, for in all the countries around they have no other oil."

If Marco Polo were alive today, he could still write that people come "vast distances" to get oil from the Middle East. Huge tankers from Japan, the United States, and Western Europe now come for this oil. Nearly half of all the world's oil comes from the Middle East and North Africa. Study the diagram on page 261.

The first modern oil well in the Middle East was drilled in 1908 in Iran, which was still called Persia. Years later oil in that country was still considered news. A writer in 1922 reported that "Persia is looked on as a new petroleum-producing country of unusual importance."

Modern oil wells began producing oil in Iraq in 1928. The great oil deposits in the countries around the Persian Gulf were not discovered until the 1930s. By that

PETROLEUM: FROM CRUDE OIL TO CONSUMER PRODUCTS

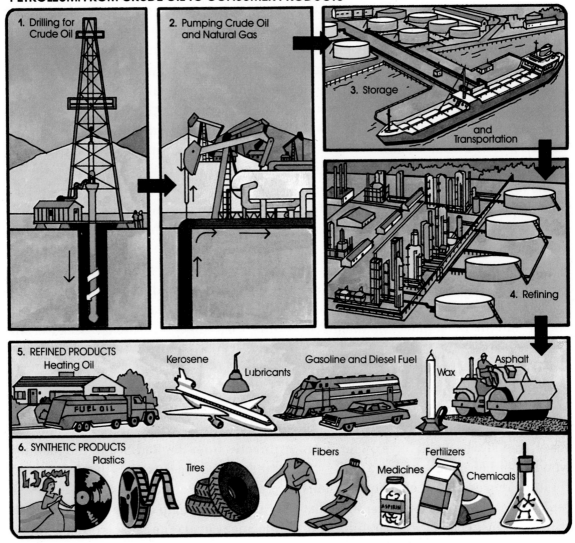

1. Drilling for Crude Oil
2. Pumping Crude Oil and Natural Gas
3. Storage and Transportation
4. Refining

5. REFINED PRODUCTS
Heating Oil
FUEL OIL
Kerosene
Lubricants
Gasoline and Diesel Fuel
Wax
Asphalt

6. SYNTHETIC PRODUCTS
Plastics
Tires
Fibers
Medicines
ASPIRIN
Fertilizers
Chemicals

Oil wells produce crude oil and natural gas. The gas is used for heating and other energy needs. Crude oil is made into fuel products and other consumer products.

time people were searching for oil throughout the whole area. Oil was later found in Saudi Arabia and in the North African countries of Algeria and Libya. In recent years oil has been discovered in Syria and in smaller countries along the Persian Gulf. These modern oil discoveries have brought great changes to the countries of the Middle East and North Africa. You will read more about these changes in another chapter.

A renewable resource that was not renewed   Forests are a **renewable resource.** This means that although trees in a forest are cut down, new trees may replace them. Unlike forests, oil is not a renewable resource. Once oil is pumped from the ground, more oil does not replace it.

The fact that forests are renewable does not mean that they have always been renewed. In general, people have used up

261

forests faster than they could be replaced. People have cut down far more trees than they have planted. Even when people have replanted forests, they have usually planted fast growing conifers in place of slow-growing deciduous trees. Fir and pine trees now grow where oak and walnut trees once stood.

Most of the forests that covered much of the Middle East and North Africa were used long ago. Nine tenths of these forests that were cut down in the Middle East and North Africa were never renewed.

The most important forests found in the Middle East and North Africa today are in the Atlas Mountains in northwestern Africa and in the Elburz Mountains in Iran.

The forests of Lebanon were famous in ancient times. Egyptians imported cedar wood from Lebanon to make coffins for the pharaohs. Solomon, a king of ancient Israel, traded wheat and olive oil for cedar wood from Lebanon.

Little remains of Lebanon's famous cedar forests today. Those cedar trees that still grow in Lebanon are carefully protected. The people of Lebanon are proud of their cedars. The flag of modern Lebanon has a cedar tree on it to remind people of this ancient renewable resource.

People used the forests because wood is such a useful material. It can be used for buildings, furniture, and tools. It makes a good fuel, and people burned it faster than it grew. They burned fully grown trees, small trees, and wild shrubs. Trees and shrubs grow slowly in dry lands. New growth could not keep up with the need for fuel.

To make matters worse, people raised sheep and goats on the land where trees and shrubs grew. In an earlier chapter you read how goats and sheep stripped the hills and mountains of Greece. These animals did the same thing in many places in the Middle East and North Africa. Wood, the renewable resource, too often had little chance to be renewed.

Where three continents meet   Trade routes between Africa, Asia, and Europe have crossed in the Middle East for thousands of years. At one time a road from China crossed Asia all the way to the Mediterranean Sea. The Romans called this road the "Silk Road" because silk from China came to Europe along this route.

Ships from East Africa, Southeast Asia, and India sailed to ports on the Persian Gulf and the Red Sea. Ships could not sail directly from the Red Sea to the Mediterranean Sea because of the Isthmus of Suez.

Look at the map on page 249 and locate the Suez Canal. The canal is on an isthmus, or a **land bridge** between Africa and Asia. A land bridge is a narrow piece of land that connects two larger pieces of land. The Isthmus of Suez separates the Red Sea from the Mediterranean and is 75 miles (121 km) wide.

The ancient Egyptians found a way to connect the Red Sea and the Mediterranean. They dug a canal between one branch of the Nile River and some saltwater lakes on the Isthmus of Suez. They then dug another canal between the lakes and the Red Sea. Ships from the Mediterranean could sail up the Nile, through the

A large freighter slowly makes its way through the Suez Canal in Egypt.

first canal to the salt lakes, then through the second canal to the Red Sea. This long, roundabout route never seems to have been too popular, and the canals were filled in during the Middle Ages.

It was not until 1854 that a man from France named Ferdinand de Lesseps (də lā seps') got Egypt's permission to build a canal across the Isthmus of Suez.

It took years to dig the Suez Canal. The first ships did not sail through it until 1869. When it was completed, a new all-water route connecting the Far East, Europe, and East Africa crossed through the Middle East.

In more recent years still other means of transportation have crossed this region where three continents meet. Today

pipelines carry oil more than 1,000 miles (1,609 km) from the Persian Gulf to the Mediterranean. Pipelines now cross deserts where once only camel caravans traveled. Canals and pipelines have changed the way goods are carried, but the Middle East is still a place where people and goods come together.

CHECKUP

1. How have people in the Middle East and North Africa made living in hot, dry lands more comfortable?
2. Why have camels been important in the Middle East and North Africa?
3. How was petroleum used in the Middle East during ancient times and in Marco Polo's time?
4. What kinds of travel routes have crossed the Middle East?

263

KEY FACTS

1. North Africa and the Middle East have a variety of climates although most of the region is quite dry.

2. The surfaces of the Caspian Sea and the Dead Sea are below sea level.

3. People have known about oil in the Middle East since ancient times, and the area is now a major oil-producing region.

4. With skill and knowledge, people can farm dry lands and live in hot climates.

5. Camels are well suited to survive in dry lands and are a useful means of transportation in the Middle East and North Africa.

6. Forests are a renewable resource, but most of the forests in the Middle East and North Africa were not renewed.

7. Important trade and travel routes cross the Middle East because it is located where three continents meet.

8. A Bedouin is an Egyptian sailor.

9. Asphalt forms in some places where oil seeps to the surface of the earth.

10. A nomad is a person who moves from place to place.

VOCABULARY QUIZ

Read the following statements. Decide which are true and which are false. Write your answers (**T** or **F**) on a sheet of paper.

1. Deserts are dry lands that usually get less than 10 inches (25.4 cm) of precipitation a year.

2. It is so hot near the Dead Sea that some water in it evaporates.

3. Petroleum is a renewable resource.

4. Water in a slowly moving river is known as groundwater.

5. A *qanat* is a person who digs irrigation ditches in Iran.

6. A dromedary is a camel with one hump.

7. A Bactrian camel is any camel used for carrying loads.

REVIEW QUESTIONS

1. Which seas touch the coasts of the Middle East and North Africa? Name an important desert in this region. What mountain ranges are found in the Middle East and North Africa?

2. Why does northwestern Africa receive more precipitation that the rest of North Africa?

3. Describe two ways people in the Middle East and North Africa get water for irrigation.

4. Why is the story of oil in the Middle East both ancient and modern?

5. Why were camels so useful in the Middle East and North Africa?

6. Why have trade and travel routes crossed in the Middle East?

ACTIVITIES

1. A tree usually adds a layer of growth every year. Each layer is called a tree ring. By counting the number of tree rings in a tree stump or a section of a tree trunk that has been cut, you can tell how many years it took that tree to grow. See if you can find a tree stump or part of a tree trunk that has been cut. Count the number of tree rings to find out how old the tree was.

2. Make a list of the ways we use petroleum. After you have made your list, look up *petroleum* in an encyclopedia to see if you can find still other ways petroleum is used.

12 / SKILLS DEVELOPMENT

USING PHYSICAL AND POLITICAL MAPS

PLACE GEOGRAPHY ON PHYSICAL AND POLITICAL MAPS

Each of the following exercises lists the maps you will need to find the information to answer the true and false statements that follow. Use a sheet of paper for your answers—**T** for true and **F** for false.

SKILLS PRACTICE: Part I

Use the map of the Middle East and North Africa on page 249 to find the answers to the first five statements.

1. Turkey has a coast on the Caspian Sea.
2. The Atlas Mountains lie north of the Sahara.
3. If you sailed from the Mediterranean Sea through the Suez Canal, you would reach the Dead Sea.
4. Syria has a coast on the Mediterranean.
5. Iran is a peninsula.

SKILLS PRACTICE: Part II

Use the Atlas maps of North America on pages 458 and 459 and the map of the Middle East and North Africa on page 249 to find the answers to the next set of statements. Use the lines of latitude on the maps to help you find the places mentioned in the statements.

1. Ankara, Turkey, is farther north than Washington, D.C., in the United States.
2. Riyadh, Saudi Arabia, is farther south than Mexico City, Mexico.
3. The northernmost coast of Africa is farther north than the southernmost coast of the United States.
4. Jerusalem, Israel, is as far south as Miami, Florida.

5. If you flew straight east from New Orleans, Louisiana, you would cross Morocco in North Africa.

SKILLS PRACTICE: Part III

Use the Atlas map of Eurasia on pages 466 and 467 and the map of the Middle East and North Africa on page 249 to help you with the following statements.

1. If you flew straight to the North Pole from Mecca, Saudi Arabia, you would pass over Finland.
2. The Middle East is west of India.
3. The Caspian Sea is northeast of the Red Sea.
4. Ankara, Turkey, is farther north than Tokyo, Japan.
5. Tehran, Iran, is farther north than Paris, France.

SKILLS PRACTICE: Part IV

Use the rainfall map on page 25 to help you with the following statements. In order to find the countries named, use the map of the Middle East and North Africa on page 249.

1. Western Europe gets more rainfall than most of the Middle East and North Africa.
2. Northwestern Africa gets more rainfall than northeastern Africa.
3. On the whole, the Arabian Peninsula gets less rain than Iran.
4. On the whole, Turkey gets more rain than the southeastern part of the United States.
5. The lands along the eastern coast of the Mediterranean Sea get more rain than the lands along the Persian Gulf.

The Birthplace of Three Religions

```
┌─VOCABULARY──────────────┐
│  ancestor        pilgrim        │
│  Torah           Allah          │
│  prophet         hegira         │
│  shrine          mosque         │
└──────────────────────────┘
```

Three religions and their holy books
The Middle East has long been a meeting place for people and ideas as well as a crossroads for trade. Three of the world's great religions began in the Middle East. These religions are Judaism, Christianity, and Islam. People who believe in these religions are called Jews, Christians, and Moslems. Judaism, Christianity, and Islam spread from the Middle East to all parts of the world. Today there are millions of Jews, Christians, and Moslems living all over the world.

Each of these religions has its own holy book. Jews call their holy book the Bible. The word *bible* comes from a Greek word meaning books. Christians also call their holy book the Bible, but it is not exactly the same as the Jewish Bible. Moslems call their holy book the Koran.

The Jewish Bible contains books of law, history, poetry, wise sayings, and other things. The Christian Bible has books from the Jewish Bible plus 27 other books. Christians call the books from the Jewish Bible the Old Testament. They call the other 27 books in the Christian Bible the New Testament.

The holy books of Judaism, Christianity, and Islam are very old. The most recent one, the Koran, was written over 1,300 years ago.

The Israelites and their law   The Jewish Bible tells the history of the Israelite (iz′ rē ə līt) people who lived in the Middle East a long time ago. These people believed that their **ancestor** Abraham came from Mesopotamia. An ancestor is a person from whom a family or a group of people descends.

The Jewish Bible also tells the history of a leader named Moses. He taught the Israelites that God had given them laws. One set of laws is called the Ten Commandments.

The laws are found in the first five books of the Jewish Bible. Jews call these books the **Torah** (tôr′ ə), a word that means *the law*. The Torah has been studied for hundreds of years. It is still studied today.

The kingdom of the Israelites   The Israelites conquered a land in the Middle East known as Canaan (kā′ nən). This is

Moslem pilgrims travel from all parts of the world to visit the Kaaba, the most sacred shrine in all of Islam. The Kaaba is in Mecca.

roughly the same land where the modern state of Israel is.

The Jewish Bible tells about the kings who ruled the Israelites. The books tell the story of David, a shepherd boy who became a great king. David increased the size of the kingdom. He captured the city of Jerusalem (jə rü′ sə ləm) and made it his capital. David wanted to build a temple at Jerusalem where the Israelites could worship. He never built the temple, but his son Solomon did.

The years when Solomon ruled are remembered as ancient Israel's time of greatness and glory. Solomon built the great temple at Jerusalem and also a fine palace. He traded with the rulers of other lands. People admired Solomon's wealth and said he was very wise. The Book of Proverbs in the Jewish Bible contains wise sayings believed to have come from Solomon. One of the sayings of this king who was both wealthy and wise is "How much better it is to get wisdom than gold."

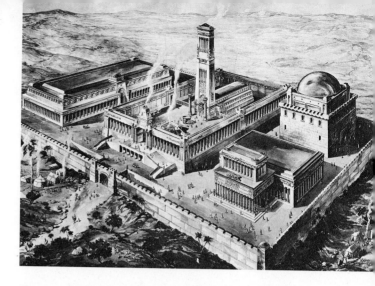

No one knows exactly what Solomon's temple looked like, but artists have created pictures of the temple based on what they have read about it. The original temple was destroyed ca. 586 B.C.

The roots of Christianity   Christianity today claims more followers than any other single religion in the world. Christians think of their religion as growing out of ancient Judaism. Jesus, the founder of Christianity, was a Jew. He was born in the land once ruled by David and Solomon. He knew the Jewish law and the writings of Judaism. He repeated them in his

This time line covers more than 3,000 years of history in the Middle East. How does the time line show that this part of the world was a land of conquerors?

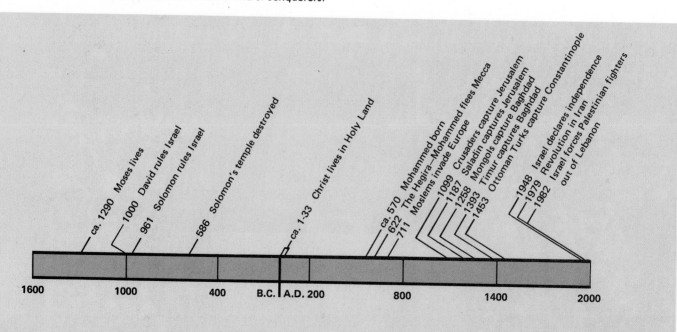

ca. 1290 Moses lives
1000 David rules Israel
961 Solomon rules Israel
586 Solomon's temple destroyed
ca. 1–33 Christ lives in Holy Land
ca. 570 Mohammed born
622 The Hegira—Mohammed flees Mecca
711 Moslems invade Europe
1099 Crusaders capture Jerusalem
1187 Saladin captures Jerusalem
1258 Mongols capture Baghdad
1393 Timur captures Baghdad
1453 Ottoman Turks capture Constantinople
1948 Israel declares independence
1979 Revolution in Iran
1982 Israel forces Palestinian fighters out of Lebanon

1600   1000   400   B.C. A.D. 200   800   1400   2000

own teachings. Much of the Christian Bible is the same as the Jewish Bible.

Who Jesus was Jesus lived when Rome ruled much of the Middle East. He was born during the time of the Roman emperor Augustus. As you learned in Chapter 2, much of the world today numbers years from the birth of Jesus.

Jesus wrote no books. Most of what we know about his life was written down by his followers. Four of the books in the New Testament tell about the life of Jesus. These books are called the Gospels.

The followers of Jesus called him a teacher, but he did not teach in a regular school. He taught in the streets, by the seashore, and on the mountainsides.

Jesus often spoke about the "Kingdom of Heaven." Some people thought that he planned to rebel against the Roman government and set up a new kingdom. These people had Jesus arrested and brought before the Roman official at Jerusalem. Jesus was tried, condemned, and put to death on a cross. The followers of Jesus believe that he rose from the dead 3 days later.

Paul and the spread of Christianity A man named Paul did much to spread the new religion. Paul was a Jew from the city of Tarsus (tär′ səs) in Asia Minor. As a young man, Paul studied the books of the Greeks. He also went to Jerusalem to study the law of his people. Paul was a scholar.

Paul believed that the teachings of Jesus were for all people. He traveled throughout Asia Minor and to the cities of Greece spreading the Christian message.

Paul wrote letters to groups of Christians throughout the Roman Empire. These letters are the oldest writings in the New Testament.

Paul was only one of the Christians who helped spread Christianity. This religion became very powerful. You have already learned that Christianity was the religion of both Western Europe and Eastern Europe during the Middle Ages.

Mohammed, the prophet of Islam Moslems believe there have been a number of **prophets,** persons who are believed to have a message from God. Moslems believe Moses and Jesus were two of these prophets. But to Moslems, the greatest and last of all the prophets was Mohammed (mù ham′ uhd).

Mohammed was born in the city of Mecca (mek′ ə) around A.D. 570. Mecca is on the western side of the Arabian Peninsula.

When Mohammed was 12, he joined a caravan as a camel driver. He traveled to places where there were Jews and Christians and he learned about their religions. Mohammed later became a merchant but his greatest interest was in religion.

The people of Arabia at that time believed in many gods and goddesses. People traveled to Mecca to worship these gods at a religious **shrine** known as the Kaaba (kä′ bə). A shrine is a place that is considered to be holy. Visitors to a shrine are called **pilgrims.** The journey of a pilgrim is called a pilgrimage. The Kaaba is a gray stone building. In Mohammed's day, the Kaaba contained images of gods and goddesses that the pilgrims came to worship. Mohammed thought that the worship of images in the Kaaba was not right.

Time-Life Books

This painting shows Mohammed riding to heaven on the back of Buraq, an imaginary animal with the head of a woman, the body of a donkey, and a peacock's tail. Mohammed's face is never seen in these old paintings. It is surrounded by fire.

Mohammed liked to pray alone. One day, he said, an angel spoke to him. He said the angel told him there was only one God, who had chosen Mohammed to be the last prophet. The Arabic word meaning "the God" is **Allah** (al′ ə).

Mohammed believed that he received messages from Allah. He taught these messages to his followers, who learned them by heart. These followers later wrote down the messages and gathered them into the Koran. This holy book of Islam also lays down laws for living. Some of these laws are like those in the Torah.

Mohammed called his religious teachings Islam, which means "surrender to God." A person who follows Islam is known as a Moslem, which means "one who has surrendered to God." The first belief of a Moslem is, "There is no God but Allah and Mohammed is His prophet."

Mohammed—the leader of the Arabs Mohammed told people in Mecca about his messages. Many of the city's leaders thought Mohammed was dangerous. Mohammed decided that he must seek a new home for his family and followers. In A.D. 622 he left Mecca to go live in Medina (mə dē′ nə), another city on the Arabian Peninsula. The trip from Mecca to Medina is called the **hegira** (hi jī′ rə). Moslems number their years from the hegira, that is, from the year A.D. 622 by the Christian calendar.

Mohammed became the leader of Medina. War broke out between Medina and Mecca. Mohammed led his people in battle and defeated his enemies from Mecca. When he entered his home city, he told the people of Mecca that they would not be harmed if they gave up their old religion.

270

Other cities and groups of people in the Arabian Peninsula later accepted Mohammed as their religious and political leader. Within 10 years after the hegira, he had brought almost all of Arabia under his rule. The one-time merchant from Mecca had become both the prophet and the ruler of the Arabs.

Mecca—the city of pilgrimage   Mohammed cleared the Kaaba of all the images of the old gods and goddesses, but the Kaaba remained a shrine. It became a place where people came to worship Allah. Mohammed taught his followers to turn toward the Kaaba and pray five times every day. Today there are more than 500 million Moslems all over the world. Every day millions of Moslems turn in the direction of the Kaaba when they pray. A Moslem place of worship is called a **mosque** (mosk). Mosques are always built to face the Kaaba in Mecca.

Mohammed also taught that all Moslems who could possibly do so should visit Mecca at least once. More than a million Moslems crowd into this desert city every year. Before entering the city, the pilgrims change to simple clothing so that rich and poor are dressed alike. They then go to the Great Mosque in Mecca built around the open space where the Kaaba stands.

CHECKUP

1. Who were Moses, David, and Solomon?
2. Why do Christians say that their religion grew out of ancient Judaism?
3. Which writings tell of the life of Jesus?
4. Who was Mohammed and how do we know about his teachings?

Conquests and Empires of the Past

VOCABULARY

caliph	sultan

Stories from the Middle East   The Jewish and Christian bibles and the Koran are three holy books that came from the Middle East. Other books have also come from the Middle East—books that have very little to do with religion.

Do you know the story of Aladdin and his magic lamp? Have you read about Ali Baba, who could open the door of a treasure cave with the magic words, "Open Sesame!"? Have you heard of a magic carpet that carried people through the air? Do you know about Sinbad the Sailor, who was shipwrecked seven times? If you know any of these stories, you know about another book that came from the

In the story of Ali Baba and the forty thieves, Ali Baba discovered the secret words that would open the way to a great treasure cave.

Middle East—a book called *Arabian Nights*. All the stories named above are in *Arabian Nights*.

Arabian Nights was written in Arabic during the Middle Ages. The book has many stories, all supposedly told by a princess named Scheherazade (shə her ə zäd′). But Scheherazade was not a real person. She was only one of the imaginary people in *Arabian Nights*.

The stories that Scheherazade told are all in *Arabian Nights*. These stories actually come from many parts of the world—from Persia, India, Egypt, Turkey, Greece, and other lands. The book shows that people not only traded goods in the Middle East, but also met and traded stories and ideas as well.

Lands of the Arabic language and alphabet   Arabic is the language of most people in the Middle East and North Africa today. The 28-letter Arabic alphabet is even more widely used.

You can see what written Arabic looks like by looking at the sample printed on this page. The lines read from right to left instead of from left to right as in our books.

Books printed in Arabic are not set up like our books. The *last* page in this book would be the *first* page in an Arabic book. It seems to us that an Arabic book goes from back to front, but an Arab would say the same thing about this book. It is simply a matter of how you look at it.

Why the Arabic language spread
The spread of Arabic was connected with the spread of Islam. Mohammed was an Arab and the Koran is in Arabic. As Islam

Arabic writing reads from right to left. Notice how the first sentence in the paragraph below the drawing is indented on the right. This picture is actually a page from a story about Columbus's three ships and his voyages to America.

spread throughout the Middle East, so did the language of Islam—Arabic.

After Mohammed's death, the Arab Moslems conquered a large empire. The map on page 274 shows the Arab conquests. The Arabs conquered lands on three sides of the Mediterranean Sea. They took the lands that are today divided into the countries of Syria, Lebanon, Israel, and Jordan. These lands are on the eastern side of the Mediterranean. Before the Arabs took these lands, they were ruled by the emperor at Constantinople. You will remember that Constantinople was the capital of all that was left of the old Roman Empire. Historians call this later empire the Byzantine (biz′ ən tēn) Empire. The Byzantine Empire lasted throughout the Middle Ages, but it grew smaller and smaller.

Arab armies swept across lands south of the Mediterranean. They conquered Egypt and North Africa as far west as the Atlantic Ocean. When one of the Arab leaders reached the shores of the Atlantic, he rode his horse into the water and shouted, "If my course were not stopped by this sea, I would still go on to the west."

The Moslems invaded Europe in 711. They conquered Spain and Portugal and crossed the Pyrenees Mountains into France. You read in Chapter 7 that Charles Martel defeated the Moslems at the Battle of Tours in 732. This was 100 years after the death of Mohammed.

The Arabs conquered Mesopotamia, which they called the land of Iraq. This is still the name of that country. They conquered Iran, which was then called Persia, and pushed into Central Asia. By 712 they had captured the main cities of Turkestan (tər kə stan′). If you look at the political map of Eurasia on pages 466 and 467, you will see that Turkestan is now part of the Soviet Union.

The Arab conquests spread the use of the Arabic language throughout the Middle East and North Africa. People in the conquered lands learned Arabic because it was the language of their rulers and the language of their rulers' religion—Islam.

The Arabs did not make people become Moslems, but they showed favor to those who did. Many people in the Middle East and North Africa became Moslems. They learned Arabic because it was the language of the Koran and the language used for daily prayers.

Many of the conquered peoples became Arabic-speaking people. They were Arabs in speech, but they had no Arab ancestors. When people write about the Arab countries today, they mean the Arabic-speaking countries.

There are today different kinds of spoken Arabic. A person from one Arab country may find it hard to understand a person from a different Arab country. The differences in written Arabic are not as great. The Koran is the same everywhere. Books and newspapers printed in one country can be read in others.

The rule of the caliphs   When Mohammed died in 632, his best friend, abu-Bakr (à bü′ bäk′ er), became the leader of the Moslems. Abu-Bakr was called the **caliph** (kā′ lif). The title means "one who comes after."

Abu-Bakr was the first in a long line of caliphs. The caliphs took the place of Mohammed as the leader of the Moslems, but they were not prophets, according to the teachings of Islam.

The first caliphs lived simply in Medina as Mohammed had done. They built no palaces. They lived in simple houses of sun-dried brick. They had no fine robes or jewels. Omar, the second caliph, wore only an old camel's-hair robe that he patched himself.

Later caliphs did not live so simply. The caliph Muawiya (mü ä′ wi yä) moved the capital to the rich city of Damascus (də mas′ kəs) in 661. Damascus was an old and rich trading city in Syria (sir′ ē ə). It was a city of fine palaces and many

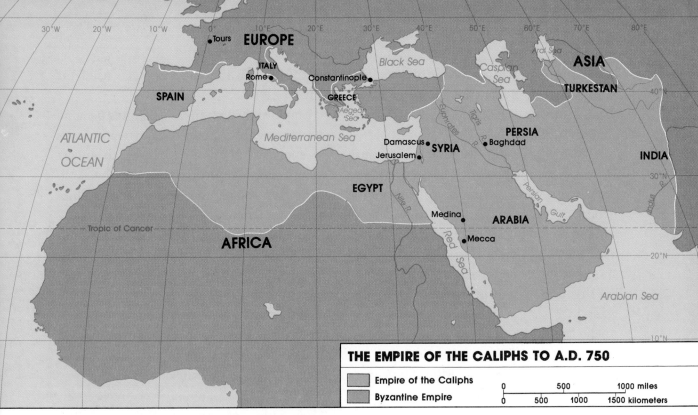

THE EMPIRE OF THE CALIPHS TO A.D. 750

▢	Empire of the Caliphs
▢	Byzantine Empire

0   500   1000 miles
0 500 1000 1500 kilometers

By the year 750, the power of Islam had spread as far east as India and as far west as the Atlantic Ocean. What European country was under the power of the caliphs?

shops. Damascus today is the capital of the modern country of Syria.

Muawiya lived more like a king than a simple Arab leader from the desert. Some Moslems did not accept him as caliph. They said that Mohammed's grandson was the true caliph. This quarrel continued for many years. It led to many wars among Moslems.

The winner in one of these wars moved the capital from Damascus to a new city he had built on the Tigris River in Iraq. The new capital was called Baghdad (bag' dad). It was a city built according to a plan. It was a round city. Three walls, one inside the other, protected Baghdad. Four main roads led from the palace to different parts of the empire. Canals were built to join the Tigris River with the Euphrates River, which ran west of the city.

Small boats brought goods into the city on the canals. The canals also supplied irrigation water for gardens within the city's great walls.

Many stories in *Arabian Nights* are about Baghdad. It was the richest and most lively city in the Middle East. Some of the stories tell about the caliph Harun al-Rashid (hä rün' äl rä shēd'), who went about the city in disguise. Harun al-Rashid was a good caliph who helped those who needed help and punished those who needed punishing.

These old stories are probably not true, but Harun al-Rashid was a real person. He was the caliph at Baghdad from 786 to 809. He may or may not have gone about the city in disguise. But the stories about him give a good picture of life in his rich capital.

The coming of the Seljuks   The empire ruled by the caliphs stretched into Central Asia. That land was the home of a number of Turkish tribes. Most of these tribes were nomads.

The caliphs found it difficult to hold their large empire together. The Turkish tribes had become Moslems, but that didn't stop them from attacking parts of the empire ruled by the caliphs. About the year 1037 a tribe of Turks known as the Seljuks (sėl jüks′) invaded Persia. These hard-riding nomads were tough and skillful fighters. The Seljuks later moved west and captured Baghdad.

The caliph was now under the power of the Seljuks. He said that their chief would be called **sultan** (sul′ tən), which means ruler.

A Seljuk leader named Alp-Arslan (älp ärs län′) became sultan in 1063. The Turks of later times remembered Alp-Arslan as a "strong and fair leader." He helped the poor and he punished dishonest officials.

Alp-Arslan and his army invaded Anatolia. Most of this land was still under the rule of the Byzantine emperor at Constantinople. Alp-Arslan's Turks defeated the Byzantine army. The Seljuks and other Turkish tribes moved into Anatolia. In time the peninsula became known as Turkey—the land of the Turks.

CHECKUP

1. How does *Arabian Nights* show that the Middle East was more than just a place where people met to trade goods?
2. Why did the Arabic language spread throughout the Middle East and North Africa?
3. Who were the caliphs?
4. Who were the Seljuks?

The Crusades

-VOCABULARY-
crusade	colony
Holy Land	

Call for a "war for the cross"   The Turkish invasion of the Middle East helped bring another invasion. This time the invasion came from Europe. The Byzantine ruler at Constantinople asked for help from Christians in Europe to fight the Moslem Turks. Thousands of people from Europe came to take part in a **crusade**— a "war for the cross."

Pope Urban (ur′ ban) II, head of the church at Rome, wanted a crusade. In 1095 he called upon the Christian knights of Europe to fight against the Moslems. Pope Urban said little about defending Constantinople. He wanted the Christians to conquer the **Holy Land**—that part of the Middle East where Jesus had lived.

The crowd that heard the Pope speak took up the cry, "It is the will of God! It is the will of God!" Thousands of men and women promised to join the crusade. They sewed crosses made of cloth on their clothes to show that they were crusaders—soldiers of the cross.

The People's Crusade   All sorts of people promised to go to the Holy Land. There were knights and feudal lords. There were people from towns and there were peasants.

The common people formed the People's Crusade. The members of the People's Crusade knew little about fighting a war. Few of the people on the crusade had weapons or had fought in battles. Yet the

Kings, nobles, knights, and ordinary foot soldiers all traveled many miles from Europe to the Holy Land to take part in the crusades.

people who went on the crusade left in high spirits.

The People's Crusade was not an army. It was a crowd of people led by a monk named Peter the Hermit and a man known as Walter the Penniless. The people on the crusade begged or stole their food as they traveled to the Middle East.

The First Crusade   It took the armies of knights a little longer to reach Constantinople. The first real army of crusaders did not arrive until 1097.

The crusaders crossed into Turkey and defeated a Turkish army. There were far more Moslems than crusaders, but the Moslems were divided. Alp-Arslan was dead, and there was no one who could take his place.

On July 15, 1099, the crusaders took Jerusalem. A priest named Fulcher (fül' cher) wrote about the taking of Jerusalem. Many people in the city were killed. "None of them were left alive," wrote Fulcher. "Neither women nor children were spared." At the time, the killings did not seem to bother Fulcher much. But later he wrote, "War is not beautiful. It is hateful to the innocent and horrible to see."

Europeans in the Middle East   The leaders of the crusade ruled the cities they conquered. They set up feudal states in the Middle East and ruled them like **colonies.** Colonies are lands ruled by people from a foreign place. Two colonies set up by the crusaders in the Middle East were the Kingdom of Jerusalem and the County of Edessa.

Some crusaders got rich from the crusade. Fulcher wrote that "Those who were poor in the west, God makes rich in this land. Those who had little money there have countless gold coins here, and those who did not have a house possess a city here."

The customs of the Middle East seemed strange to the people from Europe at first. But in time, they came to accept them and thought little about them. Some Europeans shaved their beards and dressed in clothes from the Middle East. They learned to like the foods they found in the Middle East, especially those with sugar and spices. Some crusaders learned to speak Arabic and some men from Europe married

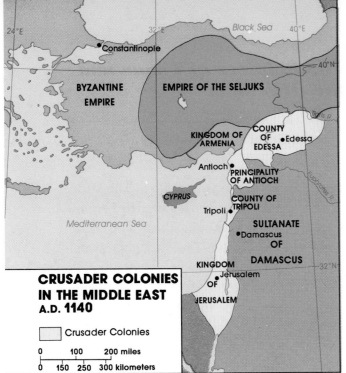

CRUSADER COLONIES IN THE MIDDLE EAST
A.D. 1140

☐ Crusader Colonies

```
0        100      200 miles
0    150    250   300 kilometers
```

The Crusader Colonies were set up near the Mediterranean Sea. These colonies were run much like the feudal fiefs in Europe.

women from the Middle East who had become Christians.

The Second and Third Crusades The crusaders from Europe found it hard to keep their colonies in the Middle East. The Seljuk Turks captured the County of Edessa in 1144. News of the loss set off a call for a new crusade. You have already learned about the Second Crusade (1147–1149) in Chapter 7. It was the crusade joined by King Louis VII of France and his lively wife, Eleanor of Aquitaine.

The Second Crusade did not help the European colonies in the Middle East very much. In the meantime, the Moslems became stronger. A new leader named Saladin (sal' a din) brought them together. In 1187 Saladin defeated a large force of Christians and captured Jerusalem.

The fall of Jerusalem caused the Europeans to send a Third Crusade (1189–1192).

Three kings led this crusade. They were Frederick I of Germany, Philip II of France, and Richard I of England. Richard was the son of Eleanor of Aquitaine. He was such a good fighter that people often called him Richard the Lion-Hearted.

There are many stories about Saladin and Richard the Lion-Hearted. Perhaps some of these stories are true. Each leader knew that the other was a brave and able soldier. Each could be generous to an enemy. Once Saladin saw Richard lose his horse in a battle. The Moslem leader sent the king other horses and a message. Saladin said that he did not like to see so fine a knight as Richard without a horse.

The crusaders won some battles, but they could not capture Jerusalem. Richard and Saladin finally agreed to make peace for 5 years. The Moslems kept Jerusalem, but Christians were allowed to visit the city.

Richard the Lion-Hearted and Saladin were both great warriors. This painting supposedly shows Richard (on white horse) and Saladin (behind Richard) battling each other.

Richard sailed away saying that he would return in 5 years to capture Jerusalem. Saladin supposedly said that if he ever did lose the city, he would rather lose it to Richard than to anyone else he knew. But the Moslem sultan and the Christian king never saw each other again. Saladin died soon after Richard left the Holy Land. King Richard had problems in Europe and never went on another crusade. Jerusalem remained a Moslem city.

The end of the crusades   There were still other crusades. One of the strangest was the Children's Crusade. Thousands of young boys and girls, led by a shepherd boy, set out for the Holy Land in 1212. Many of the young crusaders were 11 or 12 years old. Just what they had in mind is not clear. They could not fight a war. Most of them had no idea where Jerusalem was.

Groups of young people and children made their way to seaports in Europe. They seemed to think that someone would take them to the Holy Land. Slave merchants tricked them. They promised to carry the children to the Holy Land. Instead they took many children to slave markets in North Africa.

All of the crusader colonies were finally lost. The last one was taken by the Moslems in 1291. Many years later, European countries gained other colonies in the Middle East and North Africa.

CHECKUP

1. What was the purpose of the crusades?
2. What was the difference between the People's Crusade and the First Crusade?
3. What did the First Crusade do?
4. Who were Richard the Lion-Hearted and Saladin?

The Empires of Timur and the Ottomans

VOCABULARY	
magnificent	janissary

The coming of the Mongols   The Middle East continued to be invaded by people from Central Asia. Among those who came were the Mongols. The Mongols were another of the horse-riding nomad peoples. Between 1205 and 1227 the Mongols won an empire that included most of Asia and much of Eastern Europe. You will read about this Mongol empire in a later chapter.

The Mongols were cruel conquerors. They destroyed many cities and often killed all the people in any city they had to take by fighting. In one case they killed all the dogs and cats, too. A Mongol army captured Baghdad in 1258. The Mongols were not Moslems. They killed the caliph and thousands of other people.

The conquests of Timur the Lame   Timur (tē mür') was another warlike invader from Central Asia. He was the son of the chief of a Turkish tribe. Timur was wounded when he was a young man. That is why he is called Timur the Lame. Sometimes his name is written as Tamerlane (tam' ėr lān) or Tamburlane (tam' bėr lān).

Timur was a Moslem Turk, but he said he had Mongol ancestors. He had a goal in life. He wanted to become "ruler of the world." He failed to do so, but he did conquer a very large empire. It took in Central Asia, parts of India and Russia, and much of the Middle East.

This Persian painting shows Timur the Lame's soldiers attacking a stone fortress. Timur's soldiers were very fierce and greatly feared.

Timur was as terrible as the Mongols. A poet later called him "the terror of the world." The soldiers in Timur's armies were fierce and very cruel fighters. Their cruelty caused great fear and often served as a warning to other enemies.

Timur did not like to live in cities. He always felt most at home in a nomad's tent. Yet Timur wished to make his capital city of Samarkand (sam′ ər kand) in Central Asia the most beautiful city in the world. He sent many fine things from the cities his armies had captured back to Samarkand. He also sent captured artists and scholars to Sa-

markand. He wanted the artists to make beautiful things for Samarkand. He wanted the scholars to read the books and explain them to the people of Samarkand. The nomad who destroyed cities also built a fine city.

Timur once said, "Just as there is only one God in Heaven, so the earth can support only one king." We don't know if Timur really believed he could become the only king in the world, but he kept trying to take more and more land. He set out to conquer China when he was nearly 70 years old. This time death defeated him.

The empire Timur conquered did not last long after he died. People did not remember him as a ruler of the world. They mostly remembered him for the terrible way he fought wars.

The fall of Constantinople   The Ottoman Turks were another people who conquered Anatolia. The early Ottomans were Moslems. They had a spirit somewhat like that of the crusaders. They fought for religion. The Ottomans called themselves the "Swords of God."

In time the Ottomans took the place of the Seljuks as the rulers of Turkey. They also conquered much of southeastern Europe. By 1453 they had conquered every part of the Byzantine Empire except Constantinople itself. In that year Ottoman armies attacked the last bit of the old Roman Empire.

The stone walls of Constantinople had long protected the city. But the Ottomans attacked with a new type of weapon—the cannon. Neither castle nor city walls gave much protection against gunpowder and cannons.

279

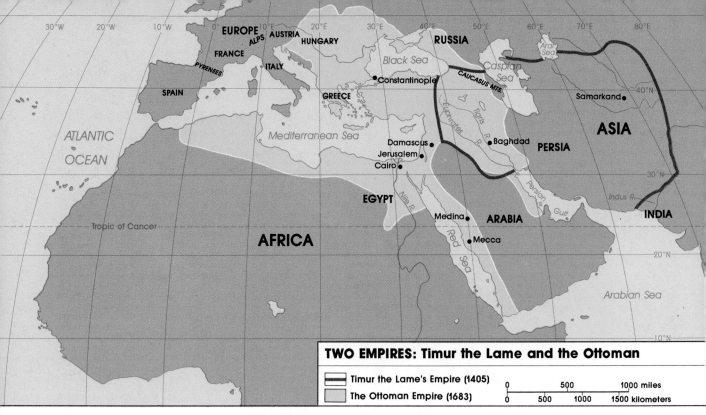

TWO EMPIRES: Timur the Lame and the Ottoman		
▬▬ Timur the Lame's Empire (1405)	0 500 1000 miles	
▨ The Ottoman Empire (1683)	0 500 1000 1500 kilometers	

Timur the Lame's empire stretched farther east than the Ottoman Empire did, but the Ottoman Empire took in parts of Europe and North Africa.

The Ottoman army had the largest cannon yet known. It shot a stone cannonball weighing 1,200 pounds (525 kg). The Ottoman attackers pounded Constantinople's stone walls with cannonballs. The walls were broken through in 54 days. Constantinople was taken. The last capital of the Roman Empire became the capital of the Ottoman sultans.

The most powerful Ottoman ruler Suleiman (sü lā man') I was the most powerful of the Ottoman rulers. He ruled from 1520 to 1566. People from Europe called him Suleiman the **Magnificent** (mag nif' ə sənt). *Magnificent* usually means great or grand, but as used here *magnificent* means rich and powerful. People from Europe did not call Suleiman

magnificent because they liked him. Most of them feared him. It seemed as if he would conquer Europe when he attacked the city of Vienna in Austria in 1529.

People from Europe called Suleiman magnificent because of the stories they heard about the way he lived. When Suleiman got up in the morning, high-ranking officials dressed him in fine robes. Every day his pockets were filled with gold and silver coins that he gave to people who pleased him. Those who displeased him might lose their lives.

Many servants brought the sultan his meals on costly dishes. He ate his meals from a low silver table. A doctor stood by to make sure nothing had been poisoned.

Suleiman slept on three red velvet mattresses covered with sheets made from

Suleiman the Magnificent ruled an empire with lands on three continents, Asia, Africa, and Europe. His capital was Constantinople.

fine cloth. His bedcovers in winter were the softest furs. Four guards kept watch as he slept, even though he changed bedrooms every night. The sultan who lived so well feared he would be killed while he slept.

Suleiman's favorite reading was *The Book of Alexander*. It was about the ancient Greek conqueror, Alexander the Great. Suleiman thought of himself as another Alexander. Like Alexander, Suleiman ruled an empire on three continents. It included southeastern Europe, all of the Middle East except Iran, and a large part of North Africa.

Training officials and soldiers The Ottoman rulers wanted well-trained officials and soldiers. They got them in a strange way. Every few years they sent government officials to the Christian villages within the empire. The officials looked for the smartest and strongest boys they could find between the ages of 10 and 14. They took these boys away to serve the sultan. They became the sultan's slaves. The Ottomans thought of this as a special type of tax.

The boys were put in Turkish homes for a few years. They were forced to become Moslems and to learn to speak Turkish. The slave boys were trained for special service to the sultan. Most of them became members of a special army knows as **janissaries** (jan′ ə ser ēz). Some rose to high rank as officers and received rich rewards. Those who did not become good soldiers were punished.

The very best slave boys were sent to a school in the palace. Here they studied with the sultan's sons under the best teachers. The boys who spent 10 or 12 years in the palace school became government officials. Some of these officials rose very high in the sultan's government. It was a strange system. The sultan's slaves became some of the most powerful people in the sultan's empire.

The end of the Ottoman Empire No other sultan ever had as much power as Suleiman the Magnificent. Later sultans could not control government officials who ruled in distant parts of the empire.

After 1830 European countries began to get colonies in parts of the empire. France, the United Kingdom, and Italy got control of most of North Africa.

Some of the people ruled by the Ottomans won their independence. Most of southeastern Europe was free by 1914 when World War I began. After the war, the Ottomans lost all their lands in the Middle East except Turkey itself.

The government of the sultan did not last much longer. In 1922 a group of army officers took over the government. The last of the Ottoman sultans slipped out of his palace early one morning. He made his way to a British ship and escaped to Western Europe.

CHECKUP

1. What was Timur's goal?
2. Who conquered Constantinople in 1453? What new kind of weapon helped the conquerors?
3. Why was Suleiman called "the Magnificent"?
4. How did the Ottomans train a special group of government officials and soldiers?

Works of Scholars and Artists

VOCABULARY

translate   observation

The House of Wisdom   The history of the Middle East is more than a history of wars and empires. Artists and scholars also played a part in the history of this region. In fact, the works of some scholars and artists from the Middle East lasted longer than the empires.

Some of the rulers in the Middle East gave help to scholars and artists. One ruler in Baghdad had the House of Wisdom built in 830. The House of Wisdom was a library and school where people could **translate** (trans lāt') books. To translate a book means to change it from one language to another. If you have read *Arabian Nights*, you have read a translation from Arabic to English. The people at the House of Wisdom translated books from Greek, Persian, and other languages into Arabic.

"Arabic" numerals from India   The scholars at Baghdad learned from books brought from India as well as Greece. They found out that people in India had a system of numerals more useful than the one used by the Greeks. You already know about this system because it is the one we use. The pages in this book are numbered with these numerals.

We call these numerals "Arabic," but the Arabs did not invent them. We call them Arabic because Europeans first learned about them from Arabic books. Arabic scholars called them Indian numerals.

Our way of writing the numerals is not exactly the same as the Arabic. But you can see how much the two ways of writing these numerals are alike by looking at the multiplication table on the next page.

The table reads from right to left and from top to bottom. Find number 1 in the upper right corner. To the left on the top line is 2 and next comes 3. To us the 2 and 3 look as if they were resting on their backs. The numerals 4, 5, 6, 7, and 8 do not look much like ours. But you can easily read 9. The 10 is simple, too, once you see that a point or a dot is used for 0.

If you take a few minutes to learn numerals 4 through 8, you will be able to translate this multiplication table.

Can you figure out what 3 × 3 is by using the table? Start at the right side of the top line. Count three spaces to your left. Now go down three spaces. What Arabic number do you find in the box? Using

١٠	٩	٨	٧	٦	٥	٤	٣	٢	١
٢٠	١٨	١٦	١٤	١٢	١٠	٨	٦	٤	٢
٣٠	٢٧	٢٤	٢١	١٨	١٥	١٢	٩	٦	٣
٤٠	٣٦	٣٢	٢٨	٢٤	٢٠	١٦	١٢	٨	٤
٥٠	٤٥	٤٠	٣٥	٣٠	٢٥	٢٠	١٥	١٠	٥
٦٠	٥٤	٤٨	٤٢	٣٦	٣٠	٢٤	١٨	١٢	٦
٧٠	٦٣	٥٦	٤٩	٤٢	٣٥	٢٨	٢١	١٤	٧
٨٠	٧٢	٦٤	٥٦	٤٨	٤٠	٣٢	٢٤	١٦	٨
٩٠	٨١	٧٢	٦٣	٥٤	٤٥	٣٦	٢٧	١٨	٩
١٠٠	٩٠	٨٠	٧٠	٦٠	٥٠	٤٠	٣٠	٢٠	١٠

This Arabic multiplication table is still used in some parts of the Middle East.

the same method, figure out the answers to 2 × 5; 10 × 3; and 7 × 8. Can you write the answers as they are written on the table? Can you write the present year using this form of Arabic numerals?

The study of diseases   Doctors in the Middle East read Greek and Indian books about diseases. They also learned about diseases by the **observation** (ob zer vā′ shən) of sick people. Observation means that they carefully watched how a disease acted on people who had it.

By observation a Persian doctor learned that measles and smallpox were two different diseases. He wrote the first book in the world describing these diseases. Another doctor observed the diseases of the eye and

In the Middle Ages, medical care in Arab lands was often considered better than medical care in Europe. Today, these modern Arab doctors work in a modern hospital in Saudi Arabia.

wrote about them. These books were translated into Latin and studied in Western Europe.

Arab doctors discovered medicines useful for treating diseases. They worked out better ways to sew up wounds. The crusaders found that the doctors in the Middle East were better than the doctors they had known at home.

Some of the cities in the Middle East had hospitals. Doctors learned about diseases by observing people in the hospitals just as doctors do today.

The art of beautiful handwriting
Have you ever thought of handwriting as an art like painting pictures? Moslems considered handwriting the greatest of the arts. It was the art used to make copies of the Koran, and Moslems believed that the Koran was the word of God. No art could be greater than one that spread God's word. The Koran praises those who "teach by the pen."

Reading the Koran is an important duty of every Moslem. Some older Korans were handwritten and decorated with beautiful designs.

284

Moslems also believed that copying the Koran was a religious act. It was like saying a prayer. They thought it was good to copy God's words.

One man made 42 copies of the Koran and kept them in a box. He copied the words of the Koran with great care, using inks of different colors. He made one copy entirely in gold. He did not make these copies of the Koran to show to other people. He asked that all 42 copies be buried with him when he died. It is good that not all such works of art were buried.

The Moslems developed many of the arts connected with bookmaking. Skilled artists bound the pages of books together between covers of soft leather. The artists often marked the covers with gold and silver.

Painters and carpet makers Some Moslems did not believe it was right to make pictures of living things. They would not paint or draw a picture of people, animals, or even plants. They made no statues and they had no pictures in their books. They did, however, fill the pages with colorful designs.

Not all Moslems thought the use of pictures was wrong. Persian and Turkish Moslems had pictures in books and in their homes. But they did not allow pictures or statues in their mosques.

Carpet makers in the Middle East made rugs with beautiful colors and designs. People used carpets in many ways. Carpets covered walls as well as floors in palaces and in the houses of rich people. Carpets were spread over floors of mosques. Moslems remove their shoes before entering a mosque. Even nomads like Timur had carpets in their tents.

This Persian prayer rug shows the detailed work for which carpet makers in the Middle East are famous. Many of these carpets have lasted for centuries.

The carpets are usually made of wool but some have silk in them, too. The threads are tied tightly together. A carpet maker may tie as many as 320 knots for each square inch (49 knots per sq cm) of carpet.

Carpets from the Middle East are used all over the world today. Perhaps you have seen some. They are beautiful and last a long time. The art of carpet making and the other arts that developed in the Middle East lasted longer than the empires did.

CHECKUP

1. What was the House of Wisdom?
2. Where did the numerals we use come from?
3. How did doctors in the Middle East learn about diseases?
4. How did the religious beliefs of Moslems affect their arts?

285

13 / CHAPTER REVIEW

KEY FACTS

1. Three of the world's major religions—Judaism, Christianity, and Islam—began in the Middle East.

2. Arab conquests spread Islam and the Arabic language throughout the Middle East and North Africa.

3. Christians from Western Europe invaded the Middle East during the crusades and set up colonies there.

4. Nomads from Central Asia conquered the Middle East from time to time.

5. The Ottoman Turks ruled southeastern Europe as well as much of the Middle East and North Africa.

6. Scholars in the Middle East passed on knowledge from three continents.

VOCABULARY QUIZ

Choose the correct word for each meaning. On a sheet of paper write the number of each meaning. Next to the number write the letter of the word that best fits the meaning.

1. Leader of the Moslems: (**a**) caliper (**b**) caliph (**c**) caloric

2. People who do not live in one place: (**a**) nomograms (**b**) nomads (**c**) nominees

3. Turkish leader: (**a**) sulky (**b**) sulpher (**c**) sultan

4. War for the cross: (**a**) crusade (**b**) crucible (**c**) cruiser

5. Land settled or ruled by foreigners (**a**) colonel (**b**) coliseum (**c**) colony

6. Great or grand: (**a**) magnetic (**b**) magnolia (**c**) magnificent

7. Special Turkish soldiers: (**a**) Januaries (**b**) janitorials (**c**) janissaries

8. To change from one language to another: (**a**) transplant (**b**) translate (**c**) transport

9. To watch carefully (**a**)observe (**b**) obscure (**c**) obtain

10. A Moslem place of worship: (**a**) mask (**b**) mosaic (**c**) mosque

REVIEW QUESTIONS

1. Why did Arabic become the language of most people in the Middle East and North Africa?

2. Who were the caliphs? What cities served as their capitals?

3. Who were the Seljuks and what did they do?

4. How were the People's Crusade and the Children's Crusade different from the other three crusades discussed in this chapter?

5. In what ways were Richard the Lion-Hearted and Saladin alike?

6. What did Timur want to do and how did he try to do it?

7. Who were the Ottomans? What important city did they capture in Turkey? Who was their most powerful ruler?

8. What method did the Ottomans use to get and train some of their important officials?

9. What did Middle Eastern scholars get from Greece? What did they get from India?

10. Why did Moslems think that handwriting was the greatest art?

ACTIVITIES

1. Read a story from *Arabian Nights* and make it into a play that you and your friends can act out in class.

2. Write the following years in the form of the Arabic numerals used on the multiplication table on page 283: 1492, 1776, 1865, 1900, 1932, the year you were born.

13/SKILLS DEVELOPMENT

USING HISTORICAL MAPS

PLACE GEOGRAPHY ON HISTORICAL MAPS

All maps show facts about places. Historical maps show facts about places at *particular times*. The map on page 274 shows facts about North Africa and the Middle East in the year 750. It gives the boundaries of the caliph's empire at that time.

Listed below are four sets of statements based on the historical maps in this chapter. Study the maps as directed and decide which statements are true and which are false. On a sheet of paper write the part number for each set of statements. Under the part number write the number of each statement and a **T** for true or **F** for false.

SKILLS PRACTICE: Part I

Study the map of the caliph's empire on page 274 to help you with the following.
1. Constantinople was within the caliph's empire.
2. The caliph's empire reached beyond 70°E and 40°N.
3. The caliph's empire was larger than the Byzantine Empire.
4. Mecca was closer to the center of the caliph's empire than Damascus was.
5. The caliph's empire took in all the lands around the Mediterranean Sea.

SKILLS PRACTICE: Part II

Study the map on page 280. This map shows the Middle East and North Africa at *two different times*. It shows Timur's empire in 1405 and the Ottoman Empire in 1683.

1. Timur's empire lay entirely in Asia.
2. The most southern part of the Ottoman Empire was in Europe.
3. Timur's empire reached farther east than the Ottoman Empire did.
4. Both empires included Constantinople.
5. The Ottoman Empire stretched from the Persian Gulf to the Atlantic Ocean.

SKILLS PRACTICE: Part III

Compare the historical maps on pages 274 and 280 to help you with the following.
1. The caliph's empire was larger than the Ottoman Empire.
2. The caliph's empire stretched farther west than the Ottoman Empire.
3. All four empires included Mecca.
4. All four empires included the mouth of the Nile River.
5. Samarkand was in Timur's empire.

SKILLS PRACTICE: Part IV

Compare the map of the crusader colonies on page 277 with the map of the Middle East and North Africa on page 249.
1. The crusaders conquered lands on the eastern shore of the Mediterranean Sea.
2. The crusaders conquered only a small part of the Middle East and North Africa.
3. The crusader colonies included part of what is now Lebanon.
4. The crusader colonies included part of what is now Iran.
5. The crusader colonies included part of what is now Syria.

How Revolutions Changed Turkey and Iran

---VOCABULARY---
concession	shah

A time of change Turkey was once part of the Ottoman Empire. During World War I, the Ottoman Empire fought on the side of Germany. As you read in Chapter 8, Germany was defeated in World War I. The Ottoman Empire was also defeated. It lost most of its lands, except Anatolia. The government became very weak and was overturned by a revolution led by army officers in 1922.

As you learned in Chapter 10, a revolution is a complete change in government, a way of life, or a way of thinking. The Turkish Revolution of 1922 destroyed what was left of the old Ottoman Empire and set up the new republic of Turkey.

The revolution was led by a Turkish army general named Mustafa Kemal (mùs tä fä' kə mäl'). Mustafa Kemal not only changed Turkey's government, but also tried to change the way people in Turkey lived and thought.

Mustafa Kemal wanted to make Turkey into a modern country. He wanted the people of Turkey to give up their old ways and to follow the ways of Western Europe. Compared to Turkey, most of the countries of Western Europe were rich and powerful. "Learn how to take from the West," Mustafa Kemal told his people.

You read in Chapter 5 that a republic is a "people's affair." When we think of a republic today, we usually think of a government of the people. But the people in Turkey did not have too much to say about how the new republic of Turkey would be run. The country was controlled by Mustafa Kemal and other army officers. Mustafa Kemal was elected president, but he was in fact a dictator—a person who has complete control over a country.

Mustafa Kemal's changes Mustafa Kemal made many changes in the way the people of Turkey lived. He wanted his people to be able to read and write so they could get new ideas. He thought that reading Turkish was hard because the language was written in the Arabic alphabet. Mustafa Kemal ordered that the Roman alphabet used in Western Europe also be used to write Turkish. All newspapers, books, and signs had to be printed in the Roman alphabet. People who could read the old Arabic letters had to learn how to read all over again.

At the time of the revolution, most people in Turkey did not have family names

Camels and oil storage tanks are common sights in the desert surrounding Dubai, one of the United Arab Emirates. What two bodies of water are near Dubai?

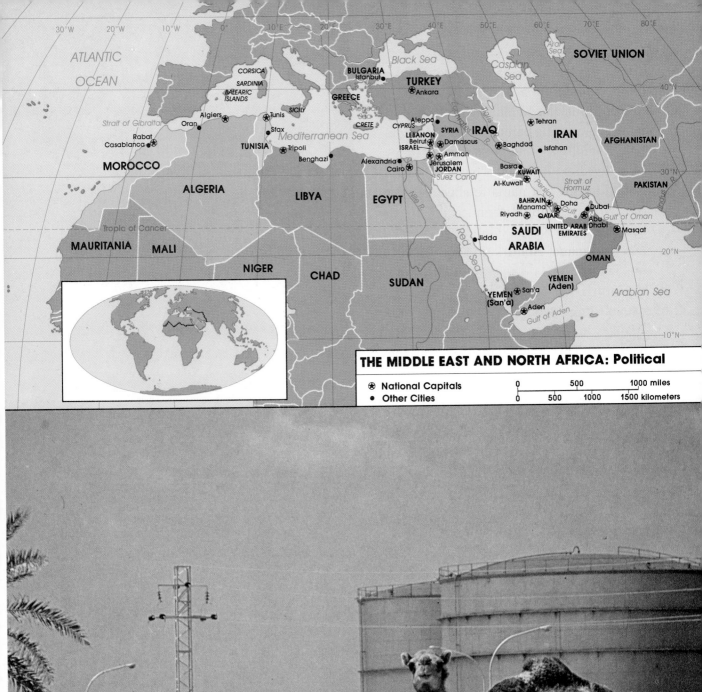

THE MIDDLE EAST AND NORTH AFRICA: Political

⊛ National Capitals
• Other Cities

0		500		1000 miles
0	500	1000		1500 kilometers

the way people in Western Europe did. A family name is a last name, such as Smith. Mustafa Kemal himself had no family name. His parents called him Mustafa. Kemal was a nickname given to him by a teacher. It means "exact." Mustafa Kemal took a last name to show his people what he wanted them to do. He became Mustafa Kemal Ataturk (ä tä turk′). His new name, Ataturk, means "father of the Turks."

Ataturk thought if people took last names they would also accept other changes in the way they lived. He wanted people in Turkey to change the way they dressed. He believed if they changed their way of dressing they would also change their way of thinking. Men in Turkey wore a small round hat called a *fez.* Ataturk ordered Turkish men to wear hats like those worn by men in Western Europe. The *fez* was banned. Women in Turkey wore veils to hide their faces. Ataturk said that veils could no longer be worn.

Ataturk wanted women to change more than the way they dressed. He said that in a modern nation men and women should be equal. Girls in Turkey had not gone to school in the past. Ataturk ordered them to do so. Women also got the right to take jobs in business and government. Women were given the right to vote. Their votes did not count for much, but neither did those of the men because the republic of Turkey was not run by the people.

Ataturk wanted his people to think of themselves as Turks rather than Moslems. The government made laws that limited the powers of religious leaders. It closed religious schools and opened

Mustafa Kemal Ataturk examines letters from the Roman alphabet written on a chalkboard in a park in Istanbul. Ataturk wanted the Roman alphabet used instead of Arabic.

schools run by the government. People were not allowed to read the Koran on the radio. Sunday was made the official day of rest in Turkey, not Friday as in other Moslem lands. Calls to prayer, made five times a day from mosques, had to be in Turkish, not Arabic.

Ataturk died in 1938. His followers ruled Turkey for a time. But changes took place after World War II. People in Turkey finally had choices when voting. Turkey became more of a government of the people.

Some of the changes Ataturk had made were not liked. Most Turks were Moslems and they wanted the government to support their religion. Schools began to teach religion. The government repaired old mosques and built new ones. Once again, calls to prayer were made in Arabic. Readings from the Koran were broadcast over the radio.

However, many of Ataturk's other changes were kept. Women did not go back to wearing veils. They still went to school, voted, and kept their jobs. Turks still use the Roman alphabet.

Turkey today   Modern Turkey is less than half as large as the old Ottoman Empire. But modern Turkey has many more people than the Ottoman Empire did. Turkey has a rapidly growing population. Many people still live in farm villages. Thousands of other people have left their villages and moved into Turkey's cities. Istanbul (is təm bül') is Turkey's largest city. This city was called Constantinople when it was the capital of the old

After the revolution led by Ataturk, the ancient city of Constantinople had its name changed to Istanbul.

Ottoman Empire. It had a million people before Ataturk's revolution. Today it has more than twice that many people and is larger than Ankara (ang' kə rə), the capital of modern Turkey.

Turkey is an agricultural country. The people of Turkey usually grow enough food to feed the country's population. Farmers also raise large crops of cotton and tobacco, two of Turkey's major exports.

Turkey's industries are expanding. Among these are food processing, textiles, and mining. Modern Turkey is the world's fourth largest producer of chromium (krō' mē əm). There is also much coal in Turkey. This coal is used in Turkey's growing steel industry.

One of Turkey's problems is that it does not have enough jobs for all its people. Many people from Turkey have taken jobs in Western Europe, where the people from Turkey are called "guest workers."

Europeans in Iran   Iran was known as Persia for many years. Persia once had a great empire. You read about the ancient Persian Empire in Chapter 4. Both Iran and Persia are old names, but Iran has been the official name of the country since 1935. The language of the people of Iran is still called Persian.

Iran was never a colony of a European country, but people from Europe did have **concessions** (kən sesh' ənz) in Iran. A concession is the right for a company from one country to carry on business in another country. Many times in the past, if a company from one country got a concession in another country, it was the *only* company allowed to carry on that business. No companies from other countries could get concessions in the same business.

Iran was ruled by a **shah** (shä). *Shah* is another word for king. The shah sold concessions as a way to make money. For example, one British company paid the shah for the right to open a bank in Iran. Another British company bought an oil concession. This gave the company the right to look for oil in Iran. If any oil were found, the shah was to receive some of the money made from the sale of the oil. Selling concessions made money for the shah, but put many businesses in Iran in the hands of people from other countries.

The British were not the only foreigners who had an interest in Iran. The Russians did, too. They had a fishing concession on the Caspian Sea and had also taken lands in Central Asia that had been part of Iran.

The British feared that the Russians might make Iran into a Russian colony. The Russians feared that the British might make Iran a British colony. Actually, neither made Iran into a colony, but both the Russians and the British sent troops into Iran during World War I.

The general who became shah   Iran was neutral in World War I, but the weak government of the shah could not stop the British and the Russians from sending troops into the country. It was this weakness that led to a revolution against the shah in 1921.

The revolution was led by an Iranian army general named Reza Khan (ri zä' kän). Reza Khan wanted to make his country into a modern nation, but he did not set up a republic. Instead he became the new shah. General Reza Khan was crowned Reza Shah in 1925.

Reza Shah made many changes in Iran, much like those made by Ataturk in Turkey. He built railroads and started modern industries. People had to wear Western dress and take family names. The shah took the name Pahlavi. Persian words replaced Arabic words in the written language. Like Ataturk, Reza Shah believed that the Moslem religion kept people from adopting new ideas. He set up government schools to take the place of religious schools.

Reza Shah hoped that if Iran became a modern country it would remain free of foreign control. But during World War II, the Soviet Union, Britain, and the United States sent troops into Iran. They said they did so to keep the Germans from taking over Iran.

Many Iranians who helped to overthrow the shah in 1979 supported religious leaders such as the Ayatollah Khomeini, pictured on this poster.

In 1941, Reza Shah's son, Mohammed Reza Pahlavi became the new ruler. He was friendly with the United States, so America provided Iran with arms and other aid. But many Iranians, particularly Moslem religious leaders, opposed the shah. In 1979, a revolution overthrew his government. A religious leader, Ayatollah Khomeini (ī yä tō′ lä kō mä′ nē), took control of the country. His government did away with many of the changes the shah had introduced.

Some Iranians thought the United States should be punished because it had supported the shah. In November, 1979, a group of Iranians took over the United States embassy in Tehran, the capital of Iran. The Americans in the embassy were held as prisoners for more than 14 months.

In the meantime, Iran became involved in a war with Iraq. Both countries claim control of the waterway through which the Tigris and Euphrates rivers flow into the Persian Gulf.

Iran today　　Iran is one of the largest countries in the Middle East and North Africa. It is larger than any country in Europe except the Soviet Union. You can compare the size of modern Iran with the old Persian Empire by looking at the maps on pages 83 and 289. Is modern Iran larger or smaller than the ancient Persian Empire?

Much of Iran is desert, but the country produced most of its own food before 1960. Wheat and rice are the main crops, but Iran is famous for its melons, nuts, and fruits.

Iran does not produce enough food to feed all of its own people today because

Although Iran has become rich from the sale of oil, life in some villages has not changed very much. Donkeys are still a common means of transportation.

the population of the country has grown so rapidly. The number of people in Iran doubled between 1950 and 1978. As the population grew, Iran imported more and more of its food.

Iran paid for food and other imports with money made from selling oil. Iran is one of the world's leading producers of oil. The government of Iran now owns the oil industry in the country.

Some of Iran's oil money was used to build schools, hospitals, and new industries. Much of the money was spent to build a modern army and air force.

Money made from selling oil made Iran richer, but many of its people remain poor. People in farm villages still live and work much as they have in the past. There was no real revolution in the village way of life.

Oil production at one of the world's largest oil refineries in Abadan, Iran, (top) fell drastically after the city was attacked (bottom) during the war between Iraq and Iran, which began in 1980.

Almost half of Iran's population now lives in cities and towns. Many of these people work in the country's oil industry. The people living in Iran's cities face all the problems of crowded city life. There is too much traffic and not enough housing. In becoming a modern nation, Iran got modern problems.

CHECKUP

1. What changes did Mustafa Kemal Ataturk make in Turkey?
2. How did Turkey change after Ataturk died?
3. How were the revolutions of Ataturk and Reza Khan similar? How were they different?
4. How did the oil industry affect life in Iran?

Conflict and Oil Bring Change in the Middle East

┌─VOCABULARY─────────────────┐
Knesset   private owner
Palestinian   emir
└────────────────────────────┘

The beginnings of modern Israel The modern country of Israel takes in much of the same land as the ancient kingdom of Israel. You read about ancient Israel in Chapter 13. After ancient Israel was destroyed, Jewish people settled in many parts of the world. But many of these people felt their homeland was the land once ruled by ancient Israel.

This land became known as Palestine (pal' ə stīn). Over the years, it was ruled by the Romans, the Arabs, and finally by the Ottoman Turks.

During World War I, some Arab leaders helped the British fight the Ottomans in Palestine. The British promised that the Ottoman Empire would be broken up after the war. The Arabs thought this meant they would rule themselves. But the British also promised support for "a national home for the Jewish people in Palestine." These promises to Arabs and Jews caused troubles after the war.

In 1919 most people in Palestine were Arabs. Less than 10 percent were Jews. In the following years, more and more Jews moved to Palestine. The number of Jews seeking new homes grew even more after Adolf Hitler came to power in Germany. You read about Adolf Hitler and the Jews in Chapter 8. Even more Jews came to Palestine after Germany was defeated in World War II. Many Arabs did not want so many Jews coming to Palestine. They did not see why people from Europe should crowd into this small part of the Middle East.

The British controlled Palestine from 1919 until 1948. In 1921, Jordan was created out of most of Palestine. In 1948, Israel was formed out of another part of Palestine. War broke out between Israel and the neighboring Arab countries. Israel won the war in 1949, but that did not end the struggle between Israel and its Arab neighbors. Three other Arab-Israeli wars followed—in 1956, 1967, and 1973—but Israel kept its independence.

Life in Israel   Not all the people in Israel are Jews. About 15 percent of the population is Arab. Both Arabic and Hebrew are official languages in Israel.

Israel is a democratic republic. There are a number of political parties. The people elect members of the **Knesset** (knes' et), which is somewhat like the British Parliament.

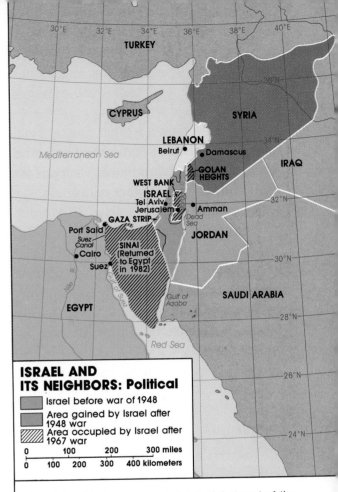

ISRAEL AND ITS NEIGHBORS: Political

- Israel before war of 1948
- Area gained by Israel after 1948 war
- Area occupied by Israel after 1967 war

| 0 | 100 | 200 | 300 miles |
| 0 | 100 | 200 | 300 | 400 kilometers |

The state of Israel was created out of that part of the Middle East once known as Palestine.

Jerusalem is a holy city to Jews, Christians, and Moslems. Before the 1967 war, Jerusalem was divided between Israel and Jordan. Israel has ruled the entire city since 1967.

Israel is a small country, and much of it is desert. The people of Israel proudly say that they have "made the desert bloom." By this they mean that they have turned much of the desert into farmland. Farmers in Israel have learned to grow crops that do best in Israel's soil and climate. Among these crops are oranges and lemons. Israel grows about three fourths of its own food and exports certain special crops. For example, Israel exports flowers to the United States.

Israel has no great deposits of minerals, but the country has done well with what it does have. The salty water of the Dead Sea has minerals in it. The people of

295

Israel have built a plant that evaporates the salty water and leaves the minerals behind.

Israel has factories that make such things as shoes, textiles, tires, and machinery. Israel also makes weapons for itself and for sale to other countries.

The people of Israel have had much help from the people of other countries. The early settlers received money from Jews in the United States and Europe. Israel continues to get help from Jewish groups outside of Israel and from friendly countries such as the United States.

Jordan   Israel's neighbor, Jordan, is mostly desert. As its name suggests, the country lies along the Jordan River. Part of Jordan actually lies on the western side of the river. This part of Jordan has been under Israel's control since the Arab-Israeli war of 1967.

Jordan was part of the Ottoman Empire before World War I. The British controlled the country after the war. Jordan got some control over its own affairs in 1928, but did not get complete independence until 1946. Jordan is now ruled by a king, but the people elect a parliament that has some power.

The official language of Jordan is Arabic. Over 90 percent of the people in Jordan are Moslems. The rest are mostly Christians. More than half of the people in Jordan live in small farming villages. Although mostly desert, Jordan is an agricultural country. Farmers raise crops of grapes, olives, and citrus fruits on irrigated plots of land mostly in the Jordan River valley. Jordan exports some of these crops and imports manufactured goods.

Many people in Jordan have moved into its cities and towns. The largest city in the country is the capital, Amman (a män').

Since the first Arab-Israeli war in 1948, Jordan has been the home of many Arabs who fled Palestine during the fighting. These people are often called **Palestinians** (pal ə stin' ē ənz). The king of Jordan has promised to give these Palestinians a homeland on the part of Jordan that is now occupied by Israel.

Syria   Syria is larger than Israel and Jordan put together. The Mediterranean Sea borders Syria on the west, and the country stretches as far east as the Tigris River. The eastern part of Syria is very important because it has rich deposits of oil.

Almost half of Syria's people live in small farming villages. Farming is important in Syria. Two major crops are cotton and wheat. Industries have been growing in Syria, especially textiles and oil refining. Syria's cities have been expanding and its capital, Damascus, has more than 1 million people.

France controlled Syria between World War I and World War II. Syria became an independent country in 1946. Officially, Syria is a republic, but one major political party controls the government. Syria is partly a Socialist country. Do you remember what Socialist means? If not, look back to the section on socialism in Chapter 10.

The government of Syria owns the country's large industries and some large farms. But most of the land in the country is owned by **private owners** and not controlled by the government.

Lebanon   About half the people in the Arab country of Lebanon are Christians and half are Moslems. Lebanon is an important trading country in the Middle East. It imports manufactured goods and oil. It exports agricultural products, especially citrus fruits.

France controlled Lebanon from the end of World War I until 1943 when it became an independent nation. The French built schools there, and many people spoke French. Students from other Arab countries came to study in Lebanon. European and American banks and businesses had offices in Beirut (bā rüt′), the capital city. Beirut was sometimes called "the Paris of the Middle East."

When Lebanon became independent, there were more Christians than Moslems in the country. But later the number of Moslems increased more rapidly. This was partly because many Moslem Palestinians came to Lebanon during the Arab-Israeli wars. A civil war between Moslem and Christian groups broke out in 1975, causing much destruction in Beirut. Other Arab countries sent troops into Lebanon to try to stop the fighting.

Other troubles also disturbed the peace of this small country. Some groups of Palestinians used Lebanon as a base for armed raids into Israel. In 1982 Israel invaded Lebanon and attacked villages and cities where the Palestinians had bases. Beirut was attacked, and more of "the Paris of the Middle East" was left in ruins. The Israelis stopped their attack only when the armed Palestinians agreed to leave Lebanon. The troubles in Lebanon threaten the future of all the Middle East.

Iraq   The word *Iraq* (i räk′) means "the well-rooted country." This suggests that the country has had a long history. The country is located in that part of the Middle East that was once known as Mesopotamia. You read about the early history of Mesopotamia in Chapter 3.

Beirut, Lebanon, (left) was one of the most beautiful cities in the Middle East until 1975, when civil war began in Lebanon and left much of Beirut in ruins. The picture on the right shows destruction left by Israel's attacks on Beirut in 1982.

The people of ancient Mesopotamia depended on the waters of the Tigris and Euphrates rivers to irrigate the crops they raised. Farmers in modern Iraq still depend on the waters from these rivers to irrigate their farm fields of wheat, beans, and vegetables.

Some of the fields in Iraq that once grew crops no longer do so. As irrigation water evaporates, it leaves behind salts and minerals in the soil. The amount of salt builds up from year to year if there are no heavy rains or floods to wash it away. Land that has been irrigated for many years sometimes gets too salty to grow crops.

Although almost half the people in Iraq still make their living from farming or herding, the country's most important industry is oil production. Oil wells are found in many different parts of Iraq. Oil from Iraq is shipped by pipeline to ports in Lebanon and sold to many countries in the world.

Iraq was under British control from after World War I until 1932, when it became an independent kingdom. In 1958 army officers revolted against Iraq's king and set up a republic. But real power in Iraq belongs to army officers, not the people.

Iraq's population has increased rapidly in recent years. The country had just under 3 million people in 1920. Today there are more than four times that many people living in Iraq. Baghdad, the capital of Iraq, is the country's largest city.

Saudi Arabia A reference book in 1929 reported that Arabia's exports were "of little importance." At that time, Arabia produced little that the rest of the world wanted. This situation changed in the next 50 years. Great amounts of oil were discovered under the deserts in Arabia. This oil became very valuable to the rest of the world. Japan, Western Europe, and the United States came to depend on oil from the Arabian Peninsula.

Saudi Arabia is the largest country on the Arabian Peninsula. It has been ruled by kings from the Saud (sä üd') family since 1925. That is why the country is known as Saudi Arabia. The Saudi kings have ruled the country very strictly according to the teachings of Islam. The people of Saudi Arabia do not elect a parliament. The king chooses government officials. Many of these officials are members of the royal family.

The money made from selling oil has made the government of Saudi Arabia very wealthy. Some of this money has been used to build highways, railroads, schools, and hospitals. Some money has been spent to build new industries, such as a glass-making plant and a steel-rolling mill. The Saudis do not want to depend only on oil for income in the future. For this reason, the Saudis have also bought land and businesses in Western Europe and in the United States.

Oil wealth has brought about changes in the way people live in Saudi Arabia. A growing number of people live in cities such as Riyadh, the capital. Oil has even changed life for the Bedouin nomadic herders living in Saudi Arabia. Some of the Bedouins now have jobs in the oil fields. Others still move about with their herds in search of pastures. Some of the money made from selling oil has been

Life is changing in Saudi Arabia. Riyadh, the capital, is a bustling city, and modern Bedouins may ride to the local well in pickup trucks instead of on camels.

used to dig deep wells that provide more water for Bedouin herds. The Bedouins now raise more sheep and goats than camels. The growing cities are good markets for cheese made from goat milk and meat from sheep. Many Bedouins now drive pickup trucks instead of riding camels.

Saudi Arabia has changed in many ways in a very short time. But Saudi leaders believe that their people do not want everything changed. One government official has said that new hospitals and industries are fine, but they can not take the place of mosques and religion. According to this official, "The price we will not pay for development is our religion." What do you think the official meant by this? How does this view differ from that of Ataturk?

Other lands on the Arabian Peninsula Saudi Arabia is not the only country on the Arabian Peninsula. There are also several other countries along the peninsula's coasts. Some of these are quite small, but they are important because most of them have oil.

Kuwait (kə wāt′) is a small country at the northern end of the Persian Gulf. It is one of the world's leading oil producers. Money from the selling of oil has made Kuwait very rich. It has one of the highest per capita incomes in the world. Much of Kuwait's riches has been spent on hospitals, schools, and roads.

A desert land, Kuwait gets very little rainfall. Providing enough fresh water for all its people has been one of the major problems facing this small country. In the past, boats brought water to Kuwait from Iraq's rivers. To get more fresh water, the government has built the world's largest plant for turning seawater into fresh water.

Bahrain (bä rān′) is a small island in the Persian Gulf. It has some oil. It also has a large oil refinery, which processes oil brought by underwater pipeline from Saudi Arabia.

The United Arab Emirates (ə mir′ its) are a group of seven small lands on the Persian Gulf. Each of these lands is ruled by an **emir** (ə mir′). *Emir* is an Arabic word that means "prince" or "chief." The land

Much of the world's oil supply is carried by tankers traveling through the narrow Strait of Hormuz located between Iran and Oman.

ruled by an emir is called an *emirate*. The United Arab Emirates are rich in oil. In order to sell this oil more easily, the seven emirates joined together to act as one government.

The small country of Qatar (kät′ ər) borders the United Arab Emirates on the northwest. At one time, Qatar was known for pearl fishing. Today oil brings in more wealth than pearls ever did.

The country of Oman (ō män′) is on the southeastern part of the Arabian Peninsula. Oman is a very hot desert country. The northernmost tip of Oman comes very close to southern Iran. A narrow waterway known as the Strait of Hormuz (hôr′ məz) connects the Persian Gulf and the Gulf of Oman here. At its narrowest point the strait is 24 miles (38.6 km) wide. Many tankers carrying oil to Western Europe and the United States pass through this narrow strait.

You read in Chapter 12 of two countries called *Yemen* on the southwestern edge of the Arabian Peninsula. The larger Yemen has a seacoast along the Gulf of Aden (äd′ ən). The official name of the country is the People's Democratic Republic of Yemen. The capital of this Yemen is the city of Aden, and the entire country is usually called Yemen (Aden).

The other Yemen has a seacoast along the Red Sea. You read about this Yemen in Chapter 12. Its capital is San′a, and the country is often called Yemen (San′a).

Yemen (San′a) gets enough rainfall to make farming an important industry in that country. Yemen (Aden) is much drier. It gets only about 3 inches (7.6 cm) of rain a year. Oil refining is the most important industry in Yemen (Aden).

CHECKUP

1. How was the modern country of Israel created?
2. Who are the Palestinians?
3. How has oil changed life in Saudi Arabia?
4. In addition to Saudi Arabia, what other countries are located on the Arabian Peninsula?

Egypt and North Africa

VOCABULARY

shelter belt	phosphate
oasis farming	Berber

Revolution in Egypt　After the Suez Canal was completed in 1869, the British and French took a great interest in Egyptian affairs. The British were especially interested in keeping the canal open for British ships. The canal provided the shortest water route between the United Kingdom and India. India was part of the British Empire. The British called the Suez Canal the "lifeline" of their empire.

Egypt was officially part of the Ottoman Empire until the beginning of World War I in 1914, but British troops stationed in Egypt protected the Suez Canal. The entire country came under British protection in World War I. Egypt got its independence in 1922. It became a kingdom with its own king, but British troops remained in the country to protect the canal.

The British remained in Egypt until a group of Egyptian army officers revolted against the Egyptian king in the early 1950s. The king was forced to leave the country. The British troops also left the country. Egypt became a republic in 1953, but real political power was in the hands of the army officers who led the revolution against the king.

Egypt today is a republic in which the president of the country has a great deal of power. The people elect a People's Assembly, but the president can sometimes rule the country on his own. The people of Egypt think of their country as one of the Arab nations. The official name of the country is the Arab Republic of Egypt. Egypt joined the other Arab nations in their wars with Israel.

Crowded land along the Nile　Egypt is not a small country, but most of its people live on only about 4 percent of the land. This land is along the Nile River valley and in the delta of the Nile River. People in ancient Egypt also crowded into the Nile River valley and delta where they raised crops on the rich soil. But there are at least ten times as many people living in these areas now.

The Nile River valley has rich soil. In ancient times farmers in the valley raised enough food to feed the people of Egypt. This is no longer true. Egypt today imports 40 percent of its food from other food-producing countries.

As Egypt's population grew, many people could not make a living farming the small amount of land that was good for farming. As a result, many people in Egypt have moved into the country's growing cities. Cairo (kī′ rō), the capital of Egypt, more than doubled its population between 1960 and 1980. Cairo is the largest city in North Africa and the Middle East. It is also one of the most crowded cities in the world.

The people of Egypt have tried to increase the amount of land used for farming. They have taken more water for irrigation from deep wells and from the Nile. But Egypt's growing cities and industries have taken over land used for farming about as fast as new land can be irrigated.

301

It is now against the law to put an industrial building on land that can be used for crops. The government of Egypt has begun to build new industrial cities in the desert. Deep wells are drilled to supply water for these new cities. Rows of trees have been planted near these cities to protect them from desert winds. These strips of trees are called **shelter belts.**

There is another type of farming carried on in the desert region of Egypt and the other countries of North Africa. This farming is called **oasis farming,** or oasis agriculture. An oasis is a place in a desert where groundwater comes to the surface of the land or can be reached by digging wells. Water at an oasis makes it possible for deep-rooted trees to grow and for some crops to be raised. People can live at an oasis and farm the land. There are many oases in the Sahara and other deserts in North Africa.

The Aswan dam   The people of Egypt built a large dam on the Nile River at Aswan (a swän') to help both industry and farming. The Nile River behind the Aswan dam forms a lake 300 miles (483 km) long.

The Nile River flows through Cairo, the capital of modern Egypt. Cairo is located at 30°N, 31°E and is the most populated city in Africa.

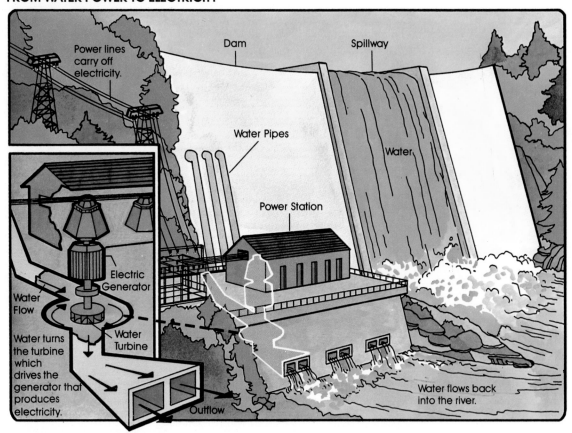

Part of the power station is drawn in detail at the left to show how electricity is made.

The lake provides irrigation water for new cropland. The dam also prevents the Nile from flooding the valley below the dam. In the past, floods covered the lowlands along the river below the dam during the summer months. Now that the river does not flood, farmers can plant an extra crop every year.

The high dam provides waterpower to make electricity. Electric power means more industries and jobs. The largest aluminum plant in the region uses electricity from the Aswan dam.

The Aswan dam has been good for Egypt in some ways, but it has also caused some problems. For centuries, the Nile floods had fertilized the land along the river. The Nile left rich silt on the fields after the water from the flood went down. Since there are no more floods, farmers must now buy fertilizers to take the place of the silt.

Water from the Nile is still used to irrigate lands used for farming. This irrigation water contains some minerals and salts. If the salts are not washed away, they build up and can ruin farmland. In the past, the yearly floods washed away the built-up salts. Now that there are no floods, the salts build up year after year.

The dam also affects fishing at the mouth of the Nile in the Mediterranean Sea. The floods carried plants and other materials on which the fish fed. Since

303

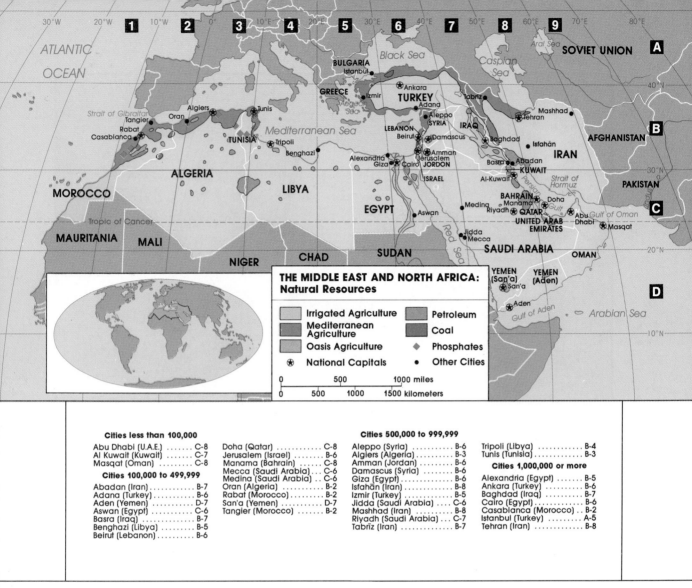

THE MIDDLE EAST AND NORTH AFRICA: Natural Resources

Legend:
- Irrigated Agriculture
- Mediterranean Agriculture
- Oasis Agriculture
- ⊛ National Capitals
- Petroleum
- Coal
- ◆ Phosphates
- • Other Cities

0   500   1000 miles
0   500   1000   1500 kilometers

Cities less than 100,000

Abu Dhabi (U.A.E.) C-8
Al Kuwait (Kuwait) C-7
Masqat (Oman) C-8

Cities 100,000 to 499,999

Abadan (Iran) B-7
Adana (Turkey) B-6
Aden (Yemen) D-7
Aswan (Egypt) C-6
Basra (Iraq) B-7
Benghazi (Libya) B-5
Beirut (Lebanon) B-6

Doha (Qatar) C-8
Jerusalem (Israel) B-6
Manama (Bahrain) C-8
Mecca (Saudi Arabia) ... C-6
Medina (Saudi Arabia) .. C-6
Oran (Algeria) B-2
Rabat (Morocco) B-2
San'a (Yemen) D-7
Tangier (Morocco) B-2

Cities 500,000 to 999,999

Aleppo (Syria) B-6
Algiers (Algeria) B-3
Amman (Jordan) B-6
Damascus (Syria) B-6
Giza (Egypt) B-6
Isfahān (Iran) B-8
Izmir (Turkey) B-5
Mashhad (Iran) B-8
Riyadh (Saudi Arabia) ... C-7
Tabrīz (Iran) B-7

Tripoli (Libya) B-4
Tunis (Tunisia) B-3

Cities 1,000,000 or more

Alexandria (Egypt) B-5
Ankara (Turkey) B-6
Baghdad (Iraq) B-7
Cairo (Egypt) B-6
Casablanca (Morocco) .. B-2
Istanbul (Turkey) A-5
Tehran (Iran) B-8

Oil is by far the most valuable natural resource in the Middle East and North Africa today. Near what body of water are most of the oil deposits in the Middle East found?

---

there are no more floods, there is less food for fish, and therefore there are fewer fish.

The building of the Aswan dam shows some of the difficulties in making changes. The dam made some things better and some things worse. The question is, were the gains greater than the losses? So far, people do not agree on the answer to this question.

Libya Like Egypt, Libya is mostly a desert land. But unlike Egypt, Libya has no great river like the Nile. As a result, most people in Libya live along the Mediterranean coast, which receives winter rains. Libya's two major cities, Tripoli (trip′ ə lē), the capital, and Benghazi (ben gäz′ ē), are on the coast.

Libya was an Italian colony before World War II. After the war, Libya became an independent nation with its own king. In 1969, officers in the Libyan army revolted against the king and set up a republic. The people of Libya today have little say in how the country is run. Real power is in the hands of the military.

Libya was a poor country when it became independent. The discovery of oil brought the country quick riches. Libya is now richer than the other countries of North Africa.

Tunisia Tunisia is on the northernmost part of the continent of Africa. The Atlas Mountains stretch into the northern part of the country and the Sahara covers the southern part.

Most people in Tunisia live in the north near the Mediterranean Sea. This part of Tunisia gets more rainfall than the rest of the country. Most of Tunisia's cities are in the northern part of the country, including the capital, Tunis.

The Soviet Union produces more oil than any other country in the world. However, the total production of oil by countries in the Middle East and North Africa is more than double that of the Soviet Union and almost three times as much as the oil produced by the United States.

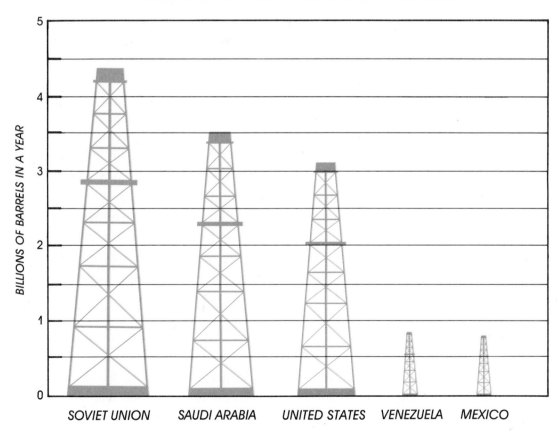

WORLD OIL PRODUCTION BY LEADING COUNTRIES

BILLIONS OF BARRELS IN A YEAR

SOVIET UNION   SAUDI ARABIA   UNITED STATES   VENEZUELA   MEXICO

Most of Tunisia's farms are also in the north. Tunisia is basically an agricultural country. Its farmers usually produce enough food to feed the country's population. The farmers raise wheat, barley, and citrus crops.

Tunisia has few mineral resources but it does mine and export **phosphates** (fos′ fāts). Phosphates are materials that are used to make fertilizers and detergents. Detergents are soaplike products used for cleaning. Tunisia also has some oil, but not as much as its neighbor Libya.

Tourism is a big business in Tunisia. The country makes as much money from its tourists as it does from oil. Thousands of visitors come from Europe to lie on Tunisia's sunny Mediterranean beaches and to visit the ruins of ancient cities. The sign at the Tunis-Carthage airport reminds travelers that they have come to a land that was important in ancient Roman history. Carthage was the city of Hannibal, the general who fought against Rome.

Arabic is the official language of Tunisia, but French is widely spoken. For 75 years, Tunisia was part of the French empire. Tunisia won its independence in 1956.

Tunisia is a republic, but voters have little choice in Tunisia's elections. There is only one political party and Tunisia's first president has been made president for life.

Algeria   Most people in Algeria live in the northern part of the country along the Mediterranean coast. This part of Algeria has a climate much like Greece, southern Italy, and the eastern coast of Spain. Crops grow well in this part of Algeria. Farmers raise oranges, lemons, and olives. Grapes are also raised, and Algeria is one of the major wine producers in the world.

The French conquered Algeria in the 1830s. For many years, the French said that Algeria was part of "Greater France." People from France and other parts of Europe settled in Algeria but never made up more than 11 percent of the population. Many settlers from France lived in Algiers, which looked much like a city in southern France. Today, Algiers is the capital of Algeria.

Most Algerians did not feel that Algeria was part of France. One Algerian put it this way: "Islam is my religion. Arabic is my language. Algeria is my country."

A civil war broke out in 1954 in Algeria between those people who wanted to keep the area under French rule and those who wanted it to be independent. After 8 years of fighting, the government of France asked the people of Algeria to vote on Algeria's future. The people decided that Algeria should be a separate, independent republic.

Freedom from France did not mean freedom for all the people of Algeria. One political party chooses who will run for office. The government controls what is printed and broadcast.

The Sahara covers much of southern Algeria. Oil and natural gas have been discovered beneath the surface of the desert. Algeria exports both oil and natural gas to many countries. The United States is one of Algeria's best customers.

Algeria's population is growing rapidly, even more rapidly than that of Egypt.

RECOGNIZING GENERAL AND SPECIFIC STATEMENTS

GENERAL STATEMENTS SAY THINGS ABOUT GROUPS

The following sentence is a general statement: *The countries of the Arabian Peninsula are desert countries.* It is called a **general statement** because it says something about the countries in general—as a group. It is a **true** general statement because what it says about the countries is true. Some general statements are not true. For instance: *The countries of the Arabian Peninsula are arctic countries.* This is a **false** general statement. None of the countries of the Arabian Peninsula are arctic countries.

SOME STATEMENTS ARE NOT GENERAL

Some statements are true about most members of a group, but not all. These statements are not general statements. They are specific statements. They say things about parts of groups or about individual cases. For example: *Islam is the main religion in the Middle Eastern lands.* This statement is not true of the whole group because it is not true of Israel, which is one of the Middle Eastern lands. We say that Israel is an **exception** to this statement, which makes it a specific statement. An exception is anything that differs from the other members of the group.

SKILLS PRACTICE

Listed below are a number of statements about the Middle East and North Africa.

Some are true general statements.

Some are true statements but not general statements. (For example: Ankara is the capital of Turkey. This is a true statement, but it is not a general statement.)

Some of the statements are general statements but they are not true.

Read each statement and on a sheet of paper write if the statement is:

TG—True General Statement
FG—False General Statement
NG—Not a General Statement

All of the statements are about the Middle East and North Africa.

1. Governments never change.
2. Mustafa Kemal led a revolution in Turkey.
3. Revolutions were led by army officers.
4. Populations have grown rapidly.
5. Turkey adopted the Roman alphabet.
6. People crowded into cities.
7. Ways of living never change in desert countries.
8. Oman is on the Arabian Peninsula.
9. Cairo is the largest city in the Middle East.
10. The Arab lands were once part of the Ottoman Empire.

5/UNIT REVIEW

1. The Middle East and North Africa are in the middle of a great land-mass formed by the continents of Asia, Africa, and Europe. — *Why does the name* Middle East *suggest a European view of the world? Look up the words* oriental *and* occidental. *How do these words also reflect a European view of the world?*

2. Much of the Middle East and North Africa is desert, but some mountainous areas receive plentiful rainfall. — *Name two deserts in the Middle East and North Africa. Name two mountainous areas that receive plentiful rainfall.*

3. The people in the Middle East and North Africa have developed ways to make life more comfortable in hot lands and ways to farm dry lands. — *What are some of the ways people in the Middle East and North Africa have made life in hot lands more comfortable? What are some of the things they have done to farm dry land?*

4. Oil is one of nature's gifts to the Middle East and North Africa. — *Name five countries in the Middle East and North Africa that have important amounts of oil.*

5. The spread of Islam also spread the use of the Arabic language and alphabet throughout the Middle East and North Africa. — *What is the connection between Islam and Arabic?*

6. The Middle East was invaded by Christian crusaders from Europe during the Middle Ages. — *Why did Europeans fight "wars for the cross"? Were the wars successful?*

7. Much of the Middle East and North Africa was invaded by peoples from Central Asia. — *Name three empires that were set up in this region.*

8. The countries of the Middle East and North Africa have become independent nations since World War I. — *Name 18 independent countries in this region.*

9. Many revolutions in the Middle East and North Africa were led by army officers. — *What kinds of changes did these revolutions bring about?*

10. Oil has brought great changes to the Middle East and North Africa. — *Give some examples of the changes that have come about in the Middle East and North Africa because of the oil industry in this region.*

Africa South of the Sahara

The Land and Climate

VOCABULARY

traditional	vegetation
rural	savanna
urban	expedition

Land of contrasts   Africa is a continent of great contrasts. There are many different ways of life, old and new. Large modern cities and **traditional** villages can be found only a few miles apart. "Traditional" means having things the way they have been for years and years. Almost every country in Africa has modern factories as well as very old ways of doing things. Most farming is done in traditional ways with hoes and other hand tools. In some places, plows are drawn by horses, water buffalo, or other animals. Some of the countries also have some very modern farms.

Throughout Africa's history, most people have lived in **rural** areas. A rural area is the countryside, away from the cities. Cities are **urban** areas. Today, eight out of ten people are in rural Africa, where they live mostly by farming and herding. But some groups of Africans have lived in cities for hundreds of years. These people have been merchants and traders. Today, Africa's old and new cities are growing very quickly.

Contrasts in the land and climate of Africa are also great. There are rain forests and grasslands where people farm and herd. There are desert areas where no people at all live. You have already read about the Mediterranean coastlands and deserts of North Africa.

In this unit, you will learn about Africa from the great Sahara south to Cape Agulhas (ə gəl′ əs) and the Cape of Good Hope. The western shore of the African continent is along the Atlantic Ocean. Africa's eastern coastline is the Indian Ocean. The southernmost tip of Africa is Cape Agulhas, where these two oceans meet. This chapter is about the land and some of the peoples who have lived between and along these shores.

A continent divided by a desert   The world's largest desert—the Sahara—stretches across northern Africa. This desert, which is nearly as large as the United States, reaches from the Atlantic Ocean to the Red Sea. The Sahara separates the coastlands of North Africa from the rest of the continent.

Before modern times, people crossed the great Sahara by camel caravan. You will remember from Chapter 12 that James Richardson was one such traveler who journeyed from North Africa south

The picture on the next page is a view looking south to the Cape of Good Hope and the Atlantic Ocean. Find this cape at 34°S, 18°E on the map at the right.

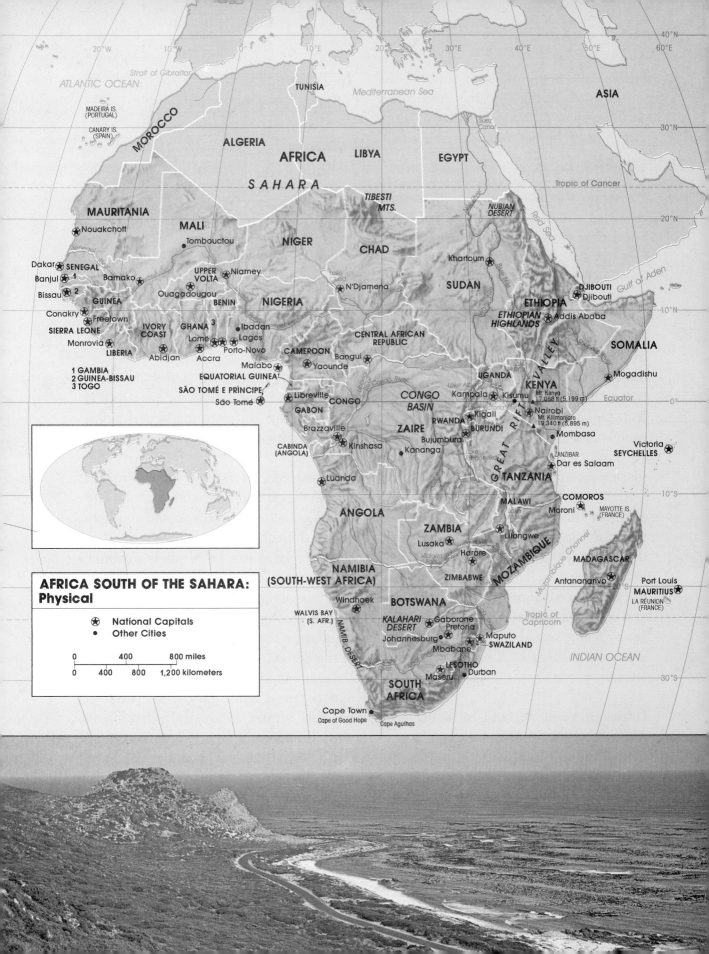

ATLANTIC OCEAN

Strait of Gibraltar

MADEIRA IS.
(PORTUGAL)

CANARY IS.
(SPAIN)

Mediterranean Sea

TUNISIA

MOROCCO

ALGERIA

AFRICA

LIBYA

EGYPT

Suez Canal

ASIA

SAHARA

Tropic of Cancer

MAURITANIA

MALI

NIGER

TIBESTI MTS.

CHAD

NUBIAN DESERT

Red Sea

Nouakchott

• Tombouctou

Senegal

Dakar • SENEGAL

Banjul 1

Bissau 2

UPPER VOLTA

Niamey

Lake Chad

Khartoum

SUDAN

DJIBOUTI

Gulf of Aden

Djibouti

GUINEA

Bamako •

Ouagadougou

BENIN

• N'Djamena

ETHIOPIA

Conakry •

• Freetown

SIERRA LEONE

IVORY COAST

GHANA 3

Lomé

Ibadan •

Lagos •

NIGERIA

CENTRAL AFRICAN REPUBLIC

ETHIOPIAN HIGHLANDS

• Addis Ababa

Monrovia

LIBERIA

Abidjan

Accra

Porto-Novo

CAMEROON

Bangui

SOMALIA

1 GAMBIA
2 GUINEA-BISSAU
3 TOGO

Malabo

EQUATORIAL GUINEA

SÃO TOMÉ E PRÍNCIPE

• Yaounde

UGANDA

Lake Albert

KENYA

Mt. Kenya 17,058 ft (5,199 m)

• Mogadishu

São Tomé

Libreville

CONGO

GABON

CONGO BASIN

Congo River

Lake Victoria

Kampala •

Kisumu •

Nairobi

Mt. Kilimanjaro 19,340 ft (5,895 m)

Equator

Brazzaville

ZAIRE

RWANDA

Kigali

BURUNDI

Bujumbura

Mombasa

Kinshasa

Kananga •

Lake Tanganyika

GREAT RIFT VALLEY

ZANZIBAR

• Dar es Salaam

Victoria

SEYCHELLES

CABINDA (ANGOLA)

• Luanda

TANZANIA

ANGOLA

MALAWI

Lake Malawi

COMOROS

Moroni

MAYOTTE IS. (FRANCE)

ZAMBIA

Lilongwe

Lusaka •

Zambezi River

Victoria Falls

Harare •

MOZAMBIQUE

MADAGASCAR

Antananarivo

Port Louis

MAURITIUS

LA RÉUNION (FRANCE)

NAMIBIA
(SOUTH-WEST AFRICA)

ZIMBABWE

Mozambique Channel

Windhoek

BOTSWANA

Tropic of Capricorn

WALVIS BAY (S. AFR.)

KALAHARI DESERT

Gaborone

Pretoria

Maputo

SWAZILAND

INDIAN OCEAN

NAMIB DESERT

Johannesburg •

Mbabane

Orange River

LESOTHO

Maseru

• Durban

SOUTH AFRICA

Cape Town •

Cape of Good Hope

Cape Agulhas

AFRICA SOUTH OF THE SAHARA: Physical

⊛ National Capitals
• Other Cities

0	400	800 miles
0	400	800	1,200 kilometers

through the many different lands of the desert. Most of the land that he crossed gets less than 8 inches (20 cm) of rain a year. Some parts of the Sahara get less than 1 inch (2.5 cm).

When Richardson reached the dry grasslands south of the Sahara, he discovered that summer is when the rain falls. Sudden rainstorms could be dangerous. One day the caravan made camp in a dry wadi as usual. You will remember that a wadi is a dry streambed. Late in the afternoon, Richardson heard people crying, "The wadi is coming! The wadi is coming!" He looked out of his tent and saw "a broad white sheet of foam advancing between the trees of the valley." Richardson and the drivers hurriedly moved their camels and supplies to higher ground. In 10 minutes the dry wadi had become a roaring river that uprooted trees.

Richardson had reached the country south of the Sahara at the beginning of the rainy season. The hills turned green. It was a very different scene from what he had seen during the weeks in the desert. He wrote in his journal: "Here and there are scattered numerous trees, many of considerable size, giving the surface of the valley something of a park-like appearance."

Different kinds of land on a big continent Richardson saw different scenes in his journey from north to south. But Africa has still other kinds of land. Africa is a large continent, second only to Asia in size. It has about 20 percent of the world's land area, and is three times the size of Europe. The Equator crosses Africa from the country of Gabon on the west coast to

AREAS OF THE WORLD'S CONTINENTS (Figures are rounded)		
Continent	Area (sq mi)	Area (sq km)
Asia	17,179,000	44,493,000
Africa	11,696,000	30,293,000
North America	9,442,000	24,454,000
South America	6,887,000	17,838,000
Antarctica	5,396,000	13,975,000
Europe	3,956,000	10,245,000
Australia	2,966,000	7,682,000

Somalia on the east coast. Yet Tunis in North Africa is closer to Norway than it is to the Equator.

The map on page 316 shows the different kinds of **vegetation,** or plants, that grow in the different parts of Africa. Much of Africa has only desert vegetation. South of the Sahara there are two other large deserts in Africa. They are the Namib Desert and the Kalahari (kal ə här´ ē) Desert, which meet near the southern end of the continent.

A very large part of Africa is **savanna.** Savanna land is covered with coarse grass and, sometimes, scattered trees and bushes as shown on the next page. The grasslands that Richardson found south of the Sahara were one kind of savanna.

Savannas are usually fairly dry. They receive most rain during the summer months. Winter is usually a dry season with little or no rain. In the savannas north of the Equator, summer comes in June, July, and August. In the savannas south of the Equator, summer falls in the months from December through March. Study the precipitation map on page 25 to find how much rain falls in Africa's savannas. Farming is done in much of the

Africa's Varied Wildlife

An alphabetical list of African animals would begin with *aardvark* and end with *zebra*. The list would include the biggest, tallest, and fastest land animals on earth. African elephants are the biggest. Giraffes are the tallest. A large cat, the cheetah, holds the animal speed record. Ostriches are the world's largest living birds. Unlike most of Africa's nearly 2,300 different species of birds, ostriches do not fly. Africa also has lions, leopards, rhinoceroses, hippopotamuses, antelopes, wild oxen, monkeys and apes, and many other kinds of animals.

Africa's wildlife is one of the continent's valuable natural resources. To save the wild animals, some African countries have set aside large parks and game reserves. People come from all over the world to see the animals. Tourism is an important industry for many countries in Africa.

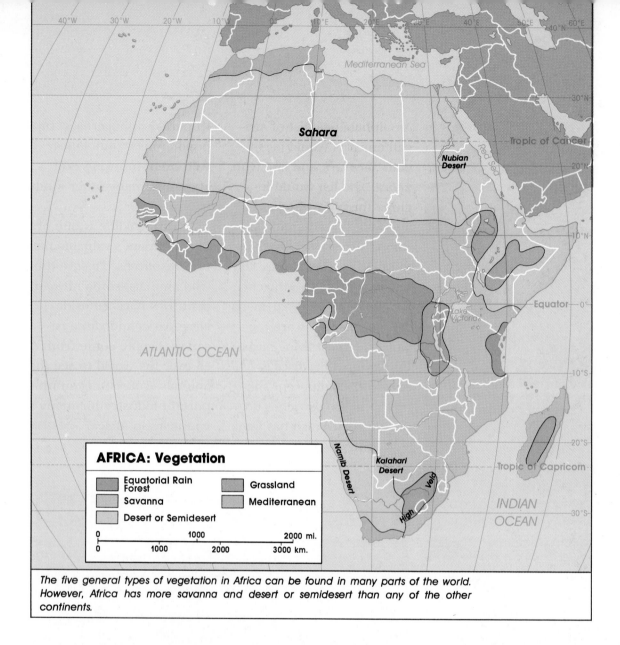

Equatorial Rain Forest

Savanna

Desert or Semidesert

Grassland

Mediterranean

| 0 | | 1000 | | 2000 mi. |
| 0 | 1000 | 2000 | 3000 km. | |

The five general types of vegetation in Africa can be found in many parts of the world. However, Africa has more savanna and desert or semidesert than any of the other continents.

savanna even though the soil is rarely good. Tobacco, cotton, sugarcane, corn, and other grain crops grow in some places.

Africa also has large forests. Most of the forests are rain forests. As you can see on the vegetation map, they are in central and western Africa near the Equator. These are hot lands that receive at least 50 inches (127 cm) of rain a year.

The southern and northern coasts of Africa are about the same distance from the Equator. South Africa has a climate much like that of the lands on the Mediterranean. You read in Chapter 6 that a Mediterranean climate has dry summers and rainy winters. You will remember from Chapter 1 that in southern Africa summer begins in December instead of June as in North Africa.

Highlands and mountains The vegetation map shows certain areas of Africa as grassland. These grassy areas are

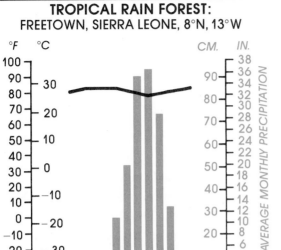

TROPICAL RAIN FOREST:
FREETOWN, SIERRA LEONE, 8°N, 13°W

AVERAGE MONTHLY TEMPERATURE

°F °C

100
90 — 30
80
70 — 20
60
50 — 10
40
30 — 0
20
10 — -10
0 — -20
-10
-20 — -30

CM. IN.

90 — 38
— 36
— 34
80 — 32
— 30
70 — 28
— 26
60 — 24
— 22
50 — 20
— 18
40 — 16
— 14
30 — 12
— 10
20 — 8
— 6
10 — 4
— 2

AVERAGE MONTHLY PRECIPITATION

J F M A M J J A S O N D
MONTHS

This climograph shows the average monthly temperature and precipitation throughout the year for Freetown, Sierra Leone. The total annual rainfall is about 157 inches (399 cm). Which months are the wettest?

somewhat like the Great Plains of the United States. Most of these lands are used for growing corn and grasses or for grazing sheep. Some grasslands are near the Equator, but they are not particularly hot. You will discover why if you compare the vegetation map with the physical map of Africa on page 462 in the Atlas. The grasslands are also highlands. You may remember that places with high elevations are cooler than lowlands.

Much of Africa south of the Sahara is more than 2,000 feet (610 m) above sea level. The southern two thirds of the continent is a plateau that rises from the sea.

There are high mountains on the plateau. Find Mount Kenya on the Equator in eastern Africa. In spite of its location, snow covers Mount Kenya throughout the year because of its high elevation. South of Mount Kenya is Mount Kilimanjaro (kil ə mən jär' ō), the highest mountain in Africa. Mount Kilimanjaro is 19,340 feet (5,895 m) high. It is taller than any of the mountains of Europe. Mount Kilimanjaro is also always covered with snow.

Lakes and rivers   A deep valley runs north and south on the plateau in eastern Africa. It is called the Great Rift Valley. A series of lakes have formed in the deepest part of the Great Rift. Find Lakes Malawi (mə lä' wē), Tanganyika (tan gən yē' kə), and Albert on the map on page 313.

Lake Tanganyika is the deepest of these lakes. If you dropped a rock at the deepest place, it would fall nearly a mile before reaching bottom.

These people are drying their fishnets on a beach by Lake Tanganyika. The fish caught in Africa's lakes of the Great Rift Valley are marketed and eaten locally.

Lake Victoria is not so deep as Lake Tanganyika, but it is the largest lake in Africa. It is a little larger than the state of West Virginia, in the United States. Lake Victoria is on the eastern African plateau. The lake covers over 200 miles (322 km) north and south and 150 miles (241 km) east and west.

Lake Chad is a very different kind of lake. It is located between the Sahara and the savanna. It is not very deep and it is fed by rivers that flow toward the desert rather than toward the sea. The size of Lake Chad varies from year to year. In a year with unusually heavy rains, it will be three times as large as during a dry year.

The longest river in Africa is also the longest river in the world. It is the Nile, which has its source in Africa's moun-

tainous lakeland near the Equator. The Nile flows north 4,160 miles (6,693 km) through the eastern savanna and the Sahara to the Mediterranean Sea. It is the river of the ancient Egyptians, whom you studied in Chapter 3.

All of Africa's other major rivers are south of the Sahara. Most of them descend from the plateau over waterfalls and rapids. The Congo River flows over 32 waterfalls less than 200 miles (320 km) from its mouth. The Zambezi (zam bē′ zē) River in eastern Africa begins nearly a mile (1.6 km) above sea level. On its way down to the Indian Ocean, the Zambezi flows over Victoria Falls, one of the largest waterfalls in Africa. Victoria Falls is twice as wide and nearly twice as high as Niagara Falls in North America.

The first four of Africa's longest rivers flow to the seas. The Shebelle ends in a swamp near the Equator in southern Somalia, a country in eastern Africa.

Victoria Falls is located at 18°S, 26°W, on the Zambezi River, which forms the border between Zambia and Zimbabwe.

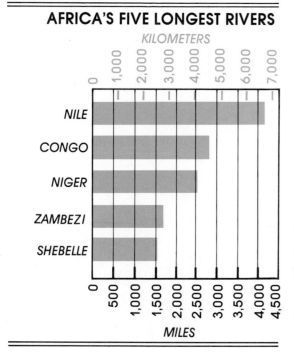

AFRICA'S FIVE LONGEST RIVERS

KILOMETERS

0 · 1,000 · 2,000 · 3,000 · 4,000 · 5,000 · 6,000 · 7,000

NILE
CONGO
NIGER
ZAMBEZI
SHEBELLE

0 · 500 · 1,000 · 1,500 · 2,000 · 2,500 · 3,000 · 3,500 · 4,000 · 4,500

MILES

The Niger River is the longest river in western Africa. The Niger begins in the far western bulge of Africa and follows a long, indirect route to the Atlantic Ocean. Trace the Niger with your finger on the map at the beginning of the chapter. It first flows northeast toward the Sahara. It then makes a great loop and flows across the savanna and through the rain forest, and finally forms a delta as it empties into the Atlantic. The Niger divides into many channels in the delta. Early explorers had a hard time deciding which was the main channel.

Exploring Africa   It took a long time for people from other places to learn about the vast interior of the African continent. Africa's rivers do not provide easy routes inland. Boats cannot travel up rapids and waterfalls. Although Africa is about three times as large as Europe, it has a shorter coastline. Africa has fewer deep bays. No great peninsulas jut into the oceans. No arms of the sea reach into the continent. The mouths of the rivers do not form long natural harbors as do the rivers of Western Europe.

These facts about the African continent made it a difficult land in which to travel. The Sahara and other parts of the interior also made it difficult. But about a hundred years ago, there were many explorers other than James Richardson who were eager to find out about the continent.

Between 1874 and 1877 Henry Stanley led an **expedition** across central Africa. An expedition is a group formed to carry out a trip of exploration. Stanley was a British newspaper writer who also worked for a newspaper in the United States. Stanley journeyed to parts of Africa very different from those crossed by James Richardson. Stanley described Africa's great lakes, mountains, deep forests, and fast-moving rivers.

Stanley's newspaper stories told readers in London and New York about the lands and streams he "discovered." By a "discovery" Stanley meant visiting a place never before visited by a European or American. Of course, what Stanley "discovered" was well known to Africans who lived and traveled in the area.

Some Africans found it hard to understand what Stanley wanted in their homeland. Someone asked Stanley's African guide why the white man had come. The guide said that Stanley had "come to see, that's all."

"To see! See what?"

"To see the river," the guide replied.

"What for?"

"Who knows?" said the guide. "The white men do such strange things. They put it down in a book, and that is all I know that ever becomes of it."

Journeying to Lake Victoria   Stanley's expedition set out from the narrow plain along the coast of eastern Africa. He described the coastlands as "green as an English lawn." People along the coast grew rice, sweet potatoes, and many kinds of vegetables.

The expedition soon began to climb up to the eastern African plateau. They reached a thick growth of thorny trees. Stanley called it a "bush jungle." There was no trail or road. The expedition had to push its way by scrambling and crawling along the ground. It was slow, hard

This village in the highlands near Mount Kenya has many homes made of wood with fenced-in vegetable gardens.

toria, which looked like "a vast sea" on the plateau. Stanley and a crew sailed or rowed the boat all along the shores of this largest of Africa's lakes.

East of Lake Victoria Stanley saw the open savanna. He wrote in his account: "The country is one continuous plain with low hills rising here and there." Stanley noted that the people on this plain kept "vast herds" of cattle. This was also the home of many kinds of wildlife, including antelopes, giraffes, zebras, rhinoceroses, leopards, lions, elephants, baboons, and hundreds of different birds.

Stanley saw a stream that flowed out of Lake Victoria. An earlier explorer had discovered that this was one source of the Nile. The world's longest river ran all the way from Lake Victoria in eastern Africa to the Mediterranean Sea.

The expedition left Lake Victoria and traveled farther into the continent. Stanley saw mountains with snow on them. He later learned that the snow did not

work, especially for the men carrying supplies. Some carried sections of a 24-foot (7.3-m) boat. The boat was made in sections so that it could be taken apart and carried overland. The sections could be bolted together when the expedition reached a lake or river. Stanley called the boat the *Lady Alice,* shown below.

Stanley was glad to have the *Lady Alice* when the expedition reached Lake Vic-

Under sail in the Lady Alice, Stanley is welcomed on the shores of Lake Victoria. There to greet him are people from the village and King Mtesa's bodyguard in full dress. The Lady Alice could be taken apart and carried in sections across the distant hills.

remain throughout the year as it did on Mount Kilimanjaro.

Into the rain forest down the Congo River West of the mountains the expedition entered a rain forest. From a distance the forest looked like a soft "robe of green" covering the earth. Close up the scene was very different. Beneath tall trees there was a tangled undergrowth of bushes, vines, thorns, and grass. Stanley told his readers that "the grasses are coarse and high and thick. Their spearlike blades wound like knives and their points like needles."

The bushes that looked so pretty in the distance were filled with sharp thorns and many wild creatures. Chimpanzees, gorillas, monkeys, buffalo, and wild pigs lived in the thick forest. The rain forests are also the homes of many snakes and the largest frog in the world, which grows to weigh as much as 10 pounds (4.5 kg).

The forest had thousands of insects. Some were beautiful, such as the butterflies that landed on Stanley's notebook as he wrote. Others were not so pleasant. Mosquitoes, stinging bees, wasps, and hornets swarmed about a traveler's head. If a person stood still for a few moments, an army of stinging ants crawled up the person's legs. Stanley wrote in a newspaper story: "It is all beautiful—but there must be no sitting or lying down on this seething earth. It is not like your pine groves and dainty woods in England." In the rain forest, "you must keep moving."

In the forest the expedition reached a large river that flowed north. Earlier explorers had thought that the stream must flow into the Nile. Stanley did not think so. He guessed that this was the Congo River. He believed that at some place downstream the river must turn west and flow toward the Atlantic Ocean. If you look at the map on page 313, you will see that Stanley guessed right. The Congo does flow north out of the highlands west to Lake Tanganyika. Trace the river with your finger and you will see that after running north, the Congo makes a great loop and flows into the Atlantic.

But Stanley had no map of the river. There was no way to learn the river's course except to travel downstream.

The trip down the Congo was difficult and dangerous. The Congo tumbles over many rapids and waterfalls. Some members of the expedition lost their lives trying to float through rapids. Some of the waterfalls were so high that they had to drag the boats around them. To do this they had to cut broad trails through the forest. Stanley wrote of this part of his journey: "It is bad by river and it is bad by land."

After many weeks the expedition finally made its way to the Congo's mouth. Stanley had guessed right about the river's course. From central Africa, they had followed the river to the Atlantic Ocean.

CHECKUP

1. What is meant by the statement "Africa is a continent of great contrasts?"
2. What are the five main vegetation regions of Africa?
3. Do all places on the Equator in Africa have a hot climate? Explain your answer.
4. Why have Africa's rivers not served as easy routes into the continent?
5. What did Henry Stanley see in his journey across central Africa?

People Use the Land

Gathering food in the Kalahari Desert Africans have used their different kinds of land in many ways. Africans have grown crops, kept livestock, hunted, and gathered food. Some groups of people, such as the Bushmen of southern Africa, learned to live in places where most people would starve.

The Bushmen live in the Kalahari Desert in the country of Botswana. Today most of them work for cattle ranchers. But in the past the Bushmen lived by hunting and gathering their food.

The Kalahari has areas of desert grass and bushes and some trees. Most people could not find very much to eat there, particularly during the long dry season. But the Bushmen know where to look.

The men used poisoned arrows to hunt antelopes and other desert animals. But meat was not the main food for the Bushmen. They ate mostly plants, which the women gathered. At the end of the short rainy season, they picked small juicy melons that grow wild. The Bushmen not only ate the melons, they roasted and ate the seeds. If they had any meat, they would boil it in the juices of the melons.

The women also gathered small wild cucumbers after the rains. Later they searched for sour red berries that grew on bushes.

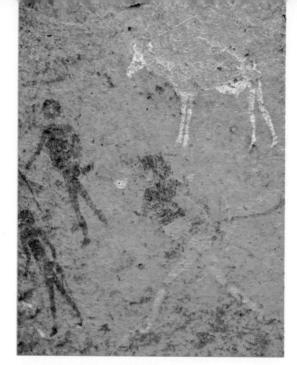

This rock painting by Bushman artists is in southern Africa, where they have lived for thousands of years. It shows Bushmen hunting an antelope with a bow and arrow.

During the long dry season the Bushmen depended mostly on eating roots. They knew that certain vines stored water in thick roots. Eating these roots provided people with both food and water.

The Bushmen had to keep moving about in the search for food. They soon used up the roots and melons in any one place. The Bushmen built no cities nor permanent homes. But they had the knowledge and skill to use land where other people could not survive.

Farming in the forests The soils of the rain forests are not rich soils. When the land is cleared for crops, the heavy rains quickly wash away the minerals and materials that feed plants. But Africans found a way to grow crops on the forestland. Locate the rain forests on the vegetation map on page 316.

Today, African farmers in the rain forests live and work mostly as they have for centuries. Forest farmers first clear small patches of land. Next they burn the dead trees and bushes on the ground. Before planting, they break up the ash-covered soil with hoes. The ash helps to make the soil fertile. They plant different crops side by side rather than in separate plots or fields. Corn, peanuts, beans, yams, **cassava** (kə sä′ və), and **okra** (ō′ krə) all grow together in the forest clearing. Cassava, also called manioc (man′ ē ok), is a plant with a large root that is made into meal or flour. Cassava flour made into porridge is one of Africa's important foods. Okra is a plant with green pods that are eaten in stews and soups. Corn is not native to Africa. Seeds were brought there from America and corn is now one of Africa's most important crops.

Forest farmers do not use the same patch of land for more than 2 or 3 years because the soil wears out so quickly. Instead of planting the same patches, they clear others. The old patches are left to grow back as forest. This way of farming is called **shifting cultivation.**

The forest grows back quickly, but it takes a long time for the soil to build up again. Leaves and other materials fall on the ground and decay. Trees and bushes draw minerals from deep in the soil. After 20 years a patch may be cleared and burned again. The minerals are spread on the surface in the ashes. For another few years crops will grow well.

Forest farming is very hard work. Farmers must use hoes rather than plows to dig among the stumps and roots of the cleared land. Machines cannot be used to harvest crops that grow side by side and ripen at different times.

This village in the rain forest of western Africa is by the St. Paul River, which flows into the Atlantic Ocean near Monrovia, Liberia. Find the river on page 313.

This person is clearing a field in the dense rain forest of the country of Ivory Coast in western Africa.

There must be a great deal of land when farmers shift from field to field every year or two. In recent times the number of people has grown. More people need more food. Farmers re-clear the land every few years instead of waiting 20 years or more. The forest does not have time to build up the soil. Some land has become so poor that it will grow neither crops nor trees. The heavy rains wash away the soil. Too much farming in the forest makes it nearly useless.

Growing cash crops   Farmers in and out of the forest grow food for themselves or to trade with neighbors. During the past century Africans have been growing more **cash crops.** A cash crop is one sold for money rather than used by the grower. They are often grown for sale in other lands. For example, cotton and peanuts grown in the country of Sudan on the upper Nile are sold to countries in Europe and the Middle East.

Africa's forestlands are well suited for growing tree crops, such as oil palms, coconut, rubber, and **cacao** (kə kā′ ō). These are valuable cash crops in western and central Africa and in some parts of eastern Africa.

The cacao tree produces the beans from which chocolate and cocoa are made. If you eat chocolate candy, you may eat one of Africa's cash crops. About 60 percent of the world's cacao beans come from western Africa.

You may also have eaten African coconut. You almost surely have used something made from coconut oil. It is used in foods and in soaps. Palm oil is another important cash crop of the forest-lands. Africa produces most of the world's palm oil.

Various cash crops are grown on the plateaus of eastern and southern Africa. Wheat and corn are produced for the world market. These parts of Africa have also become important producers of tea and tobacco. Farms in eastern Africa grow about two thirds of the world's **sisal** (sis′ əl). Sisal is a plant with strong fibers used for making rope and twine.

Coffee is grown on the slopes of Mount Kenya as well as in parts of western and central Africa. Africa now produces one fourth of the world's coffee.

1.

3.

2.

Raising livestock   Much of Africa is too dry for crops, so Africans use these lands in other ways. You read in Chapter 12 how some people in North Africa raise camels to use for food, work, and travel in the Sahara. Africans south of the Sahara make use of the dry savannas by raising cattle. Sheep also are raised in semidesert and grassland areas near the Sahara and in southern Africa. Find these regions on the vegetation map on page 316.

Africans were raising cattle long before Henry Stanley saw "vast herds" on the east African plateau. The cattle-herding people usually have permanent villages. Some groups that raise cattle are nomadic herders, such as the Masai (mä sī') in eastern Africa. They keep their cattle near their homes during the rainy season. But during the dry season the men and boys must move about with the herds. There are rainstorms now and then during the dry months. But the rains are scattered and there is no way to know

These women in the country of Niger are shaking leaves from the trees to feed their herd of goats.

1. *In the picture at the left, young oil palm trees are planted in pots at a palm nursery.* **2.** *Above, a farmer uses a hooked knife attached to a long pole to harvest clusters of oil palm nuts. A mature tree bears about 10 clusters of 200 nuts each.* **3.** *The clusters are delivered to a store house such as that shown at the top. Individual palm oil nuts are about the size of dates. The flesh is crushed to make a thick oil used as butter, and to manufacture soaps, chocolates, cosmetics, and candles. Inside the flesh of the nut is a hard kernel, which is also crushed to make oil used in margarine. Africa produces about half of the world's palm kernels.*

just where they will fall. Herders must follow the rains to find pastures.

Women and girls usually remain in the villages throughout the year. They take care of the crops. They grow various vegetables, but **sorghum** (sôr' gəm) is the main crop. Sorghum is a grain that can grow in dry climates and is used mostly for livestock feed. The grain, or seeds, of sorghum are also ground into meal, which is used as flour. Africans were the first people to grow sorghum, but it is now one of the world's important crops.

Today there are cattle ranches in Africa that produce animals for market. But this is not the way of most Africans who herd cattle. Traditional groups do not raise their cattle for sale. Like the Masai, they live off their herds. They drink milk and eat milk products. Only now and then do they kill an animal for meat. The size of a family's herd is the size of its wealth.

Much of the savanna across central Africa is not suited for raising cattle because of tsetse flies. These insects live in the thick undergrowth of forestlands near the savanna. The flies carry a disease known as sleeping sickness that kills cattle when they are bitten by the flies.

Wealth from under the soil   In 1497 a Portuguese sailor named Vasco da Gama (vas' kō dä ga' mə), rounded the southern tip of Africa and headed up the east coast. When Da Gama returned to Europe, he told people that Africa had great deposits of precious stones. He said he had heard of places where precious stones were "so plentiful that there was no need to buy them because they could be picked up in baskets."

Vasco da Gama had not actually gathered basketfulls of precious stones. He was simply telling one of those stories that travelers like to tell about faraway places. But there are precious stones and other great mineral resources in Africa. Early kingdoms in eastern, western, and southern Africa found gold, copper, and iron in the ground. These metals were made into tools and fine works of art that were either used or traded.

Today southern Africa produces more than two thirds of the world's diamonds. It also has deposits of garnets, emeralds, and other precious stones. Southern Africa also produces about three quarters of the world's gold and cobalt. Cobalt is a metal used for making other metals.

Africa produces large amounts of many of the world's mineral and agricultural products. The figures below stand for Africa's share of the total world output.

IMPORTANT PRODUCTS OF AFRICA

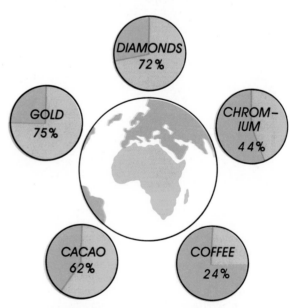

The figures and the orange part of each pie graph stand for Africa's share of the total world output.

This dam on the Volta River in Ghana is similar to hydroelectric plants built on rivers in many parts of Africa. Electricity is produced by generators powered by the flow of water from the dam.

Parts of Africa have important deposits of copper, uranium (yū rā′ nē əm), manganese, and asbestos. Asbestos is a valuable resource for many different uses because it does not burn even in an open fire.

Do you have anything that is chrome-plated? If so, you probably have something made with metal from southern Africa. This part of Africa is one of the world's main sources for chromium ore.

There is gas and petroleum south of the Sahara under the delta of the Niger River. Find the Niger River delta in the country of Nigeria on the map at the beginning of this chapter. Petroleum has become an important export for Nigeria, as it is for most countries in North Africa.

More than one way to use a river Falls and rapids made it difficult to travel on Africa's rivers. Stanley had discovered this on his trip down the Congo River.

But falling water has other uses. It may be used to make electricity. The falls that make it impossible to travel by boat on the lower Congo now provide waterpower for an electric plant.

There are many places on Africa's rivers that can be used to make electricity. It is said that 40 percent of all the waterpower in the world is in Africa. Waterpower is a good way to make electricity because it is a renewable resource. Only part of it is being used now. In the future, waterpower may become Africa's most important source of energy.

CHECKUP

1. How are forest farmers able to grow crops on the forestlands?
2. What is a cash crop? What are some of Africa's cash crops?
3. How have people in Africa made use of deserts and dry savannas?
4. What wealth does Africa have under the soil?
5. What use can be made of Africa's rivers?

15/ CHAPTER REVIEW

KEY FACTS

1. The Sahara divides North Africa from Africa south of the desert.

2. Most Africans live in rural areas.

3. Africa is a large continent with a variety of lands, wildlife, vegetation, climate, and ways of life.

4. Most of the southern two thirds of Africa is a plateau that rises from the sea.

5. Rivers do not serve as easy routes into Africa south of the Sahara because of waterfalls and rapids.

6. Africans found ways to make use of different kinds of land and climate.

7. Forest farmers cleared and burned patches of land in the forest to grow crops.

8. In recent times Africans have grown more cash crops.

9. Cattle herders make use of the dry savanna.

10. Africa has abundant mineral wealth and waterpower.

VOCABULARY QUIZ

Read the following statements. Decide which are true and which are false. Write your answers (**T** or **F**) on a sheet of paper.

1. Forest farming is a traditional way of life in Africa.

2. Okra is a camel driver.

3. Sisal is a kind of African cattle.

4. Vegetation is the kind of plants that grow in an area.

5. A rural area has many cities.

6. An expedition is a type of river boat.

7. Cash crops are products made in factories.

8. Flour is made from cassava roots.

9. Chocolate comes from the cacao tree.

10. Sorghum is an American plant which was taken to Africa.

REVIEW QUESTIONS

1. What are some of the contrasts in ways of living in Africa?

2. What are the different vegetation regions in Africa?

3. How does elevation affect climate and rivers south of the Sahara?

4. How did the Bushmen make use of the Kalihari Desert?

5. How were forest farmers able to keep growing crops in the rain forests where the soil wore out quickly?

6. What are some of Africa's cash crops?

7. How did Africans make use of savannas?

8. How are cattle used in Africa? What is one way that cattle are used today that is not traditional?

9. What kinds of mineral wealth does Africa have south of the Sahara?

10. Why are Africa's rivers valuable resources?

ACTIVITIES

1. Make up 10 true-false questions about the material in this chapter. Exchange questions with another member of the class. Try to answer the other person's questions.

2. Make a report on the life of the Masai of eastern Africa, the Swazi of southern Africa, or the Yoruba of western Africa. Use an encyclopedia or other books for information.

3. Trace the outline of Africa from the map on page 313. Find out what wildlife Africa has today and draw or label the animals on the map in the areas where they live. Use information from the chapter and other books.

4. Make a graph that presents the information from the table on page 314. Choose the type of graph that will work best.

15/SKILLS DEVELOPMENT

USING PRIMARY SOURCES

PRIMARY SOURCES ARE FIRSTHAND VIEWS

James Richardson's journal is called a primary source because it gives a firsthand account of his trip across the Sahara. A primary source is written by someone who either saw or took part in an event. Richardson's journal is a primary source because he took part in the trip across the desert. A secondary source is written by someone who did not see or take part in the event described. Secondary sources are based on what others have written or said. This book is a secondary source, as are encyclopedias.

FIRSTHAND VIEWS FROM A JOURNAL

There are many ways to express an idea. For example, Richardson wrote, "The wind followed exactly behind us as we pursued our south-west course." If you were to tell about his trip, you might write, "The wind blew from the northeast." That would be another way to say the same thing. This is called paraphrasing. Your account of Richardson's trip would be a secondary source because you were not there.

SKILLS PRACTICE

Listed below are other passages from Richardson's journal. Each passage is followed by two statements. Choose the one you would use to paraphrase what Richardson wrote. Write on a sheet of paper.

1. "No herbage for camels is found in these parts."
  a. Nothing grew in those parts of the desert.
  b. There was no place to shelter a camel.

2. "We feel little of the sun's power."
  a. The weather was hot.
  b. The weather was cool.

3. "The face of the cliffs of the plateau was blackened as with the smoke of a huge furnace."
  a. There was a huge fire below the cliffs.
  b. The plateau had black cliffs.

4. "The houses are not whitewashed, but retain the dirty hue of unburnt brick and mud with which they are built."
  a. The houses were made of unpainted mud brick.
  b. The houses were dirty.

5. "We noticed a small black bird with a white throat. But all through this desert we listen in vain for some songster."
  a. They saw a black and white songbird in the desert.
  b. They saw a black and white bird but heard no songbirds in the desert.

6. "The lightning flashed, sometimes above, sometimes between the isolated hills, showing them like long black tents pitched here and there on the plain."
  a. They pitched their tents among the black hills during a lightning storm.
  b. Flashes of lightning made it possible to see the hills scattered on the plain.

7. "There cannot be a doubt that occasionally an immense quantity of rain falls in every region of this great desert."
  a. All parts of the desert got rain at some time.
  b. It was doubtful if some regions of the desert got any rain.

16 History of Africa South of the Sahara

Africa in 1500

┌─VOCABULARY─────────────────┐
│ monsoon   porcelain │
│ Swahili   │
└────────────────────────────┘

Europeans begin to learn about Africa   The history and ways of life in Africa were very little known to Europeans before the fifteenth century. European mapmakers filled in empty spaces of their maps with drawings of imaginary animals, people, and cities. Most of what Europeans knew came from travelers and soldiers who either came from or had gone to African lands.

In 1415 Prince Henry of Portugal captured a city on the coast of North Africa. In the city, the Portuguese prince learned that gold came by caravan from the lands south of the Sahara.

Prince Henry knew that Portugal was too small a country to capture the caravan routes. But he had another idea. Could the Portuguese reach the rich lands south of the Sahara by sailing along the African coast? This question raised still another question. Would it be possible to sail all the way around Africa to the Asian countries of India and China? Merchants in Europe wanted to find an all-water route to carry on trade with these lands. Prince Henry sent expeditions to explore the African coast. His ships sailed farther and farther south. Piece by piece, the mapmakers in Portugal filled in their maps of the African coast.

In 1444 one of Henry's ships reached the mouth of the Senegal River. This river flows into the Atlantic Ocean along the westernmost coast of Africa. At that time, Europeans knew so little about Africa that the sailors thought the Senegal was a branch of the Nile. If you look at the map on page 313, you will see how mistaken they were. The Portuguese tried to sail up the Senegal. But, as on so many African rivers, rapids blocked the way.

Prince Henry the Navigator died in 1460. He had learned that it was indeed possible to reach the lands south of the Sahara by sea. But it was not until 1488 that a Portuguese captain named Bartholomeu Dias (bar′ tü lü mā ủ dē′ əsh) sailed around the Cape of Good Hope and Cape Agulhas. Locate these two capes on page 313.

Almost 10 years later, Vasco da Gama, another Portuguese captain, sailed around the capes and then north along the east coast. In one city along the east coast of Africa he hired a sailor who knew the trade routes to India. In a 23-day sail Da Gama completed the trip by sea to India. It was the first time that Europeans had sailed around Africa to Asia.

The contrasts of new and old can be seen in this picture of modern Kano, one of the cities in western Africa that has been a center of trade for many centuries. Camel caravans passed through Kano, carrying trade goods across the Sahara to and from North Africa.

An African writes about Africa By 1520 European mapmakers had been able to chart much of Africa's coastline, based on the reports of Portuguese sailors. But Europeans still knew very little about the interior of Africa south of the Sahara. For this reason, people in Rome were much interested in the stories told in their city by a newcomer named Al-Hasan ibn Mohammed (äl ha san′ ib′ n mù ham′ məd). Al-Hasan said that he had traveled through 15 kingdoms in "the land of the Blacks" south of the Sahara.

Al-Hasan was a Moslem from Morocco, a country in northern Africa. He had been captured at sea by Italian pirates and taken to Rome. There Al-Hasan was made a servant of Pope Leo X. The pope took a special interest in Al-Hasan when he learned that Al-Hasan was a scholar who had traveled widely.

Al-Hasan became a Christian and took a new name, Leo Africanus—Leo from Africa. Pope Leo paid Leo Africanus a salary and urged him to write a book about Africa.

Leo Africanus wrote *The History and Description of Africa.* He told about the places he had seen. He also wrote about what others had told him.

Cities south of the Sahara Leo Africanus wrote about cities south of the Sahara. One of the most interesting was Tombouctou (tōm bük tü′). This city was located on the southern edge of the desert near the great bend of the Niger River. If you look at the map of Africa on page 349, you will find Tombouctou in the modern country of Mali. You will sometimes find the name of this city spelled Timbuktu.

Trade in Tombouctou There is an old saying that "Tombouctou is the meeting place for all who travel by camel or canoe." It was the place where caravans from North Africa met traders who came by boats from lands farther south.

Tombouctou had its own king. Leo Africanus said that he knew the king's brother. The king was very rich because

In which century did trading centers develop in western Africa? In eastern Africa?

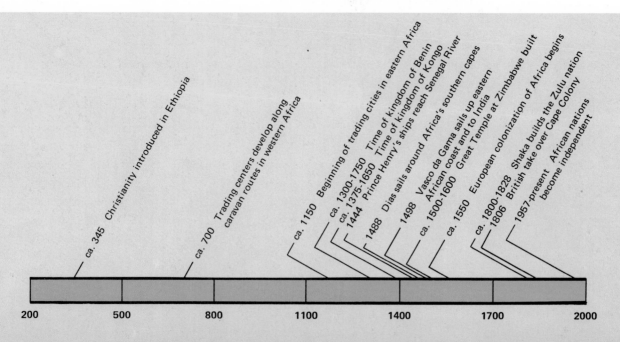

ca. 345 Christianity introduced in Ethiopia

ca. 700 Trading centers develop along caravan routes in western Africa

ca. 1150 Beginning of trading cities in eastern Africa

ca. 1300-1750 Time of kingdom of Benin

ca. 1375-1650 Time of kingdom of Kongo

1444 Prince Henry's ships reach Senegal River

1488 Dias sails around Africa's southern capes

1498 Vasco da Gama sails up eastern African coast and to India

1500-1600 Great Temple at Zimbabwe built

ca. 1550 European colonization of Africa begins

1800-1828 Shaka builds the Zulu nation

1806 British take over Cape Colony

1957-present African nations become independent

| 200 | 500 | 800 | 1100 | 1400 | 1700 | 2000 |

A caravan approaches Tombouctou, as shown in this mid-nineteenth-century drawing. For centuries the city was a center of trade and learning in western Africa.

of the trade that passed through his city. Even the dishes in his house were made of gold.

Workers wove cotton and linen cloth in Tombouctou, but it was mainly a trading town. Traders from the north came with silk cloth, brasswork, steel weapons, salt, and fine leather goods. Merchants in Tombouctou traded ivory, gold, copper, and slaves. There were slaves in Africa as well as in some other parts of the world in those days. The salt sold in the market came from mines in the Sahara worked by slaves.

Salt was needed for cooking and to keep food from spoiling. Salt was so valuable in some parts of Africa south of the Sahara that it was used as money. Control over the salt trade brought a great deal of wealth and power to the merchants and rulers of Tombouctou.

Tombouctou seems to have been a lively place. Leo Africanus said that people "spend a great part of the night in singing and dancing through all the streets of the city."

Tombouctou was a great center of learning as well as trade. The people of Tombouctou were Moslems. The picture above shows the towers of mosques rising above Tombouctou. When Leo Africanus visited the city, scholars taught in the mosques. Leo said that the caravans from North Africa brought many books to the city. They "sold for more money than any other mechandise."

Leo visited a number of other cities south of the Sahara. He told of other kings who had much gold. One king was so rich even his dogs wore gold chains.

Benin, a kingdom in the forest   Leo Africanus's book does not mention the kingdoms in Africa's forestlands. Leo had not visited them, but there were such kingdoms in his time.

Benin was located in the forest of the country now called Nigeria. Find Nigeria on the map of Africa on page 349. You will notice that one of Nigeria's neighbors now calls itself Benin. Modern Benin lies west of the old kingdom.

The king of Benin wore this royal ivory mask around his neck as a symbol of his religious authority.

The people of Benin grew crops in the forest. As you read in Chapter 15, these farmers used shifting cultivation, cutting new fields in the forest. From year to year, they moved their crops to new fields, as forest farmers still do. They gathered fruit and nuts from different kinds of palm trees. The palms provided them with food, oil, and drink. They also used the nut of the kola tree to chew and to flavor drinks. This is the same nut now used to make cola drinks.

The chief town of Benin was surrounded by an earthen wall. Houses lined the streets, which were laid out on an orderly plan.

The king's house stood in the middle of the town. Nearby were the houses of the officials of the kingdom. People who did the same kind of work usually lived on the same street within the city. For example, there was one street for woodcarvers and another for metalworkers.

Metalworkers were among the most skilled people in Benin. Other artisans worked in clay, stone, or ivory. The mask shown at the left was carved from a single piece of ivory elephant tusk.

The wooden pillars in the king's house were covered with bronze plates that showed famous people and events of the past. These plates served as a kind of history book. Benin had no written language, but it had a record of the past.

King and people help each other

The king of Benin was the chief priest as well as the ruler. The people of Benin worshiped a number of different gods and goddesses. The king performed important religious services that were thought to please the gods. Each family also worshiped the spirits of their ancestors. Their home had shrines and altars.

Each village in the kingdom had to give a part of what it produced to the king. It was a way to pay taxes. The king did not

Metalworkers in modern Nigeria use methods developed centuries ago in kingdoms of western Africa. The metal is heated and then shaped with hammers and other tools.

pay salaries to the officials or to the workers who made bronzes and other fine goods. Instead the king provided food and the other things they needed.

There were other forest kingdoms besides Benin. South of the Equator lay the larger kingdom of Kongo in the country now called Angola. Kongo had excellent blacksmiths who made the iron tools so useful in clearing forestland for crops.

A kingdom in Ethiopia Ethiopia is a high, mountainous country. It has always been a hard place to reach. That is one reason why the Arab Moslems did not conquer Ethiopia. As you read in Chapter 13, they invaded the rest of North Africa.

The people of Ethiopia say that the history of their country goes back thousands of years. They believe that one of their queens is mentioned in the Bible. She is called the Queen of Sheba, who visited Solomon's kingdom. Scholars do not all agree that the Queen of Sheba came from Ethiopia, but they do agree that Ethiopia has a long history. In 345, more than 1,600 years ago, a king of Ethiopia adopted Christianity.

Father Francisco Alvarez (äl′ və rəsh), a Portuguese priest, made his way into Ethiopia in 1520. This is the time when Leo Africanus was writing his book in Rome. Father Alvarez also wrote a book about what he saw in Africa.

Perhaps because he was a priest, Father Alvarez wrote much about Ethiopia's Christian religion. The Ethiopians had a Bible written in the ancient Ethiopic alphabet and language. The land had many monks and nuns. Father Alvarez saw churches in many of the villages.

The most unusual churches that Father Alvarez saw, such as the one shown below, were carved out of solid rock. He thought

This church was shaped and hollowed out from the solid rock of the hill surrounding it.

there was nothing like them in all the world. This church was not *built* with blocks of stone; it was *carved* out of the solid stone of the hillside. The people who made the church had to carve away great layers of rock in such a way as to leave a large block. Next they cut doors and windows into the block and hollowed it out. Designs were then carved on both the inside and outside walls. Father Alvarez wrote at length about these churches be cause he had "a great desire to make known this splendor to the entire world."

Father Alvarez wrote about things other than churches in Ethiopia. Ethiopia was ruled by a king. The king had large farms and estates in different parts of the kingdom. But he had no permanent capital city. Instead, the king and his officials moved about the country so that they could keep watch on it.

Father Alvarez visited the royal camp. The tents were always laid out the same way with regular streets and lanes. The king's large white tent stood in the middle of the camp. Four lions were chained at the entrances of the royal tent. There were two chapels nearby, one for the king and one for the queen. Around the royal tents were the tents of the high officials. Less important officials and soldiers pitched their tents still farther out, around the edge of the camp.

Trading cities on the Indian Ocean
Winds called **monsoons** greatly affected the history of eastern Africa. Monsoons are seasonal winds that blow steadily from one direction. The summer monsoon off the east coast of Africa blows from the

This sailing vessel, called a dhow, is the same kind of boat that sailed with the monsoons, carrying trade goods between eastern Africa, Arabia, and India.

southwest from May to September. From November to March the winter monsoon blows from the northeast.

Sailors in ancient times learned to make use of the regular monsoon winds. The summer monsoon carried their ships from Africa to Arabia or across the Indian Ocean to India. The winter monsoon brought them back to eastern Africa.

People came by sea from Arabia to Africa's east coast. Some settled there and married Africans. Most of these people were Moslems. They usually spoke Arabic and **Swahili** (swä hē′ lē). Swahili is an African language that has many Arabic words.

Footprints in Stone

Many of the same kinds of plants and animals that are in Africa today were there more than 2 million years ago. We know about life in the long-ago time because of fossils. Fossils are stone-like remains of a plant or animal. A fossil may be a piece of bone or tooth or even the impression of a leaf in a piece of coal. Some of the most interesting fossils in eastern Africa have been found in the country now called Tanzania.

About 3,600,000 years ago a volcano erupted and scattered a thin layer of ashes over a plain in what is now Tanzania. Rain moistened the ash layer so that animals walking on it left tracks, much as a dog leaves pawprints in the wet concrete of a new sidewalk. The layer of ashes hardened and in time was covered by more ashes and dirt.

In 1975 a group led by Dr. Mary Leakey were searching for fossils on the plain. As they dug away the upper layers of dirt and rock, they discovered the hardened tracks of creatures that had walked on the damp ashes 3,600,000 years ago. They found the tracks of elephants, giraffes, hares, gazelles, guinea fowls, and ostriches—creatures still found in eastern Africa. They also found the tracks of animals that no longer exist, such as the saber-toothed cats. But the most exciting discoveries of all were footprints that looked as if they had been made by a small human being. By 1978 Dr. Leakey's group had uncovered 70 such footprints. They also found teeth and pieces of skull and jawbone. Dr. Leakey believes that these bones are the remains of those who made the footprints 3,600,000 years ago.

Discovering remains of Africa's past is nothing new for Dr. Mary Leakey. For many years she and her husband Dr. Louis Leakey dug for such remains at Olduvai Gorge in Tanzania, about 30 miles (48.3 km) north of the plain. They discovered many stone and bone tools. In 1959 Mary Leakey dug up a piece of a skull and some teeth. The next year she found more bones and teeth in the same layer where they had found stone tools. The Leakeys believed the skull belonged to one of the early toolmakers.

Discoveries by the Leakeys and others in Africa have led many scholars to believe that Africa was probably the first inhabited continent.

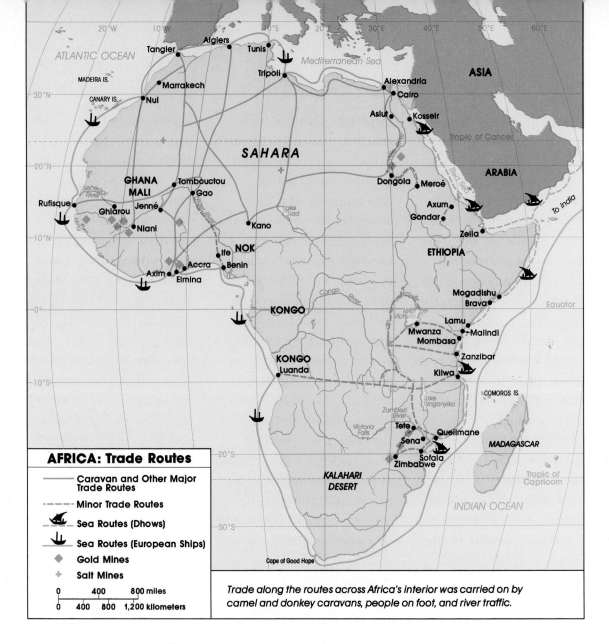

AFRICA: Trade Routes

— Caravan and Other Major Trade Routes
- - - Minor Trade Routes
⛵ Sea Routes (Dhows)
⛵ Sea Routes (European Ships)
◆ Gold Mines
✛ Salt Mines

| 0 | 400 | 800 miles |
| 0 | 400 | 800 | 1,200 kilometers |

Trade along the routes across Africa's interior was carried on by camel and donkey caravans, people on foot, and river traffic.

Cities grew up along the African coast where there were harbors for traders' ships. The traders took Africa's gold, ivory, copper, and iron to India and the Middle East. They brought back silks, glassware, and other fine goods. They even brought **porcelain** that was made in China. Porcelain, which is a fine type of ~~pottery~~ used for cups and dishes, is called ~~china~~ or chinaware.

~~Each trading~~ city had its own ruler, and ~~sometimes~~ times made war on each other.

Mombasa (mäm bäs′ ə) and Zanzibar (zan′ zə bär) were two of the most powerful cities. You can locate both of these cities on the modern map of Africa on page 349.

About 400 years ago, one visiting sailor said the cities reminded him of towns in Portugal. Of Mombasa he wrote, "It is a very fair place, with lofty stone and mortar houses." The nearby coast was "a land very full of food." People grew rice, vegetables, oranges, lemons, and figs. They

Modern Zimbabwe is named after the kingdom of old Zimbabwe that built these stoneworks.

kept "very fine sheep, cattle in great plenty, and many fowls, all of which are exceedingly fat."

The stones of old Zimbabwe The merchants from the cities on the east coast traded with people who lived farther inland. Much of the country now called Zimbabwe (zim bäb′ wē) was then ruled by a king. Modern Zimbabwe takes its name from the place where the king lived.

The picture on this page shows part of what is left of old Zimbabwe. Its walls were made of cut stone fitted tightly together without mortar. The walls are thick, about 17 feet (5.1 m) at the base and 3 feet (.9 m) at the top. Inside the walls is a cone-shaped tower that still stands. It, too, is made of solid stone and is about 34 feet (10.4 m) high. It must have taken the work of many people to build the walls and tower of old Zimbabwe. Only a powerful king could have had so many people to do this work.

Old Zimbabwe was far from the cities on the Indian Ocean, but the people of this inland kingdom had goods that came from those cities. Among the old ruins of Zimbabwe, modern scholars have found glass beads from India and broken pieces of Chinese porcelain.

There are remains of stone buildings from other kingdoms in southern Africa. But none are so large or so famous as those in old Zimbabwe. The people of modern Zimbabwe named their country after the old kingdom to honor the history of their land.

CHECKUP

1. What kind of business went on at Tombouctou?
2. What are some of the things Leo Africanus would have seen if he had visited Benin?
3. Why did the king of Ethiopia have no permanent capital city? Did the Ethiopians know how to build permanent buildings?
4. How did the monsoons affect eastern Africa?
5. Why do we know that there was contact between old Zimbabwe and the trading cities of eastern Africa?

Africa Becomes a Continent of Colonies

—VOCABULARY—

plantation   impi
veld

Europeans come to trade   As Portuguese sailors worked their way along the African coast, they traded with the peoples they met. They traded silk cloth, guns, wine, and other European products for gold, ivory, and pepper.

Trade with western Africa grew. The Portuguese wanted to build a fort on the coast of what is now the country of Ghana. The fort would be a place where traders could live and store their goods. The Portuguese asked the king of that

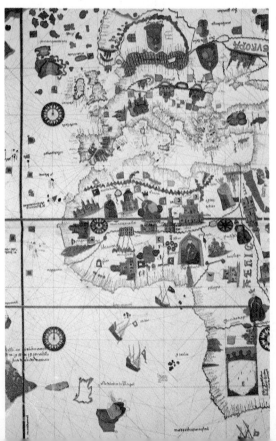

When this map was made ca. 1500, Europeans had charted much of Africa's coastline, but little of the interior.

land for permission to build. One of the king's advisers said that it would be better for the Portuguese to trade from ships and not stay in Africa. He pointed out, "Friends who meet occasionally remain better friends than if they are neighbors."

The king did not take this wise advice. He allowed the Portuguese to build a fort large enough for 60 armed guards.

Other Europeans followed the Portuguese to western Africa seeking trade. In time other countries had trading forts on the coast.

Europeans and the slave trade
Europeans came to trade for more than just African products. They also came to buy people—slaves. As you have read, Africans had some slaves. In war, the victors often made slaves of those they captured just as the Greeks and Romans had done in ancient times. Rulers sometimes enslaved criminals as a punishment. Children of slaves were also slaves.

Most slaves were servants. They worked around the owner's house or in the field. Slaves generally did not work in large groups except in a few places such as the Sahara salt mines. There were no large farms that grew cash crops at that time in the African forests. Even African rulers did not have large numbers of slaves. They had no need for them.

The coming of the European traders changed this. The traders wanted large numbers of slaves for **plantations** in the West Indies and the Americas. Plantations are large farms that use workers to grow cash crops.

Europeans usually did not capture the slaves. Instead they bought them from

This fort in Ghana is one of many built by European nations to carry on trade in Africa.

Africans. As the demand for slaves increased, they became more valuable. Some Africans sold their servants and tried to replace them by getting more slaves. Lawbreakers were made slaves in larger numbers. Rulers began to make war mainly to capture prisoners to sell to the slave traders.

Slavery was common in Africa even before European traders came to buy slaves. The drawing shows slaves carrying firewood and harvesting rice on an African farm.

Some Africans well understood the harm of the slave trade. A king of Kongo wrote the king of Portugal about the cruel business. He asked that the Portuguese not come to Africa to buy its people. But neither king any longer had the power to stop the slave trade. There were too many Africans, as well as Portuguese, who were deep in the business.

Selling slaves became the most valuable part of European trade. European traders began selling guns to African slave raiders. This made it easier for the raiders to capture people who had only spears and bows to defend themselves.

The slave trade went on for 300 years. During that time millions of people were taken from their homeland to the Americas.

Dutch settlers come to South Africa Ships from other European countries followed Vasco da Gama's route around Africa to Asia. In 1648 the Dutch

341

ship *Haarlem* was wrecked off the coast of southern Africa near the Cape of Good Hope. The crew got to land safely and even managed to save most of the cargo.

Knowing that it might be months before another ship passed by, the crew prepared for a long wait. They traded part of the cargo to the Hottentots for sheep and cattle. The Hottentots were the African people who lived in the southernmost part of Africa. Most of them were cattle raisers. The Dutch crew planted crops with the seeds they had saved from the *Haarlem*. The crops grew well. Hunting and fishing also were good, so the shipwrecked crew made out well.

After a time, the crew of the *Haarlem* was picked up and returned home. They told people about the land and climate at the southern tip of Africa. They said that the Dutch trading company should establish a small settlement there. The settlement could produce food for the growing number of ships that made the long trip around to Asia.

Several years later the Dutch sent out three ships to establish a supply post at the Cape of Good Hope. The little group faced numerous difficulties during the first few months. They found the cape to be far less pleasant than the descriptions given by the *Haarlem's* crew. The group arrived in April, which was autumn south of the Equator. Their first crops failed. They found it hard to trade for cattle. The Hottentots grew less friendly when they saw the Dutch building a fort. They rightly guessed that the Dutch had come to stay.

As the number of settlers increased, so did troubles with the Africans. The Europeans were outnumbered, but they had guns, which won out against the Hottentots' spears and bows. Even more danger-

Hottentots were farmers living in southern Africa when Europeans arrived. Below some Hottentots are shown building a home. What else is happening in this picture?

Zulus and other Bantu people who live in rural areas often build their homes in this traditional way. The homes are arranged in a small cluster called a kraal.

ous than guns were the diseases the Europeans brought to southern Africa. Large numbers of Hottentots died of smallpox. Those who were left could do little but go to work as herders for the Europeans, who were taking over the best land. The area became a Dutch colony.

Black Africans worked for the whites on farms and ranches. Many blacks were slaves. Even free African blacks were treated not much better than slaves.

Cape Colony becomes British   In 1806 during a war in Europe, the British navy took over Cape Colony. The British government put an end to slavery in all parts of the British Empire in 1834. Slave owners were paid for their slaves, but the Dutch settlers said they got only a small part of what the slaves were worth.

The Dutch settlers, who were called Boers, did not like British rule. A number of Boers decided to leave the British-ruled cape and moved farther inland. They moved to the open grasslands called the high **veld.** Find the veld shown in the vegetation map of Africa on page 316.

On the veld the Boers came into conflict with other groups of black Africans known as Bantu people. This was the land of one such group called the Zulus. The Zulus were a cattle-raising people, too. They did not want to have the white ranchers moving onto the grasslands.

Shaka builds a Zulu nation   In the early nineteenth century, Shaka (shak′ ə) became king of the Zulus. He had a great desire for power. Shaka began to build a new kind of army. He put his men into groups called **impis** (im′ pēz), or regiments. He trained the men until they were strong, brave fighters. Zulu regiments could journey 50 miles (80 km) a day over rolling African hills. Shaka also improved the Zulu weapons. He invented a short thrusting spear. He taught his men to use it. As yet the Zulus had few guns.

343

Shaka holds the traditional Zulu assagai, or long spear.

Shaka was a hard and cruel man. People feared him with good reason. He used his army to conquer other Bantu tribes. Many ran away to neighboring lands. Other Bantu tribes were forced to join the growing Zulu nation. Shaka also tried to send officials to London so that the British government would work with the Zulus against the Boer settlers. By the time of his death, Shaka had built a nation.

Dingaan (din' gän), the next Zulu king, used the strong army against the Boer settlers. There were wars on the veld much like the wars between the Native Americans and the European settlers on the American frontier. Although Dingaan led the Zulus to victory against the Boer settlers, they lost in the end. In 1838, the Boers won control over the veld country at the well-named battle of Blood River.

European empires in Africa The British spread their control northward in southern Africa. When the Boer settlers left Cape Colony, they hoped that they had left everything British behind them. But the British later took control of the high veld country, too. The British also took over the lands of the Zulus and other Bantu people who lived in the eastern part of southern Africa.

At the time the British were colonizing larger parts of Africa, other European countries were dividing up the whole continent. The map on page 345 shows European control of African lands in 1920, after World War I.

The Portuguese had been the first Europeans to explore south of the Sahara. They were also the first to gain colonies. Portugal still had the large colonies of Angola and Mozambique (mō zəm bēk') in 1920. They lay near the mouths of two great African rivers. Angola extended south from the mouth of the Congo. Mozambique in eastern Africa stretched along the coast on both sides of the Zambezi River.

Britain and France between them held the largest part of Africa in 1920. The British controlled lands from the modern country of South Africa to Egypt. It was said that Britain ruled Africa from the Cape of Good Hope to Cairo in Egypt. The British Empire also included the important western African country of Nigeria.

The French empire in 1920 included most of northwestern and western Africa. The French held a large part of the Sahara lands. They also had wide stretches of savanna and forestlands south of the Sahara. In addition, France ruled the large island of Madagascar in the Indian Ocean, 300 miles (483 km) off the coast of eastern Africa. Madagascar is the fourth largest island in the world.

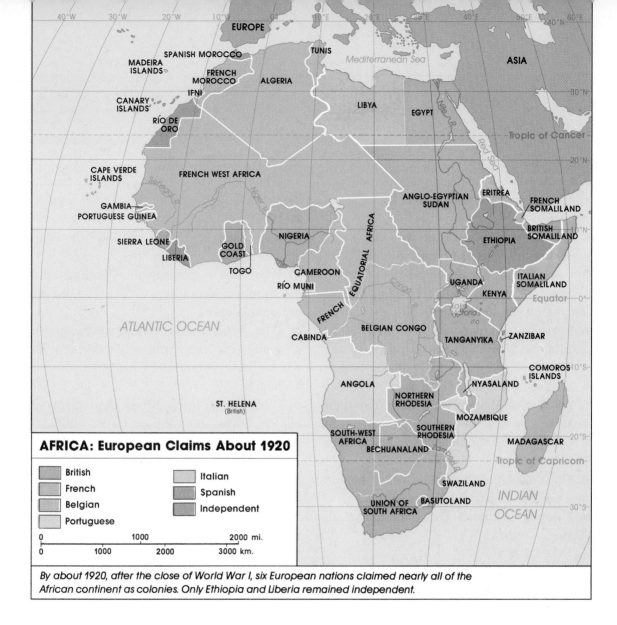

AFRICA: European Claims About 1920

British   **Italian**

French   **Spanish**

Belgian   **Independent**

Portuguese

0	1000	2000 mi.
0	1000	2000	3000 km.

By about 1920, after the close of World War I, six European nations claimed nearly all of the African continent as colonies. Only Ethiopia and Liberia remained independent.

The small European country of Belgium ruled a large country in Africa in 1920. At an earlier time, a Belgian king, Leopold II, organized a company to develop the lands drained by the Congo River. King Leopold was head of the company that, for a time, actually ruled the land which Europeans called the Congo. Later the Congo became a Belgian colony even though it was 77 times the size of Belgium.

The European empires in Africa did not last. Most African people and lands became independent nations after World War II. You will read about some of these nations in the next chapter.

CHECKUP

1. Why did the demand for slaves grow after European traders came to Africa?
2. Why did the Dutch start a settlement at the Cape of Good Hope? How did this affect Africans?
3. Who was Shaka and what did he do in Africa?
4. Which European countries controlled parts of Africa south of the Sahara in 1920?

345

KEY FACTS

1. In 1500 Europeans were just beginning to learn about the different lands of Africa south of the Sahara.

2. The Portuguese were the first Europeans to explore the coast of Africa and to sail from Europe to Asia.

3. There were rich trading cities like Tombouctou on the southern edge of the Sahara.

4. There were skilled workers in such forest kingdoms as Benin and Kongo.

5. The monsoons made it possible for traders to sail regularly from Asia to eastern Africa.

6. Millions of Africans were taken from their homeland by slave traders.

7. Europeans settled in southern and eastern Africa.

8. Shaka built a Zulu nation, which he and later kings led against the Boer settlers.

9. European countries controlled almost all of Africa in 1920.

VOCABULARY QUIZ

On a sheet of paper write the letter of the group of words that correctly completes each statement.

1. A monsoon is (**a**) a seasonal wind, (**b**) a forest crop, (**c**) a city in eastern Africa.

2. Porcelain is (**a**) a type of ship used in the Indian Ocean, (**b**) a person from Portugal, (**c**) fine earthenware such as china dishes.

3. Swahili is (**a**) a forest kingdom, (**b**) an African language with many Arabic words, (**c**) a trading city on the coast of eastern Africa.

4. Veld is (**a**) an open grassland, (**b**) a Boer settlement, (**c**) a building carved in solid rock.

5. A plantation is (**a**) a ship, (**b**) a colony in some faraway part of the world, (**c**) a large farm where workers raise cash crops.

REVIEW QUESTIONS

1. Who was Henry the Navigator and what did he do?

2. What did Europeans learn from Leo Africanus's book about African cities like Tombouctou?

3. What kind of government and religion did the people of Benin have? What kind did the Ethiopians have?

4. What African cities and kingdoms carried on trade with other parts of the world? With whom did they trade and what products were exchanged?

5. What can be learned from the remains of old Zimbabwe about the people who built it?

6. Why did the coming of European traders to Africa increase the demand for slaves? Who became slaves?

7. Who were the Bantu people? How did Shaka change life among the Zulus?

8. Which parts of Africa were under the control of the following European countries in 1920: Portugal, Britain, France, Belgium?

ACTIVITIES

1. Listed below are African cities or states important in history. Write a report about one of them: Gao, Ghana Empire, Ife, Jenne, Kongo, Kush, Mali Empire, Nok, Songhai Empire.

2. Make a map to show trade between African lands and other parts of the world during the fifteenth and sixteenth centuries. First trace the map of the world from the Atlas on pages 452 and 453. Label the different countries, kingdoms, and cities that carried on the trade. Then use symbols to stand for what was traded, and draw lines to show the different trade routes.

COMPARING MAPS/REVIEWING TIME

PHYSICAL AND POLITICAL MAPS GIVE DIFFERENT KINDS OF INFORMATION

Political and physical maps give different kinds of information about places. For example, the physical map of Africa in the Atlas on page 462 shows the surface of the land and the elevation. The political map of Africa on page 463 shows the boundaries of countries and locations of capitals and other important cities.

To complete the statements below so that they are correct, you may have to look at *both* the political and physical maps.

Example: In the country of Chad there (**a**) is a low coastal plain, (**b**) are mountains in the desert, (**c**) is little difference in elevation from one part of the country to another.

To choose the correct answer, you first locate Chad on the political map. You then locate that area on the physical map. You see that the Tibesti Mountains of the Sahara are in northern Chad. So the correct answer is **b**.

SKILLS PRACTICE

Write on a sheet of paper the correct answer for each statement below.

1. As the Portuguese sailed south from the Canary Islands along the coast to the Senegal River, they saw mostly (**a**) high mountains, (**b**) a high plateau rising sharply to more than 1,000 feet (300 m) above the coast, (**c**) low flat land along the coast.

2. Ethiopia is mostly (**a**) mountainous highlands, (**b**) a great river basin, (**c**) a gently sloping land.

3. Which of the following countries in western Africa is the most mountainous? (**a**) Guinea, (**b**) Benin, (**c**) Ghana.

4. The basin of the Congo River lies mostly in (**a**) Zaire, (**b**) Angola, (**c**) Gabon.

5. The most mountainous part of South Africa is (**a**) along the Atlantic coast, (**b**) north of the Vaal River, (**c**) along its eastern coastline.

6. Madagascar is (**a**) a low, flat island, (**b**) an island with some land of more than 2,000 feet (600 m) elevation, (**c**) an island with mountains that rise over 10,000 feet (3,000 m).

7. Which of these capital cities has the highest elevation? (**a**) Lagos, Nigeria, (**b**) Luanda, Angola, (**c**) Nairobi, Kenya.

8. If you followed the Nile River from Uganda to the middle of the Sudan, you would (**a**) climb to a higher elevation, (**b**) descend to a lower elevation, (**c**) remain at the same elevation.

9. Botswana is a country with (**a**) the highest mountains in Africa, (**b**) a broad plain along the coast, (**c**) both a desert and a swamp.

SKILLS PRACTICE: Reviewing Terms About Time

Review the material about the numbering of centuries in Chapter 2 on page 35. On a sheet of paper, write the century in which each of the following events took place:

1. A king of Ethiopia adopted the Christian religion, ca. 345.

2. Bartholomeu Dias sailed around the southern African capes, 1488.

3. Leo Africanus published his book called the *History of Africa,* 1526.

4. The Dutch established their first settlement at Cape of Good Hope, 1652.

5. British did away with slavery in all parts of their empire, 1834.

6. What does *ca.* mean in **1** above?

17 Africa Today South of the Sahara

Western and Central Africa

> **VOCABULARY**
>
> Commonwealth
>   of Nations   drought
> economy   famine
> landlocked   cobalt

The changing map of a changing continent The names of many lands have changed on the map of Africa since 1920. What used to be Gold Coast is now the country of Ghana. Northern Rhodesia has become the country of Zambia (zam′ bē ə), and the Belgian Congo has become the country of Zaire (zä ir′). The city of Léopoldville, named for a Belgian king, is now called Kinshasa (kin shäs′ ə).

The changes of names are signs of still greater changes. In 1920 European countries controlled almost all Africa. The continent was divided between the French, British, Belgian, Portuguese, and Spanish empires. After World War II, people all over Africa decided to throw off the rule of outsiders. African people and their leaders decided to do whatever was necessary to become independent. Today, most of Africa is made up of independent countries. Namibia, Cabinda, the Madeira Islands, the Canary Islands, and a few other islands are not yet independent.

There are more than 50 independent countries in Africa today. No other continent has so many nations. The African nations changed their names to show that they were no longer colonies of Europe. Some of the new names came from African kingdoms in the past.

Freedom from European rule has not always meant that Africans became free to elect their own governments. Many countries are governed by leaders chosen by the people. But many African countries are ruled by military leaders who have used the armies to gain and hold power. Some of these military leaders rule as dictators and allow no one to speak out against their rule.

This chapter tells about some of the different kinds of countries south of the Sahara. You will find all of the countries listed in the tables starting on page 486.

Empires go but languages and trade remain European empires no longer rule Africa, but African countries still use European languages as well as African languages. In the tables mentioned above, there is a list of languages used in each country. French is the official language in the countries that France once ruled. Portuguese remains the official language

Most countries in Africa south of the Sahara became independent of their European rulers between 1957 and 1980. Ghana became independent in 1957—an event honored by this arch in Ghana's capital.

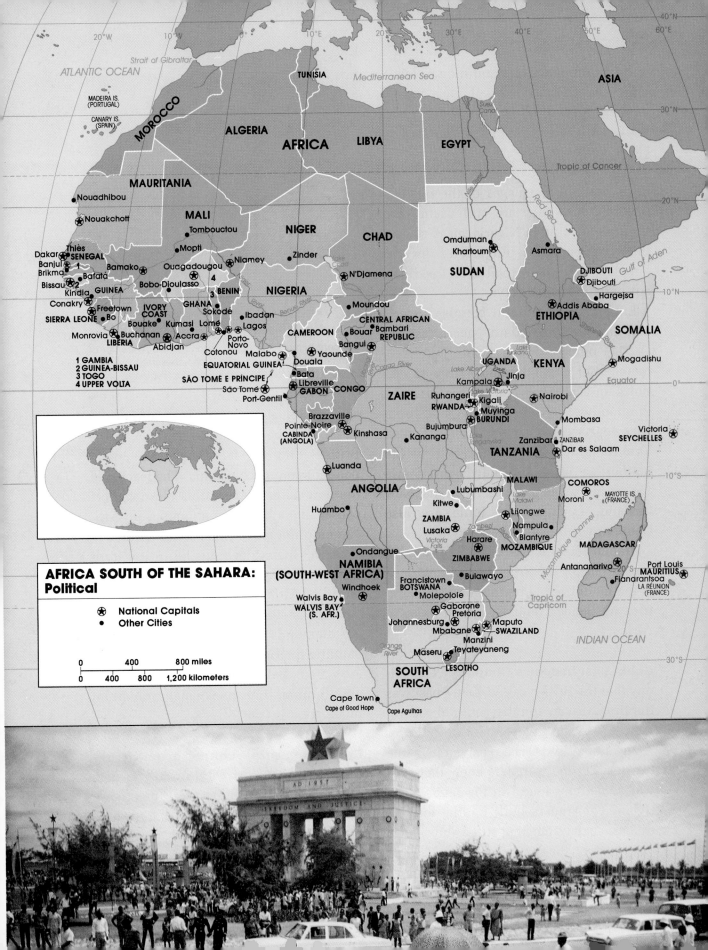

ATLANTIC OCEAN

Strait of Gibraltar

MADEIRA IS.
(PORTUGAL)

CANARY IS.
(SPAIN)

MOROCCO

MAURITANIA

Nouadhibou

Nouakchott

MALI

Tombouctou

Mopti

Thiès SENEGAL
Dakar
Banjul 1
Brikma Bamako
Bissau 2 Bafatá
Kindia GUINEA
Conakry
Freetown
SIERRA LEONE Bo
Bouake
Monrovia Buchanan
LIBERIA Abidjan

1 GAMBIA
2 GUINEA-BISSAU
3 TOGO
4 UPPER VOLTA

Niamey
Ouagadougou
4
Bobo-Dioulasso
3 BENIN
GHANA
Sokodé
Kumasi Lomé
Accra
Porto-
Novo
Cotonou

ALGERIA

AFRICA

TUNISIA

LIBYA

Mediterranean Sea

EGYPT

ASIA

Tropic of Cancer

NIGER

CHAD

Zinder

N'Djamena

NIGERIA

Ibadan
Lagos

Moundou

CAMEROON

CENTRAL AFRICAN
REPUBLIC

Bouar

Bambari

Bangui

Malabo
Douala
Yaounde

EQUATORIAL GUINEA

SÃO TOMÉ E PRÍNCIPE

São Tomé
Port-Gentil

Bata
Libreville
GABON

Omdurman
Khartoum

SUDAN

CONGO

Brazzaville
Pointe-Noire
CABINDA
(ANGOLA)

Kinshasa

ZAIRE

Kananga

Luanda

ANGOLA

Huambo

Ondangue

NAMIBIA
(SOUTH-WEST AFRICA)

Windhoek

Walvis Bay
WALVIS BAY
(S. AFR.)

ZAMBIA
Lusaka

Lubumbashi

Kitwe

MALAWI

Lilongwe

Asmara

DJIBOUTI
Djibouti

Hargejsa

Addis Ababa

ETHIOPIA

SOMALIA

Mogadishu

UGANDA
Kampala
Jinja

Ruhangeri
RWANDA Kigali
Muyinga
BURUNDI
Bujumbura

KENYA

Nairobi

Equator

Mombasa

Zanzibar ZANZIBAR
Dar es Salaam

Victoria
SEYCHELLES

TANZANIA

COMOROS
Moroni

MAYOTTE IS.
(FRANCE)

Nampula
Blantyre

MOZAMBIQUE

MADAGASCAR

Antananarivo

Port Louis
MAURITIUS

Fianarantsoa
LA RÉUNION
(FRANCE)

Harare

ZIMBABWE

Bulawayo

Francistown
BOTSWANA
Molepolole

Gaborone
Pretoria
Johannesburg
Mbabane
Maseru
Teyateyaneng
LESOTHO

Manzini
SWAZILAND

Maputo

SOUTH
AFRICA

Cape Town
Cape of Good Hope

Tropic of Capricorn

INDIAN OCEAN

Cape Agulhas

AFRICA SOUTH OF THE SAHARA:
Political

⊛ National Capitals
• Other Cities

0   400   800 miles
0   400   800   1,200 kilometers

in Angola and Mozambique (mō zəm bēk′), which were Portuguese colonies. Nigeria has not been ruled by Britain for years, yet English is still official and is the language taught in the schools.

Most independent African countries have kept the languages of the old empires because they are still useful. For example, people in Nigeria speak several different languages. English is the one language best understood in all the different parts of the country.

English is also useful because Nigeria still has ties with Britain. Nigeria, as well as 11 other African countries, is a member of the **Commonwealth of Nations.** In Chapter 8 you learned that the Commonwealth is an association of countries that were once part of the British Empire. It includes not only such African nations as Zambia, Malawi, and Sierra Leone, but others as well. Australia, New Zealand, Canada, and India are also Commonwealth countries.

French remains useful to countries no longer part of the French empire. France is the main trading partner of such countries as Senegal and Gabon in western Africa.

Gold Coast becomes Ghana   The colony that the British called Gold Coast was the first African country south of the Sahara to become independent of its European rulers. Gold Coast received its name because European traders knew that gold was sometimes found in the sands of its rivers. The traders built trading forts or castles, such as one that still stands in the city of Accra, the capital of Ghana. The fort is now used for government offices.

The central market in Accra, Ghana, is a busy center of commerce. Food, cloth, and other consumer products are sold here. Make a list of the products you see.

In 1957, about 100 years after Gold Coast had been made a colony of the British Empire, it became the independent country of Ghana. The leaders of the new nation gave it this old name because Ghana had been a famous old African empire on the Niger River. Although modern Ghana does not lie in the territory of old Ghana, this name reminds the world of Africa's great past.

There is still gold in Ghana, and there are diamonds as well. Large deposits of bauxite, the ore that contains aluminum, are also valuable. The smelting of aluminum is one of Ghana's important modern industries.

Chocolate and coffee from Ivory Coast   The early European traders who came to western Africa wanted ivory as well as gold. Ivory comes from the long teeth, or tusks, of elephants. One land came to be called Ivory Coast by the Europeans who traded for ivory there.

The French later took over this country and made it a colony. When the colony became independent in 1960, the new nation kept the old name.

If Ivory Coast were named today, it might be called "Chocolate and Coffee Coast." The country's greatest wealth now comes from cacao trees and coffee bushes rather than elephants' ivory tusks. Ivory Coast is the world's largest producer of cacao and the fourth largest producer of coffee.

Ivory Coast farmers are generally better off than those in other countries of western Africa. The government works to help farmers. Ivory Coast has small farms of 10 and 12 acres (4 and 5 ha). Many have a few cacao trees or coffee bushes along with food crops. Some small farms and plantations grow cacao, coffee, bananas, and hardwood trees for cash crops.

Shipping is a big business in countries that have good harbors and carry on an active trade with other countries. Ivory Coast and Ghana ship cacao, coffee, and other products to many parts of the world.

1. *A mature cacao tree, such as that shown at the left, bears between 20 and 40 fruit pods, which grow on the trunk and main branches.* **2.** *A pod, shown cut open, contains as many as 40 seeds, known as cocoa beans.* **3.** *The beans are fermented for 3 to 10 days and then dried in the sun, as shown in the bottom picture. The beans are then ready to be roasted, ground, and pressed to make cocoa powder, chocolate, and cocoa butter.*

1.

2.

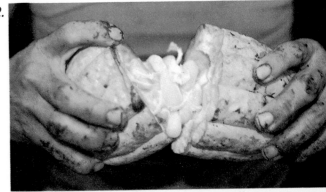

3.

The making of Nigeria   The British invented the name Nigeria for several lands they ruled along the lower Niger River. Different groups of people lived in these lands. They spoke different languages and had different ways of life.

When Nigeria became independent in 1960, it was hard to hold together the different parts of the country. It was said at that time, "West and East Nigeria are as different as Ireland from Germany." And northern Nigeria is also very different from the rest of the country.

Differences within the country brought on a civil war between 1967 and 1970. Thousands of people were killed. When fighting finally stopped, the people stayed together as one country. Today many Nigerians want to forget that terrible time. They tell visitors who ask about the different groups, "We are all Nigerians now!" Nigeria has more people than any other African country. The use of English in the schools helps to make one nation out of a country that has many other languages.

Oil from the "oil rivers" in Nigeria
The Niger River flows through many channels in its large delta. The British used to speak of these channels as separate streams. They called them the "oil rivers" because so much palm oil was shipped through the delta.

Today another kind of oil comes from the delta of the "oil rivers"—petroleum. Petroleum was first found in Nigeria in 1958. Since then the country has become one of the world's leading petroleum producers. Nigeria sells much of its petroleum to other countries, particularly to the United States.

Petroleum brought great changes to Nigeria, as it did in the Middle East. Lagos, the capital, has become a large and very crowded city. There are tall office buildings along with thousands of newly built houses and apartment buildings. Traffic fills the streets at rush hour. Nigerians call a traffic jam a "go slow."

Many Nigerians have left the rural areas for jobs in the city. At one time Nigeria

Lagos, Nigeria's capital city, is a busy center of government, business, education, worship, and other aspects of life and national culture.

Nigeria is the largest producer of petroleum in Africa. This refinery is at Port Harcourt, which is located on the delta of the Niger River at 4°N, 7°E.

Automobiles and the Old Wall of Kano

More than 460 years ago, Leo Africanus visited Kano, a trading city south of the Sahara. Among the things that Leo saw and described was the thick wall that enclosed the city. The wall was made of sun-dried brick and covered with mud plaster. It was 40 feet (12 m) thick at the base and sloped toward the top. In places the wall was 50 feet (15 m) tall.

The old wall is still one of the interesting sights of modern Kano in northern Nigeria. But, like old buildings in many places, it gets in the way of automobiles. Modern Kano has grown. The old wall is within the city rather than around it. The old gates were too narrow for automobiles, so they were made wider. Broader streets have been built in the old city, and new gates have been cut where there were none. In Kano, as in other parts of the world, people tear down old buildings to make room for automobiles and other new developments.

produced all of its food. Now it imports much food from other countries. Lagos has become an important port for ships that bring food, other consumer goods, and machinery into the country.

Nigeria has one of the most modern **economies** in Africa south of the Sahara. The economy of a country is its use of workers and resources to produce goods and services. Nigeria's wealth has increased with greater production of goods and services. Manufacturing of cloth and other goods has grown. The country's income from oil has increased rapidly. But so has its population. The number of people has doubled since 1958. As a result per capita income is not as high as in rich countries in other parts of the world.

Dry years in dry countries   The French empire in Africa was divided into 14 independent countries in 1960. Three of these countries, Mali, Niger, and Chad, are **landlocked** countries. A landlocked country is one that has no outlet on the sea. Africa has more landlocked countries than any other continent.

Mali, Niger, and Chad have a dry climate, and some years are drier than usual. In the 1970s, this part of Africa suffered a series of terrible **droughts.** A drought is an unusually dry season. Some places had no rain for years.

Many farmers did not have water to irrigate their crops. Nomads could not find pasture for sheep and cattle or even for camels. At least half of the livestock in

353

This mosque, which still stands in Tombouctou, was seen by Leo Africanus during his visit ca. 1516.

Niger died during those years. There was **famine** in the dry lands. A famine is a great lack of food. Large numbers of people had to move to camps where they were given food brought from other lands. For example, the United States sent grain and powdered milk.

Diseases spread among people crowded into the camps. Famine and disease took many lives. It was reported that as many as 100,000 people died in Mali alone.

The city of Tombouctou is in Mali. Leo Africanus said that Tombouctou was a rich city when he visited it more than 460 years ago. Visitors today no longer find a rich city, although some find the old mosque and other buildings interesting. Mali and its neighboring lands on the south edge of the Sahara are among the poorest countries in the world.

Congo becomes Zaire   Before 1960 Zaire was a Belgian colony known as the Congo. The colony was far larger than the European country that ruled it—77 times larger. The peoples who lived in this large land had not been united into a single nation. They spoke different languages. It was the Belgians who drew the boundaries and called the Congo a single land.

When Belgian rule ended in 1960, it looked as if the Congo would break apart. The people had no practice in working together in a government. The Belgians had ruled, and now they were gone. Civil war broke out.

An army officer, General Joseph Mobutu, took control of the Congo in 1965. He changed the country's name to Zaire. He said that Zaire was the true African name for the river that Europeans had wrongly called the Congo. Cities named after Europeans were given African names. Léopoldville and Stanleyville became Kinshasa and Kisangani (kē sən gān′ ē). The general changed his own name from Joseph Mobutu to Mobutu Sese Seko.

The official language was not changed. The Belgians had used French, and French remains the language of the government. It is one language understood by leaders in all parts of a country in which groups have different languages.

Zaire is Africa's second largest country. Sudan is the largest, but much of that country is desert and dry grassland. Zaire is twice the size of Nigeria, but Nigeria has twice as many people. Which country has higher population density?

Zaire's mines   Zaire supplies the world with useful minerals. Two thirds of the world's **cobalt** comes from Zaire. People have used cobalt since ancient times to

Africa is rich in mineral resources. Many valuable deposits are still undeveloped.

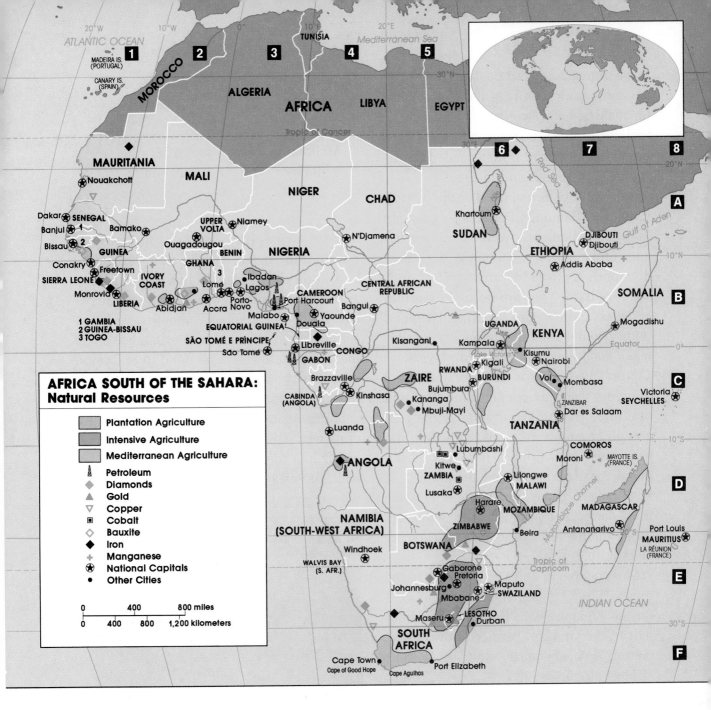

AFRICA SOUTH OF THE SAHARA: Natural Resources

Legend:
- Plantation Agriculture
- Intensive Agriculture
- Mediterranean Agriculture
- Petroleum
- Diamonds
- Gold
- Copper
- Cobalt
- Bauxite
- Iron
- Manganese
- National Capitals
- Other Cities

0   400   800 miles
0   400   800   1,200 kilometers

Map labels:

ATLANTIC OCEAN
MADEIRA IS. (PORTUGAL)
CANARY IS. (SPAIN)
MOROCCO
ALGERIA
TUNISIA
Mediterranean Sea
LIBYA
EGYPT
AFRICA
Tropic of Cancer
MAURITANIA
MALI
NIGER
CHAD
SUDAN
Red Sea
Gulf of Aden
Nouakchott
Khartoum
DJIBOUTI
Djibouti
Dakar
SENEGAL
Banjul
Bamako
UPPER VOLTA
Niamey
N'Djamena
ETHIOPIA
Addis Ababa
Bissau
GUINEA
Ouagadougou
BENIN
NIGERIA
SOMALIA
Conakry
GHANA
Mogadishu
SIERRA LEONE
Freetown
IVORY COAST
Lome
Ibadan
CENTRAL AFRICAN REPUBLIC
Monrovia
LIBERIA
Abidjan
Accra
Porto-Novo
Lagos
CAMEROON
Port Harcourt
Bangui
UGANDA
KENYA
1 GAMBIA
2 GUINEA-BISSAU
3 TOGO
Malabo
Yaounde
Douala
Kampala
Kisangani
Kigali
Kisumu
Nairobi
EQUATORIAL GUINEA
SÃO TOMÉ E PRÍNCIPE
Libreville
CONGO
ZAIRE
RWANDA
BURUNDI
Voi
São Tomé
GABON
Brazzaville
Bujumbura
Mombasa
Equator
CABINDA (ANGOLA)
Kinshasa
Kananga
ZANZIBAR
SEYCHELLES
Victoria
Luanda
Mbuji-Mayi
Dar es Salaam
TANZANIA
Lubumbashi
COMOROS
ANGOLA
Kitwe
Moroni
MAYOTTE IS. (FRANCE)
ZAMBIA
Lilongwe
MALAWI
MADAGASCAR
Lusaka
Antananarivo
NAMIBIA (SOUTH-WEST AFRICA)
Harare
MOZAMBIQUE
Port Louis
MAURITIUS
ZIMBABWE
Beira
LA RÉUNION (FRANCE)
Windhoek
BOTSWANA
Tropic of Capricorn
Gaborone
Pretoria
INDIAN OCEAN
WALVIS BAY (S. AFR.)
Johannesburg
Maputo
SWAZILAND
Mbabane
SOUTH AFRICA
Maseru
LESOTHO
Durban
Cape Town
Cape of Good Hope
Cape Aguilhas
Port Elizabeth

Cities less than 100,000

Banjul (Gambia) A-1
Bujumbura (Burundi) C-5
Djibouti (Djibouti) A-7
Gaborone (Botswana) ... E-5
Kisumu (Kenya) C-6
Malabo (Equatorial
   Guinea) B-3
Maseru (Lesotho) E-5
Mbabane (Swaziland) ... E-6
Moroni (Comoros) D-7
São Tomé
   (São Tomé e Príncipe) . C-3
Victoria (Seychelles) C-8
Voi (Kenya) C-6
Windhoek (Namibia) ... E-4

Cities 100,000 to 499,999

Antanandrivo
   (Madagascar) D-7
Bamako (Mali) A-2
Bangui (Central
   African Republic) B-4
Beira (Mozambique) D-6
Bissau (Guinea-Bissau) . A-1
Brazzaville (Congo) C-4
Conakry (Guinea) B-1
Douala (Cameroon) B-3
Freetown (Sierra Leone) . B-1
Kampala (Uganda) B-6
Khartoum (Sudan) A-6
Kigali (Rwanda) C-5
Kisangani (Zaire) B-5

Kitwe (Zambia) D-5
Libreville (Gabon) B-3
Lilongiwe (Malawi) D-6
Lome (Togo) B-3
Luanda (Angola) C-4
Lubumbashi (Zaire) D-5
Maputo (Mozambique) .. E-6
Mbuji-Mayi (Zaire) C-5
Mogadishu (Somalia) ... B-7
Mombasa (Kenya) C-6
Monrovia (Liberia) B-1
N'Djamena (Chad) A-4
Niamey (Niger) A-3
Nouakchott (Mauritania) . A-1
Ouagadougou
   (Upper Volta) A-2

Port Elizabeth
   (South Africa) F-5
Port Harcourt (Nigeria) .. B-3
Port Louis (Mauritius) ... E-8
Porto-Novo (Benin) B-3
Yaounde (Cameroon) ... B-4

Cities 500,000 to 999,999

Abidjan (Ivory Coast) ... B-2
Accra (Ghana) B-2
Cape Town (South Africa) F-4
Dakar (Senegal) A-1
Dar es Salaam
   (Tanzania) C-6
Durban (South Africa) .. E-6
Ibadan (Nigeria) B-3

Harare (Zimbabwe) D-6
Kananga (Zaire) C-5
Lusaka (Zambia) D-5
Nairobi (Kenya) C-6
Pretoria (South Africa) .. E-5

Cities 1,000,000 or more

Addis Ababa (Ethiopia) .. B-6
Johannesburg
   (South Africa) E-5
Kinshasa (Zaire) C-4
Lagos (Nigeria) B-3

355

make blue glass and porcelain. But cobalt has more important uses today. It is used for making hard steel needed for cutting tools such as drills, saws, and tools used in medicine. Cobalt is also needed for the steel in jet engines and magnets.

Zaire produces one third of the world's industrial diamonds. Perhaps you thought that most diamonds were used in rings and other jewelry. Actually, far more diamonds are used in industry. Diamonds are very hard. They are needed for grinders, glass cutters, and oil drills. Diamond points do not wear down quickly, so they make good needles for record players.

Zaire has deposits of other important minerals, such as copper, zinc, tin, and uranium. During World War II the first atomic bombs were made with uranium from this land. Copper is a very useful metal that has been used for more than 5,000 years. Today, most copper is made into electrical equipment and wires because the metal is very good for carrying electricity.

Most people in Zaire do not work in the mines. They are farmers. Zaire is located on the Equator. Rain forests cover about half of the country. Farmers grow coffee, cotton, rice, bananas, and other hot-climate crops.

CHECKUP

1. Why are European languages still used as official languages in a number of African countries? Give examples.
2. Name at least one farming, mining, or manufacturing product that each of the following countries produces: Ghana, Ivory Coast, Nigeria, Zaire.
3. Why did the leaders of Ghana and Zaire adopt those names for their countries?

Southern and Eastern Africa

```
┌─VOCABULARY──────────────────┐
│  Afrikaans        guerrilla   │
│  minority         pyrethrum   │
│  apartheid                    │
└──────────────────────────────┘
```

South Africa—the leading industrial country in Africa   The first Africans and European settlers to live in southern Africa were farmers and herders. A century ago the descendants of the first Dutch settlers were called *Boers*, a Dutch word meaning "farmer." The land that they settled became the country called the Republic of South Africa, or South Africa.

South Africa has a variety of lands and climates. The south near the cape is much like the Mediterranean lands. It is well suited for growing citrus fruits, wheat, and grapes. Wine was the first

The Mediterranean climate in South Africa's southern cape makes the area well suited for growing grapes.

important product exported from South Africa. The low land along the east coast near the city of Durban is sugarcane country. Most of the corn is grown in an inland area south of Pretoria, the capital. This land is shown as veld and savanna on the vegetation map on page 316.

Africans raised livestock in South Africa before the first European settlers arrived. South Africans still raise cattle and sheep. About 90 percent of the farmland is pasture. Wool is a leading export.

Although farming and ranching remain important, South Africa is now a modern industrial country. It is a rich nation and the leading industrial country in Africa. The tall buildings of the city of Cape Town and Johannesburg (jō han′ əs bərg), the largest city, look much like those in Western Europe and North America. South African factories make such products as steel, automobiles, farm machinery, tires, plastics, and electrical goods.

A treasure of minerals under the ground South Africa exports 54 different minerals. It has been said that the country "sits on a treasure of wealth

Cape Town is one of Africa's busiest harbors and business centers. As the city grows, it spreads nearer and nearer the steep cliffs of Table Mountain. The three buildings in the distance are circular apartment towers with views of the mountain and the city.

under the ground." The growth of the mining industry began with the discovery of diamonds and gold.

There is a story that diamonds were discovered about 1866 by children playing on the banks of the Orange River. The children took some pebbles home, not knowing that one was a diamond. Later someone discovered that the pebble could scratch glass. This is one test of a diamond, since it is the hardest stone known.

Hundreds of thousands of people work in South Africa's gold mines and mills, which produce nearly three times as much gold as any other country. Workers are shown melting gold to make bars that are 99.99 percent pure.

This diamond mine, the first dug in South Africa, is called the Big Hole. South Africa produces more gem diamonds than any country in the world.

News of diamonds brought people to South Africa. Mining camps grew into towns, and diamond mining became an important industry. It is still an important industry. Most of the diamonds used in jewelry today come from South Africa. South Africa also produces industrial diamonds.

South Africa leads the world in the production of gold. Johannesburg began as a gold rush town. It is located on a rocky ridge that Boer settlers believed was too poor for farming. In 1886 word spread that a man had found gold in a rock that he had kicked out of the ground on the ridge. Soon thousands of people came from Europe and elsewhere to dig for gold.

Diamonds and gold are not the only minerals in South Africa's earth. There are large deposits of copper, chromium, silver, and platinum. The world demand for platinum has grown lately because it is used in automobile engines to help reduce pollution.

European descendants in South Africa The Europeans who came to South Africa 300 years ago came to stay. They were like the Europeans who came to North America at the same time.

European settlers in South Africa differed from the few Europeans who lived for a time in the colonies of western and central Africa. Europeans in those colonies never thought of themselves as Africans. They went to the colonies for business and to run the governments. For them "home" was in Europe.

Descendants of the early Dutch, French, and German settlers in South Africa called themselves Afrikaners (af rə kä′ nərs). They speak a language known as **Afrikaans.** Afrikaans came from Dutch. During the last 300 years in Africa, Dutch became a separate language that includes words from English, French, German, and Bantu languages.

British settlers came to South Africa after Britain took over the Dutch colony. The number of settlers increased rapidly after the discovery of diamonds and gold.

About 17 percent of the total population in South Africa are white people whose ancestors were Europeans. Afrikaners make up 60 percent of this population. The others are called English because they descend from British settlers. Both Afrikaans and English are official languages. Many people speak both.

Bantus and other peoples in South Africa Black Africans make up the majority of people in South Africa. A majority is more than half of a group or nation. They make up 70 percent of the population. Most black South Africans are Bantus, who speak one of the Bantu languages. Many Bantus also speak Afrikaans or English. Bantus belong to different groups, sometimes called tribes or nations. Each group has its own ways and history.

About 10 percent of South Africa's population are called Coloureds. In South Africa *Coloured*, which is the British spelling of *colored*, means a person of mixed

South Africa is ruled by a small group—about 17 percent—that is made up of descendants of European settlers.

POPULATION OF SOUTH AFRICA

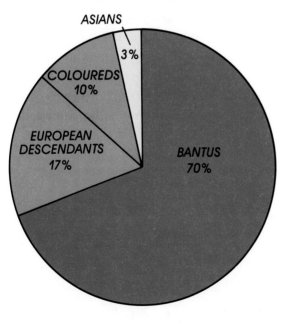

ASIANS 3%

COLOUREDS 10%

EUROPEAN DESCENDANTS 17%

BANTUS 70%

South Africa's Bantus and Coloureds make up most of the work force for the country's mines, factories, farms, and fishing fleets.

black and white origins. Most Coloureds speak Afrikaans or English.

South Africa also has a group of people whose ancestors came from India or other Asian countries. They are called Asians even though they were born in South Africa and live there. About 3 percent of the population are Asians, most of whom speak English.

European descendants rule in South Africa   In South Africa, the government is ruled by a small **minority** of the country's total population. A minority is a group that is smaller than half of a larger group or nation. The minority that runs the government in South Africa is made up of the white descendants of the Europeans. The country has an elected government, but only the white descendants of Europeans are allowed to vote or to

hold office. Neither the Bantu majority nor the Coloured and Asian minorities can take part in the government. The European descendants make the laws that all groups of people must follow.

The government says that it is better for everyone if each group of people lives in its own way. The government has laws to keep the Bantus, whites, Coloureds, and Asians apart. This plan is called **apartheid**

This home, built in a popular cape Dutch style, is in a community reserved for European descendants.

These homes are in an urban township reserved for Bantus. Men and women who live here work in the homes of European descendants or in factories and other jobs in the city nearby. Bantu townships are located near most cities.

South Africa's apartheid laws require most Bantus to live in rural areas of the country called homelands. These women and men, who live in one of the homelands, are building a traditional house made of mud bricks. Most soil in the homelands is not well suited for farming.

(ə pärt′ hāt), a word meaning "apartness." Each group has a certain district, or part of the country, in which it must live. But most of the land, the best farms, and the factories and big businesses are owned by the European descendants. Because they run the government, they have been able to keep everything that way.

Although all the non-European groups must live in their own districts, they work in the mines, factories, and farms owned by the European descendants. Bantu workers help produce the wealth that makes South Africa the richest country in Africa south of the Sahara.

People all over the world have said that apartheid is not fair. Some of the white European descendants in South Africa agree. It is pointed out that nonwhite workers receive lower wages than whites. Both Bantus and Coloureds have been forced to move from their old homes in order to create separate districts. The amount of money spent for each pupil in the schools differs greatly. For example, in 1980 about $900 was spent per pupil

for European descendants, $300 for Coloureds, and only $95 for Bantus.

Zambia and Zimbabwe Two other African countries in which Europeans settled are Zambia and Zimbabwe. But the European settlers in these lands were an even smaller minority than the European settlers were in South Africa.

Until 1964, Zimbabwe and its neighbor Zambia were known as Southern and Northern Rhodesia (rō dē′ zhēə). The Rhodesias were named after Cecil Rhodes, a European leader in southern Africa.

Cecil Rhodes wanted Britain to rule Africa from the Mediterranean Sea to the southern tip of the continent. He called for an empire reaching "from the Cape to Cairo." Rhodes formed a trading company that sent armed settlers into the lands that they named Southern Rhodesia and Northern Rhodesia. Black Africans tried to keep the settlers out, but the settlers had better weapons. Guns won over spears. But Rhodes's empire never came to be.

Zambia is the world's fourth largest copper producer. This factory for smelting copper is near Kitwe, located at about 13°S, 28°E. Notice the communities around the factory.

Few Europeans went to live in Northern Rhodesia. Most of them settled on the farmlands of Southern Rhodesia. But at no time did they make up more than 4 percent of the total population.

Independence in southern Africa   In 1964 Northern Rhodesia became the independent country of Zambia. After that, Southern Rhodesia was known simply as Rhodesia.

Many of the Bantu people in Rhodesia were no longer willing to accept rule by the minority who were European descendants. In the 1970s groups of Bantus began a **guerrilla** (gə ril′ ə) war against people who supported the government. A guerrilla war means a "little war" carried on by small groups that attack and hide. The Rhodesian army and police fought for 7 years against groups that were hard to find. Although it was called a "little war," it cost the lives of 27,000 people.

The government finally agreed to an election in which all people, black and white, could vote. Bantu leaders won. In April of 1980 they took over the country and called it Zimbabwe. Cecil Rhodes's name disappeared from the map. Three months later the new government took down Rhodes's statue in the capital city. The leaders of Zimbabwe did not wish to honor the man who had once taken their land for the British Empire.

Zimbabwe and Zambia are mostly farmlands, but both countries have other valuable resources. The Zambezi River, which forms their shared border, provides hydroelectric power. Zambia is the world's fourth largest producer of copper. Zimbabwe also manufactures many consumer goods, including automobiles and tobacco products. Both countries are landlocked, so they need the aid of their neighbors to get products to and from shipping ports on the Indian Ocean.

Kenya—a country in the eastern highlands Nairobi (nī rō′ bē), the capital of Kenya, is about 80 miles (129 km) south of the Equator. But Nairobi does not have a hot climate because it is located on the Kenya highlands. You read about these highlands and snow-covered Mount Kenya in Chapter 15.

When Kenya was made part of the British Empire in 1895, Nairobi was only a water hole for cattle herders. The name means "cold water." There was no town or city there until the railroad came in 1899.

The British built a railroad across Kenya to connect Lake Victoria with Mombasa, the chief port city on the Indian Ocean. It was difficult to build a railroad across such a highland, as you can see from the diagram on page 364. This cross section shows the elevation of the land along the railroad route. For example, it shows that a train must climb 2,000 feet (610 m) while going 100 miles (161 km) from Mombasa to Voi. A train must climb above 5,000 feet (1,524 m) before reaching Nairobi, 330 miles (531 km) from the coast. How much higher

You can see that some of Kenya's roadways are used for more than travel by foot, bike, and automobile. Cattle herding has been a way of living for centuries in Kenya.

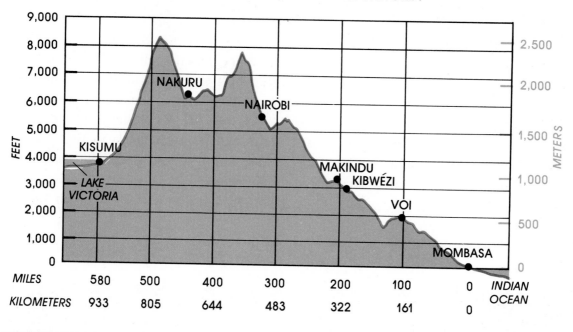

A CROSS SECTION OF KENYA'S RAILROAD ROUTE:
FROM THE INDIAN OCEAN TO LAKE VICTORIA

This railroad has made it easier to move people and products to and from the highlands.

must a train climb before beginning the steep descent to Kisumu on Lake Victoria? At its highest point, the train will have reached an altitude of more than 1.5 miles (2.4 km) above sea level.

The railroad brought new groups of people to Kenya. Workers from India came to build the railroad. Indian merchants followed. European settlers came to farm on the highlands. Europeans called the highlands "empty lands" because it seemed to them that the African herders made such little use of the land.

The settlers who came to Kenya intended to stay, as Europeans had done in South Africa. One farmer who had lived 35 years in Kenya wrote: "We are Africans—white Africans—and Africa is our home and our country as much as it is the country of black Africans."

Yet the number of white Africans was small. They remained a minority of less than 1 percent, although they had 25 percent of the best land.

Independence for Kenya   The black Kenyans believed that their land had been taken from them unfairly. They said that the highland had never been truly "empty lands." The cattle herders had used the land in the African way. They had moved about with their cattle seeking the best pasture. They had cultivated small patches to raise the food they needed.

The black Africans believed that Kenya was their country. They wanted their own government rather than white rule. Guerrilla war broke out. In 1963 Britain agreed to let all the people of Kenya vote on their future. They chose independence.

The people of Kenya elected Jomo Kenyatta as the first president. Kenyatta had led the struggle against the British. But he invited whites and Indians to stay in Kenya and build a new nation. Some people stayed, although others left.

The large farms of the European settlers were divided into smaller farms and sold. Today Kenya is mostly a farming country. Coffee and tea are the most important crops grown for export. **Pyrethrum** (pī rē′ thrəm) is Kenya's most unusual cash crop. Pyrethrum is a daisylike

Tea farms, such as this one, make up an important part of Kenya's economy. Kenya is mostly a farming country, which also grows large crops of coffee, sisal, sugarcane, corn, wheat, and pyrethrum.

Jomo Kenyatta reviews the presidential honor guard of Kenya. He became the first president of Kenya in 1963, after leading the long struggle for independence from Britain.

plant used to make insect poison. Kenya produces most of the world's supply of pyrethrum.

Kenya became a member of the Commonwealth of Nations. English remains an official language, but people running for office must also know Swahili. Swahili is the African language most commonly spoken in Kenya.

A few descendants of the Europeans have held office in Kenya since independence. In 1979 a European descendant was elected to the assembly. He was a true white African. He had been born in Kenya as had his father before him.

The end of European empires in Africa   The Portuguese were the first Europeans to build trading forts on the African coast. They were the first to claim colonies, and Portugal was the last country to give up its African empire.

The two largest lands held by Portugal were Angola and Mozambique. Both countries became independent in 1975 after years of guerrilla war.

Angola is on the southwestern coast of Africa. It also includes Cabinda, a small territory north of the Congo River. Cabinda is separated from the rest of Angola by a strip of Zaire's territory. Cabinda looks small when compared with the rest of Angola, but it is an important part of the country. Angola's most important petroleum field is located in Cabinda. It also has valuable forests.

Since Angola's independence, changes in the economy have strengthened the country. Most people still farm, but minerals have become the chief exports. New industries also have helped Angola to grow.

Mozambique is on the southeastern coast of Africa. It lies along the Indian Ocean north and south of the mouth of the Zambezi River. Exports from Mozambique include cashew nuts, sisal, and other farm products. The cashew nut tree was taken from America to Africa by the Portuguese about 400 years ago.

Most of the French colonies became independent countries in 1960. You can see which countries these are by comparing the map on page 345 with the political map of Africa on page 349. But France continued to control Djibouti until

Today there are more than 50 independent countries in Africa. Most of them were colonies of European countries until winning independence during the past three decades.

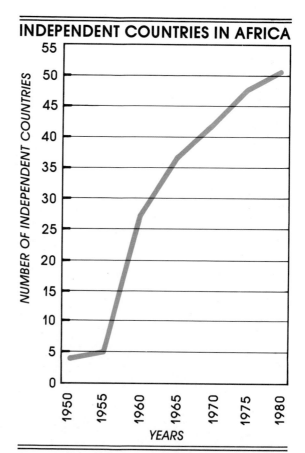

INDEPENDENT COUNTRIES IN AFRICA

This painting is in the headquarters of the Organization of African Unity. It shows the flags and leaders of the independent nations in Africa that formed the group in 1963.

1977. Djibouti is a small and very poor country. It has no oil, gold, or diamonds. It is very dry and does not grow enough food to feed its people. The country's one important resource is its location. Djibouti is on the narrow strait that leads to and from the Red Sea. It serves as a port for the region. A railroad runs from Djibouti to Addis Ababa, the capital city of Ethiopia.

Djibouti became independent 20 years after Ghana. In those years more than 30 other countries south of the Sahara also became independent. The European empires that had grown up over many years broke up in a short time. Today, most African countries are members of the Organization of African Unity, which has its headquarters in Addis Ababa. The organization supports freedom for all African people. Through the organization, African countries work for peace and cooperation so that they can help each other to build strong nations.

CHECKUP

1. Who are the different groups of people in South Africa?
2. What was the name of Zimbabwe before it became independent?
3. Why did Europeans come to Kenya?
4. Which European colonies south of the Sahara were the last to become independent?

KEY FACTS

1. Most European colonies in Africa became independent countries between 1957 and 1980.

2. White minorities in South Africa, Zimbabwe, and the highlands of Kenya are the descendants of European settlers.

3. Many independent African countries use both African and European languages.

4. Nigeria has more than twice the population of any other country in Africa.

5. Zaire has rich deposits of minerals.

VOCABULARY QUIZ

Listed below are the meanings of 12 words. Each is followed by 3 words that look somewhat alike. On a sheet of paper, write the letter of the word that fits the meaning.

1. An unusually dry season. (**a**) draught, (**b**) drudge, (**c**) drought.

2. A "little war." (**a**) gorilla, (**b**) guerrilla, (**c**) gargle.

3. An element used in making hard steel. (**a**) cobalt, (**b**) copra, (**c**) cobra.

4. A great lack of food. (**a**) fanfare, (**b**) famine, (**c**) familiar.

5. A country with no outlet to the sea. (**a**) landward, (**b**) landlocked, (**c**) landmarked.

6. An association of countries once part of the British Empire. (**a**) Commonwealth, (**b**) Commune, (**c**) Committee.

7. Language used in South Africa. (**a**) Afrikaner, (**b**) Afrikander, (**c**) Afrikaans.

8. Less than half of a group or nation. (**a**) majority, (**b**) majesty, (**c**) minority.

9. A plan to keep groups separated in South Africa. (**a**) apparition, (**b**) apartheid, (**c**) apparatus.

10. A daisylike plant used in making insect poison. (**a**) pyrethrum, (**b**) pyrite, (**c**) python.

REVIEW QUESTIONS

1. The following names were once used for certain African countries. Give their present names: Gold Coast, Belgian Congo, Southern Rhodesia, Northern Rhodesia.

2. Why are some European languages still used as official languages in some African countries?

3. Where are the "oil rivers" and what kinds of oil are exported from that region?

4. What minerals are mined in Zaire? In South Africa?

5. How have some African countries gained independence? How are different countries ruled?

6. Why was Zimbabwe once called Rhodesia? Why was the name changed?

7. Why was it difficult to build a railroad from Lake Victoria to the African east coast?

8. Which African countries did Portugal rule?

ACTIVITIES

1. Suppose you were a radio or television news reporter who had to prepare a report entitled "Africa in the News." Collect stories from recent newspapers that would provide material for the report. Write a script that a newscaster could read on the air.

2. Suppose an airline offered a free trip to any country in Africa for the best letter explaining why the writer would like to go there. Which country would you like to visit? Write a letter explaining why. Use a reference book to learn more about what you could see and do there. Choose a committee of the class to read the letters and decide which should win.

3. Make a drawing of the flag of one or more countries of Africa south of the Sahara. You can find pictures of flags in reference books.

17/ SKILLS DEVELOPMENT

LOOKING FOR CAUSES

ASK *WHAT* AND *WHY* EVENTS HAPPEN

When we learn about an event, we want to know *what* happened and *why* it happened.

The first four exercises state events described in Chapter 16. Each statement about an event is followed by three other statements. Each of the three statements is true, but only one tells why the event happened. Only that statement gives the cause of the event.

SKILLS PRACTICE: Part I

On a sheet of paper, write the letter of the statement that makes each sentence tell what happened and why. The page numbers tell where the event is described in Chapter 16.
Example: Regular trade between eastern Africa and India grew because (page 336)
   a. of the monsoon winds.
   b. people in eastern Africa spoke Swahili.
   c. each city had its own ruler.
Both **b** and **c** are true statements, but only **a** tells why trade grew.
1. The Arabs did not conquer Ethiopia because (page 335)
   a. it was a Christian country.
   b. it is hard to reach and mountainous.
   c. the Queen of Sheba visited Solomon's kingdom.
2. The slave trade grew after Europeans came to western Africa because (page 340)
   a. large numbers of slaves were wanted for plantations in the Americas.
   b. the Portuguese were the first to build trading posts.
   c. the king of the Kongo wrote to the king of Portugal.
3. The Dutch established a settlement at the Cape of Good Hope because (page 342)
   a. the British took the cape during a war.
   b. the Hottentots lived there.
   c. they wanted a supply station for ships.
4. The Boers moved to the high veld because (page 343)
   a. they did not like British rule.
   b. the Zulus lived there.
   c. the Zulus raised cattle.

SKILLS PRACTICE: Part II

The questions in the second part of this exercise are about events described in Chapter 17. You are to answer each question with a *complete sentence that tells what happened and why it happened.* Your sentences will probably include such words as "because," "in order that," "for the reason that." The page numbers tell where the event is described.
Example: Why were European settlers able to take over land they called Rhodesia? (page 361)
   A complete sentence telling *what* happened and *why* could read, "European settlers took over Rhodesia because they had better weapons than the Africans living there."
Write your answers on a sheet of paper.
1. Why was English chosen as the language for schools in Nigeria? (pages 350 and 352)
2. Why are farmers of Ivory Coast better off than farmers in other countries of western Africa? (page 351)
3. Why has the per capita income of oil-rich Nigeria not risen rapidly? (page 353)
4. Why have people all over the world said that South Africa's apartheid is unfair? (page 361)
5. Why did the Africans in Kenya believe that the lands taken by European settlers were not "empty lands"? (page 364)
6. Why were the names of some African countries changed? (pages 350, 354, and 362)

6/UNIT REVIEW

1. Africa is divided by the Sahara. — *Why did people cross the Sahara during many centuries of Africa's past?*

2. Africa has a variety of lands and climates. — *Describe the kinds of lands you would see if you were to fly from North Africa to Cape Agulhas.*

3. Most of the southern two thirds of Africa is a plateau. — *Why is it difficult to travel by riverboat into the interior?*

4. Africans learned to use different lands in different ways. — *How did Africans make use of the deserts, rain forests, and dry grasslands?*

5. Before 1500 there were cities on the edge of the Sahara and kingdoms in the forests and on the Ethiopian plateau. — *List one thing a traveler in 1500 could have seen in each of the following places: Tombouctou, Benin, Ethiopia. Suppose you were an artist who visited Africa's cities and kingdoms in 1500. What would you have drawn in your sketchbook?*

6. European traders came to the African coast seeking gold, ivory, and slaves. — *Why did the demand for slaves increase at this time?*

7. Almost all of Africa became colonies under the rule of European empires. — *Which countries in Europe had African territories in 1920? What were some of the different reasons that European countries wanted colonies in Africa? Where did Europeans settle in Africa?*

8. Most countries of Africa are now independent. — *Why were the following names chosen for each of these countries: Ghana, Ivory Coast, Nigeria, Zaire, Zimbabwe?*

9. South Africa is ruled by its white minority. — *Name the other groups of people in South Africa. Where do they live and work, and what part do they take in the government? How have groups been kept separate?*

10. Some African countries have important mineral resources. — *What are some mineral resources of the following: Ghana, Zaire, South Africa?*

11. There have been wars within certain African countries since World War II. — *What was the difference between the wars in Nigeria and Zaire and those in Zimbabwe and Kenya?*

12. European empires in Africa came to an end in the 1970s. — *Which European country was the last to give up large territories in Africa?*

South Asia, East Asia and Australia

What Nature Gave South and East Asia

┌─VOCABULARY─────────────────┐
│ interior   causeway │
│ subcontinent   │
└────────────────────────────┘

The world's largest continent   It is very hard to take a detailed look at the lands and peoples of Asia because Asia has one third of all the earth's land and most of the world's people. Asia is so large that almost anything you can say about any land in the world is true of some part of Asia.

Are there mountains in Asia? Yes, the highest in the world. Are there lowlands? Yes, some parts of Asia are below sea level. Some parts of Asia are very wet, yet Asia has some of the world's largest deserts. Some parts of Asia are very hot, but other parts are very cold. On the average, Asia is the coldest continent on which people live.

You have already read about parts of this large continent. The Soviet Union stretches across northern and central Asia. The countries of the Middle East are actually part of southwestern Asia. In this unit you will learn about the lands and peoples of South and East Asia. You will also learn about Australia and New Zealand. Both these lands are in the Southern Hemisphere. Australia is the only inhabited continent that lies entirely south of the Equator.

Mountains and plateaus divide Asia
The physical map of Eurasia on pages 464 and 465 in the Atlas shows an important fact about Asia. A belt of mountains and plateaus stretches northeast from the Persian Gulf all the way across the continent.

The world's highest mountains, the Himalayas (him ə lā′ əz), form part of this belt. The highest mountain in the world, Mt. Everest (ev′ ər ist), is in the Himalayas. Mt. Everest is more than 5 miles high (29,028 feet or 8,848 m). It is hard to climb so high a mountain because of the cold winds and the lack of oxygen. No one climbed Mt. Everest until 1953, when Sir Edmund Hillary from New Zealand and Tenzing Norgay (ten zing′ nor gā′) from Nepal (nə pol′) reached the top. Since then, Everest has been climbed a number of times. The first woman climbed it in 1970.

Mountains such as the Himalayas and the Hindu Kush (hin′ dü kush) form a steep wall between South Asia and the rest of the continent. But there are passes through this mountain wall. One of the most important passes is the Khyber (kī′ bər) Pass through the Hindu Kush between Pakistan (pak i stan′) and Afganistan.

Some of the world's highest mountains and longest rivers are in South and East Asia. Australia's mountains are not as high, and it has few rivers.

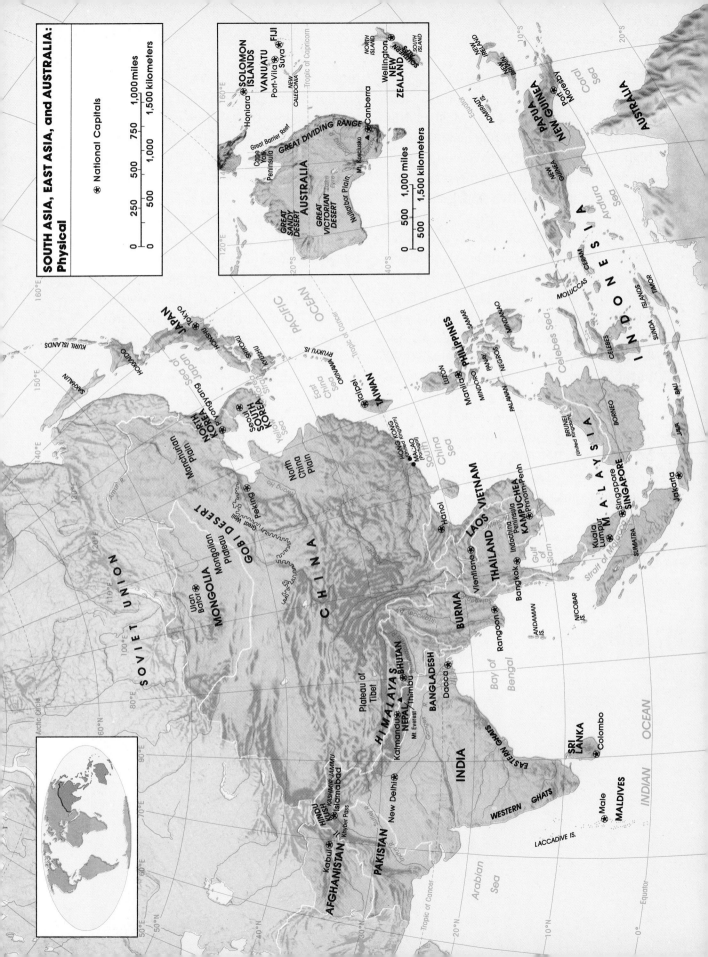

SOUTH ASIA, EAST ASIA, and AUSTRALIA: Physical

⊛ National Capitals

0   250   500   750   1,000 miles
0   500   1,000   1,500 kilometers

0   500   1,000 miles
0   500   1,000   1,500 kilometers

SOLOMON ISLANDS
VANUATU
FIJI
Honiara
Port-Vila
Suva
NEW CALEDONIA
Wellington
NEW ZEALAND
NORTH ISLAND
SOUTH ISLAND
Canberra
Mt. Kosciusko
GREAT DIVIDING RANGE
Cape York Peninsula
Great Barrier Reef
AUSTRALIA
GREAT SANDY DESERT
GREAT VICTORIAN DESERT
Lake Eyre
Nullabor Plain

SOVIET UNION

JAPAN
Tokyo
HOKKAIDO
HONSHU
SHIKOKU
KYUSHU
KURIL ISLANDS
SAKHALIN
Sea of Japan
NORTH KOREA
Pyongyang
SOUTH KOREA
Seoul
Yellow Sea
East China Sea
OKINAWA
RYUKYU IS.
TAIWAN
Taipei

PACIFIC OCEAN

Manchurian Plain
MONGOLIA
Ulan Bator
Mongolian Plateau
GOBI DESERT
Great Wall
Peking
North China Plain
CHINA
Plateau of Tibet
HIMALAYAS
Mt. Everest
Ganges R.
Huang Ho (Yellow R.)
Yangtze R.

HONG KONG (United Kingdom)
MACAO (Portugal)
South China Sea

PHILIPPINES
Manila
LUZON
MINDORO
PANAY
NEGROS
SAMAR
MINDANAO
PALAWAN

Celebes Sea

INDONESIA
BORNEO
CELEBES
MOLUCCAS
CERAM
SUNDA ISLANDS
TIMOR
BALI
JAVA
SUMATRA
Jakarta
Arafura Sea

PAPUA NEW GUINEA
NEW GUINEA
NEW IRELAND
NEW BRITAIN
Port Moresby
ADMIRALTY IS.
Coral Sea

AUSTRALIA

Equator
Tropic of Capricorn

HINDU KUSH
AFGHANISTAN
Kabul
Khyber Pass
KASHMIR-JAMMU
Islamabad
PAKISTAN
Indus R.
New Delhi
NEPAL
Katmandu
BHUTAN
Thimbu
BANGLADESH
Dacca
INDIA
WESTERN GHATS
EASTERN GHATS
Bay of Bengal
Colombo
SRI LANKA
Male
MALDIVES
LACCADIVE IS.

BURMA
Rangoon
ANDAMAN IS.
NICOBAR IS.
LAOS
Vientiane
THAILAND
Bangkok
Gulf of Siam
VIETNAM
Hanoi
KAMPUCHEA
Phnom-Penh
Indochina Peninsula
Mekong R.
MALAYSIA
Kuala Lumpur
BRUNEI (United Kingdom)
SINGAPORE
Singapore
Strait of Malacca

Arabian Sea
INDIAN OCEAN
Tropic of Cancer
Equator

Arctic Circle

The plateau of Tibet (tə bet') forms part of the great belt of mountains and plateaus that divides Asia. Most of this plateau is more than 10,000 feet (3,048 m) high. Even though Tibet is very high, people do live there. It is sometimes said that the people of Tibet live "on the roof of the world."

Mongolia (män gōl yə) is a country located on a plateau northeast of Tibet. Mongolia is not as high as Tibet, but it is still called a "mile-high land." The Gobi (gō' bē) Desert is in Mongolia. People who think that all deserts are sandy and hot would be surprised if they crossed the Gobi in the winter. The Gobi is a stony desert. Sand covers only about 3 percent of it. Winter temperatures drop to −30°F (−34°C) and sometimes lower. Summers are hot, for the Gobi is like much of Asia's **interior**, or inland area. You will recall reading in Chapter 9 that the Soviet lands in Asia's interior have a continental climate. They are hot in summer and cold in winter.

Most people in Asia live south and east of the belt of mountains and plateaus. Much of the land west and north of the belt is dry, and, in winter, very cold.

The monsoons and climate The monsoons that carried sailing ships between eastern Africa and Asia greatly affect Asia's climate. The summer monsoon picks up moisture as it blows over the Indian Ocean. The moisture falls as rain on South Asia. Different parts of South Asia get different amounts of rain. Rainfall is heavy in the foothills south of the mountain wall. One village in northeast India once received a record 366 inches (930 cm) of rain in a single month. Usually the village gets about half that amount. How does this compare with the amount of rain that falls where you live?

The highest mountains in the world, the Himalayas, are high above this river valley in the mountain country of Nepal.

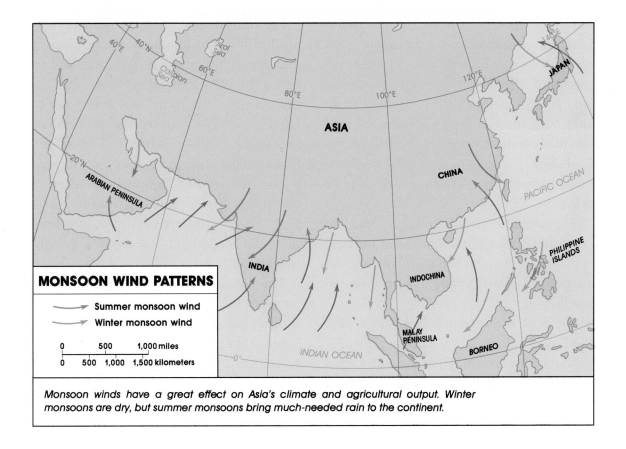

MONSOON WIND PATTERNS

→ Summer monsoon wind

→ Winter monsoon wind

| 0 | 500 | 1,000 miles |
| 0 | 500 | 1,000 | 1,500 kilometers |

Monsoon winds have a great effect on Asia's climate and agricultural output. Winter monsoons are dry, but summer monsoons bring much-needed rain to the continent.

The winter monsoon blows from Asia's dry interior. Winters in South Asia are sunny and dry. The spring months before the start of the summer rains are the hottest time of the year.

In East Asia the summer monsoon blows from the east off the Pacific Ocean. It, too, brings moisture from the ocean. Heavy summer rains fall, particularly in Southeast Asia. Winters are drier in East Asia, since the winds usually blow from Asia's interior.

Peninsulas and islands The Indian **subcontinent** is a large peninsula that stretches into the Indian Ocean. It is called a subcontinent partly because of its size, and partly because it is separated from the rest of Asia by the highest part of the mountain wall. The Indian subcontinent is larger than Western Europe.

The Eastern Ghats (gots) are mountains along the eastern coast of the Indian subcontinent. The Western Ghats are mountains along the western coast of the subcontinent. When Vasco da Gama sailed east from Africa in 1498, the first part of Asia he saw was the Western Ghats.

The Indian subcontinent is only one of Asia's peninsulas. The Malay (mə lā′) Peninsula is another. It is a long, narrow neck of land that separates the Indian Ocean from the South China Sea.

The island of Singapore (sing′ gə pōər) lies just off the tip of the Malay Peninsula. Singapore is so close to the peninsula that the island has been joined to the mainland by a **causeway**. A causeway is a raised roadway across water. Both a railroad and a highway cross the causeway between Singapore and the Malay Peninsula. Singapore is located on the shortest sea route from the coast of South Asia to East Asia. Because of its location, Singapore became one of the world's great seaports.

The islands off the coast of Asia are considered part of the continent because they are so close to the mainland. About 13 percent of all Asians live on these islands.

Some of these islands are on or near the Equator. Look at the map on page 373. Find the Sunda (sən' də) Islands, Sri Lanka (srē län' kə), and the Philippine (fil' ə pēn) Islands. These are lands near the Equator that have a hot climate and a summer rainy season.

The islands of Japan are also considered part of Asia. They are farther north than the other islands, and east of the Korean peninsula. Hokkaido (hä kīd' ō), the northernmost of the main Japanese islands, is as far north of the Equator as France is. Honshu (hän' shü) is the largest Japanese island. Ocean winds bring rains to Japan throughout the year. Forests grow on the mountainous Japanese islands. Most of the land is too rugged for farming.

River plains and valleys Much human history has taken place along rivers. City life began on the plains of the Tigris and Euphrates rivers in ancient Mesopotamia. The ancient Egyptians lived in the valley and on the delta of the Nile.

For centuries people have grown crops, built cities, and fought wars on the river plains of South and East Asia. The Indian subcontinent's first cities were built on the plains of the Indus (in' dəs) River in what is now the country of Pakistan. The Indus begins high in the Himalayas and flows across a large dry plain on its way to the Arabian Sea. People built cities on the Indus Plain more than 4,000 years ago. These cities, like those in Mesopotamia, depended on river water for irrigation.

The Ganges (gan' jēz) River starts not far from the Indus in the Himalayas, but it flows east to the other side of the Indian subcontinent. The Ganges begins with water from a melting glacier 10,000 feet (3,048 m) above sea level. The Ganges flows across a plain made rich with silt washed down from the mountains and hills. Before flowing into the Bay of Bengal (ben gol'), the Ganges and the Brahmaputra (bräm ə pü' trə) rivers join each other and form a large delta. The delta is larger than some countries.

Millions of people have lived along the Ganges and grown crops on its rich plain. Many millions live there today. It is one of the most densely populated areas in the world. Millions of people visit the Ganges because they believe it is a holy river.

The ancestors of the Chinese people built the first cities of East Asia on the plain of the Hwang Ho [Hwang He]. (The name in brackets is the way the Chinese pronounce the name of this river. Throughout the following chapters, the Chinese pronunciation of place-names will be given in brackets after the old Chinese place-name.)

A boat carrying religious worshipers along the Ganges River in India passes by the Hindu holy city of Varanasi. Thousands of Hindus visit the Ganges every year.

The Hwang Ho makes its way down from Tibet and flows across a plain of fine yellow soil. Rain washes the soil into the river, giving it a muddy yellow color. The Hwang Ho is also called the Yellow River.

The Hwang crosses the flat North China Plain. In the past, when the waters of the Hwang rose, the river spread over its banks, destroying crops and homes on the plain. Because of such floods, the Chinese called the Hwang "China's sorrow." When the floods went down, they left rich silt on the land. The silt-covered fields made it possible for farmers to grow enough food to support the people who built cities.

The Yangtze (yan' sē) [Chang] River also begins in Tibet. The Chinese call the Yangtze the "long river." It is a good name, for it is the longest river, not only in China, but in all of Asia. The Yangtze carriers much silt along its long course. Much of this silt is deposited at the Yangtze's delta, which grows about a mile (1.6 km) every 64 years or so.

The longest river in Southeast Asia is the Mekong (mā kon'). Millions of people live in the valley of the Mekong. Like the Hwang and the Yangtze, the Mekong begins in Tibet. It then flows south through Laos (laùs), Kampuchea (kam pù' chē ə), and Vietnam (vē et nam') to the South China Sea.

CHECKUP

1. Describe the belt that divides South and East Asia from the rest of the continent.
2. How do the summer and winter monsoons affect South and East Asia?
3. Name some of the islands usually considered part of Asia.
4. What are the two largest rivers of the Indian subcontinent?

377

Using the Land in South and East Asia

┌─VOCABULARY─────────────────
│ cultivate   mechanization
│ terrace   waterlogged
│ compost
└────────────────────────────

Farming changes the land   People in South and East Asia learned how to **cultivate** the land thousands of years ago. To cultivate land means to prepare and use it for growing crops.

As people use the earth, they change it. The very first farmers, like farmers today, dug up and threw away plants they did not want so they could raise plants they did want. Later they dug ditches to irrigate land that was too dry, or to drain land that was too wet for farming.

People in South and East Asia also changed hillsides to make more land for farming. Some hills were too steep for regular fields, so people built **terraces** (ter′ is iz). Terraces are flat areas built up like staircases on the sides of hills. Crops are planted on each terrace, so that even steep hills can be used to grow food.

It takes skill and hard work to build terraces. It also takes work to keep them in good shape and to grow crops on them. The terrace builders did not use machines. They changed the shape of the land with hand tools and muscle power.

Skilled farmers of the past   Over the centuries, farmers in South and East Asia learned a great deal about cultivating the land. They were the first to grow rice, one of the world's most important grains. They learned how to raise crops that came from other parts of the world. They discovered how to grow more than one crop on the same field at different times of the year.

Travelers to Asia told about the skilled work of its farmers. A visitor from Africa in 1345 wrote: "China is the best cultivated country in the world. There is not a spot in the whole extent of it that is not brought under cultivation."

Almost 600 years later, in 1910, an American agricultural expert visited China to see how people farmed. What this scientist saw "instructed, surprised, and amazed" him. The Chinese farmers were among the most skilled farmers in the world at that time.

Farmers in South China grew two crops of rice a year. Farmers in North China grew different crops on the same fields each year. They planted wheat in the fall

Terraced hillsides are found in many countries in South and East Asia. Terraces provide more land for farming in this part of the world.

Rice is the major grain crop in South and East Asia. Planting rice shoots in flooded fields is very hard work.

and harvested it in the spring. Then they planted a summer crop of soybeans or sweet potatoes, which would be harvested before it was time to plant wheat again. Soybeans were first grown in East Asia. Today they are called "the most important beans in the world." They are used as food by people and animals. They provide vegetable oil, which is used in cooking and in industry.

To grow so much on their land, the Chinese farmers had to fertilize it often. They let nothing go to waste. Almost everything went into **compost** heaps. Compost is a mixture of leaves, grass, plants, and other materials—almost anything that will decay and make fertilizer. Farmers gathered garbage and wastes from cities and towns for compost heaps. They

pulled water plants from streams and ponds to throw on the heaps. When they harvested wheat, they pulled the stalks out of the ground. They shook off the soil from the roots so that it could be used to grow new crops. Then they cut off the roots and threw them on the compost heaps.

The American visitor said that Chinese farmers knew how to build up the soil. They dug soil from the bottom of canals and spread it on the fields. They planted clover from time to time because they knew that clover makes land fertile.

The American decided that the skilled farmers of East Asia knew a great deal about the care of the land. He thought they had something to teach farmers of the whole world in 1910.

Using new ways to farm In some places in Asia today, farmers work the land just as farmers did 2,000 years ago. One writer visited farm village "where the clock stuck 20 centuries ago." What do you think he meant by that?

But the clock is not stuck everywhere in Asia. Another writer visited a farmer on the Ganges Plain who worked differently than the farmer's father had worked 20 years ago. The modern farmer had an electric pump in a deep well that provided more water for irrigation than his father had. The modern farmer planted new kinds of seed. He sprayed insecticide on his fields to kill insects and other pests that once destroyed much of the crop. By using a lot of fertilizer and irrigation water, the farmer grew four crops a year.

There have also been great changes in the farming villages of Japan. Most people in Japan worked on the land 40 years ago. This is no longer true. Most people in Japan today are not farmers, but the land is still carefully cultivated. Fewer people do the same amount of work as more people once did because of the **mechanization** (mek ə nə zā′ shən) of Japan's farms. Mechanization means the use of machines. The Japanese do not usually have the large tractors and other machines used on American farms. But most farmers in Japan do have small two-wheeled machines that can be used for plowing, harvesting, and threshing.

Some Japanese farmers now have rice-planting machines. Planting rice can be hard, backbreaking work. When planting rice without a machine, a person must stand bent over in a flooded field and stick each rice plant into the muddy soil, one at

Many farmers in Japan have small hand-operated machines to help them plant rice.

a time. A machine makes planting both easier and faster.

Using machines does not necessarily mean that more food will be produced. Better seed and good fertilizer do more to increase the size of a crop. But machines help people do more work. One farmer with a machine can do as much work as four farmers without machines. People who in the past would have worked the land now work in factories making manufactured goods.

Using and controlling rivers Farmers have used the waters of the Indus River for at least 4,000 years. In ancient times they dipped buckets into the river to get water to irrigate gardens and fields near the river. Later they dug canals that carried water to large parts of the Indus Valley.

Today the water of the Indus is used to irrigate an area larger than some countries in Europe. Canal irrigation increased the amount of land that can be farmed. But canal irrigation also created some problems. A lot of water seeped from the canals and some lowlands became **waterlogged**. Land is waterlogged when it is soaked with too much water. In low areas groundwater seeped to the surface, evaporated, and left a salty crust on the land. This made it necessary to find ways to drain water from the waterlogged land. Building canals to help irrigate the land helped solve the problem of how to turn dry land into farmland. But, as is often the case, solving one problem created another.

People in North China tried long ago to solve the problem of floods along the Hwang Ho. They built dikes made of earth along the river to hold back high water. The floods had spread silt over the land. After the dikes were built, the silt settled to the bottom of the river. As the river bottom got higher because of the silt deposits, the level of the river rose. Dikes had to be built still higher. When a dike breaks, as it sometimes does, a hugh flood pours out over the land. At such times the Hwang Ho does, indeed, become "China's sorrow."

The use of animals   Raising animals is one way to make use of the land. Animals eat plants and supply milk, meat, and hides.

Pigs were probably first raised in Southeast Asia. Pigs are very useful animals. They eat many types of food and do not take much space. They provide meat and their skin can be used to make leather. Today more than one third of all the pigs in the world are raised in China.

India has more cattle than any other country in the world, but most Indians do not eat beef. They believe it is against their religion to kill cattle. You will read more about this religion in the next chapter. People in India use oxen to pull loads and for plowing. Cows are used to supply milk.

Most of the belt of mountains and plateaus that crosses Asia is too rugged and dry for farming. But herders make use of this land. There are millions of sheep, cattle, and horses on the dry grasslands of Mongolia north of the Gobi Desert. Like the herders in Africa and the Middle East, the Mongolian herding peoples are nomads. They move with their animals in search of pastures.

On the high plateau of Tibet people raise yaks. Yaks are long-haired animals that can live in the high, cool land. People ride yaks and use them for carrying loads. Yaks also supply milk and meat. Their tails are valued as fly whisks.

Water buffalo are used in South and East Asia. Water buffalo are not the same as American bison, which are often called buffalo. American bison are not used in farming or to give milk.

Water buffalo are strong, useful animals. They pull plows in muddy rice fields where other animals are of little use. They do not move fast, but they can pull a heavy load. Buffalo provide meat and milk. In fact, water buffalo give almost twice as much milk as cows.

Water buffalo do not need good pastures to survive. These animals eat straw

Water buffalo are valuable animals in parts of Asia.

as they spun and wove cotton and wool. Marco Polo described how they made the cloth white: "They put it into a fire and let it stay there about an hour, when they draw it out uninjured by the flame." We call this material asbestos (as bes' təs). It is still mined in China today.

Asia has other useful minerals. One of these is tin. Two thirds of the world's supply of tin comes from Southeast Asia. Much of our food is packed in what we call "tin cans." Actually, "tin cans" are made of steel, but they are coated with tin to keep the steel from rusting.

and grass that is too dry and poor for other cattle. One writer has called the water buffalo "a tractor that provides meat and cheese."

People in some parts of Asia have put elephants to work. Elephants are useful for lifting logs in the lumber industry in Burma and Sri Lanka.

Wealth under the land   In Chapter 12 you read about Marco Polo, the traveler from Italy who saw fountains of oil in Iran in 1272. Marco Polo traveled on to China where he saw other wonders. One of these wonders was "black stones" that burned. The black stones, of course, were coal. Asia has large deposits of this useful fuel. China today is the third largest producer of coal in the world.

Marco Polo not only saw stones that burned, but also cloth that did not burn. People made this cloth from "fibers not unlike wool." They dug these fibers from the mountains. They spun the fibers into thread and wove the thread into cloth just

Using the forests   Asia, like other continents, once had more forests than it does today. Farms, pastures, towns, and cities have taken the place of much forestland. As the forests were cut down, the number of trees left grew smaller and smaller and there was less wood to use.

There was no shortage of wood when Marco Polo visited China 700 years ago. But Marco Polo thought that the wood supply would run out because there were so many people in China. It took a lot of wood to cook so many meals, warm so many homes, and heat so much bath water. Marco Polo said that the Chinese liked to bathe often, sometimes once a day. That may not seem strange to us, but people in Europe in Marco Polo's time did not take so many baths.

Marco Polo was partly right. The Chinese did use up wood faster than trees grew. Parts of China were stripped of trees. In recent years, the Chinese have planted a large number of trees.

Forests are important in other countries in Asia. About half the land on the

Crowded cities such as Hong Kong are common in South and East Asia. Hong Kong is located at 22°N, 114°E.

mountainous Japanese islands is covered with forests. The Japanese use more wood than their forests supply. Japan now imports large amounts of wood from North America.

Southeast Asia and the islands off the Asian mainland have valuable rain forests. Much timber is cut in this part of Asia.

Crowding the land   Asia has many resources, but it also has many people. Most of the world's people live in Asia, and most of these people live in South and East Asia.

The number of people in Asia has been growing rapidly. Marco Polo thought China had many people when he was there. Today it has more than eight times as many people as it did in Marco Polo's time.

Asia's population has doubled in the past 50 years. The population densities are highest in the warmer parts of Asia. There is an average of 1,678 people per square mile (648 per sq km) in the coun-

try of Bangladesh (bän glə desh'). The island of Java (jäv' ə) in Indonesia (in də nē zhə) has a population density of 1,742 people per square mile (672 per sq km). The population density for India as a whole is 562 people per square mile (218 per sq km), but it is far higher in the Ganges Valley. By comparison, the population density of the United States is 63 people per square mile (24 per sq km).

In the past 4,000 years, people in South and East Asia have shown great skill in using the land. But there are now many more people than ever living in these lands.

CHECKUP

1. What are some of the old ways used by Asian farmers to make use of the land? What are some of the new ways?
2. Name some of the animals used in Asia. How are they used?
3. What did Marco Polo learn about minerals in China?
4. How has the population of South and East Asia changed recently?

383

Australia and New Zealand

The world's smallest continent On a map of the world, Australia looks like the largest island off the coast of Asia. But Australia is not considered part of Asia. It is a separate continent—the world's smallest. But since it is all one nation, Australia is also one of the world's largest countries. The distance from east to west across Australia is about the same as the distance between the Atlantic and Pacific coasts of the United States.

The world's largest coral reef, the Great Barrier Reef, lies off the northeastern coast of Australia. Corals are small ocean animals with hard skeletons. Corals live in shallow ocean water, where they form large colonies. Live corals grow on the remains of dead corals building up, over the years, into reefs or ridges near the surface of the water. The Great Barrier Reef stretches for almost 1,300 miles (2,092 km). A belt of shallow water separates the Great Barrier Reef from the Australian shoreline.

The northern part of Australia is close to the Equator. The southeastern part of the continent is as far away from the Equator as the Mediterranean countries of Europe are. Northern Australia has a hot climate with rainy summers and dry winters. The southeast has a climate much like that of the Mediterranean lands.

Australia's largest cities are along its coasts. Most Australians live in the southeast. Most of Australia's interior is either dry grassland or desert.

Flat, grass-covered plains in the state of Queensland, Australia, serve as a backdrop for this sheep station, or ranch.

Australia has no great rivers. No large stream flows through the heart of the continent. There are no rivers like the Danube in Europe or the Nile or Congo in Africa. The Murray River in the southeast is Australia's largest river. It is about one-third as long as the Nile.

Much of Australia is flat. A belt of mountains and highlands called the Great Dividing Range rises near the eastern edge of the continent. This belt divides the narrow coastal plains from the open lands of the interior. Most people live east of the Great Dividing Range. Australians call the land west of this range the **outback**. They talk about the outback the way Americans once talked about "the West."

The highest mountains in the Great Dividing Range are in the southeast. Mt. Kosciusko, the tallest peak, rises 7,330 feet (2,230 m). There is a group of bare rock mountains called the Macdonnell

Range in the center of Australia. Ayers Rock—one huge mass of stone that rises more than 1,000 feet (304 m) from a flat desert—is south of the Macdonnell Range.

The mountainous island of Tasmania (taz mā′ nē ə) is just south of the continent and seems small when compared with Australia. But Tasmania is larger than some of the countries of Europe.

Australia before Europeans came
In 1770 Captain James Cook, an English explorer, claimed the eastern part of Australia for England. At that time, there was not a single city, town, or farm on the whole continent of Australia. There were probably only about 300,000 people in all of this land. These people were known as the **Aborigines** (ab′ ə rij′ ə nēz). The word *aborigines* means "earliest known inhabitants." It may refer to the earliest inhabitants of any place. But when *Aborigines* is spelled with a capital A, it usually means "the earliest inhabitants of Australia."

The Aborigines were not farmers. They got their food by gathering it or by hunting. They understood this way of life very well. They knew where to find fruits, berries, birds' eggs, nuts, and even insects that could be eaten. They gathered certain types of grass seed and made the seed into little flat cakes that they baked in hot ashes. They hunted wild animals and birds. They speared fish and gathered shellfish and crabs.

When the Aborigines hunted in places where there were no streams or springs, they knew how to get moisture from the roots of certain plants. They also cut into the bark of the paperback tree and got as much as 2 cups (½ L) of water in about 10 minutes.

The search for food kept the Aborigines on the move. They never built permanent houses or villages. Instead, they made huts of sticks, grass, and bark, which they left behind them as they moved from place to place.

The Aborigines made all their tools and weapons from sticks, stones, shells, and bones. They made stone knives and stone scrappers, and they made a wooden spear thrower, which was like a handle for a spear. By using the spear thrower they could send a spear through the air with great speed.

The most unusual weapon of the Aborigines was a curved throwing stick called a boomerang. Skillful hunters could throw one kind of boomerang in such a way that, if it hit nothing, it circled

Aborigine children at a school in Pine Island, Australia, are descendants of the first known inhabitants of Australia. Australian Aborigines make up a small part of the country's population.

and returned to the thrower. The Aborigines also had a heavy war boomerang. This boomerang would not return, but could hit a person or animal more than 100 yards (91.4 m) away.

The Aborigines made no pottery, but they wove baskets so tightly that they held honey or even water. These people made no cloth. When it was hot, they needed little clothing. When it was cooler, they wore animal skins.

There were no empires, kingdoms, or republics in Australia in 1770. The Aborigines lived in tribes. Each tribe usually had its own area where it hunted and gathered food. The older men who knew the ways of their ancestors ruled the tribes. Since the Aborigines had no system of writing, knowledge was passed on to younger people by word of mouth.

The islands of New Zealand Australia and New Zealand are about 1,200 (1,931 km) miles apart, but to some people Australia and New Zealand are always thought of together. The Soviet Union is closer to Spain than New Zealand is to Australia. Northern Australia is much closer to Indonesia than southeastern Australia is to New Zealand.

New Zealand has two main islands, which are called simply North Island and South Island. North Island has a warmer climate than South Island because North Island is closer to the Equator. This is because New Zealand, like Australia, is in the Southern Hemisphere.

No part of New Zealand is far from the ocean. The ocean has an effect on the climate. Winters are mild in New Zealand, and summers are cool. Of course, since

New Zealand is south of the Equator, the seasons are the opposite of those in the lands north of the Equator. July and August are winter months in New Zealand, and January and February are summer months.

Ocean breezes also bring rain to New Zealand, and there are no deserts in the country as there are in Australia.

The highest mountains in New Zealand are on South Island. Europeans named these mountains the Southern Alps because their rugged peaks reminded the Europeans of the Alps in Europe. Snow covers the highest peaks in the Southern Alps all year long. Sir Edmund Hillary, one of the first two men to climb Mt. Everest, learned how to climb mountains in New Zealand's Southern Alps.

The high rugged mountains of South Island in New Zealand reminded early settlers of the Alps in Europe. Today these "Southern Alps" attract tourists from all over the world.

This Maori village in New Zealand was built by the descendants of the early Maori tribes to show how the Maori lived before the Europeans came.

The Maori   People named the Maori (mä′ ō rē) have lived in New Zealand for hundreds of years. They were there when the first Europeans came to the islands. The ancestors of the Maori came to New Zealand from other islands in the Pacific. The Maori sailed the ocean in large double canoes joined together with wooden planks. These sea canoes were probably about the same size as the boats sailed by the Vikings.

The Maori hunted and fished for food, but they also raised crops such as taro and sweet potatoes. They built houses of reeds and wood that lasted longer than the huts of the Aborigines.

The Maori made mats from the fibers of plants. They fastened the mats together to make clothing. They also made beautiful robes of feathers. Maori chiefs wore these robes at special times.

The Maori were divided into tribes that were ruled by chiefs. The tribes some-times fought wars, so the Maori built their villages on cliffs and other places that were hard to attack.

The Maori had no written language. Older people passed on their knowledge to younger people by word of mouth.

There are still Maori in New Zealand and Aborigines in Australia. But both groups are far outnumbered by people whose ancestors came from Europe. In a later chapter you will read why the settlers came from Europe and how they made use of the land.

CHECKUP

1. Where do most people live in Australia?
2. What skills and knowledge did the Aborigines have before Europeans came to Australia?
3. What are some of the differences between New Zealand and Australia?
4. Who are the Maori? Where did their ancestors come from?

KEY FACTS

1. Asia, the world's largest continent, has almost every kind of land and climate.

2. A belt of mountains and plateaus separates South and East Asia from the rest of the continent.

3. Monsoons affect Asia's climate.

4. Asian farmers know how to make use of Asia's land and rivers.

5. Raising animals is one way to make use of the land.

6. Most of the world's people live in Asia, and most Asians live in South and East Asia.

7. Australia is the smallest continent but one of the world's larger countries.

8. Most Australians live in the southeastern part of the continent.

9. The Aborigines lived in Australia before Europeans came there.

10. The Maori lived in New Zealand before Europeans came there.

VOCABULARY QUIZ

Match each word in the list with the correct meaning below. Write your answers on a sheet of paper.

a. interior	**f.** compost
b. subcontinent	**g.** mechanization
c. causeway	**h.** waterlogged
d. cultivate	**i.** outback
e. terraces	**j.** aborigines

1. Inland area

2. Australian term for land west of the Great Dividing Range

3. The use of machines

4. Earliest known inhabitants

5. A raised roadway across water

6. Flat areas built up on the side of a hill or slope

7. Soaked with too much water

8. A large area, but not as large as a continent

9. To prepare and use land for crops

10. A mixture of decayed plant and other materials used for fertilizer

REVIEW QUESTIONS

1. What are some of the high mountains and plateaus that divide Asia?

2. How do monsoons affect Asia?

3. Name two of Asia's peninsulas and five important islands or groups of islands.

4. What river valleys or plains have been important in India's history?

5. What river valleys or plains have been important in China's history?

6. What were some of Asia's farmers doing in 1910 to make use of their land?

7. What has happened to Asia's population in the last 50 years?

8. Where do most Australians live?

9. Who were the Aborigines and how did they live? Who were the Maori and how did they live?

10. What are the two main islands of New Zealand? Which has the warmer climate?

ACTIVITIES

1. Find out the elevation of the place you live in and compare it with the elevation of Mt. Everest in the Himalayas. You may find the elevation of your town by looking in an almanac, the local fact section of your telephone directory, or publications put out by your city or chamber of commerce, or by looking at a physical map of your state.

READING FOR FACT AND OPINION

STATEMENTS OF FACT CAN BE PROVEN

Some statements that you read or hear are statements of *fact*. Others are statements of *opinion*. A statement of fact is true. It can be proven. A statement of opinion tells what the writer or speaker thinks or feels. The following statements show the difference:

1. Three strikes in baseball make an out. (fact)
2. Baseball is a more interesting game than basketball. (opinion)

The first statement can be proven by either reading a rule book or watching a baseball game. The second statement cannot be proven. It tells what the writer thinks or feels.

Books usually contain statements of both fact and opinion. The statements below come form a book entitled *Our World* by Mary L. Hall. It is a schoolbook written over 100 years ago in 1873. (fact) It is very interesting. (opinion)

STATEMENTS OF OPINION ABOUT FACTS

Read each statement below and decide if it is a fact or an opinion. Some statements give the author's opinions about facts. For example: "In the slimy mud, on the edge of the Nile River, creep huge, horrible-looking creatures, called crocodiles." It is a fact that there are crocodiles on the Nile. But it is the author's opinion that they are "horrible-looking." Consider such a statement to be an opinion.

SKILLS PRACTICE

Write your answers on a sheet of paper. Use **O** for opinion and **F** for fact.

1. "The whole country of Greece is cut up by small ridges of mountains or hills, with valleys between, watered by many little rivers, and shaded with groves of dark, old olive trees."

2. "It was a strange idea of the Greeks, that their gods loved, hated, married, and fought, just like human beings."

3. "The people who live in this dreary land are called Eskimos. . . .They make houses of snow that look like great ovens, with only a little hole for a door. . . ."

4. "The Greeks often had public games or races in honor of some god, when all the Greeks came from every part of the land to sacred groves. The [most important] of these were called the Olympic Games."

5. "Here in the Alps are the grandest glaciers, the prettiest little villages, and in the midst of the high valleys, the loveliest lakes in the world."

6. "You may well think that Siberia is not a very pleasant country to live in, much less to travel in; and yet there are people who have homes here. Even some Englishmen and Americans sometimes go to this dreary place."

7. "The manners and the ways of living of the Chinese people are very different from ours. They use no forks, but put food into their mouths with two little rounded sticks called chopsticks."

8. "The rest of Spain is not so fair and pleasant. Things do not generally look so bright and cheerful as in France."

9. "The high tops of the Himalaya [s] . . . are always covered with snow. From their sides many streams rush down—some of them large rivers, and some of them torrents pouring through the mountain gorges in foaming waterfalls."

10. "The river Ganges is called a holy river by the Hindus who worship horrible idols of wood and stone."

CHAPTER
19 Early Times in South and East Asia

The Indian Subcontinent

VOCABULARY

granary	caste
Hinduism	Buddhism
class	

Cities on the Indus River plain   About 4,000 years ago a dog chased a cat in a city on the Indus River plain. We are sure of this because both the dog and the cat left pawprints on a mud brick that had not dried. Thousands of years later, scholars found this brick. Judging by how deep the prints are, both animals were moving very quickly.

The paw-marked brick is only one of thousands of bricks scholars have dug up on the Indus Plain. These bricks are what is left of cities where people lived between 2500 B.C. and 1500 B.C. The cities on the Indus Plain were nearly as old as the cities of ancient Mesopotamia and Egypt.

The two largest Indus cities were at places now called Mohenjo-Daro (mō hen jō där′ ō) and Harappa (hə rap′ ə). No one knows what the people who once lived in these cities called them. Both cities were deserted long ago and forgotten until scholars discovered the buried brick walls of Mohenjo-Daro in 1922. Since then the remains of more than 150 other towns and villages have been found.

History from old bricks   The people of the Indus cities left no books. They had a system of writing, but no one can now read what they wrote. Even if scholars could read the writing of the early Indus people, we might not learn much about these early cities because the only writings found are on small carved stones. These stones were probably used to stamp marks on things people owned.

Most of what scholars know about the early Indus cities comes from studying the bricks the people used to make their cities. Scholars believe that the streets of Mohenjo-Daro were laid out in regular blocks, much like city streets today. Most of the buildings were very much alike. A number of them had baths connected to sewers. Such comforts were not common in ancient cities.

There was a large platform made of bricks and earth in one part of Mohenjo-Daro. This was probably the citadel (sit′ ə dəl), or fort. Inside the citadel was a large structure built around a pool lined with asphalt. The pool had steps leading into it much like a modern swimming pool. Scholars think that bathing in the pool may have been part of a religious ceremony.

One of the largest buildings at Mohenjo-Daro seems to have been used

The ruins of Mohenjo-Daro on the vast flat Indus River plain in modern Pakistan are evidence that a great city once flourished here.

as a **granary** (gran' ər ē), a place for storing grain. It is likely that the city collected taxes from farmers in the form of wheat. The granary may have served as the city treasury.

Small objects found in the ruins of the Indus cities tell something of everyday life in these cities. People shaved with bronze razors and put up their hair with bronze hairpins. They played with dice and marbles. They seem to have made toys for their children. Scholars can think of no other use for a clay monkey that slides down a string or a little clay bull with a head that wiggles.

The people in the Indus Plain had a highly developed way of life much like that of ancient Mesopotamia and ancient Egypt. The people in the Indus Plain used bronze and copper to make pots, pans, and weapons. They also knew how to use silver and gold for decorating things. They traded with their neighbors to the north and south. They may even have traded with the people of Mesopotamia.

Something happened to the Indus cities ca. 1500 B.C. No one knows why the people left the cities, but they did. Scholars do know that another group of people, the Aryans (ār' ē ənz), entered the Indian subcontinent after that date. The Aryans came from the northwest through the passes in the mountains. They were herders who moved about with their cattle before they settled in the subcontinent.

The early Aryans had thousands of hymns and chants, which were later written down in books called the Vedas (vā' dəz). The language of the Vedas is Sanskrit (san' skrit). Scholars can study the Vedas because most modern Indian languages developed out of Sanskrit. Most of what we know about the early Aryans comes from the Vedas.

The beginnings of Hinduism The religion of most people in India is called **Hinduism** (hin' dü iz əm). People who follow this religion are called Hindus. The beginnings of Hinduism go back to the

Compare this time line with the one on page 268. Did the Buddha and Confucius live before or after Christ and Mohammed?

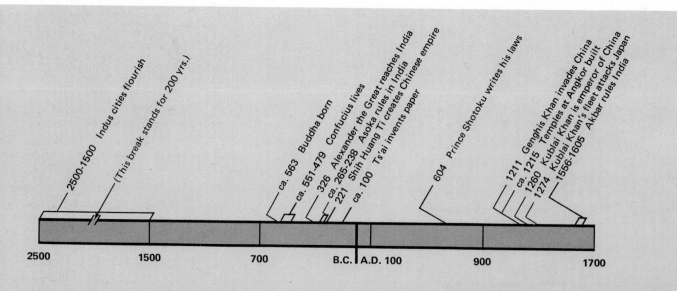

Hinduism has many gods. One of these gods is Krishna, who is seen in the center of this painting standing over a rishi, or wise man, who is shown with four heads.

Aryans. Hindus think of the Vedas as holy writings. But Hinduism is much more than the religion of the early Aryans. It is a religion that has developed in India over hundreds of years. Hinduism includes many different beliefs. Today Hindus worship many gods and goddesses not known to Aryans.

Hinduism has been connected with the growth of separate groups or **classes** of people in India. A class is a group of people who are alike in certain ways. For instance, the Aryans were divided into four main classes. Priests and their families made up one class. Families of rulers and warriors made up a second class. A large third class included farmers, merchants, and skilled workers. The lowest class of all was made up of workers who had no special skills.

In the course of time, each of the large classes divided into many smaller groups. For example, blacksmiths made up one class, and carpenters another.

A person's class depended on birth. The child of a priest belonged to the priestly class. When class depends entirely on birth, it is called **caste** (kast).

Each caste had its own customs and duties. Members of the same caste often lived in the same village or the same part of town. Children grew up with other children of the same caste. Members of different castes usually did not eat together. Most important of all, people married in their own caste.

Each caste taught its own members their duties. Hindus believe that "it is better to do one's own duty badly than to do another's duty well.

Beliefs about duty and caste were based on two important teachings of Hinduism. Hindus believe that good is always rewarded and that evil is always punished. Hindus also believe that what happens to a person after he or she dies depends on how well that person lived. Hindus believe that when a person dies, he or she is born again as another person or even as an animal. A person who lived well and did his or her duty well will be reborn into a higher caste. A person who lived badly and failed in his or her duty will be reborn into a lower caste.

In modern India, the caste system is not as strong as it once was. It is now against the law in India to deny people their right to an education, a job, or anything else because of caste. The caste system weakened over the years as people moved to cities and towns and learned new professions.

The beginnings of Buddhism The Indian subcontinent was the home of another religion, **Buddhism** (büd′ iz əm). This religion is based on the teachings of Siddhartha Gautama (sid där′ tä gä′ ü tä mä) who was born ca. 563 B.C. Gautama's followers called him the Buddha, which means the "enlightened one." They called him enlightened because they believed that his teachings were the "light" of true knowledge.

According to an old story, Gautama was a prince, the son of a rich ruler. His father tried to raise Gautama so that he would never know about suffering and pain. Gautama grew up in palaces without knowing about illness, death, or being poor. When the young prince rode outside the palace, his father's servants hid all poor and sick people.

One day the servants missed three people—an old beggar, a sick person, and a dead person. Prince Gautama saw all three and learned that there was pain and suffering in the world. After learning about these things, the prince did not

Statues of the Buddha are found in many countries in Asia. This statue is in Sri Lanka.

want to remain cut off from such suffering. He gave up his riches and high position.

Gautama wanted to find a way to free people from pain and suffering. After years of thought, he was "enlightened" with the knowledge he was looking for. Prince Gautama became the Buddha.

The Buddha became a teacher of other people. He taught that the cause of suffering is selfishness. He also taught that people should forget about themselves and the things they want. They should show "friendliness to the whole world." Buddhists believe that a person who is a friend of the whole world does not lie, cheat, steal, or kill any living thing. There is much more to the Buddha's teachings, but what he taught all began with these ideas.

A Buddhist emperor   Many different types of people have become Buddhists. One of the greatest was the Indian emperor Asoka (a sō′ ká). Asoka ruled India from ca. 265 to 238 B.C. This was long after the Buddha lived.

During the first years he ruled India, Asoka was not a Buddhist. He did not show much "friendliness to the whole world." He was a hunter who killed animals for sport. He was a conqueror who made war against his neighbors. But after a time, the suffering he caused bothered him. It began "to weigh heavily on his mind." He turned to the teachings of the Buddha. Asoka the conqueror and hunter became Asoka the peace-loving ruler.

Asoka worked for the good of the people he had conquered. He had trees planted along roads so travelers and animals might have shade. He had wells dug so people could have water. He told his officials to be "self-controlled, calm in mind, and gentle" when dealing with people. Asoka felt that the government in the past had been too slow to help people. He showed his officials how he wanted them to act by telling them, "I am ready to take care of the people's business at all hours and in all places."

Asoka became a teacher of his people as well as their ruler. He had Buddhist teachings carved in stone in different places in his empire. Some of these stones still exist. They carry messages, such as "It is not good to kill living things."

Most people in India today are Hindus, not Buddhists. But they remember and honor Asoka as one of their greatest rulers.

Moslems in the subcontinent   Over the centuries other conquerors followed the Aryans through the mountain passes into the Indian subcontinent. Alexander the Great and his soldiers reached the Indus Plain in 326 B.C. You read about Alexander in Chapter 4.

Long after Alexander's time, Moslems from Central Asia invaded the subcontinent. Among these conquerors was the great conqueror, Timur the Lame, whom you read about in Chapter 13.

The Moslems brought their religion, Islam, with them to the subcontinent. The differences between Islam and Hinduism sharply divided people. Moslems thought Hinduism was a false religion. Some Moslems destroyed Hindu temples and statues of Hindu gods. The Hindus, in turn, looked down on the Moslems. The Moslems may have ruled the land, but the Hindus considered Moslems outcastes, people beneath even the lowest castes.

The Taj Mahal was built by a Moslem ruler in India more than 300 years ago. The building shows how strong the Moslem influence was in India.

Differences between Moslems and Hindus still divide the people of the subcontinent. You will read about these divisions in Chapter 21.

A Mogul emperor Timur's empire broke up after he died. His descendants, known as Moguls, returned to India and conquered it. The Mogul rulers were called the Great Moguls. Akbar (ak' bär) was the most powerful of these rulers. He ruled from 1556 to 1605. This was about the time Elizabeth I ruled England.

The Moguls were Moslems, but Akbar respected the Hindus. He knew he could be truly powerful only if he had the support of all the people he ruled. After all, most Indians were Hindus. Akbar chose a number of Hindu officials to serve him, and he married a Hindu princess.

Akbar knew that people respect rulers only if they govern fairly. He spent much time hearing complaints from people who thought they had been treated unfairly. Akbar became well known for his fairness. It was said that people who had been treated unfairly believed that the Great Mogul would help them.

Akbar had a great deal of curiosity, a great desire to know. He collected a large library, even though he could not read. There was no need for Akbar to learn how to read. He had many people ready to read to him at any hour of the day or night.

Akbar was very interested in different types of religions. He built a Hall of Worship, where he heard Moslems and Hindues talk about religion. Akbar learned that some visitors from Portugal had brought

This painting shows the Great Mogul Akbar receiving visitors at his court. Akbar was respected as a conqueror and as a just and wise ruler.

Christian priests to India. He asked the priests to come to his Hall of Worship.

The priests were glad to come to the Hall of Worship. They hoped the Great Mogul would become a Christian. But the priests soon learned that Akbar wanted to know about many other things besides Christianity. He asked them many questions. What were the countries of Europe like? How were they ruled? Did the Europeans have ways of making cannons that were not known to the Moguls? Was it true that sailors from Europe had found a new land across the ocean? It seems that Akbar must have heard of Columbus's discovery of America. We do not know if he learned that the people in this new land had been called Indians by mistake.

Akbar did not become a Christian, but he did not remain a Moslem, either. Instead he started a new religion that combined ideas from other religions. The new religion was not popular, and it disappeared after Akbar died.

Akbar's sons and grandsons ruled after him, but they were not as fair or as wise as he was. They did not try to keep the support of the Hindus. The Moguls became less powerful. In time, their empire began to break apart. By that time, a new group of outsiders—people from Europe—had invaded the subcontinent. You will read about the Europeans in India in the next chapter.

CHECKUP

1. How have scholars been able to learn about the ancient cities of the Indus Plain?
2. How did the caste system work?
3. Why was Prince Gautama called "the Buddha"?
4. Why are both Asoka and Akbar famous rulers?

Ancient China

┌─VOCABULARY─────────────────────┐
│ diviner   lodestone   │
│ counselor   compass   │
└────────────────────────────────┘

Writing on turtle shells and ox bones
About 3,500 years ago a king of China decided to go hunting. He wondered if he would have any luck, so he sent for a **diviner** named Ku. A diviner was a person who supposedly could tell what was going to happen by asking the gods about the future.

Ku wrote the king's question on a piece of turtle shell. "Will we get anything when we hunt?" Then Ku heated a bronze rod and put it on the shell. The heat from the rod caused the shell to crack. The diviner supposedly could tell by the way the shell cracked whether the answer to his question was yes or no. In this case the answer was yes, and the king did, in fact, have good luck on the hunt. Someone later wrote on the same shell, "On that day we hunted and killed 1 tiger, 40 deer, and 164 wolves."

Diviners wrote questions on ox bones as well as turtle shells. Thousands of these bones and shells have been found. On them are written questions such as: "Should the king go to war this spring?" "Will Lady Hao be in good health after she has a baby?" People even had diviners ask, "Will it rain tomorrow?"

Writings on ox bones and turtle shells are the oldest Chinese writings that exist. It is likely that the Chinese at that time also wrote on strips of wood and bamboo. But wood and bamboo rot, so scholars who study the long history of the Chinese language begin by studying the diviners' bones and shells.

This early Chinese writing shows that the people of the Hwang Ho valley had a highly developed way of life more than 3,000 years ago. The ancient Chinese built cities at an early time, as did the peoples of Mesopotamia, Egypt, and the Indus Plain.

The Chinese system of writing Scholars today can read the diviners' questions because modern Chinese writing developed out of the system of writing used in China 3,500 years ago.

The Chinese do not use an alphabet. Instead, they have many different signs, or characters. Some characters stand for complete words. Character writing probably began with pictures that stood for the names of things. The figures below show how two modern Chinese characters developed from those used on diviners' bones and shells. The first character in the top row is a turtle. The first character in the bottom row is a tree with roots and branches. The next three figures in each row show how the two characters changed over the years. The character now used for the word *turtle* hardly looks like a turtle any more.

The diviners in ancient China used about 4,000 characters. Modern Chinese writing has about 50,000. Many characters that began as pictures of things now stand for ideas and sounds. For example, the characters for sun and moon together mean "bright." The characters for woman and child together mean "good."

Chinese writing is beautiful, but it takes time to learn its thousands of characters. The system has one advantage. People who speak in different ways can still use the same system of writing. For example, people in one part of China pronounce the word for mountain as *shan*. People in another part of China say *sa* for mountain. But both use the same character when writing the word *mountain*. People who speak European languages do much the same thing when writing numerals. The English say *three;* the French say *trois;* and the Germans say *drei*. But all write the numeral 3.

Chinese writing began over 3,000 years ago. Some of the characters or signs used in early Chinese writing served as the base for some of the modern characters.

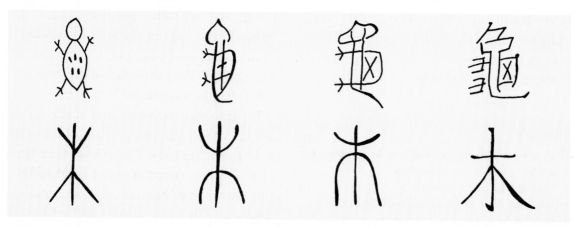

Two great Chinese teachers   Ancient China had great teachers. Confucious (con fyü′ shus), one of the greatest, lived at the same time as the Buddha. But Confucius and the Buddha lived differently and did not teach the same ideas. The Buddha began life as a wealthy prince. Confucius was a poor village boy. The Buddha gave up his high position because he did not want to be a ruler. Confucius wanted to be a **counselor**—a person who advises rulers and helps them make decisions.

In the time of Confucius, China was divided into separate kingdoms that were often at war with each other. To make matters worse, the officials of the kingdoms were usually not honest. The people of China longed for peace and fair government.

Confucius said that there could be good government only when good people governed. The improvement, or reform, of government had to begin with the reform, or improvement, of individuals. Confucius wanted to be a counselor of kings so that he could be a teacher of kings.

Confucius taught that those who wished to rule others should first learn how to rule themselves. They should learn how to control their feelings and not act in angry haste. Those in superior, or high, positions, should be truly superior persons. Superior persons, according to Confucius, were honest, courteous, and not easily bothered by difficulties. Confucius was once asked to give a single rule for a superior person to follow. He answered, "What you do not want done to yourself, do not do unto others." Can you think of another way to say the same thing?

The thoughts, teachings, and writings of Confucius still influence people living today.

Confucius said that all people should respect or honor those over them. Children should respect their parents. Young people should respect older people. The people ruled should respect rulers. And rulers should respect the gods and the "will of Heaven."

Confucius never became a royal counselor, but he taught young people who might become counselors. Many people later read the teachings of Confucius. About 400 years after Confucius died, a Chinese historian wrote, "There have been

The Teachings of Confucius

The teachings of Confucius are found in his sayings. Many of these sayings tell how a truly superior person acts.

In his writings Confucius sometimes pointed out the differences between a superior and an inferior person.

The superior person thinks of goodness; the inferior person thinks of comfort.

The superior person cares for goodness; the inferior person cares for gain.

A superior person is not one-sided.

A superior person is not quarrelsome.

Confucius also had many other teachings. Some of these were:

Do not think yourself so large as to think others small.

Do not begin or quit anything hastily.

Mechanics who wish to do their work well must first sharpen their tools.

To be respected one must first show respect.

Criticizing others is easy, but to receive criticism is difficult.

Unfair government is more terrible than tigers.

This is knowledge: when you know a thing, to know that you know it, and when you do not know a thing, to know that you do not know it.

One day when Confucius was teaching, a student fell asleep. Confucius did not wake the student, but said, *"There is no use trying to carve on rotten wood."*

many kings, emperors, and great men in history who enjoyed fame and honor but they came to nothing at their death, while Confucius, who was but a common scholar, became the master of scholars for ten generations." Confucius remained the master of scholars for many more generations.

Lao-tzu (lou′ dzŭ′) was another great teacher in ancient China. We know little about his life except that he supposedly lived during the same time as Confucius. The followers of Lao-tzu are called Taoists (tou′ ists).

Taoists believed that a wise person did not seek wealth or power. The truly wise knew that they could know nothing for sure. One Taoist told the following story to prove this point.

A wise man dreamed one night that he was a butterfly. The dream was very real. While he was dreaming, he was sure that he was a butterfly. The next day he thought that it was all a dream and that he was really a man. But how could he be sure? Was he really a man who dreamed he was a butterfly, or a butterfly dreaming he was a man?

Taoists believe that there are two main forces in life. Taoists call these forces *yin* and *yang*. Yin is a female force, and yang is a male force.

Long after the time of Confucius and Lao-tzu, travelers from India brought the teachings of the Buddha to China. Buddhist books were translated into Chinese. Many Chinese adopted the Buddhist religion.

The first Chinese empire   In 221 B.C. a ruler named Shih Huang Ti (shē′ hwäng′ tē′) brought the warring kingdoms of China together in one empire. Shih Huang Ti is really a title rather than a name. It means "the first emperor."

Shih Huang Ti was not one of the "superior persons" that Confucius wrote about. Shih Huang Ti carried on many wars, and some people said he had "the voice of a jackal and the heart of a tiger." Shih Huang Ti did not follow the teachings of Confucius. He ordered all books containing them to be burned. Some scholars hid copies of the teachings of Confucius so that they would not be destroyed forever.

In order to make one empire out of separate kingdoms, Shih Huang Ti forced people to do things the same way. All parts of the empire had to use the same kind of money. All people had to use the same weights and measures. Scholars had to write with the same characters.

This clay horse and soldier are part of the clay army buried in China during the time of Shih Huang Ti.

Shih Huang Ti forced people to build roads and canals. He made them build palaces for him when he was alive and a tomb for his body when he died. The tomb was really a palace for the dead. An army of life-sized clay soldiers were buried near the tomb. The clay soldiers held real bronze weapons. Many of the soldiers were put in real chariots attached to life-sized clay horses. Some well diggers accidently discovered this buried clay army in 1974.

The Great Wall and the Grand Canal
Shih Huang Ti's largest building project was a wall along the boundary of his empire. Some earlier kings had built shorter walls to protect their kingdoms from the peoples who lived in Mongolia.

The horse-riding herders of the dry grasslands in Mongolia raided the more settled lands of China from time to time. Shih Huang Ti connected some of the shorter walls to form the Great Wall. Emperors in later times made the Great Wall still stronger and larger.

The Great Wall stretches 1,500 miles (2,413 km) across North China. It has been called the largest structure ever built. It is so large that it is marked on maps such as those of Eurasia in the Atlas of this book. If such a wall were built in the United States, it would reach halfway across the country.

Shih Huang Ti also built canals connecting rivers. Later emperors continued this work. In time there was a series of waterways, called the Grand Canal, that connected the Yangtze and the Hwang rivers. The Grand Canal is one of the longest waterways ever built.

The Great Wall of China was actually built as a series of separate walls that were later connected during the rule of Shih Huang Ti. The walls were built to keep nomadic tribes from Central Asia out of China.

The Great Wall stretches across North China.

The empire of the Mongols The Great Wall was only as strong as those who guarded its gates. The Chinese emperors paid tribes that lived along China's border to guard the gates of the Great Wall. Some of these tribes could not be trusted. In 1211 when an army of Mongols led by Genghis Khan appeared at one of the gates, the tribe guarding the Great Wall let the army pass.

The Mongols were nomads who led a hard life as herders on the grasslands of Central Asia. Genghis Khan had brought the Mongol tribes together to form a strong army. The Mongols could ride horses well and were good fighters. They could cover long distances in a short time and catch their enemies by surprise. Each soldier had a number of horses. The Mongols did not have to carry food for these horses. The tough little Mongolian horses needed nothing but grass and water. Even when snow covered the ground, the shaggy little animals pawed through the snow to find grass.

The soldiers of Genghis Khan carried few supplies for themselves. They took what they needed from the lands and people they conquered. Each rider carried two bows, some iron-pointed arrows, and a file to keep the points of the arrows sharp. Each rider also had a pointed lance with a hook that could be used to pull an enemy off a horse.

Genghis Khan's armies conquered North China. They then went on to conquer an empire that stretched across Asia into Eastern Europe. After Genghis Khan died in 1227, his sons and grandsons conquered even more of Eurasia. You have already read how the Mongols invaded parts of the Middle East and Eastern Europe.

The Mongol empire was one of the world's largest empires. But it did not remain one empire. By 1260 it was divided into four parts. The richest part was ruled by Genghis Khan's grandson, Kublai Khan (kū' blī kän').

Genghis Khan never gave up the old Mongol way of life. He liked living in a tent rather than in a palace in a city. Kublai Khan liked cities and the Chinese ways of living. He liked living in a Chinese palace much more than living in a smoke-filled nomads' tent.

Mongol warriors were fierce and hard-fighting. They were greatly feared by the people in the countries they conquered.

Kublai Khan chose Chinese officials to carry on the business of his large empire. As a result, the rule of the Mongol emperor was much like that of earlier Chinese emperors. The Great Wall had not protected China from the Mongols. But the Mongol conquerors adopted the ways of the people they had conquered.

Choosing officials by tests People who wanted to become officials in the Chinese empire had to take tests, or examinations. Today many governments use examinations to test people who want to become government officials. But in the time of Kublai Khan, there was nothing like these examinations in any other part of the world.

Only men could become officials in ancient China. They began studying for their exams when they were very young. Girls were not usually taught to read and write. A boy wishing to become an official spent years learning how to read and write the thousands of characters in the Chinese language. He learned Chinese history and poetry. He studied the books containing the teachings of Confucius.

After many years of study, a young man took his first examination. If he passed the first test, he could then take an examination in one of China's main cities.

He came to the examination grounds the day before the test. He carried a paper stating that he had passed the first examination. He showed the paper to the gatekeeper. The gatekeeper searched the young man to be sure that he had brought no notes. If a man was caught trying to cheat, both he and his teacher were disgraced.

When the gatekeeper was certain that everything was in order, the young man went to one of the examination booths. Each booth had a stool and a plank fitted into the wall. The plank was used as a desk during the daytime and a bed at night.

Early the next morning the subject of the examination was announced. Every-

Early Chinese rockets were powered with gunpowder and called "arrows of flying fire."

one taking the examination wrote about the subject being tested. They were supposed to show that they could write well and had read the ancient books.

Those who passed the first day's examination took another on the next day. The best papers were then chosen, and the men who wrote them took a third examination. Those who passed the third examination could now hold certain government positions. They could also go to the capital city to take examinations for even higher positions.

There was no limit to the number of times a man could take the examinations. Some men spent most of their lives studying for and taking the examinations over and over again.

Four important Chinese inventions
Certain Chinese inventions affected the whole world. They changed the way people made books, fought wars, and traveled.

A man named Ts'ai (tsī) who lived ca. A.D. 100 first made paper. Ts'ai is not very well known, but he should be famous. It is hard to imagine what the world would be like without paper.

The Chinese were the first people to use carved wooden blocks to print words on paper. Later, the printing blocks were made of clay or metal. This type of printing led to the printing press and changed the way people made books.

Nearly 1,000 years ago someone invented firecrackers. Firecrackers are not very useful, but the Chinese found ways to use the gunpowder in them. Chinese soldiers put gunpowder into bamboo sticks, lighted them, and threw them at

This early Chinese compass was beautiful as well as useful.

enemies in battle. They made the first guns out of bamboo tubes. The Mongol armies had gunpowder when they invaded Eastern Europe in 1241. This was probably the first time that Europeon knights ever saw this Chinese invention.

Long ago someone in China discovered a use for **lodestones** (lōd' stōnz). A lodestone is a natural magnet. When a lodestone is cut so that it turns easily on a smooth surface, it points north. Lodestones were used to make the first **compasses**. The Chinese later learned how to make compasses with magnetic steel needles. The invention of the compass made sailing over the open seas far safer because sailors could use compasses to find out in which direction their ships were sailing.

CHECKUP

1. What are some of the things that Confucius taught?
2. Who were the Mongols?
3. How did the Chinese select government officials?
4. What were four important Chinese inventions?

405

China's Neighbors

Korea   The people of Korea are not Chinese. Their language is very different from Chinese. But since Korea is very close to China, it has been greatly affected in many ways by its larger neighbor.

Scholars from Korea studied in China where they learned the teachings of Confucius. Koreans borrowed the great teacher's ideas. The kings of Korea spoke of the emperors of China as "elder brothers." Confucius had taught that younger people should honor older people. The kings of Korea sent payments called tributes each year to their "elder brothers" in China. Their practice continued for hundreds of years.

Buddhists from China brought their religion to Korea. Buddhism became one of the most important religions in Korea.

Since scholars in Korea learned Chinese, they used the characters of the Chinese language to write Korean. Only people who spent years memorizing thousands of characters were able to write Korean. One Korean king wished to have a simpler system. He knew about using an alphabet to write a language. He invented a Korean alphabet. Most of the people who knew how to write Korean with Chinese characters would not use the new way of writing. It has only been in recent years that schools in Korea have taught everyone to use alphabetic writing for the Korean language.

Chinese ideas in Japan   About the year A.D. 593 the emperor of Japan sent a message to the emperor of China. The message began, "The emperor of the country where the sun rises sends greetings to the emperor of the country where the sun sets." Can you tell why Japan was called "the country where the sun rises" and China "the country where the sun sets"? Use the map on page 373 to help you find the answer.

The Japanese learned about Chinese ways from the people of Korea. A Korean king sent the first Buddhist books to Japan. He urged the Japanese to study Buddhism although he said, "It is hard to explain and hard to understand."

Some people in Japan became interested in the ideas of the Chinese. Prince Shotoku (shō tō′ kü), a member of Japan's royal family, learned to read Chinese books. He sent students across the sea to China to learn more about Chinese ways.

Prince Shotoku became a Buddhist and built Buddhist temples. He also learned about the ideas of Confucius.

Like Confucius, Prince Shotoku wanted to reform the government. He drew up a set of laws to guide both government officials and the Japanese people. The prince wrote that everyone should live in **harmony**—"harmony between the ruler and the ruled and between neighbor and neighbor." By harmony he meant that everyone should live in peace.

Shotoku also taught that the people should respect the emperor and his officials. "When you receive commands from the emperor, fail not to obey them," Shotoku said.

Government officials were told that they should "punish the bad and reward the good." They were also told to keep in mind that "few people are completely bad." Shotoku thought that everyone could be taught to respect the law. Confucius would probably have agreed with much in Shotoku's laws.

Feudal lords and samurai Prince Shotoku said that everyone should carefully obey the emperor's orders. But the emperor did not always give the orders that ruled Japan. Powerful nobles usually controlled the emperors and ruled in their name.

Nobles in Japan came to be much like nobles in Europe during the Middle Ages. The Japanese nobles had large estates worked by peasants. The nobles ruled their own estates, settling arguments and keeping order. The nobles defended their own estates. Sometimes there was war between the nobles. At such times, there was little of the harmony Prince Shotoku had called for.

Each noble had a group of fighting men called **samurai** (sam′ ů rī). The samurai were much like the knights of Europe. It was said that "a samurai should live and die with a sword in hand." The samurai trained for years learning how to ride, shoot a bow, and fight with a long, two-handed sword.

Originally the name *samurai* was given only to those warriors who guarded the Japanese emperor. Over the years, the use of the name spread to include other types of warriors. Eventually, *samurai* came to mean an entire class of people in Japan—the warrior class. Samurai

This early photograph clearly shows how a samurai warrior was armed and protected.

warriors believed that their honor was more important than life itself.

The samurai were very powerful in Japan. Some samurai warriors became **shoguns** (shō′ gunz)—military rulers of Japan.

The samurai fought mostly in wars between the nobles. But in 1274 they faced a new enemy, the army of Kublai Khan.

407

Kublai Khan's attack on Japan At the closest point, the islands of Japan are about 100 miles (161 km) from the mainland of Asia. The Japanese were close enough to borrow ideas from China but far enough away to remain free of Chinese rule.

Kublai Khan, the Mongol emperor of China, did not think that the narrow sea separating Japan and the mainland of Asia was large enough to hold back his forces. After all, the conquering armies of the Mongols had brought most of Asia under their rule.

Kublai Khan sent word to the Japanese that they should pay tribute to him as the Koreans did. The Japanese would not pay, so in 1274 Kublai Khan sent 450 ships loaded with soldiers to attack the islands of Japan.

The samurai were ready to fight, but they had never faced such a large and well-trained army. After the first day's fighting, neither side had won. Kublai Khan's troops returned to their ships at night. That was a mistake. A heavy storm wrecked many ships and drove the others back to the coast of Asia.

Some years later, Kublai Khan sent a much larger force to Japan. This time the Japanese were better prepared to fight. The war went on for 2 months without either side winning. Then, once again, a storm helped the Japanese. A strong **typhoon** (tī fün') hit Japan. A typhoon is a storm like a hurricane. The high winds scattered and wrecked the invaders' ships. The soldiers left on shore were quickly rounded up. The Japanese believed that their gods had sent the storms that saved their land.

Southeast Asia—a meeting place No one knows for certain how long people have lived in Southeast Asia. Some scholars have found evidence that may show that people in the part of Southeast Asia now called Thailand (tī' land) learned how to farm and use tools before people in Mesopotamia, India, and China did. Scholars are not certain about this, but they do know that people from India, China, and the Middle East came, over the years, to Southeast Asia to trade and live. These people brought their customs, languages, and religions with them. Southeast Asia has been a place where East Asia and South Asia meet.

Indian merchants went to Southeast Asia more than 2,000 years ago. Later there were Indian colonies along the Mekong River in the country we now call Kampuchea. Other Indians settled in Burma and Thailand and at the tip of the Malay Peninsula. Indian colonies were set up on the islands now known as Indonesia. Use the map on page 433 to locate these countries.

Many of the people who lived near the Indian colonies adopted the ways of the people from India, Hinduism and, later, Buddhism spread throughout Southeast Asia. The ruins of great Hindu temples still stand at Angkor (an' kôr) in modern Kampuchea. Buddhism is now the main religion in Kampuchea, Burma, and Thailand. The largest Buddhist temple is on the island of Java in Indonesia. It was built ca. A.D. 800 when Java had a Buddhist king.

People from China moved south into the country now called Vietnam. Vietnam was part of the Chinese empire from 111

The Hindu temple of Angkor Wat was built in Kampuchea about 800 years ago. It is surrounded by a moat and a long causeway leads to its main entrance.

B.C. to A.D. 939. The people in Vietnam adopted many Chinese ways during that long period of time.

When the people of Vietnam had their own kingdom they sent tribute to the Chinese emperors from time to time. Other kingdoms in Southeast Asia did the same thing. One ruler sent Kublai Khan 20 large elephants every year.

Moslem merchants came to Southeast Asia from the Middle East and India. They brought Islam and the Arabic language with them. Islam took the place of Hinduism and Buddhism in much of Malaya and Indonesia. Moslems also reached the Philippine Islands.

The different peoples who came to Southeast Asia kept their own ways of living. They kept their own religions, languages, and customs. Southeast Asia is not only a region with many people; it is also a region with a great variety of peoples. You will read more about this variety in Chapter 21.

CHECKUP

1. How did China affect Korea?
2. What were some of the ideas the Japanese learned from the Chinese?
3. In what ways were the nobles and soldiers of Japan like those in Europe during the Middle Ages?
4. Who came to live and trade in Southeast Asia?

KEY FACTS

1. The remains of cities on the Indus Plain are nearly as old as those in Egypt and Mesopotamia.

2. Both Hinduism and Buddhism began in India.

3. Differences between Hinduism and Islam have divided the peoples of India.

4. Moslem invaders spread Islam in the Indian subcontinent.

5. Chinese writing uses thousands of characters instead of an alphabet.

6. Confucius and Lao-tzu were teachers in ancient China.

7. Government officials in China were chosen after taking examinations.

8. Paper, printing, gunpowder, and the compass were Chinese inventions.

9. Chinese ideas and ways spread among countries in East and Southeast Asia.

10. Southeast Asia is a region with a great variety of peoples.

VOCABULARY QUIZ

On a separate piece of paper write the numbers of the statements below. Next to each number write the letter of the word that best fills in the blank in the statement.

a. citadel **f.** reform
b. Hinduism **g.** counselor
c. caste **h.** compass
d. Buddhism **i.** harmony
e. diviner **j.** samurai

1. The teachings of Siddhartha Gautama are known as_____.

2. The_____of Japan were like the European knights during the Middle Ages.

3. Mohenjo-Daro had a_____for defense.

4. The Chinese invented the_____, an instrument for showing directions.

5. Confucius wanted to_____the old government in China.

6. Prince Shotoku taught that people should live in_____with each other.

7. _____is a religion based on the writings in the Vedas.

8. A class based on birth in India was called a _____.

9. A_____is supposed to be able to know what will happen in the future.

10. A _____advises those who rule.

REVIEW QUESTIONS

1. How do we know about the ancient cities on the Indus Plain?

2. What is the difference between class and caste?

3. How did the teachings of the Buddha affect Asoka?

4. How did Akbar's rule differ from that of earlier Moslem rulers?

5. What was early Chinese writing like?

6. How did Confucius try to reform governments?

7. What were four important Chinese inventions?

8. Who was Kublai Khan?

9. How did the Chinese empire affect Korea?

10. What peoples came to trade and live in Southeast Asia?

ACTIVITIES

1. Prepare a written and oral report on either the Taj Mahal or Angkor Wat.

2. Suppose the Buddha or Confucius were to come to your school. Write down five questions you would ask each of them.

19/SKILLS DEVELOPMENT

PARAGRAPHING

PARAGRAPHS ARE GROUPS OF SENTENCES

A paragraph is a group of sentences on one topic. The first sentence in a paragraph usually tells what the paragraph is about. This sentence is called the *topic sentence*.

After the subject of a paragraph has been introduced by the topic sentence, the remaining sentences in the paragraph develop the subject. These sentences add details and make the idea or ideas introduced by the topic sentence easier to understand. Some paragraphs may have only one or two sentences. Other paragraphs can be longer.

The material below has been divided into two paragraphs. The topic sentence of each paragraph has been underlined.

Each village in India had its headman and council, who managed the village affairs. They saw that the ditches and ponds were kept in repair. They made whatever rules were needed for the village.

The villagers thought of their villages as a kind of large family. Often whole villages were made up of one or two families, with brothers, sisters, cousins, aunts, uncles, parents, and grandparents living together.

SKILLS PRACTICE

The following passage about India should be divided into five paragraphs. Decide what the topic sentence of each paragraph is and write each topic sentence on a sheet of paper. You should have five topic sentences.

WHEN THE GUPTAS RULED INDIA

The time when the Guptas ruled India (A.D. 320–480) was India's time of greatness. Great writers, scientists, thinkers, and artists lived in India during those years. The Indians think of that time as western people think of Greece in the time of Socrates. The Buddhists were losing strength in Gupta times, but they still had the finest schools in the land. Thousands of young people, many of them not Buddhists, attended these schools. Students even came from other lands. One Chinese traveled across the mountains and deserts of Central Asia in order to study at a famous Buddhist school. The books that the students read were made from the leaves of a certain kind of palm tree. The leaves were cut into large rectangles. Writers scratched words on them with an iron spike about the size of a new pencil. Afterwards they rubbed the leaf with brown material that colored the scratches dark brown. Holes were punched in each leaf, and they were tied together between two board covers. A finished book was something like a looseleaf notebook. Most of the books were written in Sanskrit. This was not the language that the common people spoke. It was the language of the holy writings studied by the scholars. Most people did not read, but they knew many stories. Some of the world's best stories were first told in India. Do you remember the story about the lion that caught a mouse and let it go free when the mouse pleaded for its life? Later some hunters caught the lion and bound him with strong ropes. Then it was the mouse's turn to do a favor. The mouse chewed the rope in two and saved the lion's life. The Indians tell the same story except it is about an elephant and some mice. In the Indian story the mice begged an elephant not to step on them. Later hunters caught the elephant and bound him to a tree with strong ropes. The grateful mice came and chewed the ropes and set the huge beast free.

India

┌─ VOCABULARY ──────────────┐
  factor   profit
  factory
└───────────────────────────┘

An English traveler in Mogul India
In 1615 Thomas Coryat (kor' i yat), an English traveler, walked all the way from Jerusalem to India. Coryat liked to call himself the "Leg-Stretcher." He had once made a long walking journey in Europe and had written a book about it. After his European trip he hung up his worn shoes in his hometown church so that people could remember his great feat. (Or should that be spelled *feet*?)

While in India, Coryat visited the Indian ruler, Jahangir (ja hän' gēr), the Great Mogul. Jahangir was the son of Akbar, about whom you read in the last chapter. Coryat made a speech before Jahangir, giving reasons why he had come to India. One reason was that Coryat wanted "to see your Majesty's elephants which kinds of beasts I have not seen in any other country."

Coryat got his wish. He saw the Great Mogul's elephants. He even rode one. If there had been cameras in those days, Coryat would no doubt have had his picture taken. He hoped to have a picture painted showing him riding an elephant, but as far as we know, he did not. an artist in England later drew a picture of the "Leg-Stretcher" on an elephant.

Colonies and trading posts   Thomas Coryat was one of a number of people from Europe who went to India at that time. Most of the people from Europe went to trade, not to see the sights or ride elephants. Few, if any, of the other people from Europe traveled on foot. They came by sea, following the route Vasco da Gama had taken around Africa in 1497-98.

About 12 years after Vasco da Gama first sailed to India, the Portuguese conquered the port city of Goa (gō' ə). This was one of several colonies set up by the Portuguese in South Asia. Goa remained a Portuguese colony until 1961.

In 1600 a group of English merchants formed the East India Company. The company got permission from Jahangir to trade within his empire. The English did not seek colonies at that time, but they did set up trading posts where people from England could live and carry on business. The people who traded for the companies were called **factors.** The trading posts were called **factories**, places where the factors did business.

The French formed their own East India Company in 1664. The new French

This painting shows the Great Mogul Jahangir talking to a Moslem scholar. The drawing on the bottom of the page shows Tom Coryat riding an elephant.

company set up business at the village of Pondicherry (pän də cher′ ē), on the east coast of India. Pondicherry later became France's first colony in Asia.

What the Europeans bought The trading companies from Europe wanted to buy spices such as pepper, cinnamon, ginger, and cloves. Pepper grew in India, but most of the other spices were imported from the islands of Southeast Asia.

Many people in Europe wanted spices. Some of these spices were used to help keep food from spoiling quickly. For example, meat can be kept longer in the form of a spiced sausage. Spices can also make dull-tasting foods taste better. A dash of pepper "peps up" many a dish.

Spices bought in India could be sold for high prices in Europe. Some of the early traders sold spices for three times as much as they had paid for them. A gain made from selling goods is called **profit**.

The traders also found that there were profits to be made in buying and selling cloth made in Asia. The people of India made fine cotton cloth that sold for high prices in Europe. People in Europe liked a special cloth called calico (kal′ ə kō),which came from a city in India called Calicut (kal′ i kət). This city is sometimes called Kozhikode (kō zhə kōd).

It was easier to sell Indian goods in Europe than European goods in India. The people of India did not want many of the things Europeans made. For example, Europeans made good woolen cloth, but woolen cloth was not needed in India's hot climate. People in Europe also made fine jewelry, but it was no better than that made in India. In fact, people in Europe bought many Indian jewels and gems, such as rubies, sapphires, and pearls. Merchants from Europe paid for much of what they bought with silver.

India under British rule The Great Moguls were no longer able to hold their empire together after 1707. They ruled little except their capital of Delhi (del′ ē).

This time line reflects European involvement in South Asia, East Asia, Australia, and New Zealand. The British especially were involved in all four areas.

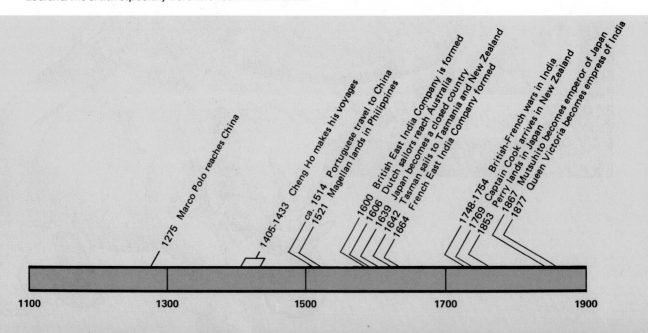

1275 Marco Polo reaches China
1405-1433 Cheng Ho makes his voyages
ca. 1514 Portuguese travel to China
1521 Magellan lands in Philippines
1600 British East India Company is formed
1606 Dutch sailors reach Australia
1639 Japan becomes a closed country
1642 Tasman sails to Tasmania and New Zealand
1664 French East India Company formed
1748-1754 British-French wars in India
1769 Captain Cook arrives in New Zealand
1853 Perry lands in Japan
1867 Mutsuhito becomes emperor of Japan
1877 Queen Victoria becomes empress of India

1100   1300   1500   1700   1900

British power in India was supported by British soldiers, some of whom pose here with an Indian elephant.

The rest of India was divided into many small kingdoms that were often at war with each other.

The European trading companies hired guards to protect their factories. As the Mogul's government grew weaker, the companies hired more guards. The British and the French East India companies had small armies that lived in company forts. Most of the soldiers in these armies were Indian. They were led by European officers who taught the soldiers how to use guns made in Europe.

Some of the Indian kingdoms that fought each other asked the trading companies for help. When the French company helped one kingdom, the British helped another. Wars between the Indian kingdoms grew into a war between Great Britain and France. France lost the war, but kept its colony at Pondicherry until 1954.

The British were left as the real rulers of India. The Moguls held their throne until 1858, and a number of Indian states still had their own governments. But the Moguls and the other Indian rulers were really under the power of the British. In 1877 Queen Victoria of Great Britain also became empress of India. Great Britain ruled the subcontinent until 1947.

The slow pace of change in the villages   The coming of traders from Europe did not greatly change the lives of most of the people of India. They still lived and worked in small farm villages, as they had before the Europeans came. The people in the villages knew little about the change of rulers. Invaders might come and empires might fall, but life for most people went on in much the same way.

Villagers spent a large part of their lives working in the fields. They plowed, planted, watered, and harvested in the same ways year after year.

The only government officials villagers knew were tax collectors. It made little difference which ruler sent the tax collectors because the taxes did not help the people in the villages. The government did not provide schools, post offices, or even village police.

Each village had its own leader and council to run village affairs. The council settled disputes and dealt with people who broke the customs of their caste or village. Village life went on whether the Great Mogul or Queen Victoria ruled.

CHECKUP
1. Why was it easier to sell Indian goods in Europe than European goods in India?
2. How did the British become rulers of India?
3. Why did changes in government have little effect on most Indians?

China

┌─VOCABULARY─────────────────┐
│ missionary   embassy   │
│ ambassador   │
└─────────────────────────────┘

Marco Polo's book   For centuries the peoples of Europe and China knew very little about each other. The belt of mountains and deserts in Central Asia made trade and travel difficult between Europe and China.

Marco Polo, a merchant from Italy, was one of the few Europeans to journey across Asia during the Middle Ages. Marco Polo reached China in 1275, when Kublai Khan was emperor. You have already read about the "fountains of oil" in Persia and the "burning stones" in China that Marco Polo saw during his trip.

Marco Polo spent 17 years in China. He told Kublai Khan and the Chinese many things about Europe. After Marco Polo returned home, he wrote a book telling the people of Europe about East Asia. The book became very popular. People thought Marco Polo's stories about far-off lands were interesting, but they did not always believe them. They thought the book was mostly a collection of traveler's tales. People in Europe knew so little about China at that time that they found it hard to believe Marco Polo's story of a great empire in the east. But Marco Polo said that he had not told half of the wonders he had seen.

Scholars today know that Marco Polo accurately described the Chinese cities he really had seen. He was not so dependable when he told of places he had only heard about. Few people are.

The voyages of Cheng Ho   The people of China learned much about the world from Chinese sailors who journeyed to South Asia. Between 1405 and 1433 Chinese emperors sent seven large expeditions to the Indian Ocean. Cheng Ho (jung' hu') was the leader of these expeditions, which brought back goods and information from South Asia, the Middle East, and East Africa.

More than 300 ships sailed in the first expedition. Cheng Ho's ship had nine masts and was 444 feet (135 m) long. It was far larger than any European ship of that time. The fleet included treasure ships loaded with gold, porcelain, and other valuable goods. To protect the treasure ships from enemies and pirates, Cheng Ho had large warships armed with cannons.

The seven trips of Cheng Ho took him to the islands of Southeast Asia and to the coasts of India and Arabia. The treasure ships returned to China loaded with rare woods, ivory, pearls, incense (a powder that gives off a nice smell when burned), and unusual animals for the emperor's zoo. Lions, leopards, ostriches, and rhinoceroses were brought back to China. One ship came back from Arabia with a dromedary, a camel with one hump. Bactrian camels with two humps were common in China, but a dromedary was a rare animal to be shown in a zoo.

Even more unusual than the dromedary was a giraffe. An Indian ruler had been given a giraffe from Africa. The Indian ruler sent the giraffe to the emperor of China. The Chinese emperor liked the giraffe so much that he sent ships to Africa to get another one.

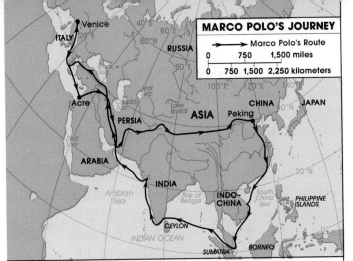

MARCO POLO'S JOURNEY

→ Marco Polo's Route

0   750   1,500 miles

0   750 1,500 2,250 kilometers

Marco Polo began his long trip to China in 1271. He left Venice with his father and uncles and traveled for more than 3 years before reaching China.

After 1433 the emperors of China sent no more expeditions to distant places. The emperors saw no reason to send ships to other lands because they thought the Chinese had whatever they needed at home. The Chinese felt that their country was the most highly developed land in the world. They felt that all other countries were inferior. This feeling of being better than other peoples and countries led to a long period of time during which China was, for the most part, cut off from much of the world.

Since the emperors felt there was nothing to be gained by sending expeditions to faraway places, the ships in the once-great Chinese fleet were not repaired or replaced. When the Portuguese arrived in East Asia in the early 1500s, China no longer had a powerful fleet.

The Portuguese trading post at Macao   The Portuguese were the first people from Europe to reach East Asia by sea. Ships from Portugal appeared along the Chinese coast about 1514, a few years after the conquest of Goa. The Portuguese wanted trading stations in China like those they had in India. But the Portuguese dared not try to set up a colony in China. The emperor's government was too powerful.

The Chinese officials did not trust the strangers from Europe and had little desire to do business with them. It was nearly 50 years before the Portuguese were allowed to have a trading factory at Macao (mə kaủ′). Macao is a very small peninsula on the south coast of China near Canton [Guangzhou]. The Chinese kept careful watch over the Portuguese, who could not leave Macao without permission. The Portuguese could go to Canton to trade only twice a year. To make sure this rule was obeyed, the Chinese built a wall across the peninsula. Within Macao the Portuguese could not put up new buildings or repair old ones without permission from Chinese officials. The Chinese wanted no foreign forts built in China.

A cannon from an old fort points over the port city of Macao. The Portuguese operated a trading post in Macao when China was a "closed" country.

A European who won respect In 1582 Matteo Ricci (mät tā′ ō rēt′ chē), a Roman Catholic priest from Europe, arrived at Macao. Ricci did not come to trade. He was a **missionary**. Missionaries are people who try to spread their religion. Ricci wanted to teach the Chinese about Christianity.

After living for a time at Macao, Ricci was allowed to move to a town near Canton.

Matteo Ricci believed that people from Europe had to win the respect of the people of China. To win respect, people from Europe would have to show respect for the people of China and their way of life. Ricci learned to speak and write Chinese. He dressed the way the people of China dressed. He ate their food and followed their customs. He even took a Chinese name.

A growing number of Chinese people visited Ricci's house. They looked at his clocks and globe. They were very interested in a map of the world that Ricci showed them. The Chinese had their own maps, but they showed China as the largest land in the world with other smaller lands around China. The Chinese called their country the "Middle Kingdom." Ricci's map showed China, but it also showed the Americas, about which the Chinese knew nothing.

Ricci pointed out that it was hard to say that any land was the "Middle Kingdom." It all depended on how a person looked at a map or globe. To make his ideas clearer, Ricci made a copy of his world map and wrote in the names of places in Chinese characters.

Matteo Ricci explained European science and mathematics to the Chinese. He

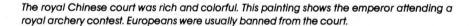

The royal Chinese court was rich and colorful. This painting shows the emperor attending a royal archery contest. Europeans were usually banned from the court.

translated Chinese books into Latin so that people in Europe could learn more about China. He worked out the first system for writing Chinese with the letters of the Roman alphabet. His system is no longer used, but we still spell the name *Confucius* the way Ricci did.

Ricci believed it would greatly help his cause if he could speak with the emperor of China. After years of waiting, Ricci got permission to go to Peking [Beijing], the capital of China. He took different types of gifts for the emperor, including two clocks from Europe. He knew that the Chinese were very interested in clocks. He gave the clocks to an official who would give them to the emperor.

Ricci waited in Peking, hoping that his gifts would please the emperor and that he would be called to the palace to meet the ruler. After waiting more than a week, Ricci finally received a message to come to the palace. Ricci thought he would now have his chance to speak to the most powerful person in China. Imagine how disappointed Ricci must have felt when he found out that he had been called to the palace not to meet the emperor but only to fix one of the clocks he had sent as a present.

Ricci never had a chance to speak to the emperor. He never got many people in China interested in Christianity. But he did win the respect of the Chinese. He was given permission to live in Peking, where he remained until he died.

The closed country   Few Europeans shared Matteo Ricci's respect for Chinese ways. Most of them were interested in trade, not earning the respect of the Chinese. And few Chinese were as interested in European ideas as those who visited Ricci's house. Most Chinese still thought of China as the "Middle Kingdom."

China was almost completely closed to foreigners. There were no foreign **ambassadors** (am bas′ ə dərz) living in Peking. Ambassadors are officials who represent their governments in foreign countries. An ambassador usually lives in a foreign country's capital city. The building where an ambassador lives and works is called an **embassy** (em′ bə sē). The Chinese emperors wanted no foreign embassies in Peking.

The emperors also did not want to trade with foreign countries. One emperor said that China "lacks no product within its own borders." However, the Chinese knew that other countries wanted to buy China's tea, silk, and porcelain. As a favor to foreigners, the emperors allowed some trade at Canton. This was the only port where people from Europe could trade with China.

The Chinese had strict rules for trading at Canton. Europeans could trade only during the winter months. They could do business only with certain Chinese merchants. Europeans could not bring their wives or families to Canton. They could live only in certain parts, or districts, in the city. They could not even walk outside of their districts except at certain times. Three times a month small groups of up to ten Europeans could visit a public park or garden, but they had to be back in their own district before it got dark. Most important of all, Europeans were not allowed to mix with the Chinese.

In spite of these difficulties, trade between Europe and China grew. Europe imported large amounts of tea and porcelain, which the Europeans called "chinaware." The Chinese sold so much chinaware that they made special teacups for the European trade. The Chinese did not use handles on their cups. Europeans liked handles, so the Chinese made cups with handles. In such small ways, trade with Europe began to affect people living inside the closed country.

An effort to open the closed country Canton was a door into the closed country. As trade grew, Europeans wanted to open still other doors.

In 1793 Great Britain sent a special ambassador to Peking. The Chinese emperor had never received a European ambassador, but he agreed to do so this time as a special favor.

At one time Canton was the only port in China open for European trade. Today Canton is a busy and important port city located on the Pearl River at 23°N, 113°E.

The British ambassador carried a message from his king asking that there be more trade. The British also asked that they be allowed to have an embassy in Peking.

The emperor replied that China did not want more trade. In a message to the king of England the emperor said, "As your ambassador can see for himself, we possess all things. I set no value on strange or clever things and have no use for your country's manufactures."

The Chinese thought the request for an embassy was a "wild idea." The Chinese thought that the British had been very rude to ask for more favors after the emperor had agreed to meet the British ambassador. To the Chinese, it seemed that their emperor was very generous to excuse such bad manners. But, of course, the Chinese considered the British to be foreigners who "knew no difference between good and bad."

The British, on their part, thought that China was a backward nation because the Chinese would not exchange ambassadors as other countries did. It was clear that the British and Chinese had different ideas about what was proper behavior.

Wars open the closed country The differences between the Chinese and the British led to quarrels. The British did not like the way the Chinese treated British merchants in Canton. The Chinese said that the British living in Canton did not obey Chinese laws.

War finally broke out between China and Great Britain in 1839. The British won the war. The Chinese were forced to open five ports. British merchants could live

Conflicts between China and the United Kingdom finally led to war. British ships bombarded Canton during this war.

Southeast Asia and Japan

Europeans and Southeast Asia   When the Portuguese first went to India looking for spices, they discovered that most spices came from the islands of Southeast Asia. The Portuguese sailed to these islands, where they built forts and trading factories.

The spice trade was profitable. One man wrote to his brother back in Portugal that in 9 months he had become "richer than you can imagine." Such reports brought other people from Europe to the islands of Southeast Asia.

Some ships from Spain reached the Philippine Islands in 1521. Although the ships were from Spain, they were led by Ferdinand Magellan, a sailor from Portugal. Magellan had sailed west across the Atlantic, around South America, and then across the Pacific to the Philippines. If you look at the map of the world in the Atlas, you will see how it is possible to sail west from Europe to reach East Asia.

Magellan lost his life in the Philippines, but one of his ships continued the journey and finally reached Europe. It was the first ship ever to sail around the world.

Spain made the Philippines part of its empire. The islands were named after King Philip II of Spain. Spain ruled the Philippines until the United States took them in 1898.

The Dutch also sent trading ships to Southeast Asia. They captured the Portuguese trading posts on the islands now called Indonesia. The Dutch ruled these

and trade in these ports. Britain took control of the island of Hong Kong, off the South China coast. Under British rule, Hong Kong grew into one of the largest cities in China. Hong Kong is still a British colony.

Once Britain opened the door, other countries increased their trade with China. France, Russia, Germany, and Great Britain became very powerful in China and actually controlled parts of the country. Japan took over Korea and Taiwan, both of which had been part of the Chinese empire. By 1900 China was no longer a country closed to foreigners. In many ways, it was a country controlled by foreigners.

CHECKUP
1. What did people in Marco Polo's time think of his book?
2. Who was Cheng Ho and what did he do?
3. How did Matteo Ricci win the respect of the Chinese?
4. Why was China a closed country for many years?

421

islands for many years. During that time, the islands were known as the Dutch East Indies.

Singapore and Indochina   The shortest sea route between India and China is through the Strait of Malacca (mə lak' ə). This is a narrow strip of water between the Malay Peninsula and the island of Sumatra (sü mä' trə). In the days of sailing ships a captain could cut 6 days off the trip from India to China by sailing through the Strait of Malacca.

The island of Singapore is at the eastern end of the Strait of Malacca. Stamford Raffles, an official of the British East India Company, realized that whoever controlled Singapore controlled a gateway to East Asia.

In 1819 Raffles sailed with a British fleet to Singapore. Only a few hundred people lived there under the rule of a chief. Raffles got the chief's permission to let the British have a base on the island.

Singapore grew rapidly from a village to a city. It was a **free port.** This means that merchants who bought goods to sell did not have to pay a **tariff.** A tariff is a tax on imports or exports.

Many people did business at the free port of Singapore. Malays came from the mainland. Chinese, Indian, and Arab merchants came to trade and many stayed to live in Singapore.

The British later ruled the entire Malay Peninsula as well as Singapore. British rule lasted until 1959.

French priests and merchants came to Vietnam as early as 1619. One of the priests developed a system for writing Vietnamese with the Roman alphabet.

The people of Vietnam still use this system.

The French began the conquest of Vietnam in 1858. They later took over Laos and Kampuchea. The French called these lands French Indochina (in' dō chī' nə). The name *Indochina* shows that these lands were where people from India and China met each other.

Europeans in Japan   Portuguese merchants were probably the first Europeans to visit Japan. Marco Polo knew of Japan, but he never saw the Japanese islands. Japan was not part of Kublai Khan's empire, although he had tried to conquer the islands.

Francis Xavier (zā' vē ər), a Christian missionary priest, was in Japan in 1549. Xavier reported that "the Japanese desire very much to hear new things." They were very much interested in European science and geography. According to Xavier, "They did not know the world is round, they knew nothing of the course of the sun and the stars, so that when they asked us and we explained to them these and other like things, such as the causes of comets, of the lightning and of rain, they listened to us most eagerly."

For a time European goods became popular in Japan. Some Japanese nobles even dressed in European styles. A few Japanese who traveled to Europe brought back clocks, watches, maps, and musical instruments.

Europeans who went to Japan found things to admire in that country, too. Don Rodrigo de Vivero (rod rē' gō dē vē vā' rō), a Spanish noble, wrote that the inside of a Japanese house "is far more beautiful" than those in Europe. He said that the streets in the city of Edo (ed′ ō) were straight and well laid out. He then added, "They are kept so clean that you might think no one ever walked on them."

While in Japan, Vivero saw a large bronze statue called the Great Buddha. Vivero wondered how he could describe the size of the huge statue when he returned home. He told a servant to climb up and measure the thumb of the statue's right hand. According to Vivero, the servant "tried to encircle the thumb with both his arms; but howsoever much he stretched, he was unable to make his hands meet around the thumb."

Japan closes its doors Japan's rulers became worried about the interest the Japanese showed in European goods and ideas. Japan's rulers knew that Europeans had set up colonies in India and in the Americas. They knew that Spain had made the nearby Philippines into a Spanish colony. Europeans who came to trade stayed to rule.

In 1639 Japan, like China, became a closed country. Most Europeans were forced to leave the country. Only a few Dutch traders were allowed to come to the port city of Nagasaki (näg ə säk′ ē). The rules for trading at Nagasaki were much like those the Chinese set up at Canton. The Dutch traders had to stay on a small island in the harbor. They could not leave the island without permission from the Japanese. All business had to be carried on by a small group of Japanese who spoke Dutch. The foreign merchants were not allowed to learn Japanese.

Japan's rulers almost closed the door to the outside world, but they did leave open

The Japanese allowed only the Dutch to carry on trade in Japan after 1639. This illustration from a Japanese scroll shows the Dutch trading station at Nagasaki.

a small crack because they wanted to know what was happening in the outside world. Every year a new Dutch captain came to take over the post at Nagasaki. The captain had to write a newsletter to the Japanese rulers telling them about the most important events of the year. The Dutch also supplied the Japanese with European books and magazines, which a few Japanese scholars could read.

Opening the closed door   A few years after China began trading with the rest of the world, some ships from the United States sailed to Japan. The year was 1853 and the leader of the American ships was Commodore (kom′ ə dôr) Matthew Perry. Among Perry's ships were three new steamships, the first ever seen in Japan.

Commodore Perry and 300 sailors and marines went ashore. Perry gave the Japanese a letter from the President of the United States. The letter said that the United States wanted to be friendly and that the Americans wanted to trade with Japan. Perry said that he would return the next year to receive the Japanese answer to the President's letter.

Early in 1854 American ships returned to Japan carrying gifts from the United States. The Americans wanted to show some of the things they had to sell. Perry gave the Japanese officials clocks, sewing machines, and steel tools. The Americans set up a telegraph line to show how rapidly messages could be sent. The gift that received the most attention was a small steam locomotive that pulled a railroad car around a short track.

Perry's visit was friendly, but the Japanese feared that in the future less peaceful fleets from other countries might come to Japan. They knew what had happened in China, and they didn't want the same thing to happen in Japan.

The Japanese decided that the best way to keep foreigners from forcing open the door to trade with Japan was for Japan

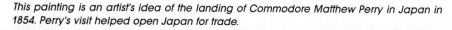

This painting is an artist's idea of the landing of Commodore Matthew Perry in Japan in 1854. Perry's visit helped open Japan for trade.

The Japanese were very interested in the products Perry's ships brought to Japan. The small steam locomotive attracted much attention.

itself to allow trade with other countries. Japan no longer kept the door to trade shut. It opened its ports to American and European trade.

A time of great change   Japan changed very rapidly after 1867 when the emperor Mutsuhito (mü tsü hē tō) came to the throne. The emperor told his people: "My country is now undergoing a complete change from old to new ideas which I sincerely desire. To speed the change, people should seek knowledge from the whole world."

The Japanese sent people to Europe and America to study and learn. A young Japanese student went to the United States Naval Academy to learn about modern navies. Young Japanese women went to American schools and colleges so that they could go back to Japan and set up schools for girls and women. A young man worked in a locomotive shop in America so that he could learn how locomotives were made. In a few years Japan had a modern railroad.

The Japanese hired foreigners to come to Japan to show the Japanese how to build and run modern factories.

The Japanese changed their government. They formed a parliament elected by the voters. They made many new laws, but they kept the emperor as the head of the government. The Japanese remained loyal to their monarch.

The Japanese also learned how to build a strong army and navy. They had seen that countries with modern armies and navies won wars. The Japanese built a modern army and navy. Japan fought a war with China in 1894. Japan won the war and took control of Taiwan and Korea. In 1904 Japan defeated Russia in another war. The victory came just 50 years after Perry's second visit to Japan. The country had changed very much in those 50 years.

New schools did much to change ways of thinking in Japan. Almost all boys and girls went to school. Many attended high school and college, where they studied mathematics, science, and modern history, among other things. They also learned about school sports.

Teachers from the United States taught the Japanese how to play baseball. It soon became a favorite game in Japan. The Japanese compared a good batter to a samurai warrior who knew how to swing a deadly sword. Some of the Japanese baseball teams became very good. In the year 1896, the First Higher School of Tokyo thought that their team was good enough to play a baseball team from an athletic club made up of Americans in Japan.

At first the Americans refused to play the Japanese team. The Americans did not think a Japanese team could possibly play "the American national game" very well. But finally the Americans agreed to play one game. The First Higher School won 20 to 4. The Americans now wanted a second game, so the teams played again. This time the First Higher School won 32 to 9. The Japanese had certainly learned how to play "the American national game."

CHECKUP

1. Which lands in Southeast Asia came under European rule?
2. Why did Japan close its doors to Europeans? Were the doors completely closed?
3. What kinds of changes took place in Japan after 1867?

Australia and New Zealand

┌─VOCABULARY─────────────────┐
│ convict   ticket of leave │
└─────────────────────────────┘

Europeans sail to Australia and New Zealand   A Dutch trading ship sailed along the coast of Australia as early as 1606. The Dutch called the land New Holland, but showed little interest in it. They thought the Aborigines were a very poor people with nothing to trade. The Dutch were looking for spices, silks, and gold.

Abel Tasman (täs' män), a Dutch ship captain, sailed south of Australia in 1642 and landed on the island that is now called Tasmania in his honor. Tasman did not see any people on the island. He thought some people were living there because he and his crew heard "certain human sounds."

Tasman then sailed east until he reached the land he called New Zealand.

This fruit orchard in Australia grows some of the great wealth of crops and other farm products produced by Australia and New Zealand today.

He named this land after the Dutch province of Zeeland, although it is spelled differently. It was a strange name for this mountainous island, which is so different from the flat lowlands of Zeeland.

While sailing along the New Zealand coast, the Dutch ship was approached by two canoes filled with Maori. The Maori called to the Dutch, but, as Tasman wrote, "We could not understand the least of it. However, we called out to them."

One of the Maori blew a few notes on a kind of trumpet. Tasman told one of his crew to take out a trumpet and "play them some tunes in reply." The two groups played for each other until it got dark, and the Maori paddled back to shore.

When Tasman returned to the Dutch trading station in Indonesia, he said that New Zealand was "a beautiful land." But he also said that he "had found no treasures or matters of great profit." The trading company was interested in profit, not beauty, so they sent no more ships to New Zealand. No one bothered the Maori for more than a century.

Captain Cook in Australia and New Zealand   More than 100 years after Tasman's trip, the British sent Captain James Cook to learn more about Australia and New Zealand.

Captain Cook landed in New Zealand in 1769. He saw that although the Maori had no spices or gold to trade, New Zealand did have good land. He believed that people from Europe could settle there, just as they were doing in North and South America.

Cook wrote that if people settled in New Zealand "they will very soon be supplied not only with the necessities but many of the luxuries of life."

The Maori cultivated part of the land, but Cook thought there was plenty of room for people from Europe. He did not ask the Maori if they thought so, too.

Cook sailed from New Zealand to the southeastern part of Australia. You read in Chapter 18 that this is the most fertile part of Australia. Cook called it New South Wales. He wrote that this land would also be good for settlers. There was enough grass for "more cattle at all seasons of the year than ever can be brought into the country." He did not think the Aborigines would cause the settlers any trouble. There were not that many Aborigines, and they had no forts where they could defend themselves.

Captain Cook took an interest in the Aborigines. He thought they were a happy people, although they did not have many of the things people from Europe thought were necessary. He reported that the Aborigines showed little interest in the cloth the British gave them. But then why should they? Cook said, "They live in a warm and fine climate and they enjoy very wholesome air, so they have little need of clothing."

British settlement in Australia   Captain Cook claimed Australia for Great Britain. For many years, the British paid no attention to the land. People looking for new homes went to America, which was closer to Europe than Australia.

The British first used Australia as a place to send **convicts.** Convicts are people who have been found guilty of breaking laws. Before the American Revolution the British had sent convicts to the American colonies. After the Americans won their independence, the British needed another place to send their convicts.

The first ships carrying convicts landed in New South Wales in 1788. After they landed, the convicts were not kept in a prison. They went to work for free settlers who were also beginning to come to Australia. If the settlers were fair, the convicts were better off than in a prison back in Great Britain.

Marsupial animals, such as this family of koala bears, are some of the unfamiliar sights that greeted Captain Cook in Australia. Kangaroos are also marsupials.

One young convict wrote home, "I have a good place at a farmhouse and I got a good master, and I am a great deal more comfortable than I expected."

After the convicts had served part of their sentences, they were usually given **tickets of leave.** These allowed them to live on their own as long as the officials knew where the convicts were.

The growing number of settlers took over the Aborigines' hunting grounds for farms and ranches. The settlers raised cattle on the hunting grounds and the Aborigines hunted the cattle. To the settlers, the Aborigines were cattle thieves. The Aborigines were pushed farther and farther into the dry interior of Australia. Many Aborigines died. As the number of settlers increased, the number of Aborigines decreased.

Europeans in New Zealand   A few Europeans settled in New Zealand before 1830. Missionaries came to teach the Maori about Christianity. The mis-sionaries worked out a written language for the Maori and printed the first books in the Maori language.

Traders came to New Zealand to exchange nails, guns, and other goods from Europe for Maori wood carvings and timber. Whalers set up bases on the coast of New Zealand. The whalers hunted whales for oil.

More settlers came to New Zealand after 1830. They wanted land for farms and ranches. The Maori did not try to stop the settlers from coming because the Maori wanted goods from Europe. The Maori used guns from Europe for hunting and in their wars. Many Maori thought the missionaries helped their people. The Maori wanted to learn how to read and write. But, in time, the settlers who wanted land caused trouble for the Maori.

As troubles grew, the British made New Zealand part of the British Empire. The British promised to protect the Maori, but war broke out between the government and the Maori tribes. It took about 12

Maori chiefs signed the treaty of Waitangi in 1840. The treaty made New Zealand part of the British Empire.

years for the British to bring the tribes under control.

In spite of the troubles, the Maori had more success in living with the people from Europe than the Aborigines did. Many Maori went to school and learned English. A few held office in the government. The Maori elected some of their own people to the New Zealand Parliament.

Today the Maori make up about 9 percent of New Zealand's population. The majority of the Maori live and work in cities. Yet the Maori keep alive the knowledge of their past, their customs, and their arts. About half the Maori in New Zealand still speak their own language.

Settlement causes change The settlers who came from Europe to Australia and New Zealand brought things with them that changed their new homelands. They brought animals, plants, insects, and diseases that were unknown in Australia and New Zealand.

Some diseases, such as measles, killed many Aborigines and Maori. The settlers from Europe did not know that measles would be such a deadly disease in Australia and New Zealand. Measles was a common disease in Europe. Over the years, people in Europe had built up natural defenses against measles, and the disease seldom killed people. But measles was a new disease to Australia and New Zealand. The Aborigines and the Maori had never had measles and had not built up a natural defense against the disease. Indeed, European diseases like measles killed more Aborigines and Maori than European guns did.

Settlers planted the kinds of trees they had raised in Europe. Oaks, elms, willows, and other European trees now grow in Australia and New Zealand.

Settlers even brought wild animals with them from Europe. They brought deer to New Zealand and rabbits to Australia. The settlers wanted to be able to hunt these animals as they had hunted them in Europe. The rabbits had no natural enemies in Australia, no animals that would hunt the rabbits and keep them from growing too numerous. As a result, the number of wild rabbits in Australia grew very rapidly. Soon there were thousands and thousands of rabbits overrunning the countryside. They ate crops and grass. The settlers who had brought the rabbits for sporting purposes had created a pest.

The settlers from Europe caused many changes in Australia and New Zealand. There were changes in government, changes in ways of living and thinking, and changes in the land itself. Were the changes good or bad? It is not easy to answer that question. But it is certain that life would never be the same in Asia, Australia, and New Zealand after Europeans settled in these lands.

CHECKUP

1. Why were the Dutch not interested in Australia or New Zealand? What was Captain Cook's view about the value of these lands?
2. Why did the British government become interested in Australia after the American Revolution?
3. What was the main reason why the Europeans quarreled with the Aborigines and Maori?
4. What did Europeans bring to Australia and New Zealand besides themselves?

KEY FACTS

1. The British came to India to trade but later ruled the country.

2. China was a closed country except for a Portuguese trading station at Macao.

3. The British forced China to open its doors to trade.

4. Many lands in Southeast Asia became European colonies.

5. Japan was a closed country until Commodore Perry's visit.

6. After Japan opened its doors, the country changed very rapidly.

7. Europeans settled in both Australia and New Zealand.

VOCABULARY QUIZ

On a sheet of paper write the numbers of the definitions given below. Next to each number write the letter of the term that best fits each definition.

a. factor
b. factory
c. profit
d. missionary
e. ambassador
f. embassy
g. free port
h. tariff
i. convict
j. ticket of leave

1. Person who traded for a trading company

2. A place where an ambassador lives

3. A person found guilty of breaking the law

4. A trading post or station

5. A tax on imports or exports

6. A permit that allowed convicts to live on their own

7. A person who tries to spread a religion

8. An official who represents his or her government in a foreign country

9. A place where merchants do not have to pay a tax on their exports and imports

10. A gain made from selling goods

REVIEW QUESTIONS

1. What was the main reason why the first Europeans came to India? How did most of them travel to India?

2. How did the British become the rulers of India? Against what other European country did the British fight a war in India?

3. To which lands did Cheng Ho sail?

4. Why were China and Japan called "closed countries"?

5. How was China finally opened to trade?

6. How was Japan finally opened to trade in the nineteenth century?

7. Which lands in Southeast Asia were taken over by the Spanish? The Dutch? The British? The French?

8. What kinds of change took place in Japan after that country opened its door to trade with the rest of the world?

9. What kinds of Europeans went to Australia and New Zealand?

10. How did Europeans change Australia and New Zealand?

ACTIVITIES

1. Europeans first went to South Asia to get spices such as pepper, cinnamon, cloves, curry, and ginger. Collect as many of these spices as you can. You probably have many of them at home in your kitchen. Try to find more spices than the ones named above. Prepare a short report on at least five different spices. In your report tell where the spices came from and how they are used in your home today.

2. Make a report about one of the following people: Marco Polo, Ferdinand Magellan, Stamford Raffles, Francis Xavier, and James Cook.

20/SKILLS DEVELOPMENT

COMPARING TIME LINES

EVENTS TAKE PLACE AT THE SAME TIME IN DIFFERENT PARTS OF THE WORLD

By comparing two or more time lines, it is possible to see what events took place at the same time but in different parts of the world. To answer the exercises below, you will have to compare the time lines from different chapters in this book. The chapters and pages given in parentheses at the end of each exercise tell you where to find the time lines.

For example:

Francis Xavier arrived in Japan 9 years before

(a) the Turks captured Constantinople

(b) Elizabeth I became Queen of England

(c) World War I was fought

(Use time lines in Chapter 20, page 414, and Chapter 7, page 142.)

If you look at the time line for Chapter 20 on page 414, you will see that Francis Xavier arrived in Japan in 1549. If you look at the time line for Chapter 7, page 142, you will see that Elizabeth I became queen in 1558 and that World War I was fought between 1914 and 1918. Therefore the correct answer for the above exercise is **b**, because 1549 came 9 years before 1558.

SKILLS PRACTICE

On a sheet of paper, write the answers to each of the following time line exercises.

1. Confucius died about 9 years before

(a) Homer created the Iliad

(b) Socrates was born

(c) Plato established the Academy

(Use the time lines in Chapter 19, page 392, and Chapter 4, page 74.)

2. Shih Huang Ti established the Chinese empire about the time that

(a) Rome established a republic

(b) Augustus became emperor of Rome

(c) Hannibal fought in the Second Punic War

(Use the time lines in Chapter 19, page 392, and Chapter 5, page 98.)

3. The Chinese admiral Cheng Ho lived at about the same time as

(a) Henry the Navigator

(b) Vasco da Gama

(c) Leo Africanus

(Use the time lines in Chapter 20, page 414, and Chapter 16, page 332.)

4. Marco Polo reached China about 10 years before

(a) the Mongols captured Baghdad

(b) Mohammed fled Mecca

(c) the Crusaders captured Jerusalem

(Use the time lines in Chapter 20, page 414, and Chapter 13, page 268.)

5. Marco Polo reached China at about the same time that

(a) Alexander the Great reached India

(b) Buddha was born

(c) Kublai Khan's fleet reached Japan

(Use the time lines in Chapter 20, page 414, and Chapter 19, page 392.)

6. The emperor Mutsuhito came to power in Japan a few years after

(a) Peter the Great founded St. Petersburg

(b) Alexander II freed the serfs

(c) Lenin led Communists to power in Russia

(Use the time lines in Chapter 20, page 414, and Chapter 10, page 204.)

The Indian Subcontinent

---VOCABULARY---

censorship	navigable river
press	

Independence and divisions The British rule of the Indian subcontinent ended in 1947 when the subcontinent was divided into India and Pakistan. The subcontinent was divided because the Moslems who lived in British India felt that they should have their own country.

Since the Moslems lived mainly in two different parts of the subcontinent, the new Moslem country of Pakistan was divided in two. West Pakistan was on the plain of the Indus River. East Pakistan lay on the other side of the subcontinent at the mouth of the Ganges River.

You will not find East Pakistan on the map today. The peoples of West and East Pakistan were separated by more than distance. They spoke different languages and had different views on government. After 24 years, a civil war broke out. East Pakistan became the independent country of Bangladesh in 1972.

Other countries in South Asia under British rule or protection also became independent after World War II. Ceylon (sə län') became free in 1948. Ceylon's name was later changed to Sri Lanka.

Nepal is a mountainous country in the Himalayas. The British had left Nepal under the rule of its kings and nobles, but the British controlled these rulers. When the British gave up control of India, they also gave up control over Nepal's rulers.

All of the countries of the subcontinent except Nepal are now republics. The Indians like to say that their country is "the world's largest democracy." The voters in India elect members of the Indian Parliament, who then choose the country's prime minister. The prime minister is in charge of the government and has great powers.

There is less **censorship** in India than in most countries in Asia. Censorship is control over what is printed in the **press.** The press is newspapers, magazines, and books. But, even in India, the prime minister's powers have been used to limit freedom of the press.

Peoples, languages, and religions The Indian subcontinent has more people than Africa, South America, and Australia together. India has by far the largest population of the subcontinent. Bangladesh is very crowded. It has more people than any country in Europe except the Soviet Union. Sri Lanka's population is about the same as Australia's.

Almost all of the countries of South and East Asia are north of the Equator. Indonesia is right on the Equator, and Australia and New Zealand are in the Southern Hemisphere.

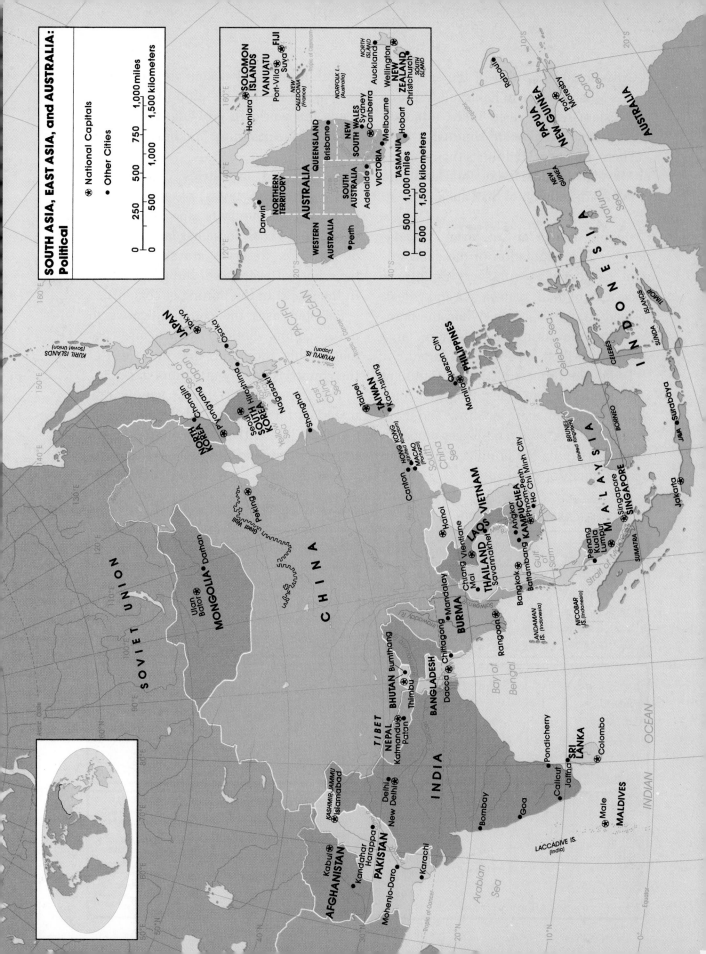

SOUTH ASIA, EAST ASIA, and AUSTRALIA: Political

⊛ National Capitals
• Other Cities

0 250 500 750 1,000 miles
0 500 1,000 1,500 kilometers

(Australia inset)

SOLOMON ISLANDS
⊛ Honiara
VANUATU
Port-Vila
Suva FIJI
NEW CALEDONIA (France)
NORFOLK I. (Australia)
AUSTRALIA
NORTHERN TERRITORY
Darwin
QUEENSLAND
• Brisbane
NEW SOUTH WALES
WESTERN AUSTRALIA
Perth
SOUTH AUSTRALIA
Adelaide
VICTORIA
Sydney
⊛ Canberra
Melbourne
TASMANIA
Hobart
Auckland
NORTH ISLAND
Wellington ⊛
NEW ZEALAND
Christchurch
SOUTH ISLAND

0 500 1,000 miles
0 500 1,500 kilometers

Main map

SOVIET UNION (Soviet Union)
KURIL ISLANDS
JAPAN
⊛ Tokyo
Osaka
PACIFIC OCEAN
RYUKYU IS. (Japan)
NORTH KOREA
Chongjin
⊛ Pyongyang
SOUTH KOREA
Hiroshima
Nagasaki
Shanghai
Yellow Sea
East China Sea
TAIWAN
Taipei
Kao-hsiung
Quezon City
PHILIPPINES
Manila ⊛
MONGOLIA
⊛ Ulan Bator
Darhan
CHINA
Great Wall
Chungking ⊛
Canton
HONG KONG (United Kingdom)
MACAO (Portugal)
South China Sea
Hanoi ⊛
VIETNAM
LAOS
Chiang Mai
Vientiane ⊛
THAILAND
Savannakhet
Angkor
KAMPUCHEA
Phnom Penh ⊛
Ho Chi Minh City
Battambang
Bangkok ⊛
Gulf of Siam
BRUNEI (United Kingdom)
BORNEO
M A L A Y S I A
Penang
Kuala Lumpur
Singapore ⊛ SINGAPORE
Strait of Malacca
SUMATRA
I N D O N E S I A
CELEBES
Celebes Sea
SUNDA IS.
TIMOR
JAVA
Surabaya
Jakarta ⊛
Macassar
NEW GUINEA
PAPUA NEW GUINEA
Port Moresby
Rabaul
Coral Sea
AUSTRALIA
Arafura Sea
BURMA
Mandalay
Chittagong
Rangoon ⊛
Irrawaddy R.
Bay of Bengal
ANDAMAN IS. (India)
NICOBAR IS. (Indonesia)
BHUTAN
Bumthang
BANGLADESH
Dacca ⊛
NEPAL
Katmandu ⊛
Patan
TIBET
Thimbu
Mekong R.
Gulf of Siam
Brahmaputra R.
INDIA
Ganges R.
Delhi
⊛ New Delhi
KASHMIR, JAMMU
⊛ Islamabad
PAKISTAN
Harappa
Kandahar
⊛ Kabul
AFGHANISTAN
Mohenjo-Daro
Karachi
Bombay
Goa
Calicut
Pondicherry
Jaffna
SRI LANKA
⊛ Colombo
LACCADIVE IS. (India)
Male
⊛ MALDIVES
Arabian Sea
INDIAN OCEAN
Equator
Tropic of Cancer
Tropic of Capricorn

Only about one third of the subcontinent's Moslems live in Pakistan. Millions of Moslems still live in India, although most people in India are Hindus.

There are fewer Buddhists than Hindus or Moslems in India today. But Buddhism is the main religion of Sri Lanka.

Growing food for a large population The population of the subcontinent has been growing very rapidly. It takes a lot of food, such as rice and wheat, to feed so many people. When the monsoons do not bring enough rain, large amounts of food have to be imported.

Today the farmers of the subcontinent raise more rice and wheat than they once did. Better seed, more fertilizer, and more irrigation have produced bigger crops. In good years India has produced more than enough food for its people.

Both India and Pakistan grow cotton. It is Pakistan's largest crop. Bangladesh leads the world in growing jute. Jute is made into ropes, rugs, and burlap cloth.

Minerals and industries India has many different types of mineral resources. The country is especially rich in iron ore and coal. India has large reserves of iron ore. Reserves are supplies that have not yet been used. India ranks fifth in the world in the mining of coal.

Pakistan uses the cotton it grows to make cotton cloth. Pakistan also has many other industries that make use of the country's supply of natural gas.

The forests of Sri Lanka supply raw materials for a number of its industries. Graphite (graf' ĭt) is the country's most important mineral. Graphite is the material used to make pencil lead.

COTTON: FROM PLANTS TO CLOTH

1. Growing and harvesting cotton.
2. Fibers are separated from seeds. COTTON GIN
3. Fibers are baled. BALER
4. Fibers are cleaned and blended. CLEANER
5. Fibers are combed and drawn into rope. BLENDER
6. Cotton rope is spun into thread. SPINNER
7. Spools of thread are bleached or dyed. DYING VAT
8. Thread is woven into cotton cloth. WEAVING MACHINE

Afghanistan—neighbor to the subcontinent Conquerors, traders, and travelers have long entered the Indian subcontinent from Afghanistan. The land routes from the Middle East, Central Asia, and China all cross Afghanistan.

Afghanistan is a high, mountainous country. Much of it is over 4,000 feet (1,219 m) above sea level. Travel across this high land is not easy unless you take an airplane. Afghanistan does not have many good roads. There are no railroads or **navigable rivers**—rivers that large ships and boats can use regularly.

In the past, Afghanistan had a king. In 1973 the country became a republic. The republic was not able to hold free and peaceful elections. The first three presidents were killed. A rebellion broke out in 1979. At that time the Soviet Union, Afghanistan's neighbor to the north, invaded the country.

Kabul (käb′ əl) is Afghanistan's capital and largest city. Most of Afghanistan's people live in the countryside. Wheat and cotton are Afghanistan's main crops. Herders keep large flocks of sheep and goats. Wool and sheepskins are two of the country's most important products. Some of the fine wool is used to make beautiful carpets and rugs.

CHECKUP

1. Which countries were formed from the lands in the Indian subcontinent that were under British control?
2. Why has it been necessary to increase food production on the subcontinent? What crops other than food crops are raised?
3. Name some of the minerals mined in the subcontinent.
4. Why is Afghanistan's location important?

East Asia

Revolutions and wars in China The years between 1910 and 1950 were not peaceful in China. A revolution in 1911 overthrew the emperor's government. A republic was set up in 1912, but the new government could not control the country. Local leaders called warlords actually ruled much of China. The warlords had their own armies much like the feudal lords had in Europe.

Wars between the Chinese government and the warlords weakened China. In 1931 Japan invaded China and occupied the northeastern part of the country known as Manchuria (man chúr′ ē ə). To **occupy** a land means to take it over.

In 1937 Japan began a conquest of the rest of China. The United States opposed Japan's actions. Japan became an ally of Germany and Italy. Japan attacked United States bases in Hawaii and the Philippines in 1941. With that attack, Japan's war in China became part of World War II. The war did not end until Japan **surrendered**, or gave up, in September 1945.

The end of World War II did not bring peace to China. For 4 more years, two Chinese groups fought for control of the country. The republic's government was under Chiang Kai-shek (jəäng′ kī shek′) and the Nationalist party. The Chinese Communist party, led by Mao Tse-tung (mou′ dzü′ dùng) [Mao Zedong] fought against the Nationalists. By 1949 the Communists had control of mainland China.

435

The Nationalists retreated to the island of Taiwan (tī wän′) and set up a capital at the city of Taipei (tī′ pā′).

The Communists call their country the People's Republic of China. Its capital is at Peking. The government on Taiwan calls itself the Republic of China. Both the Communists and the Nationalists claim to be *the* rightful rulers of all of China.

China under Communist rule   The People's Republic of China is controlled by the Communist party. No other political parties are allowed in China.

People who have opposed the Communists have been called "enemies of the people." Many were killed. Many more were forced to do hard labor.

When the Communists took over China, they said that all the land belonged to the people. By this they meant that no individual farmer could own land. All farmers had to join large groups called **communes** (kom′ yünz). Members of a commune worked the land together as a team.

The communes were supposed to be a new way of life. People ate together in large dining halls, not in their own homes. Small children were put into day-care centers so that both their parents could work full time.

So many people did not like this way of life that the government had to make changes. Farmers now own their own homes and live as families. People of a village must still work as a team on the

A Chinese farming commune has its own fields, its own school, and its own repair shop. Commune families can raise crops for sale on their own small private plots.

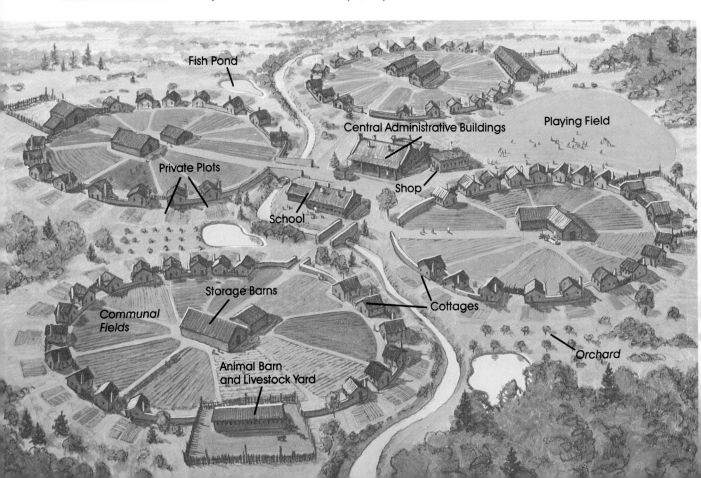

commune land, but a family may also have a small plot of land for itself. Farmers may grow vegetables on their little piece of land or raise a pig or two. They are free to sell anything they raise on their own land.

China today leads the world in the production of rice and vegetables. Chinese farmers also grow wheat, corn, and cotton. China has more pigs than any other country.

Industries in China The government took over all industries and businesses when the Communists came to power in China. For a time the government tried to do away with all private ownership of businesses.

Workers were told that they were building a "new China." Workers who turned out more goods were honored and given such things as banners and red stars. After a time the government decided that people would work harder for extra money than for banners and red stars. In recent years, workers who do more work get more money. People who do poor work are given lower-paying jobs.

The government still owns large industries in China. The managers of these industries are now allowed more power over running them than was once the case. People are also allowed to own small businesses.

China ranks third in the world in the production of coal. Only the United States and the Soviet Union produce more coal than China. More and more iron ore is being mined in China, and this iron ore is used in China's growing steel industry. China is now the world's fifth largest producer of steel.

This modern steel mill in China shows how the Chinese are trying to modernize their industries. The steel industry in China is growing.

The Chinese are working to **modernize** (mod′ ər nīz) their industries. To modernize means to use up-to-date methods and machinery to produce more goods and services. Some industries in China still have very old equipment.

The most heavily populated nation on earth More people live in China than in any other country on earth. When the Communists took over the country in 1949, China had 500 million people. In 33 years this number has doubled. In 1982 China finished another count of its population. It now has 1 billion people.

Most Chinese live in farm villages and country towns. But China has a number of very large cities. There are at least 15 cities in China with a population of 1 million or more. Shanghai (shang hī′) is the largest city in the world.

A large population is good in one way—it provides many workers for China's farms and industries. But having

437

a large population can bring problems when it comes to providing homes, food, and clothing for so many people. The government of China is trying to keep down the population of the country by asking people to have smaller families.

Change in China   For many years Mao Tse-tung was the leader of China. He was the chairman, or leader, of the Chinese Communist party. His pictures were everywhere—in homes, schools, factories, and on the outsides of buildings. Mao's writings were called "the greatest truth ever known."

Mao Tse-tung died in 1976. The leaders who got control of the government believed that Mao had made some mistakes. In time they took down many of his pictures. One of the new leaders told the people, "There have been too many portraits, quotations, and poems of Chairman Mao in public places."

Life in Taiwan   Taiwan has a much smaller population than the People's Republic of China. But Taiwan is small compared to the rest of China and the population density of Taiwan is far greater than that of the People's Republic.

When the Nationalists came to Taiwan, the government limited the amount of land any one person could own. Anyone who had more land than the limit had to sell it to the government. The government then sold the land to farmers who had no land of their own.

The Nationalists' plan created many small farms worked by their owners. In 13 years, the amount of food grown on Taiwan doubled.

So many people were crowded on Taiwan after 1949 that they had to do more than just farm the land. There wasn't enough farmland for everyone. Many people went to work in factories and industries. The Chinese on Taiwan

The production of television sets is an important industry in Taiwan.

built factories that now turn out all sorts of manufactured goods—shoes, clothing, television sets, and many other products.

Hong Kong and Macao   Portugal and the United Kingdom still have small territories in China. Portugal has Macao and the British have Hong Kong. Both Macao and Hong Kong are very crowded. The population density of Hong Kong is one of the highest in the world.

There is a guarded border between Hong Kong and the People's Republic of China, but relations between Hong Kong and China are friendly. Hong Kong serves as a major port for South China.

Macao is about 40 miles (64 km) west of Hong Kong. Most of the people who live in Macao are Chinese. Tourism is Macao's most important industry.

Tibet and Mongolia   The Chinese emperors claimed Tibet as part of their empire, but the Chinese did not really have control over this high plateau country. The real rulers of Tibet were the heads of Buddhist monasteries and a small group of noble families.

When the Communists came to power in China they said that Tibet was part of the country and they invaded it. The Communists did away with all the Buddhist monasteries. The lands of the monasteries and the nobles were turned into communes. Chinese officials came to Tibet in increasing numbers. Today about half of the people in Lhasa (läs' ə), the capital of Tibet, are Chinese.

Mongolia is divided into two parts by the Gobi Desert. The northern part of the land is now called the Mongolian People's Republic. It is a Communist-rule land located between two much larger Communist countries, the People's Republic of China and the Soviet Union. The Mongolian People's Republic is sometimes called Outer Mongolia. Ulan Bator (ü lan' bä' tor) is the capital of Outer Mongolia and its largest city.

The southern part of Mongolia is called Inner Mongolia and is part of the People's Republic of China. Only one person in ten in Inner Mongolia is a Mongol. Most people in Inner Mongolia are Chinese who have moved there since the Communists came to power in 1949.

Both Outer and Inner Mongolia have broad grasslands. Many Mongols still raise herds of goats, sheep, cattle, and horses, as they did in the time of Genghis Khan. There are more livestock in Outer Mongolia than people.

The two Koreas   Japan ruled Korea before World War II. When Japan lost the war in 1945, the Soviet army moved into northern Korea, and the United States Army occupied southern Korea. It was agreed that both armies would stop at the 38th parallel (38°N), which crossed Korea.

The Communist and non-Communist forces could not agree on what type of government Korea should have. As a result, the country was divided at the 38th parallel. North Korea became a Communist country. South Korea remained non-Communist.

In 1950 Communist North Korea invaded South Korea. The United States and some other countries helped the South Koreans against the Communists. The Chinese Communists fought for North

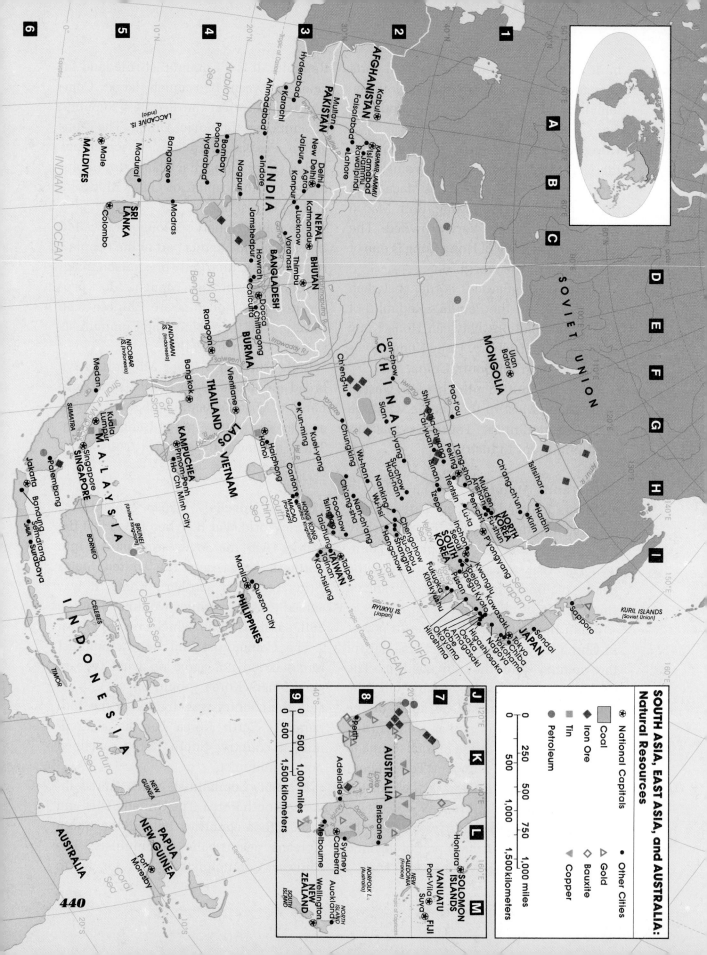

SOUTH ASIA, EAST ASIA, and AUSTRALIA: Natural Resources

Cities less than 100,000

Honiara (Solomon Islands) L-7
Islamabad (Pakistan) .. B-2
Male (Maldives) B-5
Phnom-Penh (Kampuchea) E-4
Port-Vila (Vanuatu) M-7
Suva (Fiji) M-7
Thimbu (Bhutan) C-3

Cities 100,000 to 499,999

Canberra (Australia) ... L-8
Jammu (Kashmir-Jammu) B-2
Jamshedpur (India) C-3
Katmandu (Nepal) C-3
Kuala Lumpur (Malaysia) E-5
Macao (Portugal) F-3
New Delhi (India) B-3
Port Moresby (Papua-New Guinea) . I-6
Ulan Bator (Mongolia) .. E-1
Vientiane (Laos) E-4
Wellington (New Zealand) M-9

Cities 500,000 to 999,999

Adelaide (Australia) ... K-8
Agra (India) B-3
Amagasaki (Japan) H-2
Anshan (China) G-1
Auckland (New Zealand) M-8
Ch'ang-ch'un (China) .. G-1
Ch'ang-sha (China) F-3
Chengchow (China) ... G-2

Chiba (Japan) I-2
Chittagong (Bangladesh) D-3
Colombo (Sri Lanka) .. C-5
Faisalabad (Pakistan) .. B-2
Foochow (China) F-3
Hangchow (China) G-2
Higashiosaka (Japan) . H-2
Hiroshima (Japan) H-2
Howrah (India) C-3
Huai-nan (China) F-2
Hyderabad (Pakistan) . A-3
Inchon (S. Korea) G-2
Indore (India) B-3
Jaipur (India) B-3
Kabul (Afghanistan) ... A-2
Kirin (China) G-1
K'un-ming (China) E-3
Kwangju (S. Korea) G-2
Kuei-yang (China) E-3
Lan-chow (China) E-2
Lo-yang (China) F-2
Lucknow (India) C-3
Madurai (India) B-5
Medan (Indonesia) D-5
Multan (Pakistan) B-2
Nagpur (India) B-3
Nan-ch'ang (China) F-3
Okayama (Japan) H-2
Palembang (Indonesia) E-6
Poa-t'ou (China) E-1
Pen-ch'i (China) G-1
Perth (Australia) J-8
Poona (India) B-4
Quezon City (Philippines) G-4
Rawalpindi (Pakistan) .. B-2
Semarang (Indonesia) . F-6

Sendai (Japan) I-2
Shih-chia-chuang (China) F-2
Su-chou (China) G-2
Su-chow (China) F-2
Taejon (S. Korea) G-2
Taichung (Taiwan) G-3
Tainan (Taiwan) G-3
T'ang-shan (China) F-2
Tsinan (China) F-2
Tsitsihar (China) G-1
Tzepo (China) F-2
Varanasi (India) C-3
Wu-hsi (China) G-2

Cities 1,000,000 or more

Ahmadabad (India) B-3
Bandung (Indonesia) ... E-6
Bangalore (India) B-4
Bangkok (Thailand) E-4
Bombay (India) B-4
Brisbane (Australia) ... L-8
Calcutta (India) C-3
Canton (China) F-3
Ch'eng-tu (China) E-2
Chungking (China) E-3
Dacca (Bangladesh) ... D-3
Delhi (India) B-3
Fukuoka (Japan) H-2
Fu-shun (China) G-1
Haiphong (Vietnam) ... E-3
Hanoi (Vietnam) E-3
Harbin (China) G-1
Ho Chi Minh City (Vietnam) E-4
Hong Kong (United Kingdom) F-3

Hyderabad (India) B-4
Jakarta (Indonesia) E-6
Kanpur (India) C-3
Kao-hsiung (Taiwan) ... G-3
Karachi (Pakistan) A-3
Kawasaki (Japan) H-2
Kitakyushu (Japan) H-2
Kobe (Japan) H-2
Kyoto (Japan) H-2
Lahore (Pakistan) B-2
Luta (China) G-2
Madras (India) C-4
Manila (Philippines) ... G-4
Melbourne (Australia) .. L-8
Mukden (China) G-1
Nagoya (Japan) H-2
Nanking (China) F-2
Osaka (Japan) H-2
Peking (China) F-2
Pusan (S. Korea) G-2
P'yongyang (N. Korea) . G-2
Rangoon (Burma) D-4
Sapporo (Japan) I-1
Seoul (S. Korea) G-2
Shanghai (China) G-2
Sian (China) E-2
Singapore E-5
Surabaya (Indonesia) .. F-6
Sydney (Australia) L-8
Taegu (S. Korea) G-2
Taipei (Taiwan) G-3
T'ai-yuan (China) F-2
Tientsin (China) F-2
Tokyo (Japan) H-2
Tsingtao (China) F-3
Wu-han (China) F-2
Yokohama (Japan) H-2

Many countries in South Asia and East Asia are rich in a variety of natural resources. The western part of Australia has deposits of iron ore, tin, and gold.

Korea. The Soviet Union sent North Korea supplies. After 3 years of fighting, both sides accepted the division of Korea. A truce line near the 38th parallel marked the boundary between the two Koreas.

South Korea has changed a great deal since the end of the Korean War. In 1953 most South Koreans lived and worked in farm villages. Now most South Koreans live and work in cities. Seoul (sōl), the capital of South Korea, is a very large and crowded city. Factories in South Korea make many different products. Although many people in South Korea moved away from their farms, food production has grown. South Korea set the world record for the highest average yield of rice per acre (.4 ha).

North Korea has more land but fewer people than South Korea. The North Koreans have built modern industries and raised food production.

Japan after World War II   Japan suffered great losses during World War II. Most of its factories were destroyed or damaged by bombing. One atomic bomb dropped on the city of Hiroshima (hir ə shē′ mə) destroyed two thirds of the city and killed about 70,000 people.

But the Japanese rebuilt their cities and replaced their factories. By 1953 the Japanese were producing more goods than they had in 1941 when the war began. Japan is today one of the leading industrial countries of the world.

441

Japan is one of the world's leading producers of automobiles. Robots do most of the work on this assembly line near Tokyo.

Japan's government changed after World War II. Japan kept its emperor but took away most of his powers. Today the power to make laws and govern Japan belongs to an elected parliament.

"The ability to make things" Japan is not a large country. The Japanese islands are beautiful, but much of the land is too mountainous for farming. Japan does not have many minerals—not nearly enough to supply its industries.

How are so many people able to make a living on these islands? A Japanese merchant explained it this way: "We have no oil, no iron, almost no coal. All we have to sell is our ability to make things."

What kinds of things do the Japanese make? All sorts of things. They import coal and iron to make steel and they use the steel to make everything from giant oil tankers to tiny watch springs. Japanese industries make automobiles, airplanes, watches, computers, cameras, television sets, and many other products that need highly skilled workers.

People born in Japan before World War II have seen great changes take place. The country has grown much richer. Rapidly growing cities have taken the place of farming villages. One man who grew up near the city of Osaka (ō säk′ ə) remembered that when he was in elementary school, there were some farm children in his classes. But by the time he got to high school, there were none. "There were no farms left—only city."

CHECKUP
1. What changes did the Communists make in China?
2. Why are there two Koreas?
3. How did Japan become an important manufacturing country?
4. How has manufacturing changed living patterns in Japan?

442

Southeast Asia

War in Vietnam   France ruled Vietnam before World War II. Japan occupied the country during the war. After Japan lost the war, the French returned to Vietnam. Many Vietnamese did not want a return of French rule. A Communist leader named Ho Chi Minh (hō′ chē′ min′) led a war to throw off French rule. From 1946 to 1954, the French fought to keep control of Vietnam. Finally the French were defeated and Vietnam was divided. The Communists ruled the northern part of the country, and a government opposed to Communism ruled the south. Hanoi (ha noi′) was the capital of North Vietnam, and Saigon (sī gän′) was the capital of South Vietnam.

Dividing Vietnam did not bring peace. War broke out between the two Vietnams. The United States helped South Vietnam. At one time the United States had more than 500,000 soldiers fighting in Vietnam. The United States kept forces there until 1973. The war continued until 1975 when the Communists took control of all of Vietnam. Hanoi became the country's capital. Saigon was renamed Ho Chi Minh City in honor of the Communist leader.

Changes in Southeast Asia   The lands once called French Indochina are now three separate countries —Vietnam, Laos, and Kampuchea. All have Communist governments. The long war in Vietnam did great damage and cost many lives, but the population in these lands grew larger.

The population of Vietnam more than doubled between 1946 and 1979.

Most people in these countries are farmers whose main crop is rice. The valley and delta of the Mekong River have some of the richest land in all of Asia. Find the Mekong on the map on page 433. In which country is the Mekong Delta?

Burma and Thailand   Burma (bər′ mə) was controlled by the British until 1948, when it became an independent country. Rangoon (ran gün′) is Burma's capital and chief port.

The kingdom of Thailand (tī′ land) was known as Siam (sī am′) before 1939. Thailand means "land of the free." Thailand was never part of any European empire. Bangkok (ban′ käk) is Thailand's capital and the largest city in Southeast Asia.

Both Burma and Thailand are rice-growing countries. Both countries also have forests that produce valuable timber. Teak is one of these valuable woods. It is very hard. The center of a teak log is so hard that even termites will not eat it. Teak beams in some temples in Burma are more than 1,000 years old.

Malaysia and Singapore   Malaysia (mə lā′ zhə) is a country divided by 400 miles (644 km) of ocean. Western Malaysia is on the southern part of the Malay Peninsula. Eastern Malaysia consists of part of the island of Borneo. These lands were controlled by the British before they united to form an independent country in 1963. Eastern Malaysia is larger than western Malaysia, but more people live in the western part of the country.

443

Workers in a tin smelting plant in Malaysia are protected by special face masks. Malaysia is the world's major producer of tin.

Today tin and rubber are Malaysia's most important products. Its mines produce more tin than any other *two* countries in the world.

Southeast Asia produces about 90 percent of the world's natural rubber, and half of it comes from Malaysia. Natural rubber is the sap collected from rubber trees. Before World War II almost all tires, hoses, and other rubber products were made from natural rubber. Today two thirds of the rubber we use is **synthetic** (sin thet′ ik) rubber. Synthetic rubber is made from oil and other materials.

Singapore is both a large city and a small country—the smallest in Asia. It is an island with an area of 226 square miles (586 sq km). It has a large population. It has more people than Outer Mongolia, which is many times larger.

Singapore was part of Malaysia, but it became a free republic in 1965. Although Singapore is a very small country, it is not poor. As measured by per capita income of its citizens, Singapore is the richest country in all of Southeast Asia.

Indonesia Find Indonesia on the Atlas map on pages 466 and 467. It is made up of a chain of islands stretching about 3,200 miles (5,149 km) along the Equator.

Indonesia has more people than any other country in Southeast Asia. In the world, only China, India, the Soviet Union, and the United States have larger populations.

The population of Indonesia is not spread evenly over the islands. A very great number of people live on Java, one of the most heavily populated places on earth. Jakarta (jə kärt′ ə), the capital of Indonesia, is on Java. With a population of about 4½ million people, Jakarta is the second largest city in Southeast Asia.

When the Netherlands ruled this chain of islands, they were known as the Dutch East Indies. Indonesia became independent in 1949.

Indonesia is a farming country. Rice and rubber are its main crops. Indonesia also has mineral wealth. It is fourth among the world's producers of tin, and it has more oil than any other country in Southeast Asia.

The Philippines The people of the Philippines are called Filipinos. The country has three official languages—Pilipino, Spanish, and English. The use of three languages reflects the country's history. Spain ruled the Philippines for more than 300 years. In 1898 the United States and Spain fought a war. The causes of the war had nothing to do with the Philippines, but the United States occupied the islands. The Philippines remained an American territory for almost 50 years. The Philippines became independent in 1946. Manila is the capital.

Many Filipinos are farmers, raising corn, rice, and vegetables. Coconut trees provide the most important exports—coconut oil and the dried coconut meat known as **copra** (kop′ rə).

CHECKUP

1. Why were there two Vietnams at one time?
2. What are Malaysia's two major products?
3. Name three countries in Southeast Asia that have Communist governments.
4. How do the three official languages of the Philippines reflect the history of the country?

Australia and New Zealand

```
┌─VOCABULARY──────────────────┐
│  industrialized    geothermal │
└─────────────────────────────┘
```

The people of Australia   Most Americans visiting Australia would probably feel quite at home. Australians and most Americans speak English even though they pronounce words somewhat differently, and Australians have some words of their own. In Australia a ranch is called a station and a friend is a mate. To an Australian, a herd of sheep is a mob of sheep and a cowhand is a jackaroo.

Even though Australia is an entire continent, it does not have a large population. The whole country has fewer people than Taiwan, although Australia is 200 times larger than Taiwan.

Most Australians or their ancestors came from the British Isles. It was only after World War II that many people came from other countries in Europe. The Aborigines now make up less than 2 percent of the population.

Australia's cities   When people think of Australia, they often think of the country's large sheep and cattle ranches—or stations. Actually more than 85 percent of Australia's population lives in cities. Most of the largest cities are on the southeastern part of the continent. Turn to the map on page 433. Locate Adelaide, Melbourne, Sydney, and Brisbane.

Sydney is the largest city in Australia. One fifth of the continent's population lives

Melbourne, Australia, has a marine climate. This means that Melbourne's climate is greatly affected by its closeness to the ocean.

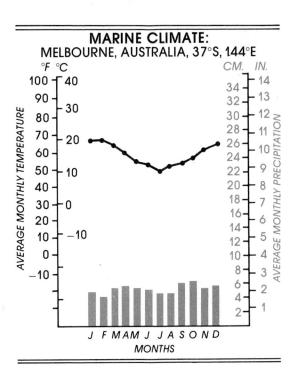

MARINE CLIMATE:
MELBOURNE, AUSTRALIA, 37°S, 144°E

The Opera House in Sydney, Australia, juts out into Sydney Harbor. Sydney is a bustling, busy port and the largest city in Australia.

Australia has great mineral wealth. Gold was discovered in the country in the 1850s and is still an important export. The world's largest lead mine is in Australia. The country also has vast deposits of silver, copper, and zinc. Australia leads the world in the production of bauxite, which is used to make aluminum. The country ranks second in the world in the mining of iron ore.

Australia's government Australia is one of the oldest members of the Commonwealth of Nations. It is an independent country, but the British ruler appoints a governor-general to represent the British in Australia.

The country is divided into six states and two territories. One of the states is the island of Tasmania. The country's capital, Canberra, is not located within any state but is one of the territories.

The Australian Parliament makes the country's laws and chooses the prime minister, who is the leader of the country. Parliament is divided into two houses. One is called the House of Representatives, and the other is called the Senate. Members of both houses are elected by the people.

in this one city. Perth is the main city in western Australia, and Darwin is the only city of any size on Australia's north coast. But Darwin is a fairly small city.

Australia's farms and industries Although most Australians live in cities, the country's farms and ranches provide three of Australia's most important exports—wool, wheat, and meat.

Australia's crops vary from one part of the continent to another. The crops and fruits raised in the southeast are much like those grown in Western Europe. Along the northeastern coast, tropical crops such as sugarcane and pineapples are raised.

Australia is a highly developed, **industrialized** country, a country that has developed its mines and factories. Australians make automobiles, tractors, machinery, and many other kinds of products.

People and cities of New Zealand New Zealand is a long way from the United Kingdom, yet for many years New Zealand was called "the most British" of the Commonwealth countries. Most of the settlers in New Zealand came from the British Isles.

At one time the Maori population of New Zealand was decreasing, but this is no longer true. In the last 50 years the

Maori population has increased at a faster rate than the population of New Zealand as a whole. One out of every 12 New Zealanders is a Maori.

North Island is slightly smaller than South Island, but 70 percent of the people of New Zealand live on North Island. Wellington, the capital, is on North Island. Christchurch is the largest city of South Island.

The importance of trade   Millions of cattle and sheep are raised on New Zealand's green pastures. It is often pointed out that livestock in New Zealand outnumber people by 25 to 1. The livestock supply New Zealand's important food-processing industries. Cheese making and meat packing are examples of food-processing industries.

Butter, cheese, meat, and wool are New Zealand's chief exports. New Zealanders also use their own products. They eat more butter and meat per person than do people in any other country in the entire world.

Sources of energy in New Zealand New Zealand does not have much coal and oil, but there are other sources of energy on these islands. The waterpower of mountain streams is used to make most of the country's electricity. The best places for plants that generate electricity using waterpower are on mountainous South Island. These plants also supply part of the electricity used on North Island.

New Zealand also has **geothermal** (jē ə thėr' məl) energy. Geothermal means heat from the earth. The heat comes from steaming hot springs on a volcanic plateau in North Island. Steam from the springs is used to make electricity. About 8 percent of New Zealand's electricity is produced by geothermal energy.

New Zealand's government   Like Australia, New Zealand is an independent nation, but it also has a governor-general appointed by the British ruler.

New Zealand has a single-house Parliament elected by the people. New Zealand was the first country in the world to let women vote in national elections.

CHECKUP

1. Why might an American feel at home in Australia?
2. Where do most people in Australia live?
3. What kinds of governments do Australia and New Zealand have?
4. What kinds of energy sources does New Zealand use to make up for its lack of coal and oil?

Looking Back

What you have read about   In this book you have read about the people who live on four continents. All together they make up 86 percent of the human race. You have read about where these peoples live, the crops they grow, the things they make, and the ideas they have.

Now that you have reached the end of the book, it may be useful to remember—not all that you have learned—but the *kinds of things* you have learned. Listed below are some of the important ideas about the material you have read. As you look at these important ideas, try to remember some particular examples that illustrate each one.

What people do depends partly on where they live There are many different kinds of places where people live on these four continents. There are deserts, forests, river valleys, mountains, and plains. There are different climates ranging from hot to cold and from wet to dry. People have had to work out different ways of living for such different lands and climates. Can you think of some of these different ways? Can you think of different ways to live in the same kind of place— for example, different ways to live in a desert? Can you remember where in this book you read about deserts?

People have the ability to use—and sometimes destroy—the gifts of nature In order to live in any place, people have to use nature's gifts. Sometimes people have used these gifts wisely, making life better for themselves and for people in the future. But at other times people have wasted and even destroyed resources so that little is left for the future. Can you think of cases in which people used nature's gifts wisely and others in which they wasted resources by the changes they made?

What people do is connected with what people did in the past You have read about people of many different times. Some lived more than 4,000 years ago, others much more recently. Can you remember examples of something done at one time that affected people in a later time? Can you think of anything done by different groups of people in the past that affects your reading the words in this sentence?

People have both harmed and helped each other The story of what people have done is not always a happy one. You have read about killings, conquests, slavery, and other dreadful things. Some of these events happened long ago; some happened recently.

But you have also read of how people have made life better both in their own times and in later times as well. You should know about examples of both harmful and helpful actions of the past because they are both part of the human story.

The ways people live keep changing You have read again and again about changes that have taken place. There have been changes in the ways people make a living, changes in the ways they are governed, and changes in the ways they think. Can you recall some of these different changes?

Even more important than knowing about changes in the past is to know that changes never stop. Between the writing of these words and your reading them, there will be changes in the lands you have read about. Changes will continue long after you have finished this book.

You will be better able to understand these changes because of what you have been learning. You will know about the places where people live. You will know something about how they live. You will look for connections between what has happened in the past and those changes in the future. As you think about future changes, you may discover that you remember more of what you have read than you thought you did.

KEY FACTS

1. After British rule ended, the Indian subcontinent was divided into India and Pakistan. East Pakistan later became Bangladesh.

2. The People's Republic of China has more people than any other country in the world.

3. Japan is a leading industrial nation even though it has few natural resources.

4. All the lands of Southeast Asia that had been part of European empires became independent after World War II.

5. Both Australia and New Zealand export food and wool.

VOCABULARY QUIZ

On a separate sheet of paper, write the letter of the word in the list that best fills each of the blanks in the statements that follow.

a. censorship
b. press
c. navigable
d. occupied
e. surrender

f. communes
g. modernize
h. synthetic
i. industrialized
j. geothermal

1. Hot springs provide _____ energy.

2. In 1931 Japan _____ Manchuria.

3. Japan's _____ ended World War II.

4. There is little water transportation in Afghanistan because it has no _____ rivers.

5. In countries where there is little freedom, there is often _____ of the news.

6. After the Communists took over China, farmers had to join _____.

7. Newspapers and magazines are known as the _____.

8. The Chinese government wants to _____ old-fashioned industries.

9. An _____ country is one that has developed factories and mines.

10. Oil is used to make _____ rubber.

REVIEW QUESTIONS

1. Why was the Indian subcontinent divided into two countries in 1947? Why are there three countries now?

2. Name some agricultural and industrial products of the subcontinent and Sri Lanka.

3. Why is Afghanistan's location important?

4. What are the political and geographic differences between the Republic of China and the People's Republic of China?

5. How did North and South Korea become two separate countries?

6. How did Japan become an industrial nation while lacking many natural resources?

7. How did the Communists come to power in Vietnam?

8. What role did the United States play in the history of the two Koreas and Vietnam?

9. What are some of the important natural resources in the countries of Southeast Asia?

10. What are some products of Australia and New Zealand?

ACTIVITY

The English language contains a number of words taken from Asian languages. Some dictionaries give the origin of words, including the language from which the words came. The words below came from Hindi (India's official language), Tibetan, Chinese, Japanese, and Malay. Write the words on a separate piece of paper. Look up each word and next to it write its origin.

1. bamboo
2. dungaree
3. judo
4. polo
5. tea

6. catsup
7. jungle
8. pajamas
9. shampoo
10. thug

449

21/SKILLS DEVELOPMENT

SUMMARIZING

PUTTING THINGS TOGETHER

The last section of Chapter 21 lists some important ideas and asks a number of questions, such as *Can you think of different ways to live in a desert?* To answer this question, you must put together two or more sets of facts. You must think about things you read in more than one place. You can answer the question if you review the material in Chapter 12 and in Chapter 15.

MAKING SUMMARIES

It helps to put things together if we write summaries. A summary should give the main facts or ideas in a few words. In order to make a summary, we have to decide just which facts or ideas are main ones. A summary about different ways to live in deserts could read as follows:

> *The people who live in the Sahara and the Kalahari have worked out different ways to live in deserts. The people of the Sahara herd animals and grow crops. They keep camels and goats that can live on desert plants. They irrigate small fields and gardens with groundwater from wells. The Kalahari people gather food. They hunt wild animals and gather desert plants such as roots. The desert affects the ways both groups live, but they do not live in the same way.*

WRITING PARAGRAPHS

Summaries are usually written in paragraphs. A paragraph is a group of sentences on one topic. A paragraph usually includes the following:

1. A topic sentence that tells what the paragraph is about

2. Supporting sentences that give details to support, or back up, the main idea in the topic sentence

3. A summary sentence that sums up the main idea

SKILLS PRACTICE

In the sample paragraph at the left, pick out the topic sentence, the supporting sentences, and the summary sentence. Write them on a piece of paper.

Listed below are questions from the last section of Chapter 21. You should base your answers on what you have read in this book. With the questions are the numbers of pages that you may want to review in order to put your ideas together. Answer at least two questions. Put your answers in the form of a paragraph.

1. What are some of the different ways people have worked out to live in different places? (Chapter 9, page 190; Chapter 12, page 257.)
2. How do people make use of nature's gifts? (Chapter 3, page 60; Chapter 14, page 302.)
3. How have people wasted and even destroyed gifts of nature? (Chapter 6, page 129; Chapter 12, page 261.)
4. What ancient inventions were used in writing this book? (Chapter 2, page 30; Chapter 5, page 114; Chapter 13, page 282.)
5. What are some ways in which people have improved life for others? (Chapter 5, page 117; Chapter 19, page 395.)
6. How have people done harm to others? (Chapter 13, page 278; Chapter 16, page 340.)
7. Where have great changes taken place in recent times? (Chapter 14, page 298; Chapter 17, page 348; Chapter 21, page 441.)

7/UNIT REVIEW

1. Most Asians live south and east of a broad belt of mountains and high plateaus that stretch across Asia. — *How does the belt affect Asia's climate? How does the climate affect where Asians live?*

2. Australia is the world's smallest continent and much of its interior is dry grassland and desert. — *How did the Aborigines use the land before the coming of the Europeans? How do modern Australians use the land?*

3. The Indian subcontinent was the homeland of Hinduism and Buddhism. — *What do Hinduism and Buddhism teach about how people should live?*

4. Chinese ways and teaching were copied by their neighbors in Korea, Japan, and Southeast Asia. — *What are some of the things visitors to China could have seen in the days of Kublai Khan? What teachings could they have learned about?*

5. Southeast Asia has been a meeting place for peoples from India and China. — *What are the modern countries of Southeast Asia?*

6. A century ago European empires ruled most of South and Southeast Asia. — *Which countries had colonies in Asia before World War I (1914 – 1918)?*

7. China and Japan were closed countries that were forced to open their doors to the outside world. — *Why did China and Japan wish to be closed countries? What happened in each country after the doors were opened?*

8. So many Europeans moved to Australia and New Zealand that these lands are much like Western European countries. — *Why, do you think, did Europeans move to Australia and New Zealand rather than to India or China?*

9. Almost all of the European colonies in South Asia and East Asia became independent countries after World War II. — *Name the countries of the subcontinent and of Southeast Asia. It has been said that a people would rather be badly ruled by themselves than well ruled by others. Can you think why?*

10. There have been great changes within the countries of East Asia since World War II. — *What changes took place in China? What changes in Japan? In Korea?*

11. The populations of Asian countries have increased rapidly since World War II. — *How has population growth affected the development of countries?*

Atlas

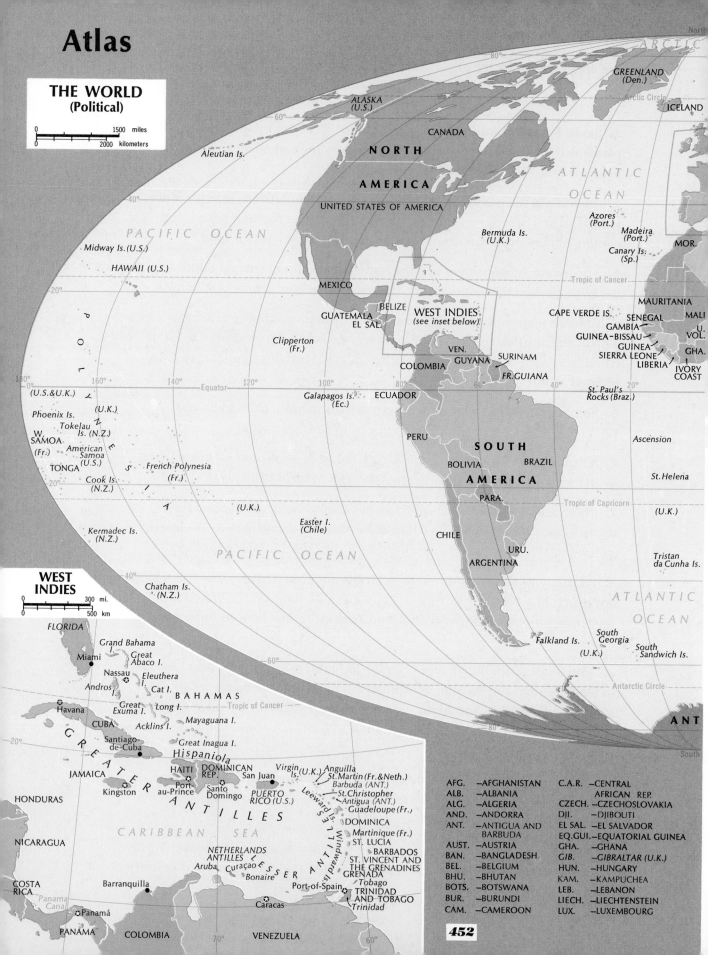

ARCTIC

North

GREENLAND
(Den.)

Arctic Circle

ICELAND

ALASKA
(U.S.)

CANADA

NORTH

AMERICA

ATLANTIC

OCEAN

Aleutian Is.

UNITED STATES OF AMERICA

PACIFIC OCEAN

Bermuda Is.
(U.K.)

Azores
(Port.)

Madeira
(Port.)

MOR.

Midway Is.(U.S.)

Canary Is.
(Sp.)

HAWAII (U.S.)

Tropic of Cancer

MEXICO

CAPE VERDE IS.

MAURITANIA

WEST INDIES
(see inset below)

BELIZE

MALI

GUATEMALA

SENEGAL

EL SAL.

GAMBIA

U.
VOL.

Clipperton
(Fr.)

GUINEA-BISSAU

GUINEA

GHA.

VEN.

SIERRA LEONE

COLOMBIA

GUYANA

SURINAM

LIBERIA

IVORY
COAST

Galapagos Is.
(Ec.)

ECUADOR

FR. GUIANA

Equator

St. Paul's
Rocks (Braz.)

P
O
L
Y
N
E
S
I
A

Phoenix Is.
(U.K.)

PERU

SOUTH

Ascension

Tokelau
Is. (N.Z.)

W.
SAMOA
(Fr.)

American
Samoa
(U.S.)

BOLIVIA

BRAZIL

St. Helena

TONGA

AMERICA

French Polynesia
(Fr.)

Cook Is.
(N.Z.)

PARA.

Tropic of Capricorn

(U.K.)

(U.K.)

Easter I.
(Chile)

CHILE

Tristan
da Cunha Is.

Kermadec Is.
(N.Z.)

URU.

ARGENTINA

PACIFIC OCEAN

ATLANTIC

Chatham Is.
(N.Z.)

OCEAN

Falkland Is.
(U.K.)

South
Georgia

South
Sandwich Is.

Antarctic Circle

South

ANT

FLORIDA

Grand Bahama
I.

Miami

Great
Abaco I.

Nassau

Eleuthera
I.

Andros

Cat I.

BAHAMAS

Havana

Great
Exuma I.

Long I.

Tropic of Cancer

CUBA

Acklins I.

Mayaguana I.

Santiago-
de-Cuba

Great Inagua I.

Hispaniola

JAMAICA

HAITI

DOMINICAN
REP.

Virgin
Is.

(U.K.)

Anguilla

St. Martin (Fr.&Neth.)

Kingston

Port-
au-Prince

Santo
Domingo

San Juan

Barbuda (ANT.)

St. Christopher

Antigua (ANT.)

PUERTO
RICO (U.S.)

Leeward Is.

Guadeloupe (Fr.)

GREATER ANTILLES

HONDURAS

CARIBBEAN

SEA

NETHERLANDS
ANTILLES

LESSER ANTILLES

DOMINICA

Martinique (Fr.)

ST. LUCIA

BARBADOS

ST. VINCENT AND
THE GRENADINES

NICARAGUA

Aruba

Curaçao

Bonaire

GRENADA

Windward Is.

Tobago

COSTA
RICA

Barranquilla

Port-of-Spain

TRINIDAD
AND TOBAGO

Panama
Canal

Trinidad

Panamá

Caracas

PANAMA

COLOMBIA

VENEZUELA

AFG.	—AFGHANISTAN	C.A.R.	—CENTRAL
ALB.	—ALBANIA		AFRICAN REP.
ALG.	—ALGERIA	CZECH.	—CZECHOSLOVAKIA
AND.	—ANDORRA	DJI.	—DJIBOUTI
ANT.	—ANTIGUA AND	EL SAL.	—EL SALVADOR
	BARBUDA	EQ.GUI.	—EQUATORIAL GUINEA
AUST.	—AUSTRIA	GHA.	—GHANA
BAN.	—BANGLADESH	GIB.	—GIBRALTAR (U.K.)
BEL.	—BELGIUM	HUN.	—HUNGARY
BHU.	—BHUTAN	KAM.	—KAMPUCHEA
BOTS.	—BOTSWANA	LEB.	—LEBANON
BUR.	—BURUNDI	LIECH.	—LIECHTENSTEIN
CAM.	—CAMEROON	LUX.	—LUXEMBOURG

452

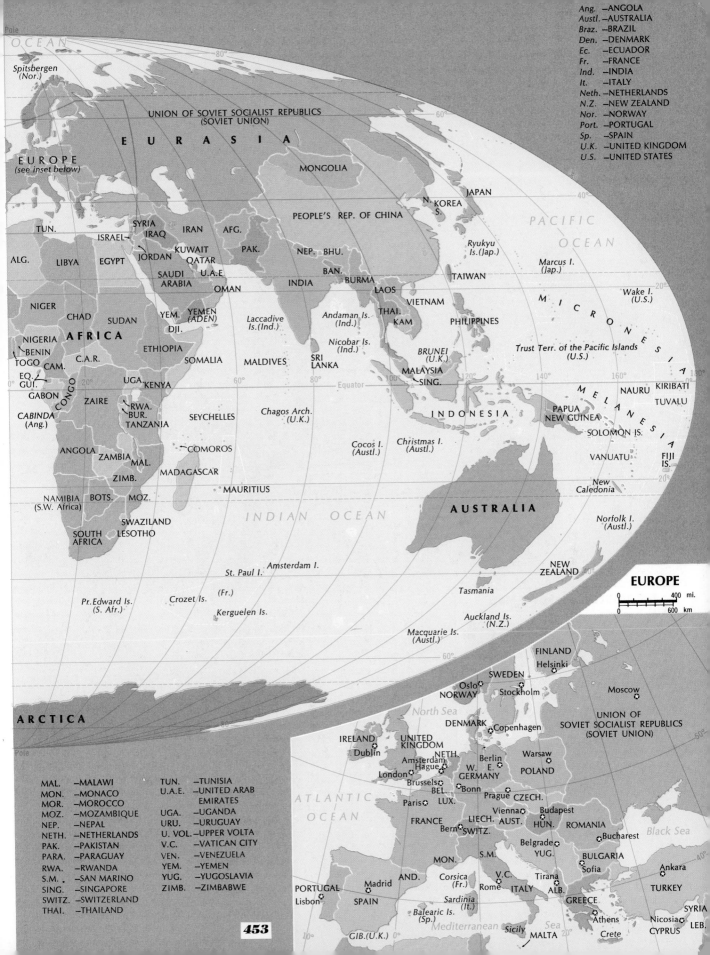

THE WORLD: A Physical Map

Above 10,000 ft.	Above 3,000 m
5,000–10,000 ft.	1,500–3,000 m
2,000– 5,000 ft.	600– 1,500 m
500– 2,000 ft.	150– 600 m
0– 500 ft.	0– 150 m
Below sea level	Below sea level

Land under ice

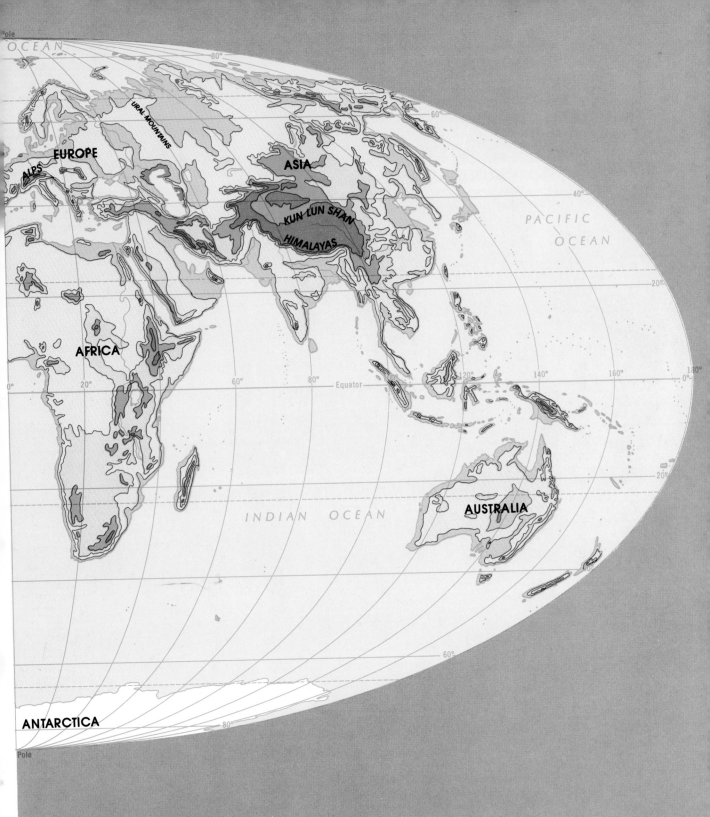

OCEAN

URAL MOUNTAINS

EUROPE

ALPS

ASIA

KUN LUN SHAN

HIMALAYAS

PACIFIC

OCEAN

AFRICA

Equator

INDIAN   OCEAN

AUSTRALIA

ANTARCTICA

Pole

455

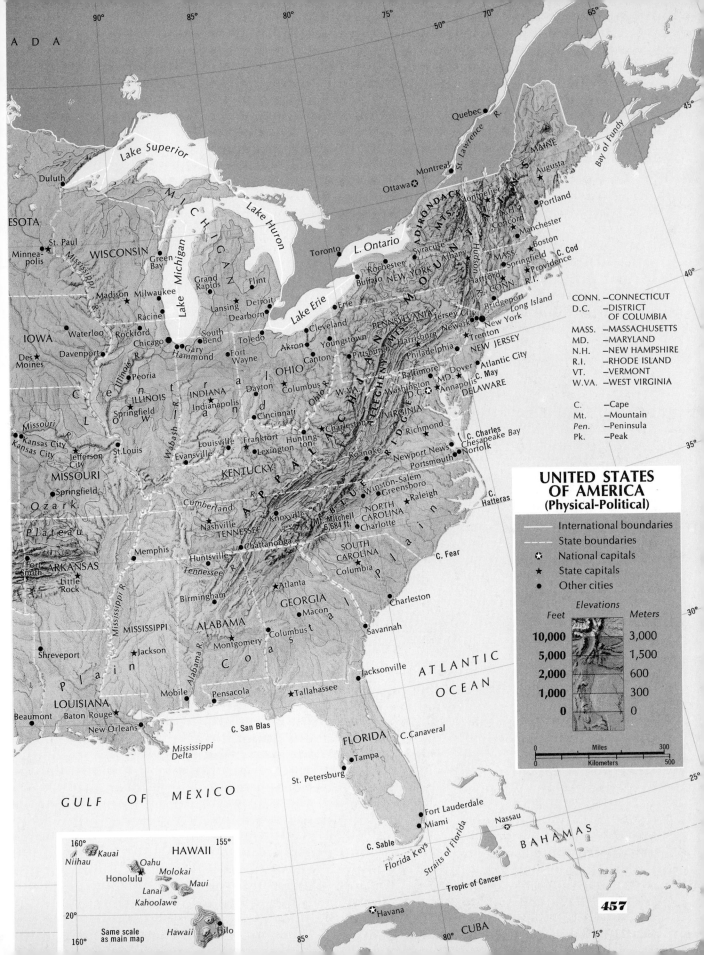

ADA

90°   85°   80°   75°   50°   70°   65°   45°

Quebec   St. Lawrence R.

Lake Superior

Duluth

MICHIGAN

Lake Huron

Montreal

Ottawa ⊛

MAINE

Bay of Fundy

Augusta

Montpelier   N.H.   Portland

ADIRONDACK MTS.   VT.   Concord   Manchester

ESOTA

St. Paul

Minne-   apolis

WISCONSIN   Green Bay

Madison   Milwaukee

Racine

Grand Rapids   Flint

Lansing   Detroit   Dearborn

Lake Michigan   Lake Erie

Toronto   L. Ontario

Rochester   Syracuse   Albany   Boston

Buffalo   NEW YORK   MASS.   Springfield   Providence

Hartford   CONN.   R.I.

Erie   Bridgeport   Long Island

APPALACHIAN MOUNTAINS   Hudson R.   New York

Jersey City   Newark

IOWA

Waterloo   Rockford

Davenport   Chicago   Gary   Hammond

South Bend   Toledo   Cleveland

Fort Wayne   OHIO   Akron   Youngstown   Canton   Pittsburgh

PENNSYLVANIA   Harrisburg   Philadelphia   Trenton   NEW JERSEY

Des Moines   Peoria

ILLINOIS   INDIANA   Dayton   Columbus   Ohio R.

Springfield   Indianapolis   Cincinnati

Baltimore   MD.   Dover   Atlantic City

Washington   D.C.   C. May

Annapolis   DELAWARE

Missouri R.

Kansas City   Kansas City

Jefferson City   St. Louis

MISSOURI

Springfield

Ozark

Plateau

Fort Smith   ARKANSAS   Little Rock

Evansville   Louisville   Frankfort   Hunting-   ton

Lexington   KENTUCKY

Nashville   TENNESSEE   Knoxville

Chattanooga

Charleston   W.VA.

VIRGINIA   Richmond

Roanoke   BLUE RIDGE

C. Charles   Chesapeake Bay

Newport News   Norfolk

Portsmouth

C. Hatteras

Memphis

Huntsville   Tennessee R.

Birmingham

MISSISSIPPI

Jackson

Shreveport

LOUISIANA

Beaumont   Baton Rouge

New Orleans

Mobile   Alabama R.

Montgomery   ALABAMA   Columbus

GEORGIA   Macon

Pensacola

Tallahassee

Winston-Salem   Greensboro

NORTH CAROLINA   Raleigh

Mt. Mitchell   6,684 ft.   Charlotte

SOUTH CAROLINA   Columbia

C. Fear

Charleston

Savannah

Jacksonville

Coastal Plain

ATLANTIC OCEAN

UNITED STATES
OF AMERICA
(Physical-Political)

—— International boundaries
----- State boundaries
⊛ National capitals
★ State capitals
● Other cities

Elevations
Feet   Meters
10,000   3,000
5,000   1,500
2,000   600
1,000   300
0   0

Miles   300
Kilometers   500

CONN. —CONNECTICUT
D.C. —DISTRICT
        OF COLUMBIA
MASS. —MASSACHUSETTS
MD. —MARYLAND
N.H. —NEW HAMPSHIRE
R.I. —RHODE ISLAND
VT. —VERMONT
W.VA. —WEST VIRGINIA

C. —Cape
Mt. —Mountain
Pen. —Peninsula
Pk. —Peak

GULF   OF   MEXICO

C. San Blas

Mississippi Delta

FLORIDA   C. Canaveral

Tampa

St. Petersburg

C. Sable

Fort Lauderdale   Miami

Nassau

Florida Keys   Straits of Florida   BAHAMAS

Tropic of Cancer

Havana   CUBA

160°   155°   HAWAII

Kauai   Oahu

Niihau   Honolulu   Molokai   Maui

Lanai

Kahoolawe

20°

160°

Same scale
as main map   Hawaii   Hilo

457

NORTH AMERICA
(Physical)

Arch. —Archipelago
C.   —Cape
G.   —Gulf
Mt.   —Mountain
Pen. —Peninsula
Pt.   —Point
RA.   —Range
Str. —Strait

Elevations		
Feet		**Meters**
10,000		**3,000**
5,000		**1,500**
2,000		**600**
1,000		**300**
0		**0**

Miles 0 — 500
Kilometers 0 — 800

458

ARCTIC OCEAN

PACIFIC OCEAN

ATLANTIC OCEAN

GULF OF MEXICO

CARIBBEAN SEA

Bering Sea

Beaufort Sea

Baffin Bay

Hudson Bay

Labrador Sea

Davis Str.

Greenland

Iceland

Queen Elisabeth Is.

Knud Rasmussen Land

Victoria I.

Baffin I.

Barrow Str.

Southampton I.

Nunivak I.
St. Lawrence I.
Alaska Pen.
Kodiak I.
Gulf of Alaska
Alexander Arch.
Queen Charlotte Is.
Vancouver I.

Bering Str.
Pt. Barrow
ALASKA RA.
BROOKS RANGE
Yukon R.
Mackenzie R.
Great Bear Lake
Great Slave Lake
Peace R.
Athabasca R.
Arctic Circle

Mt. Rainier 14,410 ft.
C. Mendocino
San Francisco
Pt. Conception
Los Angeles
Guadalupe I.
Eugenia Pt.
False Cape
Guadalajara
Mexico City
Citlaltepetl 18,700 ft.

CASCADE RA.
COAST RANGE
SIERRA NEVADA
Mt. Whitney 14,495 ft.
Mt. Elbert 14,431 ft.
Great Salt Lake
Great Basin
Colorado Plateau
Columbia R.
North Platte R.
South Platte R.
Colorado R.
Rio Grande
Lower California
G. of California
Madre
SIERRA MADRE OCCIDENTAL
SIERRA MADRE ORIENTAL

ROCKY MOUNTAINS
Canadian Shield
Saskatchewan R.
Lake Winnipeg
North
South
Black Hills
Central Lowlands
Ozark Plateau
Mississippi R.
Red R.
Ohio R.
Missouri R.
Houston

Lake Superior
L. Michigan
L. Huron
L. Erie
L. Ontario
Chicago
Detroit
Montreal
St. Lawrence R.
LAURENTIAN HIGHLANDS
APPALACHIAN MTS.
Mt. Mitchell 6,684 ft.
Coastal Plain
New York
Philadelphia
Washington
Long I.
C. Cod
Chesapeake Bay
C. Hatteras
Nova Scotia
Newfoundland
Labrador

Florida Pen.
Florida Keys
C. Canaveral
Bahama Islands
Bermuda Is.
Tropic of Cancer
Cuba
Hispaniola
WEST INDIES
Greater Antilles
Lesser Antilles
Leeward Is.
Windward Is.
Yucatan Pen.

CENTRAL AMERICA

SOUTH AMERICA

C. Farewell

West longitude

NORTH AMERICA
(Political)

Den.	—DENMARK
Fr.	—FRANCE
Neth.	—NETHERLANDS
Mex.	—MEXICO
U.K.	—UNITED KINGDOM
U.S.	—UNITED STATES

International boundaries
National capitals
Other cities

0   500 miles
0   800 kilometers

ASIA

ARCTIC OCEAN

Barrow

ALASKA (U.S.)

Fairbanks
Anchorage
Dawson
Juneau

Gulf of Alaska

Bering Sea

Beaufort Sea

Arctic Circle

Port Radium

Great Bear Lake

Great Slave Lake

Thule

GREENLAND (Den.)

ICELAND

Pond Inlet

Baffin Bay

Godthaab

C A N A D A

Churchill

Hudson Bay

Labrador Sea

Edmonton
Victoria
Vancouver
Calgary
Seattle
Spokane
Portland
Regina
Winnipeg

Lake Winnipeg

Goose Bay

Seven Islands

Gander
St. John's

PACIFIC OCEAN

San Francisco

Salt Lake City
Denver

UNITED STATES OF AMERICA

Minneapolis
St. Paul
Milwaukee
Omaha
Chicago
Detroit
Cleveland
Kansas City
St. Louis
Cincinnati
Pittsburgh

Great Lakes

Quebec
Montreal
Ottawa
Toronto
Buffalo
Boston
New York
Philadelphia
Baltimore
Washington
Norfolk

Halifax

Los Angeles
San Diego
Phoenix

Memphis

Dallas
Atlanta

Bermuda Is. (U.K.)

Guadalupe I. (Mex.)

El Paso

San Antonio
Houston
New Orleans

Tropic of Cancer

Monterrey

MEXICO

Guadalajara

GULF OF MEXICO

ATLANTIC OCEAN

Miami

Grand Bahama I.
Great Abaco I.
Nassau
Eleuthera I.
Andros I.
Cat I.
BAHAMAS
Long I.
Gr. Exuma I.
Acklins I.
Mayaguana I.
Gr. Inagua I.

Havana

CUBA

Mexico City
Orizaba

Belmopan
BELIZE

GUATEMALA
Guatemala
San Salvador
EL SALVADOR

HONDURAS
Tegucigalpa

NICARAGUA

Managua

San José

COSTA RICA

Santiago-de-Cuba

JAMAICA
Kingston

HAITI
Port-au-Prince

DOMINICAN REPUBLIC
Santo Domingo

PUERTO RICO (U.S.)

Virgin Is. (U.K.)
(Fr.)

Guadeloupe (Fr.)
DOMINICA
Martinique (Fr.)
ST. LUCIA
Neth. Antilles
ST. VINCENT AND THE GRENADINES
GRENADA

CARIBBEAN SEA

Panama Canal
Panamá

PANAMA

SOUTH AMERICA

TRINIDAD AND TOBAGO

459

CARIBBEAN SEA

Guajira Pen.
Margarita I.
Tobago
Caracas
Trinidad
L. Maracaibo
Orinoco R. Delta
G. of Panama
Orinoco R.
L L a n o s
Angel Falls
GUIANA HIGHLANDS
Devils I.
C. Orange
Malpelo I.
Mt. Tolima 19,049 ft.
Cauca R.
Meta R.
Magdalena R.
Bogotá
Orinoco R.
Rio Negro
Amazon R. Delta
A M A Z O N
Marajó I.
Equator
Mt. Chimborazo 20,561 ft.
Japura R.
Amazon R.
C. São Roque
Gulf of Guayaquil
Marañón R.
Juruá R.
B A S I N
Tapajóz R.
Xingu R.
Tocantins R.
Aguja Pt.
Purus R.
Madeira R.
Araguaia R.
Parnaíba R.
Ucayali R.
Mt. Huascarán 22,205 ft.
Beni R.
Mamoré R.
Mato Grosso Plateau
Tocantins R.
São Francisco R.
Lima
Mt. Ancohuma 21,490 ft.
Lake Titicaca
B R A Z I L I A N
Brasília
L. Poopó
Paraguay R.
Mt. Bandeira 9,452 ft.
PACIFIC OCEAN
Gran Chaco
Paraná R.
H I G H L A N D S
San Felix I.
San Ambrosio I.
São Paulo
C. Frio
Rio de Janeiro
Tropic of Capricorn
A N D E S
Salado R.
Paraná R.
Uruguay R.
ATLANTIC OCEAN
Mt. Aconcagua 22,834 ft.
Juan Fernández Is.
Santiago
P a m p a s
Buenos Aires
Montevideo
Rio de la Plata
M O U N T A I N S
Colorado R.
Blanca Bay
Chiloé I.
Patagonia
San Matías Gulf
Valdés Pen.
Chonos Arch.
Taitao Pen.
Gulf of San Jorge
C. Tres Puntas
Grande Bay
Strait of Magellan
Strait of Magellan
Falkland Is.
Cape Horn
Tierra del Fuego

Arch. — Archipelago
C. — Cape
G. — Gulf
Mt. — Mountain
Pen. — Peninsula
Pt. — Point

SOUTH AMERICA
(Physical)

Elevations
Feet — Meters
10,000 — 3,000
5,000 — 1,500
2,000 — 600
1,000 — 300
0 — 0

Miles
0 — 500
Kilometers
0 — 800

460

Barranquilla
Cartagena
Maracaibo
Valencia
Caracas
Port-of-Spain
TRINIDAD AND TOBAGO
Barquisimeto
Cúcuta
San Cristóbal
VENEZUELA
Orinoco R.
Georgetown
Paramaribo
Cayenne
Medellín
Bucaramanga
Bogotá
GUYANA
SURINAM
FRENCH
GUIANA
(Fr.)
Malpelo I.
(Col.)
Cali
COLOMBIA

Col. —COLOMBIA
Fr. —FRANCE
U.K. —UNITED KINGDOM

Quito
ECUADOR
Guayaquil
Iquitos
Manaus
Belém
São Luis
Equator
Fortaleza

Trujillo
PERU
Recife
Maceió
BRAZIL

Callao Lima
Cuzco
Arequipa
La Paz
BOLIVIA
Sucre
Brasília
(Federal
District)
Salvador

PACIFIC
OCEAN
Belo
Horizonte

Chuquicamata
PARAGUAY
Rio de Janeiro
São Paulo Niterói
Santos
Tropic of Capricorn
Antofagasta
Asunción
Curitiba

San Felix I.
(Chile)
San Ambrosio I.
(Chile)
Tucumán

CHILE
Córdoba
Santa
Fe
Paraná
Pôrto Alegre
Valparaiso
Rosario
URUGUAY
Santiago
Buenos Aires
Montevideo
Juan Fernández Is.
(Chile)
La Plata
Rio de la Plata
ATLANTIC
OCEAN
Concepción
ARGENTINA
Mar del Plata
Bahía Blanca

Lake
Titicaca
Paraná R.

Falkland Is.
(U.K.)
Punta Arenas
Strait of
Magellan

SOUTH AMERICA
(Political)

International boundaries
⊛ National capitals
● Other cities

0   500 miles
0   800 kilometers

461

80° 70° 60° 50° 40°
West longitude

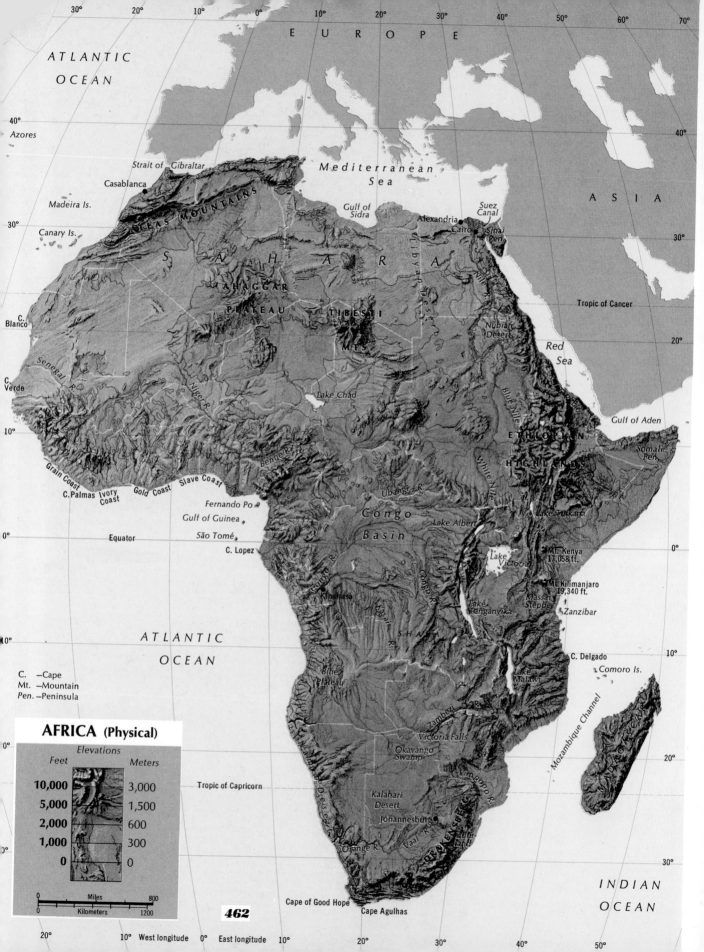

ATLANTIC
OCEAN

EUROPE

Azores

40°

Mediterranean
Sea

Strait of Gibraltar

Casablanca

Madeira Is.

30°

ATLAS MOUNTAINS

Gulf of
Sidra

Suez
Canal

ASIA

Alexandria

Cairo

Sinai
Pen.

Canary Is.

S   A   H   A   R   A

Libyan Desert

Tropic of Cancer

C.
Blanco

AHAGGAR
PLATEAU

TIBESTI

Nubian
Desert

20°

MTS.

Red
Sea

Senegal R.

Lake Chad

Niger R.

Gulf of Aden

10°

Grain Coast

Benue R.

ETHIOPIAN

Somali
Pen.

C. Palmas
Ivory
Coast

Gold Coast

Slave Coast

HIGHLANDS

Blue Nile

Lake Rudolf

Fernando Po

Ubangi R.

White Nile

Gulf of Guinea

Congo
Basin

Lake Albert

Mt. Kenya
17,058 ft.

0°

Equator

São Tomé

C. Lopez

Congo R.

Lake
Victoria

Mt. Kilimanjaro
19,340 ft.

0°

Congo R.

Kinshasa

Massai
Steppe

Zanzibar

Kasai R.

Lake
Tanganyika

ATLANTIC

KATANGA

C. Delgado

10°

OCEAN

Bihé
Plateau

Lake
Malawi

Comoro Is.

AFRICA (Physical)

Zambezi R.

Mozambique Channel

Elevations

Victoria Falls

Feet   Meters

Okavango
Swamp

10,000   3,000

Tropic of Capricorn

Limpopo R.

20°

5,000   1,500

Kalahari
Desert

2,000   600

Desert

1,000   300

Johannesburg

0   0

DRAKENSBERG

Vaal R.

Zululand

Orange R.

Miles

C. —Cape
Mt. —Mountain
Pen. —Peninsula

0   800

Kilometers

INDIAN

0   1200

Cape of Good Hope

Cape Agulhas

OCEAN

30°

462

20°   10° West longitude 0° East longitude 10°   20°   30°   40°   50°

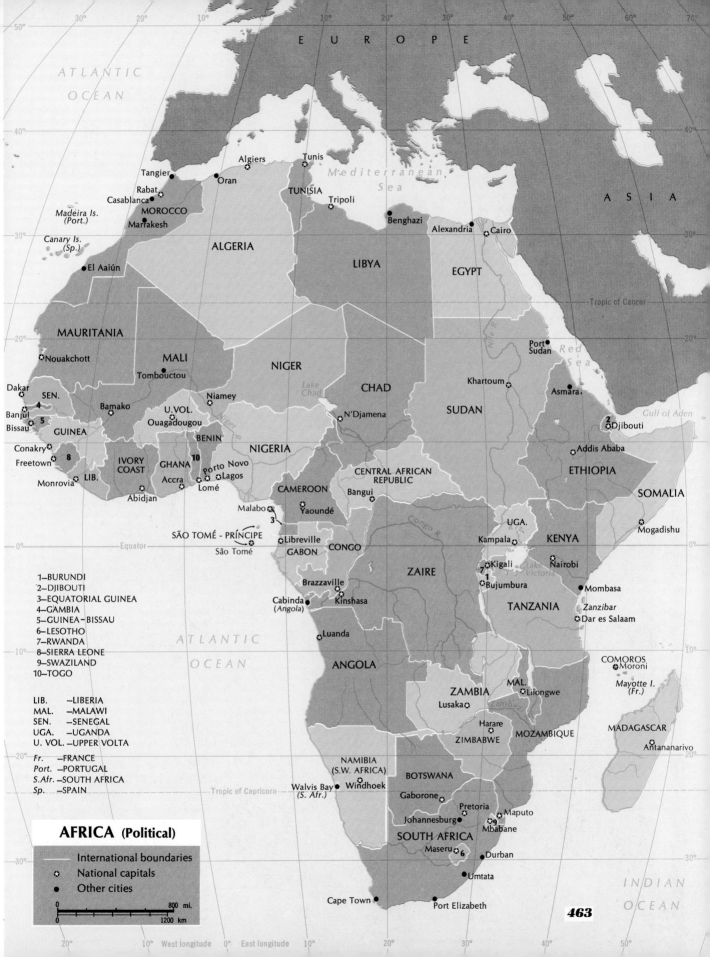

EUROPE

ATLANTIC
OCEAN

Mediterranean Sea

ASIA

Tangier •
Algiers •
Tunis •
Oran •
Rabat ⊛
Casablanca •
MOROCCO
Marrakesh •

Tripoli •
Benghazi •
Alexandria •
Cairo ⊛

*Madeira Is.
(Port.)*

TUNISIA

*Canary Is.
(Sp.)*

El Aaiún •

ALGERIA

LIBYA

EGYPT

Port
Sudan •

*Red
Sea*

Tropic of Cancer

MAURITANIA

Nouakchott ⊛

MALI
Tombouctou •

NIGER

CHAD

SUDAN

Khartoum •

Asmara •

Gulf of Aden

Dakar ⊛
SEN.
4
Banjul ⊛
5
Bissau
GUINEA

Bamako ⊛

U. VOL.
Niamey ⊛
Ouagadougou ⊛
BENIN

Lake
Chad

N'Djamena •

2
Djibouti ⊛

Conakry ⊛
8
Freetown ⊛
Monrovia ⊛
LIB.
IVORY
COAST
GHANA
10
Accra ⊛
Abidjan •
Porto Novo ⊛
Lagos •
Lomé ⊛

NIGERIA

CENTRAL AFRICAN
REPUBLIC

Bangui •

Addis Ababa ⊛

ETHIOPIA

SOMALIA

Malabo ⊛
SÃO TOMÉ - PRÍNCIPE
São Tomé •

3
CAMEROON
Yaoundé •

Mogadishu •

Libreville ⊛
GABON
CONGO
Brazzaville ⊛
Kinshasa ⊛

Cabinda
(*Angola*) •

Congo R.

ZAIRE

UGA.
Kampala ⊛

KENYA

7 Kigali ⊛
1 Bujumbura ⊛

Lake
Victoria

Nairobi ⊛

Mombasa •

Equator

0°

ATLANTIC
OCEAN

Luanda ⊛

TANZANIA

Zanzibar •
Dar es Salaam •

1—BURUNDI
2—DJIBOUTI
3—EQUATORIAL GUINEA
4—GAMBIA
5—GUINEA-BISSAU
6—LESOTHO
7—RWANDA
8—SIERRA LEONE
9—SWAZILAND
10—TOGO

ANGOLA

ZAMBIA
Lusaka ⊛

MAL.
Lilongwe ⊛

COMOROS
Moroni ⊛

*Mayotte I.
(Fr.)*

Zambezi

LIB.   —LIBERIA
MAL.   —MALAWI
SEN.   —SENEGAL
UGA.   —UGANDA
U. VOL. —UPPER VOLTA

Harare •
ZIMBABWE

MOZAMBIQUE

MADAGASCAR

Antananarivo •

Fr.   —FRANCE
Port. —PORTUGAL
S.Afr. —SOUTH AFRICA
Sp.   —SPAIN

Tropic of Capricorn

NAMIBIA
(S.W. AFRICA)

BOTSWANA

Walvis Bay
(*S. Afr.*) •
Windhoek •

Gaborone ⊛

INDIAN
OCEAN

AFRICA (Political)

Pretoria ⊛
Johannesburg •
Maputo ⊛
9 Mbabane ⊛

━━━━ International boundaries
⊛ National capitals
• Other cities

SOUTH AFRICA

Maseru ⊛ **6**
Durban •

Umtata •

0 ┣━━━━┫ 800 mi.
0 ┣━━━━┫ 1200 km

Cape Town •
Port Elizabeth •

463

West longitude   0°   East longitude

ATLANTIC
OCEAN

20°

Madeira

30°

Str. of Gibraltar

IBERIAN
PENINSULA
Tagus R.
Madrid

PYRENEES

ALPS

Balearic
Is.

Corsica

Sardinia

Tyrrhenian
Sea

Rome
R. Tiber

Adriatic Sea

Maltese
Is.

Ionian
Sea

Aegean
Sea

Crete

Cyprus

Mediterranean Sea

0°

20°

Tropic of Cancer

10°

AFRICA

0°

20°

Equator

10°

10°

30°   40°   10°   50°   East longitude   60°   70°   80°

464

Arctic
Circle

BRITISH ISLES

London

Paris
Loire R.

Seine R.

Hamburg
Elbe R.
Berlin

Danube R.

CARPATHIAN

North Sea

North European Plain

Baltic Sea

Baltic Plains

R. Vistula

Dnieper R.

Don R.

Black Sea

Istanbul

ASIA MINOR

CAUCASUS

Euphrates R.

Syrian Desert

Baghdad
Mesopotamia

Sinai Pen.

HEJAZ

ASIR

Red
Sea

ARABIAN
PENINSULA

Hadhramaut

Gulf of Aden

Socotra

SCANDINAVIA

Stockholm

Leningrad

Moscow

Dvina R.

Volga R.

Kama R.

Ural R.

Volga R.

URAL MOUNTAINS

Kirgiz Steppe

Caspian Sea

Plateau
of
Iran

ZAGROS MOUNTAINS

Tehran

Persian Gulf

Gulf of Oman

Karachi

Arabian Sea

Laccadive Is.

ARCTIC

Spitsbergen

80°

50°   60°   70° 80° 90° 100°

North
Land

OCEAN

Novaya Zemlya

Kola Pen.

Barents
Sea

Dz.

Kara Sea

Yamal Pen.

Taymyr

Yenisey R.

West
Siberian
Plain

Ob R.

Ob R.

Irtysh R.

Ishim R.

Kazakh
Uplands

Aral
Sea

Lake
Balkhash

Syr Darya

Turan Lowland

Amu Darya

HINDU
KUSH

TIEN SHAN

Tarim Basin

KUNLUN

Plateau
of
Tibet

HIMALAYA

Mt. Everest
29,028 ft.

Indus R.

Sutlej R.

Indian
Desert

Delhi

Ganges R.

Ganges
Plain

Deccan
Plateau

Godavari R.

Bombay

WESTERN GHATS

EASTERN GHATS

Madras

Sri Lanka

Maldives

INDIAN

120° 130° 80° 140° 150° New Siberian Is. 70° 60° Bering Sea 50° Aleutian Is. 40° 30° Sunday International Date Line Monday 170°

Laptev Sea

Central Siberian Plateau

Lower Plateau

Lena R.

Tunguska R.

Angara R.

Baikal L.

Shilka R.

MTS.

Kamchatka Peninsula

Tropic of Cancer 180° 20°

170°

Sea of Okhotsk

Sakhalin

Kuril Islands

Hokkaido

Sea of Japan

Honshu

Tokyo

Kyoto Fujiyama 12,388 ft.

EURASIA (Physical)

Elevations
Feet   *Meters*

10,000	3,000
5,000	1,500
2,000	600
1,000	300
0	0

0   Miles   800
0   Kilometers   1200

Mt. —Mountain
Pen. —Peninsula
RA. —Range
Str. —Strait

Mongolian Plateau

The Gobi

GREAT KHINGAN MTS.

Manchuria Plain

Harbin

Shenyang

Great Wall

Peking

Tientsin

Dairen

Yellow Sea

North China Plain

Shanghai

Shikoku

Kyushu

Korea Strait

East China Sea

Okinawa

Ryukyu Islands

Philippine Sea

PACIFIC OCEAN

NAN SHAN

Chungking

Yangtze R.

BOHEAN HILLS

Canton

Hong Kong

Taiwan

Luzon Strait

Philippine Islands

Luzon

Manila

Samar

Hainan

South China Sea

Mindoro

Panay

Negros

Mindanao

Admiralty Is.

New Ireland

New Britain

Equator 0°

Calcutta

Brahmaputra

Bay of Bengal

INDOCHINA PENINSULA

Mekong R.

Ho Chi Minh City

Palawan

Celebes Sea

Halmahera

MOLUCCAS

SNOW MTS.

New Guinea

10°

Andaman Is.

Andaman Sea

Gulf of Siam

Nicobar Is.

Str. of Malacca

Malay Pen.

Natuna Is.

Borneo

Celebes

Buru

Ceram

Aru Is.

Coral Sea

OCEAN

Sumatra

Mentawai Is.

Bangka

SUNDA ISLANDS

Java Sea

Jakarta

Bali

Lombok

Sumbawa

Sumba

Flores

Timor

Arafura Sea

AUSTRALIA

20°

90° 100° 110° 120° 130° 140°

465

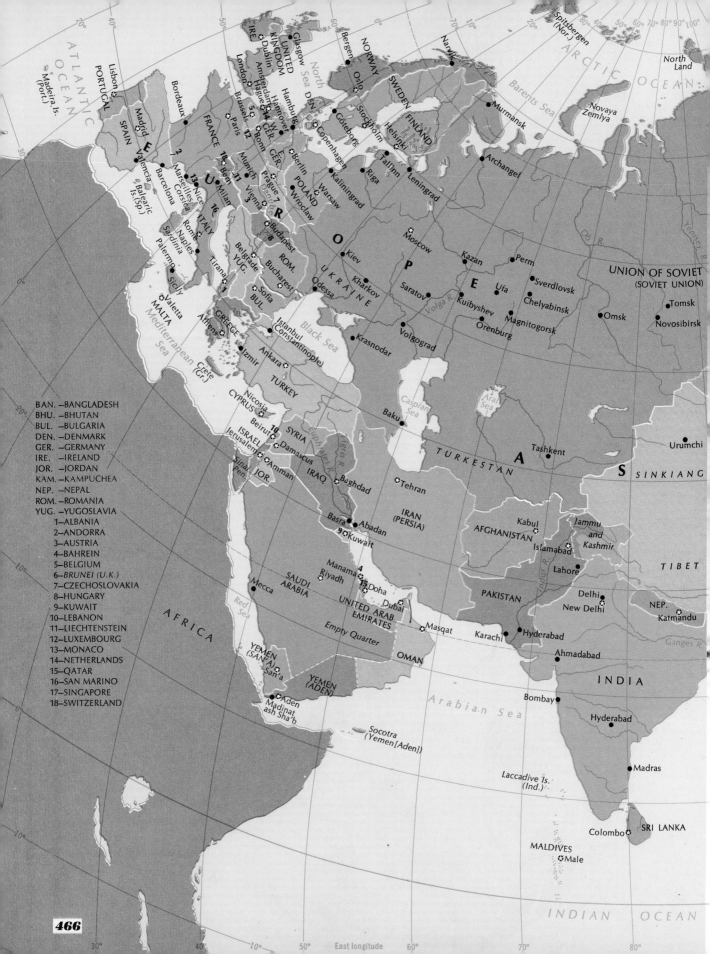

ATLANTIC OCEAN

ARCTIC OCEAN

Spitsbergen (Nor.)

North Land

Novaya Zemlya

Barents Sea

Murmansk

Archangel

NORWAY SWEDEN FINLAND

Narvik

UNITED KINGDOM

IRE. Dublin
Glasgow
London
Amsterdam
Hamburg
Hannover
Bremen
Berlin
GER.

Oslo
Göteborg
Stockholm
Helsinki
Tallinn
Riga
Leningrad
Kaliningrad

Bergen
North Sea DEN.
Copenhagen

PORTUGAL Lisbon
Madeira Is. (Port.)

SPAIN Madrid
Valencia
Balearic Is. (Sp.)
Barcelona

Bordeaux
FRANCE Paris
Marseilles
Corsica
Nice
Milan
ITALY
Rome
Sardinia
Naples
Palermo
Sicily

Brussels
Bonn
Munich
Bern
Vienna
Prague
Budapest
POLAND Warsaw
Wrocław
E U R O P E

Moscow
Kazan
Perm
Sverdlovsk
Chelyabinsk
Magnitogorsk
Tomsk
Novosibirsk
Omsk

UNION OF SOVIET (SOVIET UNION)

Kiev
Kharkov
UKRAINE
Odessa
Saratov
Kuibyshev
Orenburg
Ufa

Volgograd
Krasnodar

MALTA
Valetta
Athens
GREECE
Crete (Gr.)
Izmir
Tiranë
YUG.
Belgrade
Bucharest
ROM.
Sofia
BUL.

Istanbul (Constantinople)
Black Sea
Ankara
TURKEY
Nicosia
CYPRUS
Beirut
ISRAEL
Jerusalem
Damascus
SYRIA
Amman
JOR.
IRAQ
Baghdad

Caspian Sea
Baku
Aral Sea
Tashkent

T U R K E S T A N

Urumchi

SINKIANG

Tehran
IRAN (PERSIA)
Basra
Abadan
Kuwait

AFGHANISTAN
Kabul
Islamabad
Lahore

Jammu and Kashmir

TIBET

Manama
Riyadh
Doha
Dubai
Masqat

SAUDI ARABIA

Mecca

AFRICA

Red Sea

Empty Quarter

UNITED ARAB EMIRATES

OMAN

PAKISTAN
Karachi
Hyderabad

Delhi
New Delhi
NEP.
Katmandu

Ahmadabad

INDIA

Bombay

Hyderabad

YEMEN (SAN A)
San'a
YEMEN (ADEN)
Aden
Madinat ash Sha'b

Socotra (Yemen [Aden])

Arabian Sea

Laccadive Is. (Ind.)

Madras

SRI LANKA

Colombo

MALDIVES
Male

INDIAN OCEAN

BAN. —BANGLADESH
BHU. —BHUTAN
BUL. —BULGARIA
DEN. —DENMARK
GER. —GERMANY
IRE. —IRELAND
JOR. —JORDAN
KAM. —KAMPUCHEA
NEP. —NEPAL
ROM. —ROMANIA
YUG. —YUGOSLAVIA
1—ALBANIA
2—ANDORRA
3—AUSTRIA
4—BAHRAIN
5—BELGIUM
6—BRUNEI (U.K.)
7—CZECHOSLOVAKIA
8—HUNGARY
9—KUWAIT
10—LEBANON
11—LIECHTENSTEIN
12—LUXEMBOURG
13—MONACO
14—NETHERLANDS
15—QATAR
16—SAN MARINO
17—SINGAPORE
18—SWITZERLAND

East longitude

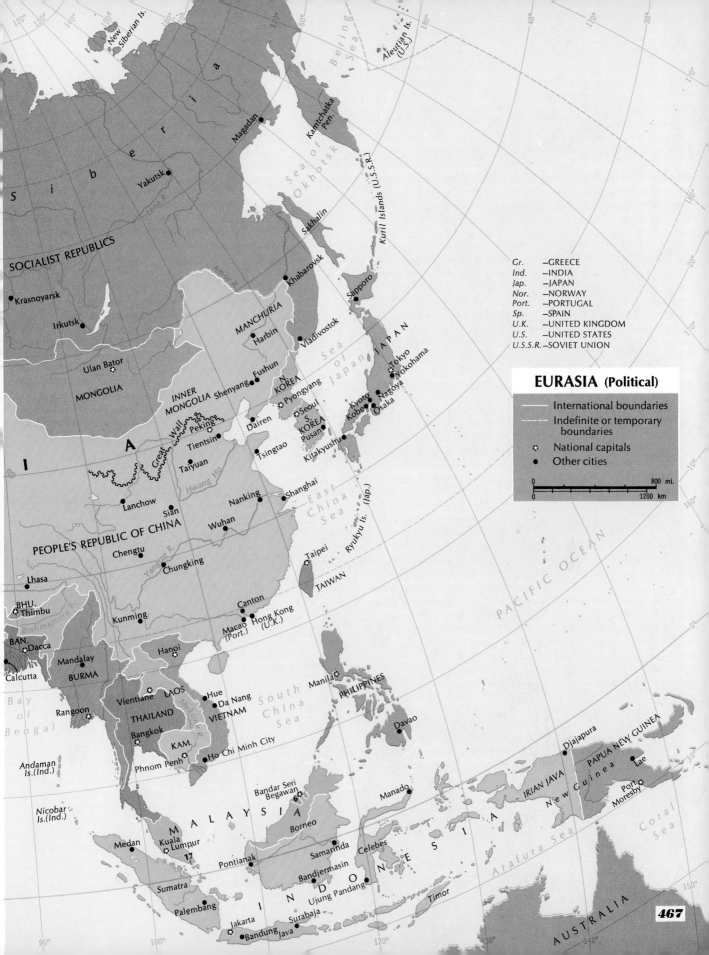

EURASIA (Political)

Gr.	—GREECE
Ind.	—INDIA
Jap.	—JAPAN
Nor.	—NORWAY
Port.	—PORTUGAL
Sp.	—SPAIN
U.K.	—UNITED KINGDOM
U.S.	—UNITED STATES
U.S.S.R.	—SOVIET UNION

EURASIA (Political)

International boundaries
Indefinite or temporary boundaries
⛛ National capitals
● Other cities

800 mi.
1200 km

EUROPE (Physical-Political)

Elevations
Meters
3,000
1,500
500
200
0

Feet
10,000
5,000
1,650
650
0

Miles
Kilometers

ASIA

ARCTIC OCEAN

Barents Sea

Caspian Sea

Baku

CAUCASUS MOUNTAINS
Mt. Elbrus (18,480 ft.; 5,633 m)

UNION OF SOVIET SOCIALIST REPUBLICS
(SOVIET UNION)

Kuibyshev
Ural R.
Volgograd
Volga R.
Don R.
Rostov
Gorki
Voronezh
Moscow
Kharkov
Dnepropetrovsk
Donetsk
Dnieper R.
Zaporozhye
Kiev
Crimea
Odessa
Dniester R.

Black Sea

CYPRUS
Nicosia

FINLAND
Leningrad
Helsinki
Riga
Minsk

Gulf of Bothnia

Baltic Sea

North European Plain

Pripet R.

SWEDEN
Stockholm

Warsaw
Łódź
POLAND
Vistula R.
Oder R.

Copenhagen
DENMARK
Hamburg
Elbe R.
Berlin
EAST GERMANY
Prague
CZECHOSLOVAKIA
CARPATHIAN MTS.
Budapest
HUNGARY
Hungarian Plain
Danube R.
ROMANIA
Bucharest
BULGARIA
Sofia
RHODOPE MTS.
Aegean Sea
Mt. Olympus (9,570 ft.; 2,920 m)
GREECE
Athens
Crete (Gr.)
Rhodes (Gr.)

NORWAY
Oslo

NORTH Sea

NETHERLANDS
Amsterdam
Ghent
BELGIUM
Cologne
WEST GERMANY
Rhine R.
LUXEMBOURG
Munich
Vienna
AUSTRIA
LIECHTENSTEIN
ALPS
SWITZ.
Zurich
Matterhorn (14,690 ft.; 4,478 m)
Mt. Blanc (15,780 ft.; 4,810 m)
Monte Como
Monte Rosa (15,200 ft.; 4,630 m)
SAN MARINO
Adriatic Sea
YUGOSLAVIA
DINARIC ALPS
Belgrade
Tirana
ALBANIA

North Sea

Faeroe Is. (Den.)
Shetland Is. (U.K.)
Orkney Is. (U.K.)

Outer Hebrides (U.K.)

Glasgow
Birmingham
London
UNITED KINGDOM

IRELAND
Dublin

English Channel

Paris
FRANCE
Seine R.
Loire R.
Rhone R.
Garonne R.
MONACO
Marseilles
Corsica (Fr.)
Sardinia (It.)
VATICAN CITY
ITALY
APENNINES
Naples
Sicily (It.)
Mediterranean Sea
MALTA

Bay of Biscay

PYRENEES
Pico de Aneto (11,170 ft.; 3,404 m)
ANDORRA
Barcelona
Balearic Is. (Sp.)

ICELAND
Reykjavik

Norwegian Sea

ATLANTIC OCEAN

SPAIN
Madrid
Meseta
PORTUGAL
Lisbon
Gibraltar (U.K.)

AFRICA

Mediterranean Sea

East longitude
West Longitude

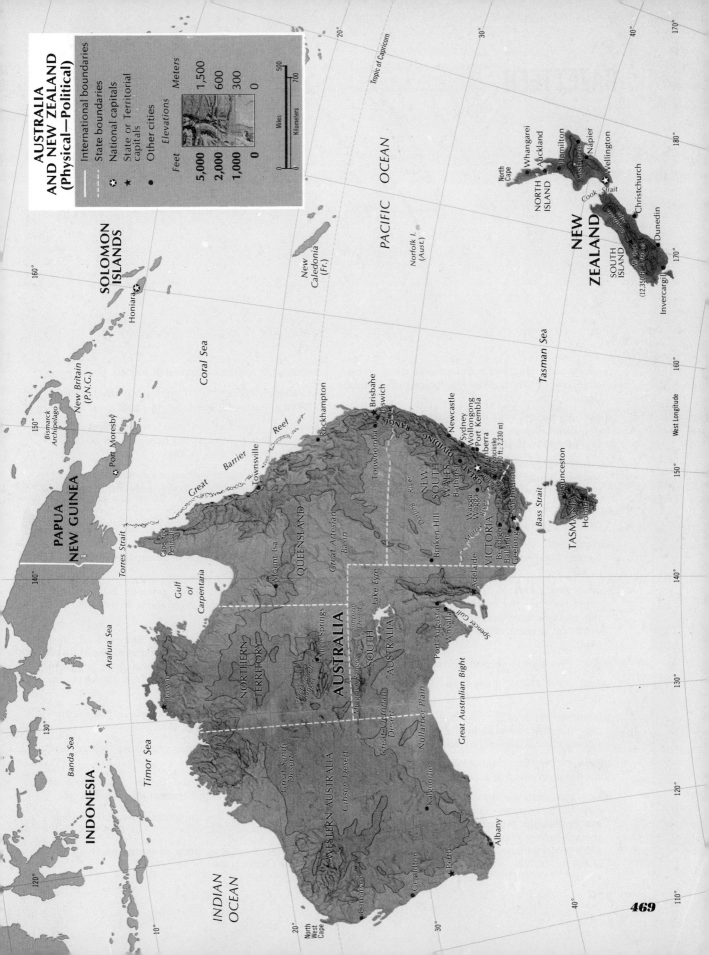

INDONESIA

Banda Sea

Timor Sea

PAPUA NEW GUINEA

Arafura Sea

Bismarck Archipelago

New Britain (P.N.G.)

Port Moresby ⊛

SOLOMON ISLANDS

Honiara ⊛

Coral Sea

PACIFIC OCEAN

New Caledonia (Fr.)

Norfolk I. (Aust.)

Torres Strait

Cape York Peninsula

Gulf of Carpentaria

Great Barrier Reef

Townsville

Rockhampton

Toowoomba

Brisbane
Ipswich

Darling River

NEW SOUTH WALES

Mount Isa

QUEENSLAND

Great Artesian Basin

Newcastle
Sydney
Wollongong
Port Kembla

GREAT DIVIDING RANGE

Bathurst

Canberra ⊛

Kosciusko
(7,310 ft.: 2,230 m)

Broken Hill

Wagga Wagga

Murray River

Melbourne

VICTORIA

Bendigo
Ballarat
Geelong

Bass Strait

Launceston

TASMANIA

Hobart

Darwin ★

NORTHERN TERRITORY

Alice Springs

Macdonnell Ranges

Musgrave Ranges

SOUTH AUSTRALIA

AUSTRALIA

Simpson Desert

Lake Eyre

Port Augusta
Whyalla

Adelaide ★

Spencer Gulf

Great Australian Bight

Great Sandy Desert

WESTERN AUSTRALIA

Gibson Desert

Great Victoria Desert

Nullarbor Plain

Kalgoorlie

Geraldton

Perth ★

Albany

North West Cape

Carnarvon

INDIAN OCEAN

Tasman Sea

NEW ZEALAND

North Cape

Whangarei
Auckland
Hamilton
Gisborne
Napier
Wellington ★

NORTH ISLAND

Cook Strait

Christchurch

SOUTH ISLAND

Mt. Cook
(12,350 ft.: 3,760 m)

Dunedin

Invercargill

West Longitude

Tropic of Capricorn

GAZETTEER

The Gazetteer is a geographical dictionary. It shows latitude and longitude for cities and certain other places. Latitude and longitude are shown in this form: 36°N/84°W. This means "36 degrees north latitude and 84 degrees west longitude." The page reference tells where each entry may be found on a map.

Accra (6°N/0° long.). Capital of and most populated city in Ghana. Port city located on Atlantic Ocean. p. 355.

Addis Ababa (9°N/39°E). Capital of and most populated city in Ethiopia. Located at an elevation of 7,900 ft (2,408 m). p. 355.

Adelaide (35°S/139°E). Capital of the Australian state of South Australia. Located near a gulf of the Indian Ocean. p. 469.

Aden (13°N/45°E). Capital of Yemen (Aden). Located on the Gulf of Aden. p. 304.

Adriatic Sea. An arm of the Mediterranean Sea located between Italy and the Balkan Peninsula. p. 123.

Aegean Sea. Part of the Mediterranean Sea located between the eastern coast of Greece and the western coast of Turkey. Bounded on the north by Greek mainland and on the south by Crete. p. 123.

Africa. The earth's second largest continent. p. 18.

Akkad (33°N/45°E). Ancient city in Mesopotamia. p. 49.

Alexandria (31°N/30°E). Second most populated city in Egypt. Located in the Nile Delta. It was founded by Alexander the Great in 332 B.C. p. 100.

Algiers (37°N/3°E). Capital of Algeria. Located on the Mediterranean Sea. p. 304.

Alps. Mountain system extending in an arc from the Mediterranean coast between Italy and France through Switzerland and Austria and into the northwest coast of Yugoslavia. The highest peak is Mont Blanc, with an elevation of 15,771 ft (4,807 m). p. 123.

Amman (32°N/36°E). Capital of Jordan. p. 304.

Amsterdam (52°N/5°E). Capital of the Netherlands. Connected to the North Sea by canal. p. 179.

Anatolia. Peninsula on which Asian Turkey is located. This peninsula lies between the Black and Mediterranean seas. p. 464.

Angkor (13°N/104°E). Ancient city located in present-day Kampuchea. Today only ruins are left. p. 433.

Ankara (41°N/33°E). Capital of Turkey. Located in central Anatolia. p. 304.

Antarctica. The earth's third smallest continent. p. 18.

Antwerp (51°N/4°E). Chief port of Belgium. Located on the Schelde River about 50 miles (80 km) from the North Sea. p. 179.

Apennines. Mountains in Italy. They extend from northwest Italy near Genoa to the southern tip of the Italian Peninsula. Its highest peak is Monte Corno, with an elevation of 9,560 ft (2,914 m). p. 123.

Aquitaine. One of the largest fiefs in France during the feudal period. p. 145.

Arabian Peninsula. Large peninsula located east of the Red Sea. p. 249.

Arabian Sea. Part of the Indian Ocean located between India and the Arabian Peninsula. p. 249.

Arctic Circle. A line of latitude located at 66½° north latitude. p. 11.

Arctic Ocean. Large body of water north of the Arctic Circle. p. 18.

Asia. The earth's largest continent. p. 18.

Asia Minor. Asian peninsula on which most of Turkey is located. It is bounded on the north by the Black Sea, on the west by the Aegean Sea, and on the south by the Mediterranean Sea. p. 75.

Aswan (24°N/33°E). City on the Nile River. Site of Aswan High Dam. p. 49.

Athens (38°N/24°E). City-state in ancient Greece. Today, the capital of and largest city in modern Greece. p. 179.

Atlantic Ocean. Large body of water separating North and South America from Europe and Africa. p. 18.

Atlas Mountains. Located in Morocco, Algeria, and Tunisia, along northern edge of the Sahara. The highest peak is Djebel Toubkal, with an elevation of 13,665 ft (4,165 m). p. 249.

Australia. The earth's smallest continent. p. 18.

Babylon (33°N/44°E). Ancient city in the country of Mesopotamia. It was located on the Euphrates River. Its ruins are near the present-day city of Baghdad, Iraq. p. 49.

Baghdad (33°N/44°E). National capital of and most populated city in present-day Iraq. Located on the Tigris River. One-time capital of the empire of the caliphs. p. 304.

Baku (40°N/50°E). Large city in the Soviet Union. Located on a peninsula in the Caspian Sea. Center of rich oil field. p. 234.

Balkan Mountains. Range of mountains stretching east-west across Bulgaria. Highest point is Botev Peak, with an elevation of 7,793 ft (2,375 m). p. 187.

Balkan Peninsula. Peninsula in southeast Europe between the Adriatic and Ionian seas on the west and the Aegean and Black seas on the east. Usually thought to consist of Greece, Albania, Bulgaria, Romania, and European Turkey. p. 123.

Baltic Sea. Part of the Atlantic Ocean, south and southwest of Sweden. p. 123.

Bangkok (14°N/101°E). Capital of and most populated city in Thailand. Located on the Chao Phraya (river). p. 440.

Barcelona (41°N/2°E). Large important port city in northeast Spain on the Mediterranean Sea. p. 179.

Barents Sea. Part of the Arctic Ocean north of Norway and European U.S.S.R. It is bounded by Spitsbergen and Franz Joseph Island on the north, by Novaya Zemlya on the east, and by the Norwegian Sea on the west. p. 123.

Bay of Bengal. Part of the Indian Ocean between the east coast of India and the Malay Peninsula. p. 373.

Beirut (34°N/36°E). Capital of Lebanon. Located on the eastern shore of the Mediterranean Sea. p. 304.

Belgrade (45°N/21°E). Capital of Yugoslavia. Located where the Sava River joins the Danube River. p. 234.

Benghazi (32°N/20°E). Port city in Libya. p. 304.

Berlin (53°N/13°E). Formerly the capital of Germany. Today a divided city located in East Germany. East Berlin is the capital of East Germany. West Berlin, although surrounded by East Germany, is a part of West Germany. p. 172.

Bern (47°N/7°E). Capital of Switzerland. Located on the Swiss Plateau. p. 179.

Birmingham (53°N/2°W). The second most populated city in the United Kingdom. p. 179.

Black Sea. Large sea located on the southern divide between Europe and Asia. p. 123.

Bordeaux (45°N/1°W). Large city in France, located on the Garonne River. p. 123.

Bosporus. Narrow body of water separating European Turkey from Asian Turkey. Connects the Black Sea and the Sea of Marmara. p. 199.

Brahmaputra River. Rises in southwestern Tibet. Joins the Ganges River near Dacca, India, before flowing into the Bay of Bengal. In China this river is called the Tsangpo. p. 373.

Brisbane (28°S/153°E). Capital of the Australian state of Queensland. Port city located on the east coast of Australia. p. 469.

Bucharest (44°N/26°E). Capital of Romania. Located on a tributary of the Danube River. p. 234.

Budapest (48°N/19°E). Capital of Hungary. Located on both sides of the Danube River. p. 234.

Cabinda. Part of Angola separated from the rest of the country by part of Zaire. p. 349.

Cairo (30°N/31°E). Capital of Egypt. Most populated city in Africa. Located on the east side of the Nile River. p. 304.

Calicut (11°N/76°E). City in India that gave its name to a cloth called calico. Today, the city is also known as Kozhikode. p. 433.

Canberra (35°S/149°E). Capital of Australia. Located in southeastern Australia. p. 469.

Canton (23°N/113°E). Chief port of south China. Located in the delta of the Hsi River. p. 440.

Cape Agulhas (35°S/20°E).   Southernmost point of Africa. It is located at 20°E longitude, which serves as the dividing line between the Indian and Atlantic oceans. p. 313.

Cape of Good Hope (34°S/19°E).   Located on southwest coast of South Africa. p. 313.

Cape Town (34°S/18°E).   Seaport city on southwest coast of South Africa. p. 355.

Carpathian Mountains.   They stretch from the Alps in the west to the Balkans in the east. Highest peak is Gerlachouka Peak, with an elevation of 8,737 ft (2,663 m). p. 187.

Carthage (37°N/10°E).   Ancient city and nation once located on coast of north Africa near present-day city of Tunis, Tunisia. p. 100.

Caspian Sea.   Largest totally inland body of water in the world. Except for its southern shore, which borders Iran, the Caspian is completely within the Soviet Union. p. 187.

Caucasus Mountains.   Very high mountains in the Soviet Union. They form part of the southern divide between Europe and Asia. Highest peak is Mt. Elbrus, with an elevation of 18,481 ft (5,633 m). p. 187.

Christchurch (44°S/173°E).   City in New Zealand. Located on South Island. p. 469.

Congo River.   One of the world's longest rivers. Rises in southeast Zaire as the Lualaba River. Flows into Atlantic Ocean at Matadi, Zaire. p. 313.

Constantinople (41°N/29°E).   Built by Emperor Constantine in A.D. 325 on the site of the ancient Greek city of Byzantium. p. 274.

Copenhagen (56°N/13°E).   Capital of and largest city in Denmark. An important port. p. 179.

Corinth (38°N/23°E).   City-state of ancient Greece. p. 75.

Crete.   Largest island in Greece. Located in the Mediterranean Sea. Ancient Minoan civilization developed here. p. 75.

Crimea.   Peninsula in the Black Sea. Located in Soviet Union. p. 187.

Dacia.   Part of ancient Roman Empire. Today an area in Romania. p. 100.

Damascus (34°N/36°E).   Capital of Syria. p. 304.

Danube River.   Second longest river in Europe. It begins in the Alps and flows into the Black Sea in Romania. The Danube passes through or borders eight European countries. Three capitals are located on it. p. 468.

Dardanelles.   Narrow strait in Turkey connecting the Sea of Marmara and the Aegean Sea. p. 199.

Darwin (12°S/131°E).   Capital of Northern Territory, Australia. Port city on the Timor Sea. p. 469.

Dead Sea (32°N/36°E).   Salt lake located on the border between Israel and Jordan. p. 295.

Delhi (29°N/77°E).   City in India. Located on the Jumna River. Once the capital of Mogul India. p. 440.

Djibouti (12°N/43°E).   Capital of the country of Djibouti. Located on the Gulf of Aden. p. 355.

Dnieper River.   Located in the Soviet Union. It rises in Valdai Hills and flows into Black Sea. p. 187.

Don River.   Located in the Soviet Union. Rises south of Moscow and flows into the Sea of Azov, which is part of the Black Sea. Connected by canal to Volga River. p. 187.

Dresden (51°N/14°E).   Industrial city in East Germany. Located on the Elbe River. p. 234.

Durban (30°S/31°E).   Seaport on east coast of South Africa. p. 355.

East Berlin (53°N/13°E).   Capital of East Germany. Communist part of the divided city of Berlin. p. 234.

Eastern Ghats.   Mountains located along eastern coast of India. Highest peak is Dodabetta, at an elevation of 8,640 ft (2,633 m). p. 373.

Eastern Hemisphere.   The half of the earth east of the Prime Meridian. p. 10.

Ebla (36°N/37°E).   Ancient city built about 4,000 years ago. Located in what is today the nation of Syria. p. 49.

Elbe River.   Rises in northwest Czechoslovakia and flows through Czechoslovakia, East Germany, and West Germany into the North Sea. p. 187.

Elburz Mountains.   Located in northern Iran. They separate the Iranian Plateau from the Caspian Sea. Highest peak is Mount Damāvand, with an elevation of 18,386 ft (5,604 m). p. 249.

Equator.   0° latitude. A line drawn on maps that circles the earth halfway between the North Pole and the South Pole. p. 11.

Euphrates River.   Rises in mountains in eastern Turkey and flows through Syria into Iraq where it joins with the Tigris River near Al Qurna to form the Shatt-al-Arab, which flows into the Persian Gulf. p. 49.

Eurasia.   The name often given to the total area covered by Europe and Asia. p. 464.

Europe.   The earth's second smallest continent. p. 18.

Fertile Crescent. Stretch of land from Jericho to Ebla through Mesopotamia. p. 49.

Florence (44°N/11°E). City in Italy located on the Arno River at the base of the Apennines. p. 163.

Ganges River. Sacred river of India. Rises in the Himalayas. Joined by the Brahmaputra near Dacca before flowing into the Bay of Bengal. p. 373.

Gaul. Historical name for area that is part of the present-day country of France. p. 100.

Gdańsk (54°N/19°E). City in Poland. Located on Baltic Sea. Formerly called Danzig. p. 234.

Gdynia (55°N/19°E). City in Poland. Located on Baltic Sea. p. 234.

Goa (15°N/74°E). Former Portuguese colony on west coast of India. Today the site of Indian city of Panaji. p. 433.

Gobi Desert. Dry area located in Mongolia. p. 373.

Gold Coast. Located along Gulf of Guinea between Ivory Coast and Slave Coast. Named for large amounts of gold once mined in the area. p. 462.

Great Barrier Reef. World's largest deposit of coral. Located in the Coral Sea off the northeast coast of Australia. p. 469.

Great Dividing Range. Mountain area of Australia. Extends from north to south near most of the east coast. Highest peak is Mt. Kosciusko, at 7,305 ft (2,226 m). p. 469.

Greenland. Large island between Canada and Iceland. Belongs to Denmark. p. 458.

Greenwich. A place in London, England, designated as 0° longitude. The Prime Meridian runs from the North Pole through Greenwich to the South Pole. p. 11.

Gulf of Aden. Part of the Arabian Sea located between Africa's Somalia Peninsula and the Arabian Peninsula. p. 249.

Gulf of Oman. Part of the Indian Ocean located between the Arabian Peninsula and southeast Iran. p. 249.

Gulf Stream. Warm ocean current flowing from the Gulf of Mexico to the North Atlantic Ocean. p. 18.

Hamburg (54°N/10°E). Busy port city on the Elbe River in West Germany. p. 179.

Hanoi (21°N/106°E). Capital of Vietnam. Located on the Red River. p. 440.

Harappa (31°N/73°E). Site of ancient city in the Indus Valley. p. 433.

Hastings (51°N/1°E). William the Conqueror defeated King Harold here in A.D. 1066. p. 145.

Himalayas. The world's highest mountain system. Located in central Asia. Mt. Everest, at 29,028 ft (8,848 m) the highest peak in the world, is located in the Himalayas. p. 373.

Hindu Kush. Very high mountain range located mostly in Afghanistan. Highest point is Tirich Mir, with an elevation of 25,260 ft (7,699 m). p. 373.

Hiroshima (34°N/132°E). Industrial city in Japan. On August 6, 1945, the city was destroyed by an atomic bomb. This was the first time an atomic bomb was ever used in warfare. p. 440.

Hobart (43°S/147°E). Capital of the Australian state of Tasmania. p. 469.

Ho Chi Minh City (11°N/107°E). City formerly called Saigon. Name was changed in 1975 following the Communist takeover of South Vietnam. p. 440.

Hokkaido. Northernmost of the four main islands of Japan. p. 373.

Hong Kong (22°N/114°E). British Colony in southeast China. p. 433.

Honshu. Largest of Japan's four major islands. p. 373.

Hungarian Plain. Located mostly in Hungary. The Danube River crosses this plain. p. 187.

Hwang Ho. Chinese river that starts in the mountains of Tibet and flows into the Yellow Sea. p. 373.

Iberian Peninsula. European peninsula southwest of Pyrenees. Spain and Portugal are on this peninsula. p. 123.

Indian Ocean. Large body of water between Africa and Australia. p. 18.

Indus River. Rises in Tibet and flows into the Arabian Sea in Pakistan near its border with India. p. 373.

Inner Mongolia. Part of China. Bounded on the north by the nation of Mongolia. Partially bounded on the south by the Great Wall. p. 467.

Irkutsk (52°N/104°E). City in Siberia. Located near Lake Baikal and the Lena River. p. 234.

Iron Gate (45°N/23°E). Pass, or gorge, between Carpathian and Balkan mountains through which the Danube River flows. p. 187.

Istanbul (41°N/29°E). Turkish name for city of Constantinople. Most populated city in Turkey. Located on both sides of the Bosporus. Part of the city is in Europe and part is in Asia. p. 304.

Isthmus of Suez. Narrow piece of land that separates the Red and Mediterranean seas. p. 249.

Ivory Coast. Coastal region of western Africa, along the Gulf of Guinea between the Gold Coast and the Grain Coast. p. 462.

Jakarta (6°S/107°E). Capital of Indonesia. One of the world's most populated cities. Located on the northwest coast of Java. p. 440.

Java. Island that is part of Indonesia. Located between the Java Sea and the Indian Ocean. p. 373.

Jericho (32°N/35°E). One of the world's first cities. Was located near present-day Jerusalem. p. 49.

Jerusalem (32°N/35°E). Capital of Israel. Holy city for Jews, Christians, and Moslems. p. 295.

Johannesburg (26°S/28°E). Most populated city in South Africa. p. 355.

Jordan River. Rises in Syria and flows south through the Sea of Galilee and into the Dead Sea. p. 295.

Jutland Peninsula. Peninsula located between the North and Baltic seas. Denmark and part of West Germany are located on it. p. 123.

Kabul (35°N/69°E). Capital of and most populated city in Afghanistan. p. 440.

Kalahari Desert. Dry plateau region located in Botswana, South Africa, and Namibia. p. 313.

Kano (12°N/9°E). City in Nigeria. p. 338.

Karnak (26°N/33°E). Today a village on the east bank of the Nile River. Site of Egyptian temple at Thebes in ancient Egypt. p. 49.

Kazan (56°N/49°E). Mongol city in the Soviet Union. Located near the Volga River. p. 209.

Khyber Pass (34°N/71°E). Narrow pass through the Hindu Kush along border between Pakistan and Afghanistan. p. 373.

Kiev (50°N/31°E). One of the oldest cities in Soviet Union. Today a large city located on the Dnieper River. p. 209.

Kinshasa (4°S/15°E). City in Zaire. Located on the Congo River. Formerly known as Leopoldville. p. 355.

Kisangani (1°N/25°E). City in Zaire. Located on Congo River. Formerly known as Stanleyville. p. 355.

Kisumu (0° lat./35°E). Port city in western Kenya on Lake Victoria. p. 364.

Kyushu. Most southern of the four main islands of Japan. p. 373.

Lagos (6°N/3°E). Capital of and most populated city in Nigeria. Located on Gulf of Guinea. p. 355.

Lake Albert. Located between Uganda and Zaire. Also known as Albert Nyanza. p. 313.

Lake Baikal. (Sometimes spelled Baykal.) The world's deepest lake. It is 5,712 ft (1,741 m) deep. Located in Soviet Union. p. 187.

Lake Chad. Located on borders between Niger, Chad, Nigeria, and Cameroon. Size of this lake varies depending on season. p. 313.

Lake Malawi. Located between Malawi, Tanzania, and Mozambique. Formerly known as Lake Nyasa. p. 313.

Lake Tanganyika. Four African nations—Tanzania, Zaire, Zambia, and Burundi—have coastlines on this lake. p. 313.

Lake Victoria. One of the largest bodies of fresh water in the world. Located in eastern Africa. Kenya, Uganda, and Tanzania all have coastlines on this lake. p. 313.

Leipzig (51°N/12°E). Industrial city in East Germany. p. 234.

Lena River. Rises near Lake Baikal and flows north into the Arctic Ocean. p. 187.

Leningrad (60°N/30°E). Second most populated city in the Soviet Union. Located on the Gulf of Finland. Once called St. Petersburg. Formerly the capital of the Russian empire. p. 234.

Lhasa (30°N/91°E). Major city in Tibet. It is the second highest city in the world. Its elevation is 12,002 ft (3,658 m). p. 467.

Lisbon (39°N/9°W). Capital of Portugal. Mainland Europe's westernmost port city. p. 179.

London (52°N/0° long.). Capital and most populated city in the United Kingdom. Located on the Thames River. p. 179.

Macao (22°N/113°E). Portuguese colony located in southern China on the South China Sea. p. 433.

Macdonnell Range. Mountains in central Australia. Highest peak is Mt. Ziel, with an elevation of 4,953 ft (1,510 m). p. 469.

Macedonia. Part of ancient Greece once ruled by Alexander the Great. It was located in northern Greece. p. 75.

Madagascar. Island located in the Indian Ocean off the southeast coast of Africa. Excluding Australia it is the world's fourth largest island. The nation of Madagascar is on this island. p. 462.

Madrid (40°N/4°W). National capital of Spain. Second most populated city in Europe. p. 179.

Malay Peninsula. Located in Southeast Asia. Parts of Malaysia and Thailand are on this peninsula. p. 465.

Manchuria. Part of China located in northeast China. p. 467.

Manila (15°N/121°E). Capital of and most populated city in the Philippines. Located on Manila Bay on the island of Luzon. p. 440.

Marathon. Plain about 20 miles (32 km) from Athens. The Greeks won an important battle against the Persians here in 490 B.C. p. 75.

Mecca (21°N/40°E). Birthplace of Mohammed. Holy city for Moslems. Located in Saudi Arabia. p. 304.

Medina (24°N/40°E). City in Saudi Arabia. Mohammed's trip from Mecca to Medina in A.D. 622 is called the Hegira. p. 304.

Mediterranean Sea. Large body of water surrounded by Europe, Africa, and Asia. It is the largest sea in the world. p. 13.

Mekong River. River in Southeast Asia. Rises in Tibet. Forms most of the boundary between Thailand and Laos. Flows into the South China Sea in southern Vietnam. p. 373.

Melbourne (38°S/145°E). Capital of the Australian state of Victoria. Located near the coast in southeastern Australia. p. 469.

Memphis (30°N/31°E). City in ancient Egypt. Land north of Memphis was known as Lower Egypt. Memphis was located about 15 miles (24 km) south of the present site of Cairo. p. 49.

Mesopotamia. Region between the Tigris and Euphrates rivers. p. 49.

Meuse River. Rises in northeast France and flows north through Belgium and the Netherlands into the North Sea. In the Netherlands it forms a common delta with the Rhine River. p. 123.

Milan (45°N/9°E). Industrial city in northern Italy. Second most populated city in Italy. p. 179.

Mohenjo-Daro (28°N/69°E). Site of ancient city in the Indus Plain. p. 433.

Mombasa (4°S/40°E). Seaport city on east coast of Kenya. p. 355.

Mont Blanc. Located in the French Alps, near the border with Italy. The highest peak in the Alps. Its elevation is 15,771 ft (4,807 m). p. 123.

Montreal (46°N/74°W). Most populated city in Canada. Located on Montreal Island in the St. Lawrence River. p. 459.

Moscow (56°N/38°E). Capital of the Soviet Union. The most populated city in Europe. p. 234.

Mount Ararat (40°N/44°E). Highest point in Turkey. Its elevation is 16,945 ft (5,165 m). p. 249.

Mount Damāvand (36°N/52°E). Highest peak in Iran. Located in Elburz Mountains. Its elevation is 18,368 ft (5,604 m). p. 249.

Mount Everest (28°N/87°E). Highest peak in the world. Located in the Himalayas at an elevation of 29,028 ft (8,848 m). p. 373.

Mount Kenya (0° lat./37°E). Located in central Kenya. Second highest point in Africa, with an elevation of 17,058 ft (5,199 m). p. 313.

Mount Kilimanjaro (3°N/37°E). Highest mountain peak in Africa. Its elevation is 19,340 ft (5,895 m). Located in northeast Tanzania near the Kenyan border. p. 313.

Mount Kosciusko (36°S/148°E). Highest peak in the Australian Alps. Located in southeast Australia. Its elevation is 7,305 ft (2,226 m). p. 469.

Mount Olympus (40°N/22°E). Highest peak in Greece. It has an elevation of 9,570 ft (2,917 m). In ancient Greek mythology it was supposed to be the home of the gods. p. 75.

Mount Vesuvius (41°N/14°E). Only active volcano on the European mainland. Located near Naples, Italy. p. 100.

Murray River. Most important river in Australia. Rises in the Great Dividing Range. Flows into the Indian Ocean near Adelaide. p. 469.

Nagasaki (33°N/130°E). Industrial city and seaport in Japan. Located on island of Kyushu. Was destroyed by an atomic bomb near the end of World War II. p. 433.

Nairobi (1°S/37°E). Capital of and most populated city in Kenya. p. 355.

Namib Desert. Dry area along coast of Namibia. p. 313.

Naples (40°N/14°E). Important port city in Italy. Located on part of the Mediterranean Sea called the Tyrrhenian Sea. p. 179.

New Delhi (29°N/77°E). Capital of India. Located on the Jumna River. p. 440.

Nice (44°N/7°E). Resort city on Mediterranean coast of France. p. 179.

Niger River. Rises in Guinea near Sierra Leone border. Flows into Gulf of Guinea in Nigeria. p. 313.

Nile River. The longest river in the world. Flows into the Mediterranean Sea at Alexandria, Egypt. p. 462.

Nippur (32°N/46°E). Ancient city located on the Euphrates River about 4,000 years ago. Today its ruins can be seen in Iraq. p. 49.

Normandy. Region of France located on the English Channel. p. 145.

North America. The earth's third largest continent. p. 18.

North Atlantic Drift. Warm ocean current formed by the joining of the Gulf Stream and Labrador Current. p. 18.

North China Plain. Large plain located in eastern China. p. 373.

North European Plain. Large area of flat land stretching from southwestern France through Belgium, the Netherlands, the Germanies, and Poland into the Soviet Union. The southeastern part of the United Kingdom is also part of this plain. p. 468.

Northern Hemisphere. The half of the earth that is north of the Equator. p. 10.

North Island. Northernmost of the two major islands of New Zealand. p. 469.

North Pole. Located at 90° north latitude. The most northern place on the earth. p. 10.

North Sea. Part of the Atlantic Ocean between Great Britain and the European continent. p. 123.

Novgorod (59°N/31°E). One of the oldest cities in Soviet Union. It is located on the Dnieper River. p. 209.

Ob River. Rises in the Altai Mountains and flows north into the Arctic Ocean. Located in the Soviet Union. p. 187.

Oder River. Rises in Czechoslovakia and flows north through Poland. Near Frankfurt, East Germany, it is joined by the Neisse River. It then flows north to the Baltic Sea, forming the boundary between Poland and East Germany. p. 187.

Olympia (38°N/22°E). City in ancient Greece. Located in western Peloponnesus. Site of the ruins of the temple of Zeus. Ancient Greeks held their Olympian Games here every 4 years. p. 75.

Orange River. Longest river in South Africa. Part of it forms the boundary between South Africa and Namibia. Flows into the Atlantic Ocean at Alexander Bay. p. 313.

Osaka (35°N/136°E). Second most populated city in Japan. Major seaport located on Osaka Bay on Honshu Island. p. 440.

Oslo (60°N/11°E). National capital of Norway. Located on Oslo Fjord. p. 179.

Ostrava (50°N/18°E). Industrial city in Czechoslovakia. p. 234.

Pacific Ocean. The earth's largest body of water. It stretches from the Arctic Circle to Antarctica and from the western coast of North America to the eastern coast of Asia. p. 18.

Paris (49°N/2°E). National capital and most populated city of France. Located on the Seine River. p. 179.

Peking (40°N/116°E). Capital of China. Fourth most populated city in the world. p. 440.

Peloponnesus. Peninsula in southern Greece. p. 75.

Persia. Ancient kingdom in the area that today is called Iran. p. 83.

Persian Gulf. Arm of the Arabian Sea. Separates Iran and Saudi Arabia. Connected with the Gulf of Oman and Arabian Sea by the Strait of Hormuz. p. 249.

Perth (32°S/116°E). Capital of the Australian state of Western Australia. Located on the west coast of Australia. p. 469.

Pik Kommunizma (39°N/72°E). Highest point in Soviet Union. Located in the Pamirs. It has an elevation of 24,590 ft (7,495 m). Formerly called Stalin Peak. p. 187.

Pilsen (50°N/13°E). Industrial city in Czechoslovakia. p. 234.

Plataea. (38°N/23°E). City in ancient Greece near Thebes. Ancient Greeks won an important battle here against the Persians in 479 B.C. p. 75.

Ploieşti (45°N/26°E). City in Romania. Located in a large oil field. p. 234.

Po River. Longest river in Italy. Starts in Alps and flows into the Adriatic Sea south of Venice. p. 123.

Pompeii (41°N/15°E). Ancient Roman city at the base of Mt. Vesuvius. Destroyed in A.D. 79 by an eruption of Mt. Vesuvius. p. 100.

Pondicherry (12°N/80°E). Former French colony on east coast of India. This was France's first Asian colony. p. 433.

Prague (50°N/14°E). Capital of Czechoslovakia. Located on the Vltava River. p. 234.

Pretoria (26°S/28°E). Capital of South Africa. Located on tributary of Limpopo River. p. 355.

Prime Meridian. 0° line of longitude that passes through Greenwich, England. It divides the earth into Eastern and Western hemispheres. p. 11.

Pyrenees. Mountains along border between France and Spain. Highest peak is Pico de Aneto, 11,168 ft (3,404 m). p. 123.

Rangoon (17°N/96°E). Capital of and most populated city in Burma. Located on the Rangoon River. p. 440.

Red Sea. Large sea separating part of eastern Africa from Asia. p. 13.

Rhine River. Starts in the Alps in Switzerland. Flows north into the North Sea in the Netherlands. p. 123.

Rhodes. Greek island in the southeast Aegean Sea. p. 75.

Rhone River. Starts from a glacier in the Alps in Switzerland and flows through France and into the Mediterranean Sea near Marseilles, France. p. 123.

Riyadh (25°N/47°E). Capital of Saudi Arabia. p. 304.

Rome (42°N/13°E). Capital and most populated city in Italy. Located on the Tiber River. Most important city in the Roman Empire. p. 179.

Sahara. The largest desert in the world. Located in North Africa. p. 462.

St. Petersburg (60°N/30°E). City in Russia built by Peter the Great in 1703. Located on the mouth of the Neva River. Today the city is called Leningrad. p. 209.

Salamis (38°N/23°E). Greek island in the Saronic Gulf near Piraeus. Ancient Greeks won an important naval battle near here over the Persians in 480 B.C. p. 75.

Samarkand (40°N/67°E). Capital of Timur's empire. Today a city in the Soviet Union. p. 280.

San'a (15°N/44°E). Capital of Yemen (San'a). Located on a plateau at an elevation of 7,750 ft (2,362 m). p. 304.

Sarajevo (44°N/18°E). City in Yugoslavia. Site of 1984 Winter Olympics. p. 234.

Scandinavia. Consists of the countries of Norway, Sweden, Denmark, and Iceland. p. 123.

Sea of Marmara (41°N/28°E). Body of water between European Turkey and Asian Turkey. Connects the Bosporus and the Dardanelles. p. 199.

Senegal River. Rises in Guinea. Flows into the Atlantic Ocean at Saint-Louis, Senegal. Forms boundary between Senegal and Mauritania. p. 313.

Seoul (37°N/127°E). Capital of South Korea. One of the world's most populated cities. p. 440.

Shanghai (32°N/122°E). The world's most populated city. Located on the delta of the Yangtze River in China on the East China Sea. p. 440.

Shikoku. Smallest of the four main islands of Japan. p. 373.

Sibir (58°N/69°E). Once a Mongol town in Russia. Conquered by Russians in 1581. p. 209.

Siberia. Part of the Soviet Union covering much of the area between the Ural Mountains and the Pacific Ocean. p. 234.

Sicily. Largest island in the Mediterranean Sea. Part of Italy. p. 123.

Silesia. Located in Poland and Czechoslovakia. An important European coalfield. p. 234.

Sinai Peninsula. Peninsula in eastern Egypt separated from Egypt by the Suez Canal. p. 249.

Singapore (1°N/104°E). City on the island of Singapore. Also the capital of the nation of Singapore. One of the world's busiest ports. Located on Singapore Strait. p. 440.

Sofia (43°N/23°E). Capital of Bulgaria. p. 234.

South America. The earth's fourth largest continent. p. 18.

South China Sea. Part of the Pacific Ocean west of the Philippines and Borneo. p. 373.

Southern Alps. Mountain range on South Island in New Zealand. Highest peak is Mt. Cook, with an elevation of 12,349 ft (3,764 m). p. 469.

Southern Hemisphere. The half of the earth that is south of the Equator. p. 10.

South Island. Largest of New Zealand's islands. p. 469.

South Pole. Located at 90° south latitude. The most southern place on the earth. p. 10.

Sparta (37°N/22°E). City-state in ancient Greece. Today a small town on the Eurotas River on the southern part of the Peloponnesus peninsula. p. 75.

Stonehenge (51°N/2°W). Remains of prehistoric structure near Salisbury, England. The original structure was built about 4,000 years ago. p. 164.

Strait of Gibraltar (36°N/6°W). Narrow neck of water separating the Iberian Peninsula from North Africa. It connects the Mediterranean Sea with the Atlantic Ocean. p. 123.

Strait of Hormuz (27°N/56°E). Narrow body of water connecting the Persian Gulf and the Gulf of Oman. p. 249.

Strait of Malacca. Narrow channel of water between the Malay Peninsula and the island of Sumatra. p. 373.

Suez Canal (30°N/33°E). Waterway that joins Red and Mediterranean seas. Construction started in 1854 and completed in 1869. p. 249.

Sumatra. Large island in Indonesia. p. 373.

Sunda Islands. Group of islands in Southeast Asia. They include Sumatra, Java, Borneo, Celebes, Bali, and Timor. p. 373.

Sydney (34°S/151°E). Capital of the Australian state of New South Wales. Most populated city in Australia. Port city located on Tasman Sea, which is part of the Pacific Ocean. p. 469.

Taipei (25°N/122°E). Capital of and most populated city in Taiwan. p. 440.

Tasmania. Island off the coast of Australia. Also one of Australia's states. p. 469.

Tehran (36°N/51°E). Capital of Iran. Located at base of Elburz Mountains. p. 304.

Thames River. River in Great Britain on which London is located. p. 164.

Thebes (26°N/33°E). City in ancient Egypt. Site of ancient temple at Karnak. Located on the Nile River. p. 49.

Thebes (38°N/23°E). City-state in ancient Greece. p. 75.

Thermopylae (39°N/22°E). Narrow pass in eastern Greece where ancient Greeks fought Persians in 480 B.C. p. 75.

Tiber River. River in Italy. It rises in the Apennines and flows through Rome to the Mediterranean Sea. p. 100.

Tibet. High mountainous area in China near border with India and Nepal. p. 373.

Tigris River. Rises in Turkey and flows into Iraq, where it joins with the Euphrates River near Al Qurna to form the Shatt-al-Arab, which flows into the Persian Gulf. p. 49.

Tirana (41°N/20°E). Capital of Albania. p. 234.

Tokyo (36°N/140°E). Capital of Japan. Located on the island of Honshu on Tokyo Bay. Second most populated city in the world. p. 440.

Tombouctou (17°N/3°W). Town in Mali. Located near the Niger River on the southern edge of the Sahara. Once a city with 1,000,000 people. p. 338.

Tours (47°N/1°E). Charles Martel defeated the Moors here in A.D. 732. Today it is a large city in France. p. 145.

Tripoli (33°N/13°E). Capital of Libya. Port city on the Mediterranean Sea. p. 304.

Trondheim (63°N/10°E). City in Norway on Trondheim Fjord. Ancient capital of Norway. p. 123.

Tropic of Cancer. A line of latitude located at 23½° north latitude. p. 11.

Tropic of Capricorn. A line of latitude located at 23½° south latitude. p. 11.

Troy (40°N/26°E). Ancient city on the coast of Asia Minor. p. 75.

Tunis (37°N/10°E). Capital of Tunisia. Seaport located on the Mediterranean Sea. p. 304.

Ukraine. Part of the Soviet Union. Wheat grows well in the rich black soil of the area. p. 466.

Ulan Bator (48°N/107°E). Capital of Mongolia. p. 440.

Ur (31°N/47°E). Ancient Sumerian city built about 5,000 years ago. p. 49.

Ural Mountains. Located in the Soviet Union. They form the east-west divide between Asia and Europe. p. 187.

Uruk (32°N/46°E). Ancient Sumerian city built about 5,000 years ago. p. 49.

Victoria Falls (18°S/26°E). Located on the Zambezi River on boundary between Zambia and Zimbabwe. More water flows over these falls than over any other in Africa. p. 313.

Vienna (48°N/16°E). Capital of and largest city in Austria. Located on the Danube River. p. 179.

Vistula River. Longest river in Poland. Rises in Carpathians and flows into the Baltic Sea near Gdańsk. p. 187.

Vladivostok (43°N/132°E). City in the Soviet Union. Eastern end of the Trans-Siberian Railroad. Located on the Sea of Japan. p. 234.

Voi (3°S/39°E). Town in Kenya. Located on the rail line between Mombasa and Nairobi. p. 364.

Volga River. Longest river in Europe. Rises in the Valdai Hills. Flows into Caspian Sea at Astrakhan. p. 187.

Volgograd (49°N/44°E). City in the Soviet Union. Located on the Volga River. Formerly called Stalingrad. p. 234.

Wales. One of the four major political divisions of the United Kingdom. p. 164.

Warsaw (52°N/21°E). Capital of Poland. Located on the Vistula River. p. 234.

Wellington (41°S/175°E). Capital of New Zealand. Located on North Island and Cook Strait. p. 469.

West Berlin (53°N/13°E). West German city located in East Germany. Part of divided city of Berlin. p. 179.

Western Ghats. Mountains located along western coast of India. Highest peak is Anai Mudi at an elevation of 8,841 ft (2,695 m). p. 373.

Western Hemisphere. The half of the earth west of the Prime Meridian. p. 10.

White Sea. Inlet of Barents Sea, which is part of the Arctic Ocean. p. 187.

Yakutsk (62°N/130°E). City in the Soviet Union. Located on the Lena River. p. 187.

Yangtze River. One of the world's longest rivers. Rises in Tibet. Flows into East China Sea near Shanghai, China. p. 373.

Yenisei River. Located in the Soviet Union. One of the world's longest rivers. Rises in the Sayan Mountains. Flows into Kara Sea, which is part of Arctic Ocean. p. 187.

Zagros Mountains. Mountains that stretch from northwest Iran to near southern end of Persian Gulf. Highest peak is Zardeh Kuh. Its elevation is 14,921 ft (4,548 m). p. 249.

Zambezi River. Rises in Angola. Flows into the Indian Ocean in Mozambique. Forms boundary between Angola and Zimbabwe. p. 313.

Zanzibar (6°S/39°E). Island belonging to Tanzania. Located in the Indian Ocean off the coast of Tanzania. Also the name of the chief city on the island. p. 313.

GLOSSARY

abbot. The head or leader of a monastery. p. 150.

abolish. To do away with. p. 211.

aborigine. The earliest known inhabitant of a place. p. 385.

abundance. A quantity that is more than enough. p. 129.

Afrikaans. A South African language of Dutch origin but with words from English, German, French, and Bantu languages. p. 359.

Allah. An Arabic word meaning "the God." p. 270.

ally. A country or government that has united with another for defense. p. 83.

altitude. Height above sea level. Altitude is usually measured in feet or meters. p. 5.

ambassador. An official who represents his or her government in a foreign country. p. 419.

ancestor. A person from whom a family or a group of people descends. p. 266.

ancient. Relating to a period long past. p. 36.

annex. *v.* To add territory to a state or nation. p. 225.

anno Domini. Latin words that mean "in the year of the Lord." Usually shortened to the letters A.D., the words are used to mark the years (time) after the birth of Jesus. p. 33.

apartheid. Racial segregation in the Republic of South Africa. Apartheid means "apartness." p. 360.

apprentice. A person learning a trade or an art. p. 149.

aqueduct. A structure or an artificial channel used to transport water. p. 105.

artisan. A skilled craftworker. p. 191.

asphalt. A substance formed from a combination of oil, sand, and rock. p. 260.

astronomy. The scientific study of the sun, moon, planets, and other stars. p. 2.

authority. Power to enforce obedience. p. 204.

autocrat. A ruler with complete power. p. 210.

Bactrian camel. A camel with two humps. p. 258.

barometer. An instrument used to record air pressure. p. 23.

Bedouin. A wandering Arab herder. p. 259.

Berber. A person from Morocco whose ancestors lived in northwest Africa before the Arabs conquered it. p. 307.

bishop. A clergyman of high rank. p. 205.

boundary. The extent or limit of the borders of a country or state. p. 232.

Buddhism. A religion founded by Siddhartha Gautama in India in the sixth century B.C. p. 394.

cacao. The tree and the seeds from which cocoa and chocolate are made. p. 324.

calendar. A system that fixes the beginning, length, and divisions of the year. p. 34.

caliph. The Arabic title given to Moslem religious leaders. p. 273.

candidate. A person who seeks to be elected to office. p. 230.

caravan. A group of people traveling together, usually on animals or in vehicles. p. 250.

cartographer. One who makes maps. p. 5.

cash crop. A crop that is grown for sale rather than for the use of the grower. p. 324.

cassava. A tropical plant with a large root that can be eaten and from which flour is made. p. 323.

caste. A way of separating people into groups, or classes, based on birth. p. 393.

catholic. General or universal. Member of the Roman Catholic Church. p. 205.

causeway. A raised roadway across a body of water. p. 376.

censorship. Control of what is published, filmed, or broadcast. p. 432.

century. A period of 100 years. p. 35.

circa. The Latin word meaning "about" or "approximately" used especially to refer to dates. p. 34.

citadel. A protected, walled-in part of a city. A fortresslike protected area. p. 50.

citizen. A member of a city or nation. p. 77.

civil war. A war between two or more groups of people within a country (as opposed to a war between two different countries). p. 101.

class. A group of people who are alike in certain ways. p. 393.

climate. The average condition of weather at a place, over a period of years, as shown by such things as temperature and precipitation. p. 25.

cobalt. A hard, shiny, silver-white, magnetic metal that occurs only in combination with other metals like iron and nickel. p. 354.

collective. A farm that a group of people operate together to produce and to share the products. p. 218.

colony. A settlement in one land ruled by the government of another country. p. 276.

Colosseum. A large arena in Rome where spectators watched Roman games. p. 110.

Commonwealth of Nations. An association of countries that were once part of the British Empire. p. 350.

commune. Land that is worked together by a team of people. p. 436.

communism. A social and economic system in which most property is owned by the government and shared by the governed. p. 214.

compass. An instrument used to find direction. p. 405.

compost. A mixture of rotted plant materials used as a fertilizer. p. 379.

concession. The right for a company to carry on a business in another country. p. 291.

conifers. Evergreen trees that have cones. Pine, fir, and spruce are conifers. p. 128.

consul. Annually elected chief magistrate of the Roman republic who was given the powers of a king. p. 96.

consumer goods. Things that are grown or made by producers and used by people. p. 226.

continent. A very large body of land: North America, South America, Europe, Africa, Asia, Australia, and Antarctica. p. 18.

continental climate. A climate with extreme changes of temperature with hot summers and cold winters. Continental climates are typical of the interiors of continents. p. 190.

convent. Building or buildings in which a group of nuns live. p. 150.

convict. A person who has been found guilty of breaking a law. p. 427.

copra. Dried coconut meat. p. 445.

counselor. A person who advises and helps someone make decisions. p. 399.

crusade. A Christian military expedition to recover the Holy Land from the Moslems. p. 275.

cultivate. To prepare and use land for growing crops. p. 378.

cuneiform. A form of writing with wedge-shaped symbols that was used in Mesopotamia. p. 53.

curiosity. The desire to know or learn. p. 90.

decade. A period of 10 years. p. 35.

deciduous. Dropping off; losing leaves at the end of a growing season. p. 128.

delta. Land formed by mud and sand in a river mouth. p. 58.

democracy. A government in which power is held by the people. p. 78.

desert. An area of land with very little rain and therefore little plant life. p. 248.

dictator. One who has absolute power of rule in a country. p. 96.

dike. A wall or bank built to control or hold back the water of a river or sea. p. 176.

diviner. A person who supposedly can predict the future by consulting the gods. p. 397.

dromedary. A camel with one hump. p. 258.

drought. A long dry period with no rain. p. 353.

economy. The use and management of workers and resources of a country to produce goods and services. p. 353.

elevation. The height of something. The elevation of land is its distance above or below sea level; usually measured in feet or meters. p. 5.

embassy. The buildings where the ambassador of a country lives and works. p. 419.

emir. Arabic word that means "prince." p. 299.

empire. Many different lands brought under the rule of one government. p. 55.

engineer. A person who designs or builds machines. p. 154.

Equator. An imaginary line of latitude that circles the earth, exactly halfway between the North Pole and the South Pole. It is shown on a map or a globe as the east-west line numbered 0° latitude. p. 10.

era. A period of years counted from a set point in time. p. 33.

evaporate. To pass off, or disappear, in the form of a gas or vapor. p. 254.

expedition. A group formed to carry out a trip of exploration. p. 319.

export. *n.* An article that is sent out of a country for sale in another country. *v.* To send out for sale. p. 164.

fable. A story that teaches a lesson. p. 90.

factors. People who traded for a company. p. 412.

factory. A trading post. A modern industrial plant. p. 412.

famine. A very great shortage of food. p. 354.

feudalism. The system of mutual rights and duties between lords and vassals that existed in Western Europe in the Middle Ages. p. 144.

fief. Land granted by a lord to his vassal in return for military service. p. 144.

flint. A very hard, brittle stone, that makes a spark when struck against a hard surface. p. 135.

foreign aid. The sending of economic or scientific help to another country. p. 231.

free port. A port or place with no taxes on imports or exports. p. 422.

frigid. Extremely cold. The frigid zones are near the North and South Poles and are usually called the high latitudes. p. 19.

front. The imaginary line between cold and warm air masses near the earth's surface. p. 24.

geography. The science that deals with the earth and its life. p. 8.

geothermal. Relating to heat from the earth. p. 447.

gladiator. A person who fought another person or an animal for the entertainment of an audience in ancient Rome. p. 111.

granary. A place for storing grain. p. 392.

graph. A diagram or drawing on which data is shown. p. 38.

grid. A network of lines that forms a pattern of crisscrosses. p. 9.

groundwater. The water under the earth's surface. p. 256.

guerrilla. A person who engages in hit-and-run warfare, harassment, and sabotage. p. 362.

guild. An organization of people in a craft or trade. p. 148.

harmony. An agreement of feelings, ideas, and actions. Peaceful interaction. p. 406.

hegira. Mohammed's flight (journey) from Mecca to Medina in A.D. 622. p. 270.

hemisphere. Half the earth or globe. The Equator divides the world into a Northern Hemisphere and a Southern Hemisphere. p. 10.

Hinduism. One of the world's oldest living religions. Hinduism is practiced by most of the people of India. p. 392.

Holy Land. The place where Jesus lived. p. 275.

humidity. The amount of water or dampness in the air. p. 21.

hygrometer. Instrument used to measure humidity, or the dampness in the air. p. 23.

immigrant. A person from one country who comes into another to live there. p. 78.

impi. A group or regiment of Zulu soldiers. p. 343.

import. *n.* An article that is purchased outside a country and brought into the country. *v.* To bring in from another country. p. 164.

independence. Freedom from the control of another country, group, person, or thing. p. 232.

independent. Not subject to control by another power or government; self-governing. p. 77.

industrialized. Having an economy in which the major sources of wealth and income are trade, business, or manufacturing. p. 446.

inhabit. To live somewhere. p. 91.

interior. Inland area or inner part. p. 374.

irrigate. To bring water to crops, usually through canals, ditches, or pipes. p. 60.

isthmus. A narrow strip of land connecting two larger bodies of land. p. 19.

janissary. A member of the special army of the Turkish sultan. p. 281.

journal. A daily written account. p. 250.

justice. The ideal or concept of giving each person that which rightfully belongs to that person. p. 117.

khan. A Mongol ruler. p. 206.

Knesset. The Israeli parliament. p. 295.

knight. An armed soldier who fought on horseback during the Middle Ages. p. 144.

kremlin. The old Russian word for a fortress. Today when people speak of the *Kremlin,* they mean the Soviet government. p. 227.

land bridge. Narrow strip of land that connects two larger pieces of land. p. 262.

landlocked. Having no outlet to the sea. A country that is landlocked is surrounded on all sides by other countries. p. 353.

latitude. Distance measured north and south in degrees from the Equator to the earth's poles. Lines of latitude are imaginary lines used to locate places on the earth. p. 9.

lodestone. A natural magnet. Lodestones were used to make the first compasses. p. 405.

longitude. Distance measured east and west from the Prime Meridian in degrees. Lines of longitude are imaginary circles that go around the earth and pass through the North and South Poles. p. 9.

magnificent. Great or grand. p. 280.

Magyar. Member of the chief group of people living in Hungary, whose language is Hungarian. p. 237.

majority. More than half. p. 81.

manor. A large medieval farm. p. 145.

mature. To reach full growth or development. p. 132.

mechanization. The use of machines. p. 380.

Mediterranean climate. A warm, temperate climate, occurring on the western margins of continents in the latitudes 30° to 40°, and marked by hot, dry, sunny summers and moist, warm winters. p. 178.

meridian. An imaginary line of longitude running in a north-south direction on a map or globe. The number on the line shows how far the line is east or west of the Prime Meridian. p. 11.

military alliance. An agreement between two or more countries to join together for the purpose of defense in times of war. p. 222.

minority. A group that is smaller than half of a larger group or nation. p. 360.

missionary. A person who tries to spread his or her religion. p. 418.

modern. Relating to present or to recent times. p. 36.

modernize. To change over to the use of up-to-date ways of doing things. p. 437.

monarchy. A government headed by one ruler, usually a queen or king. p. 78.

monastery. Building(s) where monks live together. p. 150.

Mongol. A member of an Asian people living in Mongolia and parts of China and Siberia. p. 206.

monk. A man who is a member of a religious group and lives in a monastery. p. 33.

monopoly. The exclusive possession or control of a commodity or service. p. 148.

monsoon. Seasonal wind that blows from the land to the water in one season and from the water to the land in the other. p. 336.

mosque. A Moslem place of worship. p. 271.

nationality. Membership in a nation. p. 177.

natural resources. Things made by nature that people use, such as trees, water, soil, and minerals. p. 16.

navigable river. A river that large ships and boats can sail on. p. 435.

navigate. To steer a course through water or air, or on land. p. 74.

neutrality. Not taking sides. p. 174.

nomad. A person who moves from place to place. p. 259.

oasis. Green places in a desert where wells provide water. p. 250.

oasis farming. Farming in that part of a desert where water is available. p. 302.

obelisk. A four-sided stone pillar that is usually carved out of a single piece of rock. p. 65.

observation. Keeping careful watch on something. p. 283.

occupy. To take over. p. 435.

oil reserve. The amount of oil known to be still in the ground in a country. p. 39.

okra. A plant with green pods that are eaten in stews, soups, and other dishes. p. 323.

oligarchy. Government by a few. p. 78.

Olympiad. The four-year intervals between the athletic contests (Olympian Games) by which time was measured in ancient Greece. p. 32.

ore. A material containing the mineral for which it is mined. p. 136.

orthodox. That which is held to be right or true. p. 204.

outback. The hot, dry lands to the west of the Great Dividing Range in Australia. p. 384.

Palestinian. Person who lived in the land once known as Palestine. p. 296.

papyrus. A tall reed that grows in the Nile Valley, the pith (spongy center part) of which was used to make a paperlike substance. p. 61.

parallel. An imaginary line of latitude running in an east-west direction on a map or globe. The number on the line shows how far the line is north or south of the Equator. p. 10.

Parliament. The lawmaking body of the United Kingdom. p. 162.

patrician. Member of one of the original citizen families of ancient Rome. Member of the upper class. p. 98.

pedestrian. A person who travels on foot. p. 186.

peninsula. A piece of land extending out into the water from a larger body of land. p. 19.

per capita income. The amount of income (money received) each person in a country would have if the country's total income were divided equally among all of its people. p. 170.

permafrost. Permanently frozen ground. p. 185.

permanent. Lasting a very long time. p. 190.

petroleum. An oily liquid found in the earth, from which gasoline and many other products are made. p. 260.

pharaoh. Egyptian word for "Great House"; a ruler of ancient Egypt. p. 62.

phosphate. A mineral used in making fertilizers and detergents. p. 306.

pilgrim. A person who travels for religious reasons, often to visit holy places. p. 269.

plantation. A large farm where cash crops are grown. p. 340.

plebeian. One of the common people. p. 98.

plot. A small piece of land. p. 227.

pollution. The unclean condition of the earth's soil, air, and water. p. 133.

pope. The head of the Roman Catholic Church. p. 180.

population density. The average number of people living in a unit of land area. p. 16.

porcelain. Very fine earthenware. p. 336.

precipitation. Moisture that falls on the earth's surface; rain, snow, sleet, hail. p. 21.

press. Newspapers, magazines, books, and often radio and television news services. p. 432.

Prime Meridian. The line of 0° longitude that passes through Greenwich, England. p. 11.

private owner. An individual (as opposed to a government) who owns property. p. 296.

process. To put an item being manufactured through a special treatment. p. 171.

profit. The gain made from selling a product or service over the cost of producing or purchasing the product or service. p. 414.

projection. The representation on a map of all or part of the earth's grid system. p. 15.

prophet. A person who was believed to have a message from God. p. 268.

pyramid. A massive four-sided structure built on a broad base, and narrowing gradually to a point at the top. p. 56.

pyrethrum. Plant used to make insect poison. p. 365.

qanat. A well and tunnel in Iran. p. 256.

raw materials. Natural materials that can be processed into finished products. p. 164.

reform. A change made to improve something. p. 114.

reign. Period of time a king or queen rules. p. 30.

Renaissance. "A new birth"; refers to the great revival of art and learning in Europe in the 1300s, 1400s, and 1500s. p. 154.

renewable resource. A replaceable thing produced by nature, such as grass or timber. p. 261.

rent. Money paid for the use of property. p. 153.

republic. A government in which citizens choose representatives to run the country. p. 96.

revolt. An attack on a ruler or government by the governed. p. 78.

revolution. Complete, often violent, change in government, in a way of thinking, or in a way of life. p. 213.

Romance language. Any language that grew out of Latin; Spanish, Portuguese, French, Italian, and Romanian. p. 115.

rural. Having to do with the country. p. 312.

samurai. The military class in feudal Japan. p. 407.

savanna. Land covered with coarse grass and, sometimes, scattered trees and bushes. p. 314.

scroll. Sheet of papyrus or paper in a long roll. p. 61.

scrub. Stunted trees, bushes, and brushwood. p. 129.

sculptor. A person who makes statues. p. 154.

serf. A person who lived and worked on a manor. Serfs could not leave the manor without the permission of the lord of the manor. p. 146.

shah. A Persian word meaning "king." p. 292.

shelter belt. Rows of trees planted to protect an area from desert winds. p. 302.

shield money. A form of tax paid by vassals to their king or queen. p. 152.

shifting cultivation. Clearing a piece of land, farming it until it is no longer productive, and then moving on to another piece of land to clear and farm it in the same way. p. 323.

shogun. A military leader in feudal Japan. p. 407.

shrine. A place considered to be holy. p. 269.

silt. Fine particles of earth that are carried and deposited by water and wind. p. 46.

sisal. A plant with strong fibers used for making rope. p. 324.

Slav. A member of a group of peoples in eastern, southeastern, and central Europe, whose languages have something in common. Poles, Russians, Czechs, Slovenes, Slovaks, Yugoslavs, and Bulgarians are Slavs. p. 202.

Slavic Languages. A group of languages spoken by Slavic peoples, including Russian and Polish. p. 222.

socialism. A system that calls for ownership of land and industry by the government. p. 214.

soil. The top layer of the earth where plants grow. p. 129.

sorghum. Any of a group of tall, grassy plants that look somewhat like corn, used mostly for livestock feed. p. 326.

source. A place where something—such as a river—begins. p. 195.

sphere. A three-dimensional figure that is round or nearly round. p. 4.

steppe. One of the belts of grassland in Europe and Asia, somewhat like the prairie of North America. There are also steppes in Africa. p. 193.

strait. A narrow waterway connecting two larger bodies of water. p. 199.

subcontinent. A landmass of great size but smaller than the continents. p. 375.

subject. A person under the power or control of another person or a government. p. 77.

sultan. Ruler of a Moslem country. p. 275.

surrender. To give up. p. 435.

Swahili. A Bantu language of eastern and central Africa. p. 336.

symbol. Something that stands for something else; a sign. p. 4.

synthetic. Made by people, not by nature, and often made from chemicals. p. 444.

taiga. The great coniferous forest region of northern and western Soviet Union. p. 192.

tannery. A place where animal hides are prepared for clothing and other uses. p. 107.

tariff. A tax on imports or exports. p. 422.

tax. Money paid to a ruler or government and spent on providing government services. p. 152.

temperate. Having moderate temperature. The temperate zones of the earth are usually called the middle latitudes. p. 19.

terrace. A flat, wide ledge on the side of a hill or mountain created in order to make farming possible in steep areas. p. 378.

ticket of leave. Permission granted to convicts to live on their own after part of their sentences has been served. p. 428.

time line. A line representing a period of time, on which dates and the order of events are shown. p. 36.

token. An object or disk used to represent something of value. p. 52.

Torah. The first five books of the Jewish Bible; also known as The Law. p. 266.

torrid. Very hot; the torrid zones of the earth are near the Equator and are usually called the low latitudes. p. 19.

tourism. The industry that serves people who travel for pleasure. p. 174.

traditional. Having things the way they have been for a long time. p. 312.

translate. To change from one language to another. p. 282.

tribe. A social group held together by family ties, geography, or custom. p. 98.

tribute. A payment given by subjects to rulers or by the ruler of one nation to another as a tax or for protection. p. 83.

tsar (czar). Title of the rulers of the Russian empire. p. 208.

tundra. A rolling plain without trees, found in the Arctic area of the high latitudes. p. 184.

typhoon. A tropical storm accompanied by strong winds and heavy rain. p. 408.

urban. Having to do with the city. p. 312.

vassal. A person who promised to obey and fight for another person. p. 144.

vault. Place for storing valuable things. p. 237.

vegetation. Plant growth. p. 314.

veld. A grassland of South Africa with few bushes and very few trees. p. 343.

wadi. The bed of a stream that is dry most of the time. p. 250.

waterlogged. Soaked with water. p. 381.

TABLE OF COUNTRIES

AFRICA

COUNTRY	TOTAL AREA	POPULATION AND POPULATION DENSITY	CAPITAL CITY AND POPULATION	LANGUAGE(S)	OTHER FACTS
Algeria	919,595 sq mi (2,381,741 sq km)	20,000,000 22 per sq mi (8 per sq km)	Algiers 903,530	Arabic*, French, Berber	The Sahara Desert covers 7/8 of Algeria. Most Algerians live along the Mediterranean coast.
Angola	481,354 sq mi (1,246,700 sq km)	6,800,000 14 per sq mi (5 per sq km)	Luanda 475,328	Portuguese*, Bantu	*Welwitschia mirabilis*, a plant that can live for 100 years, grows on the parched land of southwest Angola.
Benin	43,484 sq mi (112,622 sq km)	3,700,000 85 per sq mi (33 per sq km)	Porto-Novo 104,000	French*	Dugout canoes are "school buses" for children who live in the lagoon villages.
Botswana	231,805 sq mi (600,372 sq km)	900,000 4 per sq mi (1 per sq km)	Gaborone 33,142	English*, Setswana	Okovango Basin is a large, inland swamp in northwest Botswana. The tsetse fly lives in this swamp.
Burundi	10,747 sq mi (27,834 sq km)	4,400,000 409 per sq mi (158 per sq km)	Bujumbura 78,810	French, Kirundi*	Watusi adults can grow to be 7 ft (213 cm) tall. Pygmy adults are about 4½ ft (137 cm) tall.
Cameroon	183,569 sq mi (475,442 sq km)	8,900,000 48 per sq mi (19 per sq km)	Yaoundé 274,399	French*, Ewondo, English*, Donala, Foulbé, Mungaka, Bamiléke, Bassa	As much as 400 in. (1,000 cm) of rain can fall each year in some parts of the coastal rain forest.
Cape Verde	1,557 sq mi (4,033 sq km)	300,000 193 per sq mi (74 per sq km)	Praia 21,494	Portuguese*	Cape Verde is a series of 10 main and 5 tiny volcanic islands in the North Atlantic Ocean.
Central African Republic	240,535 sq mi (622,984 sq km)	2,400,000 10 per sq mi (4 per sq km)	Bangui 301,793	French*, Sango	This is a poor country with no railroads and many roads that wash out during the rainy season.
Chad	495,755 sq mi (1,284,000 sq km)	4,600,000 9 per sq mi (4 per sq km)	N'Djamena 281,000	French*, Massa, Sara, Arabic, Kanembou, Gorane, Ouddai	The major form of transportation through this country is by river. Lake Chad has no outlet to the sea.
Comoros	838 sq mi (2,171 sq km)	400,000 477 per sq mi (184 per sq km)	Moroni 12,000	French*, Arabic, Swahili	The Comoros Islands were formed by volcanoes in the Indian Ocean. Mont Karthala is an active volcano.
Congo	132,047 sq mi (342,000 sq km)	1,600,000 12 per sq mi (5 per sq km)	Brazzaville 298,967	French*, Lingala, Kokongo	More than half of this hot, humid country is covered with thick forests where only wild animals live.
Djibouti	8,494 sq mi (22,000 sq km)	500,000 59 per sq mi (23 per sq km)	Djibouti 62,000	Arabic*, French, Afar, Somali	Djibouti has one of the driest and hottest climates in the world. Its capital is an important seaport.
Egypt	386,662 sq mi (1,001,449 sq km)	44,800,000 116 per sq mi (48 per sq km)	Cairo 6,818,318	Arabic*	The very dry air has preserved the pyramids and temples of ancient Egypt.
Equatorial Guinea	10,830 sq mi (28,051 sq km)	300,000 28 per sq mi (11 per sq km)	Malabo 37,237	Spanish*, Fang, Bubi	Snowflake, the world's first known white gorilla, was found here. The world's largest frog, about 34 in. (86 cm), lives here.
Ethiopia	471,778 sq mi (1,221,900 sq km)	30,500,000 65 per sq mi (25 per sq km)	Addis Ababa 1,242,555	Amharic*, Galligna, Tigrigna	The Red Sea ports of Mitsiwa and Aseb are two of the hottest places in the world.
Gabon	103,347 sq mi (267,667 sq km)	700,000 7 per sq mi (3 per sq km)	Libreville 186,154	French*, Bantu	This country is an important source of ebony and mahogany lumber.
Gambia	4,361 sq mi (11,295 sq km)	600,000 138 per sq mi (53 per sq km)	Banjul 45,604	English*, native languages	Gambia was a slave-trading center in the 1700s. Peanuts are the most important export product.
Ghana	92,100 sq mi (238,537 sq km)	12,400,000 135 per sq mi (52 per sq km)	Accra 564,194	English*, Twi, Fanti, Ga, Ewé, Dagbani	Ghana was called the Gold Coast by Europeans because Portuguese explorers found much gold there.
Guinea	94,926 sq mi (245,857 sq km)	5,300,000 56 per sq mi (22 per sq km)	Conakry 197,267	French*, Malinke, Susu, Fulani	Guinea has rich deposits of bauxite, gold, diamonds, and iron. It also has very rich soil.
Guinea-Bissau	13,948 sq mi (36,125 sq km)	800,000 57 per sq mi (22 per sq km)	Bissau 109,500	Portuguese*, Crioulo	Most people of Guinea-Bissau are farmers. The main crops are peanuts and rice.
Ivory Coast	124,504 sq mi (322,463 sq km)	8,800,000 71 per sq mi (27 per sq km)	Abidjan 560,000	French*	There are more than 60 languages spoken here. The Europeans came here to trade for ivory.
Kenya	224,961 sq mi (582,646 sq km)	17,900,000 80 per sq mi (31 per sq km)	Nairobi 835,000	Swahili*, English, Bantu, Kikuyu	Kenya is known for its variety of wildlife. Mt. Kenya is the second highest mountian in Africa.
Lesotho	11,720 sq mi (30,355 sq km)	1,400,000 119 per sq mi (46 per sq km)	Maseru 45,000	English*, Sesotho*	2/3 of the school children are girls because the boys start herding livestock by the age of 5 or 6.
Liberia	43,000 sq mi (111,369 sq km)	2,000,000 47 per sq mi (18 per sq km)	Monrovia 171,580	English*, tribal dialects	In 1847, Liberia became an independent state for freed American slaves.
Libya	679,362 sq mi (1,759,540 sq km)	3,200,000 5 per sq mi (2 per sq km)	Tripoli 551,477	Arabic*	Al-Kufrah is a huge underground lake in southeast Libya. The Sahara covers 90% of Libya.
Madagascar	226,658 sq mi (587,041 sq km)	9,200,000 41 per sq mi (16 per sq km)	Antananarivo 400,000	Malagasy*, French*	Madagascar, world's leading producer of vanilla beans, was a haven for pirates in the 1600s and 1700s.

*Official language(s)

486

TABLE OF COUNTRIES

AFRICA

	COUNTRY	TOTAL AREA	POPULATION AND POPULATION DENSITY	CAPITAL CITY AND POPULATION	LANGUAGE(S)	OTHER FACTS
	Malawi	45,747 sq mi (118,484 sq km)	6,600,000 144 per sq mi (56 per sq km)	Lilongwe 102,924	Chichewa*, English*, Nyanja, Yao, Tumbuka	In Malawi tribes, women are heads of the families. Family land belongs to all family members.
	Mali	478,767 sq mi (1,240,000 sq km)	7,100,000 15 per sq mi (6 per sq km)	Bamàko 400,022	French*	Mali, where the old trading city of Tombouctou is located, was part of 7 ancient African kingdoms.
	Mauritania	397,956 sq mi (1,030,700 sq km)	1,700,000 4 per sq mi (2 per sq km)	Nouakchott 134,986	French*, Arabic, Tucolor	Most of the people in this large country lead a nomadic life, living in the desert and grasslands.
	Mauritius	790 sq mi (2,045 sq km)	1,000,000 1,266 per sq mi (489 per sq km)	Port Louis 144,412	English*	Mauritius is an island nation that is smaller than Rhode Island but has a larger population.
	Morocco	172,414 sq mi (446,550 sq km)	22,300,000 129 per sq mi (50 per sq km)	Rabat 367,620	Arabic*, Berber, French, Spanish	Morocco leads the world in exporting phosphates. It ranks 7th in world olive production.
	Mozambique	302,330 sq mi (783,030 sq km)	12,700,000 42 per sq mi (16 per sq km)	Maputo 354,684	Portuguese*, Bantu, English	Traditional and modern farming is done. Major crops are cashews, coconuts, cotton, and sugarcane.
	Namibia (South-West Africa)	318,251 sq mi (824,292 sq km)	1,100,000 3 per sq mi (1 per sq km)	Windhoek 64,700	Afrikaans*, English*, German, tribal dialects	Namibia's most valuable product is diamonds. The Namib Desert stretches for 1,000 mi (1,609 km) along the coast.
	Niger	489,191 sq mi (1,267,000 sq km)	5,800,000 12 per sq mi (5 per sq km)	Niamey 225,314	French*, Fulani	Almost ½ of Niger receives less than 4 in. (10.2 cm) annual rainfall. It is a landlocked nation.
	Nigeria	356,669 sq mi (923,768 sq km)	82,300,000 231 per sq mi (89 per sq km)	Lagos 1,060,848	English*, Hausa, Yoruba, Ibo (about 245 other languages)	Most Nigerians speak more than one of the 245 languages. This nation ranks 10th in population, worldwide.
	Rwanda	10,169 sq mi (26,338 sq km)	5,400,000 531 per sq mi (205 per sq km)	Kigali 117,749	French*, Kinyarwanda*	Although near the equator, this nation's climate is cool and pleasant because of high plateaus.
	São Tomé e Príncipe	372 sq mi (964 sq km)	100,000 269 per sq mi (104 per sq km)	São Tomé 17,830	Portuguese*	The islands are formed from extinct volcanoes. In the 1500s it was the center for slave trade.
	Senegal	75,750 sq mi (196,192 sq km)	5,900,000 78 per sq mi (30 per sq km)	Dakar 798,792	French*, Wolof, Serer, other tribal dialects	This is the westernmost country in Africa. Before modern times, it was the site of many kingdoms.
	Seychelles	108 sq mi (280 sq km)	100,000 926 per sq mi (357 per sq km)	Victoria 23,000	English*, French*, Creole	Coco de mer, a double coconut that can weigh as much as 50 lbs (22.7 kg), grows only here.
	Sierra Leone	27,669 sq mi (71,740 sq km)	3,700,000 163 per sq mi (52 per sq km)	Freetown 214,443	English*, Krio, tribal languages	This is the world's leading exporter of *piassava*, a fiber from the raffia palm used in making brushes.
	Somalia	246,201 sq mi (637,657 sq km)	4,600,000 19 per sq mi (7 per sq km)	Mogadishu 400,000	Somali*, Arabic, English	The nomadic people of this easternmost country of Africa seek water and pasture for their herds.
	South Africa	471,445 sq mi (1,221,037 sq km)	30,000,000 64 per sq mi (25 per sq km)	Cape Town 825,752 Pretoria 543,950	Afrikaans*, English*, Bantu	South Africa ranks 1st in the world production of gold and gem diamonds.
	Sudan	967,500 sq mi (2,505,813 sq km)	19,900,000 21 per sq mi (8 per sq km)	Khartoum 333,906	Arabic*, English, tribal dialects	Sudan is the largest country in Africa. The Nile River forms where the White and Blue Nile meet.
	Swaziland	6,704 sq mi (17,363 sq km)	600,000 89 per sq mi (35 per sq km)	Mbabane 24,000	English*, Siswati*	Many large rivers provide hydroelectric power and irrigation.
	Tanzania	364,900 sq mi (945,087 sq km)	19,900,000 55 per sq mi (21 per sq km)	Dar es Salaam 870,000	English*, Swahili*, Bantu, Arabic	Kilimanjaro, formed from a volcano, is the highest mountain in Africa at 19,340 ft (5,895 m).
	Togo	21,622 sq mi (56,000 sq km)	2,800,000 129 per sq mi (50 per sq km)	Lomé 229,400	French*, Ewé, Mina, Kabyé, Cotocoli	Togo has one of the world's largest phosphate reserves.
	Tunisia	63,170 sq mi (163,610 sq km)	6,700,000 106 per sq mi (41 per sq km)	Tunis 550,404	Arabic*, French	Tunisia ranks 5th in world production of olives and 2nd in phosphate production.
	Uganda	91,134 sq mi (236,036 sq km)	13,700,000 150 per sq mi (58 per sq km)	Kampala 330,700	English*, Swahili, Luo, Luganda, Ateso	Lake Victoria is the largest lake in Africa.
	Upper Volta	105,869 sq mi (274,200 sq km)	6,700,000 63 per sq mi (24 per sq km)	Ouagadougou 168,607	French*, tribal dialects	Herding cattle, sheep, and goats on the grasslands is the most important part of its economy.
	Zaire	905,568 sq mi (2,345,409 sq km)	30,300,000 33 per sq mi (13 per sq km)	Kinshasa 2,443,876	French*, Ishiluba, Kikongo, Lingala, Swahili, (local languages)	1/3 of Zaire is covered by one of the world's largest and thickest tropical rain forests.
	Zambia	290,586 sq mi (752,614 sq km)	6,000,000 21 per sq mi (8 per sq km)	Lusaka 641,000	English*, Bantu (8 major tribal languages)	Zambia ranks 4th in the world production of copper. Most of Zambia is a high plateau.
	Zimbabwe	150,804 sq mi (390,580 sq km)	8,000,000 53 per sq mi (20 per sq km)	Harare 654,000	English*, Chishona, Sindebele *Official language(s)	Victoria Falls, one of the world's natural wonders, sends up a cloud of spray that can be seen for 10 miles.

487

TABLE OF COUNTRIES

ASIA

COUNTRY	TOTAL AREA	POPULATION AND POPULATION DENSITY	CAPITAL CITY AND POPULATION	LANGUAGE(S)	OTHER FACTS
Afghanistan	250,000 sq mi (647,497 sq km)	15,100,000 60 per sq mi (23 per sq km)	Kabul 913,164	Pashto*, Dari*	The Afghan hound, used for hunting gazelles, leopards, and hares, was first raised in Afghanistan.
Bahrain	240 sq mi (622 sq km)	400,000 1,667 per sq mi (643 per sq km)	Manama 88,785	Arabic*, English, Persian	The discovery of oil in 1932 turned Bahrain into one of the richest countries in the gulf area.
Bangladesh	55,598 sq mi (143,998 sq km)	93,300,000 1,678 per sq mi (648 per sq km)	Dacca 1,679,572	Bengali*, English	Bangladesh ranks eighth among all countries in population. It produces more jute than any other country.
Bhutan	18,147 sq mi (47,000 sq km)	1,400,000 77 per sq mi (30 per sq km)	Thimbu 8,922	Dzongkha*, Drukke, Nepali	Most Bhutanese are descendants of Tibetan settlers. They practice Lamism, a branch of Buddhism.
Burma	261,218 sq mi (676,552 sq km)	37,100,000 142 per sq mi (55 per sq km)	Rangoon 2,050,365	Burmese*, English	Rice and teakwood are Burma's chief exports. Burma produces the world's finest jade.
China	3,691,523 sq mi (9,561,000 sq km)	1,000,000,000 270 per sq mi (105 per sq km)	Peking 7,570,000	Chinese*	China has a written history that goes back 3,500 years. It ranks as the world's oldest living civilization.
India	1,269,346 sq mi (3,287,590 sq km)	713,800,000 562 per sq mi (218 per sq km)	New Delhi 301,801	*(all official) Hindi, English, Assamese, Bengali, Gujerati, Kannada, Kashmiri, Malayalam, Marathi, Oriya, Punjabi, Sanskrit, Sindhi, Tamil, Telegu, Urdu	Over 200 languages are spoken in India. India has the world's largest film-making industry.
Indonesia	578,119 sq mi (1,497,320 sq km)	151,300,000 262 per sq mi (101 per sq km)	Jakarta 4,576,009	Bahasa Indonesia*, Dutch, English, various Malayo-Polynesian languages	The Komodo dragon, the world's largest lizard, is protected by law on the Indonesian island of Komodo.
Iran	636,296 sq mi (1,648,000 sq km)	41,200,000 65 per sq mi (23 per sq km)	Tehran 4,498,159	Farsi (Persian)*, Turkish, Kurdish, Arabic, Azerbaijani	The name *Iran* means "land of the Aryans." The poems of the 12th century Persian poet Omar Khyyam are world famous.
Iraq	167,925 sq mi (434,924 sq km)	14,000,000 83 per sq mi (32 per sq km)	Baghdad 1,745,328	Arabic*, Kurdish, Persian, Turkish	The ancient ruins of Babylon and Nineveh in ancient Mesopotamia are a great tourist attraction.
Israel	8,019 sq mi (20,770 sq km)	4,100,000 511 per sq mi (197 per sq km)	Jerusalem 366,600	Hebrew*, Arabic*, English	The *Dead Sea Scrolls*, the oldest-surviving biblical documents, were found in the caves of Qumran in Israel.
Japan	145,711 sq mi (377,389 sq km)	118,600,000 814 per sq mi (314 per sq km)	Tokyo 8,646,520	Japanese* English	Japan has about 1,500 earthquakes a year, though few do much damage. It produces 60% of the world's raw silk.
Jordan	37,738 sq mi (97,740 sq km)	3,500,000 93 per sq mi (36 per sq km)	Amman 732,587	Arabic*, English	Jordan has many ruins of historical and biblical fame. Jericho, one of its oldest cities, dates back to 8000 B.C.
Kampuchea (Cambodia)	69,898 sq mi (181,035 sq km)	6,100,000 87 per sq mi (34 per sq km)	Phnom Penh 393,995	Khmer*, French, Vietnamese, Chinese	The temples of Angkor Wat, now in ruins, are masterpieces of Khmer sculpture that date back to about A.D. 600.
Korea (North)	46,540 sq mi (120,538 sq km)	18,700,000 402 per sq mi (155 per sq km)	Pyongyang 1,500,000	Korean*, seven major dialects of Korean	Students in North Korea must work for the state 2 months each summer beginning after their fifth year in school.
Korea (South)	38,025 sq mi (98,484 sq km)	41,100,000 1,081 per sq mi (417 per sq km)	Seoul 7,823,195	Korean*	In relation to its size, South Korea has one of the world's largest armies—a force of almost 600,000.
Kuwait	7,768 sq mi (20,118 sq km)	1,500,000 193 per sq mi (75 per sq km)	Al-Kuwait 80,405	Arabic*, English	Due to an increase in the number of immigrants, today less than half the population is made up of Kuwaitis.
Laos	91,429 sq mi (236,800 sq km)	3,700,000 40 per sq mi (16 per sq km)	Vientiane 176,637	Lao*, French, English	Most roads in Laos are passable only in the dry season. In many areas, goods can be transported only by airplane.
Lebanon	4,015 sq mi (10,400 sq km)	2,700,000 672 per sq mi (260 per sq km)	Beirut 474,870	Arabic*, French, English	Its beauty, climate, and impressive Phoenician, Roman, and Crusader ruins attract many tourists to Lebanon yearly.

*Official language(s)

488

TABLE OF COUNTRIES

ASIA

	COUNTRY	TOTAL AREA	POPULATION AND POPULATION DENSITY	CAPITAL CITY AND POPULATION	LANGUAGE(S)	OTHER FACTS
	Malaysia	127,316 sq mi (329,749 sq km)	14,700,000 116 per sq mi (45 per sq km)	Kuala Lumpur 451,728	English*, Malay*, Chinese, Tamil	Over half the people in Malaysia are under 15 years of age. Islam is the official religion of Malaysia.
	Maldives	115 sq mi (298 sq km)	200,000 1,739 per sq mi (671 per sq km)	Male 29,555	Divehi*, English	Most of the people of Maldives—the smallest independent country in Asia—are descendants of people from Sri Lanka.
	Mongolia	604,250 sq mi (1,565,000 sq km)	1,800,000 3 per sq mi (1 per sq km)	Ulan Bator 402,300	Mongolian*	During the 1200s, under Ghengis Khan and Kublai Khan, the Mongols built one of the largest land empires in history.
	Nepal	54,362 sq mi (140,797 sq km)	14,500,000 258 per sq mi (99 per sq km)	Katmandu 332,982	Nepali*	Nepalese gurkhas (soldiers) won fame for their bravery while fighting for the armies of India and Great Britain.
	Oman	82,030 sq mi (212,457 km)	900,000 11 per sq mi (4 per sq km)	Masqat 5,080	Arabic*	A major oil producer, Oman has no agriculture. The Shuhu, an Islamic sect in northern Oman, are cave dwellers.
	Pakistan	310,404 sq mi (803,943 sq km)	93,000,000 300 per sq mi (116 per sq km)	Islamabad 76,641	Urdu*, Baluchi, Punjabi, Pushtu, Sindhi, English	The area that is now Pakistan was once the site of the Indus Valley civilization which dates back at least 4,500 years.
	Philippines	115,831 sq mi (300,000 sq km)	51,600,000 445 per sq mi (172 per sq km)	Manila 1,454,352	Pilipino*, English, Spanish, (dialects: Tagalog, Visayan)	In the 1970s scientists in the Philippines found the Tasadays, a tribe of Stone-Age cave-dwellers.
	Qatar	4,247 sq mi (11,000 sq km)	300,000 71 per sq mi (27 per sq km)	Doha 50,000	Arabic*, English	Before the discovery of oil in 1939, people depended on camel raising, fishing, and pearl diving to make their livings.
	Saudi Arabia	831,313 sq mi (2,153,090 sq km)	11,100,000 13 per sq mi (5 per sq km)	Riyadh 666,840	Arabic*	Saudi Arabia exports the most oil of any nation. Islamic law regulates even such things as traffic rules in Saudi Arabia.
	Singapore	224 sq mi (581 sq km)	2,500,000 11,161 per sq mi (4,303 per sq km)	Singapore 2,413,945	Chinese*, English*, Malay*, Tamil*	About 40,000 ships enter and leave the island port of Singapore every year.
	Soviet Union (see Europe)					
	Sri Lanka	25,332 sq mi (65,610 sq km)	15,200,000 600 per sq mi (232 per sq km)	Colombo 616,000	Sinhali*, Tamil*, English*	The name Sri Lanka means "beautiful island" and has been the official name of the country since 1972.
	Syria	71,498 sq mi (185,180 sq km)	9,700,000 136 per sq mi (52 per sq km)	Damascus 836,668	Arabic*, Kurdish, Armenian, Turkish, Circassian	The first alphabet was developed by the Phoenicians in Syria in 1500 B.C.
	Taiwan	13,885 sq mi (35,961 sq km)	18,500,000 1,332 per sq mi (514 per sq km)	Taipei 2,196,237	Chinese* (Mandarin)	The name Taiwan means "terraced bay." Taiwan trades mostly with the United States and Japan.
	Thailand	198,457 sq mi (514,000 sq km)	49,800,000 251 per sq mi (97 per sq km)	Bangkok 4,870,000	Thai* (Siamese), Chinese, English	The Siamese cat and Siamese twins received their name from Thailand, which was once known as Siam.
	Turkey	292,261 sq mi (756,953 sq km)	47,700,000 163 per sq mi (63 per sq km)	Ankara 2,203,729	Turkish*	Mt. Ararat, where Noah's Ark is said to have landed after the biblical flood, is an extinct volcano in Turkey.
	United Arab Emirates	32,278 sq mi (83,600 sq km)	1,200,000 37 per sq mi (14 per sq km)	Abu Dhabi 22,023	Arabic*	The discovery of oil in the late 1900s changed the UAE from a poor area to one of the world's richest countries.
	Vietnam	128,402 sq mi (332,559 sq km)	56,600,000 441 per sq mi (170 per sq km)	Hanoi 2,570,905	Vietnamese*, English, French, Chinese, Russian	Vietnam has one of the most productive rice growing areas in Southeast Asia.
	Yemen (Aden)	128,560 sq mi (332,968 sq km)	2,000,000 16 per sq mi (6 per sq km)	Aden 285,373	Arabic*	Yemen (Aden) was once part of the British Empire. The most important industry in Yemen (Aden) today is oil refining.
	Yemen (San'a)	75,290 sq mi (195,000 sq km)	5,500,000 73 per sq mi (28 per sq km)	San'a 447,898	Arabic*	The legendary Queen of Sheba ruled the Yemens in the 900s B.C. She is said to have visited King Solomon in 950 B.C.

*Official language(s)

TABLE OF COUNTRIES

AUSTRALIA & OCEANIA

COUNTRY	TOTAL AREA	POPULATION AND POPULATION DENSITY	CAPITAL CITY AND POPULATION	LANGUAGE(S)	OTHER FACTS
Australia	2,966,139 sq mi (7,682,000 sq km)	15,000,000 5 per sq mi (2 per sq km)	Canberra 234,700	English*	Cut off from other continents for millions of years, Australia developed a unique animal population.
Fiji	7,055 sq mi (18,272 sq km)	700,000 85 per sq mi (33 per sq km)	Suva 63,622	English*, Fijian, Hindustani	This South Pacific country is made up of over 800 islands that were formed by volcanoes.
Nauru	8 sq mi (21 sq km)	9,000 (1,125 per sq mi (429 per sq km)	Yaren 8,000	English*, Nauruan*	The government pays the tuition of students who attend college abroad.
New Zealand	103,747 sq mi (268,704 sq km)	3,100,000 30 per sq mi (12 per sq km)	Wellington 137,000	English*, Maori	New Zealand has no snakes, but it is the home of the tuatara—a native prehistoric reptile.
Papua New Guinea	178,260 sq mi (461,691 sq km)	3,300,000 19 per sq mi (7 per sq km)	Port Moresby 122,761	Pidgin English, Chinese	The people of Papua New Guinea speak over 700 languages. Many houses are built on stilts.
Solomon Islands	10,983 sq mi (28,446 sq km)	200,000 18 per sq mi (7 per sq km)	Honiara 14,993	English*, Pidgin English	More than 80 different languages are spoken in the Solomon Islands, and no one language is commonly spoken.
Tonga	270 sq mi (699 sq km)	90,128 334 per sq mi (129 per sq km)	Nukualofa 19,882	Tongan*	The government owns all the land, which it rents to males over 16. The population of Tonga is mostly Methodist.
Vanuatu	5,699 sq mi (14,763 sq km)	112,304 20 per sq mi (8 per sq km)	Vila 3,072	Bilama*, French*, English*	Vanuatu is a nation of 80 islands in the southwest Pacific Ocean. Its national anthem is "Yumi, yumi, yumi" ("We, we, we").
Western Samoa	1,097 sq mi (2,842 sq km)	200,000 182 per sq mi (70 per sq km)	Apia 32,201	Samoan*, English*	The noted writer Robert Louis Stevenson was a resident of Samoa. Most Samoans live in extended families.

EUROPE

COUNTRY	TOTAL AREA	POPULATION AND POPULATION DENSITY	CAPITAL CITY AND POPULATION	LANGUAGE(S)	OTHER FACTS
Albania	11,100 sq mi (28,748 sq km)	2,800,000 252 per sq mi (97 per sq km)	Tirana 192,000	Albanian*	Turkish customs have influenced Albanian culture and dress. Many men wear Turkish trousers and hats.
Andorra	175 sq. mi (453 sq km)	28,348 162 per sq mi (63 per sq km)	Andorra la Vella 12,800	Catalan*, French, Spanish	The postal system in Andorra is free, being paid for by the sale of stamps to collectors around the world.
Austria	32,374 sq mi (83,849 sq km)	7,600,000 235 per sq mi (91 per sq km)	Vienna 1,567,500	German*, Serbo-Croatian, Magyar, Slovene, Czech, Slovak	Some of the world's greatest musical composers—Haydn, Mozart, and Strauss, to name a few, were Austrian.
Belgium	11,781 sq mi (30,513 sq km)	9,900,000 840 per sq mi (324 per sq km)	Brussels 143,957	Dutch*, French*	The transportation system consists largely of inland waterways. A Belgian instrument maker invented the saxophone.
Bulgaria	42,823 sq mi (110,912 sq km)	8,900,000 208 per sq mi (80 per sq km)	Sofia 1,047,920	Bulgarian*	Damask roses from central Bulgaria provide much of the rose oil used in the making of perfume.
Cyprus	3,572 sq mi (9,251 sq km)	600,000 168 per sq mi (65 per sq km)	Nicosia 117,100	Greek*, Turkish, English	Cyprus has been known since the earliest times for its mineral wealth. In fact, the name Cyprus means "copper."
Czechoslovakia	49,371 sq mi (127,869 sq km)	15,400,000 312 per sq mi (120 per sq km)	Prague 1,193,345	Czech*, Slovak*, Hungarian	Czechoslovakia, a highly industrialized eastern European country, has a high standard of living.
Denmark	16,629 sq mi (43,069 sq km)	5,100,000 307 per sq mi (118 per sq km)	Copenhagen 505,982	Danish*	One of Denmark's well-known writers is Hans Christian Andersen, who wrote the famous fairy tales for children.
Finland	130,120 sq mi (337,009 sq km)	4,800,000 37 per sq mi (14 per sq km)	Helsinki 484,879	Finnish*, Swedish*	In the northernmost part of Finland (above the Arctic Circle), the sun shines 24 hours a day for much of the summer.
France	211,208 sq mi (547,026 sq km)	54,200,000 257 per sq mi (100 per sq km)	Paris 2,299,830	French*	French wines are world famous. The Louvre in Paris is one of the largest art museums in the world.
Germany (East)	41,768 sq mi (108,178 sq km)	16,700,000 400 per sq mi (154 per sq km)	Berlin (East) 1,133,854	German*	The Trade Fairs held in Leipzig date back to the Middle Ages and attract business people from everywhere.
Germany (West)	95,934 sq mi (248,468 sq km)	61,700,000 643 per sq mi (248 per sq km)	Bonn 285,200	German*, Sorb	West Germany, the most highly industrialized European country, ranks second, worldwide, in total value of trade.

*Official language(s)

490

TABLE OF COUNTRIES

EUROPE

COUNTRY	TOTAL AREA	POPULATION AND POPULATION DENSITY	CAPITAL CITY AND POPULATION	LANGUAGE(S)	OTHER FACTS
Greece	50,944 sq mi (131,944 sq km)	9,800,000 192 per sq mi (74 per sq km)	Athens 867,023	Greek*	The first European civilization developed in Greece over 2,000 years ago.
Hungary	35,919 sq mi (93,030 sq km)	10,700,000 298 per sq mi (115 per sq km)	Budapest 2,060,000	Hungarian*	Hungary's mineral water baths are well known for their medicinal qualities. Goulash is a popular Hungarian stew.
Iceland	39,769 sq mi (103,000 sq km)	200,000 5 per sq mi (2 per sq km)	Reykjavik 83,376	Icelandic*	Iceland has over 250 thermal springs that supply homes and businesses with hot water and steam heat.
Ireland	27,136 sq mi (70,283 sq km)	3,500,000 139 per sq mi (50 per sq km)	Dublin 544,586	English*, Irish (Gaelic)	Raising livestock is important to Ireland's economy. Shaw, Wilde, and Beckett are three famous Irish writers.
Italy	116,314 sq mi (301,253 sq km)	57,400,000 493 per sq mi (191 per sq km)	Rome 2,916,414	Italian*, German, French, Slovene	By law, movie theaters in Italy must show Italian films for at least 25 days every 3 months.
Liechtenstein	61 sq mi (157 sq km)	25,808 423 per sq mi (164 per sq km)	Vaduz 4,892	German*	Liechtenstein is one of the smallest countries in the world. Its stamps are prized by stamp collectors everywhere.
Luxembourg	998 sq mi (2,586 sq km)	400,000 401 per sq mi (155 per sq km)	Luxembourg 76,500	French*, German*, Letzburgesch	Luxembourg, a highly industrialized country, was the scene of the Battle of the Bulge in World War II.
Malta	122 sq mi (316 sq km)	400,000 3,279 per sq mi (1,266 per sq km)	Valletta 14,042	Maltese*, English*	Malta is the Mediterranean headquarters of NATO. Tourists come to Malta to view its many historical buildings.
Monaco	0.58 sq mi (1.49 sq km)	25,029 43,153 per sq mi (16,798 per sq km)	Monte Carlo 9,948	French*	By a 1918 treaty, if Monaco's ruling family had no male heirs, the country would come under French rule.
The Netherlands	15,892 sq mi (41,160 sq km)	14,300,000 900 per sq mi (347 per sq km)	Amsterdam 716,919	Dutch*	The Netherlands is known for its dairy products, as well as its tulips and other bulb flowers.
Norway	125,182 sq mi (324,219 sq km)	4,100,000 33 per sq mi (13 per sq km)	Oslo 454,823	Norwegian*, Lapp dialects	The oldest Norwegian literature is a body of legends written by the Vikings in old Norse.
Poland	120,725 sq mi (312,677 sq km)	36,300,000 301 per sq mi (116 per sq km)	Warsaw 1,567,600	Polish*	Despite government opposition, the Roman Catholic Church is the strongest social institution in Poland.
Portugal	35,553 sq mi (92,082 sq km)	9,900,000 278 per sq mi (108 per sq km)	Lisbon 829,900	Portuguese*	One half of the world's total cork supply comes from Portugal's special cork oak forests.
Romania	91,699 sq mi (237,500 sq km)	22,600,000 246 per sq mi (95 per sq km)	Bucharest 1,832,015	Romanian*	Sandy beaches, sunny climate, and modern hotels make Romania's Black Sea coast a popular vacation resort.
San Marino	24 sq mi (61 sq km)	20,400 850 per sq mi (334 per sq km)	San Marino 4,628	Italian*	San Marino is the second smallest republic in the world. Its chief sources of income are tourism and postage stamps.
Soviet Union	8,649,500 sq mi (22,402,000 sq km)	270,000,000 31 per sq mi (12 per sq km)	Moscow 7,831,000	Russian*	Aeroflot, the national airline, makes the longest nonstop flight between two cities (Moscow and Havana).
Spain	194,885 sq mi (504,750 sq km)	37,900,000 194 per sq mi (75 per sq km)	Madrid 3,267,664	Spanish*, Castilian, Basque	Bullfighting is the most popular spectator sport in Spain. Leading matadors become national heroes.
Sweden	173,732 sq mi (449,964 sq km)	8,300,000 48 per sq mi (18 per sq km)	Stockholm 647,220	Swedish*	The safety match was invented in Sweden. Sweden has the highest standard of living in the world.
Switzerland	15,941 sq mi (41,288 sq km)	6,300,000 395 per sq mi (153 per sq km)	Bern 141,300	German*, French*, Italian*	Switzerland is renowned for its watchmaking industry. Its banks attract wealthy customers from everywhere.
Turkey (see Asia)					
United Kingdom	94,251 sq mi (244,108 sq km)	56,100,000 595 per sq mi (230 per sq km)	London 6,696,008	English*, Welsh, Scottish, Gaelic	The British Empire was once the largest of any in history. There were British colonies on every inhabited continent.
Vatican City State	0.17 sq mi (0.44 sq km)	231 4,300 per sq mi (1,661 per sq km)		Italian*	Vatican City, the smallest independent country in the world, is the headquarters of the Roman Catholic Church.
Yugoslavia	98,766 sq mi (255,804 sq km)	22,600,000 229 per sq mi (88 per sq km)	Belgrade 1,445,000	Serbo-Croatian*, Slovenian*, Macedonian*	Until the 1800s the Yugoslavs handed down their culture orally. Today the country has an 85% literacy rate.

*Official language(s)

491

INDEX

Key to Pronunciation

a	hat, cap							
ā	age, face	i	it, pin	ou	house, out	zh	measure, seizure
ã	care, air	ī	ice, five	sh	she, rush	ə	represents:
ä	father, far	ng	long, bring	th	thin, both		a in about
ch	child, much	o	hot, rock	ŦH	then, smooth		e in taken
e	let, best	ō	open, go	u	cup, butter		i in pencil
ē	equal, see	ô	order, all	ù	full, put		o in lemon
ėr	term, learn	oi	oil, voice	ü	rule, move		u in circus

The Key to Pronunciation above is reprinted from *The World Book Dictionary* © 1981 by permission of J. G. Ferguson Publishing Company, Chicago, IL 60601.

A

Abadan, Iran, 294
Abbot, 150
Aborigines, 385 – 386, 426 – 429
Abraham, 266
Abu-Bakr (caliph), 273
Academy of Plato, 92
Accra, Ghana, 350
Acropolis, 87
  pollution damage to, 133 – 134
Addis Ababa, Ethiopia, 367
Adelaide, Australia, 445
Aden, Yemen, 300
Aden, Gulf of, 300
Adriatic Sea, 124
Aegean Sea, 19, 74, 124, 199
Aesop's fables, 90
Afghanistan, 192, 231, 372, 435
Africa, 12, 18 – 19, 312 – 367
  central, 316, 321, 322 – 324, 326, 353, 356, 366
  colonization of, 340 – 345
  eastern, 312, 315, 317, 318, 319 – 321, 325, 326, 361 – 367
  European exploration of, 330 – 339
  farming and industry of, 322 – 327
  land and climate of, 312 – 321
  southern, 312, 316, 322, 325, 326, 327

356 – 362, 366
  western, 316, 319, 322 – 324, 326, 350 – 353, 366
  See also Middle East and North Africa.
Africanus, Leo, 332
Afrikaans, 359
Afrikaners, 359
Agora, 79
Agriculture. *See* Farming and agriculture.
Agulhas, Cape, 312, 330
Air currents, 126
Air pollution, 133 – 134
Air pressure, 23
Akbar (Mogol emperor), 396 – 397
Akkad, 48, 55
Albania, 198, 222, 241 – 242
Albert, Lake, 317
Alexander the Great, 85 – 86, 93, 100, 395
Alexander II (Russian tsar), 211
Alexandria, Egypt, 2 – 4, 85 – 86
Algeria, 252, 261, 306 – 307
Algiers, Algeria, 306
Ali Baba, 271
Allah, 270
Allies, in World War I, 172
Alma-Ata, Soviet Union, 197
Alp-Arslan (Seljuk sultan), 275

Alphabet, 72, 114 – 115, 206, 222, 239, 335, 406
Alps, 99, 126, 134 – 135, 174, 175, 180
  Austrian, 174
  Italian, 180
  Swiss, 175
Altitude, 5
  climate and, 25
Aluminum, 225, 239, 350, 446
Alvares, Francisco, 335 – 336
Ambassadors, 419
Amman, Jordan, 296
Amsterdam, Netherlands, 177
Anatolia, 275, 279, 288
Anatolian peninsula, 253
Anatolian Plateau, 253
Anaxagoras, 91
Ancestor, 266
Ancient History, by Cellarius, 140
Ancient times, 36
Andersen, Hans Christian, 171
Andorra, 178 – 180
Androcles, 111
Angkor, Kampuchea, 408
Angola, 335, 344, 350, 366 – 367
Animals of Africa, 315
Ankara, Turkey, 291
Anne (Russian empress), 190
Anno Domini (A.D.), 33
Antarctica, 19

Antwerp, Belgium, 177
Apartheid, 360 – 361
Apennines Mountains, 180
Aphrodite, 88
Apollo, 88
Appian Way, 107
Apprentices, 149
Aqueducts, 27, 105 – 106, 116
Aquitaine, France, 149
Arabian Nights, 271 – 272, 274
Arabian Peninsula, 248, 252, 299 – 300
Arabic language, 272, 336
Arabic numerals, 282 – 283
Ararat, Mount, 253
Arc de Triomphe, 173
Arctic Circle, 124
Arctic Ocean, 19, 194, 195
Ares, 88 – 89
Aristotle, 26, 80, 92 – 93
Armenians, 197
Artisans, 191
Aryans, 392 – 393
Asbestos, 327, 382
Asia, 18 – 19, 74, 189, 248, 372 – 373, 390 – 426, 432 – 445
  Burma and Thailand, 443
  China, 397 – 405, 416 – 421, 435 – 439
  Hong Kong and Macao, 439
  Indian subcontinent,

CREDITS

8 9 10—RRD—91 90 89 88 87